ANOTHER LENS

How did we get here? As the twenty-first century unfolds, several seemingly unprecedented phenomena evoke ghosts of past histories that suggest we may have been here before. Forms and arguments gone acquire new relevance, as retrospective signposts for the contemporary. **India Since the 90s** assembles texts and images from diverse academic disciplines and cultural practices, to look again at the millennial turn that is shaping our present.

Series Editor
Ashish Rajadhyaksha

IN THE SERIES

VOLUME 1 The Hunger of the Republic: Our Present in Retrospect
Editor: **Ashish Rajadhyaksha**

VOLUME 2 Improvised Futures: Encountering the Body in Performance
Editor: **Ranjana Dave**

VOLUME 3 The Vanishing Point: Moving Images After Video
Editor: **Rashmi Sawhney**

VOLUME 4 Another Lens: Photography and the Emergence of Image Culture
Editor: **Rahaab Allana**

VOLUME 5 Cities on the Ground: The New 'Urban' Experience
Editors: **Solomon Benjamin and the Frozen Fish Collective**

VOLUME 6 Ghosts of Future Nations: Gods, Migrants and Tribals in the Late-Modern Museum
Editor: **Kavita Singh**

Set up in 2010, **West Heavens** (http://westheavens.net/) is an integrated cross-cultural exchange programme aiming to disentangle and compare the different paths of modernity taken by India and China. It promotes several layers of interaction across intellectual and art practices, and social thought, between the two countries. In its ten years of existence, the project has organized numerous forums, exhibitions, film screenings and workshops, and has published more than twenty books.

India Since the 90s

ANOTHER LENS

PHOTOGRAPHY AND THE EMERGENCE OF IMAGE CULTURE

edited by
RAHAAB ALLANA

Tulika Books

WEST HEAVENS

India Since the 90s is a collaborative bilingual project between

Tulika Books, New Delhi and **West Heavens**, Shanghai

Tulika Books

WEST HEAVENS

supported by **Moonchu Foundation**, Hong Kong

會金基教文周夢
Moonchu Foundation

Another Lens: Photography and the Emergence of Image Culture

First published in India in 2024 by
Tulika Books
44 (first floor), Shahpur Jat, New Delhi 110 049, India · tulikabooks.in

ISBN: 978-81-958394-9-0

supported by **The Alkazi Foundation for the Arts,** New Delhi

The Alkazi Foundation
for the Arts

Design, visual concepts, montages: Kinshuk
Layout design: Gauri Nagpal
Copy-editing: Smriti Vohra

Printed in India by Naveen Printers, New Delhi 110 020

INTRODUCTION TO THE SERIES

Another Lens: Photography and the Emergence of Image Culture is the fourth in our series of six volumes titled *India Since the 90s*. The series is published bilingually, in English and Chinese, and is intended to provide a historical frame for our present. As with the other volumes, the texts and images here are not new, in that they have not been produced for this book. Indeed, this particular volume carries some of the most famous photographic images made in post-Independence India, alongside numerous others that are equally significant, if not so well known.

What is *new* here, apart from their choice of selection and their assemblage into this particular order, is their *re-presentation*. The form is intended to give these works an afterlife. It attempts both estrangement and refamiliarization, as we seek to re-describe an era that is our very recent past and, in some instances, our actual present.

Previous volumes in this series include *The Hunger of the Republic*, *Improvised Futures* and *The Vanishing Point*, which in their own ways sought to provide different vantage points to address what seemed to be an overarching question for this series as a whole: how the past produces our present. If in a way the continuous invention of a mythical past becomes part of the ideological dynamics of present-day power, the reverse appears also to be true, namely, how the present takes us relentlessly and compulsively back to other moments similar to our 'now', moments that too might have once encountered their own 'new normal'. This is not a return to origins. Rather, it is the discovery, in such moments, of the ghosts of other moments. Today's stories, however things pan out, cannot be told without recognizing in them the spectres of the 1990s, the decade that launched globalization whose end might well be signalled in 2020. And the 1990s cannot in turn be comprehended without accessing yet another equally 'new' moment in history – the 1940s – when the Indian state was imagined, politically and administratively.

So far in these volumes the inquiry has expanded from social sciences theory to performance and body art, and thence to technologies of the moving image that brought what was once cinema into a new ecosystem of data storage and circulation. On the way, we encountered diverse kinds of repositories of memory, from the garbage heaps and recycled second-hand markets that have become the natural archives of our present, to the embattled body as it stood in the crosshairs of past-meeting-present. Future volumes will take this inquiry into museums (*Ghosts of Future Nations*) and constantly mutating urban space (*Cities on the Ground*).

The present volume addresses photography as central to the making of a modern image culture. It produces immediacy and also casts a wider net than the previous volumes have done in defining this visual culture, returning to the armatures defining late colonialism and the modern Indian state. Photography becomes particularly significant at a moment when we are incessantly reminded of the ghosts of history. Even as our capacity to imagine stable utopian futures drains away, our present is reinvigorated by a textual prescience, as texts and images produced in other times and other places begin to reveal things that could never have been anticipated at the time they were made. Indeed we have discovered, it seems, an entirely new ability to read uncanny significances. As clarity slowly emerges around our 'new normal', to use the phrase of the moment, it also occasionally lifts the cover-ups of normalcy to give us a glimpse into what lies beneath.

This volume includes maps, producing from on high perhaps the definitive visual intervention of the modern nation state: the line defining a national border (and in the subcontinent's history a somewhat arbitrary one) that split a continent into nations and sub-nations. Here it triggered not only the violence we associate with the Partition, but also a history of popular map-making, barefoot cartographers using multiple iconographies as they entered a new zone of national spatiality. It includes multiple bodies upon whom these national imaginations are inscribed, from Gandhi's 'superbody' to those of the victims of the 1943 Bengal Famine. It defines the spaces of modernity, especially urban spaces, and the modes of popularizing these through print journalism.

The book includes several experiments with the apparatus of the camera by painters, media artists, political activists and photojournalists. These produce vastly varying concerns of such history-making, moving from postmemory on the one extreme to the relentless here-and-now of the political debacle on the other. They move into the domain of ethical doubt, into vexed questions of authenticity and fidelity to source, and diverse kinds of artistic experiment pushing the limits of both the medium and its capacity for verisimilitude.

A central component of the book is its recognition of the fact that photography, as a founding component in the modern public domain, has in recent years developed an uncanny new capacity: one where it impacts a putative *citizenship* upon its subject within what Israeli-Palestinian author and curator Ariella Azoulay has famously named the 'civil contract of photography'. Nothing marks a date, a time and a place of a recording than the specific moment when a photograph is taken, and we well know that such a marking includes moments of major national, even planetary, significance. What such a marking also includes, she argues, is a condition of *governance*, that exists analogous to, if independent of, state functioning. In a very real sense, the relationship of the photographer to the person or object photographed is *governed*: there is an imagined political equality between the two, but it is one that has to be actually produced in the work. Such an equality becomes especially significant when the object photographed is literally stateless or without juridical rights.

The relationship of photography both to the apparatus of the modern state and its flip side, the practice of human rights – together with the legal status of photographed truth as legally admissible evidence, and the photographer as a privileged eyewitness – is well documented. Less discussed perhaps is the way such a right gets further bestowed upon the subject of the lens. It is this definition of the photographed subject, in turn the subject of a political gaze, that becomes an overarching concern in this book.

Each of the volumes exists on its own, as conceived by its editor. A common feature across the texts has been to introduce a glossary of keywords. Several are from Indian languages, some are names of people, yet others are acronyms or abbreviations, while others are English words used in India in ways that divert sharply from dictionary definitions. All are being re-presented here, by way of explanation and for purposes of estrangement and refamiliarization.

An important element of commonality across the titles, apart from their interest in the period following the 1990s in India, is their shared interest in the triad of concepts that we may name *politics*, *space*, *technology*. The pendular movement of the political spaces, until recently spaces of public existence, increasingly turned into spaces of negotiation between *state* and *planet*, a twenty-first-century variation of the old local–global divide, defining both virtual and physically occupied space. Technology is apparatus, frame, mode of mediation and surveillance. Three further terms, in turn, produce the *habitus* for these concepts: *democracy*, the *body* and the *text*. Even as key democratic concepts such as freedom need to be defined anew in times when bodies – both physical and virtual – occupy complex political domains, the text – as *prescient*, as *re-interpreted* and as *meme* – too finds itself bearing new responsibilities.

Ashish Rajadhyaksha
Series Editor
Bangalore, December 2023

CONTENTS

Introduction

| Rahaab Allana

> A product of technology, the camera can still be used to retreat from society changing under its impact into a sheltered aestheticism. Or the camera can be used to comment on life, to alert against disruptions of tradition, to welcome desirable modulations. The social concern for the cameramen seeking to re-forge Salon art's link with life is also an important aspect of modern India. And for the integral image of India sought to be presented in this exhibition, their work has been chosen as sole medium.
>
> – K.K. Nair[1]

In January 1987, the Ministry of Tourism, Government of India, installed *Pratibimba* (Hindi: 'Reflections'), a large exhibition of photography from India, at The Pushkin State Museum of Fine Arts in Moscow. This gesture of cultural diplomacy was an outcome of the consolidation of Indo-USSR relations in 1987–88.[2] The exhibition also travelled to Tatarstan and Azerbaijan. It presented diverse modes of Indian photographic work of the 1980s, much of it generally hosted by state-funded ventures which sought to represent a homogenous sovereign 'nation' striving towards a desired international standard of 'modernity'.

That exhibition remained an example of the habitual reliance on government sponsorship for big arts events in the post-Independence decades. The trend would soon shift. By the 1990s, Indian photographic production had become a significantly more autonomous strand of cultural discourse, with complex and layered re/definitions of both 'nation' and 'modernity'. There was a clear renunciation of the influence of classic European photography. Photographers from India, of Indian origin or working in India, had begun to capture the contemporary moment through a local rejection of exoticism. New lens-based practices began scrutinizing the 'everyday' in their representations of the bazaar, the street, the folk and popular culture, even as the 'nation' itself, once immured within socialist logic, was being aggressively coerced by globalization and capital investment to mutate into a more diverse and 'modern' political entity.

The radical, whole-scale liberalization of the Indian economy in the 1990s induced rapid changes in every visual sphere.[3] More specifically, it provided a prologue not only to new lens-based practices, but also to the legitimization of documentary imaging that would be canonized as a form of social 'truth'. Based on the conviction that the postcolonial 'nation' could efficiently accommodate the fixed traditions of its past within a fluctuating cosmopolitan present, many photography initiatives of the time reinforced a sort of 'national' faith in India's 'modern' hybrid, liberalizing culture cautiously seeking its place within the new world order.

By the 1990s, dial-up Internet connections, CD ROMs, Motorola pagers, FM radio stations and the expanded regional press had begun connecting Indians across national and social boundaries. A vast underprivileged demographic had much more access to simple forms of new media. At the other end, elite and upper-middle classes benefiting from privileged, borderless cosmopolitanism were able to consume, support and disseminate globalized culture. As information technology witnessed larger public/private investment, national cultural institutions began to assert their capacity as instruments of international soft power.

Another Lens: Photography and the Emergence of Image Culture examines various contexts around lens-based practices leading up to the 1990s and thereafter, thus tracing new directions for photography from the subcontinent within a wider South Asian visual-cultural orbit. It presents the 1990s as the decade that enabled new sites of articulation, including subaltern realities. Inserting themselves into novel spaces within newly proliferating globalized arts discourses, progressive artists everywhere in India felt the need to communicate with different audiences, and to deploy a combination of media and experiments with the image (installation works by Rummana Hussain, Navjot Altaf and many others) as they responded to major national and social crises such as the Bombay riots of 1992–93 in response to the Babri Masjid demolition, or the Pokhran-II nuclear tests in 1998. There were also responses to the abhorrent symbiosis of mytho-religious supremacism and toxic 'othering' of minorities through legislation, discrimination, micro-aggressions and lethal assault. In parallel, art critics and art historians consciously turned their focus on images of dissent, as seen for example in Chaitanya Sambrani's *Edge of Desire: Recent Art in India* (2005)[4] that featured artists' responses to the unconscionable, politically fuelled communitarian violence of 1992 (Ayodhya) and 2002 (Gujarat).[5]

The texts in this volume both dissect and suture the trajectories of post-Independence lens-based practices. They look at street photography, cinema, journalism, contemporary arts and the archive to capture multi-nodal ways by which a new public received and consumed images. This introductory essay draws a chronological arc through a complex period of cultural production. It delineates how local, state-supported, private as well as international lens-based work from the late 1980s through the 1990s coalesced into a dynamic art form even as it began eliding with an emergent new media culture. Paralleling this expansion was the exponential rise in competitive galleries, and international practitioners and curators working within the flexible, profit-oriented ethos of globalization.

Through the 1990s, the arts (including media arts) in India claimed increasingly diverse national audiences and also actively began courting non-Indian ones. These publics saw a growing appreciation and exposure of international art within the subcontinent, as well as of Indian art at prestigious foreign venues.[6] Over the next three decades, the grand narrative of post-Independence modernism would be deconstructed through radical, critical, technology-driven modes that both exposed and manipulated meta-relationships between symbolic language, medium, form and site. Taking cognizance of these four categories, *Another Lens* is divided into four distinct sections: pre- and post-Independence/Partition narratives which had an exerting impact on subsequent art/activist practices; the interregnum of the 1960s/1970s culminating in the Emergency which shaped the politics of the 1990s; the 1990s and post-liberalization refrains; and lastly, practices after the 1990s, and the new millennium through the voice of practitioners. Each section and its constituent chapters are arranged so that they are continually in dialogue with other sections and their constituent chapters, throughout.

Individually and collectively, the interwoven texts of *Another Lens* examine photographic and visual work that pivots around the following themes:

(1) the late colonial and postcolonial metropolis, Partition and famine-related imagery, and the subsequent transformation of urban spaces as the Nehruvian socialist paradigm transitioned into economic liberalization, with India's gradual entry into linked/hyperlinked global cultures that included new formats of production, curation, dissemination and critique of the visual arts, photography, printmaking, film and new media;

(2) the expansion of image spectra, exhibition practices and viewership in relation to journalism, documentary, video, visual/conceptual/new media art;

(3) innovative aesthetic practices that singly and collaboratively deconstruct and re-read canonized notions of 'nation', 'nationality' and 'nationhood';

(4) representational strategies that navigate the unstable, tactical politics of art activism – art as witnessing and testimony, art as dissent, art as resistance – and confront the state and self-appointed conservative/vigilante censorship; and

(5) curatorial and artistic methodologies that diffract the complex micro-histories of suppressed and disenfranchised subjects through the prisms of gender, ethnicity, sexuality and identity.

As an addition to the essays in *Another Lens*, which revisit and re-orient the scholarship on arts practices anew though juxtaposition, this introductory essay includes an analysis of major state-endorsed photographic cultural projects, such as the seminal photography biennales of 1989 and 1993 organized by the Lalit Kala Akademi[7] and some significant photography exhibitions hosted by the private gallery, Art Heritage (est. 1977),[8] that together support the claims made above as they set a new curatorial paradigm in Delhi and plausibly the wider Indian art world.

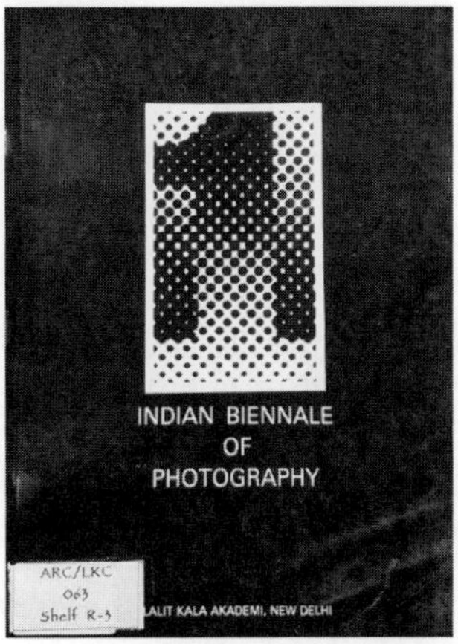

Catalogue cover, First Indian Biennale of Photography, 1989, Lalit Kala Akademi

Entering the 1990s

> In the decades after Independence, many vanguard painters, breaking away from both British academic models and traditional Indian styles, adopted Western modernism as the appropriately progressive style for a new nation. And in the form of a versatile, readily personalized, often semi-abstract figuration, it maintains its currency in India today, though its cachet has faded in the West.
>
> – Holland Cotter[9]

Across the post-Independence decades, India saw several exhibitions defining influential trajectories of modernist photographic arts. One example was *Images of India* (1960), realized in response to the massive *The Family of Man* (1955) exhibition.[10] The latter was a feature of American cultural diplomacy in the Cold War era. This mega-display was shown at Bombay's Jehangir Art Gallery and other Indian cities (1956–57) and toured the world in different editions. While *The Family of Man* was international in its scope and ambition, *Images of India* asserted the significance of the 'Indian' practitioner. A sudden surge in photographic 'salons' (the European term for exhibitions) focused on demonstrating the craft of photography through pictorialism.[11] There was also a corresponding surge in local organizations supporting amateur and professional practitioners in metro cities, such as the Federation of Indian Photography, established in 1952 by doctor-photographer G. Thomas and others, renowned in the photographic circles of Mysore. By the 1960s, the Bombay-based Photographic Society of India (est. 1937) had the largest membership (about 500 practitioners).[12] Small photo clubs such as *L'Avenir* in Calcutta were also flourishing, and there was the beginning of state-sponsored exhibitions such as *India '58*, held in New Delhi in 1958, that presented photography on a large scale for the first time and featured works by Sunil Janah, R.J. Chinwalla, B.F. Ferreira, Richard Lannoy and Jitendra Arya, among others.[13]

In terms of broader South Asian visual culture, the 1970s presented a pivotal moment for some non-mainstream, subversive print cultures that became transnational networks for underground printing and publishing. Bypassing (or tactically navigating) 'official' constraints, these 'solidarity publications' were often dedicated to the spread of liberal, revolutionary, anarchist thought, and in multiple strategic ways shaped political and artistic concerns into resistance narratives within right-wing and imperialist regimes and within established democracies.[14] In India these publications invoked flourishing cultural initiatives of the 1960s supported by figures such as, to take one example, Baroda-based artists Gulammohammed Sheikh and Bhupen Khakhar, founders of the arts and literary magazine *Vrishchik* ('Scorpion').[15] Sheikh was a participant in the important experimental photography group show *Painters with a Camera* (1968) mounted at the Jehangir Art Gallery, Bombay. Another was the avant-garde, iconoclastic little magazine *damn you*, launched in 1965 by Allahabad-based author Arvind Krishna Mehrotra, with his friends Alok and Amit Rai (grandsons of Munshi Premchand).[16] Artist-activist groups also included the Indian Radical Painters and Sculptors Association (associated with the Faculty of Fine Arts, M.S. University, Baroda),[17] active between the mid- and late 1980s but committing to Left politics when Prime Minister Indira Gandhi declared the repressive national Emergency in 1975.[18]

Subsequently, the 1980s saw some grand 'national' cultural events that attempted to chart a postcolonial trajectory in terms of Indian arts and international viewership. As a possible precedent, after Independence, artefacts from various Indian museums were displayed for the first time outside India in the show *Exhibition of Indian Art* held at Burlington House, London in the winter of 1947–48.[19]

Three decades later the Festival of India was held in 1982 in the UK.[20] It presented nineteen exhibitions over eight months. These included the works of contemporary Indian artists at the Royal Academy of Arts, London, Indian artists settled in Britain were shown at the Barbican, and four modern Indian artists selected by Howard Hodgkin were shown at the Tate.[21] *The Indian Experience* (1982)[22] was also held in London, produced with the support of the Lalit Kala Akademi, National Book Trust and National Institute of Design, and was more aligned to a neoliberal expansionist model for art. These perhaps set a precedent for the large exhibitions of 1997 designed to mark fifty years of India's Independence, and organized in the United States at the MET, and at the Sackler Gallery and the Smithsonian Institution in Washington DC. Other large showings outside India of contemporary Asian art, organized by the Asia Society, for instance, reinforced subcontinental themes.

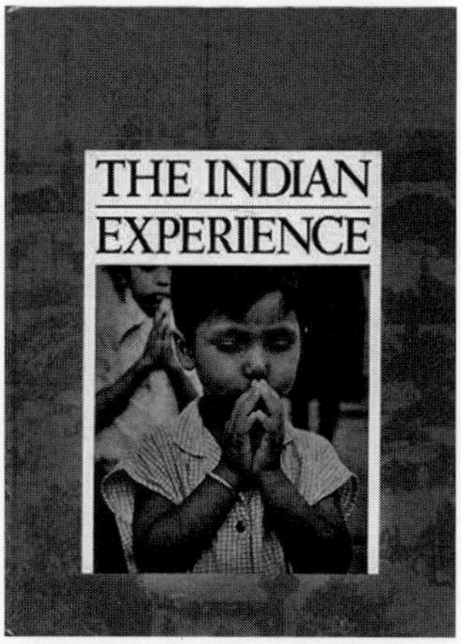

Catalogue cover, *The Indian Experience*, 1982

A fair number of exhibitions of the 1980s and early 1990s included Raj nostalgia. For instance, as part of the Festival of India, an exhibition of Raja Deen Dayal's photography was organized in collaboration with Air India and installed at the Swiss Cottage Library.[23] Actively supported by the Deen Dayal family and facilitated by the British Council, it was previously exhibited in Poona and Bombay.[24] Augmented with compelling text by Ray Desmond and Pauline Rohatgi from the British Library, the exhibition possibly included a number of original and reproduced images from the Deen Dayal family archive, and from the Library's own collection.

Several of these exhibitions have also been critiqued for their somewhat one-dimensional framing of the idea of the nation-state. Whatever their limitations, such shows nevertheless unsettled the embedded colonial genealogies of subcontinental photography in the way they acknowledged the 'Indian' practitioner. To his credit, Desmond attempted to create a more balanced image spectrum by foregrounding local photographers, and thus stimulating the wider interest in (and market for) vintage and modern photography from India. Festival of India texts became worthy precedents to exhibitions and catalogues of the 1990s, such as curator-writer Yaduendra Sahai's *Maharaja Sawai Ram Singh II of Jaipur: The Photographer Prince*, published in 1996.[25] And perhaps it was in response to these private efforts/investments that state cultural institutions began to build their own photo archives in the late 1980s – seen, for instance, in the Indira Gandhi National Centre for the Arts, Delhi acquiring glass plates by Deen Dayal & Sons, and prints of Henri Cartier-Bresson and Sunil Janah.

As part of the Festival of India programming in London, among other venues such as the National Theatre (London) and the Central Art Gallery in Wolverhampton, was an exhibition mapping India's photographic legacy and trends hosted in 1982 at the Photographers' Gallery.[26] Featuring two survey exhibitions, 'Photography in India since 1858' (researched by Partha Mitter among others) and 'Indians Here and There', the enterprise presented both Indian and European photographers. The former showcased antiquarian works, including those by Raja Deen Dayal and Johnston and Hoffmann, as well as contemporary works by Raghu Rai and film stills from James Ivory and Satyajit Ray productions. The latter included the works of photographers Mark Edwards and Peter Harrap commissioned by the Photographers' Gallery, showcasing images of Indians in Britain and those taken in India between the mid-1970s and early 1980s, in an effort to express the 'positive side of race relations'.[27]

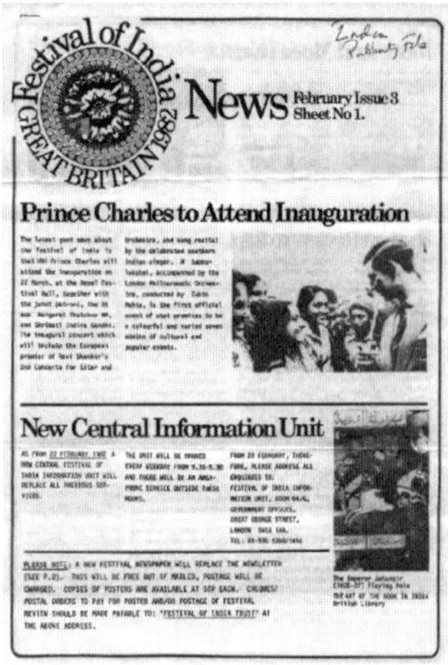

Festival of India GREAT BRITAIN 1982

News February Issue 3 Sheet No 1.

Prince Charles to Attend Inauguration

New Central Information Unit

Press announcement for the Festival of India in the UK, 1982

In the late 1980s, there was a significant upsurge in the representation of photography from all parts of India. *Pratibimba*, mounted in Moscow in 1987, was selected by a jury of painters, theatre personalities and experimental filmmakers such as Mani Kaul, Govind Nihalani, R.K. Laxman and Tyeb Mehta, as well as photojournalists such as T.S. Nagarajan.[28] The experienced organizers included scenographer and producer Nissar Allana, S.K. Misra from the Ministry of Tourism and art historian Saryu Doshi, who was later to become Director, National Gallery of Modern Art, Mumbai.[29] Also participating were non-official members such as artists M.F. Husain and Haku Shah, the former creating an independent space with his own photographs overlaid with acrylic paint. The catalogue text by journalist K.K. Nair highlighted the 'everyday' nature of 'Indian' photography and the inclusion of a large number of professional artists, hobbyists and photojournalists, chosen through a combination of an open call and by nomination. The images focused on the minutiae of daily life, experimenting and playing with form, turning the lens outward on to street and rural themes.

Pratibimba's display had section breaks comprising text by prominent Marathi poet and filmmaker Dilip Chitre, whose short descriptive and interpretive passages attempted to make distinct connections between traditional life and modern times.[30]

This exhibition significantly opened out the practice of 'modern' Indian photography and was the impetus for other large ventures that followed – for instance, the First Indian Biennale of Photography (1989), organized by the Lalit Kala Akademi in Calcutta. Divided into 'General', 'Invited' and 'Special' sections, it included well-known practitioners T.S. Satyan, Raghu Rai, Shukdeo Singh and R.A. Acharya.[31] In his Preface to the catalogue, the sculptor Sankho Chaudhuri asserted that Indian photographers had not thus far received the status of 'artists': 'The terms of reference in photographic criticism ... have not as yet crystallized ... in a manner which can be compared to other established fine arts such as painting, printmaking and sculpture.'[32] In his jury report, the curator T. Kasinath, president of the India International Photographic Council and a senior figure in the Photo Division of the Ministry of Information and Broadcasting, declared that the Biennale had received only a few entries due to the overall lack of interest in pictorial work and because no cash prizes were accorded. Kasinath was critical of 'aim and shoot' snapshot photography, declaring it inferior to the pictorial method: 'Computerized cameras' with fully automatic controls were generating innumerable hobbyists or 'button pushers'. Declaring that this deplorable state was due to lack of facilities, absence of photo-literacy and of governmental support, he lauded the efforts of privately sponsored photographic societies whose legacy went back to the nineteenth century.[33]

Any discussion of the post-Independence genealogy of these large 'national' exhibitions will benefit from Nancy Adajania's critique of the 'ambivalent fate' of Triennale India.[34] Organized in 1968 by the Lalit Kala Akademi in New Delhi, it was marked by sharp ideological fissures between participating artists, art historians and cultural luminaries. Adajania notes that the history of any such exhibition 'cannot be studied in isolation, as though it were pertinent only to a specific regional history. It must, in fact, be evaluated in the context of its entanglements with other histories of the global biennale culture as it then existed.' The 'official understanding of culture in the early decades of Independence as a subject worthy of policy and state patronage, arising from the Indian nation-state's self-image as simultaneously the inheritor of an ancient tradition and the vehicle of an unfolding modernity', produced a dual claim as 'a troubled and schizophrenic condition since official rhetoric has long attempted to render the two emphases into a seamless unity, instead of acknowledging the categorical difference between them'. Adajania asks whether it was even possible to bring complex political issues into a state-sponsored arts framework – 'not only to illustrate political reality through the medium of painting or score a polemical point, but also to activate the public sphere with urgent questions'.[35]

Twenty years later, *Artists Alert* was held at Rabindra Bhavan in New Delhi in 1989, shaped by a very different purpose.[36] It was a response to the public murder of activist-playwright Safdar Hashmi, a prominent member of the Communist Party of India (Marxist) and co-founder of Jana Natya Manch, a group committed to the practice of political street theatre.[37] On 1 January 1989, Hashmi and Nepali migrant worker Ram Bahadur were savagely assaulted in a labourers' settlement in the industrial belt of Sahibabad in full view by thugs (allegedly hired by politicians) during a performance of *Halla Bol!* (Hindi: 'Raise Your Voice!'), a street play on the theme of trade unions striking for workers' rights. Ram Bahadur died on the spot. The next day Hashmi, 34, succumbed to his injuries. Hundreds of people stood vigil outside the hospital, and thousands accompanied his funeral procession. Two days later, Hashmi's wife Moloyashree, herself a theatre actor, returned to the same location and defiantly performed the same play in full. The artist collective Safdar Hashmi Memorial Trust (Sahmat)[38] was founded in his memory, with a mission to generate public discourses on the function of art for the enunciation of dissent when democratic rights are threatened by the state. To this day, for practitioners across the arts spectrum in India, Hashmi remains a potent symbol of passionate conviction and anti-authoritarian courage.[39]

The lethal assault on Hashmi saw swift mobilization of the artists' and writers' communities. Sahmat organized an exhibition and auction of Indian art, sculpture and photography at Rabindra Bhavan, under the direction of artists Krishen Khanna, Manjit Bawa, Ram Rahman, Madan Gopal Singh and Vivan Sundaram.[40] *Artists Alert* was a formal tribute to Hashmi, and served as the keystone for the cohering of a certain cosmopolitan activist art in larger Indian cities. It featured over a hundred photographers, photojournalists and artists. Some overlapped with both *Pratibimba* and the First Biennale of 1989.[41] It opened the possibility of semi-institutional and non-governmental organizations collaborating to build an aesthetic, diverse modes of social documentary and fine art to produce a new, expansive image spectrum. As noted by Geeta Kapur,

> ... an artist's right is taken for granted in a democratic society, both because it is a publicized feature of liberal culture and because artists are rendered innocuous anyway, in that culture. Can the artist say anything that can upset money and State power? ... The question is to

> make your identity and your practice sufficiently complex so that it is not easily appropriated nor easily destroyed by antagonist forces.[42]

Money from the sales of exhibited works went to support activities like *Janotsav* (Hindi: 'People's Festival') that Hashmi had been planning. Through the 1990s, Sahmat engaged in various Left-leaning creative projects that used photography centrally in pamphlets and posters, and to document actions around the demand for social justice, with many artists remaining anonymous. This continues into the present through discussions, songs, films, performances, publications and exhibitions, and through sharing ideas with the public through accessible adult literacy programmes. Designer and photographer Parthiv Shah composed posters for Sahmat's project *Images and Words* (1991–92) that involved over 400 painters, writers and photographers coming together to express the ideology of secularism, and travelled to thirty cities and forty schools.[43] Shah conducted a workshop in which he gave cameras to fifty children to shoot their local environments and then develop, process and print their images, to be later exhibited at the National Centre for Performing Arts, Mumbai.[44]

Other noteworthy activist arts and photography events channelled the ideologies of dissent and resistance in a sustained manner through the 1990s. In Mumbai, the festival/programme *Artists Against Communalism* (1992), a response to the demolition of the Babri Masjid in Ayodhya by Hindu fundamentalist mobs, developed into a long-term project, its visual arts section organized by photo-artist and performer Pushpamala N., displayed on modular structures designed by artist and graphic novelist Orijit Sen, and featuring photos by Mukesh Parpiani.[45] Photographers built a critique of the religious fundamentalism and supremacism that had brazenly appropriated national politics, and responded strongly to the Babri Masjid violence (a temple in its place inaugurates in early 2024), now associated with an iconic photograph by Praveen Jain that showed a montage of Gandhi images.[46] Artists such as Manjit Bawa and Paramjit Singh reacted to the politico-religious violence by producing canvases on the subject of syncretism and secularism, and Sahmat developed the initiative *Hum Sab Ayodhya* (Hindi: 'We Are All Ayodhya'), exhibited at the Nehru Memorial Museum and Library in Delhi, featuring photos by Ram Rahman and Samar Singh Jodha.[47] Other significant activist projects of that decade include *Tribute to Gandhi* (1994) featuring photos by Habib Rahman and Sunil Janah, and *Manas Bana* (part of *Artists Against Communalism*) wherein Vivan Sundaram and Amanlal Paliwal produced a montage work related to Gandhi's protest marches during India's freedom struggle.[48]

The Early 1990s

> Photography has, it is said, reshaped and re-invited the human mind. Photography has become a Pandora's box sending out a stream of images – unending messages that bombard us, shaping our myths, our beliefs and our lives. Today there are more photographs than there are bricks in the world.
>
> – Satish Sharma[49]

In 1993, the Second Indian Biennale of Creative Photography was initiated under B.P. Kamboj, secretary of the Lalit Kala Akademi. The exhibition received 238 entries with 912 photos, of which 153 works were selected, in 'General/Competitive' (83 entries) and 'Invited' (70 entries) categories. Most of the artists were from Delhi, Calcutta, Bombay and Ahmedabad, followed by Chandigarh and Chennai, suggesting that, predictably, large cities were the centres of photography practice.[50] This Biennale included experimental photography as well as realist documentary, social testimony and pictorialism.[51] Kamboj[52] remarked optimistically:

> One thing is certain, that photography has immense potential as the most revolutionary medium of documentation and expression, and hence a great role to play – be it as a documentation device or as a form of pure art, or for promoting the cause of trade and industry. In all its roles, now or in the future, the element of art in photography will never lose its significance. And may this attribute of it remain to be its main driving force ...
>
> The exhibition has a varied range in style, content and technique, full freedom was allowed to the participants as well as selectors. It is hoped that the exhibition might be reflecting the state of photography in India today to some extent.[53]

Satish Sharma, associated with 'discovering' photographers such as Homai Vyarawalla,[54] and who wrote the catalogue essay for the Biennale, invoked French poets Paul Valéry and Charles Baudelaire; mentioned English painter and critic Roger Fry of the Bloomsbury group as 'the archbishop of art criticism'; noted that photography should be considered the 'handmaiden of science and industry'; and asserted that contemporary practitioners with their individual aesthetic should be respected as artists in their own right. Sharma expressed his dismay at the quality of the previous biennale, the lack of critical discourse and historical perspective:

> The first photography Biennale was ample proof of our stagnation; amateur Sunday photographer offerings faithfully echoed archaic 19th-century definitions of art in photographs that were pleasant, pretty, artificial pictures made in the superficial spirit of minor 19th-century painters by photographers who had not yet realized that painting itself was revolutionized by photography. That photography's invention had redefined concepts of Art. Photography had, in Picasso's words, 'liberated painting from the literary, from the anecdote and even from the subject'.
>
> Photographers are defining photography's territory, through the formalist exploration and formulation of photography's own aesthetic, away from the aesthetics and tradition of painting. Yet in India, photographers still painfully aspire to the status and styles of painters. Hidebound in ancient notions of Art and Artist, they fail to realize that their approach to photography needs to be more modernistic and holistic. Photography is not merely or just a fine art. It is too powerful a medium to be confined to such a role ...
>
> Photographers need to think of the role of photography in society and the effect of its images in the mass media. How they shape our lives. How advertising and movie images influence our idea ... much more than any simplistic, even powerful, photojournalism. How this never-ending flood of pictorial propaganda messages moulds our minds.[55]

Photography had always been integral to journalism, but it now developed a meaningful role as a professional 'leisure' activity pursued by talented amateurs sharing images in private venues and salons.[56] Professional photographers had begun teaching it as a formal discipline in educational, cultural, and art and design institutions. The later careers of several featured artists at the Second Biennale confirms the extent to which photography had become an established field, and the extent to which newer templates had enabled an overlap of trajectories. The exhibition featured work by Aloke Mitra, chief photographer of *The Telegraph* newspaper in Calcutta, known for his coverage of the Bangladesh War of 1971, and subsequently for his reportage of the Babri Masjid demolition in 1993.[57] Also featured were Harbans Mody who later produced the exhibition *She* (1996) that examined notions of femininity, reviewed in both the English-language and regional press; Neeraj Paul, son of veteran photojournalist S. Paul and later senior photo editor at the *Times of India* newspaper; and Rohit Chawla, later group creative editor at the *India Today Group* of news magazines and *Open* magazine.

Photography and the Press

India's print media in general underwent a dramatic change after Independence. We see a growing space for the newspaper, the tabloid, the magazine, and also what would be called the 'vernacular' press. Noteworthy publications which had a substantial impact included the *Illustrated Weekly of India*, *Life Magazine* and *Amrita Bazaar Patrika*. The Press Council of India, set up in 1966, became a self-regulatory body – today, regrettably, not as effective in terms of its original mandate. A few major photo studios such as Mahatta, Delhi Photo Studio and Kinsey Brothers also participated in press-related work in Bombay, Bangalore and Calcutta.[58]

In general, the photojournalistic histories of South Asia have been inadequately charted. We know of the work of Henri Cartier-Bresson, Margaret Bourke-White, Shambhu Saha and Sunil Janah, who became renowned for his stark documentation of the 1943 Bengal Famine that killed three million people.[59] Less discussed is the work of photojournalists working in the (mostly) English-language press with cameras such as the Speed Graphic, Rolleiflex or Leica. Homai Vyarawalla, Baldev Kapoor, R. Satakopan, T.S. Nagarajan, P.N. Sharma, Ram Dhamija, Raghubir Singh and Kulwant Roy, among others, began to be recognized mainly through the photo-dense *Illustrated Weekly of India*.[60] Following them, the extraordinary images of Kishor Parekh, S. Paul, Raghu Rai, Pramod Pushkarna and Prashant Panjiar came to represent a bold new kind of practitioner.[61]

Photography at this time also transitioned to colour, a shift most evident in Raghubir Singh, then working for *National Geographic*, who received film rolls from its international patrons. Generations of post-Independence practitioners were inspired by the methods of Robert Frank, Walker Evans, Paul Strand, Robert Capa, William Klein, Josef Koudelka, William Eugene Smith, Bruce Davidson, Robert Adams and Weegee.[62] With colour, Indian photographers started moving from realist documentary and journalism to other forms of lens-based practice including conceptual art. Ed Ruscha and Minor White seemed to influence Raghubir Singh, Ram Rahman, Ketaki Sheth, Sunil Gupta and Dayanita Singh, who also worked closely for some time with American photojournalist Mary Ellen Mark.[63] In the late 1980s, some of these practitioners were able to engage with the biggest names in cutting-edge contemporary photography in Europe/America – Garry Winogrand, William Eggleston, Lee Friedlander, Diane Arbus, Nan Goldin and Daidō Moriyama.

The journalism boom of the 1990s, coupled with television news, led to the demise of important image-oriented publications such as the *Illustrated Weekly of*

India, which closed in 1993. A new virality was established with images sent from the field via dial-up connections. This was how the press received Prashant Panjiar's frames of the demolition of the Babri Masjid in Ayodhya, for example.[64] Both English and regional-language media expansion were reinforced by major Indian newspaper houses such as the Times of India Group (Bombay), the Hindustan Times Group (New Delhi), the Eenadu Group (Hyderabad) and the Jagran Group (Kanpur), all driving India's 'economic miracle' of the 1990s and 2000s.[65] A major source of revenue for journalism, especially in print, was advertising (today accounting for over half the required funds), often used by the government to push its agenda. Print readership had increased, but was under increasing threat from cable networks. To keep pace, offset printing machines were imported, new photo-composition programmes and computerized techniques were developed, enabling the regional-language press to catch up with the privileged, resource-rich metros, and to expand their local reach. A surge in information consumption, increased literacy, new technology and private capital saw foreign direct investment in the Indian media sphere expand from the 26 per cent limit[66] to 100 per cent for niche, elite, photo-rich English-language glossies such as *Vogue*, *Marie Claire* and *Rolling Stone*.

This was not yet the time of citizen journalism, and it was perhaps for these reasons that pogroms such as the Gujarat riots or the Kargil War[67] seemed to have been less critically covered, and the question remains whether journalism at this time harmed rather than helped the so-called secular social fabric.

The Late 1990s

A major photography initiative of the 1990s was *India: A Celebration of Independence 1947–1997*, a collaboration of the noted American photography journal *Aperture* and the Philadelphia Museum of Art.[68] The exhibition travelled within the US and India (National Gallery of Modern Art, New Delhi; Lalit Kala Akademi, Chennai; and Victoria Memorial, Calcutta). It showcased the work of twenty-one photographers, many based outside India but frequent visitors documenting politics, daily life, cultural heritage, urban 'development' and India's complex elision of history and mythopoesis. There was growing international interest in the photographic construction of an India that, despite rapid change under the coercive pressures of globalization and neoliberal capitalism, 'lives outside time, in a kind of space that has never been usurped by alien forces', as the exhibition text remarked.[69]

Unlike the artists represented in earlier biennales and local exhibitions who consciously wove activism into their art, the image spectrum in this project was more experimental. The frank visual language consciously shifted away from the aesthetic of both abstraction and pictorialism, and instead drew upon social history and anthropology in order to meld the objectively staged image with the documentary thrust of photojournalism.[70]

The 1990s also saw India featured in two other important international photography exhibitions in the US: *Out of India: Contemporary Art of the South Asian Diaspora* (1997–98) at the Queens Museum of Art, New York, and *Women Artists of India: A Celebration of Independence* (1997) at 'A Gallery' in Chelsea, New York; both exhibitions recognized and validated internationalism in the South Asian artist community.[71] *Out of India* featured twenty-seven artists, the majority born in India but less than half of that group actually resident in the country. Other featured photographers were of Indian descent, and extendedly from Myanmar, Uganda, Ireland and the US. Some featured artists were already well-established internationally, including Satish Sharma, Pablo Bartholomew and Dayanita Singh, and had participated in the aforementioned biennales in India. Both exhibitions offered a dynamic array of themes – a re-visioning of colonial-era images (Ayisha Abraham),[72] documentary shots of the Indian diaspora in the US (Pablo Bartholomew), photomontages of Indian presence in the UK (Sunil Gupta), the interiors of power stations (Zarina Bhimji),[73] family portraits (Mohini Chandra),[74] Indian transvestites (Poulomi Desai),[75] religion-fuelled violence (Vijay Kumar), and from Pakistan, the image of a woman awaiting her lover (Shahzia Sikander).[76]

Other significant work themed around gender saw some women practitioners speak through performance and satiric staging. In the pioneering work of Pushpamala N., the photographer in costume is her own subject, i.e. both the gazer and the gazed upon. She produced themed series such as *Phantom Lady* (1996–98) and *Sunehre Sapne* (Hindi: 'Golden Dreams', 1998), and also extensively imaged familiar tropes from Indian cinema.[77] Anita Dube[78] developed a socio-political critique of gender through her work. Sonia Khurana[79] produced her video/photo series *Bird* (1999) which audaciously imaged the naked female body, while photographer and filmmaker Naveen Kishore created *Performing the Goddess: The Chapal Bhaduri Story* (1999),[80] a biography of the last female impersonator in Bengali theatre.

> The new, liberalized mode of citizenship was one in which the energies of public participation should be seen as coming from below rather than from the 'commanding heights' of the Planning Commission. It

> located the nation's destiny less in the heroic agency of a leader and more in the embodied and embedded impulses of everyday life. The language of faith and tradition, of consumerist desire, and of regionally chauvinist identifications might still at times trouble the sovereignty of the national project, but they attained, in this period, a new image of authenticity, the dignity of affective truth as compared to the alienating abstractions, the grand schemes of the Nehru years.[81]

Sheba Chhachhi[82] had consistently worked with women for decades, inscribing gender issues through the mode of social documentary and installation. Her work expanded in the 1990s when aspects of new media were merged with more traditional forms of representation.[83] In 1990–91, Chhachhi invited seven women activists to collaborate on developing a series of staged portraits around the women's movement in Delhi. Countering central, embedded notions such as the 'lie of objectivity', and the favoured concepts of the Western canon more generally, this project focused on recording and relaying an intimate, individualized sense of history. Photographer and subject in each case together built *mise-en-scène*s across radically diverse sites in Delhi, ranging from the steps of the Supreme Court of India to a single-room dwelling in a resettlement colony to the interior of a local bus:

> Each woman chose a place, a posture, materials and objects that she felt could speak of her and tell her story. Apa brought a small hut, meticulously made from a shoebox, glue and tinsel paper: 'my story is a shanty-town story'. Shanti borrowed an axe, spread wheat on the floor, opened her diary. ... A quasi-fictional representational method emerges, which draws on vernacular practices. ... Multiple selves appear, each woman includes a previous photograph within the setup, refusing to be contained within the essentializing unique portrait.[84]

These images offer a studied engagement with the protagonists, *their* particular agency, as the latter gaze at the viewer with determination and defiance, guiding their audience with the objects laid out before them, in locations selected by them. The subject-as-author approach presents alternatives to standard compositional methodologies of activism so as to present the underprivileged female citizen as multivalent, hybrid and emancipated. It draws upon a broader reading of pre- and post-Independence protests as well as the bazaar tradition of posed studio photography, including indigenous feminisms, the rural, and the poetic and devotional dimensions of historical figures.

Positioning the Private/Public Gallery

> Photography was to be taught under the Applied Arts department and as a two-year certificate course. It was later reduced to a subsidiary subject in the Applied Arts department – students of the Department of Painting, such as Bhatt and Katpitia, were never taught photography formally, and thus depended on the benevolence of Narendra Mehta, and his assistant, Ramachandra Kadam, for use of the dark rooms.
>
> – Diva Gujral[85]

As critical discourse around the arts rapidly evolved in the 1990s, scholars such as Nancy Adajania and Beth Citron theorized that the 1960s and 1970s had been 'context-changing' decades for the arts. This was because new technology enabled a blurring of genres and a hybrid aesthetic, as seen in exhibitions such as the group show, *Painters with a Camera* (1968).[86]

Yet for almost five decades post-Independence, photography had rarely been taught as a discipline in its own right, and many artists developed their lens-based practices without explicit training in the medium, often coming to it as part of a wider curriculum, for instance in the fine arts pedagogy of the renowned Maharaja Sayajirao University, Baroda.[87] Relevant to this history was the Aurobindo Ashram photo-school in Pondicherry, established after Henri Cartier-Bresson's visit in 1950.[88] The school provided a much needed platform for amateur photographers who were passionately experimenting with composition and technique, stepping away from pictorialism to create a personal narrative style which contrasted with the more mainstream journalistic mode for which Cartier-Bresson is acclaimed. In 1955 Robi Ganguli, an Ashram practitioner, organized the Pondicherry International Photography Exhibition, which received many fine entries.[89]

While the 1990s witnessed a swift expansion of the arts world in general, this decade also encouraged initiatives with a sharper digital and technological focus. Raqs Media Collective,[90] formed in 1992, is one example: its members were trained in mass communication and documentary film, but chose to enter the field of art and to develop a conceptual arts practice that often uses the photograph as a source or reference point.

The development of photography in India in the 1990s saw a deepening discursive relationship with the medium, along with more experimentation and greater technical sophistication. Display formats also underwent changes, with new photography categories in the biennales and in the general art exhibitions in state venues such as Rabindra Bhavan. There was also an expansion of photography along with the traditional media that had dominated Indian submissions to international large arts festivals.[91] In terms of systematic support, the 1990s reinforced a major gap: the valorization of the urban practitioner while marginalizing the arts practitioner based outside the metropolis, and categorizing the rural/folk artist as 'craftsman' or 'artisan'. Within the urban arts ethos, there was an accompanying proliferation of smaller, bazaar-based, cottage-industry initiatives in spaces dedicated to accommodating the regional 'artisan', such as Dilli Haat which opened in the capital in 1994.[92] This growth accompanied the worth of vintage textiles and 'exotic' handicrafts, together with high-end artworks. Boutiques and antique outlets, progressive bookshops and smart cafés sprang up in traditional areas such as Delhi's Hauz Khas village and Shahpur Jat, their once-provincial character now targeting tourists, the cosmopolitan elite and upper middle-class urban consumers. With them one also found small, sophisticated art galleries that sponsored, hosted and curated photography exhibitions.[93]

Although the festival and biennale models were a Western import, these were rapidly grafted on to the Indian arts scaffolding, as exhibition practices struggled to be cast as original rather than imitative. Until the 1990s, much of modern Indian art was seen as primarily decorative, and not credited with ideological depth or iconoclastic energy. It was the dedicated intellectual effort of scholars and critics which eventually led to the exponential growth of art and cultural studies pedagogy in India.[94] Art-historical and curatorial discourses also led international auction houses to seriously consider the 'modern' movement in Indian art, and to embrace Indian art as a complex and marketable commodity. Both the gallery and the auction house became quasi-academic spaces in their own right, influential venues through which to address artistic schools and styles, reinforcing the fact of Indian art now being negotiated on international terms, and seen as growing and succeeding in tandem with similar trends in other regions of South Asia.

An important venue here that consistently displayed photography through the late 1980s–90s was the Art Heritage gallery established by Roshen and Ebrahim Alkazi, and extendedly, at a slightly later time in the late 1990s, Sepia International, another gallery established in New York also by the same collector/connoisseur.[95] Art Heritage presented work by, among others, Mitter Bedi, who focused on industrial photography; Arun Kumar Mukherjee, who used Rolleiflex, Leica and 16 mm movie cameras for films; and Yog Joy, whose exhibition texts were composed by writer Mulk Raj Anand, and who served as president of the North India Accredited Press Photographers Association.[96] Works by many of the artists showcased in

India: A Celebration of Independence (1997) were shown in private galleries before being selected for international display. There were notable exceptions who we see presented at Art Heritage – Homi Kharas (whose mother Shirin was an active pre-Independence photographer) was not entirely recognized as a lensman in his own right, despite serving as editor of the well-known Agfa Photo Gallery magazine from 1955 to 1983. R.K. Bhardwaj, who later held that post, eventually became editor of *Photography Today*, India's first full-colour magazine, and was awarded honorary associateship of the India International Photographic Council.[97] The talented Shambhu Saha, known for his industrial photography, and O.P. Sharma (whose mentor was the pioneering Jehangir Unwalla), whose images were part of several books written in Hindi, including the influential *Rasa-Bhaava Darshan* (Hind Pocket Books, 1998), did not receive due international exposure and were unable to enter the art market, and hence today remain largely unacknowledged.[98]

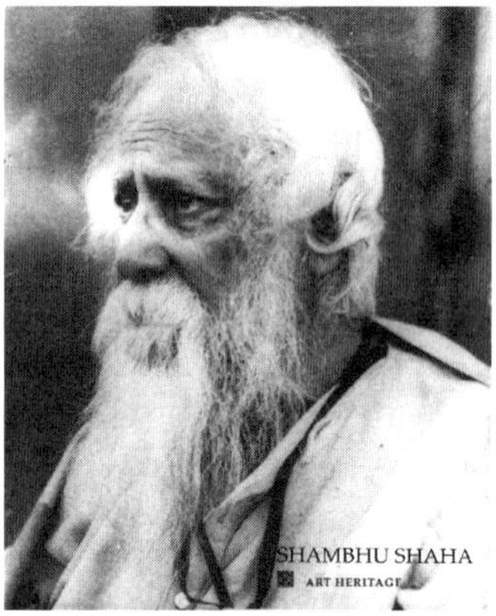

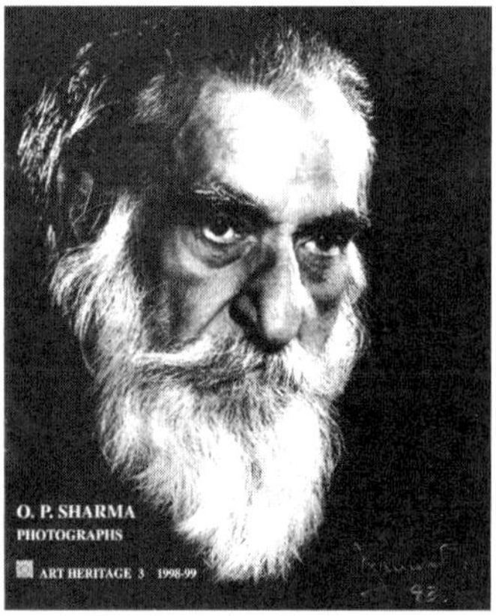

Shambhu Saha, 1996–97, O.P. Sharma, 1998–99, Art Heritage catalogues

Contextualizing his interview of international photographer Pamela Singh[99] for a late 1990s exhibition catalogue for Art Heritage, curator Peter Nagy of the Nature Morte gallery in Delhi identifies key figures involved in the deconstructive crossover paradigms that stimulated 'the Pictures Generation, 70s and 80s NY':

> Photographic work re-appropriated to painting and sculpture: David Salle, Robert Longo, Jack Goldstein, Thomas Lawson; on the other hand you had Richard Prince and Sherrie Levine, who were re-photographing other people's photos. Women artists such as Cindy Sherman, Louise Lawler, Barbara Kruger, Sarah Charlesworth and Laurie Simmons used semiotics, Psychoanalysis and Marxism.[100]

Nagy also quotes art critic Thomas McEvilley's view that India was post-modern *before* it turned modern. It was both a curious, if oblique, affirmation of the apparent deviation from entrenched Eurocentric grand narratives, and a reinforcement of 'vernacular' photography practices. This seemed to be evidenced by several private exhibitions in the 1990s that became catalysts for new lineages of practice as emerging from cultural theory. For instance, in his discussion of the work of Ketaki Sheth, critic Sadanand Menon invokes Indian professional photographers (Sooni Taraporevala, Mahendra Sinh, Raghubir Singh) along with renowned international adepts (August Sander, Diane Arbus, Bill Brandt, Brassaï, Weegee, Helen Levitt, Cartier-Bresson, Robert Frank, Lee Friedlander).[101] Artist Jyoti Bhatt writes about the work of Bindi Sheth. Artist K.G. Subramanyan writes about the work of Jyoti Bhatt, etc. And Sanjeev Saith,[102] who composes his own texts, embeds himself in his description of the predicament of the professional artist trying to negotiate an open market:

> [I have] begun to question what I photographed, how I photographed it, even why I photographed at all. I paused in an effort to distance myself from my past work, to pull my photographic idiom decisively away from the compulsion to speak a universally cogent language, and instead, to bring my own grammar as close as I could to the way I related to the common detail in my life, and in the lives of others about me. The episode was yet another example of the power that photography wielded in constructing my own personal equations. ...
>
> The danger lay in another direction as well. My photography was now straying beyond 'usage'. Till now, there had been no divergence between what I shot for myself, and what managed to appeal to others. This fortunate state had possibly been a result of the deference that I had accorded to my subject – always empathizing, always looking for good in it, never diluting the aesthetics of what lay before me by the imposition of my own will. Perhaps it was this positivism that had granted me with a continuing vocation. Now, with my visual *bhagyajanani* (Hindi: 'fortune maker') prompting me to address unease, conflict and distress, I faced what appeared to be two mutually exclusive compulsions: that of making a personally meaningful image, and that of making a living.[103]

Subramanyan meanwhile emphasized the need to support indigenous artisan traditions, to preserve India's priceless arts/crafts heritage and to protect it from the pressures of heavy commercialism and internationalism:

> At one time one fondly hoped that, in a mixed economy like ours, the artisan traditions and household arts will have a chance to survive, however precariously. And this could educate the new generation of artists and artisans. Even lead, perhaps, the powers-that-be to think in terms of a more human and value-based plan of development. But this seems unlikely; the government and the trading community are taking a great leap forward to hook up with the world economic forces. What concerns them most are export earnings, not human refinement; this makes one recall, with a tinge of sadness, William Blake's well-known lines: When nations grow old, the Arts grow cold / and Commerce sits on every tree ...
>
> In these circumstances the least we can do is to visually record the whole heritage, collect object specimens of the best kind, document methods of fabrication and use and house these objects and data in museums and archives region by region, speciality by speciality.[104]

Clearly, Subramanyan speaks for many fellow artists in this urging of the community to commit to effective custodianship of the arts traditions in order to produce locally relevant work in the era of globalization; and, equally, to resist the seductions of the profitable international art market as well as the cosmopolitan demand for a suitably 'Indian' view of the world.

Within India, leading artists were actively nurturing a closer relationship between modes and mediums. A prominent example is the late Vivan Sundaram, who in the early 1970s had started to examine his important personal archive of family photographs, primarily taken by Umrao Singh Sher-Gil; his maternal aunt was the acclaimed modernist painter Amrita Sher-Gil.[105] Sundaram often used photographs as compositional aids to pose his figures, drawing upon Amrita Sher-Gil's methods as a painter; though his pastel works from the mid-/late 70s in response to the Emergency are purely based on fine-art principles.[106] Along with Gulammohammed Sheikh, Sundaram proposed an Amrita Sher-Gil exhibition at the National Gallery of Modern Art in Delhi; this materialized instead at Rabindra Bhavan in 1972–73, with the images reproduced as large silver gelatin prints (almost 4 x 6 feet) by Navroze Contractor of the National Institute of Design, Ahmedabad.[107] In the 1980s, Sundaram began to rely on photographs as blueprints for his own paintings, and to develop his own prints. Lens-based media was evolving through Photoshop and other software, and even practitioners associated purely with fine art, such as Akbar Padamsee, were beginning to experiment with photography in their practice.[108]

Sundaram's work *Stone Column Enclosing the Gaze* (1992) that juxtaposed quotes by Roland Barthes with images by Ram Rahman, Dayanita Singh, Ketaki Sheth, Satish Sharma and Amit Bari, among others, testifies to his fascination for the photographic medium.[109] In 1994, he successfully organized an exhibition of photographs of Sher-Gil's works in Budapest, and this enabled him to orchestrate a similar exhibition at the Hungarian Arts Centre, New Delhi in 2000. This was also the year when Sundaram began to catalogue his collection of family photographs and consistently use this material in his own practice. This methodology underpinned several major exhibitions of his work, including *Re-take of Amrita* (2001), an immersive re-reading of the family archive.[110]

The late 1990s saw many independent photographers and artists producing more experimental work, and state cultural institutions expanding their presence – for instance, the Indira Gandhi National Centre for the Arts (IGNCA), New Delhi mounted the exhibition *Kashmir: A Passage in Time* (2005),[111] its images sourced from government archives and from the collections of the Associated Press and the Directorate of Advertising and Visual Publicity, under the aegis of the Ministry of Information and Broadcasting. Curated by Gayatri Sinha, the works were installed at the Mati Ghar on the grounds of the IGNCA. Among other hallmark shows curated by Gayatri Sinha were, *Woman/Goddess* (1998–2001)[112] and *Middle Age Spread: Imaging India 1947–2004*,[113] exhibited during the fifty-seventh year of Independence. Both were intended to push modern Indian photography from its early static, prescriptive and formal tenor into something more diverse, jagged, equivocal, self-conscious and satirical.

The curation of photography is still a relatively new field in India, led by researchers, practitioners and scholars, yet with the need for more formal training in the subject. In tracing photo-genealogies and linking these to the current moment, curators tend to merge formal roles with newly acquired positions of cultural mediator or arts pedagogue. Photographers now often prefer to curate their own shows, augmented by new technologies in exhibition practices. Before the digital explosion and its omnivorous allure of reproducibility, immediacy, simultaneity and mass circulation, it was the 'white cube' that contributed to the fetishization of the photograph as a singular art object. Dedicated photo galleries such as Tasveer (now closed) and Photoink[114] played (and continue to play) a vital role in showcasing contemporary work, even as practitioners such as Srikanth Kolari, Ryan Lobo, Swapan Nayak, Sohrab Hura, Kapil Das, Dhruv Malhotra, Madhuban Mitra and Manas Bhattacharya, among others, began to actively participate in the new global networks of image production and circulation.

In crucial ways, the internet, an apparently borderless photo gallery–library–archive, albeit with overt and covert control mechanisms, mandates and terms of engagement, has radically reduced practitioner dependence on the traditional gallery. However, earlier photographic cultures could not have survived, let alone flourished, without the physical gallery; and it remains indispensable in the contemporary arts scenario as well, despite the digital options to normative exhibition spaces.

The displaying of themed works by successful Indian photographers in both 'national' and private exhibition spaces also raises issues about the legacies of contemporary photo-artists and how these are valued by our cultural institutions. In the past, the National Gallery of Modern Art in Delhi had acquired classic colonial-era works as well as certain iconic contemporary works by Raghubir Singh, Raghu Rai, Dayanita Singh and Prabuddha Dasgupta.[115] Some of these practitioners draw on their background in photojournalism even as they also produce more densely symbolic, allusive, meta-textual, cross-media works as photo-artists in their own right.

Regional Photographic/Image Cultures in the 1990s

> To decolonize in the twenty-first century we need to historicize twentieth-century decolonization itself. What will this look like? Where will it anchor its questions: in the national modernities/and histories of postcolonial nation states? In the global geopolitics of decolonization and the Cold War? Should it be in the locational, vernacular registers of thought, movements and experience? Or perhaps in the global circuits of thoughts and movements?
>
> – Sanjukta Sunderason[116]

India's swift assimilation of the economic and social forces of globalization in the 1990s also led to a new vocabulary and symbolic grammar in the arts. These changes need to be understood in relation to the wider geopolitical solidarities and alliances being developed within and beyond postcolonial South and Southeast Asia, and other parts of the global South. One such optimistic ideological junction was the landmark Bandung Conference (1955),[117] and later the Afro-Asian People's Solidarity Association, where the agenda focused on reinforcing newly-won political sovereignty and self-determination, human rights, and reducing reliance on Western nations in terms of economic and cultural cooperation. Following the Bandung vein of internationalism, as a counter-narrative to the hegemonic Cold War discourses of the 1970s, I would also like to acknowledge the works of artists in the subcontinent such as the versatile Chittaprosad, who, like Sunil Janah was a member of the Communist Party of India, and documented the Bengal Famine of 1943.[118] In a recent interview, curator-critic Geeta Kapur, author of the seminal study *When Was Modernism: Essays on Contemporary Cultural Practice in India* (2000), re-contextualizes that historic conference, noting that a 'relatively recent revival' of the histories of Bandung and of the Non-Aligned Movement (formed in 1961, based on Bandung principles) 'has generated a dialogue around the idea of a new humanism developed during the founding moment of postcolonial consciousness', and that 'real politics and discursive re-evaluations need to acknowledge the historical conditions in which choices are made, whether utopian or pragmatic':

> If, for instance, developmentalism or the degree and kind of modernization are now subject to a more precise critique, it is only in hindsight – with a better understanding of capitalism's million maneuvers and a greater scientific knowledge of ecology.
>
> Even if the institutions of nation, state, and democracy have unraveled in negative ways, a critique that is irreversible produces a morbid impasse. Equipped to subsume the aspirations of a restless demos, capital produces spectres signaling 'lack' across all fronts except those that endorse its own triumphant expansionism. Even more so, then, troubled histories ... *need not* be considered demonstrations of some fundamental lack ... it may just be that lack itself provides the impetus for artists to call forth an avant-garde in displaced locations and diverse contemporalities.[119]

Affirming that 'the avant-garde depends on the particular historical conjuncture and the degree of responsiveness in the face of exigent forces', Kapur clarifies that she does 'not want to relativize this convergent force out of existence but rather to endorse radical claims from places and situations obscured by the hegemonic status of culture so easily assumed by both regressive and benign ideologies'.[120]

Along with India, other South Asian countries underwent huge changes in the 1990s under the pressure of globalization. These nations saw the emergence and consolidation of activism-oriented artists, art collectives and non-state cultural initiatives committed to presenting subaltern voices, and to offering creative and alternative responses to socio-political events as a form of resistance to state oppression. For instance, in Sri Lanka, the collective Theertha became prominent in 2000 after a decade of formative work, with the voices of artists from all walks of life responding to civil war atrocities perpetrated by the army.[121] Despite state censorship, the searing images of that violence found a platform through the work of international photojournalists reporting on the war, and through active practitioners in the field such as Stephen Champion.[122] The artist-collector-gallerist Dominic Sansoni regularly exhibited photography from the region, providing an incentive for other artists in his own space, also complemented through the Harold Pieris Gallery in the Lionel Wendt Centre in Colombo.[123]

One of the earliest established exhibition spaces in Nepal, the Siddhartha Art Gallery was opened in 1987, and under the pioneering guidance of Sangeeta Thapa showcased the works of Thomas Laird and Nicole Aquarone in 1993.[124] The adept lensman Kiranman Chitrakar, employed by Nepal's national television, formalized into a trust his family archive consisting of nineteenth- and early twentieth-century images taken by family members who were photographers for the Ranas, the dynastic rulers of Nepal.[125] These images are a stark contrast to late twentieth-century photography in Nepal which was often dominated by images documenting the prolonged and violent Maoist struggle against the state, seen also in publications such as Gopal Chitrakar's *People Power* (1992). Extensive work in this area was also produced by foreign correspondents/photojournalists such as Philip Blenkinsop.[126] In the case of Myanmar, after the 1988 student uprising the military junta targeted and jailed many dissident artists throughout the 1990s. Today, within the ethos of dictatorship one is concerned about the work and longevity of New Zero Art Space, for instance, established in Yangon in 2008 by performance artist Aye Ko who was inspired by the group show *Modern Art 90* that showcased the work of fifteen Burmese artists in 1990.[127]

The story was quite different, radically more expansive and inclusive, in Bangladesh during the 1990s. Under the direction of photographer-activist Shahidul Alam along with writer and anthropologist Rahnuma Ahmed, the Dhaka-based cultural organization and archive Drik provided a rich spectrum of media services including web development, photography/video/print production and exhibitions.[128] Through Alam's vision Drik came into wider focus when, in 1993, it mounted an exhibition of photos by international press photographers. This was inspired by a 1990 show based on images of the 1971 War of Liberation, the birth of Bangladesh as an independent nation, by veteran photographers Manzoor Alam Beg, Bijon Sarkar, Jahangir Kabir, Naib Uddin Ahmed, Mohammad Ali Salim, Shafiqul Alam Kiron and Rashid Un Nabi.[129] *Out of Focus* (1997), Drik's eighth annual exhibition, consisted entirely of images by amateur 'working-class' photographers, thus breaking with the tradition of featuring 'established' practitioners, i.e. professionals who use the medium to make a living.[130] Pathshala: The South Asian Institute of Photography (later renamed South Asian Media Institute) was established in Dhaka in 1998.[131] *Chobi Mela*, another image-focused cultural project, was initiated in Dhaka in 2000.[132]

In Bangladesh, which now hosts the Dhaka Art Summit, one of Asia's largest arts platforms for exhibiting international art and architecture, the 1990s were a vital moment of arts expansion, when

> Mahbubur Rahman, Tayeba Begum Lipi and Dhali Al Mamoon acquired skill in these [arts] technologies without formal training, and played a major role in encouraging younger artists to experiment. Artist-led collectives such as Shomoi, Britto Arts Trust, Only God Can Judge Me (OGCJM), Porapara and Santaran were instrumental in shaping a network and community of new media and installation artists, securing more visibility for multi-media and experimental art forms.[133]

There was also an exponential rise in the Pakistani art scene in the 1990s, with a focus on popular culture. Iftikhar Dadi's[134] iconic photographs of Karachi streets from the early 1990s - cinema hoardings, signage, political campaign advertisements, markets - present an otherworldly intensity of colour and a mesh of filmic trajectories. This provoked artists such as Shahzia Sikander to move on to animation and installation projects in which lens-based work played an essential role.[135] Iftikhar and Elizabeth Dadi's *Urdu Film* series (1994–2009), a suite of photographs of Urdu-language films shown on state-controlled television in the 1970s, examined television as a way of imagining and shaping collective ideas of 'success' or 'urban modernity' as exemplified by the projected interiors, fashion, personae and gestures.[136] This series influenced Huma Mulji and Rashid Rana's approaches to photography in the early 1990s, with the latter, trained in traditional painting techniques, eventually turning to digital media and photography in the mid-1990s.[137]

India too saw new film-inspired themes emerge in the photography of the 1990s, based on popular culture, the emergence of the nuclear family and the remake of historical/period narratives. There were practical reasons, as author William Mazzarella points out elsewhere, including the growth of an overseas market wherein production houses like Yash Raj Films opened offices in the

UK and the US, expanding the viewer demographic.[138] However the 1990s also witnessed the expansion of censorship within film, with both state and private interests entrenching and negotiating their stands as necessary, and with the heavy hand of the state often prevailing.[139] Key Bollywood films subjected to state and media scrutiny for their content included *Bandit Queen* (1994) and *Bombay* (1995), the latter based on the appalling religion-fuelled riots in that city in 1992–93.[140] Also on the list were *Kama Sutra: A Tale of Love* (1996) by Mira Nair, and the trilogy of *Fire* (1996), *Earth* (1998) and *Water* (2005) by Deepa Mehta, all declared socially offensive by cultural and political conservatives.[141] State censorship was extended to other art forms, including literature: Salman Rushdie's *The Satanic Verses* (1988),[142] banned in the Islamic world and in India, generating violent public protest and driving the author into hiding with an Iran-issued *fatwa* on his head; Taslima Nasreen's Bengali novel *Lajja* (Hindi: 'Shame', 1993),[143] written in response to the anti-Hindu riots in Bangladesh perpetrated shortly after the destruction of the Babri Masjid in Ayodhya by Hindu fundamentalist mobs in 1992. Dedicated to 'the people of the Indian subcontinent', this audacious text created a religio-political furore in Bangladesh. Facing death threats, Nasreen fled into exile, spending substantial periods in Sweden, Europe, the US and India.

Progressive practitioners, scholars, critics, activists and cultural figures in the subcontinent have always been aware of the need to contribute through their work to the strengthening of a democratic movement across South Asia, one that protects existent secular cultures and advocates for their reinforcement in the face of right-wing supremacist violence and suffocating hyper-nationalism. The current ethos – governmental suppression of dissent, combined with virulent nativist propaganda on the one hand and claustrophobic censorship on the other, continues to make it increasingly difficult, even dangerous, to produce the necessary image-based critique of the fundamentalist prejudice and phobia that is now infiltrating all domains of public culture, including the arts.

Perhaps the fact of state censorship being increasingly flexed in the form of overt and covert diktats in the film world was one reason many artists took to experimental video, rather than film, as a medium for activist expression in the 1990s – a trajectory that has gained incredible power in the digital age. In the later part of the decade, artists in the region actively developed new forms of documentary as social critique, using photography in a cross-pollination of perspectives, genres and techniques. A strong example of this mode of independent filmmaking is Amar Kanwar's *A Season Outside* (1997), part of a trilogy along with *To Remember* and *Night of Prophecy*.[144] Themed around the Indo-Pakistan border at Wagah in Punjab, the film intended to narrate 'the politics of aesthetics rather than the aesthetics of politics', with the film's aesthetic decisions coming from 'aesthetic dilemmas' that 'interrogate the self and the meaning of political engagement'.[145] The experimental trajectory of the 1990s extended into the next decade in terms of both form (mixed-media and installation) and content (scrutiny of the normative/status quo). This is apparent, for instance, in Kabir Mohanty's video work *Song for an ancient land* (2006),[146] which begins with photographic strips of images taken during the Mumbai riots and in the aftermath of the Ayodhya violence. Such works inscribe not just an activist commitment to social justice, but also invoke Indian artists' efforts 'to grasp subject matter obliquely in order to unfold multiple histories', to project an 'internalized understanding of the issues' and offer 'an active participation in the conditions that belie the understanding'.[147]

Since the 2000s, certain print and digital publications were committed to showcasing, supporting and studying photography, and have been crucial in generating wider public interest in the philosophical, cultural and technical aspects of image-making. Some of these were *Camerawork Delhi* (an initiative of photographers Sunil Gupta and Gauri Gill,[148] the latter focusing on the intimate documentation of local communities); *Punctum* (a South Asia-based publication managed by executive editor Lola Mac Dougall who also managed an earlier magazine, *Vislumbres*);[149] the archive of the Centre for Women's Development Studies, managed by Malavika Karlekar, co-editor of the *Indian Journal of Gender Studies*;[150] research by the Centre for Studies in Social Sciences, Kolkata;[151] and *PIX*, the theme-based independent photography initiative.

We also have to take into account three ubiquitous contemporary phenomena that have systematically blurred the demarcation of amateur and professional photography in the last two decades. First, the rise of 'citizen photography' or user-generated image content that has become influential in journalism. People record public events on cell phones and share their reportage via social media, which has become an aggressive platform for breaking news and is increasingly treated as a reliable source by the press. Second, the vast state and private surveillance industry and the innumerable security cameras that incessantly capture images of citizen activity in external and internal spaces, generate profiles, and use that data for specific ends. Third, the image as an entity *in itself* has acquired a completely new vitality and resonance through smart phones that render the internet accessible to South Asia's huge populations. Cheap instruments and data plans available for all demographics have enabled what might be termed the unstoppable and addictive 'mediatization' of subjectivity. Even illiterate or under-educated users can send voice messages, decode icons on a screen, glyphs on a keypad. Once-restricted personal horizons have radically expanded through 'selfie' culture and the uploading/forwarding of photos and videos on social media, each update already on the brink of digital obsolescence. Any user can now risk immersion in an uncensored (or self-censored) experience of image-making, editing and circulation, gradually becoming a self-appointed, intuitively self-trained, well-practised author–curator–archivist, and able to continuously reconfigure/share digital versions of the self and its realities.

Today, particularly with the sudden surge of generative AI applications on the web, the life of an image is apparently interminable, passes through innumerable hands, and is vulnerable to being ideologically and aesthetically manipulated and transmitted in any direction. To remain relevant, photographers and media practitioners are under pressure to continually adapt to the imperatives of each new digital paradigm and the ongoing expansion of digital viewership and authorship. Perhaps we are indeed moving in the direction of what the late Aveek Sen (1965–2021) astutely identified as 'a kind of intellectual and existential promiscuity, an all-absorbing hunger that is at once outwardly directed and inwardly trained' – the mode that photography must risk in order to 'break out of its documentary cage'; the practitioner 'must learn to look, as William Blake had put it (well before photography was invented), not only "with", but also "through", the eyes' – i.e. to penetrate with steady insight the personal and collective conditioning that obscures/distorts one's views and reinforces prejudices and exclusions, and to move past these mental filters to see things as they really are.[152]

Such mature, ethical practices of authentic 'looking'/seeing would no doubt add a surreal torque to the seductions and compulsions, deceptions and disruptions of contemporary lens-based practices in the context of our digital 'promiscuity', incessantly fed by the algorithmic maelstrom of pixels and packets, virtual avatars, deepfakes and chatbots – all conspiring to legally and illegally embed images at the farthest possible remove from our bygone photo-regimens of solid apparatus, fixed frames, perishable fragments and familiar visual taxonomies.

1 Midnight's Line

Sumathi Ramaswamy

2012

A FEDERATION
OF
CULTURAL ZONES
FOR INDIA

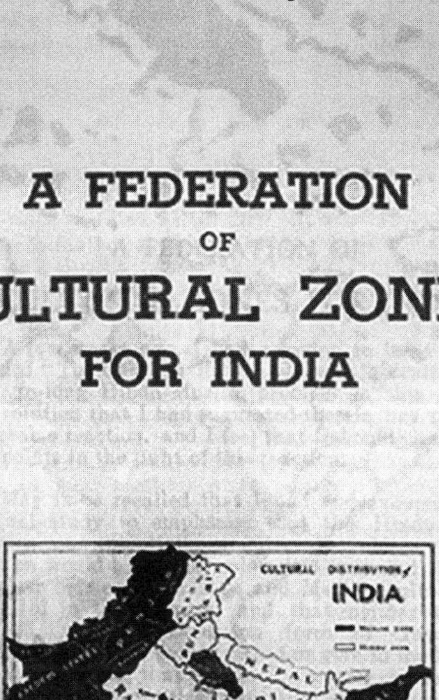

By
SYED ABDUL LATIF.

Section I
Post-Independence Paradigms

In 1947 the Radcliffe Line brutally split the Indian subcontinent into multiple nations to produce perhaps the most distinctive visual template of modern India, reconstructed over maps, photographs and other visual modes. This generated a pictorial lexicon that translates the lethal division of a land and its peoples into iconographies, both official and non-official. Such visuality further extends into administrative and popular demarcations of India's eastern and western borders, including what Sumathi Ramaswamy calls 'barefoot cartographers' working with vivid, familiar, mythical depictions of an indomitable Bharat Mata/'Mother India' alongside more familiar images of the nationalist political leadership of the subcontinent.

The depiction of nations born of the Partition thus inaugurates a political and historical visuality in India that would soon span the range of a photographic practice, transitioning from vast colonial vistas into the everyday of the postcolony.

An earlier version of this essay appeared in Iftikhar Dadi and Hammad Nasar, eds, *Lines of Control: Partition as a Productive Space*, London: Green Cardamom and Ithaca: Herbert F. Johnson Museum of Art, 2012, pp. 25–35. Grateful acknowledgements to Sumathi Ramaswamy, Iftikhar Dadi and Hammad Nasar for support.

Keywords, Names

Kashmir: Region on the borders of India, Pakistan and China with a complex and extremely disputed territorial demarcation that goes back to colonial treaties such as the Johnson Line of 1865 and the Macartney–Macdonald Line of 1899, and agreements such as the Instrument of Accession signed by Maharaja Hari Singh in October 1947 and a Ceasefire Line in 1949. The visual depictions of its borders remains a major issue of political hostility across the subcontinent. On 5 August 2019, the Government of India rescinded Article 370 of the Constitution which had accorded Jammu and Kashmir special status and allowed it the power to have a separate constitution. In 2023 the Supreme Court approved the legitimacy of this revoking of Kashmir's semi autonomy.

Radcliffe Line: Border defining boundaries of the new nations of India and East and West Pakistan, following recommendations of a commission chaired by Sir Cyril Radcliffe, a lawyer with no previous experience in cartography and who arrived in India for the first time on 8 July 1947. The border was delineated over five weeks and made public two days after Independence.

Kashmir/Kashmir insurgency, Mother India, Partition of India, see Keywords at the back of this volume.

Images

p. 1: *Cultural Distribution of India.* Cover of Syed Abdul Latif, *A Federation of Cultural Zones for India*, Hyderabad, 1938. © The British Library Board, IOR L/P&/J/8/689 f105. Reprinted with permission.

p. 9: V. Verma, *State of the Nation*, 23 January 1950: cartoon, *Organiser* (Delhi), Special Issue, 'Veer Number'. Courtesy *Organiser* (Delhi).

p. 13: Cover image of Urdu pamphlet, *Pakistan Kya He aur Kaise Banega* (What is Pakistan and How Will It Be Created), 1945; originally printed in 1939. Courtesy David Gilmartin.

pp. 16–17: (Left) *New India*, print bearing signature of Banshi, *c.* 1950 (publisher's information not decipherable); Priya Paul Collection @ Tasveer Ghar. (Right) *New India No. 2*, print bearing signature of Sushil Das, published possibly by Empire Calendar Manufacturing Co., *c.* 1950s–1960s; Priya Paul Collection @Tasveer Ghar.

> The border is the line where there is nothing to see.
>
> – Nicholas Mirzoeff[1]

Is there an inescapable hegemony of the cartographic line ushered in by the modern science of mapping, a hegemony that has transformed Earth into a geo-coded world and all those who inhabit such a bounded world into subjects of the line?[2] This is the question that provokes the reflections that follow in this essay that focuses on one specific cartographic boundary – the so-called Radcliffe Line – that began to be drawn in July 1947 and was legislated into existence a few weeks later at midnight on 14 August, with the formal end of British rule in the South Asian subcontinent. While this act of cartographic drawing marks the inaugural moment of two nation states, India and East and West Pakistan, as reconfigured geo-bodies on the face of the earth, it also set in motion a history of tense regional confrontation, war and violence that has remained with us – unresolved – to this very day. In the dash and in the line, Gunnar Olsson suggests, lies the history of cartography.[3] In the dash and in the line also lie the history of the modern nation state, and the fate of those who inhabit that bounded realm as citizen-subjects defined and controlled by the new limits materialized by scientific cartography.

Drawing the Line, Martyring the Map

> The boundary is the imaginary line that draws attention to itself by violence.
>
> – Gilberto Zorio[4]

Inspired by Michael Taussig's call to allow the image to billow out into our driving concept and to power the engines of our analysis, I begin with a striking image that appeared on the cover of *Time* on 27 October 1947, a little over two months after the British formally withdrew from their Indian empire.[5] Titled *India: Liberty and Death*, the image features a demonic four-armed naked female figure, human skulls adorning her head, wielding a bloody dagger which she plunges into her own right breast which the other hand clutches; the breast in turn is placed over that part of the map of India that a cartographically literate reader would identify as Punjab, onto which drips vivid red blood from the mutilated organ. While the outline map of 'India' (out of which the demonic figure seemingly erupts) is coloured yellow, and with Kashmir unambiguously part of it, 'Pakistan' (also left unnamed) is green, its eastern wing conforming more to the 'notional' rather than actual boundary awarded by Radcliffe's Boundary Commission.

We learn from the printed attribution that the image is the work of Ukraine-born Boris Artzybasheff, one of *Time*'s most important illustrators active between 1941 and 1965. And yet, the work might reflect not only Artzybasheff's artistic predilections for rich colours, bold design and imaginative symbolism that has been traced to Russian and Byzantine roots, but also the spirit of the accompanying cover story that it helped illustrate and that is tellingly titled 'INDIA–PAKISTAN: The Trial of Kali'. For the brutal ongoing slaughter that the subcontinent was witness to in those apocalyptic months of 1947, the editors of *Time* put Kali herself on trial. Introducing her to the magazine's readers as 'goddess of death and catastrophe, wife-conqueror of the eternal Siva, the dancer,' the cover story insisted, 'Kali, the Black One, could stand as symbol (or perhaps as scapegoat) for the horror that had [*sic*] walked hand in hand with bright liberty into India.' The essay concluded that 'the recent sin' of death and destruction 'sprang from Kali, from the dark and universal fear which rests in the slime on the blind sea-bottom of biology'.[6]

As we know, there has been a morbid fascination in the modern West with Kali, which also has its roots in the British colonial preoccupation with this figure variously described by anxious and fearful administrators as 'the goddess of death and destruction', and a 'terrible goddess' whose worship appealed to 'the grossest and the most cruel superstition of the masses'.[7] The importance of the Kali figure in the Hindu-Indic religious imagination notwithstanding, *Time*'s image is quite idiosyncratic both in associating the divine form of this particular goddess with the modern geographic form of India, and also in the visual innuendo that she had turned from attacking cosmic demons (and possibly the British colonizer) to destroying the map of the country itself. In other words, there is no precedent that I know of in the Indian pictorial archive for this particular image, and this fact itself makes it singular, but also problematic in its proposition that the catastrophic violence that accompanied the traumatic partition of the subcontinent had nothing to do with the British. Instead, some primordial force ('black grace') as embodied by this ferocious goddess had erupted from the very soil of India to destroy its people.

And yet, this was not the only provocative image of a violated map of India that *Time* published. A little over a year earlier, on 22 April 1946, it printed another cover with the provocative title *Mohamed Ali Jinnah: His Muslim Tiger Wants to Eat the Hindu Cow*.[8] Created by another famous illustrator for the magazine, the Russia-born Boris Chaliapin, this image shows two tigers attacking the map of India, their claws tearing away at the areas we know of as Punjab and Bengal, while a (British?) lion watches from the margins – possibly a sign that the empire was already retreating from the scene of impending violence; a sinister-looking Muhammad Ali Jinnah (the avowed Father of Pakistan) is in the foreground of the image, his appearance on the cover with its inflammatory title indelibly associating him – for good or bad – with the macabre scene in the background. Unlike the Artzybasheff image which to the best of my knowledge was not appropriated by the Indian media, the Chaliapin cover was republished soon after in *Chitramayi Jagat*, a Marathi-language newspaper of Hindu nationalist inclination, with a title that translates as 'From the Perspective of America: The Question of Hindustan'.[9] In this new context, the image feeds into a growing Hindu and Indian nationalist discourse about the 'vivisection' of India, and the martyrdom of its map, as we will see.[10]

Between the dates of publication of these two lurid cover images in the distant United States occurred a singular drawing event – a new all-important line made its appearance on the Indian cartographic landscape with bloody consequences. Its arrival into our already geo-coded world has been eerily, and satirically, captured in a 1966 poem titled *Partition* by W.H. Auden, which curiously leaves unnamed the line's creator as well as the land that was catastrophically divided by his cartographic act:

> Unbiased at least he was when he arrived on his mission,
> Having never set eyes in this land he was called to partition
> Between two peoples fantastically at odds
> With their different diets and incompatible gods.
> 'Time,' they had briefed him in London, 'is short. It's too late
> For mutual reconciliation or rational debate:
> The only solution now lies in separation ...'
>
> Shut up in a lonely mansion, with police night and day
> Patrolling the gardens to keep assassins away,
> He got down to work, to the task of settling the fate
> Of millions. The maps at his disposal were out of date
> And the Census Returns almost certainly incorrect,
> But there was no time to check them, no time to inspect
> Contested areas. The weather was frightfully hot,
> And a bout of dysentery kept him constantly on the trot,
> But in seven weeks it was done, the frontiers decided,
> A continent for better or worse divided.

> The next day he sailed for England, where he quickly forgot
> The case, as a good lawyer must. Return he would not,
> Afraid, as he told his Club, that he might get shot.[11]

Poem though it might be – a work of imagination – Auden captures in spirit the air of confusion, haste and melancholy that hangs over the work of Sir Cyril Radcliffe and the two Boundary Commissions – one in the west for Punjab and the other in the east for Bengal – that he was appointed to chair, soon after the announcement on 3 June 1947 that British India was indeed to be divided. That announcement itself (that most people heard over the radio at 7 p.m. Indian Standard Time or read in newspapers the following day) was unaccompanied by maps or territorial specificities. Indeed, it was not until 17 August, three days after Pakistan was born, and two days after India was created, that the new boundaries were made public knowledge to the very people whose lives were to be catastrophically transformed by this imperial act of inscription on paper and with pen. Between 3 June and 17 August, the map as artefact flickers in and out of the official records, at times a concrete object over which men pored and pondered, at other times a spectral presence, sometimes even a virtual nonentity. If we have become convinced, especially under the influence of geographer and map historian J.B. Harley, that maps anticipate and enable empire, the summer of 1947 in India should perhaps persuade us of the contrary truth: namely that empires can possibly be dismantled without the crutch of the map, or at least without the help of good ones.

Much has been made of the fact that Radcliffe, 'India's mapmaker',[12] was a career lawyer with no first-hand knowledge or experience of the subcontinent. For Radcliffe's colleagues in the colonial administration this in itself was a virtue, seemingly conferring upon him an aura of impartiality. Similarly, like him, the South Asian members of the two Boundary Commissions were lawyers, and although we can presume that modern schooling would have given them all some modicum of geographical knowledge, this does not mean that they were necessarily adept at interpreting complicated maps of the terrain they were commissioned to partition over the course of a mere six weeks. Scholarly interpretations of the available record insist that the maps placed at Radcliffe's disposal were inaccurate, inappropriate or in some cases simply unavailable.[13] Leonard Mosley, a foreign correspondent whose reminiscences of this fraught period have been used by many historians, writes that one of Radcliffe's principal worries was finding a map of suitable scale to carry out his task. 'It seems extraordinary that when you have to decide the fate of 28,000,000 people you are not even given the right map to do it with,' comments Mosley, who goes on to colourfully observe, 'With the slings and arrows of importunate Muslims, Hindus and Sikhs whistling about his ears, Radcliffe took up the largest contour map he could find and began to draw.'[14] The French journalist Dominique Lapierre quotes Radcliffe as saying, 'The equipment I had at my disposal was totally inadequate. I had no very large-scale maps.' It was not just a matter of adequacy but also of accuracy. 'The information provided on those [official maps] I did have sometimes proved to be wrong. I noticed the Punjab's five rivers had an awkward tendency to run several miles away from the beds officially assigned to them by the survey department.'[15] Locked away in his 'lonely mansion', Radcliffe had little exposure to either the land he divided up or the people who lived on it, and neither he nor members of his two committees had time to undertake detailed foot, aerial or hydrographic surveys. So in the end 'they retreated behind closed doors, working from maps using pen and paper, rather than walking the land and grasping for themselves the ways in which vast rivers, forests and administrative districts interlocked and could best be separated'.[16] Midnight's line certainly appears to have had a fraught birth, with tragically little forethought or expertise brought to bear on its drawing.

If the mighty British Raj in its last days showed a curious *lack* of map-mindedness as it went about its business of drawing lines and withdrawing from the subcontinent, its colonial subjects on the contrary demonstrated an unusual and surprising flair for the deployment of maps and faith in cartographic efficacy in the immediate years leading up to Partition, and especially in the months before and after August 1947. All of a sudden, maps began to be invoked and used in very revealing ways. Penderel Moon, a senior colonial administrator, writes of attending a meeting convened by the Muslim League in Lahore in late June in a large private home:

> On the floor and on a big table a number of maps of the Punjab were strewn about, variously coloured and chequered so as to show the distribution of the population by communities. We all fell to poring over these maps. It became plain in a very few minutes that no-one had any definite idea where we should claim that the dividing line should run ...[17]

In turn, one of the Muslim League members of the Punjab Boundary Commission, Muhammad Munir, wrote in deep suspicion of Radcliffe's secretary

Christopher Beaumont's 'distinctly pro-Hindu leanings': '... whenever I went to his office, I found him poring over a large map and was surrounded by Hindus.'[18] So much so that over the course of July 1947, the two Boundary Commissions set up by the British were inundated with petitions that resorted to maps as objects of persuasion. To be sure, the presence of maps in these 'memorials' was a response to the official request that all memoranda submitted by interested parties 'should be accompanied by such maps as may indicate the proposed line of demarcation between the two new Provinces'.[19]

Nonetheless, the fact that each of the interested parties rallied around and created maps is important to note, as is the fact that in the deliberations before the Commissions, they debated each other cartographically on the placement of various dots and dashes and lines. We do not know who actually drew these maps, nor the mechanics of their production, but it is revealing that in producing such artefacts, these men did not have access to official Survey of India maps which had been since the Second World War restricted to 'official use only'.[20]

On both sides of the projected dividing line, various individuals also resorted to the media to publish their aspirational maps of the new nation(s). Like *Time*'s lurid images, some turned to the imagery of violation and martyrdom, especially on the Indian side of the impending border. Thus on 14 August 1947, the eve of Indian Independence and the day of the birth of the new states of East and West Pakistan, the Hindu nationalist weekly *Organiser* (whose masthead continued to carry a large outline map of undivided India into the 1950s), published a cartoon to mark the event. Titled 'The Wise Pandit', the cartoon presents the body of a woman, her face contorted in pain, laid out transversely across a map of undivided India. Jawaharlal Nehru, soon to be sworn in as Prime Minister of independent India, is seated on a cushion outside the nation's geo-body, and hacks away at one of her arms (stretched out over the land that had been declared Pakistan on that day) with a sword in one hand, while his other seems to pull at her hair (laid out over the disputed territory of Kashmir); a disembodied Jinnah snarls at him. The brevity of the caption in (garbled) Sanskrit underscores the menace implicit in this illustration: 'Total destruction caused by the evil Pandit [Nehru]'.[21] Three years later, on the eve of the declaration of India as a secular republic on 26 January 1950, a cartoon captioned 'State of the Nation' showed an anthropomorphized Indian geo-body – of ambiguous gender – in tears over its dismemberment by daggers, drops of blood spilling out from the severed parts; we are not told who wields these daggers but there is an implicit suggestion that the vengeful assault is the project of Pakistan.

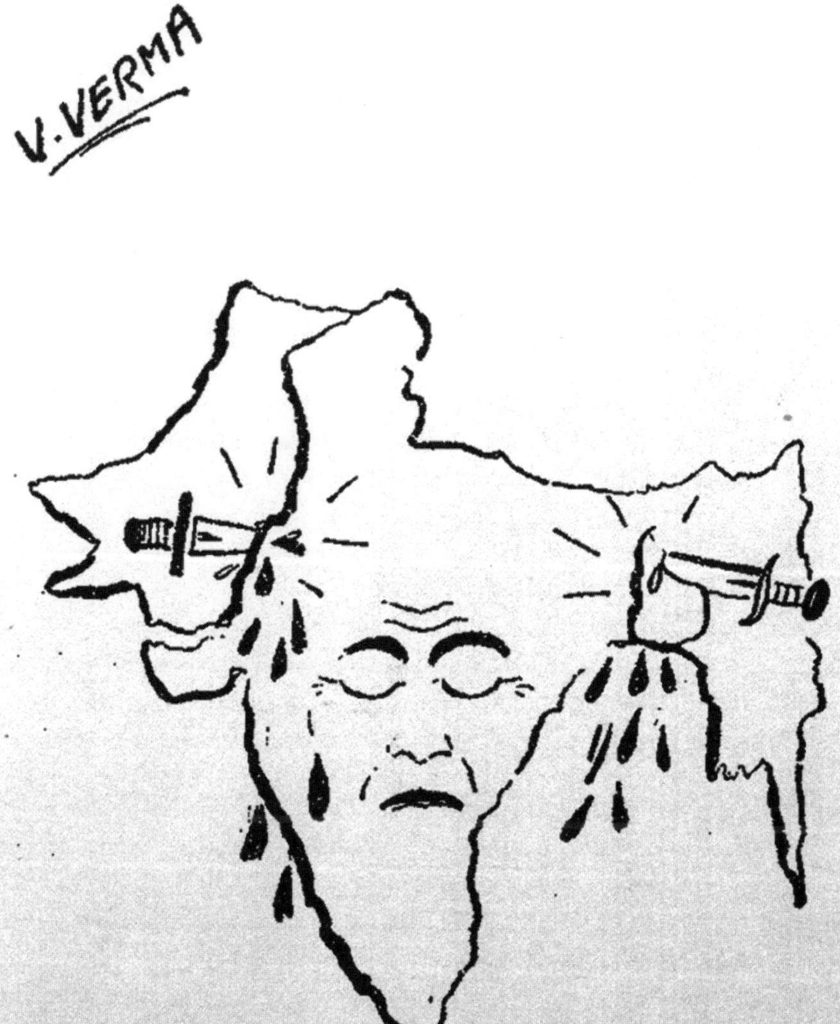
V. VERMA

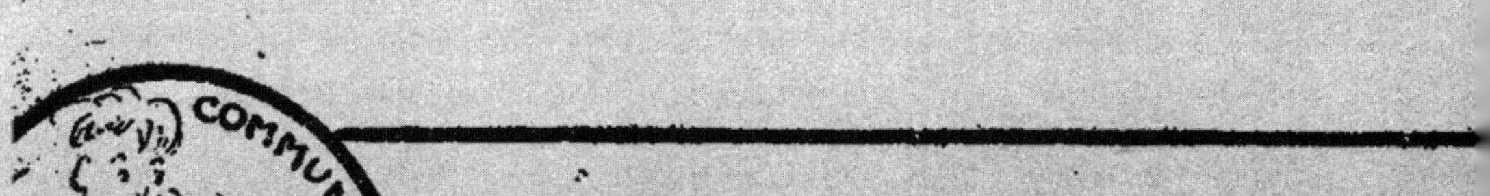

The Hindu nationalist *Organiser* is at the other end of the ideological spectrum from Gandhi, but it is worth recalling that that exponent of nonviolence used the trope of 'vivisection' (the cutting up of the body of a living organism for purposes of scientific experimentation or research) to refer to the territorial partitioning of India to which he was fiercely opposed. Even Nehru, whose secular-socialist vocabulary did not usually resort to the somatic idiom, lamented, '... but above all, what was broken up which was of the highest importance was something very vital and that was the body of India.'[22] And indeed, from at least the closing decades of the nineteenth century, the territory variously called 'Hindoostan', 'British India' or just 'India' in colonial maps and laid out as empty cartographic space within a graticule of latitudes and longitudes was also contrarily imagined by nationalists as the body of Bhārat Mātā ('Mother India'),[23] and gloriously pictured in all manner of visual media ranging from oils and acrylics to chromolithographs and cinema.[24] Thus for many involved in visual labours on the Indian side of the new border, it was not just the map of India that was being violated when midnight's line was finally announced, but Mother India herself.

Teaching the Nation's Map Form, Artfully

> We have lived within the lines we have traced, and been made the subjects we have become.
>
> – John Pickles[25]

We do not yet know of the precise mechanisms by which Indians or Pakistanis began to learn of the shape and contours of their newly formed countries, given the confusion that prevailed for several days on both sides of the border following Independence. Learning the new shape of their nation must have especially come as a shock to the citizens of Pakistan, for their country indeed more or less turned out, as Jinnah famously feared in 1944, 'maimed, mutilated, and moth-eaten',[26] divided in two parts, with hundreds of miles of hostile territory separating them. Not least of the cartographic conundrums to contend with in the years leading up to the Partition was that most of the principal sponsors behind the idea of Pakistan, including (and especially) Jinnah, were strategically vague about the shape and form of their homeland.

As David Gilmartin writes, 'The two-nation theory, the basis for the Muslim League's Pakistan demand, was a fundamentally non-territorial vision of nationality, and for most Muslims, the meaning of Pakistan did not hinge primarily on its association with a specific territory.'[27] Even the man credited with coining the term 'Pakistan' in 1933, the Cambridge-based aspiring lawyer Choudhary Rahmat Ali, who had a clearer sense than others of the territorial contours of his imagined nation, did not at first include maps in his pamphlet *Now or Never: Are We to Live or Perish for Ever?*,[28] circulated to British and Indian delegates to the Third Round Table Conference in London in November–December 1932 and released as a public appeal on 28 January 1933.[29]

In 1935, however, a two-page letter addressed to the House of Lords (which was then considering the Government of India Bill that focused on, among other complex issues, the partial reorganization of the provinces and granting them greater autonomy) included a header image of a map of British India. The parts coloured green (associated with Islam) covered Baluchistan, Sindh, the North West Frontier Province, Kashmir and Punjab, and was named 'Pakistan'; the rest was marked as India.[30] Rahmat Ali published several maps over the next decade that clearly point to the cartographic imperative at work in modern nationalist imaginations, even for those for which territorial clarity and certitude are problematic. It is clear from such images that Rahmat Ali's future 'Pakistan' would be a bounded territory that lay mostly in the north-western part of southern Asia, although its boundaries shifted over the years and across these maps.

Rahmat Ali was based in the United Kingdom, but he was not alone in generating such aspirational maps, reminding us of Thongchai Winichakul's insistence that 'a modern nation state *must* be imaginable in mapped form'.[31] We learn from Yasmin Khan that in the subcontinent in the months leading up to August 1947, Jinnah was inundated by fan mail which included 'different maps of Pakistan carved in wood'.[32] Even prior to 1947, images of wildly different, variously named geo-bodies proliferated in the public domain, all of them nevertheless resorting to the protocols of scientific cartography and the use of lines to create bounded spaces. They also without fail took the mapped form of British India as the starting point for their imaginations. It is not clear whether the creators of these maps necessarily saw their new homeland as wholly separate from 'India', even though the lines and hatchings of cartography projected the certitude of unambiguous belonging and territorial homogeneity that existed perhaps only on paper.

Thus, in 1938, Syed Abdul Latif, a retired university professor of English at Osmania University in the southern Indian princely state of Hyderabad, published a pamphlet titled *A Federation of Cultural Zones for India* whose cover image was a map titled *Cultural Distribution of India*. The dark-coloured 'Muslim zone' included territories scattered all over the map of India, in contrast to Rahmat Ali's more compact imagination.[33] Around the same time, under the patronage of Nawab Sir Muhammad Shah Nawaz Khan of the princely state of Mamdot in Punjab, a map was published showing a 'Quinquepartite Confederacy'. Constituted by various federated units, it included the 'Industan Federation' [sic] which roughly occupies the place marked Pakistan in today's maps, along with the entirety of Kashmir. Neither of these maps uses the name 'Pakistan', notwithstanding the name's appearance on Rahmat Ali's maps from slightly earlier in the decade. The word 'Pakistan' did appear in a bilingual map (in Urdu and English) that was printed on the cover of a pamphlet titled *Khilafat-i-Pakistan Scheme* in 1939, and later recycled in 1945 on the cover of another pamphlet whose Urdu title *Pakistan Kya Hai? Aur Kaise Banega??* translates as *What is Pakistan? And How Will It Be Created?*.[34] On this map, a territory called 'Pakistan Caliphate' stretched from the western edges of British India to the eastern, claiming the trans-Himalaya and much of the Hindi-/Hindustani-speaking belt of northern India; the remaining landmass was given the Arabic descriptor *'al-ard Allah'* (translating as 'God's Earth', or territory inhabited by non-Muslims but under the protection of Islam pending imminent conversion).

In retrospect, it is all too easy to dismiss such visualizations as fantasies not worthy of our contemporary attention; and indeed, little heed has been paid to such aspirational maps in the existing scholarship on the idea of Pakistan that I have read. Nations, however, yearn for territorial form, and these mapped wishes are symptomatic of that yearning, but also revelatory of what I have called the hegemony of the cartographic line. Ayesha Jalal has persuasively argued that Jinnah and his core followers, until the very eve of the actual partition, generally operated with the notion of shared sovereignty, 'which seemed the best way of tackling the dilemma posed by the absence of any neat equation between Muslim identity and territory'. Thus, the boundaries between 'India' and the proposed new homeland of India's Muslims had to be 'permeable and flexible, not impenetrable and absolute'.[35] Inevitably though, as Muslim nationalists rushed to materialize on paper their contending visions of 'Pakistan', the flexible imagination of shared sovereignty began to be undone by cartography's lines of apparent certitude.

The adherence to protocols of statist cartography is apparent as well in non-official maps of independent India, which began to appear in the bazaars and streets of that reconfigured country around and after August 1947. Such maps are primarily the work of artists who I have called 'barefoot cartographers', some of whose practices I have traced back to the closing decades of the nineteenth

كُنتُم خَيرَ اُمَّةٍ اُخرِجَت لِلنَّاسِ تَامُرُونَ بِالمَعرُوفِ وَتَنهَونَ عَنِ المُنكَرِ وَتُؤمِنُونَ بِاللّٰهِ (آل عمران ۱۱۰)

تم ان سب امتوں سے بہتر ہو جو لوگوں میں ظاہر کی جا چکی ہیں۔ کیونکہ تم نیکی کا حکم دیتے ہو بدی سے منع کرتے ہو اور اللہ پر ایمان رکھتے ہو

پاکستان کیا ہے؟

اور

کیسے بنے گا؟؟

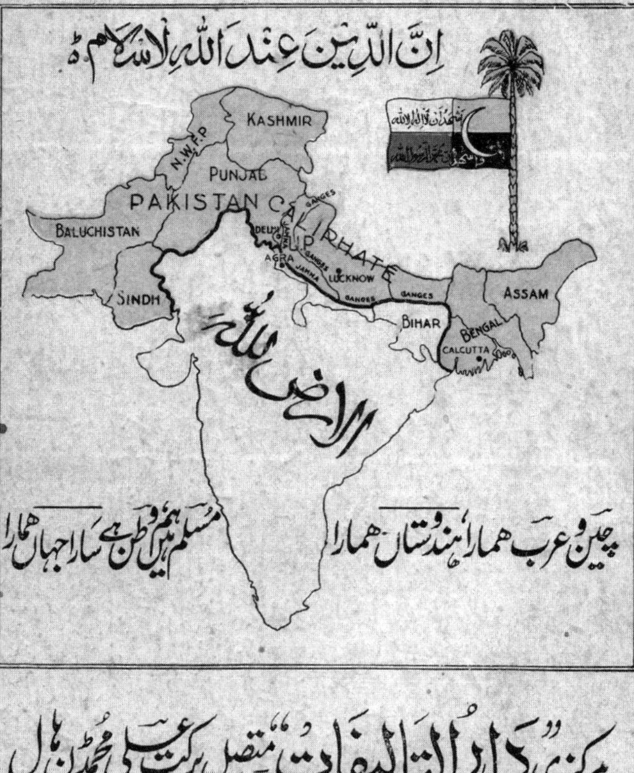

مرکزی دار التالیفات متصل برکت علی محمڈن ہال

بیرون موچی دروازہ۔ لاہور

century.[36] These 'artful' mapmakers of the street and the bazaar have a critical and constitutive role to play in producing and disseminating knowledge about the terrain of the nation among the citizenry. I would even propose that it is through the labours of barefoot cartography and such artful mapmakers – more so arguably than through the highly specialized operations of the state or science – that many Indians became familiar with the shape of national territory that they inhabited as citizen-subjects. This was especially true during the colonial period when in most schoolrooms across the country, but especially in rural India where the majority lived, geography books, atlases, maps, globes and other such artefacts were scarce objects that hardly anyone would have encountered in their daily lives. In contrast, diverse creators of mass-produced and commercially available printed and illustrated materials and goods – cheap, numerous and ubiquitous – attempted to reach the average Indian and deliver their varied image-messages. And yet, the knowledge of the terrain of the country that is disseminated through barefoot cartography and bazaar art is inflected by the somatic and worshipful, the commercial and the libidinous, so that 'India' rarely appears as empty social space as it does in normative maps marked by lines and grids. Within the vibrant templates of artfully mapped Mother India, bodies appear to matter more than boundaries, the affective more than the abstract.

Consider a print titled *New India*, possibly published sometime between Indian independence on 15 August 1947, and the so-called 'accession' and 'integration' of India's princely states between August 1947 and 1951, and the states' reorganization that began in the mid-1950s and changed the internal boundaries as well of the partitioned nation. The lion capital (the newly installed national emblem) and the tricolour national flag at the top of the print suggest that this image was possibly meant to celebrate the arrival, on the political landscape, of the Republic of India on 26 January 1950. Although 'India' is not named as such, and is instead cartographically depicted as a proliferation of numerous constitutive units, all meticulously delineated and named, the newly created Pakistan is identified (as are neighbouring new nations Nepal, Burma and Ceylon), the colour green reserved in many such maps and prints for the new Muslim country. This print adheres to the terms of state cartography in its general conformity to national boundaries as these began to be inscribed in normative maps after August 1947. And yet, what sets *New India* apart from normative maps of the country and makes this an instance of barefoot cartography, in the way I have defined it, is the presence of the heads of the leaders of the nation – the 'big men' of India – arranged in roundels around its borders. It is almost as if the newly-won national territory cannot be merely shown as empty cartographic space, marked off by geometric lines and blocks of hues, and instead needs the legitimizing presence of these faces, left unnamed but well known to any patriotic citizen as the men who had led India to freedom. These familiar faces then appear to introduce the recently configured national territory (the nation's 'geo-body') to the citizen-subject, lending their recognizable – and possibly comforting – presence to the new spatial reality that had come to fundamentally alter the lives of everyone on the subcontinent after 14/15 August 1947.

Compare this to a print titled *New India No. 2*, in which such 'big men' are displaced by the Everyman, tilling the soil of the nation to yield a rich harvest, while Gandhi smiles down on vignettes of the patriotic-bucolic (although one suspects that he might not have entirely approved of the presence of the industrial-scale technology in the fields of Nehruvian India!). This print also illustrates the contrary imperative to show Indian national territory as one homogenous whole, as opposed to *New India's* colourful mosaic, even while East Pakistan's very existence is completely disavowed.

Indeed, in such prints, the commitment to showing the Radcliffe Line – whose very drawing resulted in such displacement, unspeakable trauma and bloodshed – is inconsistent at best, and ranges from adhering strictly to its course to producing some semblance of it to completely dissolving (parts of) it.[37] Instead, the imperative appears to be to fill in empty cartographic space with all manner of activities and bodies, most often the torsos and heads of the new 'big men' of independent India: Gandhi, Nehru and others. This is because, as I have suggested elsewhere, barefoot cartography in India, even while cheekily reliant on the state's cartographic productions, also disrupts them by injecting the anthropomorphic, the devotional or the maternal into the spaces of secular science. It thus has an affective and worshipful, even idolatrous, investment in national territory, in contrast to command cartography's geometrical, instrumental, empirical grids of certitude and lines of power. This is most apparent when we turn to images where a benevolent Mother India is shown occupying the map of India. Soon after Independence, P.S. Ramachandra Rao – who had produced other such images in the past – painted a bodyscape in which Mother India's sari, clad in the new national tricolour, is arranged to suggestively approximate the shape of India in a manner that appears to leave out the new national territory of Pakistan, East and West.[38] More recently, an artist by the name of Appu painted a bodyscape where too Mother India, clad in the national tricolour, stands against a silhouette of a map of India in which both Pakistan and Bangladesh have not been incorporated.[39] All

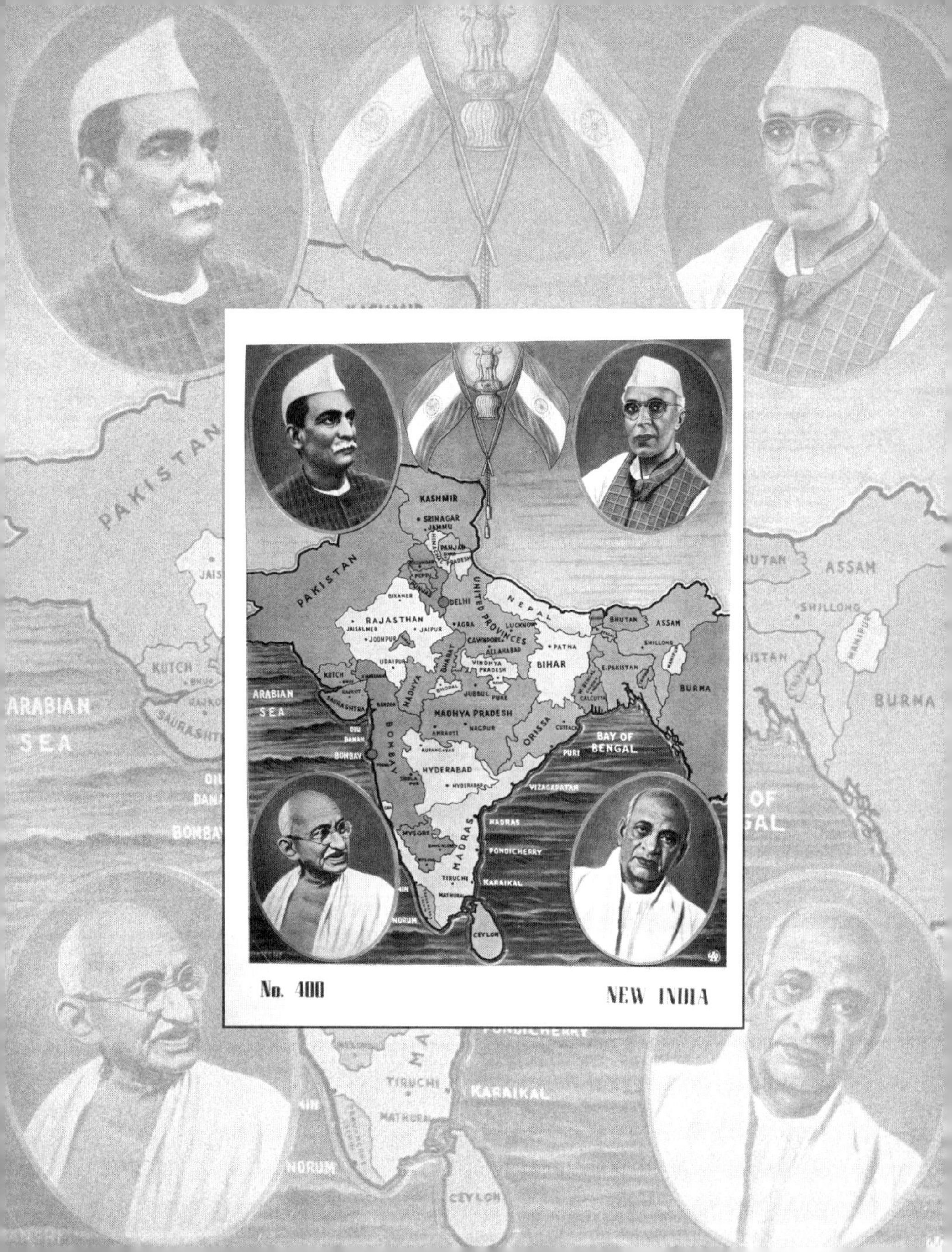
KASHMIR
SRINAGAR
JAMMU
PAKISTAN
DELHI
UNITED PROVINCES
NEPAL
RAJASTHAN
JAISALMER
JODHPUR
JAIPUR
BIKANER
AGRA
LUCKNOW
CAWNPORE
ALLAHABAD
PATNA
BIHAR
BHUTAN
ASSAM
SHILLONG
E. PAKISTAN
CALCUTTA
BURMA
KUTCH
SAURASHTRA
ARABIAN SEA
UDAIPUR
VINDHYA PRADESH
BHOPAL
JUBBULPORE
MADHYA PRADESH
NAGPUR
ORISSA
CUTTACK
BAY OF BENGAL
PURI
DIU
DAMAN
BOMBAY
HYDERABAD
VIZAGAPATAM
MADRAS
MYSORE
PONDICHERRY
TIRUCHI
KARAIKAL
MATHURAI
CEYLON
No. 400
NEW INDIA

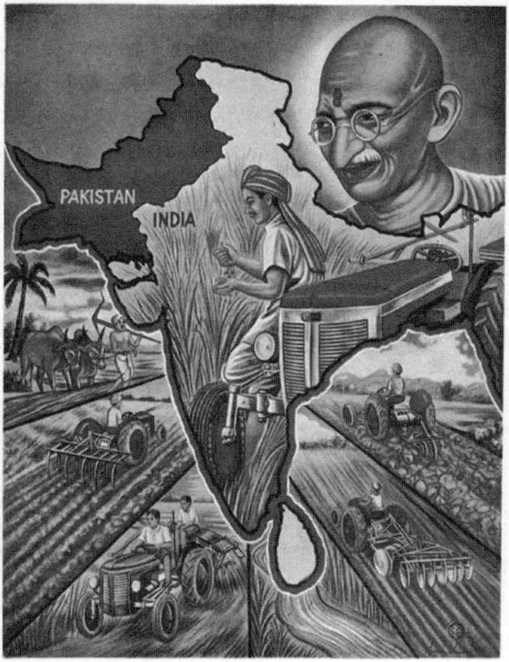

NEW INDIA No. 2
No. 700

the same, such images are in contrast to many others where, clearly, the historical fact of Radcliffe's line is denied, erased or occluded, and in which Mother India's body is deployed in various ingenious ways to defiantly claim territory that no longer belongs to independent India.

For instance, to invoke one example from a myriad of others, in an illustration that appeared in 1955 in a Tamil textbook from southern India, Mother India occupies the map of India, all critical borders to the west, east and north totally erased. The imperialist manner in which Mother India's body is deployed here is further heightened by the fact that her scarf - painted green, the colour associated with Pakistan - gracefully and seemingly innocently reaches out into Pakistani national territory: Radcliffe's critical cartographic work from a decade earlier is utterly invisible in this print.

Another image, titled *Map of India*, is an important reminder indeed that such prints may not be as benign as they look on first appearances: it shows the newly-delineated map of India in the company of Jawaharlal Nehru who looks directly out at us with a slightly weary gaze. Possibly the most striking aspect of this print is the Indian tricolour flying triumphantly over the nation's territory, the staff bearing it firmly planted on Kashmir.[40] Indeed, the most revealing acts of deletion, occlusion or incorporation in such mass-produced prints lie in the pictorial fate of the contested territory of Kashmir. In July 1947 when Radcliffe arrived in India to partition the subcontinent, his mandate did not extend to Kashmir. Within a couple of months of his cartographic deed, however, the two new states were at war over this territory - a suppurating conflict that has largely left matters unresolved until this day.[41]

Official maps of India subsume the entirety of Kashmir, disavowing the Line of Control (LOC),[42] the de facto border that separates Indian-administered Jammu and Kashmir from Pakistan-administered Azad Kashmir and the Northern Areas. Pakistani maps in turn have a stamp tersely stating 'disputed territory' marked across the region, leaving the north-eastern edge of the country 'ostentatiously unbounded - an astounding rebuttal of the universal dependence of national maps on borders'.[43] Barefoot cartography in India, by contrast, ingeniously places Mother India's head on Kashmir, the halo and the crown claiming all of the territory without question for the nationalist cause of India. In seemingly thus solving the problem of Kashmir somatically, such prints also reveal that symbolically the loss of Kashmir would amount to a decapitation of Mother India herself - implying that the disputed territory is worthy of defending by sacrificing one's own life and limb in her cause.

Anthropologist Christopher Pinney writes that 'the trauma of Partition was never visually represented by the commercial picture production industry' of India.[44] I would amend this statement by suggesting that at least some sections of this industry responded to 'the trauma' by an aggressive counter-cartography in which the new lines and boundaries that carved the body of Mother India into bits and pieces on statist maps are either realigned or entirely dissolved, and her wholeness restored back to her in the placement of her limbs, body and head, the swirl of her sari, the flow of her hair. Critically, it is the artist who worked for the mass-production image industry in the rough and tumble of the street and the bazaar – away from the elite world of gallery artists – who may have led the way in this regard, probing and challenging the legitimacy of Radcliffe's line, at least from an (Hindu) Indian nationalist perspective. If we agree with Ananya Kabir that the artist 'is the most effective vigilante of national desire', then it might be the humble barefoot cartographer – relatively unknown, even anonymous – who emerges as the midnight line's paradigmatic Indian challenger.[45]

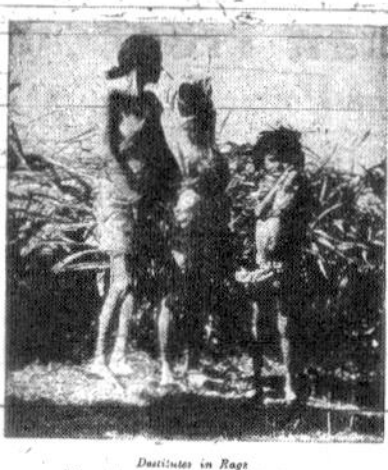

Destitutes in Rags
"Do not know where my man is," she said

★

MEN LIKE GHOSTS

A Journey Thru The Villages

A total length of 286 miles was covered in the interior of British Orissa, barring journey by railway. We travelled in palanquins, in boats and on foot. It took us a total of 17 days and nights.

WE were proceeding to the interior of the Fatehabad area (Balasore District), where the Santals live. Rai Bania village, twelve miles away, was our destination, with only a foot-track as the highway.

We were about half-way, between the villages of Ascodia and Bhalukhuan and on the bank of the river Nomonia, I turned to Sunil and said: "Look! There are vultures on the left. There must be some dead carcase there." Almost before I had finished my sentence, our guides in front shouted to us: "It is a man! It is a man!"

The body was only twenty-five yards away from where we stood. The young man had evidently been alive last night. He was half-eaten by vultures and dogs now. His stick and his earthen pot told the destitute's story all too well, especially when coupled with the dirty rag hardly three feet long which was his "dhoti"!

It was thus that we made our first acquaintance with famine-stricken Orissa.

* * * *

AT RAI BANIA village we found a "Free Kitchen" feeding nearly 8 to 9 hundred souls, most of them destitute women and helpless children under ten years of age.

"In Rai Bania there are two hundred households, and not more than thirty have any food at all. I have myself gone the

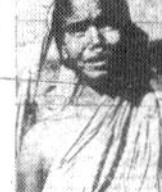

Raibari was 20 years old. She was pregnant. Lost her husband 4 months ago. Cyclone destroyed her house.

round and inspected the inside of huts and I can vouch for my statement," said the expert social worker of the Free Kitchen. I went round the village myself and made test "searches." I came to the conclusion that he must be correct.

But Rai Badin is considered a prosperous village as compared to the villages round about.

* * *

JALESHWAR is a railway station on the highway to and from Bengal. This way flowed lacs and lacs of maunds of rice out of Orissa. Jaleshwar town is on one side of the railway line. We crossed to the other side, and within fifty yards we saw fields full of hundreds of skeletons and bones—dead bodies in every stage of decomposition. It was like a battle-scarred land in which human-slaughter had been indiscriminate, and nobody had had either the time or the money to burn or bury the unfortunate dead.

On enquiry we found that those were the remains of the destitutes who had flocked to the city of Jaleshwar from the surrounding villages and even from Midnapore. Some had no doubt eaten in the "Free Kitchen," and then died of "nutritional diarrhoea," the state of exhaustion caused by starvation having been too great to allow them to recoup on the "khichdi". Others had been direct victims of the greed of the profiteers and the inefficiency of the Government—they had died from "famine".

* * * *

In the coastal belt of Bhograi, I was attracted by a village which was pitched on a hillock. They told me that its name was SUHASINI. But when we mounted the hillock a scene of desolation met our sight, a tale of woe and helpless suffering greeted our ears.

Out of 35 households only three had escaped the toll of death. Every single house had been damaged or smashed by the cyclone. Suhasini boasted of a hundred cocoanut trees. Now we could count just ten lonely sentinels. Suhasini had possessed a hundred head of cattle. Now one-fifth is dead and gone. Except the inmates of two or three households, all looked famished, weak, undernourished.

The paddy crop had miserably failed this year again. There were no cottage industries, no work at all of any sort by which people could earn a living. "Oh, yes, there are embankments to repair, and the P. W. D. will do it sometime or the other. But the ways of Government are so slow, you know!" said the headman, leaning on his stick.

It was bitter winter, but cloth was scarce. Women were half-nude and in rags; children invariably naked; men in short "langotas." Here we came across cases where the womenfolk would not come out of the huts. I thought that there was some rice hidden in them. I was pulled up in time. Between the husband and the wife there was only one piece of cloth. The husband had gone out wearing the cloth. The woman was stark naked inside. How could she come out?

This experience repeated itself over and over again, from village to village throughout the length and breadth of Orissa. What terrible misery is the lot of these peasants and labourers!

And I was told by the officials that now Orissa is no more famine-stricken, that the new harvest has solved the position, that the District Magistrates expect a surplus for export!

But it is true that the story of Suhasini and Rai Bania can be multiplied a thousandfold in the villages of Orissa. They are not exceptional villages at all, but typical of the affected parts.

* * * *

TAKE the village of Brahman Deo in the famous Chilka Lake area of Puri District. It is typical of Krishna ... a cyclone affected every hut. Out of 300 head of cattle, only fifty were left. Agents of Mahajans (money-lenders) came to the village and bought up no less than 30 cartloads of pots and pans. Every household sold. To-day, earthen pots are in universal use. Women sold even their bangles to keep the wolf from the door. Deaths have occurred in each family.

The Government undertook embankment work with forced labour from the villagers. But it so happened that embankment work clashed with the preliminary harvest work previous to the rains. Thus the peasant has lost this year's crop too.

I asked to see the Harijan quarters. A typical hut in this quarter was five feet long by seven feet broad. It was occupied by Suna, whose husband had gone away in search of work and had never returned. She had a daughter about nine years old. She had in all two earthen pots, one broken. Except for a foot long "langota", she was nude.

She lived by begging and on dried seeds of *kamal* fruit which she picked up in the pools. I saw some roots in a corner. A doctor to whom I referred told me that they were inedible. She had dug them out of some fields half a mile away. She said she had to dig a foot or so for them. This is life in the district of Puri. And the famine is said to have lifted!

LET US MEET three destitute women of Ganjam District. I met hundreds and hundreds of such in Cuttack, Puri, Balasore and Ganjam. They are going to be a real problem. Something creeps down my spine when I think of their condition to-day, when the Government is closing down free kitchens and dole centres, with no plans worth the name for relief work.

Raibari was twenty years old. She had a son four years old with her. She was in the family way, expecting to give birth in a fortnight or so. Her home had been in Binchanapalli village, but the cyclone had washed it away. Pots and pans and ornaments had been sold previously. She and her husband became destitutes. Her husband died four months back, from starvation. She was now eating in the Palur Free Kitchen. No, she had no relatives. She had nowhere to go. She would gladly give her child to the orphanage. But what would happen to her?

Adinamma was from Gopalpur. Her age must be thirty. Her husband disappeared when starvation became acute. He went in search of work. No, she has never heard from him again. She has five children of all ages, downwards from the girl of fourteen. They have now no lands, no hut, no utensils—nothing except rags on their bodies to call their own.

They were dependent on the free kitchen. There is no work at all to do. They are willing to do anything. Where should they go?

Ankolu was over fifty years old. Her blind husband was by her side. They had two sons, but both had deserted with their wives, leaving three grandchildren behind. Two of the children were dead now. They had died of swellings and sores. Food was very scarce then. Now they were eating at the Berhampore Free Kitchen. They have nothing left—no lands, no home, no utensils. They are both too old and weak to work.

"But where is work? Show me work and I shall do it," said the old woman. "Why not give the little child to the orphanage?" I asked. "Oh God! do not take my last solace from me. But if the Kitchen stops and starvation comes back again, I shall give the child away."

"Have you no daughters?" I pressed. And the old woman turned her face away. She had two, seventeen and twenty years old. She had left them with a man from Cuttack who had promised to look after them, she said. A little cross-questioning brought out the truth. The man was a pimp, and the girls had been sold to the brothels when famine was very acute.

This is Orissa as we found it, not a picture based on exceptions, but the general rule to-day.

To stop kitchens and doles in the affected areas is a crime. To say that the people are getting the "dole habit" can only be the outpouring of a blind bureaucrat. Not to offer sources of

(Continued in col. 9)

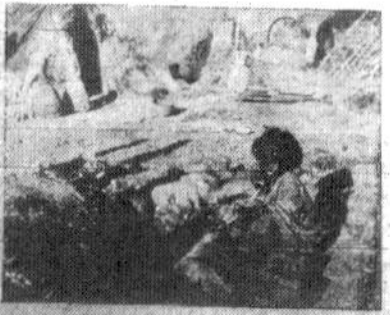

In Prayagi Village. During the cyclone Chilka lake rose and washed away the family house of this girl, now alone in the world

TOILING ORISSA FACES DEATH

by S. S. Batliwala

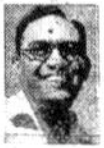

(Orissa is a[n]y province, within easy reach of enemy attack. Fo[r the] last eighteen months throughout the whole pro[vin]ce famine conditions have prevailed. If they [are] allowed to continue, not only will hundreds of th[ous]ands of Oriyas die a miserable death, but a few [bom]bing raids on a population, whose morale afte[r m]onths of starvation will have been broken, can cr[eate] tremendous havoc and suffering, and contribute [con]siderably towards disruption of the counter-off[ensive] into Burma. Comrade Soli Batliwala in these [art]icles describes the situation as he saw it on a recent [vis]it to Orissa.—Ed.)

"WHAT NATURE BEGAN, SOME MEN IN THEIR GREED COMPLETED"

THE poverty of Orissa is a commonplace in Indian politics. The vast majority of the population has always lived on a semi-starvation diet and therefore has a very small margin of resistance to disease.

The per capita consumption has been calculated to be only 15 oz. In Sindh it is 20.6 oz., in C. P., 22.8 oz. In Sindh and in C. P. the food is not wholly paddy as it is in Orissa; it is wheat with meat and eggs occasionally thrown in, along with pulses, limited though the quantity be.

Orissa again is the golden land for malaria and filaria parasites. Agriculture is very backward in most of the districts, [wi]th only one crop of paddy which [ma]terialises between November and [Ja]nuary. The plough itself is old-fashion[ed]. And on top of this, Orissa suffers [fro]m the heavy oppression of the land[lor]ds, shrivelled up trade and undeveloped [ind]ustries. Orissa is still feudal in its [trad]itions and outlook.

[Ma]ny even statistics on its life are [...]d mixed up with those of Behar and [the] Orissa native states.

In October and November 1942, [cyc]lones swept the shores of three out of [the] six districts of Orissa—Balasore, [Pur]i, and Ganjam. Houses and whole [vil]lages were washed away, the paddy [cro]ps in the fields were lost, more [tha]n 90% of the cocoanut trees and 100% of the pan-groves were destroyed. The fisherfolk lost their boats, nets, houses and all belongings. Then came the floods in 1943, spreading sand in the fields of Cuttack district, havoc in stricken Balasore. The rivers in Orissa take a toll every two or three years and nobody seems to be able to stop them. In Ganjam there was shortage of rains—came drought with its blighting tongue.

In such conditions, it would have required an efficient and honest administration fully prepared to enlist the aid of the people's organisations to stave off starvation and death. But such an administration was not there. In its place was a most unpopular Ministry, composed of the decadent aristocracy at one end and the opportunist office-seekers—seceders from the Congress—at the other.

Below the Ministry was a bureaucracy thoroughly irresponsible to public opinion, blundering and even corrupt in parts. And then there were the inevitable hoarders, at first small ones in the villages, later big province-wide hoarders indulging in the trade in human lives with the glibest tongues.

Another factor intervened to worsen the situation.

Orissa is situated to the south of Bengal. In Bengal raged a man-made famine of unsurpassed intensity. In Bengal profiteer-sharks paid fabulous prices for rice to corner all markets, to reap larger profits from the black-market. The highest price in Orissa was yet cheap for the profiteer in Bengal, even after giving a share to the Orissa hoarder-trader.

The Orissa hoarder bought rice at Rs. 4/- to Rs 7/- per maund, and sold to his Bengal counterpart at Rs. 25/- per maund. He sold to the agents of the Civil Supply Department of Bengal at Rs. 20/- a maund during the "Free Trade" period. The sharks in Orissa not only killed the poor Oriya, but helped to kill the poor Bengalee too by helping to keep rice out of his grasp in Bengal when it did arrive there.

In the pre-"Free Trade" period, eighteen lac maunds of paddy evaporated from Orissa. The Government of India intervened at this stage and helped the exporters by declaring "Free Trade". Another ten lac maunds passed out of the province. People were dying in the streets. Starvation was threatening to be universal. The Ministry was forced to abandon the "Free Trade" policy and put a ban on exports.

But Bengal gold was attracting Orissa paddy as a huge magnet would draw small iron filings. Another four and a half lac maunds of paddy, with the seal of the Ministry on them, passed out to Bengal, the Prime Minister indulging in verbal heroics to justify the permit. An unconfirmed figure which runs into lacs of maunds was spirited away without legal permits.

Rice went in railway wagons marked "bucks", rice went as bedding and head-loads, rice went surreptitiously by boat, by road and hidden in railway carriages. The corrupt railway and police officials shared a part of the profits with the trade-sharks. Paddy became "scarce" in every market in Orissa. You could buy it in Berhampore at two seers a rupee; in Jaleshwar at a seer a rupee. But for the vast majority of the poverty-stricken population of Orissa rice, their staple diet, was unavailable.

Exports by themselves had not caused the famine. The vicious policy of the hoarders in conjunction with the profiteering traders and the "incompetent" Government, was responsible for the misery of Orissa. If along with the first exports equitable distribution to distressed areas had been resorted to, if exports had been totally stopped as soon as semi-starvation conditions began to appear in non-distressed areas during the crucial months of July, August and September, the picture in Orissa would have been very different indeed.

The primary duty of feeding the people of the province first, was forgotten by the Government and its satellites in their hurry to reap profits out of the food of the poor and the semi-starved.

The Marwari and the Gujerati traders and rice-mill-owners who are in possession of 90% of the export trade, reaped huge profits as also the satellites of the Ministers. A very prominent trader frankly confessed that the profits of these six or seven odd months could not be below a crore of rupees.

What the "servants of the people," the bureaucracy, gathered in as its loaves and fishes, is not possible to estimate, though rumour in Orissa is thick with stories which involve a whole series of officials.

The Native States in Orissa had also a very important role to perform. They are, most of them, surplus rice-growing areas, and normally exported to British Orissa to keep its economy stable. They were reluctant to sell to Orissa this year, because of the higher profits which could be secured by selling to the military and to the Government agents or in Bengal. The Government of India intervened—but not on behalf of the starving British Orissa public.

It intervened on behalf of the

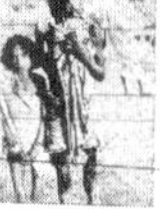

Rai Bania Village. Woman of 30, looks over 60 with her daughter.

princelings of the Native States. It allowed the Native States to sell their rice where they could reap the fattest profits, viz., outside British Orissa, while Orissa itself was starving.

Close in the wake of all this was maldistribution—Koraput and Sambalpur being held as preserves of officials.

Thus was golden hay spun while the sun scorched the starved Oriya to death. Toiling Oriyas sold everything—lands, ornaments, pots and pans—all that could be sold, and they became the inevitable homeless destitutes. Some two to three lac "Burma evacuees", pauperised labourers who succeeded in reaching safety from the Japanese in Burma, helped to swell their ranks.

What nature began, some men in their greed completed. Death, destitution, and disease have taken a terrible toll of the agricultural labourers, the fisherfolk, the town poor and even the middle peasant. To-day, a sane estimate places nearly thirty per cent of the population of Orissa as already marked out by death for its own in the coming year, over and above those who have already been claimed as its victims.

This was the Orissa to which we went for investigation.

All Photos by Sunil Janah

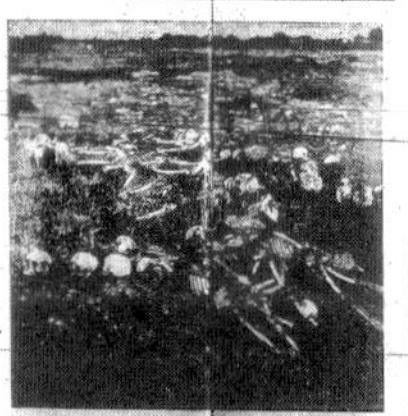

Skeletons and bones littered the places near Jaleshwar Town

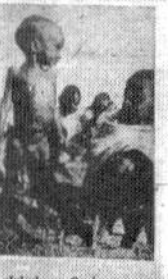

Jaleshwar Orphanage Children deserted by parents

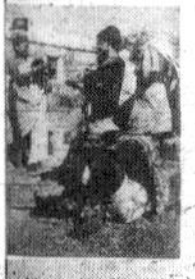

60-year old Ankolu with her blind husband.

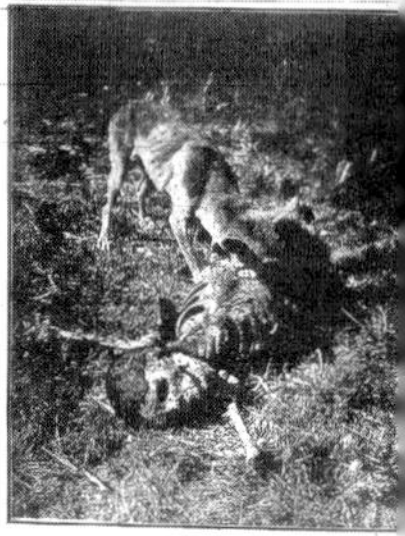

On the road to Rai Bania Village

ORISSA NEEDS YOUR HELP

Send All You Can

Orissa is dying. Although conditions there are as bad and in many places worse than in Bengal, the sufferings and horrors of Orissa are not known to wide masses of our people. Relief sent from the rest of India has been small while the need for it is very great. Here is an extract from a statement made by the Collector of Ganjam which was a rich and flourishing district before the cyclone and of how famine has laid her low.

"I have visited every nook and corner of the district and come in direct contact with the suffering population. I am not exaggerating when I say that starvation stalks this district in naked awfulness. Specially in the coastal villages thousands are going without anything like an apology for a meal. Their food is mere grass, some roots, some leaves or even worse. How can human beings live on what even animals do not relish?"

All India's patriots must answer the call of starving Orissa. Dip your hands deep in your pockets and send your contribution marked for ORISSA RELIEF WORK to:

Comrade Sarat Patnaik, Secretary,
Orissa Provincial Committee of
the Communist Party,
P. O. Chandni Chowk, Cuttack.

(Continued from col. 4)

employment and yet call the destitutes "idlers" is vicious and cowardly.

And more than all this is the toll taken by disease. Medical arrangements by the Government are so meagre that they are not worth mentioning. Quinine is a luxury for the rich. And the tale of woe for the toilers is unending.

"Sturdy labourers, who by the honest sweat of their brows have earned their modest livelihood have become emaciated devitalised bundles of bones moving about like ghosts and dropping down dead like autumn leaves," wrote a new imported Collector and District Magistrate of Ganjam District. Of course, the statement was promptly banned by the Orissa Censor. But it stands true to-day for the toiler as well as for his whole family.

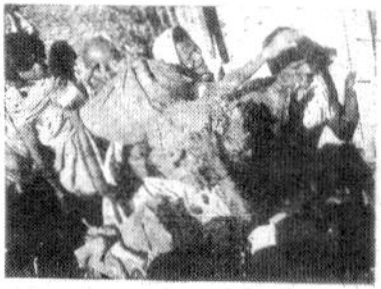

Free Kitchen door at Cuttack. They were late. No admission. Last minute struggle to get in.

2

Beyond or in Emergency?

The Emergence of Photography during the 1943 Bengal Famine: Sunil Janah

2017

Emilia Terracciano

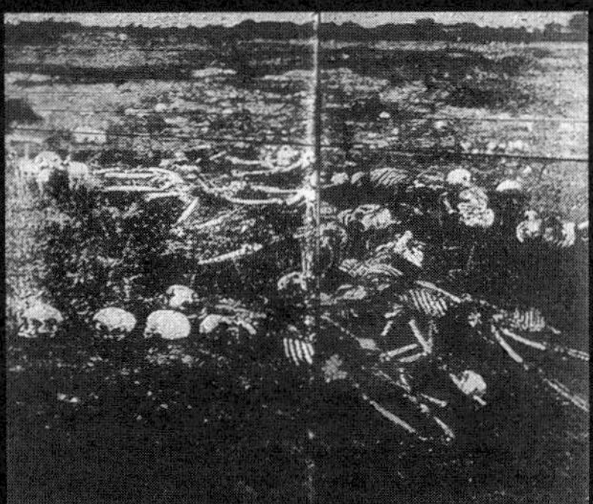
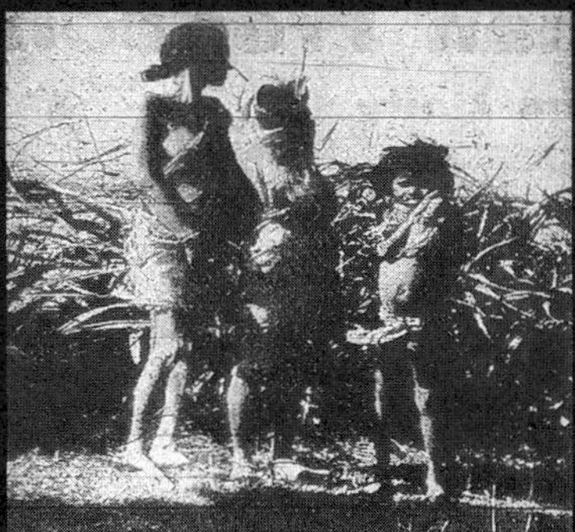
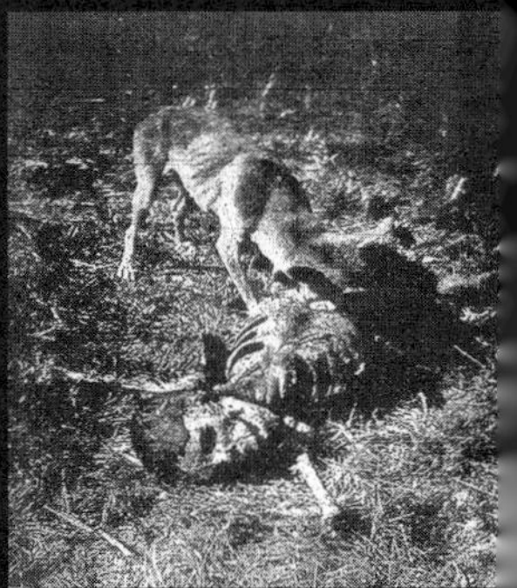

Contrasting the images of the victims of the 1943 Bengal Famine with those of other political bodies produced by the freedom struggle, Emilia Terracciano explores a 'political somatics' of spectral bodies. Some involved 'mobile and highly-crafted spectacles', others produced embodied subjects from Gandhi himself to the images of famine and hunger, to yet others of tribals and working people. Such a visual history – that Terracciano cross-references with Ariella Aïsha Azoulay's 'civil contract of photography' – is evidenced in images published in newspapers and magazines as diverse as the pro-Congress broadsheets, *The Bombay Chronicle*, *Young India*, *The Leader* and *The Hindustan Times*, Communist Party periodicals such as *People's War*, and international publications such as *Life* magazine.

The essay deals primarily with the work of **Sunil Janah**, in particular his affective images of the **Bengal Famine** (see Keywords). In parallel, the author offers a detailed analysis of **Margaret Bourke-White**'s images of Gandhi's 'superbody' that were tactically deployed for political ends. Theorizing Janah's famine photographs, Terracciano invokes Zahid Chaudhary's suggestion that the return of the 'mimesis of sympathy' haunts the medium of photography and erodes modernist narratives of progress and rationality.

This essay is a slightly abridged version of 'Beyond or in Emergency? The Emergence of Photography during the 1943 Bengal Famine: Sunil Janah', in Emilia Terracciano, *Art and Emergency: Modernism* in Twentieth-Century India, London: Bloomsbury Publishing, 2017.

Keywords, Names

Adivasi, *Civil Contract of Photography*, *Civil Disobedience Movement*, *First Indian War of Independence 1857*, *Mahatma Gandhi*, *Indian National Congress*, *Indian People's Theatre Association*, *Jallianwala Bagh massacre*, *Partition of India*, *Photographic Societies*, *Photojournalism*, *Press censorship*, *Quit India campaign (1942–44)* see Keywords at the back of this volume.

Images

p. 20: 'Toiling Orissa Faces Death', *People's War*, 1944. Courtesy the author's collection.

p. 25: Film stills from Mrinal Sen's 1980 film, *Akaler Sandhaney* ('In Search of Famine'). The actors and crew of a film-within-the-film reconstruct the 1943 famine with a visual game, trying to guess the historical moments to which different images refer.

p. 27: 'Come, let us go to the city for food', image from the Indian People's Theatre Association (IPTA) play *Nabanna* by Bijon Bhattacharya, about the 1943 famine. Published in *People's War*, 1944. Courtesy the author's collection.

p. 33: Margaret Bourke-White, *Mahatma Gandhi, April 1946, with his Charkha, or Spinning Wheel, Symbol of India's Struggle for Independence*. Margaret Bourke-White/ The LIFE Picture Collection.

pp. 36–37: 'Who Lives if Bengal Dies?', *People's War*, 1943. Courtesy the author's collection.

p. 43: Sunil Janah, *Mother and Child on a Pavement in Calcutta, Bengal Famine, 1944*, photograph, 1944.

p. 47: Sunil Janah, *Women Workers During Construction at a Thermal Power Plant in Bihar, One of Independent India's First, 1950s*, photograph, 1949.

> ... 1943 ...
> World War going on, and our country, this Bengal ...
> Neither a bullet fired, nor a bomb exploded.
> But in one year fifty *lakh*
> people died only because of starvation.
> They just starved and dropped dead.
>
> – Mrinal Sen, *In Search of Famine* (1980)[1]

Introduction

A shaft of light illuminates a mother and her suckling child, lying in the street. Muting the surrounding elements, the dramatic light focuses our attention on the two figures as though on a theatre stage. Mysterious, somewhat ghostly, the dappled rhythms of light and shade animate the scene, converging around the woman's eyes and her angular facial hollows, mouth and cheeks; a play of chiaroscuro lingers on the rag draped around her loins to sculptural effect – a *Pietà*. Although we as viewers are unaware of the history and context of this photograph, the intimate moment between mother and child that has been singled out evokes our immediate sympathy, transforming it into the very condition of being together.

To fully see and sympathize with the subjects before us, we need to turn to their particular histories. Titled *Bengal Famine, Mother and Child on a Calcutta Pavement*, the black-and-white photograph was taken by photographer Sunil Janah (1918–2012) in front of his home in Calcutta on a summer evening. The mother and child were amongst the thousands of rural refugees flooding the city in search of food and shelter in July 1943.[2] Hunger spurred people on to desert their homes, fields and families. Mothers and fathers abandoned their children or sold them into prostitution. Corpses lay rotting on the streets or in rivers. With India simultaneously gripped by World War II and famine, the colonial government refused to give the destitute the food and aid to which they were entitled according to state policy, committing instead the bulk of food resources to its military troops. Such was the magnitude of this collective catastrophe that it affected the lives of millions and dwarfed individual stories and misfortunes.

Responding to the social realist mandate that characterized artists as 'engineers of the human soul', Janah, photographer and member of the Communist Party of India (CPI), documented the conditions of famine victims for *People's War*, the Party newspaper.[3] The photograph *Bengal Famine, Mother and Child on a*

Calcutta Pavement was later integrated into a larger photographic sequence and framed by evocative descriptions of this 'exceptional' emergency in the pages of *People's War*. Circulated across India, an estimated 36,000 copies of the photo found their way into the homes of Janah's wartime viewers. The impersonal cruelty of lived hunger became a more intimate affair.

This essay engages with the photographs produced by Janah, and the spectacular affective technologies he relied upon to bring home the devastation caused by the man-made (some would argue, manufactured) catastrophe of the Bengal Famine. 'Sympathy' is but one of a number of strategies Janah exploited to convey the unfolding of this contemporary drama. In *The Theory of Moral Sentiments* (1759), Adam Smith identifies 'sympathy' as a regulatory, psychological component of the self, singling out this feeling for praise in his meditation on the economy of morality. Sympathy governs our response to the other, to ourselves, and beyond this to society, cementing social cohesion.[4] More recently, historian Zahid Chaudhary argues that the return of the 'mimesis of sympathy' haunts the medium of photography. This recurrence, he proposes, chips away at those narratives of progress and rationality which regard the emergence of the photographic medium as heralding a break with the pre-modern.[5] For this reason, a 'certain uncanniness resides at the heart of photographic mimesis itself: a strange mix of sympathetic production that is simultaneously contact and copy'.[6] Retrieving philosopher Spinoza's observations regarding affect, Chaudhary intimates that an image, whether an actual object or merely a memory, re-affirms its simultaneity with us.[7] Photography is always a 'revamped order of sympathetic mirroring'.[8] Such an understanding of the camera as 'sensory prosthetic' underscores the fact that this technology is not necessarily experienced as a discrete object detached from the body.[9] Rather, it becomes 'an area of sensitivity, extending the scope and active radius of touch, and providing a parallel to sight'.[10]

Spectral Bodies, Spectacular Hunger

The Bengal Famine catalysed the emergence of a radically committed art form of singular political import. The horror of the famine and the use of photography as a documentary tool emerged simultaneously, presaging Adorno's ideas regarding the intrinsic relationship between the modern formation of the 'mass' subject and the catastrophic.[11] For the first time in the history of Indian news media, photographs and text were interlocked in the form of a picture story to document

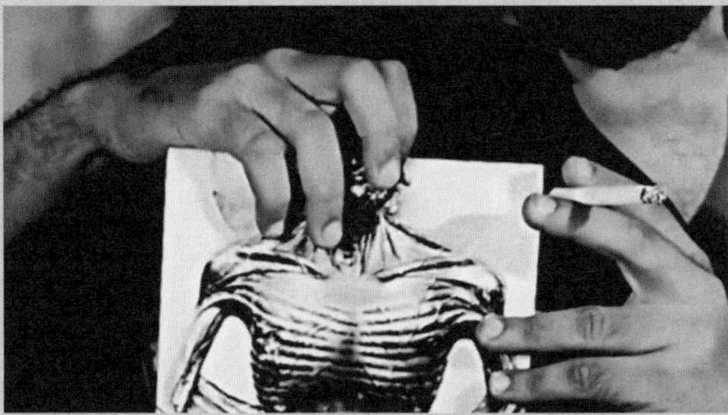
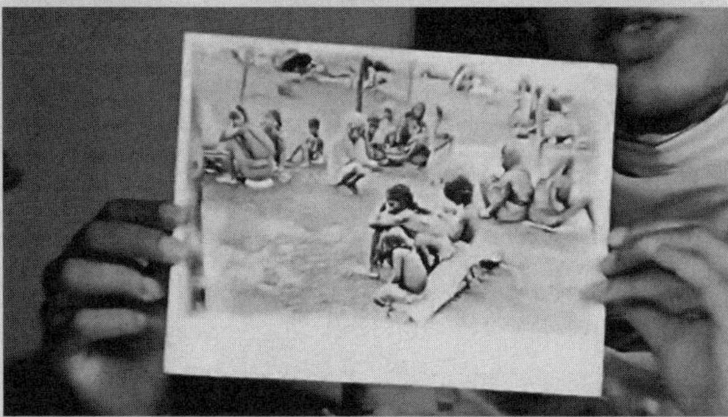
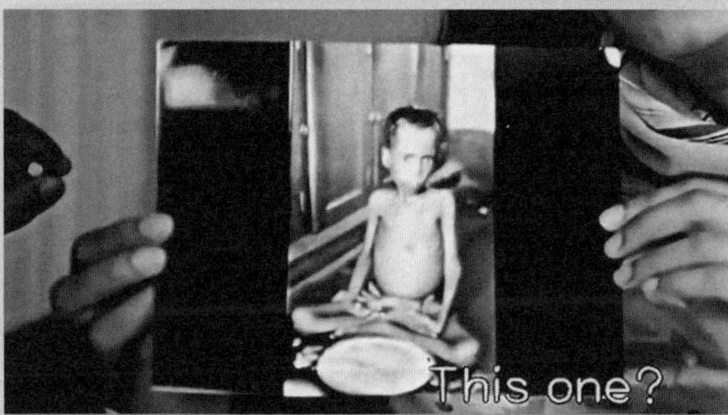
This one?
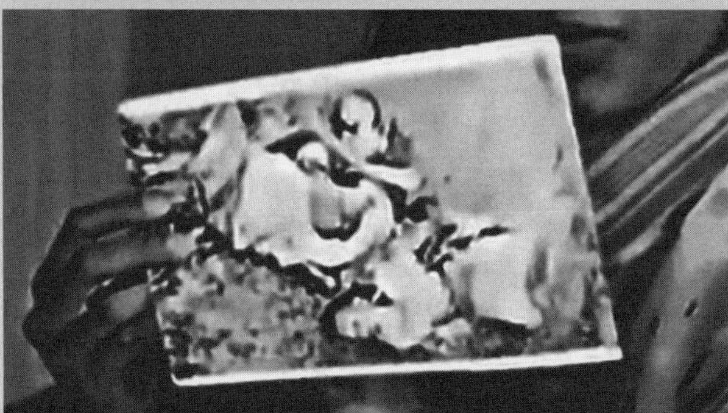
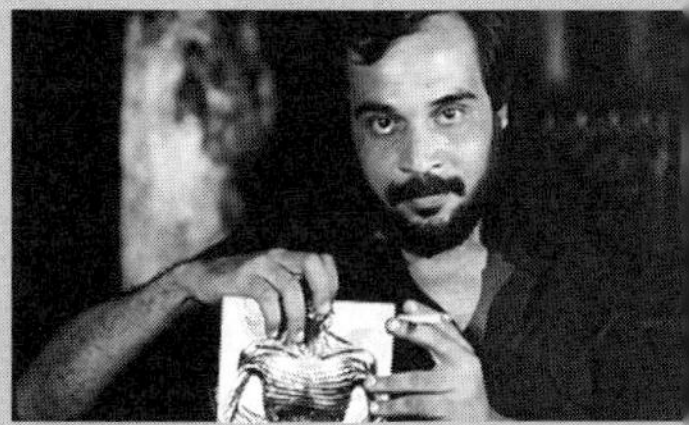
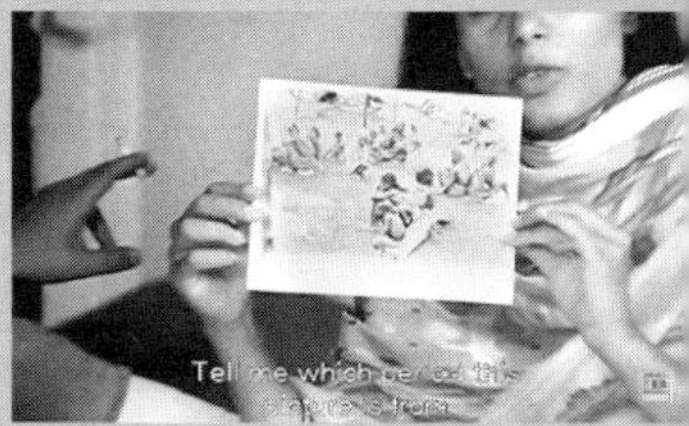
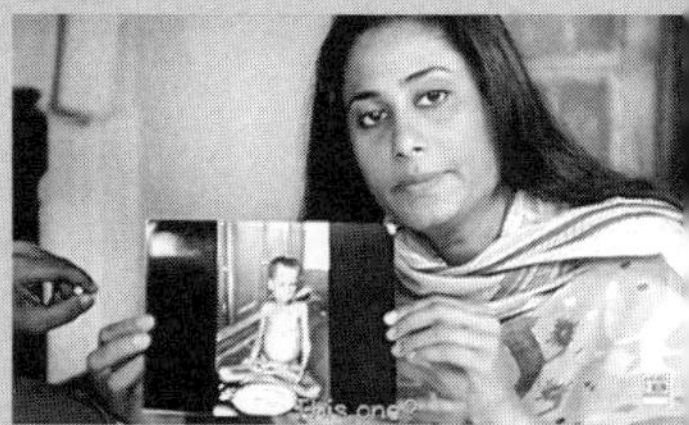
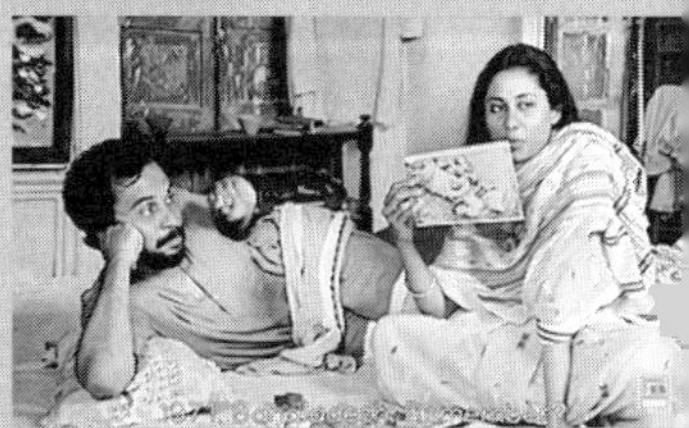
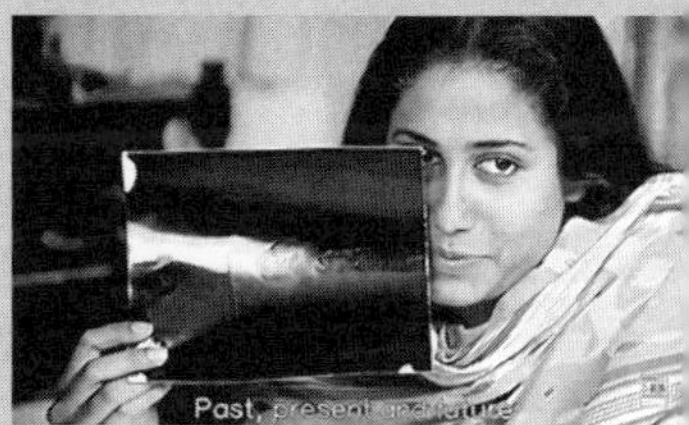

a disaster of enormous proportions. Circulated and displayed at political meetings across the country, the images brought home the impact of the famine, helping raise relief funds and promoting the Communist cause. As an image of the consequences of willful mismanagement of an ailing economy and the sacrifice of agrarian interests to those of the city and the military, the Bengal Famine provided ongoing inspiration and justification for the ending of imperial rule and the Independence movement. Images of the human destitution, hunger and suffering caused by the famine were deployed as affective rhetorical devices by the CPI not only in speaking out against political oppression and unjust deprivation but also for mobilizing resistance.[12] Through this mediatic commitment, the CPI prefigured the creation of a mass subject that is at once 'witness and victim of the catastrophic'.[13] Further, as Claude Lefort argues, the phenomenon of the 'mass subject' is nothing but a technologically mediated response to the problem of popular sovereignty. The latter, in the case of democratic regimes, is 'a vacancy, intermittently occupied and activated by virtual representations and surrogates of "the people" – a transcendental political subject that, in late modernity, transmutes into media-centered virtualized mass spectatorship'.[14] The widespread circulation of photographs of disaster and death displayed a mass subject whose spectral body could only be witnessed, not rescued.[15]

For many contemporary observers, the Bengal Famine was part of a much older story whose origins could be traced back to the beginnings of British Imperial rule in India, that is, long before the outbreak of World War II. After severe recurrent famines from 1870 through the 1880s, the 'drain theory' propounded by various Indian nationalist exponents gained prominence in the emergent rhetoric of nationalism and anti-colonial justification for 'home rule'.[16] The widespread unanimity among nationalists in blaming the British (colonial state power) had enduring repercussions on the views and ambitions of India's nascent political leaders. Mass malnutrition had compelled middle-class nationalists to consider the plight of the peasantry more carefully. As the Nobel Laureate economist Amartya Sen writes, in the eyes of many political activists the Bengal Famine represented the climax of British rule (or rather misrule), becoming 'a focal point of nationalist criticism of British imperial policy in India'.[17] For this reason, 'famine' was used by a number of political advocates as a catalyst for the Independence movement, with charged images of emaciated Indians disseminated to serve the cause of home rule.[18] Jawaharlal Nehru,[19] India's future Prime Minister, observed how the catastrophe of the Bengal Famine represented the final, tragic act in Britain's long history of 'indifference, incompetence and complacency' and therefore furnished

W/ DIA

found selling tickets. 20 weavers came all the way from Malegaon

Bombay 4.

Come, let's go to the city for food.

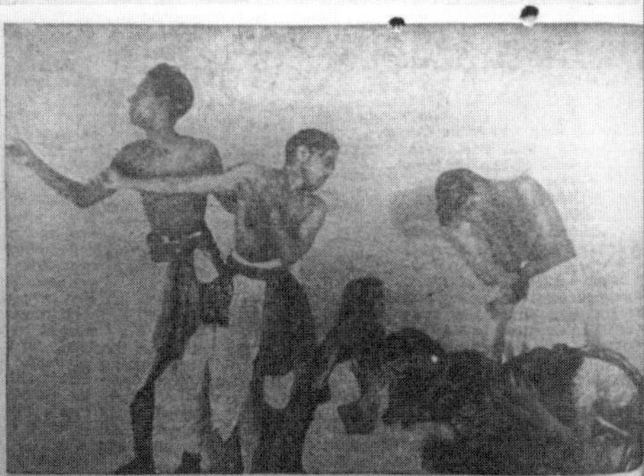

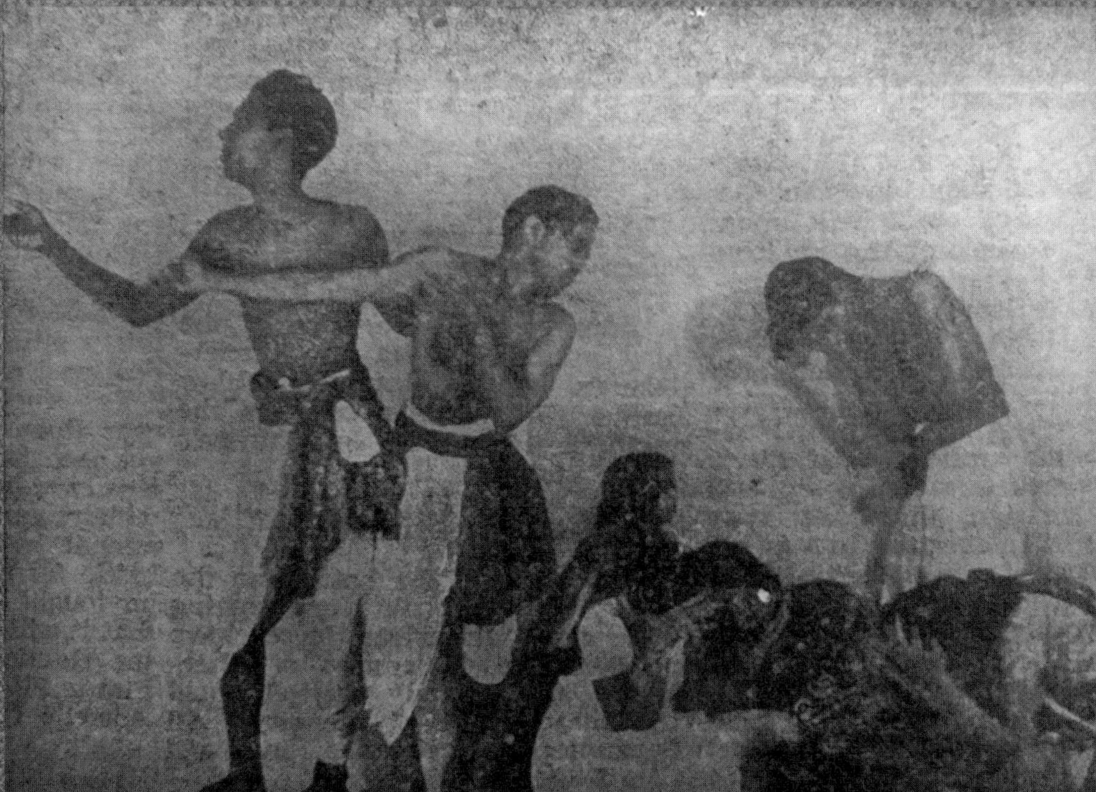

a decisive argument in the demand for self-government.[20] Writing with regard to the appalling famine mortality, Nehru was to comment: 'Obviously, if a National Government had been formed in 1942 there would have been a great deal of cooperation with the people. ... I am quite convinced that the Bengal famine could then either have been avoided or at any rate very greatly minimized.'[21]

The Bengal Famine claimed the lives of circa three million people. Its complex causes were linked to wartime exploitation of the colony, which led to privation and severe inflation. In *Triumph and Tragedy* (1953), his sixth, and final, volume of the history of World War II, former British Prime Minister Winston Churchill declared that 'no great portion of the world population' had been so 'effectively protected from the horrors and perils of the World War' as India. In his view, India had been 'carried through the struggle on the shoulders of our small island'.[22] Yet it is unlikely that this 'small island' could have survived the war without the support of the colony's two and a half million recruits, its massive industrial contribution and steady supply of food, as well as its strategic military bases. India was second only to Britain in terms of its contribution to the war effort, furnishing more than two billion pounds' worth of commodities and services.[23] This colony, moreover, was essential to the protection of British interests worldwide, positioned as it was along the communication and supply routes that stretched from Britain, via the Suez Canal, to the Cape and thereafter via the Indian Ocean to Singapore, Australia and New Zealand. For the duration of the war, ships carried provisions, troops and arms from the colonies situated around the Indian Ocean to Britain, as well as to war zones in the Mediterranean area and Southeast Asia. India was to sacrifice as much as Britain in the defence of an Empire from which it was attempting to liberate itself.

This essay proposes that during World War II, a new form of governmentality emerged in the colony. In Bengal, the plundering of material, natural and human resources led to the forced migration of millions of rural inhabitants towards Calcutta in search of nourishment, causing many to perish. Treating the colony as an occupied territory, the Government of India consigned a vast subject population to 'the status of the living dead'.[24] These crushing dynamics were exacerbated by Churchill's racial prejudice towards His Majesty's subjects. For the then Prime Minister, 'Hindus were a foul race, protected by their mere pullulation from the doom that is their due'.[25] The endorsement of 'boat denial' and 'scorched earth' policies provided Churchill the grounds for Malthusian efforts to curb the customs of an 'inferior race', whose 'breeding habits' he compared to those of rabbits. These beliefs, coupled with the need to crush national resistance and preserve internal security, were seen as a justification for Churchill's stonewalling of food shipments dispatched from countries sympathetic to the plight of starving Indians.

The propagandist policy of the CPI vis-à-vis the man-made famine was complicated on the one hand by war between the Allies and Axis powers, and on the other by the competing claims of democracy versus dictatorship. At the same time, as it posed significant challenges to the monolithic hegemony of the Indian national movement, confronting not just imperial domination but also the stranglehold of feudal-patriarchal power in the Indian countryside, the CPI found itself supporting the war effort and by extension, incongruously, the British. As a result of this policy, the CPI stood in relative isolation from the national movement as well as the mass of the people, including peasants, workers and students. Such isolation, while prompting a sense of 'militancy, self-sacrifice and idealism among cadres', placed the Party in an even more paradoxical situation, since most of the people perishing from the man-made famine were Party members.[26] Despite their conviction that colonial policies had precipitated the famine, the CPI and its artists could not, due to censorship measures enforced by the British, openly denounce its root causes.

To appreciate the novelty of Janah's photographic strategies, one ought to place his documentary series in dialogue with surviving images produced by British photographers of nineteenth-century famines. The latter failed to set up the 'civil contract' described by Azoulay; this type of colonial photography did not provoke the kind of voluntary, consensual and empathetic way of viewing atrocity that Azoulay treats as essential to photography's civic and political power. Turning to the photographs Janah made during the famine, one can see how he often resorted to theatrical measures in his effort to relay the murder of millions whilst avoiding stereotypical tropes.

In a chilling commentary published in 1943, Ian Stephens, an eyewitness and editor-in-chief of the Calcutta-based newspaper *Statesman*, described the difficulties related to delivering the 'famine story' in an editorially enticing way. In his view, the problem was primarily one of 'representation':

> Death by famine lacks drama. Bloody death, the death of many by slaughter as in riots or bombings is in itself blood-bestirring; it excites you, prints indelible images on the mind. But death by famine, a vast slow, dispirited, noiseless apathy, offers none of that. Horrid though it may be to say, multitudinous death from this cause looked at merely *optically*, regarded without emotion as a spectacle, is, until the crows get at it, the rats and kites and dogs and vultures, very dull.[27]

Janah's visibility and career as a Party photographer would turn him into one of the most sought-after photographers in the post-Independence years. The final part of this essay briefly touches upon some of his industrial commissions and studies of tribal communities; both series are haunted by the ghosts of the famine.

Gandhi's Superbody and the Performance of Political Somatics

At the turn of the twentieth century, technological advances in technology and chemistry improved the mobility of the camera and facilitated the mass distribution of photographs. The static *gravitas* associated with nineteenth-century spectacular outdoor panoramas, royal durbars, hunts and architectural sites was governed by colonial needs as much as it was linked to the heavy and complicated logistics of glass plate technology. Thus the turning away from the use of large format cameras to smaller and more compact camera models ('the camera is getting smaller and smaller', Benjamin prophetically remarked), entailed the progressive liberation of photography from 'the tableaux-like quality of the studio'.[28] But although these innovations had brought the medium within the grasp of many, eroding the pre-eminence of the professional, photography was still the exclusive preserve and hobby of British colonists. For this reason, it was mostly nurtured within the courtly domain, the bazaar and the commercial studio.[29]

From 1930 onwards, the constitution of photographic societies began to change. No longer dominated by Europeans, civilians or military, nor confined to the three Presidency cities (Bombay, Madras and Calcutta), the organization and running of small elite societies and clubs slowly shifted from British to Indian hands. Many practitioners, including Janah, regularly subscribed to the popular *Illustrated Weekly of India*, the only news magazine in India to publish photographs by amateur photographers and set up national competitions.[30] As this lavishly illustrated magazine developed and increased its circulation, its editors sought to instil a pictorial aesthetic among contributors and viewers.[31]

It was during Gandhi's Non-Cooperation Movement[32] that the camera became decisively mobile, moving beyond the studio and into the streets. The creation of smaller and more compact models such as the Speed Graphic, Rolleiflex and Leica[33] allowed press photographers attached to the state-run Press Information Bureau or to newly established independent photo agencies to move more freely and record major political events first hand.[34] This phenomenon in turn signalled the beginning of candid photography and the increased visibility of the photographer in the public arena. Once the stage where British repression had been most '*graphically* and regularly enacted', the city embodied the promise of modernity, and for this reason became an object of ambivalent craving for Indians.[35] Transformed into a set for staging political engagement, the street was the site wherein colonial hegemony appeared increasingly threatened by national unrest.[36]

In a growing trend, especially after the rise of Gandhi, who sought to reinstate the village as the fulcrum of national feeling (as opposed to the false mimicry of the colonial city), politics were no longer restricted to debate chambers or 'terrorist' alcoves. The Mahatma nonetheless believed that colonialism had to be defeated from within 'its modern fortress' and encouraged nationalist politics to overflow into the streets and openly challenge colonial rule.[37] Conversely, with his long marches on foot (*padayatras*) across the countryside, this political leader spread the nationalist idea from the city back into the villages. In so doing, he mapped out a new India, no longer demarcated by railway tracks but by the intricate, seemingly invisible networks that connected villages.[38] *Swadeshi* narratives of nationhood were carried and diffused across villages through the cheap and mobile technology of the lantern slide.[39] Grafted onto entrenched forms of popular entertainment, the form of the lantern slide was deployed to exhibit 'national' issues, while at the same time 'defining the nation'.[40] These mobile and highly-crafted spectacles momentarily united disparate individuals, encouraging each to imagine himself as part of an imagined national community to come. Visually narrating national triumphs, the lantern slide shows fostered philanthropy among communities, often denouncing the brutality of the colonial regime, as in the case of the Jallianwala Bagh series.[41]

The Congress-led agitation in the form of the Non-Cooperation Movement in the early 1920s, civil disobedience in the early 1930s, and the Quit India campaign of 1942 were all events in which processional marches, prayer meetings and public rallies became affective theatrical performances, fundamentally sabotaging the functioning of the colonial public sphere. Increasingly, confined meeting places were abandoned in favour of assemblies in public squares and parks. Gaining momentum, the movement was propelled not just by the size of its audience but by the need to project 'openness, the hint of defiance that an open public meeting granted'.[42] It was in the streets that for the first time, the formation of crowds 'allowed people to see themselves as a collective body', supplanting earlier displays of a subservient, carefully selected audience mesmerized by the composed spectacle of the imperial pageant.[43] Public space could either be strategically occupied or vacated by large crowds to sabotage colonial expectations.[44]

Whereas in South Africa Gandhi had been able to rely on local press photographers to report the dramatic burning of registration cards, and his *Satyagraha* mass campaigns, in India the 1910 Press Act and the subsequent Rowlatt Act of 1919 prevented the production and distribution of seditious photographic material.[45] Due to this vigilant censoring, the circulation of photographs touching on political issues in vernacular newspapers was very limited. Unlike other mechanically reproduced images sanctioned by the British, which allowed Indians to channel their political energies into religion, photographs were less conducive to this purpose.[46]

Political leaders as diverse as Jinnah,[47] Aurobindo Ghose,[48] Bal Gangadhar Tilak[49] and Gandhi responded defiantly to colonial press censorship by launching numerous papers, including *The Bombay Chronicle*, *Young India*, *The Leader* and later *The Hindustan Times*.[50] Hence their iconic portraits were singled out from the crowd, fostering 'new forms of recognition, memory and mass perpetuity'.[51] Gandhi was probably the first political figure to self-consciously exploit photography for political purposes. Although the leader did not court photographers, he harnessed mechanical reproduction to affirm his iconic public persona, achieving the complete integration of private and public, as well as religious and secular realms, which he so crucially advocated both in his writings and incendiary speeches.[52] The relation between the leader's asceticism and his command of mass publicity reveals how 'Gandhian body politics were not so much a technology of world-denying renunciation as the worldly condition of his communicative efficiency'.[53]

For this reason, one could argue that Gandhi's 'experiments with truth' were also 'experiments with mass publicity', and effective media strategies.[54] In any case, the leader's iconic status was crucial to his rise in 1920 to the hub of the anti-colonial struggle, leading the Indian National Congress to assume control over the all-India social movement. His powerful visual impact was reinforced by his ability to speak the language of the people, 'touching' their hearts and 'moving' hands and feet.[55] Gestural simplicity was important in communicating with the local crowds, and likewise with the imagined international audience he had fostered.[56] Yet Gandhi himself was often disappointed that the masses and the media congregated merely to see him, rather than to *hear* him speak.

From the Johannesburg certificates bonfire of 1908, to the Dandi Salt March of 1930, to the numerous 'fasts unto death' that Gandhi endured, his actions were all means to this end: the choreography of politics for both Indian and imagined, faraway, international publics. Perhaps this is why Sarojini Naidu, a distinguished poet and Congress leader who could not take seriously the Mahatma's saintly image,

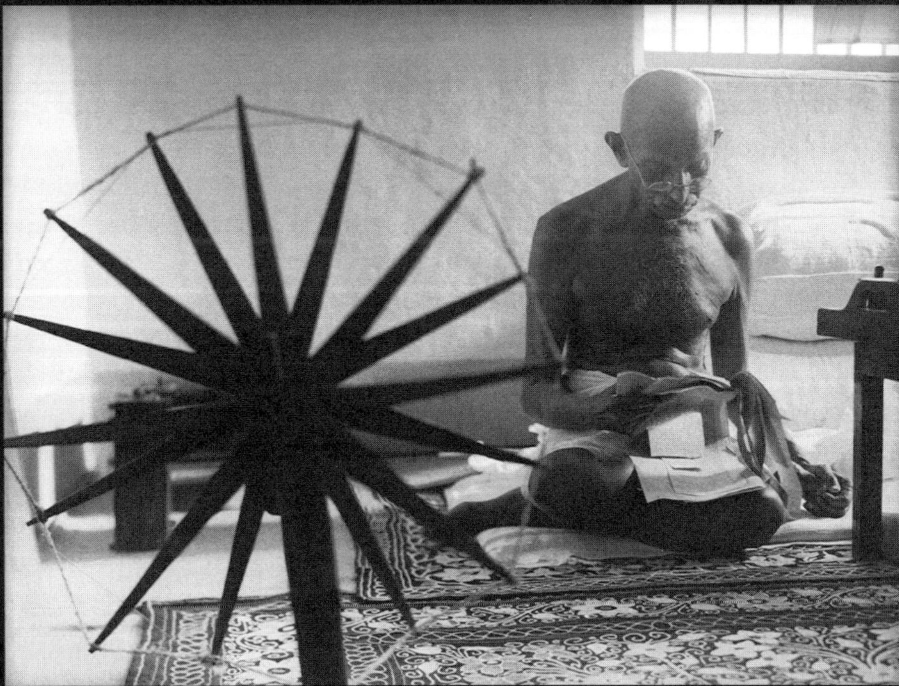

did not regard him either as a Buddha or Jesus but rather as the American cartoon character Mickey Mouse.[57] Despite Gandhi's view that the camera represented an 'inferior form' of technology when compared to the *charkha* (spinning wheel), black-and-white photography played a pivotal role in moulding and fixing his public persona. Photographs iterated and sealed his abiding sartorial code in the public consciousness: the wearing of *khadi*, a white hand-spun and hand-woven cloth.[58]

Prior to Gandhi's *Swadeshi* movement, a person's precise community and social standing could be readily ascertained from what they wore. It was 'when enhanced with the bewitching touch of colour' that the symbolism, the lavish detail and the immaculate craftsmanship of Indian textiles could be brought into relief.[59] Hence, black-and-white photography denoted 'the pristine reference of the Western photographer, scholar, critic and connoisseur', and while supplying a reliable copy of reality, it was perceived by most as disappointingly monochrome.[60] Gandhi, by contrast, harnessed the monochrome quality of photography to political advantage. Through his promotion of handmade *khadi*, which purported to signify an idealized self-reliance, a more frugal form of life, and a rebuke to the mill-made cloth produced with Indian cotton, manufactured in England, and sold back to Indians, he sought to transform the 'colonized body into an Indian body'.[61] Black-and-white photography was ideally suited to choreographing this project. As most reporters were foreigners who catered for the demands of an international market, the wearing of *khadi* conveyed a clear and simple message to the untrained eye.[62]

It was America's paramount industrial photographer, Margaret Bourke-White, who took the most iconic photograph of Gandhi.[63] Bourke-White, a fierce and intrepid individual, was primarily a 'photographer of objects, even of people as objects'.[64] At the time of the Great Depression in the United States (a period marked by profound economic decline beginning in 1929 with lasting effects into the late 1930s), Bourke-White had built her career shooting monumental steel mills, factories, dams and construction sites. By emphasizing formal attributes such as detail, repetition and pattern, the photographer glorified the visual manifestations of American industrial progress and capitalist achievement. But in India the unlikely subject of Bourke-White's focus was a human being: Gandhi, who was to become the nation's most celebrated craftsman. Indeed, no matter how taxing and busy his political schedule, Gandhi would find the time to sit (and pose before the camera) in meditative silence at his *charkha*, absorbed in the spinning he upheld and advocated as a daily practice. Although Gandhi treated modern technology with disdain, he tactically turned a blind eye to his dependence on photography and the media to propagate his message. While Gandhi the spinner maintained that the *charkha* alone symbolized the perfect 'proletarianism of science', Bourke-White retorted that the camera represented a democratically superior form of handicraft.[65]

These tensions crystallize in Bourke-White's 1946 portrait: *Mahatma Gandhi, April 1946, with his Charkha, or Spinning Wheel, Symbol of India's Struggle for Independence*.[66] A glance at the image reveals Bourke-White's continued exploitation of industrial photographic techniques as reflected in the precise rendition of form, volume and depth of interior. Her modernist ambitions recall the words of American photographer Edward Weston, the supreme artist-technician of imaging surfaces: 'The camera should be used for a recording of life, for rendering the very substance and quintessence of the living self, whether it be polished steel or palpitating flesh.'[67]

Despite the instructions of Gandhi's aides never to use flash, which was deemed disrespectful, Bourke-White necessarily employed powerful and violent flashbulbs inside the dim office. The flawless image is as much the result of Bourke-White's aggressive resolve as of her sitter's cooperation. The Mahatma, appearing serenely oblivious to the photographer, is immortalized by Bourke-White while reading intently – cropped, the giant arm of the *charkha* appears frozen in time.[68]

Agitating and Organizing: The CPI and the Role of Photography

Although Gandhi relied very much on the attention that international press photographers granted him, he never engaged a photographer to provide pictures to meet specific editorial needs. By contrast, as early as 1942 the General Secretary of the Communist Party of India, Puran Chand (P.C.) Joshi,[69] recognized the importance of photography in terms of political expediency. Decades earlier, Lenin had capitalized on photography, and particularly on a visual form of journalism that could agitate and educate millions of illiterate Russians. 'History in photos,' he remarked, is 'clear and comprehensible. No painter is able to depict on canvas what the camera sees.'[70] After Lenin's death, photography continued to play a pivotal political role in Soviet Russia. At the 1934 Congress of Soviet Writers, during Stalin's leadership, artists, writers and photographers were called upon to 'depict truthfully' and fulfil the 'needs of educating the masses in the spirit of Socialism'.[71] Joshi's enthusiastic adoption of the Stalinist policy on visual

WHO LIVES

THE MARCH OF DEATH

1. **Quitting the Village**
2. **On the Pavement**
3. **In the Relief Hospital**
4. **On the Burning Ghat**

Photos by Sunil Janah

★

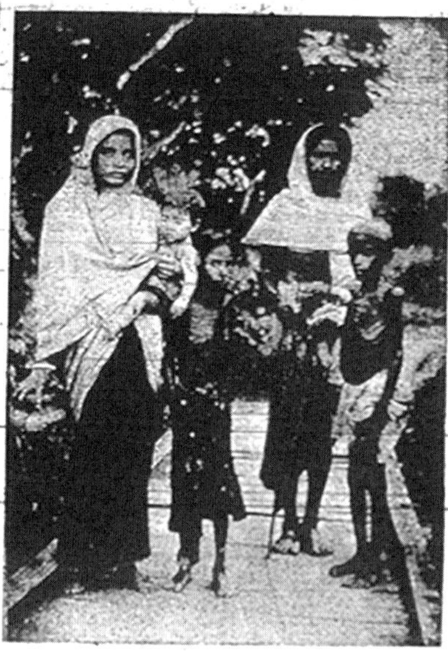

1

I know Calcutta well, I have stayed there a year and a half underground and visited it every year whenever I have been free. This time I was going there exactly after a year to study the food situation. I never realised how bad the situation was, neither from the daily press of Bengal itself, nor from the Party reports, nor the numerous press photographs

I was hardly five minutes in Calcutta when I was shaken up as I have rarely been by a voice through the window: *Ma go Babare!* I had never heard such accents nor such a tone. I would have called it the voice of the dying but it was not feeble enough for it; it was the voice of utter helplessness. Seeing me reacting strangely, Mansoor, my host told me: "A destitute is asking for rice. They are the persons who have come to Calcutta from the surrounding districts for food." I pulled aside the curtain only to see two cringing eyes over a face that looked blank, devoid of all human expression. I have lived in slum areas as a Communist organiser, I have worked in cholera infected areas as a youngster. But I had never seen such a sight before. My finger could hold the curtain no more, nor my eyes stand the sight.

The Destitute

I went round Calcutta that day and saw heaps of them, the destitutes. The Chowringhee area where the Burra Sahibs live or come to shop is alone kept clear. Otherwise they are all over Calcutta, 1,25,000 of them. The pavement is their home, their rags smell from a long distance. They sit in groups, gossip or brood if they are fresh from the village and have yet the physical and mental strength to do so or they just lie on their sides with their arms for a pillow, the whole family huddled together. There were hardly any young men among them, a very small number of old men, mostly women and children. The more I got used to the ghastly sight, the more I realised how difficult it was to understand the situation behind it.

I stayed six weeks in Bengal from mid-September onwards, spent 10 days in Chittagong, the district most affected by the crisis, heard reports from all districts in a ten days' meeting with the Provincial Party organisers, saw the League Premier Sir Nazimuddin, the Food Minister Suhrawardy, the leader of the Opposition Dr. Shyamaprasad, besides University Professors, journalists and relief workers. It was only after four weeks of seeing, listening, talking, and discussing that I got the hang of the tragic tale of Bengal today and whose living symbol is the destitute. Here is the simple story.

Bengal has a population of six crores: 5½ crores live in its villages. One crore are landless labourers and village artisans. They have been starving for the last six months at least. They struggle hard to find any job in their own village but very few peasants have rice to give them as wages and cash-wages are useless. They appeal for charity but how can this source keep the family going? And besides it is not a question of feeding a few beggars but a whole section of the village which constitutes anything from 15 to 30% of its population.

Landless Labourer

They love their village and do not want to leave it but are forced to. First the young men quit in search of jobs outside, to be able to send cash home. But they are rarely able to; the wages they get are barely enough to fill their own bellies, with the price of rice being what it is.

The family at home goes on starving, first the extremes die, the old and the children. The rest of the family holds on for a few months but the much-looked-for money-order does not come, not even a post-card, for the sons or husbands are too ashamed of themselves to write anything home when they can't send any help. The family holds counsel together and decides to sell its scanty belongings, if anything is yet left, and make for the town in search of employment and food.

Who will employ an old man or woman with children and, besides, what few jobs can a village labourer do in a town? They go round and round the town till the last flicker of hope gets extinguished and they become destitutes. They live on charity if any kind person has any food to give, or go for gruel to the Relief Kitchen if any exists and has received stocks enough to run the kitchen. Those that do not leave the village die off, one after another. Thus whole families get wiped out.

Share-cropper

Above the landless labourer are the share-croppers and poor peasants, about 1½ crores. They have been starving for the last 3 months at least. The next 3 months are going to be the worst for them. They never had rice to last the whole year; they used to scrape through during the lean months by getting rice on loan from the zamindar, jotedar (cultivating tenant-proprietor) or the mahajan. Today the mahajan, of course, does not give rice on loan nor does he advance cash.

The zamindar and the jotedar do not loan out rice either; they found it more profitable to sell it in the black-market than to reserve it to keep alive their share-croppers or peasants for the next season; they thought, looking at the growing number of destitutes inside the village, that labour power will be available. By this calculation life got cheaper! Their fate also becomes the same as that of the village labourer described above; they have also to quit the villages in search of food and the rest of the story is the same.

These 2½ crores, landless labourers and poor peasants, are being uprooted from the soil. They constitute the endless growing base of the destituted. As they become destitute and quit the village in large numbers, something happens to the village that could not feed them. With the mass exodus of the landless and poor peasants, rural economy itself has begun to crack-up.

In all the 4 districts around Calcutta acute shortage of agricultural labourers to harvest the winter aman crop is reported. That is one of the reasons why the ordinance to send them back to their villages was hurriedly promulgated. Unless they can be restored to normal strength through proper feeding and medical attention not only will they die in lacs but the aman crop will be damaged for lack of harvesters and there will be less labourers and peasants to grow food for the next year, resulting in a worse food crisis.

It is not that the village landless or poor alone are suffering starvation. A growing number of middle peasants are following close behind them. The number of transfer deeds being registered at the Sub-Registrar's office is far above the normal and is increasing month after month.

Middle Peasant

In Nilphamari (Rangpur) the number of sale-deeds was 11,915 during the last 3 months as against 4,368 last year.

In Narayanganj daily 150 to 195 sales or mortgages are registered as against the normal 10 to 15.

In Pabna between January-October 6,530 transfers took place and the daily average has now reached 100.

Land is passing from the peasants to the village rich. The rich are becoming richer, and the poor poorer.

How is it that even the middle peasant has to sell off; where did his rice go? He got humbugged by the hoarder and tempted by the high price offered. Rice was Rs. 6/- per maund in January 1942 (i.e. at the time of the last aman harvest). In November the price stood at Rs. 11/- and by January 1943 Rs. 14/- (the time to sell his aman). He had never heard of such prices before. He fell a prey to the hoarders deceitful propaganda that he would never get such good prices again. He sold off as much as he could with the hope that the price was bound to fall and he would buy back cheap in case of need.

From April the price has been rising from Rs. 24/- onwards. This is how the credulous peasant was defrauded of his stocks by the hoarder and later skinned of his cash too when he came to buy rice. This is how he began sinking to the status of the pauper.

The village middle-class that lived partly on land and partly on the money sent by the employed sons of the family did not even get a bellyful of rice when I was there. The children were fed and the rest shared out whatever was left. They have the cash but that does not buy even enough rice. When I was there the price in the mofussil was Rs. 40/- to 50/-, now it is anywhere from Rs. 50/- to 100/-. They had already begun selling jewellery, household furniture etc., and it has now come to selling houses and lands.

Nobody gets a bellyful of rice in the villages of Bengal except a small minority, the zamindars, the rich jotedars and the mahajans.

P.

Fifty lacs live in the towns; has been promised several tim[es] yet introduced. All the mofu[ssil] live on the black-market and of the lower middle-class and can be imagined. Governme[nt] send casual supplies, not eno[ugh] demand. For days in a wee[k] grains were available except at prices and in small quanti[ties]. Nazimuddin, who belongs to Nawab family, told me th[at he] received a trunk call from his [...] they were eating the grain m[...] pigeons!

Inside The Towns

In Calcutta there is no off[icial rationing], but the industrial worke[rs] employees in the priority conc[erns] most of the big firms) and [...] servants get their rations [from their] employer. But the worke[r gets] ration only for himself an[d for his] family and for them he has [to fall] back on the market. This rationing does not cover more of Calcutta's population. Th[e rest have] to depend entirely on the bl[ack-market], i.e., starve or half-starve. [...] shops give a seer of atta ea[ch] but he is lucky only if he h[as] the right place in the queue to [get it] atta before it gets exhaust[ed] other food grains are supplied there are stocks, which is not [...]

Such is the picture o[f] Bengal, its population goi[ng to] destitution and death, its rura[l economy] being destroyed. This is n[...] miserable tale.

In this very pr[ocess of] economic disintegration, [moral] degeneration is also tak[ing place] and the very foundations [of family] life are being destroyed.

Inside The Families

I heard numberless stories taking place in real life insi[de] millions. In the villages especi[ally] the poor after the young men [leave the] village in search of jobs and [starvation] reaches a worse stage, the old [...] the old woman out just to e[...] there may be one less mouth to [feed so that] he and the children may ha[ve a better] chance to live; the mother-in[-law asks] the daughter-in-law to quit or e[...] The lot of the widows is [...] Along with starvation the l[aw of the] jungle comes to prevail: Each [...]

Mothers, who, unable [to feed their] children die in their own arm[s ...]

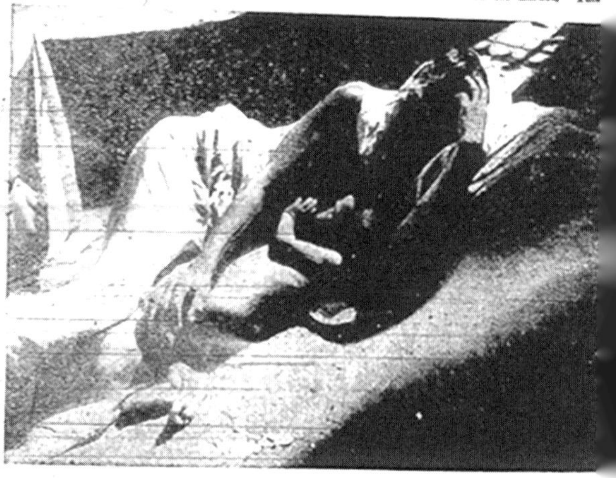

2

[ ] BENGAL DIES ?

[ ]HI

[ ]d the mutual agony or forsake [ ] the illusory hope that fate may [ ]re no more rumours or isolated [ ] mass phenomenon. I saw any [ ] destitute children myself, [ ] of course, but also looking [ ] being all alone in the wide world around.

[ ]tution is growing together with [ ] Among the destitutes of [ ]here are hardly any young [ ]ey are old women or mothers [ ] burden of children. Young [ ] unmarried girls are inside [ ]als. The story is very [ ] pimps surround the destitute [ ] it reaches Calcutta. After a [ ] knocking about, the mother [ ]nds over the daughter or [ ]-law.

[ ]planation is this. She could [ ] starve, or some cash was [ ]buy milk for the infants or [ ]der the rest (relief kitchen [ ]one meal). If one can win the [ ] of the old woman, she herself

What about millions of Bengalis who daily witness it all! Their heart bleeds but they are getting inured to it. They curse the government and themselves feel helpless. What else can we expect from the people at large when the leaders of patriotic organisations like the Congress, League and Mahasabha do not sink their differences and unite to save the very foundations of civilised life in their own homeland!

Inside Bengal humanity is being dehumanised.

Relief Kitchens

I was particularly interested in the kitchens because they mean immediate and practical relief. The latest government figures show that there are 5452 relief kitchens throughout Bengal. There are 80,000 villages, everyone of which needs relief while there is only one kitchen to every 15. In other words, existing relief has to be extended 15 times to be able to say that the relief kitchens cover all the most needy cases.

Of these 3821 are run by the Government, 1217 are subsidised and 574 are private kitchens.

The total number fed in all the kitchens put together is 30,78,886, i. e.,

[ ] comrade said that 97% of the destitutes were already pre-dropsy cases

Cholera is already raging in some districts in epidemic form and threatens to engulf the province.

Malaria was common in Bengal. But the vast majority of the people are underfed and have far less powers of resistance and so malaria has assumed the malignant form

I was one day discussing the problem of starvation, diseases and epidemics with Dr. Narayan Roy. He has done seven years in the Andamans and is a popular doctor in his locality, as the poor man's friend. His clients are from the lower and middle classes. He told me that normally he used to have one serious case in every 20, the rest such as could be tackled in a few minutes each. But for the last few months it was the other way about, 19 serious cases and only one ordinary.

He could not come home for meals in time nor did he get enough sleep; he worked as hard as he could, and yet he could not cope with the serious cases. The lower middle class no longer called the Doctor for ordinary cases. He had compared notes with other colleagues of his and their experience was the same.

famine and they don't know their basic acts.

My estimate is that 50,00,000 would die off by the end of December. I am certain it is not an over-estimate; 2¼ crores are the landless and the poor peasants alone, among whom mass starvation began from March–July. 50,00,000 would just be old men and children, the two extremes that are the worst affected by starvation, and die first.

If the situation after December does not radically improve, and the aman crop gets cornered by the hoarders next year's figures will be still more staggering.

The people of Bengal are threatened with physical extinction and moral collapse.

SEND ALL YOU CAN TO
People's Relief Committee, Bengal.
62, Bowbazar Street, Calcutta.

- Non-Party, Non-Communal Province-wide Organisation
- Has links in every rural district through the Food Committees
- Appeals to all Textile mills for cloth in view of approaching winter
- Is in dire need of medical supplies to fight cholera, typhoid, malaria, etc.

Make your cheques and drafts payable to:

PEOPLE'S RELIEF COMMITTEE, BENGAL.

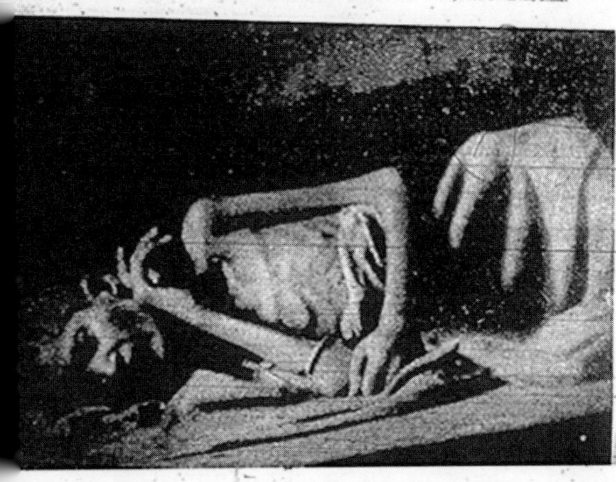

Everything to Save Bengal

Bengal is dying and it is the concern of us all.

If Bengal sinks, famine and epidemics that lay Bengal low will spread to the rest of the country and nothing will stop them. What Bengal is suffering today, all will suffer tomorrow unless we help to save Bengal now.

If famine continues to stalk Bengal it means inviting the Japs to march in. What better internal conditions could they desire—with people dying, economy cracking up, morale sagging. And the Japs are no fools.

Bose is fully exploiting the Bengal famine in his Radio broadcasts and is repeatedly announcing that he is coming with his puppet army. He has also announced the path of invasion, via Chittagong. He has moved his Provisional Government from Singapore to Rangoon. And after Bose has brought the Japs to Bengal, they will not remain content with Bengal.

To let famine rage in Bengal is to let Bengal die, to let famine invade the rest of the country and tempt the Japs to invade Bengal.

★

Bengal must not die for the sake of India and every single Indian.

If we love our family and do not want it to go to pieces like Bengal's families, we must help Bengal.

If we desire to save the honour of our wives and sisters and not lose it like Bengal's wives and sisters, we must help Bengal.

If we want our children not to die like flies as Bengal's children are dying, we must help Bengal.

If we love India we must save Bengal. If Bengal dies India cannot live.

This is how I understood the situation in Bengal after grappling with it for six weeks and with the help of the comrades there. The clearer the comprehension of the situation became, the faster disappeared my shuddering before the ghastly scenes. I left Bengal with only one determination, how to make every Indian patriot forget all differences and get together to organise maximum help for Bengal, how to make every man, woman and child pay, pay and pay for Bengal till he has not a copper left to spare.

[ ]tory amidst heart-rending [ ]mate is that about 30,000 [ ] 1,25,000 destitutes alone, [ ] the brothels, 1 in 4 of them [ ]cide. This is not likely to [ ]rivate because there are [ ] youths among them: men [ ]sh and the great majority [ ] women and children.

[De]humanised

[Am]ong our comrades reported [ ]stitution is already a pheno[menon among] the destitutes especially in [ ] far less in the villages. I [ ] evidence of this.

[ ] 28, the All-Parties Relief [ ]Netrakona rescued 12 girls [ ] sold to the prostitutes at [ ] and it expected to rehome

[ ]as I churned up inside my [ ]rts of the degradation of the [ ] was like living through a [ ] so intense my agony while [ ]t it, what unimaginable [ ]ool must have been the lot [ ] directly underwent these [ ]he first destitute I saw in [ ]diately after my arrival, [ ] and face that had given [ ], came back to mind, as [ ]orphaned children looking [ ]age, of women lying on [ ] vacantly gazing at the [ ]d been reduced to the sub-

at least one out of every thirty Bengalis is already a destitute; the figure for Calcutta is 1 in every 25; for Chittagong one in every 21; and for Contai which the Viceroy visited, 1 in every 2.

What is the food they get? They call it *khichuri*; it is a watery gruel of rice, dal and bajra. In some kitchens they don't put bajra and in others they add some vegetables to rice and dal.

The destitutes get only one meal a day from these kitchens and that too does not fill the belly. I inquired from a large number of them and learnt that what they get is only half their one meal. The Relief Kitchen therefore is not an institution that saves people but only staves off the day of death. It is but a stepping stone towards the burning ghat.

Disease And Epidemics

Long-drawn starvation, eating inedible roots, grass and even weeds from the tanks has produced stomach disorders of all sorts. Diarrhoea or dysentery, both amoebic and bacillary, are very common. The destitutes invariably suffer from these. Soon after it develops into dropsy and then over the swollen parts, festering sores appear which stink horribly. The kitchens in Calcutta are the best. While I was having a look at one of these in the Kidderpore area a Doctor

"This food crisis is going to lead to a terrible medical crisis, the whole medical system is going to collapse, unable to bear the strain."

This was his conclusion.

The Cycle Of Death

From starvation to disease and then death. Such is the cycle and it is running non-stop. The number of destitutes is growing, victims of epidemics are increasing and the death roll is mounting higher and higher. I doubt if anyone in Bengal can miss the sight of a corpse *every day*. I did not.

'Calcutta's normal death rate was 550, it is now 2000 per day. From the press reports it appears that among the starvation cases 1 dies for every 2 admitted into the hospitals in Calcutta. *The Statesman* editorially computed the weekly death-rate throughout Bengal to be 10,000 but conceded that it may well be anywhere up to 40,000. Pandit Kunzru puts the figure at 50,000 per week and I agree with him that it is a conservative estimate.

There are no official figures for total deaths by starvation. When the Government of India wanted the figures, the Bengal Government asked by turns the Civil Supplies, Home and Revenue Departments but nobody knew! These [ ] are supposed to fight the

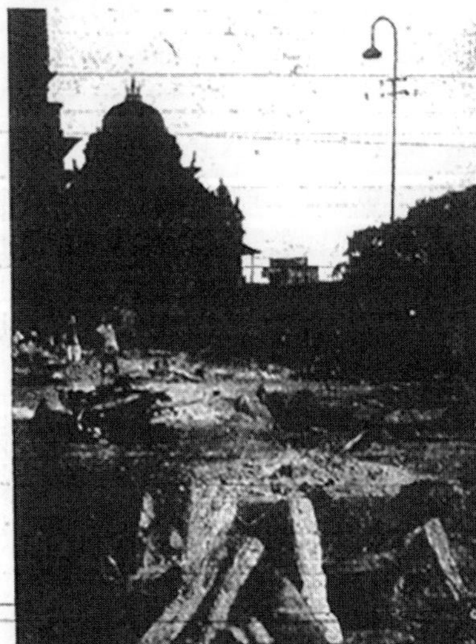

and literary propaganda strangely resonated with Bourke-White's photographic approach. Putting aside her political beliefs, Bourke-White travelled across India with the CPI and Sunil Janah to cover the 'fall of the British Empire' for the popular American picture magazine *Life*.[72]

Disillusioned with the national movement, Joshi sought new ways to achieve political and social emancipation, endorsing the need for Communist Party members to occupy all 'intellectual grounds from political parties and the press to education and cultural activities'.[73] Advocating the Gramscian role of the 'organic intellectual', Joshi believed that intellectuals operating in semi-democratic conditions were 'distinguished less by their profession, which may be any job characteristic of their class, than by their function in directing the ideas and aspirations of the class to which they organically belong'.[74] The influence of Communist thought played a greater role in India's nationalist struggle following the break of diplomatic relations between England and Russia in 1927. Intellectual debates about the social function of art and literature had emerged in the mid-1930s, culminating with the formation of the progressive cultural movement, the Anti-Fascist Writers' and Artists' Association of Bengal, in the early 1940s.[75] By 1930, as the Comintern came under the influence of the Soviet Union and Stalin, its control over Indian Communists became dysfunctional. Though largely ignorant of the political and social situation of Asia, the Comintern referred all decisions on Indian Communist directives to the English Communist Ben Bradley, representative of the Communist Party of Great Britain.[76] With no representative of its own at the Comintern headquarters in Moscow, Indian Communists experienced constant fluctuations in Comintern policy towards imperialism and the national movement.[77] Banned by the Government of India in 1934, the CPI had been reduced to less than fifty members and stood isolated from the nationalist movement and the masses. In 1935, the scattered group met in Surat and elected Joshi as General Secretary of the Party. The election occurred in a critical period, when the implementation of the Sixth Congress thesis on colonial and semi-colonial countries had reduced the CPI to a negligible existence.[78]

Despite the Soviet Central Committee diktat that all cultural endeavours should celebrate *partinost* and abide by the official doctrine of socialist realism, Joshi enjoyed relative independence on the cultural front. By 1939, the CPI had emerged as a nationalist force with key regional members as well as an independent base among workers, peasants, students and intellectuals. This was a time at which the CPI leadership had begun to think independently, grasping the importance of developing a national consciousness within the Independence movement.

Moreover, Joshi came to realize that 'Marxism was, under colonial conditions, not a negation of, but an affirmation and further extension of nationalism'.[79]

Endorsing the propagandist policies propounded by the Central Committee, Joshi was also instrumental in founding several progressive cultural movements across India to bring art and politics closer to the people: the All-India Progressive Writers' Association in 1935 and the Indian People's Theatre Association (IPTA) in 1943.[80] Moreover, Joshi was able to attract Sardar Jafri, Faiz Ahmed Faiz, P.C. Mahalanobis and Bishnu Dey, some of the most progressive cultural figures in India.[81] In 1941, under the direction of the Comintern, the CPI abandoned the united front and extended full support to the war effort and to the British Indian government.

Although the British legalized the CPI (it had continually been banned since its foundation), the Party's abandonment of the united front and betrayal of the nationalist cause was interpreted by Congress as an act of treason.[82] A pariah within Congress, the CPI now stood further isolated from the national movement and the mass of the people, comprising workers, peasants and students. But the sudden legalization granted the Party an unprecedented visibility, which it exploited by launching a new national weekly newspaper, *People's War*. By means of this publication the CPI was finally able to stage the nationalist struggle in the realm of the visual. Launching mass relief campaigns during the Bengal Famine, the CPI seized the opportunity for political expansion: by 1943, *People's War* had a national circulation of 25,000–30,000 copies, while the Party's membership had grown rapidly, to an estimated 30,000 (up from 5,000 in 1942). That of its trade union following stood at a quarter of a million.[83]

Under Joshi's leadership, Communist intellectuals, artists, actors and writers explored every available medium for the purposes of propaganda; each performed an essential mediating role in the struggle between class interests.[84] Joshi's organic vision would profoundly shape the theatre performances carried out by IPTA artists across villages and cities. Once photographed, the affective visual tropes developed for the stage became iconic, repeatable motifs that were reproduced and circulated in the press across India to inform, raise consciousness and stir up viewers.

Studying for a Master's degree in English Literature at Calcutta University, Janah had not intended to become a photographer. He lacked any professional training:

> My grandmother had bought me a Box Brownie when I was a mere boy and later a Voigtlande Brilliant camera. Within a few years, I became seriously addicted to photography. In this, I was aided and abetted by

> Shambhu Saha, a well-known photographer and friend of our family. ... He had taught me all that I knew then of photography, including darkroom work, for which he let me use his own well-equipped unit.[85]

At the time, many of Janah's friends had found temporary jobs in the wartime offices set up in Calcutta. An acquaintance suggested to Janah that he apply for a job as a photographer advertised by the Inspectorate of Scientific Stores – an establishment where scientific, specifically military, instruments supplied by colonial manufacturers were created, inspected and tested. The range of equipment comprised communications machinery, wireless receivers and transmitters, and optical instruments such as telescopes. Although Janah had no technical qualifications, his meticulous photographing of industrial objects got him the job. He recounts:

> I had to photograph 'exploded' views of these – all the components taken apart and placed one after the other in the right sequence, so that they could be accurately reassembled at the site with the help of these photographs and prepared instructions. I also had to do many other precision jobs such as making telescope graticules and gauges for various instruments photographically. These demanded precision and technical skills I had not yet acquired. Fortunately, we had an Englishman, E.J. Wender, the head of the optical section, a scientific fellow of the Royal Photographic Society, who was willing to help me understand and use the expertise needed. I learned how to make excellent, flawless prints. During the ten months that I worked there, I made up for my lack of technical training.[86]

Janah resigned from the job to prepare for his MA examinations, but, 'swallowed up' by the Communist Party, he never sat for his exams. Like many other students of his generation, he was strongly drawn towards Communist doctrines: 'Socialism, putting an end to all social injustices and the exploitation of any people, seemed to most of us the only worthwhile objective, which could be achievable only after India had won Independence.'[87]

Unlike freelance press photographers who provided an ongoing, rapid service and supply of a variety of disparate images, Janah followed specific political events, aiming in each case to create a single image that could sum up a complex narrative in its entirety and 'bring clearly before the mind the events of their time'.[88] The selection of the images, along with their arrangement, sequencing and layout was carried out in consultation with the editorial hierarchy of the Party journal.[89] The most significant difference in method between the CPI's output and other press photographs, however, concerned the text. The press photographer normally exerted no control over it and had little contact with the author. The Party photographer, on the other hand, had a tacitly understood relationship with the narrative and could often adapt and determine the function and use of the images. Despite the fact that photographic documentation was more suited to recording the changing present, Joshi also commissioned Party artists – including Chittaprosad Bhattacharya, Zainul Abedin, Gobardhan Ash, Somnath Hore, Gopal Ghose and Quamrul Hassan – to sketch the effects of the famine 'from life' with the simplest and most rudimentary of media: pen and paper.[90] Largely inspired by the contemporary Chinese example, classical and lyrical qualities were removed from this art to create graphic documents of a debased humanity.[91] This greater reliance on craft and artisanal ways of documenting the human catastrophe, as the scholar Janaki Nair observes, suggests the artists' more personal involvement with the famine phenomenon.[92]

Framing Atrocity: Sunil Janah and the Bengal Famine, 1943–44

> If you are a regular reader of *People's War*, you may have observed that our photographs tell you stories. They are not put in simply as decorations.
>
> – P.C. Joshi[93]

Once the CPI had woken up to the full horror of the famine, Joshi travelled to Calcutta from Bombay with the intention of finding and recruiting the young Communist student and amateur photographer, Sunil Janah. Seventy years later, this is how Janah describes the encounter:

> Joshi wanted to travel around Bengal to make a detailed reportage of the famine for the Party's journal. We had met a few times earlier, and he had come to know of my amateur skills from the photographs he had seen published in the *Illustrated Weekly*. When summoned by him, I turned up at the local Party office. Joshi asked me to accompany him on his projected tour across famine-ravaged Bengal, and informed me that this tour was to begin on the very next day! ... What we saw,

> travelling from village to village, was a recurrent, chilling nightmare. Unlike in the more publicized famines that have occurred in Africa in later decades, no international relief had come to the aid of the people – in fact, not even the news of the dimensions of the calamity had reached the outside world. The British-owned news agencies operating in India were chary of any detailed reporting of events in India that could be used to the disadvantage of the Allied forces. During a world war, the plight of starving Bengalis and other unfortunate Indians was not anyone's priority, or even concern.[94]

Janah's first-hand experience of the famine culminated in a photo essay published in *People's War* in November 1943, titled 'Toiling Orissa faces Death'. The photo essay comprised a written report by party member S.S. Batliwala,[95] interlocked with Janah's black-and-white photographs. Batliwala describes how the province of Orissa, situated below Bengal and within easy reach of enemy attacks on the eastern coast, had been ravaged by the famine. He attributes much of the responsibility for the famine's intensification to government corruption and, more importantly, to private speculators who purchased, hoarded and sold large quantities of rice. The situation, if allowed to continue, would not only cause the miserable death of many millions but also break the people's morale, encouraging a Japanese counter-offensive.

Janah's image *Skeletons Strewn on a Field Dumped with the Dead, Orissa Famine*, displays skulls and bones lying in an open field. The bleached skeletons follow a serpentine curve, creating a horrific tableau.[96] The theatrical quality of the image evokes photographer Felice Beato's[97] *Interior of Secundrabagh After the Massacre*, produced in 1858 and purporting to show the aftermath of the 1857 Mutiny.[98] Dug up by order of the photographer, the skeletal remains of slaughtered Indian *sepoys* and prosthetic additions of dubious provenance were arranged across the grounds of the villa's interior pavilion for a macabre photo opportunity in Lucknow.[99] Both images offer ghoulish choreographies designed to elicit horror in the viewer: Beato's panorama of disaster celebrates conflict, the advancement of political sovereignty and the triumph of British imperial might; Janah documents a harrowing example of the failure of colonial governance and indicts Empire for its extractive and irrepressible self-interest.[100]

Similarly constructed is the image *Dog Eating the Skeletal Remains of a Corpse, Orissa Famine (On the Road to Rai Bania Village)*. Janah zooms in on a dog gnawing at the semi-decomposed corpse of a famine victim; more specifically, the

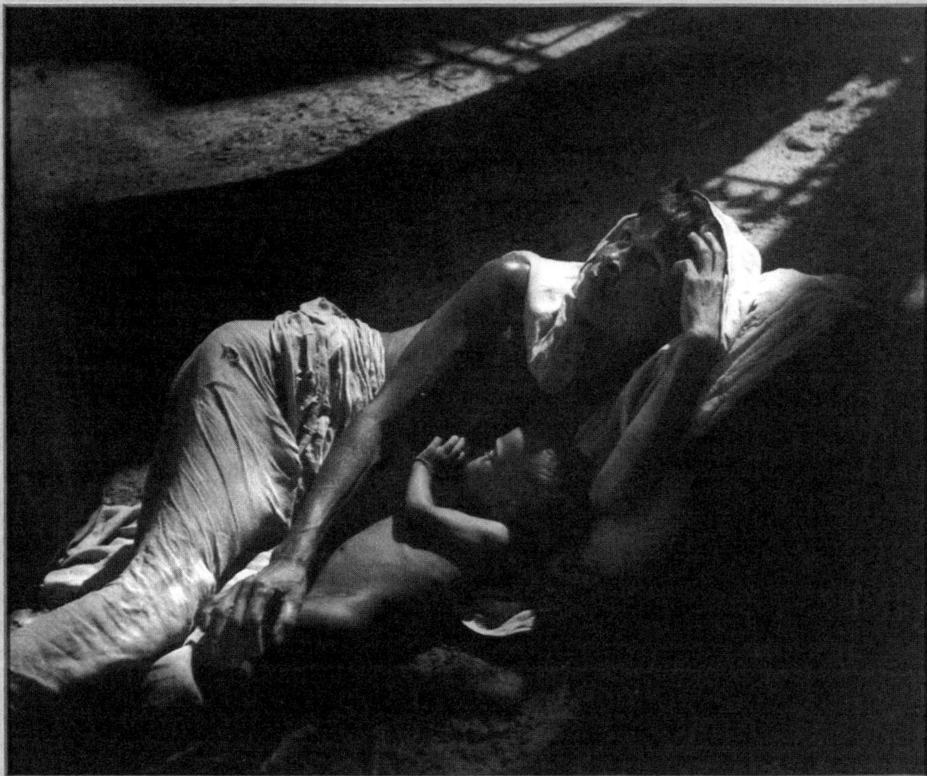

Bengal famine, Mother & child in a Calcutta pavement, 1943

Sunil Janah

remains of its lower pelvis. The stark photograph evokes the image of an emaciated Christ deposed from his cross. Below the photograph, in bold lettering, is the appeal, 'Orissa Needs Your Help Send All You Can', encouraging patriots to send money to the Orissa Provincial Committee of the Communist Party.

Shortly afterwards another photo essay, titled 'Who Lives if Bengal Dies?', was published in *People's War*. The four-sequence montage sums up with bleak realism the starving rural migrants' march towards the city: *Quitting the Village*, *On the Pavement* (which we encountered at the beginning of this essay), *In the Relief Hospital* and *On the Burning Ghat*. *Quitting the Village* depicts a family setting out on the unknown journey which will slowly but surely cause its complete disintegration. With the unfolding of each sequence, we witness the family unit's gradual collapse to the ground, metabolism slow down, and the organic processes of living and waiting to die become one. On the ground, and close to the bodies of the dying men and women, the camera shutter blinks. The same compositions and tropes resurface in the play *The March of Death*, performed by IPTA actors across India to raise awareness and generate funds for famine relief. But in the pages of *People's War*, Janah's photographic narrative and Joshi's first-hand accounts are directed towards saving the famine victims and staving off Japan's impending invasion. Patriots are urged to send money to the People's Relief Committee of Bengal: 'To let famine rage in Bengal is to let Bengal die, to let famine invade the rest of the country and tempt the Japs to invade Bengal.'[101] Responsibility for the famine is attributed to greedy private speculators, not the Government of India. To reinforce the charity appeal, the last page of the report includes Janah's photograph *Orphans Waiting for Food at a Famine Relief Centre, Orissa Famine*. Under a black sky, hundreds of emaciated orphaned children squat in a field. Janah kneels down with his camera: the affective experience of the famine becomes a communal affair.

By 1945, the Bengal Famine had spread its orbit southward, gripping large areas of southern India. That same year, the editorial board of *Life* sent Bourke-White to India to witness the 'fall of the British Empire'.[102] Struck by Janah's photographs in Calcutta, Bourke-White travelled to the CPI headquarters in Bombay to meet with him. As Janah recalls:

> I was scheduled to go down and photograph what was happening there, but joining Margaret Bourke-White on the same trail would mean that *Life Magazine* would unknowingly be paying for some of the expenses of the Communist Party of India. I travelled first class in the Railways and drove around half the South Indian peninsula in a hired car with

> a driver ... instead of travelling by bus between cities and walking the rest of the way, as had been my lot. ... We were constantly together and I found that we went about our work in a very similar manner except for one big difference, the time and materials we could expend on every photograph. When we were recording things happening and did not need to, or could do nothing to change what was before us, we both took our photographs rapidly – she with her Rolleiflex and I with my Leica. But when we found the possibilities and the time to do some rearranging of the scene we preferred to stage 'posed candids'. I would be content with shifting the position of people a little, taking a little more time to shoot three or four pictures with my Rolleiflex, which had a larger format than my 35mm Leica. But she would whip out her larger format camera, a 4x5 Linhoff Technika, put it on a tripod, grab her flash gun, attach the flash cord to her camera, and direct the people in the scene until she had them exactly as she wanted. Then she would, like an old-fashioned photographer, put her black focusing cloth over her head, and take time to focus on the ground glass. The semblance ended there, because she would then shoot four, six, eight, ten or 20 times, pulling out the tabs of her film pack in quick succession, until she was satisfied. ... Bourke-White's style of photography was monumental, the construction she built up was starkly architectural, yet the results were unfailing in the rendition of the minutest of detail. I could see for myself what stubborn persistence and effort it took to achieve that.[103]

Shooting with a handheld Rolleiflex and no flash, Janah took advantage of the better technology deployed by his American colleague. When Bourke-White's flash went off Janah photographed with a rapid shutter, using the light she provided.

The 'Immortality' of 'Bare Life'

> Neither life nor death, it is the haunting of the one by the other ... Ghosts ...
>
> – Jacques Derrida[104]

The famine images produced by Janah and the CPI artists represented the first attempt in the history of modern India to expose the plight of refugees and visually inspire resistance for the purposes of political expediency. During the final decade of India's struggle for freedom, in which genocide, famine, war and populist politics were defining factors, these images constitute one of the most compelling visual attempts to create and mobilize a mass public. Despite the threats posed to the colonial order by these images of 'bare life', there is an unsettling silence in the national narrative surrounding these visceral images that are so difficult to view, yet from which the viewer cannot look away. This tenuous legacy has barely been acknowledged in historical accounts of Indian art, with art historians skirting around it.

In 1945, as World War II drew to a close, Britain's brief flirtation with the CPI came to an end. Now a redundant ally in the fight against Fascism, CPI members 'were promptly told where they belonged'.[105] Janah continued to photograph political events for the Party up until 1947, when at the Second National Conference of the CPI, leading members declared the bankruptcy of Independence. Moving from the *People's War* ideological line back to its historical, anti-imperialist advocacy struggle, the CPI Central Committee described the post-war years in India as 'the period of unprecedented opportunity to make the final bid for power'.[106]

Mindful of the Red Army's successes, the victories in the People's Liberation War in China, and the armed struggle for independence in various colonized territories of Southeast Asia, the CPI surmised that a greater degree of insurgence against British rule in India was all the more justified. Party officials were convinced that the interests of landlords and princes were inextricably entangled with the Empire, and suspected an impending alliance between 'British big business and their India brothers'; for this reason, the CPI sought to unleash agitation on a national scale to unite the industrial workers with the peasants.[107] In 1947, however, on India's attaining Independence at the cost of the brutal Partition, the unrest ended.

Following further upheaval in the CPI in 1948, the Party splintered; former General Secretary P.C. Joshi and several members, including Janah, were expelled.[108] Their dismissal marked the dissolution of the CPI and the collapse of a movement that had radically transformed the meaning and social function of art in the decades prior to Independence. As Janah would recount:

> For many of us, the disastrous Partition of our country, and the murderous communal riots that accompanied India's Independence, were a heartbreak from which we never recovered. Independence had not brought any beginnings of a new era, nor any remarkable changes in the country, not even the promise of any. I did not rejoin the Communist Party, nor did I want to join any other party. I felt that I could never be a political activist again. ... Independence did not, of course,

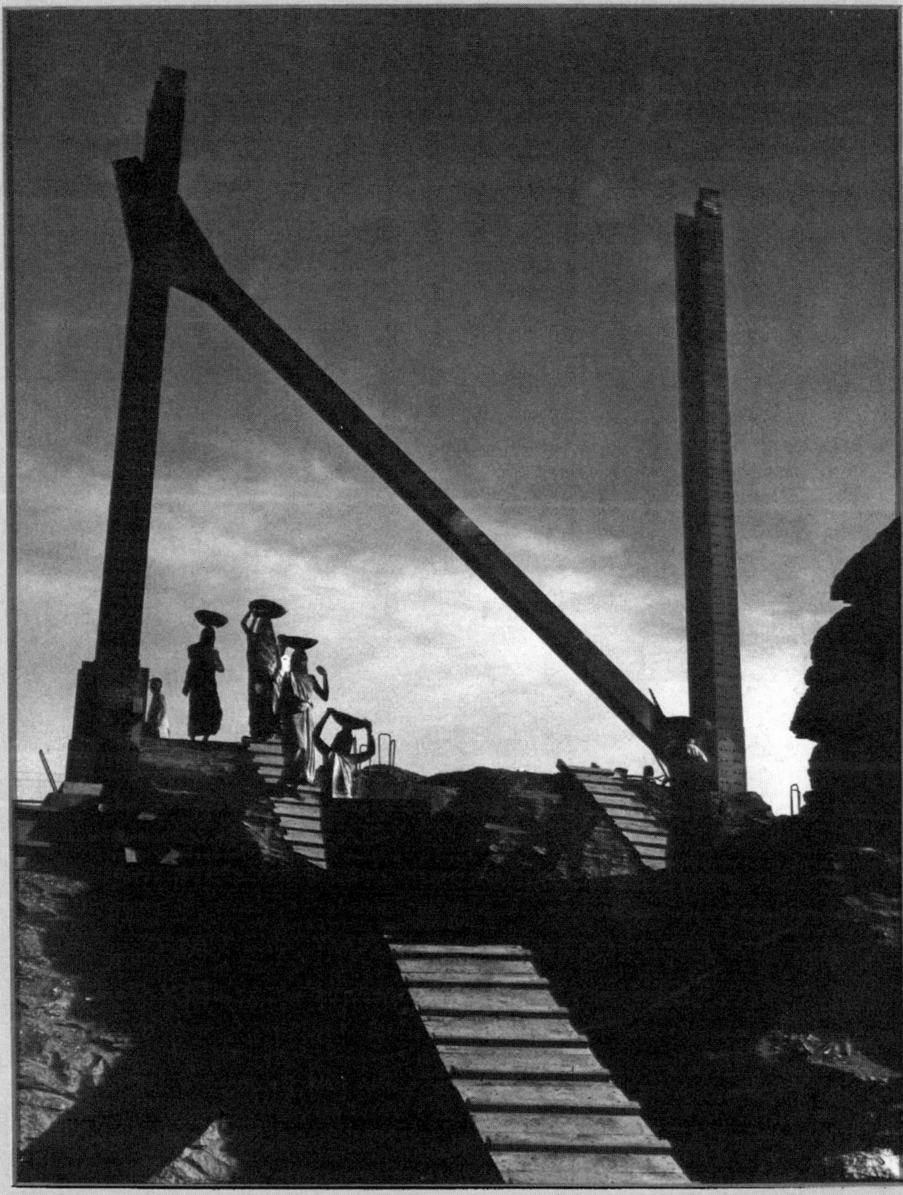

Construction of Bokaro Thermal Power Plant, 1949

Sunil Janah

> bring relief to the appalling miseries of our people, but it happened to coincide with the termination of my Communist Party days and relieved me from the onerous task of recording further miseries.[109]

A politically disillusioned Janah returned to Calcutta in 1948, where he set up a private commercial photographic studio. Completely dissociating himself from Party politics, he began to work for the Government of India. Under Prime Minister Nehru's drive for rapid industrialization during the 1950s, Janah found himself covering the country's major industrial and development ventures.[110] The projects came under the Indian Government's First Five-Year Plan, Nehru's 'new temples' of modern India. The Hindustan Steel Works, the first public sector undertaking in the steel industry, commissioned Janah to photograph the building of three of Nehru's 'temples': at Durgapur in West Bengal, Rourkela in Orissa and Bhilai in Central India. The function of photography was no longer to critique poor labour conditions and the plight of workers, but redirected toward producing lavish marketing brochures to attract interest from potential (foreign) investors. The figure of the worker appears entirely subordinated to the machine.

Up until the early 1960s Janah continually engaged with heavy industry, working for leading Indian industrialists and businessmen such as J.R.D. Tata and G.D. Birla, and for British mercantile firms.[111] In photographing the mining of coal, manganese, bauxite and aluminium, he produced images celebrating the economic foundations of postcolonial India. In this incarnation, documentary photography acquires a different propagandistic purpose. Reminiscent of Bourke-White's industrial photography, Janah glamourizes machines and industrial prowess at the expense of the workers. The industrial landscape is a 'photographic paradise', remarked Bourke-White of the Cleveland Otis Steel Mills in the early thirties.[112] Janah too delights in the novel spectacle of smokestacks, derricks and titanic machinery. In the photograph commissioned by the Tata Iron and Steel Company in Bihar, originally titled *There She Blows Setting the Jamshedpur Sky Aglow* (1957), two gigantic Bessemer converters emit toxic clouds of smoke. The converters dwarf the two workers, their faces blurred, who are casually depicted in the background.

The contrast between the scale of the human figure and the machine is further accentuated in *Steel Smelting Shop, Tata Iron and Steel Co. Jamshedpur*, from 1957. Singling out the steel-smelting area of the factory, the viewer is titillated by the play of light generated by the repetitive crates positioned on the ground. The titanic arm of a machine steers a colossal vessel along its tracks, moving towards a Lilliputian worker sporting a Nehru cap. The figure of the non-agentic factory worker resurfaces in the highly-choreographed photograph *Women Workers during Construction at a Thermal Power Plant in Bihar; One of Independent India's First, 1950s*. Spectral women Adivasi (tribal) workers descend a vertiginous staircase balancing baskets on their heads, their bodies profiled against the stark diagonal of the scaffolding.[113] The precarious and backbreaking work of indigenous women is beautifully packaged for the viewer and the potential foreign investor.

Towards the end of his photographic career, an embittered Janah began to photograph India's Adivasi communities. After meeting the well-known British former missionary and anthropologist Verrier Elwin (1902–1964),[114] with whom he formed a lifelong friendship and association, Janah spent much of his free time escaping the narrow bounds of cheerless, staid respectability in search of the communal experience of tribal life.[115] Janah's primitivist fascination with vanishing pre-industrial humanity was fuelled by the very forces of development that would eventually annihilate this humanity. This is particularly so in the case of Adivasi men and women, recruited as industrial labourers in Nehruvian India and brutally dispossessed of their lands through the construction of factories, dams and mines. Janah's glorification of the machine and upholding of the brutal, extractive postcolonial economy, parallels the sexual fetishizing of Adivasi women, as in the photograph *Younger of the Two Sisters from Poonani Village Whom I Spotted on a Beach. They Were Picking Seashells for a Lime Factory*.[116] The adolescent girl closes her eyes as she coyly offers her breasts to the voracious gaze of the camera.

Over the course of his career as a photographer, Janah moved from the turbulent arena of pre-Independence India to the intimate, personal space of the studio, and finally, towards nature, a realm seemingly untainted by industry, history and modern 'development'. Under the leadership of Joshi, the CPI played a crucial role in providing food, shelter and medical aid to the victims of the famine of 1943. Janah's photographs can be seen to contribute to this surge of relief activity during the emergency years of World War II. For this reason, they represent a peculiar moment in the history of Indian photojournalism, a history marked by the CPI's incongruous endorsement of the *People's War* line during World War II. Though the social welfare operations backed by the CPI challenged the hegemony of the Indian national movement during the 1940s, they offered no genuine political alternative. As Joshi would later put it: 'Ultimately, we failed in our basic task, namely, to explain the roots of the problems which confronted the masses.'[117] Unable to comprehend and critique the long-term economic, social and political factors which had made such a uniquely complex and diverse society so peculiarly fragile and vulnerable, the CPI failed to explain the causes underpinning the famine phenomenon: what had marked its onset, prolonged its duration, and ensured its crippling effects into the future. Janah too, while a committed Communist, was aware that mere act of taking photographs would not change the course of events:

> I do not relish, to this day, the fact that I earned my early fame from the grim business of photographing the starving, the dying and the dead victims of a dreadful famine. Joshi had impressed upon me, however, the need for bringing this hidden tragedy to light, and my only consolation had been that our reportage brought the unfortunate victims of this man-made famine some long-overdue attention, and may have prodded relief efforts.[118]

Janah's inability to lay bare the genuine causes that led to the famine can be related to CPI's precarious allegiance with the British during the war.[119] The colonial regime prevented the Party from embracing a truly revolutionary practice. As Joshi would declare in 1965: 'The historic tragedy of the Indian Revolution was that the Indian Communists were too blinded by Stalinist dogmatism to make a positive contribution in shaping the course of events.'[120] Janah's disaffection with party politics explains his reticence to describe some of these photographs. He further recounts:

> Photographs cannot make a political statement directly, but they can arouse emotions that can be harnessed for social and political causes. I did that for a time, and then, although politics was never expunged from my thoughts, I settled instead on taking photographs with no other purpose than that of pleasing myself and, perhaps, others too. These photographs captured moments from the history of our people and from the events, experiences and encounters of my lifetime, and they may have, in Susan Sontag's words from one of her essays on photography, 'conferred on them some kind of *immortality*'.[121]

Conclusion

This essay has proposed that the man-made catastrophe of the Bengal Famine precipitated the emergence of a novel form of documentary photography. The magnitude of the calamity spurred Sunil Janah to capitalize on the documentary form, developing novel ways to photograph the starved, ravaged body and foster awareness about the man-made disaster. Famines were severe and recurrent in late-nineteenth-century India, and had in part fomented the growth of a nationalist critique of colonial rule. The experience of famine and the widespread agreement among nationalists as to British responsibility had a deep impact on the aspirations and convictions of Indian leaders and their sociopolitical campaigns. The mass poverty and suffering made palpable in the phenomenon of famine forced nationalists to pay greater attention to the plight of rural populations. Hence famine was not only part of the critique of colonial rule, it became the lash with which to 'whip' the British for their oppressive and cruel regime of conquest.

The CPI built upon the ongoing indictment of British rule in India, but was also able to radically transform the meaning and social function of art. Janah's famine photographs starkly differ from surviving images of nineteenth-century famines made by British photographers. For this reason, they offer a rare and startling visual account of a collective catastrophe that impacted the lives of millions. Julian Stallabrass has suggested that fine art has a propensity to claim ownership over anything which 'is on the point of death, and photography, in particular, has a strong disposition to transform its images into *memento mori*'.[122] A similar case can be made for Janah's photographs. Two spectres – his faith in Communism and his modernist aesthetic – continue to haunt his images. Up until his ongoing engagement with remote Adivasi communities, one senses the photographer's repeated desire to capture life at the very moment of its avowed extinction, and to fix the ephemeral and transitory in a stable and stabilizing image. Viewed in such a way, Janah's images are thus more about imaging the process of annihilation than that of becoming.[123]

This impulse to fix the fleeting moment underpinned much of the early anthropological activity of bringing images and information about the 'other' to the Western viewer. James Clifford compellingly describes the activity of photographers or anthropologists who, in lamenting the extinction of the 'last x', seek to rescue it at the instant of its permanent disappearance.[124] Much of Janah's humanist photography – famine victims, Adivasi groups, flue gas stacks and crumbling ancient Indian temples – is concerned with suspending time and preserving fragments of the past; photography becomes a form of petrification: a funerary monument, an epitaph to raw and traumatic lived experiences, and perhaps, one might be tempted to add, a memorial to futures lost.[125]

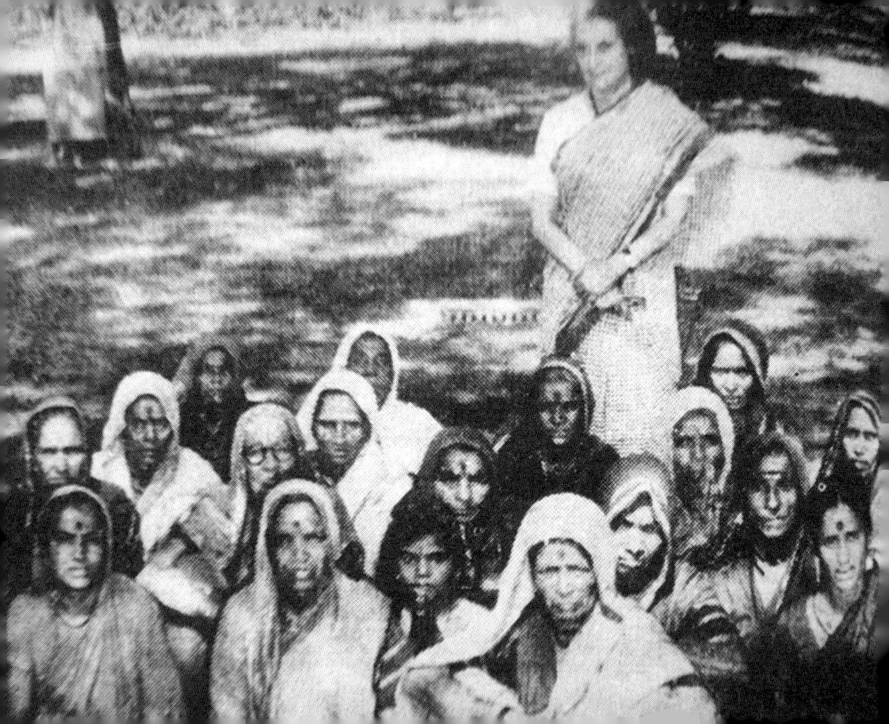

3 # Putting Women in the Picture

The Role of Photography in Mobilizing Support for the Indian Emergency 1975–77

2018

Gemma Scott

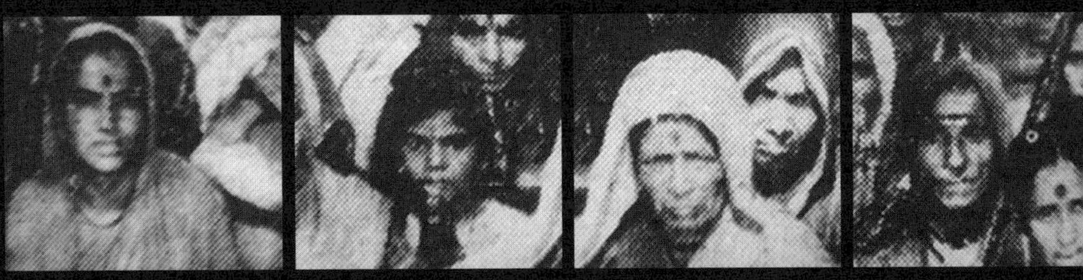

Using photographs printed during the Emergency in the Congress Party's official bulletin *Socialist India*, Gemma Scott explores how photography was used for propaganda and as instruments of political mobilization at a critical moment in modern Indian history. The bulletin tactically presented many images of women as Indira Gandhi's followers, and its strategic captioning/juxtaposition of the leader framed with women effectively positioned her as a champion of women's rights. Such images, Scott argues, were vital to the Congress Party's aggressive, and ultimately unsuccessful, manipulation of the national narrative within the turbulence of the Emergency and Indira Gandhi's ruthless suppression of dissent.

This essay was earlier published in *Photography in India: From Archives to Contemporary Practice*, eds., Aileen Blaney and Chinar Shah, © 2018 by Bloomsbury Academic. Reproduced by permission of Taylor & Francis Group.

Keywords, Names

Adivasi, Decolonization, Emergency 1975–77, Indira Gandhi, Indian National Congress, Modernism, Press censorship, see Keywords at the back of this volume.

Images

pp. 52–53: 'On 25 June, a group of pilgrims who passed through Delhi made it a point to be photographed with her – a memento to adorn their homes.' See 'The People's Tryst with the Prime Minister', *Socialist India*, 5 July 1975, 18d.

p. 59: 'An Adivasi (tribal) voter exercising her franchise', 'Spotlight on Elections', *Socialist India*, 26 March 1977, 14.

p. 65: (Above) 'Prime Minister Indira Gandhi described herself as "a sister of the people and a 'sevika' (servant) of the country" while addressing an audience in Delhi on 1 March', *Socialist India*, 5 March 1977, 3. (Below) 'A large contingent of women from the South, who passed through Delhi on 21 June in the course of their Bharat Darshan (holiday/ tourism) tour, called on the PM', 'The People's Tryst with the Prime Minister', *Socialist India*, 5 July 1975, 18c.

Socialist India images, Indian National Congress.

Introduction

This essay offers new insights into the history of India's Emergency (1975-77) by examining the state's use of photography. It analyses the ruling Congress Party's bulletin *Socialist India*, which regularly used photographs to depict the regime's popularity. In the party's representations of mass support through photographs of crowds, rallies and audiences, women dominated the bulletin's visual landscape. This is in stark contrast with women's absence from its text and their continuing absence from scholarship on the Emergency. Situated against this absence and in a discussion of how photographs function as historical sources, this chapter argues that these female-dominated images evidence the Congress government's attempts to project widespread, pan-Indian female support for Emergency measures. These photographs provide an integral means of inserting women into dominant narratives of Emergency politics.

In June 1975, Prime Minister Indira Gandhi faced crises on many fronts. The previous year witnessed numerous protest movements against the state in the midst of an increasingly precarious economic climate.[1] In response, Gandhi held state elections in Gujarat in early June 1975 and the Congress lost to the Janata Front, a coalition of opposition parties backed by prominent social reformist/activist politician Jayaprakash Narayan (JP).[2] Opposition intensified when on 12 June Justice Jagmohanlal Sinha[3] of the Allahabad High Court convicted Gandhi of corrupt election practices. This ruling bolstered the JP movement's agitations and, amidst calls for her to step down, Gandhi imposed the Emergency on 26 June. The events that followed are well known, and this remains one of the most controversial periods in independent India's history. Authorities instituted a range of measures aimed at silencing dissent and arrested opposition under preventive detention laws. Gandhi suspended elections, imposed press censorship and amended the constitution, expanding central power and restricting citizens' fundamental rights. Her government also aggressively pursued programmes of urban slum clearance and enforced sterilization. In the name of 'family planning', Emergency authorities deployed coercion and force to sterilize citizens, abandoning any focus on maternal and child health. The violations of rights that these programmes engendered have become synonymous with this period. When Gandhi called for elections in March 1977, they functioned as a referendum on Emergency rule and citizens voted overwhelmingly against it.[4]

Political commentators have long analysed these events. Recently, historians have also turned their attention to them. Bipan Chandra's and Ramachandra

Guha's studies reorient existing literature to focus on the underground resistance movement.[5] There has also been a shift towards histories from below, as seen in Emma Tarlo's scrutiny of the urban clearance and sterilization policies, focusing on how these ruthless manifestations of the Emergency affected people's daily lives.[6] The recent opening of the archived collections of the Shah Commission of Inquiry, established in May 1977 to investigate the regime's excesses, has given an impetus to historical research on the subject. Historians Patrick Clibbens and Rebecca Jane Williams draw on these records in their work on slum clearance and sterilization, respectively.[7] However, women remain absent from this existing literature. Scholars have not considered how women engaged with the state of Emergency, either in support or resistance, or how its measures affected women specifically. Some attention has been paid to the gendered dimensions of Gandhi's female leadership,[8] and a handful of women appear in accounts of resistance.[9] But what about the women who supported this regime? The Congress and Communist Party of India (the only main opposition party to initially support Gandhi's Emergency declaration) both had affiliated women's groups. Did Gandhi's government seek to mobilize their support for its increasingly authoritarian actions?

This essay begins to address these questions and analyse the nature of this support by examining the Congress's use of photography in its literature. It proceeds with a close analysis of women-dominated images that appeared in its bulletin *Socialist India*. I focus on its visual depictions of support in particular moments of crisis - the declaration of Emergency rule in June 1975 and Gandhi's sudden call for elections in January 1977.

Photographs as Historical Sources

Jennifer Tucker and Tina Campt note that the use of photography in historical enquiry 'has become a topic of urgent intellectual and cultural history around the world', as methods of shaping historical narratives continue to change 'in ways that compel attention to the employment of photographs in historiography'.[10] That historical photographs reflect and perpetuate power relations and function as sources for historians is well established. This has been a central concern in research on colonialism and the camera. James R. Ryan, for example, demonstrates the importance of photography in establishing the British Empire's imaginative geography.[11] Photographs can illuminate 'the politics of colonial perception and deterministic attempts to construct ethnicities and landscapes'. Close analysis of such images can also subvert these constructions and 'actually serve to fracture the narratives that they appear to support'.[12] Photographers have also positioned photographs as a means to resist these relations and expose the colonial gaze. Annu Palakunnathu Matthew's series *An Indian from India* (2001–03) juxtaposes images of herself with historical images of Native Americans to explore Indian identity and fracture colonial constructions of it.[13]

Describing photography as a performance of power, Paul Frosh argues that it is 'best grasped not as a medium of visual communication, but as a manifest performance of the power to make visible'. *Socialist India*'s photographs are not just visual manifestations of the Congress Party's communications. They also yield insights into its possession of the 'power to make visible', which is particularly critical given that Gandhi's institution of censorship invested this power almost exclusively with the government. The materials discussed in this chapter indicate what it chose to make visible under Emergency conditions in order to foster support and suppress dissent. Assessing Gandhi's leadership, Trina Nileena Banerjee emphasizes the importance of visual materials in the construction of Emergency power. The posters of Gandhi that proliferated in Delhi, the 'visual spectacles that marked the public space with images of Indira's supposed popularity ... formed a large part of the combined propaganda machinery that kept the Emergency juggernaut rolling'.[14] *Socialist India*'s photographs visualizing people's support for the regime contributed to this machinery.

Frosh argues, 'both the act and the material product of the act, the photographic product, generate multiple and interrelated meanings'.[15] The photographs and their material context within the party's mouthpiece are historically informative and the latter complicates our analysis beyond what these images picture. The photograph is by no means an 'objective' representation of reality. Robert Rapstein notes that 'the camera is omnivorous; our eye unconsciously selective', as all photographic data 'reflect not only the photographers' interest but also their biases and assumptions.[16] As such, Tucker and Campt observe that 'it is hard to deny that there remains, for many historians, a persisting tentativeness and even distrust about the use of visual materials as historical sources that differ from historians' scrupulous, rigorous assessments of other types of historical documents'.[17] However, for *Socialist India*'s Emergency images, the very selections that cause this distrust are historically informative. The photographer often chose to capture segregated women's sections of mass, mixed-gender crowds.[18] This is evident from some of the captions, which demonstrate that not all of these images feature snapshots of women's-only meetings or rallies. *Socialist India*'s editors made similar choices to present these women-dominated images in majority, at particular times and alongside particular text. These selections are historically significant. The photographs and their material context evidence the importance of women in the Congress government's political strategy and their attempts to project the Emergency's popularity.

Mobilizing Women's Support

In his exploration of Gandhi's final term in office, Diego Maiorano highlights that Gandhi appealed to India's 'weaker sections' for electoral support throughout her career.[19] This facet of Gandhi's political strategy was central to her discourse on and justifications for Emergency rule. She claimed that stringent measures were necessary to protect national integrity and safeguard the interests of minorities. In a speech in the Lok Sabha (Parliament's Lower House) in July 1975, she stated, 'millions of people are extremely poor and are hankering after a better life, for greater equality of opportunity, for social justice. ... Therefore, it is a question of striking a balance between the political rights of the individual and the social and economic rights of the people.'[20] Gandhi used this rhetoric about the need to alleviate minorities' sufferings to justify Emergency restrictions on individual rights. She also claimed that the nation's minorities supported the Emergency: 'at this moment all the poorer people, all the minorities, are with us'.[21] Maiorano asserts that while women constitute part of India's 'weaker sections',

> [n]o significant attempt was made by Mrs Gandhi to appeal to women nationally. Of course, she made sporadic attempts to win their support; however, it is hardly arguable that Mrs Gandhi was a feminist. This does not mean that women did not support her. Indeed, they constituted one of Mrs Gandhi's key constituencies, although no significant attempt to mobilize them was made.[22]

Maiorano is right to note that Gandhi was not a feminist and she regularly distanced herself from 'women's issues'.[23] However, she frequently aligned women with the nation's minorities. Speaking in a Rajya Sabha (Upper House) debate on a government report on their status, for instance, she referred to women as the 'biggest oppressed minority'.[24] At a public meeting in Hyderabad in December 1975, Gandhi defended Emergency measures, claimed that they were beneficial

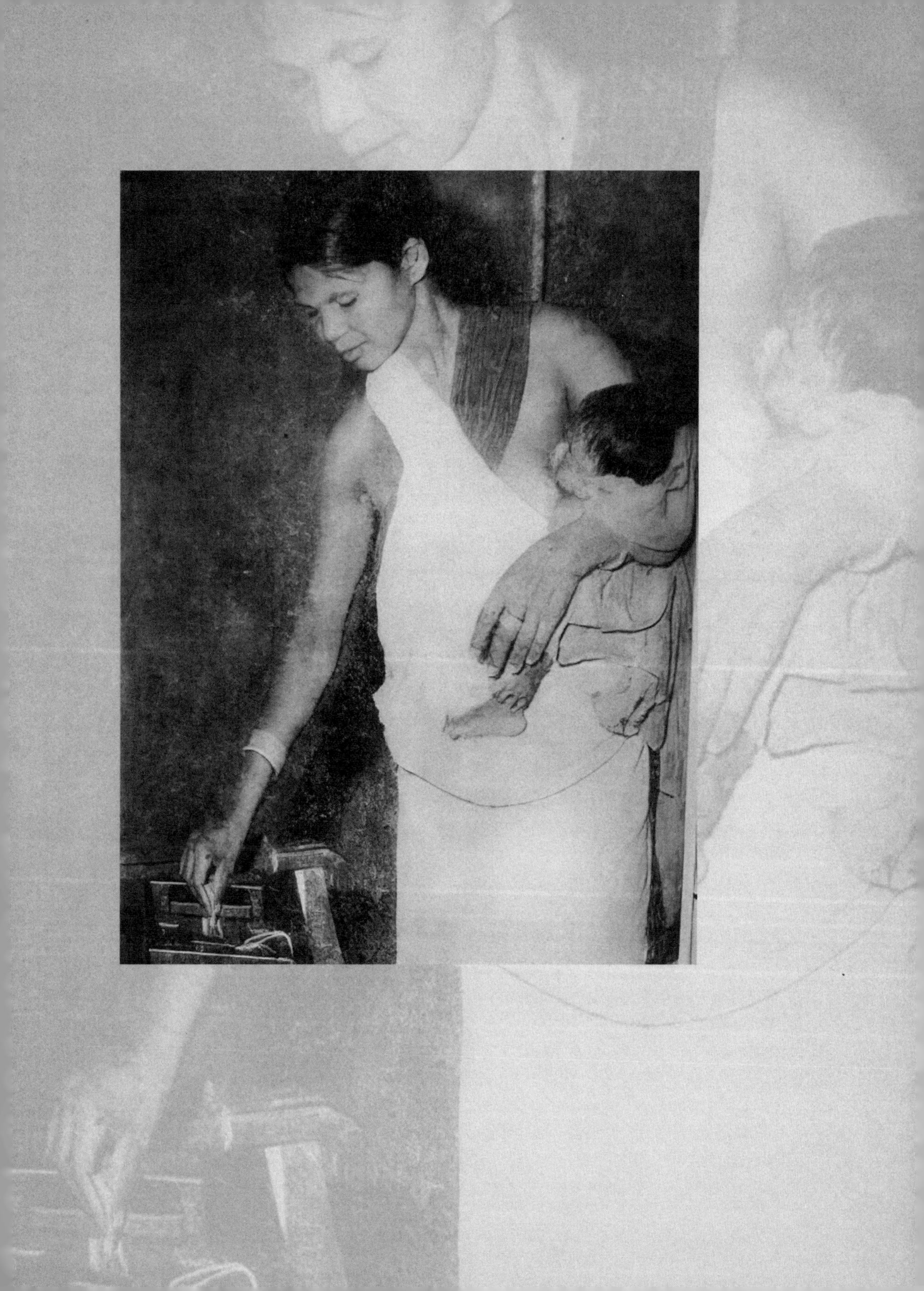

for the underprivileged and asserted that these groups supported the regime, as reported by the Congress Women's Front bulletin, *Women on the March* (*WOTM*): 'Democracy should never mean the voice of a few against the rights and liberties of the many, she said. The poor, peasants, workers and women had all stood solidly behind the Congress.'[25] This location of women alongside minority groups suggests that an analysis of the party's appeals to the weaker sections should also account for its appeals to women.

This is reiterated by *WOTM*, which evidences multiple attempts to mobilize and project women's support. It often engaged with the party's discourse on the Emergency, for example, replacing the usual cover of one issue with a pro-Emergency poster.[26] In August 1975, *WOTM* reported that the government 'called upon the women's organizations in the country to actively involve themselves in family planning work'.[27] October's editorial on Emergency measures stressed, 'women have got a very extensive role to play at this present juncture ... after the declaration of Emergency there is a new sense of discipline among the people', and exhorted readers to 'think about what women can do' to sustain this.[28] Another article underscored the need for vigilance to enforce the regime's economic programme, asserting 'women are the fittest to keep such vigilance'.[29] The Congress also presented the Emergency as a tool for women's uplift. It claimed that the International Women's Year 'saw yet another significant event for the welfare of women in this country. The event was the national Emergency'.[30] A wealth of evidence from *WOTM* suggests that women supported the Emergency and that the Congress sought to mobilize this support. In contrast, *Socialist India* rarely featured reports on this. However, women's visual presence in the latter is striking, suggesting that they formed an important part of its strategy especially at climatic moments during the Emergency.

Putting Women in the Picture

Two types of photographs appeared in *Socialist India* during this period. Some represented individuals in the upper echelons of the Emergency government, particularly Gandhi, reflecting the regime's increasing centralization of power. Those not featuring government leaders showed crowds at rallies and speeches, depicting popular support for the declaration of Emergency and its measures. Women frequently dominated these. Such images illustrated *Socialist India*'s coverage of the conflicts leading up to June 1975. Facing widespread agitations, the government dissolved the Gujarat assembly and announced elections in the state for early June.[31] Three images graced the cover of the bulletin's 'Gujarat Election Special',[32] including close-ups of Gandhi addressing a public meeting in Siddhpur (northern Gujarat), the crowd and Congress President Dev Kant Barooah[33] speaking with male Congress candidates. The close-up of the crowd depicting popular support showed only women and children, an exclusively gendered representation of public solidarity. Women, specifically mothers, embody popular support on this page. The bulletin captioned this: 'The women in the audience are seen trying to protect themselves from the scorching sun by raising a long piece of cloth over their heads.'[34] The photograph simultaneously underscored women's centrality to electoral politics and foregrounded their vulnerability, as 'raising a long piece of cloth to cover their heads' they braved the heat and sun to show their support. Strategically placing this image next to the one of Gandhi speaking, *Socialist India* suggested an affinity between her and the female audience.

This was also invoked in a Press Trust of India[35] report titled 'Women Know Their Sisters', which depicted the 'warm welcome given to the Prime Minister wherever she goes in Gujarat'. This framed a more specific discussion of her popularity among women: 'women are turning out in large numbers to see and hear Smt Indira Gandhi on a whirlwind election tour in Gujarat.'[36] The report repeated the emphasis on sacrifice and vulnerability embodied in the cover page's caption: 'Braving the severe heat they gather at roadsides sometimes with *mangal kalash* to welcome her and to have a close glimpse of the Prime Minister.'[37] Its depiction of Gandhi's interactions with these female supporters brings Maiorano's contentions that she did not seek to mobilize women into question.

At every meeting, she refers to the hardships housewives have to undergo in these difficult days with high prices and shortage. She says,

> As a mother I very much understand your difficulties. Housewives have to bear the brunt of running the house. In keeping with Indian culture and tradition you will never eat before you have fed your men and your children. If the kitchen is empty by then you might say 'today is my *upvas* (fast)'.

Smiles dance on the faces in the women's enclosure and cheers go up.[38]

Gandhi actively deployed normative tropes of gender and, more problematically, the subordinate status of women in her electoral campaign, invoking solidarity with the female crowds to rally voters.[39]

This report's reference to the 'women's enclosure' demonstrates that these meetings often segregated female audience members. Photographers chose to capture this section separately, and editors chose to use this to showcase popular support. This strategy shaped *Socialist India*'s use of photographs in its 5 July 1975 issue, which included a photo special titled 'The People's Tryst with the Prime Minister'.[40] This title invokes Jawaharlal Nehru's famous independence speech 'Tryst with Destiny' and indicates the party's intention to display Gandhi's popularity and emphasize her political lineage. Women dominate the photo special, as half of its eighteen images feature women exclusively. This is entirely disproportionate to women's presence in the bulletin's near-forty pages of text, which included only one report on Gandhi's message to the International Women's Year conference. While women hardly featured in the Congress's textual commentary on the Emergency, they occupied a significant presence in its visual depictions of mass support for its measures.

The first page of this special included three images of the prime minister and one depiction of popular support. This captured a large crowd of women and children marching with placards and signs. The women are prominent and easily identifiable by their covered heads and dress. The bulletin captioned this close-up, 'Women and children marching in hundreds to the Prime Minister's residence on the 14th'.[41] The projection of mass support on this page is distinctly gendered, embodied by women and specifically mothers. This photo depicts a march that took place on 14 June, before Gandhi imposed the Emergency. *Socialist India* used pictures retrospectively in this issue, drawing on images of crowds captured in the pre-Emergency atmosphere, when rallies and addresses dominated Delhi. However, considered alongside the rest of the issue's content (which focused almost entirely on Emergency measures), their presence here implies that these women extended their support to the newly imposed regime. Similarly, the second page of this special included three images of the party elite – the prime minister speaking, a group of journalists surrounding her and the Chief Minister of Orissa accompanying Gandhi to a rally. Again, *Socialist India* used an all-female crowd to represent popular support: 'A group of women from the hill areas in colourful costumes listening to the Prime Minister on the 18th.' The text foregrounded the female composition of the crowd in their 'colourful costumes' and stressed the fact that they were 'listening to the Prime Minister', invoking that particular solidarity between Gandhi and female supporters.[42]

Women's support continued to dominate the next page of images. One figure depicts 'a large contingent of women from the south' who called at Gandhi's residence to offer their support.[43]

Foregrounding these women 'from the south', the bulletin attempted to straddle geographical distance, suggesting pan-Indian female support and appealing to women as a category regardless of their location or other affiliations. This page also featured an image captioned, 'PM with Congress *Seva Dal* (grassroots organization) workers, who came to express their unstinted loyalty'. Although the text does not gender this audience, the image does. Depicting exclusively female workers, it pictured Gandhi standing on an elevated podium addressing the seated and smiling women, whose eyes are all fixed on her. Another image featured 'a group of elderly women singing *kirtan* (devotional songs)'. Showing Gandhi facing a group of women holding signs, the final photo on the page depicted 'Muslim women carrying placards "women's raj" and "down with men"' as they 'called on the Prime Minister'.[44] This is a more radical expression of women's mobilization, quite unlike the other visual representations of support as it allows the women an agenda outside of praising the prime minister.

Although according women visual dominance, *Socialist India* featured Gandhi first and foremost; she appears in each photograph and in the forefront, often positioned standing over groups of female supporters. Generally, the bulletin did not seek to showcase these women or their respective causes. Rather, it focused on the apparently vast dimension of female support for the prime minister and Emergency government. This continued in the final page of this special. One image showed 'a group of young college girls turned up on the 19th. Their placard hailed Smt Indira Priyadarshini Gandhi as the "*Lokpreye* (loved by the people) PM"'. Although this pictures the college girls holding a sign, Gandhi is shown in mid-utterance; *she* is the one speaking. Figure 2 shows 'a group of pilgrims who passed through Delhi' and 'made it a point to be photographed with her – a memento to adorn their homes'.[45]

The picture features a group of women but only Gandhi stands tall and dominant. The caption also genders their intention. Unlike those on the previous page campaigning via the slogan 'down with men', these women urged to be photographed with the prime minister for purely domestic purposes: creating a 'memento to adorn their homes'. The photo special also highlighted the diversity of Gandhi's followers through images of college girls, elderly women, pilgrims, Congress workers, mothers, women from the north and south, from rural and urban locations, both Hindu and Muslim. This offers a distinctly gendered representation of public support for the Emergency, whereby the government appealed to women as a singular category, transcending myriad other areas of distinction.

Such visual depictions continued in *Socialist India* throughout 1976 to 1977, most frequently at significant milestones or points of vulnerability for the party, when the need to project an image of mass support was most pressing. These dwindled during the last months of 1976 but noticeably returned when on 18 January 1977 Gandhi announced that the nation would go to the polls in March. In the subsequent election fervour, the bulletin revived the use of photographs and on 12 February again began visualizing mass support. One page covering Gandhi's election campaign included an image of 'a vast sea of humanity', a thronging crowd with barely discernible faces, reinforcing the caption's emphasis on volume. The close-up image showed only women, smiling and raising their arms in the air, actively supporting Gandhi's campaign with visually prominent gestures.[46] This same stress on female-dominated crowds saturated the 5 March issue, which was primarily concerned with supporting Gandhi's campaign. It reported on meetings and quoted from her election speeches, reproducing her reflections on the Emergency: 'though it was a bitter pill, it had its effect. There was discipline all over the country and economic stability was also achieved.' One image illustrated these speeches and depicted the crowds she addressed:[47] It superimposed a close-up of Gandhi at a microphone next to a cropped image of the large crowd, resulting in a skewed perspective that visualized only female supporters.

Socialist India's issue on election results is rife with visual representations of India's electorate foregrounding women. A report titled 'Spotlight on the Elections' featured pictures of men and women queuing in a constituency in Haryana along with an image of a woman voting.[48, 49] Although the caption remains neutral the photograph is distinctly gendered. The bulletin presented this Adivasi member of indigenous/tribal community not as a voter, but as a woman and mother, one arm in the process of casting her vote, the other supporting the infant breastfeeding.[50] Such a gendered emphasis ran throughout a photo special within the same edition, titled 'Election Cameos', where visual depictions of the election focused exclusively on women.[51] Despite the fact that these usually showed women physically casting their votes, the bulletin's presentation of the images and their captions often depoliticized them. In the above example, the Adivasi woman's motherhood is in the visual fore – she is primarily a mother rather than a member of the electorate.

Another image showed 'an official applying indelible ink on the finger of a voter at the Rae Bareli Constituency where the PM, Smt Indira Gandhi, contested'.[52] The caption suggests a connection between Gandhi and the pictured woman by drawing attention to this female assertion of franchise and relating it

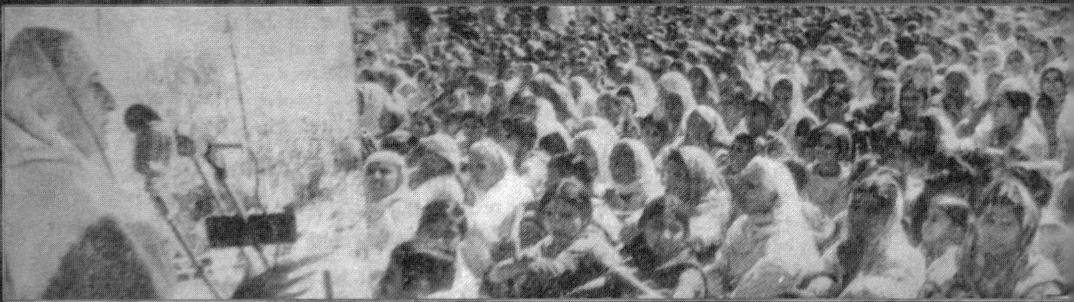

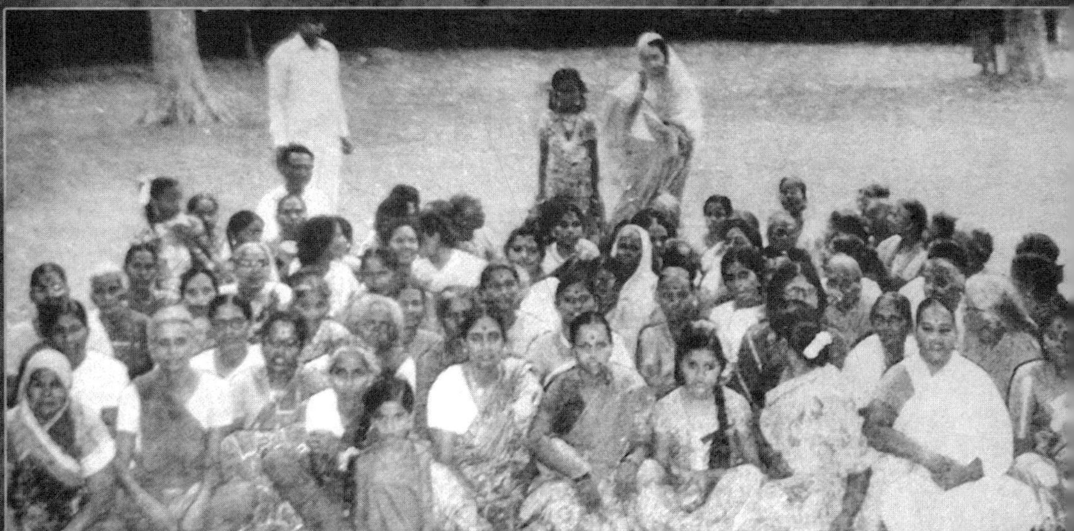

to her own constituency. Another image showed 'vote conscious tribal women in colourful attire in a booth in the north eastern region'.[53] The constant depiction of women casting their votes implies some kind of electoral agency. However, this suggestion also remained steeped in the bulletin's stress on stereotypical female identities, particularly in instances that pictured women with children or alongside comments on their 'colourful' attire.

This depoliticization of women voters continued in the final pages of this feature. Two of the pictures depict close-ups of female voters' bodies so that the rest of the voting background is not visualized.[54] The women's faces are veiled and in both instances the images show their hands placing papers into the ballot box. This contrasts to the practice, in the earlier moment of crisis following the declaration of Emergency, of visualizing large crowds of gendered support. Collectively, these isolated pictures of women voting on the regime still resonate with women as a group because of the diversity of women featured. 'Election Cameos' depicted mothers, elderly women, Adivasis, women from the North East and veiled women. While visualizing engagement from various groups, this emphasis on individual and isolated voting practices contrasted with the few visual depictions of men in this election special. It featured, for example, one image captioned 'voters on a tractor proceeding to a polling station in Rohtak'[55] and another showing 'male voters standing in a queue to cast their votes at a polling booth in Sonipat constituency in Haryana'.[56] Both images depicted male voters in masses- in a long queue, and piled overflowing onto a tractor. By representing women almost always in isolation, *Socialist India* refused to visualize their collective voting power, whereas it foregrounded this in its depiction of men's voting practices. The two images of women reinforce this sense of depoliticization as their faces appear hidden.

Conclusion

Women's dominance in *Socialist India*'s visual landscape contrasted their comparative absence from its text. Aside from brief captions, many of these images stand isolated; their origin, location or photographer not referenced. As such, the images give a distinct impression of female mass support for the party and its Emergency measures, without conveying many details of this or actually voicing women's agency. At first glance these photos, representing popular support for Gandhi's Emergency government in feminized visual form, appeared sporadically. But closer inspection suggests that *Socialist India* used these most frequently in times of political strain or importance, such as in the weeks immediately preceding and following Gandhi's declaration of Emergency rule, on its one-year anniversary, during the All India Congress Committee's annual session at Gauhati [now Guwahati] in November 1976 and in the run-up to elections in March 1977. This essay has illuminated this editorial tactic by focusing on the party's deployment of these images at two moments of state crisis. The sheer volume of these images, their proliferation in these moments of crisis and the unbalanced depiction of female crowds and popular support point to the Congress's concerted efforts to depict a large and empowered female following that augments male voter presence.

These photographs offer an important intervention in the historiography of the Emergency. They highlight a political strategy whereby the Congress government specifically sought to mobilize women in support of Emergency rule, projecting visually striking representations of that support. Anirudh Deshpande asserts that if historians choose to examine only textual sources 'they do end up limiting the scope of their enterprise. They will consciously turn their back on people who may not figure in documentary sources'.[57] These photographs help us account for women's engagements with the Emergency and their centrality in mainstream party politics. The images are also significant for debates around the use of photographs as historical sources. They demonstrate that 'biases', such as the selective choices made by photographers and editors, are historically informative in regard to these strategies of image selection. Paul Frosh notes that as 'dramatizations of the relations of power over visibility and representation, photographic practices constituted a site of social struggle as well as a mechanism of social control'.[58] While illuminating the mechanisms of Emergency power, the photographs also represent a site of struggle – specifically the struggle to move away from androcentric narratives of Emergency politics and include women in these meta-histories of the regime.

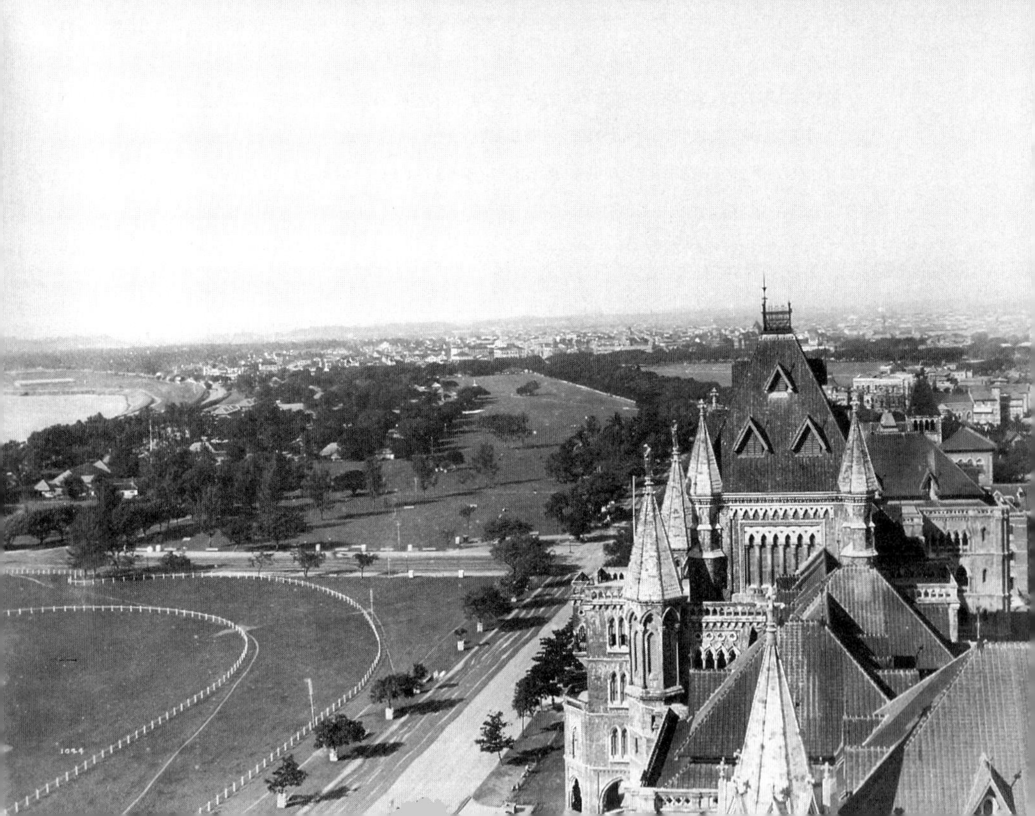

4 # The Camera Tours the City

Chronicling Practices of Photography in Urban India

2012

I **Suryanandini Narain**

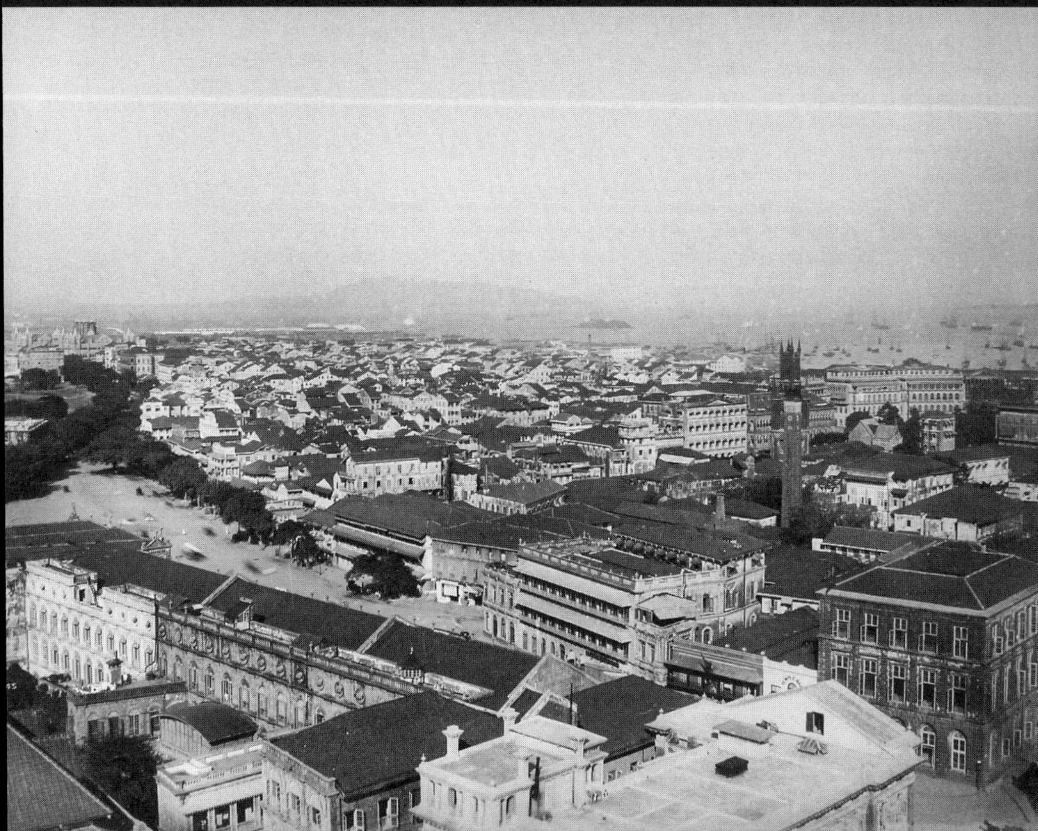

Suryanandini Narain narrates how the still camera imaged the changing urban environment and milieux over the past century, capturing 'views that observed, eulogized, critiqued and contemplated the urban issues of changed living, governance, travel and industry'. The essay moves from colonial imaginations of grandeur in the spectacle of the Delhi Durbars to the postcolonial imagination of political sovereignty, and then finally to the city as a site of violence, suppression and protest.

While some contemporary practitioners turned to the street as a dynamic source of images, others focused on interior life, gender complexities and social marginalization. New discursive interfaces were shaped through foundational critiques by prominent scholar-curators. The city as a built form enabled a spectrum of 'technological, stylistic and thematic variations in the visual realm', with digital photography posing 'perhaps the greatest contradictions in representation as realistic or mediated or imagined'.

An earlier version of this essay appeared as 'City Obscura: The Camera Tours the City', in *Depth of Field: Photography of Art and Practice in India,* edited by Rahaab Allana, *Lalit Kala Contemporary* (Special Issue on Photography), vol. 52, 2012, pp. 66–74.

Keywords, Names

Babri Masjid/Ram Janmabhoomi violence 1992, *Mitter Bedi*, *Margaret Bourke-White*, *Samuel Bourne*, *Citizenship*, *Lala Deen Dayal*, *Delhi Durbars 1903 and 1911*, *Indira Gandhi*, *Sunil Janah*, *Madan Mahatta*, *Pushpamala N.*, *Raghu Rai*, *Ketaki Sheth*, *Dayanita Singh*, *Raghubir Singh*, see Keywords at the back of this volume.

Images

pp. 68–69: Lala Deen Dayal, *Panoramic View of Bombay*, *c.* 1880. Two-part panorama, albumen print, 7.6 x 19.8 inches. Courtesy The Alkazi Collection of Photography. ACP: 98.55.0002.1/2

p. 73: *Arch of the Prince's Road at Delhi*, Historical record of the Imperial visit to India 1911 by John Murray Pub., 1914. Courtesy Wikimedia Commons.

p. 77: Sheba Chhachhi, *Shahjahan Apa Seated – Staged Portrait, Nangloi, Delhi*, 1991. Grateful acknowledgement to the artist for permission to reprint.

p. 79: Vivan Sundaram, *Prospect*, 2005–08, from the series *Trash*, pigment print. Courtesy The Estate of Vivan Sundaram.

pp. 82–83: Prarthna Singh, Interior of tent at the Shaheen Bagh protest site. Book spread from *Har Shaam Shaheen Bagh*, self-published, 2022. All copyrights belong to Prarthna Singh.

> To dream is not only a form of wish fulfillment; it is also to wake up in the middle of the night with anxious apprehensions about who you are and what may happen to you. Mumbai taught me how to dream about my hopes and aspirations, while living with my nightmares. And cities that teach you that the other side of the dream is a nightmare also teach you how to survive.
>
> - Homi K. Bhabha[1]

As a modern visual device that arrived in the subcontinent in the 1840s, the camera became the chronicler of modern urban life in rapid, spontaneous and urgent ways. Professional, amateur and personal photography responded to the nineteenth-century cityscape's socio-cultural and political transformations under the Raj, as reflected in visual markers of architecture, street life, studio aesthetics and interior living. The camera's evolving visual language shaped itself to portray the colonial city in a range of views that observed, eulogized, critiqued and contemplated the urban issues of changed lifestyle, governance, travel and industry. The lens filtered, encrusted, included and omitted from this urban landscape according to the practitioner's own history and aesthetics, with genres navigated differently by British and Indian professional and amateur photographers. Documentary, familial and street photography have responded variously to the visual matrix of the city, defining colonial and post-Independence lens-based practices in the subcontinent.

This essay lays out a broad chronology of the interrelationship between the camera and the city, leaving detailed case studies for later investigation. The nineteenth-century interest in geopolitical and cultural surveillance of the South Asian region and its people led to systematic landscape and ethnographic photography supported by the Raj. Officially supported work, such as by the Archaeological Survey of India (established in 1861)[2] under Alexander Cunningham, used sophisticated technologies and professional photographers, countered by the bazaar that used popular methods for printing images by amateur photographers producing souvenirs and albums for the tourist market. The outcome of the former was presented in sweeping picturesque format images in publications, visualizing monuments and populated towns and cities; the latter generated albums, postcards and studio portraits for personal consumption. Modernizing cities such as Bhopal under Shah Jahan Begum (r. 1868–1901) and Jaipur under Sawai Ram Singh II (1833–1880), bearing new civic amenities, educational institutions and infrastructure, were portrayed in photographs as evidence of progressive, flourishing kingdoms. The presidencies were also spaces for the generation of photographic discourse, as the Bengal, Madras and Bombay Photographic Societies[3] emerged in the 1850s to ruminate upon the medium and its possibilities. Each Society had its own journal, and held exhibitions to further the new art of the camera.

Studio practices in cities were mainstream businesses, and their numbers rose exponentially within a few decades of the camera's arrival. Samuel Bourne,[4] who worked in India during 1863–70 and established a successful studio practice in Calcutta, imaged the landscape of Kashmir and the architectural marvels of Agra and Lucknow from the perspective of the colonial gaze. Majestic views of buildings, that do not survive anymore or are in ruined/decayed state today, were photographed by Lala Deen Dayal[5] (1844-1905), such as The Residency and Alambagh Palace in Lucknow. These compositions usually had a high vantage point, the human figure dwarfed into a measure of scale, objectified in its minuteness as it seemingly navigated the built environment. The 1857 sepoy rebellion transformed the city from a complex node of high culture into a site of carnage. The camera widely documented Delhi and Lucknow, among other places that erupted during the Mutiny. That year saw Joseph Hogarth of *Art Journal* exhibiting thirty landscapes by Dr John Murray, titled 'Photographs of Indian Cities', in London, granting a premium status to pre-Mutiny images of the affected sites. Similarly, Felice Beato's portrayals of the sites of the Mutiny from 1858, focusing on the damage to historic archaeological monuments such as in Secundrabagh, became a key reference in the aftermath of India's first struggle for independence.[6] Darogha Abbas Ali's 1874 *Lucknow Album* of fifty photographs was an account of the post-rebellion geography of the city for any visitor.

The Delhi Durbars of 1903 and 1911[7] were opportune moments for the camera to document the pomp and splendour of the Raj, celebrating Britain's imperial hegemony even as demands for freedom were already on the rise. Photographed by Lala Deen Dayal and several others, these durbars re-imagined the city as a makeshift entity, with sprawling grounds hosting tents, administrative buildings, shops and spaces for celebration. As the scope of the freedom struggle widened, central figures such as M.K. Gandhi followed by leaders such as Jawaharlal Nehru filled the visual frame, embodying popular aspirations as well as political ideals. Walter Bosshard (1892–1975), Margaret Bourke-White (1906–1971), Kulwant Roy (1914–1984), Henri Cartier-Bresson (1908–2004) and India's first woman press photographer Homai Vyarawalla (1913–2012)[8] were among those who photographed this period of tumultuous change, producing stark black-and-white

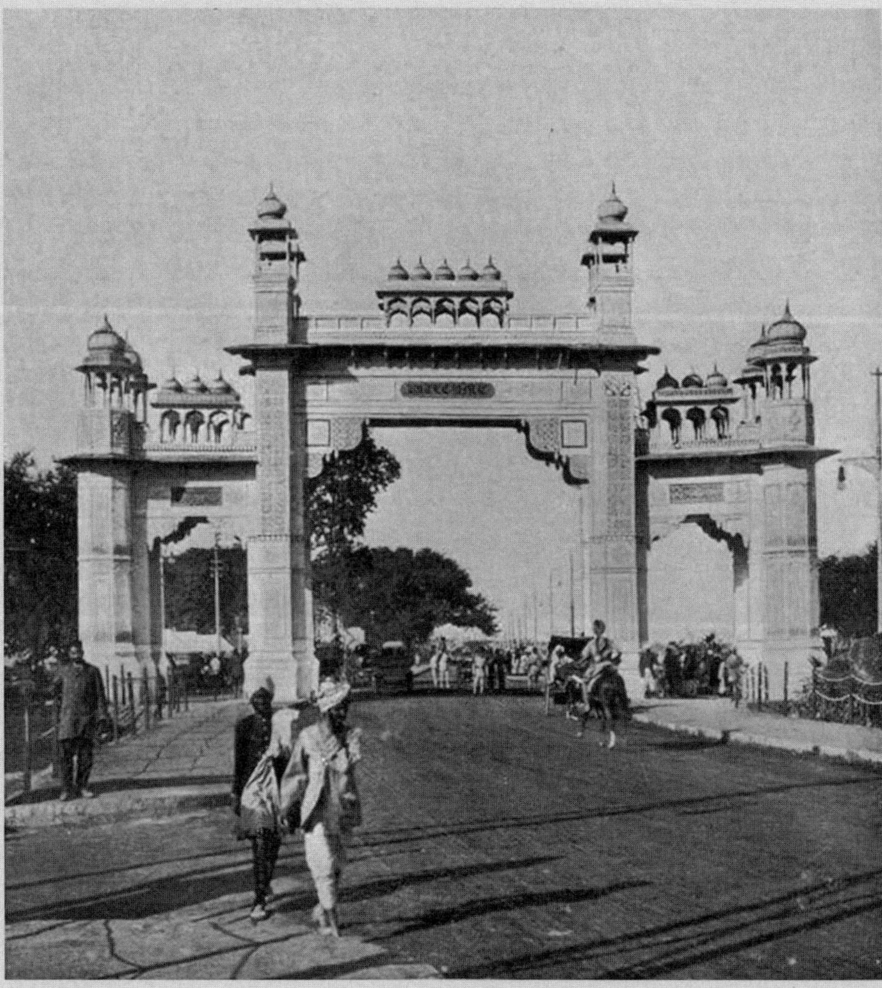

Photo Official.

AN ARCH ON PRINCE'S ROAD AT DELHI.

images of the country's leaders. In the 1930s, Gandhi's nephew Kanu Gandhi (1917-1986) photographed the Mahatma on his mission for Independence, these photos depicting the coming together of diverse rural and urban regions within the national movement. Bourke-White went on to mentor Sunil Janah (1918-2012)[9] who chronicled the Bengal Famine of 1943 for the paper *People's War* produced by the Communist Party of India, his deeply affective images challenging the ideals of urban progress that came at a heavy cost to agrarian stability.

Decades later, Kishor Parekh's book on the 1971 Bangladesh War of Liberation (*Bangladesh: A Brutal Birth*, 1972) similarly challenged emergent national discourses of development and progress in the face of violence and displacement.[10] Janah's romanticization of the rural idyll, especially of the Santal tribal community, countered the modern nation's urban aspirations, even as the integration of India's diversity into a unified Nehruvian imaginary remained central to the times. More personal views of a changing social fabric were reflected in the amateur photography of the twin sisters Debalina Mazumder (1919-2012) and Manobina Roy (1919-2001)[11]; their images from the inter-war years and beyond encompassed domestic interiors, their modernizing families, and landscapes and street views of the newly independent nation. Recently exhibited in their centenary birth year in the exhibition *Twin Sisters with Cameras* (Kolkata/Delhi, 2022-23) their work exemplified the technological possibilities of a handheld Kodak Brownie camera to which they had been introduced by their father when they were only twelve years old, taking advantage of its newfound mobility as they travelled across national borders and also extensively photographed European cities.

The traumatic division of India in 1947 and the founding of Pakistan as a sovereign nation redefined the once connected cities that now lay separated across a militarized border. The cities affected by Partition had to be reconfigured, with land given as compensation to the masses of refugees who had to be accommodated within urban spaces. The harrowing human cost, violent dispossession, forced migration and resettlement were documented by Vyarawalla, Bourke-White, Cartier-Bresson and R.D. Chopra (1915-1958), among others. Cataclysmic events such as the assassination of Gandhi in 1948 drew photographers to Delhi to mark a historic moment in India's public sphere, the aftermath of his death drawing masses to Birla House, the cremation ground and railway lines, turning Delhi into a mourning site. Photography and journalism continued to intertwine in the mapping of the changing politics of the Indian city, but outside the political space the works of Raghu Rai (b. 1942) and S. Paul (b. 1931)[12] span both ordinary and famous subjects, transcending the mandates of reportage in their depictions of urban life. Both photographers are concerned with older cities such as Delhi, Varanasi and Agra that negotiate the historical and the mythological, the sacred and the secular in parallel with the commercial interests of inhabitants; they also image ecology and labour as major victims of unplanned urban 'development'. In contrast to Rai's and Paul's documentary black-and-white images, Raghubir Singh (1942–1999)[13] infused the urban subject with colour, his frames including everyday icons such as the Ambassador car (*A Way into India*, 2002). The 1950s and 1960s also saw the documentation of massive infrastructural projects such as dams and factories as well as the visualization of smaller towns in photographs by Kulwant Roy, Mitter Bedi (1926–1985), and Madan Mahatta (1932–2014)[14] whose photographs of the capital were exhibited in the retrospective *Delhi Modern: The Architectural Photographs of Madan Mahatta* (2012), curated by Ram Rahman.[15] Urban planning saw its climactic manifestation in the city of Chandigarh, designed by Le Corbusier in the 1960s, and photographed for its modern aesthetic functionality by several Indian and foreign photographers. Newly emergent, state-supported educational chains such as the Indian Institute of Technology (IIT) and Indian Institute of Management (IIM), and the seminal National Institute of Design (NID), acknowledged for their pedagogic philosophies and excellence in producing professionals in these fields, brought cities such as Ahmedabad, Kharagpur, Kanpur, Lucknow and others into public discourse. The campuses of these institutions were photographed for their modern design; IIM Ahmedabad's archive of images by Pranlal Patel from the 1960s went on display in an exhibition titled *Not Yet 25* (2022) showcased at the campus.

A newly sovereign nation's powerful imaginings of the future influenced viewers and transformed the cinema industry, giving rise to a more expansive cultural imaginary and locations and identities for the ordinary Indian to invest with personal and collective desire. Establishing an inter-visual relationship with the still camera, cinema continued to predominantly feature the expectations of the urban middle-class, and this complex field was in turn excavated for the ruptures in its glamour by photographers such as Ram Rahman (b. 1955), Sooni Taraporevala (b. 1957) and Ketaki Sheth (b. 1957). Rahman, Satish Sharma (b. 1958)[16] and Shahid Datawala (b. 1974)[17] look outwards to the city street for the dynamic, unposed and unselfconscious underprivileged subject, the so-called 'subaltern' citizen whose life, lived in public view, in slums and temporary dwellings, under the highways connecting metropolises and in bylanes of congested colonies, had till then been mostly narrated through the same film sets where romances, historical dramas and thrillers were made. Films and photos of the city harbour humour and contradictions as objects and people crowd visual frames, suggesting rapid mobility and polyvocality. Zooming in through windows and prying open the doors of city dwellings, Dayanita Singh (b. 1961) and Datawala interrogate intimate spaces, ranging from the interiors of elite houses (*Privacy*, 2003) to the spectral zones of empty cinema halls (*Dress Circle*, 2003–05), portraying absent presences through the stark quality of black-and-white formats. Their works suggest the city's concealed spaces, secret lives within homes and abandoned buildings, where social extremes have remained hidden from public view. At the forefront of the contemporary imaging of social marginality are Sunil Gupta (b. 1953) and Sheba Chhachhi (b. 1958), their lens probing territories of sexual difference, widowhood and personal choices that are otherwise unacknowledged, stigmatized and/or 'othered'. Gupta's long engagement with the negotiation for urban public space by queer communities is seen in his series *Mr Malhotra's Party* (2008) where he poses gay men against well-known buildings in Delhi, as an alternative to the virtual or private spaces that they otherwise may be forced to inhabit. The unsettling figure of the sex worker in the shadows of urban India has drawn photographers across several decades, producing series such as Mary Ellen Mark's *Falkland Road* (1978)[18] and, more recently, *11th Road, Kamathipura* (2017) by Sudharak Olwe (b. 1966).[19]

The city as a site of violence, suppression and protest emerged as a much photographed space in the wake of the women's movement of the 1980s, its feminist leaders photographed by Sheba Chhachhi (*Seven Lives in a Dream*, 1990–91).[20] The anti-Sikh riots in Delhi[21] after Indira Gandhi's assassination by her Sikh bodyguards in 1984 marked a new chapter in communal violence, and were documented by Pablo Bartholomew, Sondeep Shankar, Ashok Vahie and Ram Rahman,[22] Divided along the lines of faith, the city erupted in fearful rage and failed to give shelter to fleeing Sikhs. Bartholomew's portrayal of a dead child being buried after the Bhopal gas tragedy in the same year also testified to the city failing to protect its inhabitants, this time from a chemical disaster. In 1992, the city of Ayodhya witnessed the demolition of the Babri Masjid,[23] the violent first step in the project of building a new Ram temple at the same site. Prashant Panjiar, Pablo Bartholomew, Raghu Rai and Nitin Rai[24] capture the fundamentalist mob violence; their images fail as evidence in court, but succeed in inscribing a dark moment in India's history of religious intolerance. More recently, the Citizenship Amendment Act[25] protests in Delhi generate innumerable photographs, condensed into works such as the photobook *Har Shaam Shaheen Bagh* (2022) by Prarthna Singh,[26] marking the city as a site of public resistance to state authoritarianism..

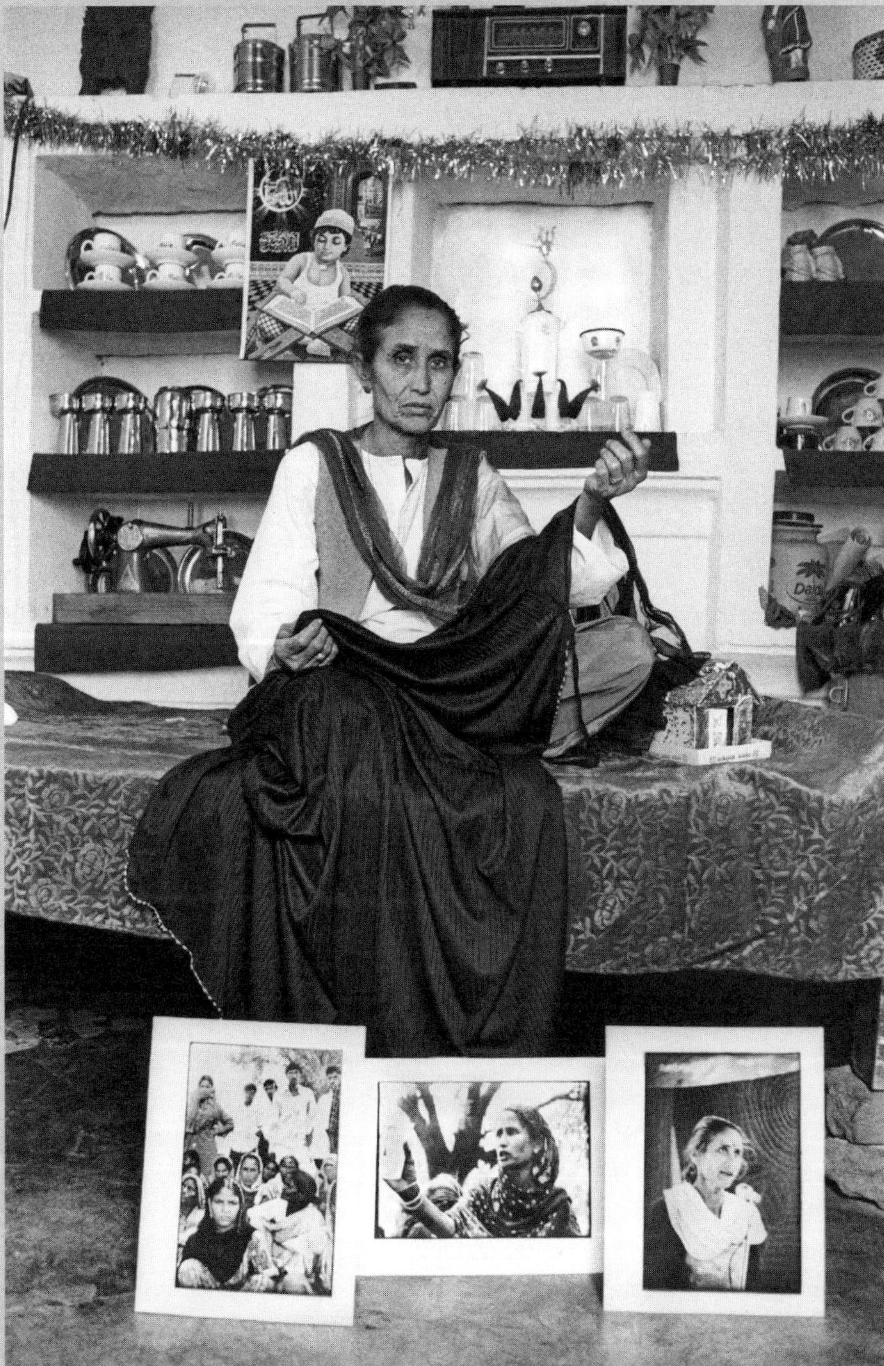

The millennial turn saw a greater proliferation of professional and personal photography, owing to the rapid improvements in digital camera technology and the mobile phone camera. Spectacles of urban living were countered by images of the underbelly of city life, the latter seen in Olwe's photographs of Mumbai conservancy workers. The environmental NGO Toxics Link, founded by photographer-activist Ravi Agarwal (b. 1958)[27] uses photography to raise awareness about the hazardous working conditions, marginalization and dehumanization of urban migrant labour, as seen in his book *Down and Out: Labouring under Global Capitalism* (Oxford University Press, 2000) and his exhibition *Of Value and Labour* (2011). The exhibitions *living.it.out.in.delhi* (2005) and *Trash* (2008) by the late Vivan Sundaram (1943-2023)[28] are deeply aesthetic visual engagements with ecological themes, including urban waste and excessive consumption. Non-biodegradable garbage, landfills and urban master plans chequered by piles of waste are collated in digital montages that form his comment on ecological damage. Night-time urbanscapes are featured in Dhruv Malhotra's *Noida Soliloquy* (2007-10) and *Sleepers* (2007-13)[29] that critique the unevenness of urban 'development' in the National Capital Region and Noida.

Themes of gender are explored in *Transportraits: Women and Mobility in the City* (2010), curated for the NGO Jagori[30] by Gauri Gill (b. 1970),[31] underscoring the drastic lack of safety for women in the city's public spaces - a social truth forced into the public conscience by the infamous Nirbhaya gang rape in Delhi in 2012[32] that shocked the country and the world. Domestic middle-class interiors where women spend much time working are seen in a series by Anay Mann[33] depicting his wife, *About Neetika* (2008), and by Bharti Kher (b. 1969)[34] who foregrounds her own body in *The Hybrids* (2003-04). The first decade of the 2000s also saw projects by photographers from India in foreign cities, including Pushpamala N.'s *Paris Autumn* (2006)[35], Sonia Khurana's *Logic of Birds* (2006)[36] shot in Barcelona and Gill's *The Americans* (2000-07), shot at different locations in the US.[37] *Body Building* (2019), a recent exhibition curated by Nada Raza at the Ishara Art Foundation, Dubai features over ninety works by artists from India, Pakistan, Sri Lanka and France, looking at architecture and the built environment in cities across South Asia and their resonance with those aspects of structures in the Gulf.

Urbanism and urban subjectivities are explored in a number of exhibitions and publications. *The City in the Archive: Calcutta's Visual Histories* (2011), curated by Tapati Guha-Thakurta, features works by Ahmed Ali (1923-2016), one of the first practitioners to image Calcutta in panoramic shots,[38] and the collection of Siddhartha Ghosh (1948-2002), author of the Bengali treatise on

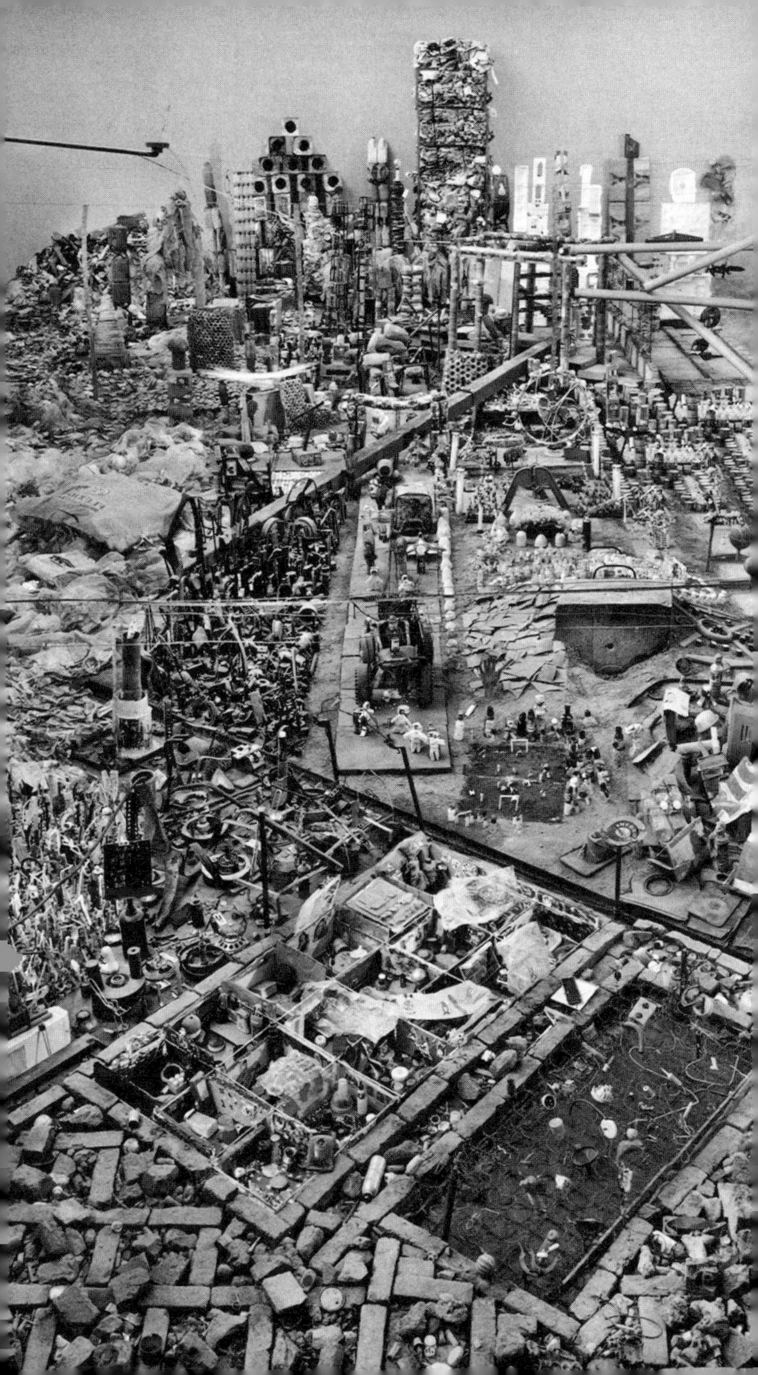

photography *Chhobi Tola: Bangalir Photography Charcha*.[39] Calcutta is also the subject of Pablo Bartholomew's *The Calcutta Diaries* (2012–13) that looked at the Chinese immigrant settlements in Tangra and Dhapa; the Alkazi Foundation for the Arts' exhibition *Calcutta: Chitpur Road and Neighbourhoods* (2016), and depicted in the book *Calcutta 1940–1970: In the Photographs of Jayant Patel* (Niyogi Books, 2017). Nishtha Jain's film *City of Photos* (2004) documents the fantasies and contradictions that manifest through the products of photo studios in Delhi, Calcutta and Ahmedabad.[40] Other metropolises reflect upon their own photographic histories, for instance Mumbai through the Matthew Foss Gallery, the first arts space dedicated to photography; its first biennale exhibition, FOCUS (2013), was displayed at different locations in the city. That same year, Madhusree Dutta published *dates.sites: Project Cinema City: Bombay/Mumbai*, a landmark multi-format mapping of the city through its cinematic legacy, accompanied by an extensive exhibition at the National Gallery of Modern Art, New Delhi.[41] The NGO Salaam Balak Trust's *Kids in the City* (2015) exhibited photographs of the lives of underprivileged children that had been taken by the children themselves.[42] Vintage and modern photographs of Delhi featured in three successive exhibitions by the Alkazi Foundation: *Historic Delhi: Early Explorations of the Camera c. 1860–1950* (2010); *Framing a Capital: Impressions of Delhi's Past, 1860–1920* (2011); and *Dawn Upon Delhi: Rise of a Capital* (2012–13). Edited by Rahaab Allana, *Delhi: Looking Out/Looking In*, a special issue of the American photography journal *Aperture*,[43] is a significant recent contribution to the discursive space being built through diverse modes of imaging the city; this space is expanding through major events such as the Delhi Photo Festival, Goa Photo and the Chennai Photo Festival that draw international participation and discussion.

The formal viewing of photography in gallery spaces is a relatively recent phenomenon in India, drawing towards itself the professional curator who was previously working with the other visual fine arts. It is no coincidence that the curatorial function in major photography projects has developed in parallel with trajectories of socioeconomic and cultural globalization in India in the 1990s. The import of camera technology was thence accompanied by the introduction of a global discourse on photography, and the urban became a mirror unto itself in various exhibitions that focused on this theme. Shows such as *Bombay/Mumbai 1992–2001*, curated by Geeta Kapur and Ashish Rajadhyaksha, part of *Century City: Art and Culture in the Modern Metropolis* (Tate Modern, London, 2001), as well as *sub-Terrain: Artworks in the Cityfold* as part of *body.city*, at the House of World Cultures (Berlin, 2003) and *SelfxSocial* at Jawaharlal Nehru University

(New Delhi, 2005), both curated by Kapur, span a range of locations, transporting one urban frame into another, creating silent dialogues of recognition between city dwellers across the world. *Middle Age Spread: Imaging India 1947–2004* (National Museum, New Delhi, 2004), curated by Gayatri Sinha, and *Public Places, Private Spaces: Contemporary Photography and Video Art* (Newark Museum, New Jersey, 2007), co-curated by Sinha and Paul Sternberger, were exhibitions of photographs and video works in which the city was an exclusive, persistent subject. These shows depicted urban life in relation to politics, violence, poverty, beauty, monumentality and state presence, and brought Indian photography to international attention. More recently, Latika Gupta's *City Cite Site* (2017) presented possible conversations between paintings, installations, photographs and video works on aspects of urban living.

The city, then, in its myriad complexities lends itself to acting as host to technological, aesthetic and thematic transformations in photography, drawing forth a range of lens-based practitioners energized by curiosity about their worlds. The digital age, more prominently since the 1990s, has further added the dimension of externalizing what may be dreams or nightmares emanating from the urban fabric. Migration, poverty, wealth, civic facilities, gender and caste dynamics are among some of the complex subjects which today extend beyond conventional portrayal into practitioners' experiments with mediated re-presentation. In a recent essay, Matias Echanove and Rahul Srivastava, co-founders of the research think tank Institute of Urbanology, discuss the ways in which the city offers itself to political and aesthetic intervention, as a fertile artistic ground amidst the counterpoints to mainstream ideologies.[44] The artist, they say, locates himself at these fault lines of resistance where the imperfections of life create rupture in the grand state plans of urbanization. These then become sites of great interest for creative interpretation and intervention by artists and activists alike who, as Echanove and Srivastava note, must collaborate as a collective voice.

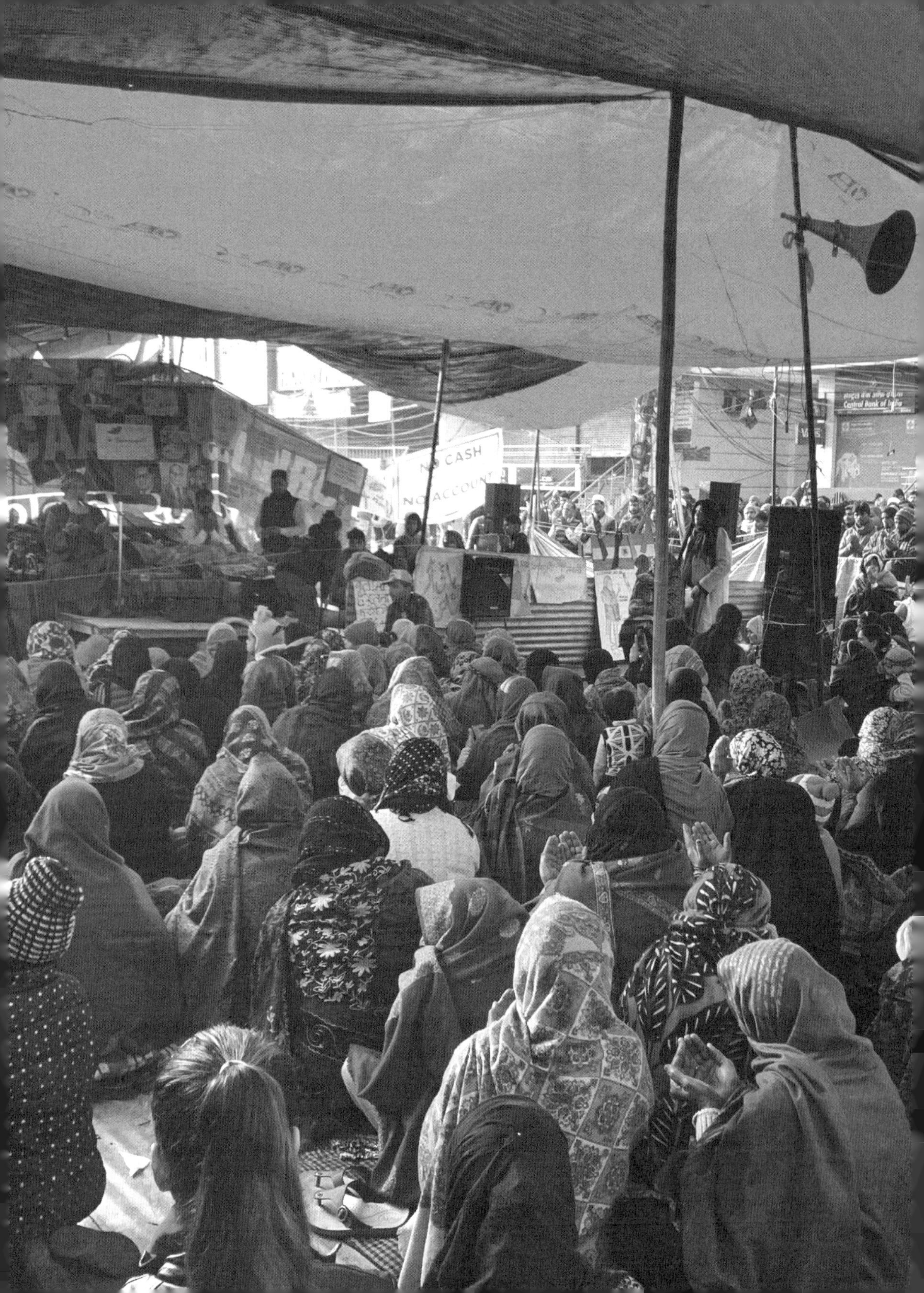
NO CASH
NO ACCOUNT
Central Bank of India

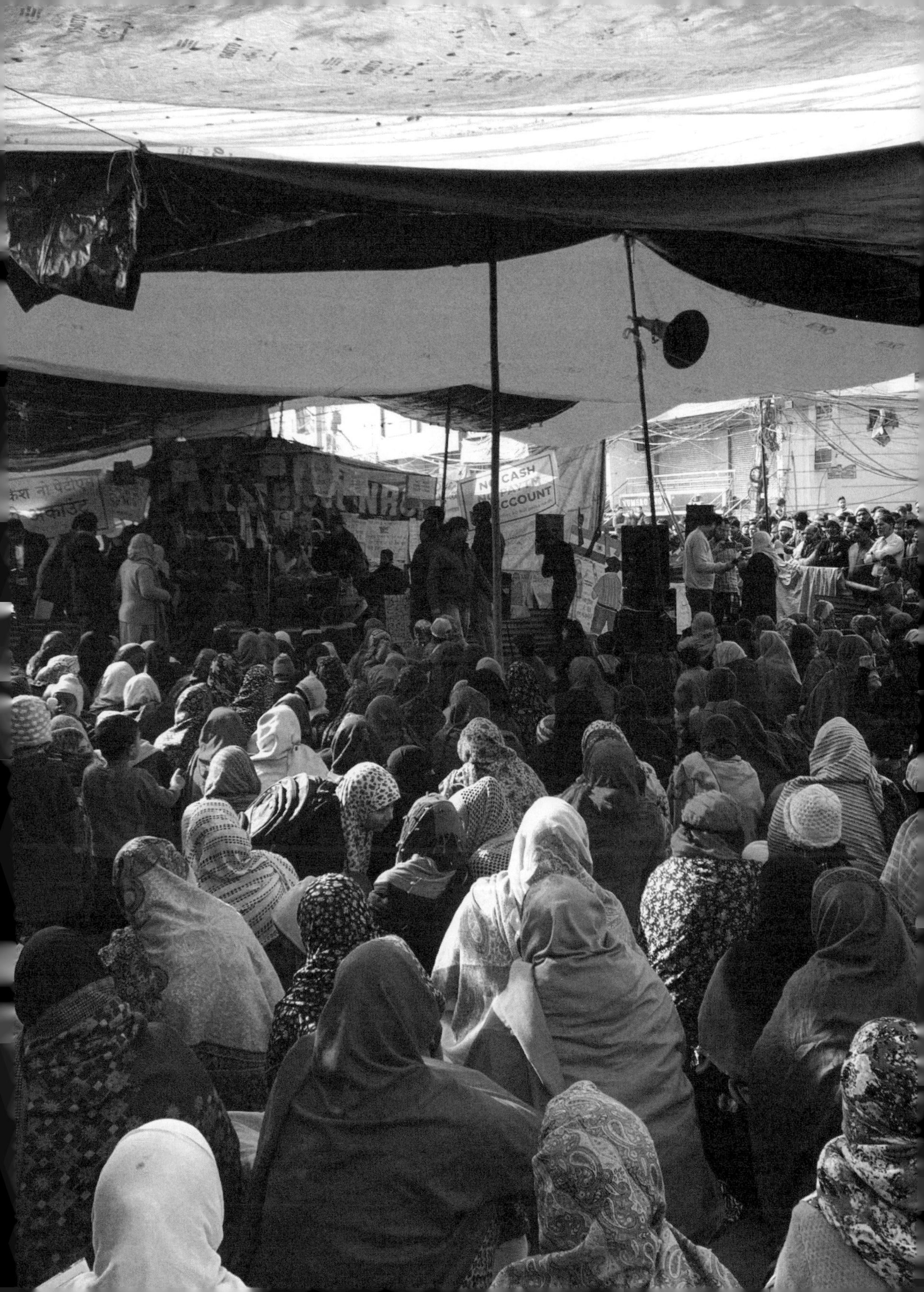
CASH
ACCOUNT

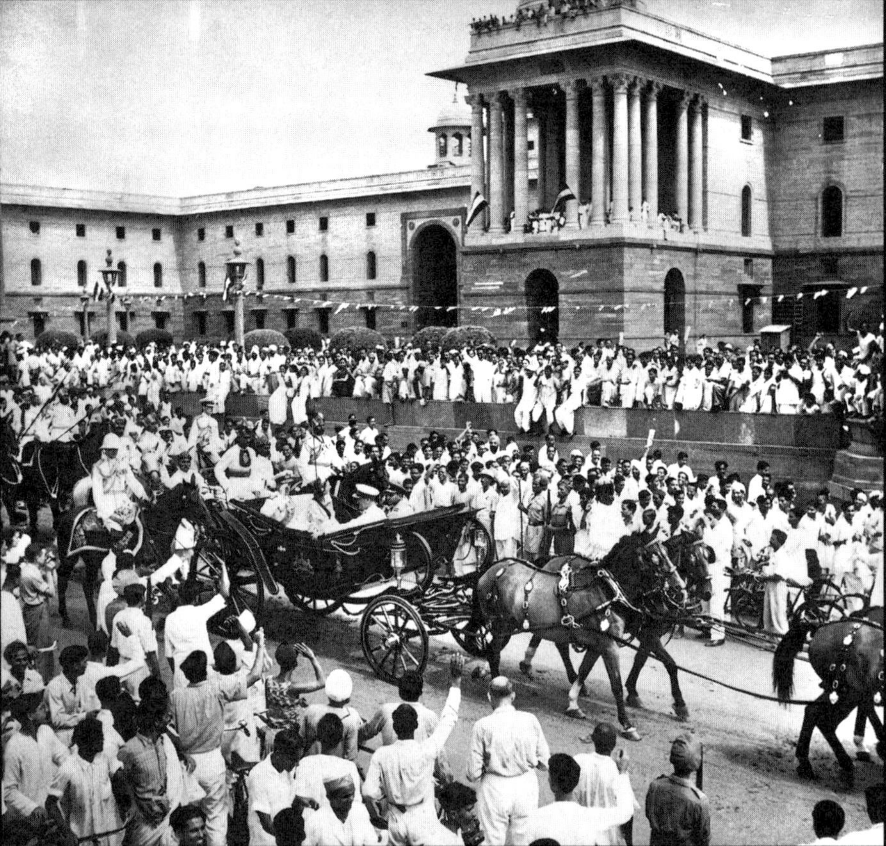

5 Journeys into Inner and Outer Worlds

Photography's Encounter with Public Space in India

2010

I Sabeena Gadihoke

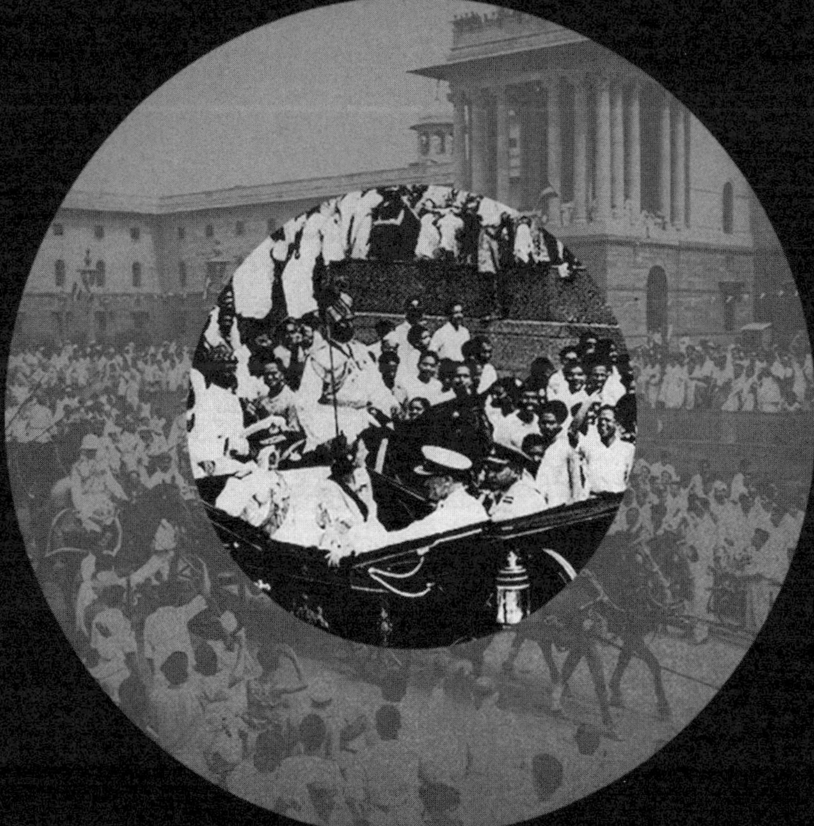

In her sweeping review of the imagining of public space, Sabeena Gadihoke looks at how early documentary photographers worked with the spectacular as well as the clichéd, the ordinary and the mundane, creating independent projects using a form of poetic realism. This was preceded by an earlier generation that saw the lingering spirit of Henri Cartier-Bresson, and then the astonishing history of photojournalism that in the pre-television era was the most important form of visual communication. In the 1940s the press photograph was marked by jubilation as well as mass suffering; in the 1960s it covered wars and the gathering clouds over a new nation while by the 1970s it was marked by images of tragedy and disaster.

Across genres, practitioners persistently imaged the material truths of an India that existed 'outside of a nationalist project that focused on politics'. This included pioneering women photographers who shaped a new symbolic idiom through a focus on themes of gender, interiority, alterity and marginalization. More recent work in the first decade of the 21st century, she suggests, refigures ways in which the outer world increasingly gets framed through the lens of the 'inside'. Gadihoke asks if these new formal strategies could recast public space with the 'subjectivities and intimacies of inner worlds, its ghosts and demons, dreams and fantasies and intangible experiences'.

Such an investment of inner feelings upon realist documentary could reveal a strange, perhaps uncanny history of photography in the subcontinent.

An earlier version of this essay was published in *Where Three Dreams Cross: 150 Years of Photography from India, Pakistan and Bangladesh* (Gottingen: Steidl; London: Whitechapel Gallery; Winterthur: Fotomuseum Winterthur, 2010), published in association with the exhibition of the same name at Whitechapel Gallery, London, 21 January–11 April 2010. Reprinted with permission of the author and the Fotomuseum Winterthur.

Keywords and Names

Pablo Bartholomew, Felice Beato, Bengal Famine, Margaret Bourke-White, Samuel Bourne, Henri Cartier-Bresson, Citizenship, First Indian War of Independence 1857, Indira Gandhi, William Gedney, Jallianwala Bagh massacre 1919, Sunil Janah, Kumbh Mela, Partition of India, S. Paul, Photojournalism, Press Information Bureau, Ram Rahman, Raghu Rai, Kulwant Roy, T.S. Satyan, Ketaki Sheth, Bharat Sikka, Dayanita Singh, Raghubir Singh, Homai Vyarawalla, see Keywords at the back of this volume.

Images

pp. 84–85: Homai Vyarawalla, *Lord Mountbatten during a ceremonial ride at Vijay Chowk, New Delhi after his swearing as Governor-General on the morning of India's Independence*, 1947. Courtesy HV Archive/The Alkazi Collection of Photography.

p. 89: Raghu Rai, *Evening Prayer at Jama Masjid, Delhi*, 1982. Photograph courtesy Raghu Rai and PHOTOINK.

p. 93: *Blitz*, October 1959, coverage of the 'Nanavati scandal', in which Naval Commander K.M. Nanavati was tried for the murder of Prem Ahuja, his wife's lover.

p. 97: Dayanita Singh, Untitled photograph from the series *I Am As I Am* (1999). Grateful acknowledgement to Dayanita Singh for permission to reprint.

> The streets of old Delhi are truly fantastic, the chaos is frighteningly real. Your eye is led from one thing to another; before it can rest your sight must move on. The movement pulls you. The crowds on all sides, wagons, bicycles, vendors, cars, cattle, a thousand shops, the curbs lined with goods, lumber carried across the street, horns blowing. Colour dashes in front of you; each street is a tunnel of movement, of frenzy. The vision is exhausting, the masses of Asia weigh down on you, you see too much, your eyes want rest.
>
> – William Gedney[1]

It is not surprising that William Gedney, who arrived in India in 1969, should express bewilderment at the excess of colour, movement and crowds on the streets of Delhi. He was articulating the problems that photographers both from and beyond the subcontinent (the insiders and outsiders) have had to contend with while shooting public space, mesmeric and anarchic. This essay revisits this meta-history of imaging through fragments; it deals with broad brushstrokes and moments, focusing primarily on post-Independence photography. Reflecting on representations of public space through the work of documentary practitioners in the last quarter of the twentieth century, it moves through other moments and genres of photography to suggest that while a realist discourse has been integral to the imaging of the exterior world, there could be other ways of accessing this experience. Posing questions about new formalistic possibilities arising from the practice of contemporary photographers and artists at the close of the first decade of this century, it asks if the subjectivities and intimacies of inner worlds, its ghosts and demons, dreams and fantasies and intangible experiences could be appropriated and recast in the imagining of public space.

Various scholars note that the private-public dichotomy that has historically existed in the West is not easily applicable to the streets in India.[2] Cognizant of these private dimensions of the public, this essay looks at how photography in the region has captured the *physicality* of public space through themes such as landscape, the streets and everyday life, crowds and demonstrations as well as other public and political events. It discusses the representation of a significant moment of 'outdoor India' through the lyrical work of documentary practitioners in the 1970s. Shifting genres and time spans, it then attends to a different mode of public visibility and citizenship through a discussion of press photography in the 1940s and 1950s. Suggesting that there were other representations of public life in print culture outside of a nationalist project that focused on politics, this section also draws attention to the capturing of everyday and urban life through social histories documented by the tabloid press and advertisements at the time. It concludes with a discussion of more recent self-conscious interventions of practitioners within public space in contemporary globalizing India. Locating each of these three moments and genres in their own context, the essay attempts to reassess both the strengths and inadequacies of realist modes of representation within a form that has been historically defined by its indexical status.

Poetic Realism and Its Discontents

> Where in India is anything in the centre? Why should it be in the centre? If you look at my works you will find all the action is in the periphery. So many elements come into play. It's about the spontaneity of the things that happen within the frame.
>
> – Raghu Rai[3]

The dilemma posed by Gedney would elicit all kinds of different responses from documentary photographers who started to create bodies of work from the 1970s onwards. While many of them eventually turned their backs on careers in the press, the ghosts of an earlier photojournalistic impulse to record persisted.[4] In the absence of other forums to showcase photographic work, their images were published in tourism-driven glossy books. It is not surprising that documentary work in the next two decades was marked by images of tragedies or disasters such as the Bhopal gas leak and anti-Sikh riots in 1984,[5] as well as pictorial photo-ethnographies about landscape, communities and iconic fairs, often inviting charges of presenting an exotic and 'unchanging' India. Engaging with the spectacular as well as the clichéd, ordinary and mundane, certain practitioners created independent projects using a form of poetic realism. Different from the more distanced ethnography of colonial photographers, *flâneur* photographers such as Raghubir Singh and Raghu Rai[6] used a traveller's gaze to photograph everyday life through lyrical photo essays. Structured as journeys along the highways, rivers, towns and cities of India, Singh's books on Benaras and Bombay were representative of this kind of photography. His last book, *A Way into India* (2002), used the Ambassador car and its contours as a moving picture frame to tell stories about small-town, urban and pastoral India.[7] With a monumental body of work to his credit and an influence over at least two generations of photographers

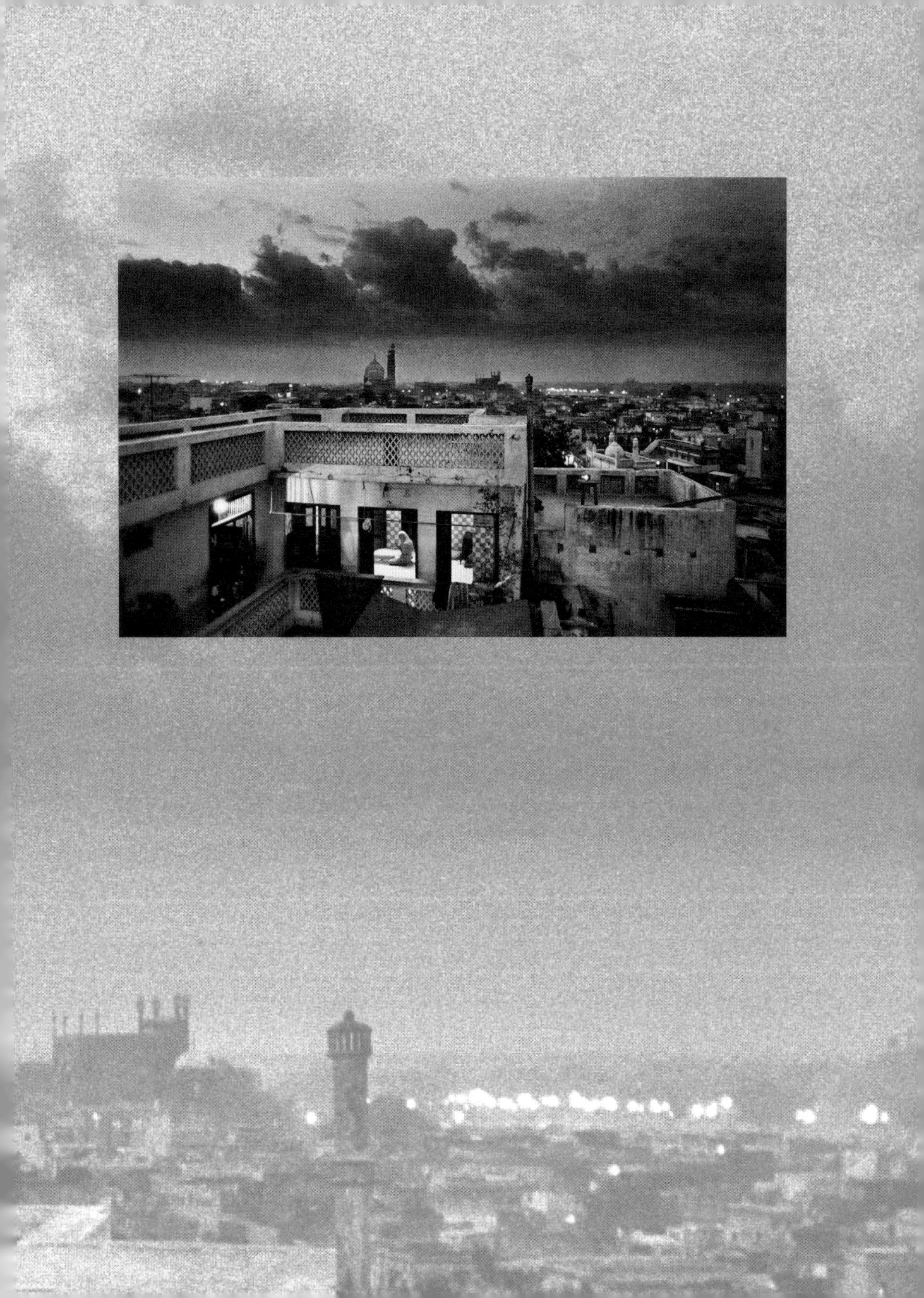

that followed, Rai remains to this day a master storyteller and poet in his ability to capture quieter and more reflective moments within the cluttered *mise en scène* of the public world.

The spirit of Henri Cartier-Bresson, who first visited India just after Independence, touched this early generation of photographers that included Mahendra Sinh and S. Paul.[8] While the spontaneous implications of Cartier-Bresson's famous 'decisive moment' could be debated in its quite calculated wait for the perfect frame, there is no doubt about its attraction for photographers of the outdoor, obsessed with capturing the ephemeral and fleeting nature of daily life in India. In the chaos of public space there would have seemed no better way to freeze this multiplicity of experiences. Many responded to their social world with a more direct snapshot-like aesthetic that played on irony and juxtaposition. Key to the imagination of the everyday and the streets was its insistent signage: posters, billboards, advertisements and graffiti. The excess of colour in India seemed to pose a dilemma for these photographers and many of them (with exceptions such as Raghubir Singh) deliberately chose to work mainly in black-and-white.

Bodies of work structured around the quintessential character of cities became another way to make sense of the experience of urban India. Raghu Rai's rooftop romance against a monsoon sky in Calcutta or his stunning images of rush-hour Bombay could be seen as examples of this kind of themed engagement.[9] A younger generation of photographers emerging from the 1980s marked both continuity and departure from this tradition of poetic realism. Like Rai, some of them created bodies of outdoor work marking the transformation of cities over decades. Among these is Ketaki Sheth's work on the streets of Bombay and Ram Rahman's social landscapes of Delhi, taken over a period of twenty years.[10] The city emerged in more oblique ways too, for instance as a rich backdrop for a photographic 'main' subject, as in Sooni Taraporevala's[11] 'insider' portraits of the Parsi community from 2000. And, if Bombay was the preferred subject as India's most modern city, another city captured the imagination of numerous other photographers for very different reasons.[12] Citing the visual excess of Benaras and its almost unchanging value from colonial times as a symbol of an amorphous Hindu-Indian essence, historian Sunil Khilnani notes, 'The Taj Mahal may be India's most photographed building but Benaras is probably its most photographed city.'[13] In an important essay he draws attention to the representational departures made in the work of Dayanita Singh[14] who chose to see the city not through the spectacle of its burning ghats and bazaars but through the secluded inner spaces of the Anandamayi ashram and its women inhabitants who live far above the city. The idea of looking at public space through the lens of inner worlds is an insight to be signposted and returned to later in this essay.

Singh's photographs of Benaras (1999) draw attention to the gendered nature of India's public spaces and the different ways in which women negotiate and navigate them. A more consciously feminist expression of this relationship came through the lens of artist Sheba Chhachhi.[15] An unofficial biographer of the women's movement in 1980s Delhi, her early photographs of the presence of women in street demonstrations and campaigns were followed by a feminist revisiting of the much-photographed Hindu festival Kumbh Mela within a work titled *Ganga's Daughters* (2001-ongoing). Photographing women who had undergone a spiritual transformation, Chhachhi's images of androgynous bodies stripped of conventional forms of femininity were transgressive and empowering, placed as they were within the massive, chaotic public space of the Kumbh where women had featured only as devotees.[16] Like diasporic photographer Sunil Gupta's performative reappropriation of the public space of the streets and monuments of Delhi by gay men in his series *Exiles* (1999), her work emerged out of a more personal investment in the politics of identity.[17] Formally schooled in photography and the arts like Gupta, Rahman, Sheth, Chhachhi and Taraporevala, Dayanita Singh focused in the early 1990s on a much photographed category of women traditionally associated with the streets: the sex worker. Marking a distinct departure from the more intrusive images taken by the American photographer Mary Ellen Mark[18] before her, Singh's photographs of distressed sex workers during the Bhandup 'rescue' by the police from the brothels of Bombay were deeply empathetic, but they also confronted her with ethical dilemmas around presenting an ethnography of 'otherness'. For Singh as for Chhachhi, disenchantment with the limitations of documentary realism and photojournalism would mark significant formalistic departures in their careers by the early 1990s towards more constructed forms of photography.

Press Photography and Its Archive of the Everyday

> News of Gandhi's assassination reaches Calcutta, 1948. That was an extraordinarily lucky accident. Nobody believes that the image was captured so perfectly. They think I superimposed the newspaper on the photograph.
>
> - Sunil Janah[19]

Domesticating the public world for private consumption in a pre-television era, the press photograph was still *the* most important form of visual communication. If some of the most striking images of the press photography from the 1960s were of wars and the gathering clouds over the new nation, those of the late 1940s were marked by both jubilation and mass suffering. Besides Independence, the other most visually iconic events of this time, Partition and the assassination of Mahatma Gandhi, were defined largely by the images of two 'outsider-insider' photographers, Henri Cartier-Bresson and Margaret Bourke-White. Some years earlier though, a photographer had captured the desperation of refugees displaced by another man-made disaster.[20] Sunil Janah, who photographed for *People's War*, a publication of the Communist Party of India, produced poignant testimony to mass suffering through unforgettable images of the 1943 Bengal Famine.[21] Other press photographers such as Kulwant Roy, T.S. Satyan and his brother T.S. Nagarajan[22] also created independent bodies of work that have yet to be properly archived. In the absence of established forums to circulate photographic work at the time, it would be interesting to explore how this generation was exposed to the work of their more famous contemporaries from Magnum and Time Life.[23]

Forgotten in a history of officialdom, and often overshadowed by other more prominent names, was the humble press photographer. Attached to the state-run Press Information Bureau or newly emerging newspapers and photo agencies, these image-makers were capturing the public world of nationalist politics and – as a result of the mass protests of the freedom movement – a much more visible presence of ordinary people on the streets. Among these professionals was India's first woman press photographer, Homai Vyarawalla,[24] who along with her colleagues had photographed the pageantry of Independence, the building of dams, steel plants and educational institutions. A deeper inquiry into the archives of these photographers reveals other kinds of visual histories, some of which are familiar, others less commonly known. Like Vyarawalla's photographs of her friend Rehana Mogul posing like a film star at a women's picnic organized by her arts school, or images of Parsi women spending leisure time at Chowpatty beach, Bombay in 1937, these images were not always panoramic in scale or compositionally strong. However, their value lies in the rich social histories of the outdoor that they documented, often in pictures that were not published.

In contrast to the more conventional press photograph, the weekly tabloids *Blitz* and its rival *Current* defined an alternative kind of portraiture. Started by Russy Karanjia in 1941, *Blitz*[25] published images of everyday life, public space and public figures but with a kind of sensationalism and irreverence that official press

BLITZ

INDIA'S GREATEST WEEKLY

EVERY SATURDAY PRICE 25 NAYE PAISE

MERCY *for* NANAVATI!

● For Mercy Petition... Page 9

REGD. NO. B. 4513

TRAGEDY OF THE ETERNAL TRIANGLE

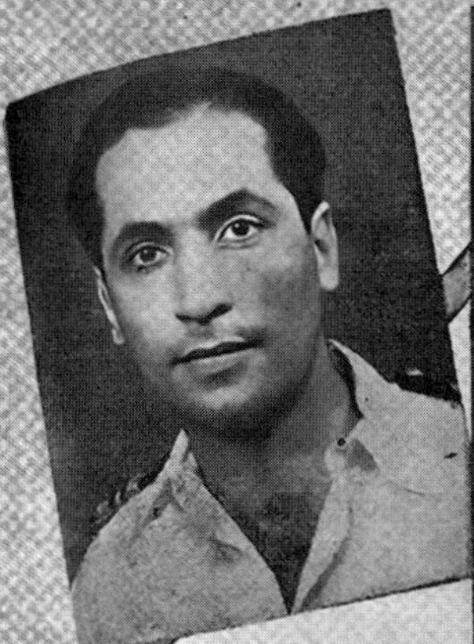

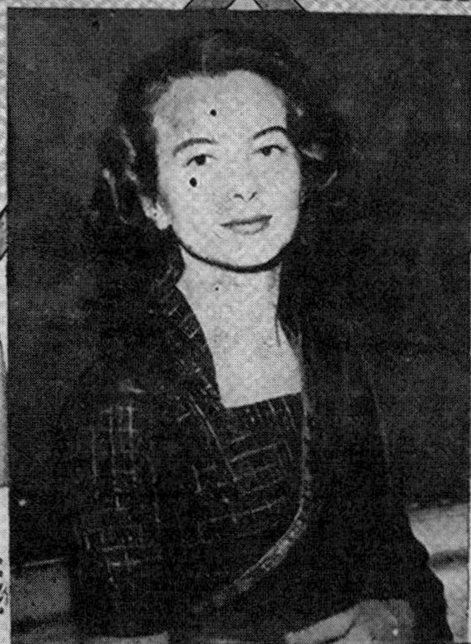

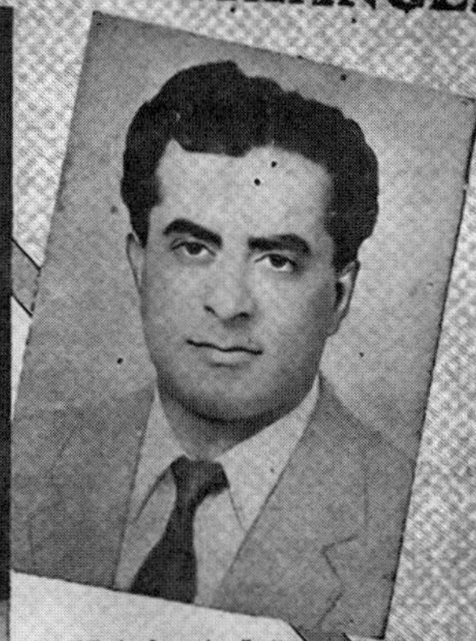

BLITZ presents the first exclusive pictures to be published of the three main characters in the latest Tragedy of the Eternal Triangle familiarly known as the sensational Ahuja Murder Trial.

On LEFT is Commander K. M. Nanavati of the Indian Navy, who is on trial for the alleged murder, at CENTRE, his beautiful English wife, Sylvia, and on RIGHT her lover, Prem Ahuja, a Bombay businessman, who was shot dead.

★ The Internationally famous Case of the Eternal Triangle, involving Commander Nanavati of the IN Flagship MYSORE (inset right), his beautiful English wife Sylvia and her lover, Bombay businessman Prem Ahuja, ended last week with the confirmation of the life sentence on the naval officer for

SYLVIA NANAVATI TELLS HER

STORY OF LOVE AND TORTURE

THREE SHOTS THAT SHOOK THE NATION

FULL PICTORIAL RECORD OF THE NANAVATI CASE

BLITZ

ASIA'S FOREMOST NEWSMAGAZINE

EVERY SATURDAY PRICE 25 NAYE PAISE

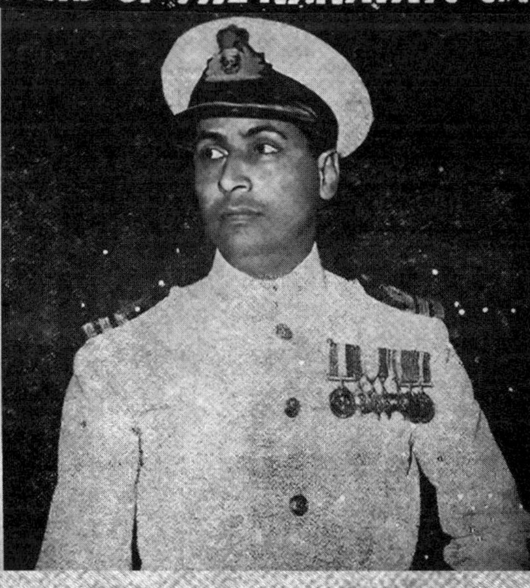

★★★ By HOMI D. MISTRY

Pics By B. K. SANIL

BANG . . . BANG . . . BANG :—Three shots ring out one by one in succession. The shrill crash of window panes is followed by a wild scream. The scene is the ultra-modernly furnished bedroom of a young Bombay businessman on the second floor of a palatial building called "Jeevan Jyot"—"the Flame of Life".

The shots shatter the peace and calm of the fashionable locality of Setalwad Road, off the Nepean Sea locality. The day is April 27, 1959; the time; late afternoon.

The Man Who Fired Three Shots

It is alleged that as the bullet-ridden body of the rich businessman, with only

the door-bell, walks through the front door, and passing the hall goes into the bedroom of his businessman friend. As he closes the door behind him, the uppermost thought in his mind is to commit suicide. What happened, however, between the minutes he closed the door of the bedroom behind him to the time three shots rang out is known only to two men.

One, Mr. Prem Bhagwandas

photography could not adopt. With its grainy photographs *Blitz* had something for everyone: news, scandals, gossip, gruesome murders, fantastic stories and pin-up girls appropriately featured on its back page. Seen as a 'low' form, the tabloid actually marked an interesting departure from the more 'objective' standards set by the conventional press. Using a playful and irreverent form of visual iconography, it questioned the 'purity' of the photograph by presenting it along with etchings, cartoons and colour, often animating the picture with leading text. The sensational pictures of *Blitz* were deeply embedded in urban life in Bombay, evoking Walter Benjamin's reference to the 'shocks and collisions' of fragmented urban living.[26] *Blitz* covered everyday life but also explored the dark side of the urban and the margins of morality through its images of crime, streetwalking and other facets of night life. Its picture stories about great love scandals such as the Roberto Rossellini–Sonali Dasgupta–Ingrid Bergman triangle (1957)[27] and the Nanavati scandal (1959)[28] exposed the deep anxieties and hypocrisies around public morality. When such salacious emotional drama occupied centre stage in the print media, it fleetingly usurped attention from larger political news.

The history of press photography in the 1940s and 1950s is incomplete without a reference to its circulation and to the rise of genres of photography that focused on other aspects of public life. Besides newspapers, the relatively staid *Illustrated Weekly of India*[29] was one of the first magazines to publish the extended picture story, thereby encouraging the careers of many amateurs and professionals. Along with popular magazines that emerged later and carried colour photographs, such as *Femina*, *Eve's Weekly* and *Filmfare*,[30] these publications printed advertisements that marked new forms of commercial photography. Using technologies ranging from scraperboard drawings to quarter-tone printing, advertisements energetically visualized new worlds of urban leisure and consumption. Advertisements for mill cloth or beauty products with models and film stars became sites for the negotiation of sexuality and self-image, and also anticipated the early beginnings of fashion photography.

Besides innovations in print technologies that enabled the mass circulation of the photograph, press photography was made possible by the increased mobility of cameras such as the Speed Graphic, the Rolleiflex and the Leica.[31] While landscapes, architectural sites, royal durbars and hunts had been a significant part of nineteenth-century colonial imagery, the static look of these outdoor spectacles was also linked to the bulk and complicated logistics of glass plate technologies.[32] From the turn of the twentieth century, the move away from the use of large-format cameras to less cumbersome models freed the image from the tableau-like quality of the studio. In 1919, Narayan Vinayak Virkar[33] took evidential images documenting the excesses of the Jallianwala Bagh massacre of Indian civilians by British troops. A studio photographer from Nasik, Virkar was more famous for his film stills and constructed portraits, and the representational shifts in his photographs of these two different spaces could not have been more striking.[34] More performative traditions of photography continued to be nurtured indoors, but the turn of the twentieth century marked the era of the candid image and its stage would definitively be the outdoors. While Virkar's images of Jallianwala Bagh were taken after the actual event, mobile technologies from the 1920s ensured the subsequent live documentation of increasingly chaotic public spaces. Christopher Pinney notes, 'If nineteenth-century Indian photography's paradigmatic location was the Himalayan foothills, in the twentieth century photography's preferred location became the street.'[35]

The Death of the Street ... ?

> You know, I really don't care how a photograph was made, whether by construction, or by suggestion or by intervention or even by photoshop. I am interested in what a photograph can do, can it transcend its inherent 'factness', can it say the unsayable? ... As long as you understand that the only 'reality' is the photographer's. It is in this 'fiction' of photography that its magical power lies, otherwise one may as well be a photocopy machine.
>
> – Dayanita Singh[36]

A century later, as the preferred location of documentary photography shifts once more, this time to urban interiors in a fast globalizing India, there are discussions on whether the streets have receded from the work of contemporary practitioners.[37] Clearly, the fractured, fluid and transforming nature of the urban terrain continues to provide new content for photographers.[38] The question to ask is whether the imaging of the exterior world, inscribed as it has been within a discourse of documentary realism, has perhaps reached an impasse in terms of representation; and if there could be different ways to revisit public space today.

A shift in economic policy in the 1990s would result in a radically transformed visual landscape in India. Independent photography was increasingly supported by the art world and given space in international biennials and museums by the end of that decade. Contemporary photography today encompasses a great diversity of work that is in continual dialogue with other kinds of art practices, including performance, video and installation; it is in this changed scenario that some of the interventions by practitioners offer interesting possibilities for a reworked sensibility.

One of the refigured ways in which the outer world gets framed increasingly today is through the lens of the 'inside'. An example of this is the title of Pablo Bartholomew's[39] recent show of photographs of urban middle-class experience taken in the 1970s, *Outside In: A Tale of Three Cities*.[40] Contemporary work that grounds itself within the ambit of the photographic print seems to take its cues from the turn toward more constructed forms of photography. A meshing of personal subjectivity with public space through performativity plays out in some of Anita Khemka's self-portraits and work by Tejal Shah.[41] Several recent bodies of work such as Gauri Gill's *Nizamuddin at Night* (2005–20) and Bharat Sikka's[42] bleak urban landscapes in *The Space In Between* (2008) focus on spaces largely devoid of people.[43] Gill's meditative images, generated within the comfort and intimacy of her own neighbourhood Nizamuddin in Delhi, can be read as a feminist reappropriation of public space at night and seems to foreground a more personal and subjective investment with public space. The intersection of the geographies of land/space with the body/self is also central to many of Sheba Chhachhi's works. Chhachhi's more abstract, immersive and sensory installations have emerged out of her interrogation of the 'truth claims' and other limitations of the 'documentary' photograph.[44] Could there be other ways of representing the experience of the exterior world that imbue it with the affective dimensions of interiority? This question has been raised by scholars in other contexts. For instance, Patricia Hayes who has worked on photographs taken by soldiers during the Namibian border war during the late 1970s has drawn attention to the inadequacies of realist forms of photography in addressing the phantasmagoria of one of the most public of events, war.[45]

This essay ends with a discussion of more recent work from photographer Dayanita Singh, who revisits public space after nearly two decades using what could be called a fictive sensibility within documentary images.

In the 1990s, Dayanita Singh's *Families* project marked a major shift in Indian photography, capturing as it did, a new globalizing India. While her images of empty rooms and museum spaces marked a significant turn to the photography of interiors through the 'absent presence' of people, later that decade she also made intriguing forays into the world outside through photographs of gigantic illusional

monuments and architectural sites created for the Durga Puja festival celebrations in Calcutta. In her most recent work, *The Blue Book* (2008), Singh returns to the exterior world of an industrial landscape - but one that acquires the quality of a haunting and melancholic reverie. Having avoided colour in the past, Singh's initial foray into this world is tentative, almost like a watercolour technique used by artists to dull its excess, but its value here is in its evocation of an emotional state. *The Blue Book* suggests departures from a realist narrative of documentary activism (her images of factory sites have no context, sense of place, captions, etc.) and the voyeurism of ethnography (there are no factory workers). Harking back to pictorial traditions and classic industrial photography, this atmospheric work is strangely intriguing because of the journey that it seems to make in crafting interiority onto a public canvas.[46]

It is in Singh's new work *Dream Villa* (2010) that some of these ideas are carried further, through the exploration of nightscapes with colour and light - this time the colours are more vivid, but all that is familiar about the outdoors seems to turn strange and uncanny, taking the work towards a far greater level of abstraction. There is a sense of the intangible unknown within the everyday quality of these photographs. Instead of documenting, the images are evocative, allowing for the meshing of the 'real' exterior world with an interiority that is emotive, dreamlike and imaginative. *Dream Villa* and some of her images in *House of Love* (2011) more clearly articulate the possibilities of the affective haunting of public events and spaces through a fictive sensibility. One of the most influential contemporary photographers in India today, Singh's new work offers another way of re-entering public space, often without people, through a different kind of journey where readers can weave their own stories about her images.

A realist documentary sensibility has always been integral in terms of style to the photography and representation of public space. The candid moment was essential to the archival and evidential nature of press photography. It was also used creatively by a generation of documentary photographers who mapped outdoor India through a poetic form of imaging. Each moment shifted certain boundaries: photographers in the 1970s were turning their back on the visual shorthand demanded by the journalistic image, while contemporary practitioners today seek to push the parameters of documentary photography further. Many of these histories will continue to overlap and run parallel. An example of this is the continuing dynamism of the work of a master photographer such as Raghu Rai.

Without pitting genres and the different imperatives of historical moments against each other, the concluding section of this essay has attempted to lay out alternative responses to the realist impulse of documentary photography. At a time when new modes of imaging make every experience of the public world a transitory spectacle, this crisis of genre and form is not limited to documentary photography. Photojournalism too finds itself stylistically appropriated by advertising and fashion photography, and its shock value overtaken by other, quicker forms such as television and the internet. While stories about wars and streets and the people who inhabit these realms still need to be told with the same urgency, we need to search for new languages to tell these stories. Those languages may emerge from the creative worlds of artists and professional practitioners. They may also emerge from other more unexpected quarters – from visual essays, personal diaries, biographies, and the pirate reportage of ubiquitous digital and mobile phone cameras. Perhaps this current moment, when there are endless possibilities of mapping the real world and yet a new unsteadiness as to what we define as 'real', is the time to make fresh beginnings.

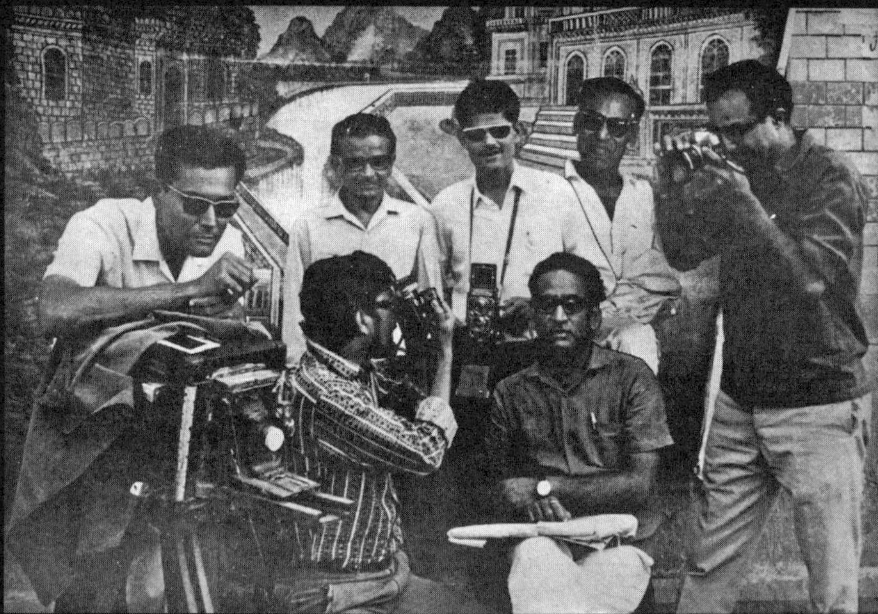

STANDING FROM L. JYOTI BHATT, VINODRAY PATEL, VINOD S. PATEL, NARENDRA MEHTA, FEROZ KATPITIA.
SEATED FROM L. GULAM SHEIKH, JERAM PATEL.

VINODRAY PATEL

Born 1933. Joined Fine Arts College Baroda — 1955. M. A. (fine) Painting 1961. Held one man show in Bombay 1963. National Award 1961 and prizes in various art Exhibitions. Participated in various exhibitions abroad. Paintings in private collections in India & abroad.

JYOTI BHATT

Born 1934, Bhavnagar (Saurashtra)
Studied painting and print making at :
Faculty of Fine Arts, Baroda;
Akademia Di Belle Arti, Naples, Italy;
Pratt Institute and Pratt Graphic Art Center, New York, U.S.A. Paintings and graphics are in private and public collections including National Gallery of Modern Art (New Delhi) and Museum of Modern Art, New York. Teaching Painting at Faculty of Fine Arts, M. S. University of Baroda.

FEROZ KATPITIA

Born at Baroda. Joined Faculty of Fine Arts, Baroda in 1950. M. A. (Fine) Degree in 1956.
Exhibited his paintings in various All India exhibitions. Executed a mural for Parliament House, New Delhi-Since 1957 on the staff of Faculty of Fine Arts, Baroda.

6 *Painters with a Camera* (1968/69)

In Search of an Indian Photography Exhibition

2019

I Diva Gujral

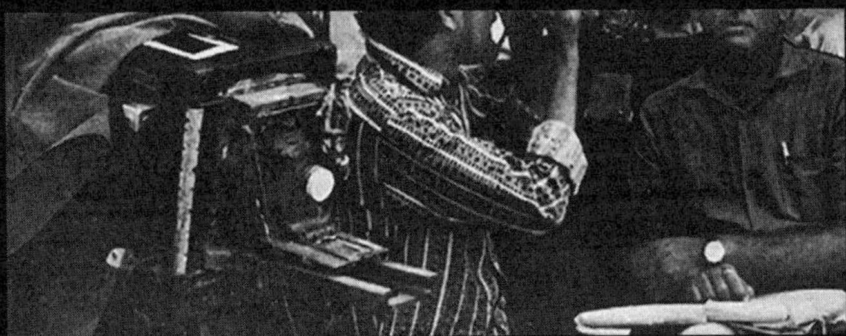

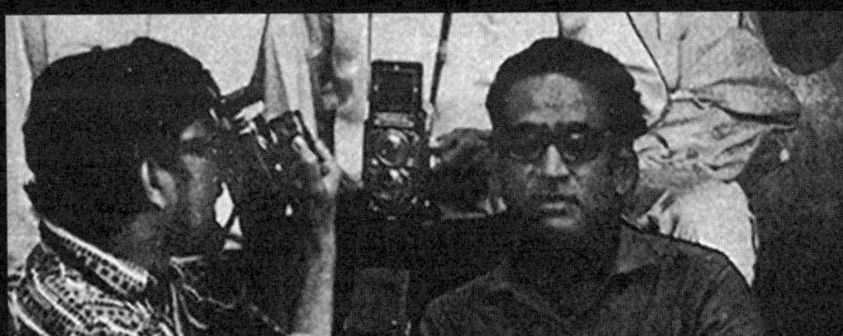

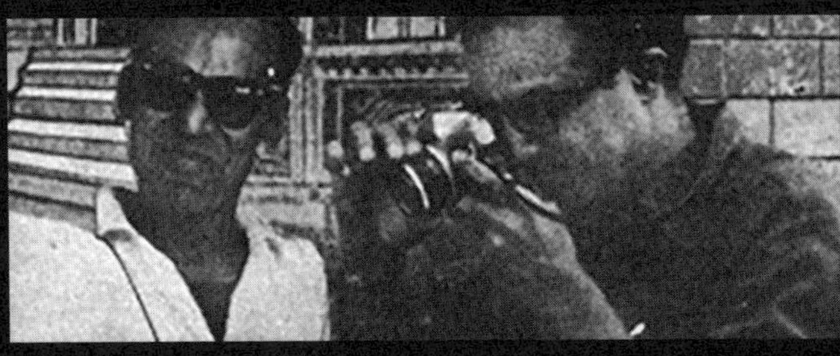

Section II
Image Spectra

In the late 1960s the **Faculty of Fine Arts in Baroda**'s venerable Maharaja Sayajirao (M.S.) University was the epicentre of a major movement in Painting, with stalwarts like K.G. Subramanyan and **Gulammohammed Sheikh** as faculty and several famous alumni. It was also a time when visual artists there, but also elsewhere, were experimenting with new media, including – as this entire section explores – photography and film.

This essay uses a specific 1968 exhibition of cross-media work, *Painters with a Camera*, mounted at the Jehangir Art Gallery, Bombay, to explore a significant movement in experimental photography. In Bombay around the same time, another major painter, Akbar Padamsee, started the **Vision Exchange Workshop** (see Keywords), which also saw painters experimenting alongside major figures in India's independent cinema with 16 mm celluloid.

An earlier version of this essay appeared in *Object*, vol. 20, 2019, pp. 33–58. Reproduced with permission of the author.

Keywords and Names

Lalit Kala Akademi, MARG, Modernism, Nasreen Mohamedi, Progressive Artists Group, Gulammohammed Sheikh, Vernacular mode, Vision Exchange Workshope see Keywords at the back of this volume.

Images

pp. 100–01: Pamphlet for *Painters with a Camera,* 1968, part II. Image courtesy Jyoti Bhatt and Asia Art Archive.

p. 105: (Above) Still from *Yet in Him We Trust* (dir. S.N.S. Sastry, 1966), produced by **Films Division** (see Keywords). Screenshot by the author. (Below) *Events in a Cloud Chamber* (dir. Ashim Ahluwalia, 2016). In 1969 the painter Akbar Padamsee made an experimental 16-mm film named *Events in a Cloud Chamber* for the Vision Exchange Workshop. That print is now lost and no copies exist. Forty years later, Ahluwalia reconstructed the film with whatever material survives of it.

p. 107: Jyoti Bhatt, *Untitled (A Face)*, *c.* 1968–69, gelatin silver print. Image courtesy the Museum of Art & Photography (MAP), Bengaluru.

p. 111: Dashrath Patel, *Untitled*, *c.*1960–65. Image courtesy Pinakin Patel and the Dashrath Patel Museum. Dashrath Patel's picture captures Jehangir Art Gallery, the same space where *Painters with a Camera* was exhibited.

p. 115: Gulammohammed Sheikh, *Untitled/ Kanwat*, 1969, still frame from 16-mm film. Sheikh made a short film using a Beaulieu R16 camera borrowed from the Vision Exchange Workshop. Shot during the Holi festival in a Kanwat village in Chhota Udaipur district of Gujarat, it features tribals dancing at the Bha(n)guriyun festival. Here young men and women came in festive clothing and silver jewellery and tied metal bells, to create a hypnotic sound. Boys assumed characters by painting faces in white dots or smeared with black paint, or by printing white circles on the body with bottle lids, to become 'tigers' or 'cheetahs' (Sheikh, private correspondence with editor). The film has only recently been recovered and surviving footage has been digitally transferred. Grateful acknowledgement to Gulammohammed Sheikh for permission to reprint and to Sanjiv Shah for digital versions.

p. 117: Vinodray Patel and Vrishchik Team, *Jorge Luis Borges*, *c.* 1971, linocut on letterpress. Image courtesy Gulammohammed Sheikh and Asia Art Archive.

Text and Context

A copy of the exhibition pamphlet for the show *Painters with a Camera* (1968), held at Jehangir Art Gallery in Bombay (now Mumbai), presents a little-known excursion into the history of experimental photography in India. The exhibition comprised of seven artists – Jyoti Bhatt, Feroz Katpitia, Narendra Mehta, Jeram Patel, Vinodray Patel, Vinod S. Patel and Gulammohammed Sheikh[1] – all of whom were teachers at the Faculty of Fine Arts, Maharaja Sayajirao University, Baroda (today Vadodara), the first art school established in independent India.[2] All, with the exception of Narendra Mehta, were young faculty members; Mehta was a former professor to a number of his fellow exhibitioners. Although only coming together for this particular exhibition, the individual artists had by now developed some amount of fame. Jyoti Bhatt, winner of the national award for painting in 1956, had already had paintings and intaglio prints accepted by the Museum of Modern Art, New York and the National Gallery of Modern Art, New Delhi; Jeram Patel's famed compositions, made with blowtorches on wood, as well as his quieter ink-on-paper compositions, had been shown widely in London; and Feroz Katpitia (although he would subsequently fall out of currency) is perhaps best known for his mural at Parliament House, New Delhi, completed in the 1950s. A shared interest in printmaking that united a number of the exhibition's constituent artists, most notably Jyoti Bhatt, Vinod S. Patel and Narendra Mehta, is alluded to in the exhibition pamphlet's title image, a fragmented portrait of Vinodray Patel made by Vinod S. Patel. Reduced to a bare network of black and white silhouettes, an elementary outline of Vinodray's face is steadily deconstructed and reconstituted across the course of the image. The faces are rendered beyond recognition, mapped out in differing swathes of positive and negative space that alternately spill into the inky black background or stand out against it.

The copy of the pamphlet, only recently discovered and archived, scanned from the archive of Jyoti Bhatt, bears a faint inscription: '1968 or 69? Or 70?'[3] Although fleeting mentions of the exhibition flicker across publications concerning the seven artists who mounted the exhibition, the details of *Painters with a Camera* have been obscured in contradictory accounts. Whereas Gulammohammed Sheikh's writing about the show dates it to 1969, leading other scholars of modern Indian art to follow in his example, a lone scan of the invitation card sent out to visitors notes 8 November 1968 as the opening day. Even less is known about the contents of the exhibition – no installation views remain as none of the photographers thought to bring along their cameras on the journey from Baroda to Bombay.[4] *Painters with a Camera* has consequently fallen out of the discourses of Indian artistic and photographic modernism. Available accounts of the exhibition confirm its objective to make an intervention in the museological and pedagogical standards of Indian institutions of display and arts education.[5] Its participants appealed for the recognition of photography as an art practice at a time when the Lalit Kala Akademi (the National Academy of Arts) and the National Gallery of Modern Art, both centres of Indian modernism and its dissemination in the postcolonial period, had not yet begun to collect or display photography, still seemingly unconvinced by the artistic efficacy and relevance of the machine-produced image.[6]

The pamphlet's precarious recuperation speaks to the condition of a wider field of experimental photographic practices in India that have disappeared from circulation and knowledge.[7] Simultaneously in Bombay, the Vision Exchange Workshop, or VIEW (1969–72)[8] became a space of fervent photographic and filmic production, such as Krishen Khanna's[9] layered photographic series *The Crows around My Studio* (c. 1975) and Akbar Padamsee's[10] intricate video works such as *SYZYGY* (1970) and the now-lost film *Events in a Cloud Chamber* (1969). Bhupendra Karia,[11] a faculty member of the Graphics Department at M.S. University, Baroda from 1964–66, set up VIEW's darkrooms, while Nasreen Mohamedi,[12] who would go on to join the Baroda faculty in the mid-1970s, was also at VIEW developing her starkly linear photographic practice.[13] S.N.S. Sastry,[14] a director at the government-funded Films Division of India, similarly exhibited a tendency towards photographic montage in experimental films such as *Yet in Him We Trust* (1966) and *Yes, It's On* (1972).[15] The abstracted, intentionally graphic turn taken by many of these artists, photographers and filmmakers in their work, and their subsequent erasure from the topographies of modernism has been attributed by Nancy Adajania to their status as 'no-context media', existing in the absence of a backdrop against which they could be 'named, identified, understood, and accepted' and of an identifiable prehistory that locates them.[16] These practices ran roughly contemporary to the Baroda scene. A symbiotic relationship was sustained by the many interlocutors between the two, such as Karia and Mohamedi, as well as by the networks of exchange provided by artist-led journals, including Gulam Sheikh and Bhupen Khakhar's[17] journal *Vrishchik*, which saw a number of contributions from Padamsee and Khanna. Although similar experimental endeavours based in Baroda have yet to be placed in this context, *Painters with a Camera*, which opened in Bombay, provides one such opportunity for reconciliation.

This essay will therefore address *Painters with a Camera* as a conduit into

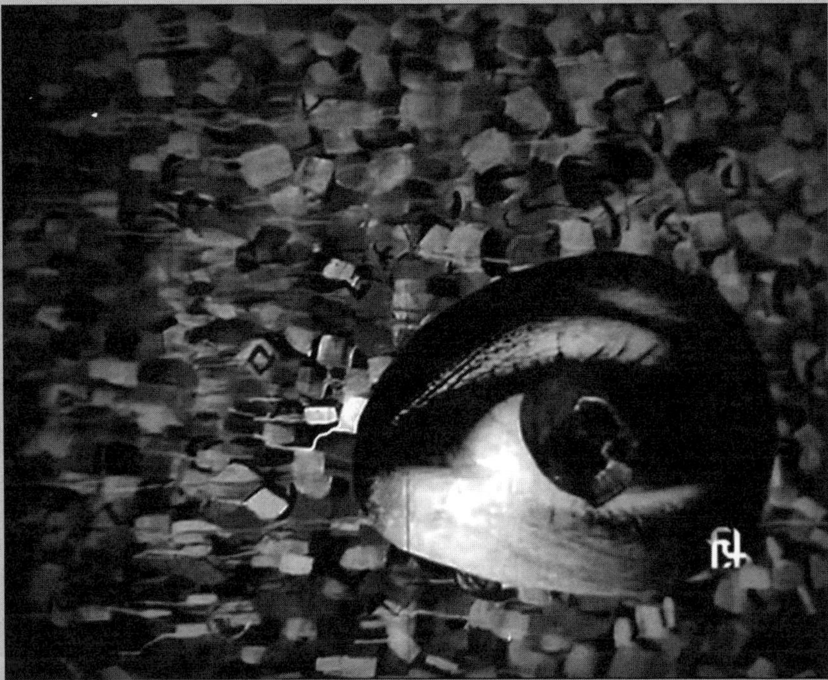

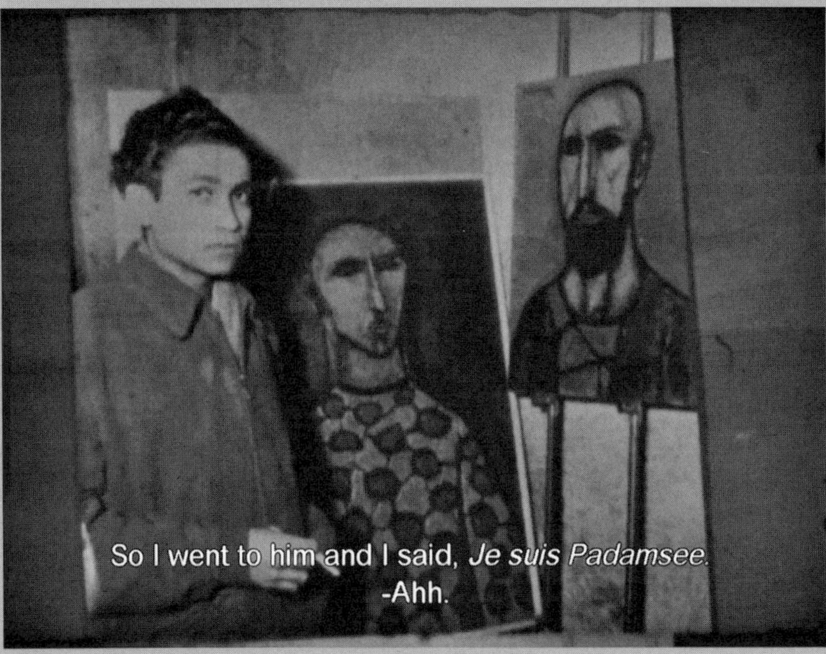
So I went to him and I said, *Je suis Padamsee.*
-Ahh.

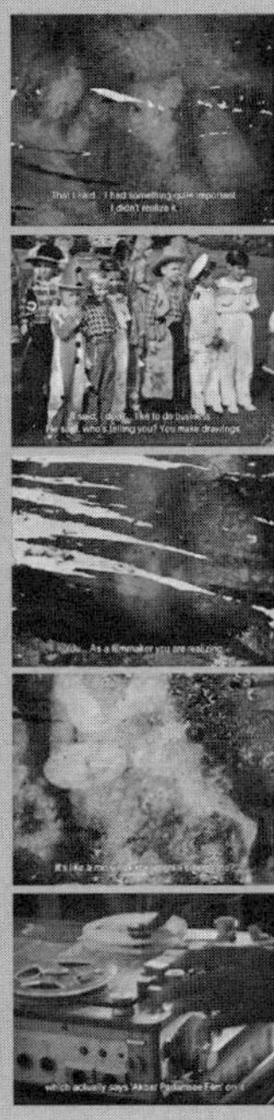

a broader study of Indian lens-based practices, their objectives and seeming disavowal of the aesthetics of postcolonial modernism. Noting a conscious turn on the Baroda artists' part to align themselves with Jehangir Art Gallery (by the 1960s an established site for the display and generation of new notions of the artistic avant-garde) I will also inquire into the networks of vision and fragmentation that play out on the exhibition's title document. As I will argue, the photograph that came to be chosen as the exhibition's title image opens up the ideological possibilities of photography with which the artists sought to align themselves. Drawing upon their varied engagements with Bauhaus photographer László Moholy-Nagy (1895–1946), I propose that the exhibitors mobilized techniques seeking to disrupt and rethink popular notions of the medium in modern India.

Constructing a Vision

In an absence of visual records of *Painters with a Camera*, its surviving participants have attempted to stitch together a description of what was on display. Jyoti Bhatt recalls that Jeram Patel's and Gulammohammed Sheikh's photographs showed resemblances to the cinematic style of the French New Wave. The rest – Bhatt himself, Katpitia, Vinodray Patel, Vinod S. Patel and Mehta – transferred their negatives onto lith film[18] and then enlarged them to create high-contrast graphic prints, in broad sweeps of black and white.[19] Bhatt included early versions of two photographs that were frequently revised over the subsequent years: *Venice 1966* (c. 1966–69) and *Untitled (A Face)* (c. 1968–69), the latter created by merging a photograph of a peacock (printed as negative) into the outline of a face (printed as positive). Sheikh provides an account of the four images he displayed as part of the exhibition, including a horse grazing in his hometown Surendranagar and a portrait of the art historian Geeta Kapur, composed by montaging a negative and positive version of the same photograph.[20]

Vinodray Patel and V.S. Patel took on the task of designing the exhibition pamphlet, consisting of a title image, brief biographies of the artists, and a studio photograph of all seven. The artists' photograph was taken at a makeshift roadside studio in Baroda. An uncropped out-take from Bhatt's personal archive (of a photograph featured in the pamphlet) provides a broader look at the photographic scene, taken by an itinerant studio photographer: an elaborately painted studio backdrop has been mounted over a doorway in the open street, its creases still visible despite the careful ropes and nails that attempt to stretch

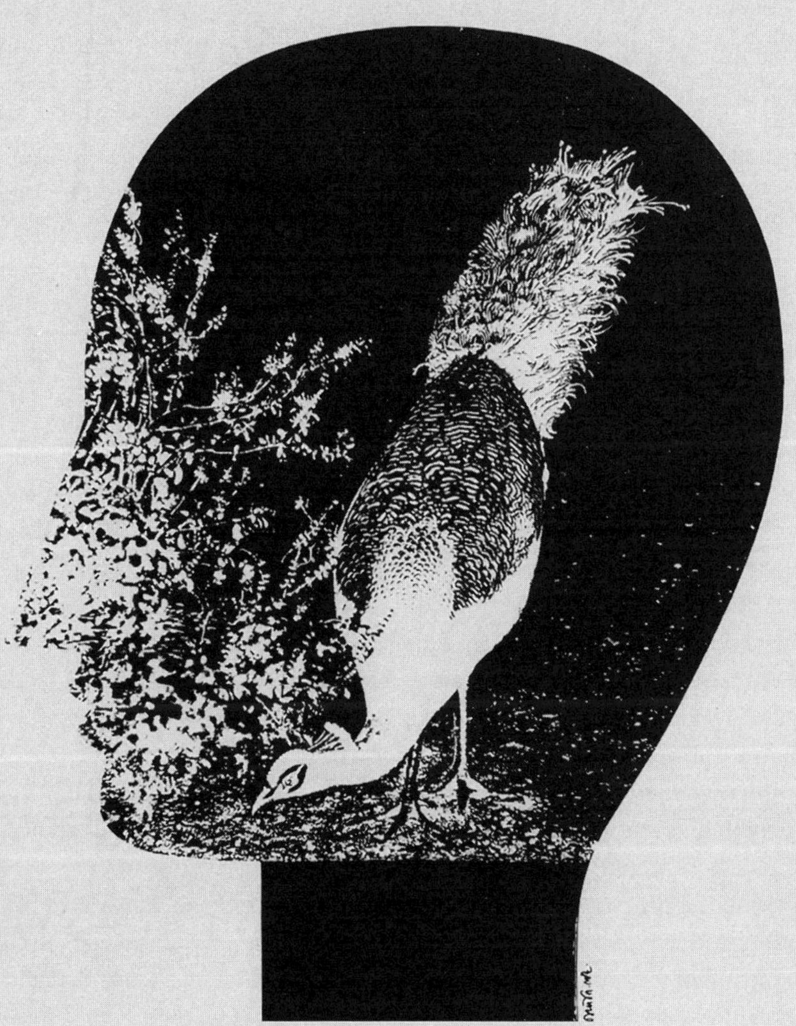

it into a realistic backdrop. In the final image, six of the photographers (sans Mehta) arrange themselves on and behind two flimsy metal chairs, where they pose with a collection of cameras, which Bhatt recalls borrowing from the studio's proprietor. The authorial photograph, and its carefully considered juxtaposition with V.S. Patel's more playful, abstracted, composite image, operates as a visual foil, rendering the work of the 'painters with a camera' distinct from that most commonly encountered iteration of the camera in everyday Indian life. The exhibition pamphlet is thus a site of legible strategy, and also a text where the ontology of experimental photography is delineated or considered. It attempts to simultaneously make the artists' experimental photography distinct from the cultural uses and production of studio portraiture, as well as from the more artisanal practice of the painted studio backdrop.

The studio photograph displays the self-assured performances of homosocial camaraderie that are often at work in photographs from early days of Baroda's art school, when young men dominated the student rolls. The comical tone of the photograph, and its injection of the group's artistic practice into the normative scheme of authorial portraiture, resembles photographic portraits of the Dadaists and suggests a considered homage. While Bhatt leans low over a vintage view camera, Sheikh and Katpitia enact a sort of photographic duel, each turned away from the studio photographer to capture the other. V.S. Patel, whose Rolleiflex points outwards from the frame, seems to challenge the studio photographer. Narendra Mehta, then their professional superior, was not invited for the fun, and was only montaged into the image later on. Although the studio image hints at the artists' own self-fashioning as photographers as they step into the medium of photography theatrically, carefully constructed photographs, such as the title image by V.S. Patel, undermine the comic tone with their precise montaged compositions.

Although there is little formal resemblance between the two photographs in the exhibition pamphlet, they are conjoined in their shared engagement with the possibilities of vision and recognition. A rich ontological concern with vision in relation to the performance of modernity exists more broadly as a field of study in modern South Asia.[21] In their theorization of the symbiotic and discursive relationship of vision to public culture, Arjun Appadurai and Carol Breckenridge assessed Indian spectatorship in relation to an 'interocular field',

> structured so that each site or setting for the socializing and regulating of the public gaze is to some degree affected by the experiences of the other sites. The interweaving of ocular experiences, which also subsumes the

> substantive transfer of ... scripts and symbols from one site to another ... is a critical feature of public culture in contemporary India.[22]

The notion of an embodied vision at the individual level, apropos Christopher Pinney, expands into a larger, loaded regime of vision in 'the vivid materiality of public visual culture'.[23] Public culture here exists in the interstices between the domestic and national spheres, 'where different social groups ... constitute their identities by their experiences of mass-mediated forms in relation to the practices of everyday life',[24] within the confines of national culture, although not unmoved by changing politico-cultural circumstances. The Baroda photographers' choice of Jehangir Art Gallery in Bombay as the venue for *Painters with a Camera* was, I argue, a purposeful act of public visual and temporal alignment with the gallery's own associations of modernity.

Situating the Modern

Designed by Durga Shankar Bajpai and G.M. Bhuta, Jehangir Art Gallery was among the first commercial, rentable, entirely extra-governmental art spaces, founded in 1952 and evolving into a democratic and dynamic space for the display of Indian art.[25] It was established in the heart of colonial Bombay's 'white' quarters, the Kala Ghoda area, flanked by the Bombay High Court, Bombay University and the Prince of Wales Museum. The gallery's centrality to the city's art world was, in part, dependent both on its affordable hire charge and the stature of the artists who chose to exhibit there in its early years, including the members of the modernist Bombay Progressive Artists' Group.[26] Print culture around the gallery offers much to the argument that Jehangir Art Gallery had, for the elite, urban echelons of public culture in Bombay, come to be considered as a theatre of an imagined and idealized modernism, both in its structure and location and in the visual culture that emerged around it. Atreyee Gupta notes a 1953 advertisement in the magazine *Art in Industry* for the Associated Cement Companies Ltd. (ACC), featuring two montaged photographs of the gallery's interior and exterior, flanked by the following text: 'For Art's Sake: India's most modern Art Gallery emphasizes the unique advantages of Reinforced Concrete for all types of construction. Beauty is wedded to strength in this modern structure which consists of Reinforced Concrete rigid frames spanning a spacious hall and projecting canopy at the entrance.'

Through montage, the advertisement strategically creates an internally logical visual constellation that marries modern architecture and modern art on the foundations of modern building techniques (reinforced concrete).[27] Tactically focusing on the interior of the gallery space, the advertisement reproduces a photograph of one of Jehangir's long, well-lit exhibition halls, unobstructed by pillars or supporting columns because of its concrete walls. What advertisements such as ACC's offer in addition to their products is, I suggest, the temptation of a Euro-American coeval modern within the gallery space, as the gallery consciously distanced itself from the surrounding Art Deco and Gothic revival buildings by staking a claim to the geographically-diffuse vocabulary of the International Style.[28]

A similar scene unfolds in multimedia artist and designer Dashrath Patel's[29] clandestine photograph taken in the same exhibition hall during his display of cubist collages. Here, the photograph proposes, viewers can partake in their own performance of cosmopolitanism, viewing, receiving and transacting with contemporary art. Each photograph - the public and the private - intentionally and unintentionally depicts an assortment of viewers in both Indian and Western dress as they peruse the paintings on display. The space of the modernist building becomes a site in which 'the face of modernity itself blasts us with its immemorial gaze'.[30] Jehangir Art Gallery comes to signify a multi-layered, heterogeneous and ultimately performative site of intervisuality, where viewers consciously partake in a modern visual transaction. That the institution was invoked in print culture as a pinnacle of Bombay's arrival into the twentieth century, and was also received as such, suggests what was at stake in the Baroda photographers choosing to display their work there.

Moreover, the gallery was no stranger to the display of photography: it was at Jehangir that the Indian iteration of Edward Steichen's[31] monumental and monumentally successful exhibition *The Family of Man* (1955), first shown at the Museum of Modern Art, New York, was put on display from 18 June–15 July 1956. This would be the only Indian art gallery where the exhibition was displayed; it was housed at an industrial fair ground in Delhi during a UNESCO Conference in November 1956, at universities in Agra and Madras, and at Ranji cricket stadium in Calcutta. It was also here that the Bombay Photography Association put up *Images of India*, a regionally-specific response to *The Family of Man*, in 1960.[32] To display at Jehangir offered purposeful alignment with its brand of syncretic modernity, as well as a means of elevating the status of the composite photograph. In the case of *Painters with a Camera*, the exhibition's disappearance from a broader history of Indian modernism makes it difficult to ascertain the success of this endeavour, and to know more about the reception of the exhibition.

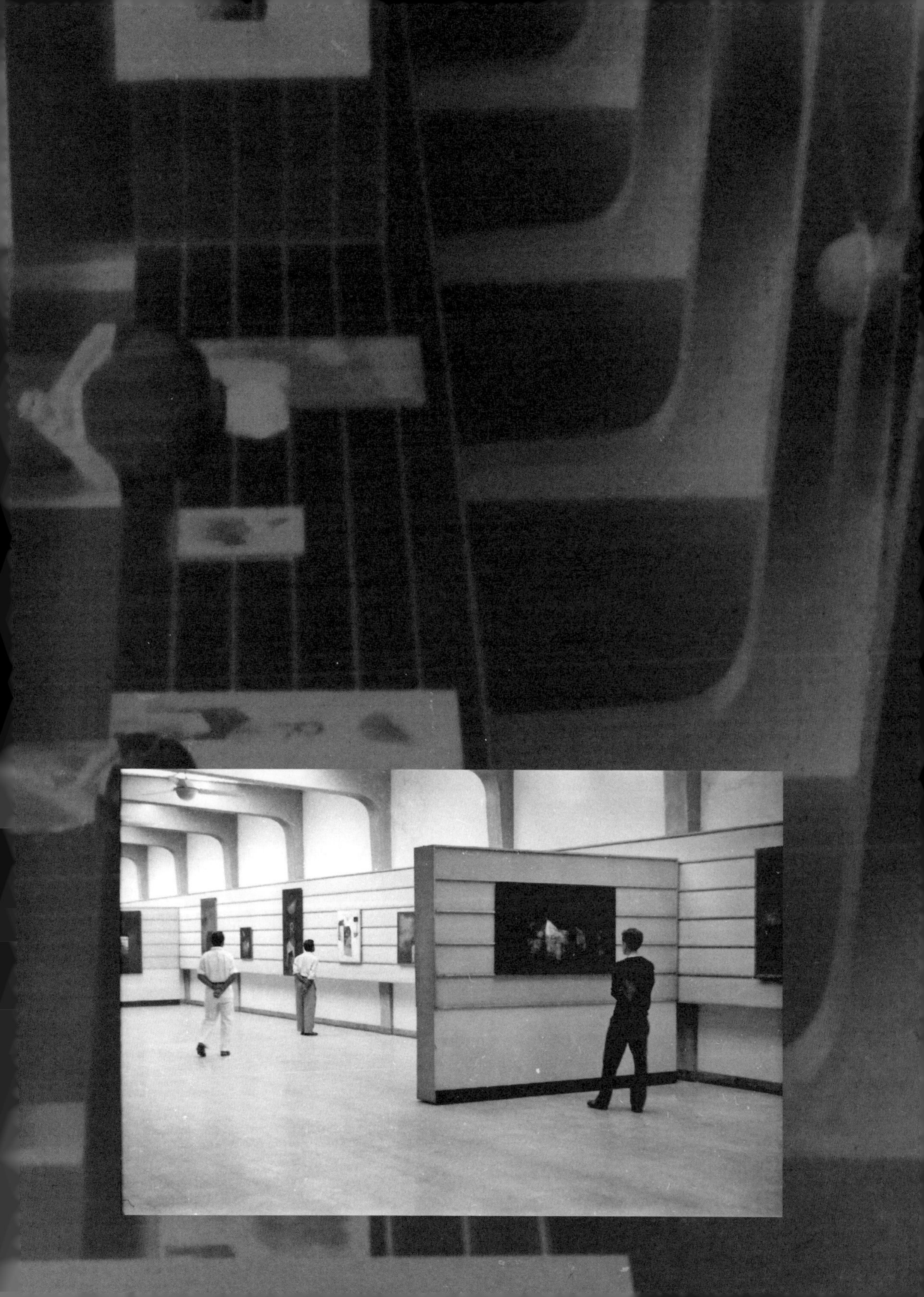

The photograph that was finally put into the pamphlet for *Painters with a Camera* equally suggests an intentional parody of the possibilities of photography and the fragmentation of ocular vision by the profusion of the camera. The authorial image with which it is paired equally creates an elaborate network of performed photographic encounters that illustrate the intervisual through the implications of multiple simultaneous authorship and viewership. The profusion of lenses in the frame is of interest; ranging from the dark or tinted glasses worn by Jyoti Bhatt, Vinod S. Patel, Vinodray Patel and Narendra Mehta, while Gulam Sheikh and Feroz Katpitia are each preoccupied by their camera viewfinders. This excess of cameras and ocular equipment is occasionally confronted in the image by the impenetrable dark glasses of the photographers and the closed lens on Bhatt's camera. In this tension between the lens as all-seeing and all-recording, with an authorial photograph that is rich with ocular potential, the photograph points both to the fragmentation and multiplication of vision and its outright denial of compositional wholeness. The image seems to stand in for the photograph's simultaneous multiplicity and fragmentation. This speaks not simply to the photographic practice of the Baroda practitioners but also to their Bombay counterparts, whose experimental explorations of composite photography were 'either ignored or grudgingly accepted as career aberrations'.[33] Here the exuberant multiplicity of machinic modes of visions among the photographers in the *Painters with a Camera* publication seems to both address and resist the dominant institutional blindness towards photography at the time.

Pedagogical Freedom

As teachers at the Faculty of Fine Arts at M.S. University, Baroda, it appears that the seven artists of *Painters with a Camera* mostly engaged with photography extraneously due to the lack of official encouragement of the medium. The Faculty was established in 1950 as the newest department within the university, formed a year previously at the behest of the Maharaja Pratapsingh Gaekwad who was acting upon the princely state's long movement towards autonomy in university pedagogy.[34] Documents from the Report from the Baroda University Committee of 1948 reveal how in their frequent negative invocations of the University of Bombay and its colonial baggage, its founders 'refashioned [the university] as a non-colonial, or rather "decolonial" weapon' in their desire to produce a specifically Indian iteration of pedagogy at Baroda.[35] It was with similar sentiment that the

Faculty of Fine Arts was founded a year later, intending to set the pace and terms for postcolonial Indian art practice.

Previously existent art schools in erstwhile British India had been intended '... to supply skilled draftsmen, designers, engravers, to meet increasing demand' in the imperial economy.[36] The art schools of Madras and Lahore, prominent in twentieth-century colonial India, were central to the mechanization of artisanal practices in their emphasis on restoring the artisan to pre-industrial excellence via industrial workshop pedagogy.[37] By contrast, the founders of the Faculty of Fine Arts sought dramatic rupture from colonial traditions, focusing on individual self-expression in a new liberal artistic climate.[38] Karin Zitzewitz notes that the Faculty was established with two models in mind: the 'post-Bauhaus American art schools' and Baroda's own Kala Bhavan, an artistic and technical institute also established by Maharaja Sayajirao in 1891, where Gujarati, the local language, was the medium of instruction.[39] The formation of the Faculty of Fine Arts gained both from the successes and personnel of its predecessor. Further, that the art school was established in a former princely state in Gujarat, far removed from the colonial cities of Bombay, Madras and Calcutta, created new lofty pedagogic preoccupations for the institution to perform 'as part of the fervour and promise of a new and independent India'.[40]

The first prospectus for the art school begins with a brief essay by Hansa Mehta, the vice-chancellor of the University of Baroda, and former diplomat and associate of Jawaharlal Nehru. Mehta writes: 'the product of this education may not become a great artist, but he certainly would acquire an intellectual understanding of art.'[41] Speaking of a thematic and formal vacuum in postcolonial India, she noted that 'we have lost our originality and either copy the Western forms of art or the ancient Indian forms' – her writing imbued with a sense of loss of the 'authentic' that the Baroda faculty sought to fill.[42] In this context many artists, such as Sankho Chaudhuri,[43] Ramkinkar Baij[44] and K.G. Subramanyan,[45] came from the Kala Bhavan at Santiniketan in Bengal, established in 1919 as an early site of trans-Asian modernism and anti-colonial protest, as well as from the new politically charged artistic climate of Bombay, including N.S. Bendre,[46] a member of the Bombay Progressive Artists' Group. Markand Bhatt, who had recently returned from the Barnes Foundation in the United States, was asked to found the faculty in 1949 and create the structure of its educational programme, where he remained until 1959.

Although early students (including most of the 'painters with a camera') were encouraged to engage with 'Oriental and Western traditional paintings', to 'study from life, mural decoration, elements of portraiture ... and were recommended the study of modern art and the comprehensive study of Indian and Western arts',[47] photography was to be taught under the Applied Arts department and as a two-year certificate course. It was later reduced to a subsidiary subject in the Applied Arts department – students of the Department of Painting, such as Bhatt and Katpitia, were never taught photography formally, and thus depended on the benevolence of Narendra Mehta, and his assistant Ramachandra Kadam, for use of the darkrooms.

The exact interest or manifestation of the Bauhaus in Baroda is debated. That Markand Bhatt was a proponent of Bauhaus pedagogy in India, although undeniable, is yet to be more specifically established with reference to the Baroda faculty's curriculum. It is, however, made manifest in the faculty's emphasis on the exploration of 'individuated, intuitive energies', and on materiality.[48] Moreover, the inclusion of the work of Moholy-Nagy in the faculty syllabi would not necessarily have spelled any explicit rupture from the Bengal school – in fact, the interest in the Bauhaus at Baroda could have been informed by an earlier legacy of the German school's allegiance with their Bengali counterparts. This was a network of friendships and solidarity with an anti-colonial cause that culminated in the Bauhaus exhibition organized by the Indian Society of Oriental Art in Calcutta in 1922, where the works of Santiniketan practitioners Rabindranath[49] and Gaganendranath Tagore[50] were shown alongside those of painters Johannes Itten and Georg Muche.[51] The Bauhaus itself, in sites such as Calcutta and Baroda, had come to connote extra-colonial modernism, a source of industrial critique and aesthetic inquiry into modernity beyond the reach of British colonial authority. Unpublished essays by Jyoti Bhatt that make reference to Moholy-Nagy's writing on photographic literacy suggest that he encountered the latter's writing in all likelihood around the Faculty of Fine Arts. Bhatt's essays and his engagement with the Bauhaus further raise the possibility that *Painters with a Camera* itself displayed a techno-optimistic interest in the camera 'as cure', producing a new system of optics – not simply a means of reproduction but also 'a way to bringing (optically) something entirely new into the world'.[52]

The Faculty of Fine Arts' pedagogical hesitation to include the study of photography in many ways mirrors the Bauhaus's late adoption of the camera, although many decades later. It is possible that the founders of the Baroda curriculum who came from Santiniketan inherited their disdain for photography from their own teachers. Nandalal Bose, the long-standing principal of Santiniketan's art school and an established anti-colonial painter from the Bengal School, wrote:

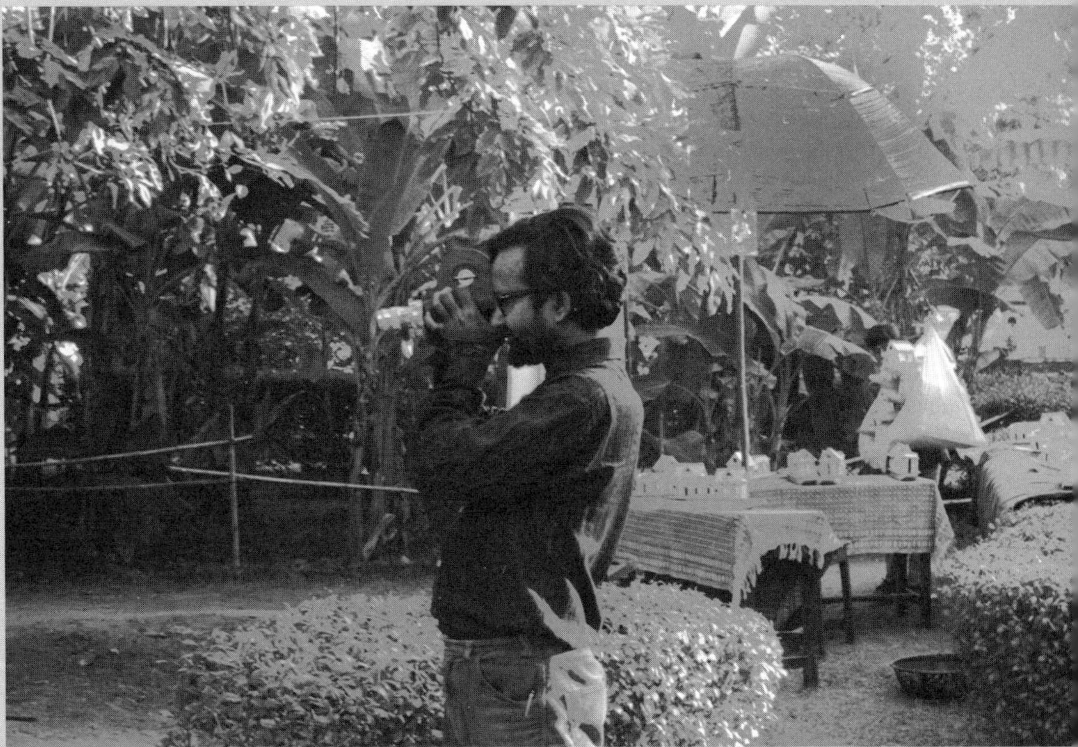

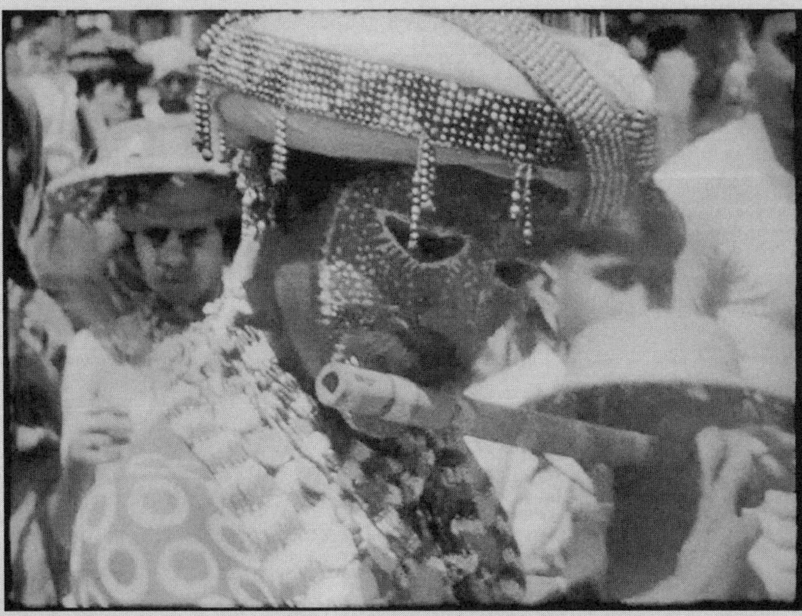

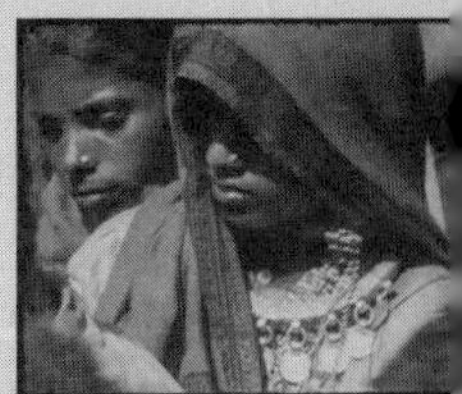

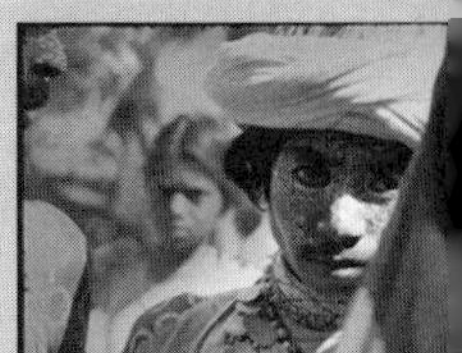

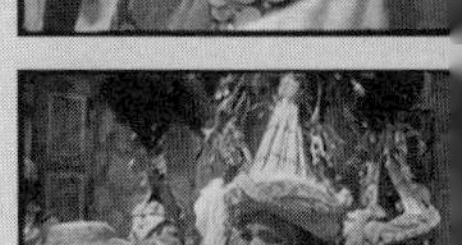

> In a photograph one can exactly reproduce the details of a natural object. But however good a photograph is, it is not a painting ... the camera is a mere tool. Since it has no heart or intellect it merely catches the exact details of whatever is in nature. While painting a scene or an object, an artist selects as much as is needed from natural objects ... not copying, but making a selection.[53]

Bose's suspicion of the camera may well have come from his teacher Abanindranath Tagore, who wrote that the photograph is capable of 'veracity but not variety'.[54]

The assumption of photography's irredeemable foreignness (uncontested even by the proponents of the medium) was an added source of anxiety for decolonial art pedagogues. An article on the history of Indian photography in the Bombay-based cultural quarterly magazine *MARG* (1960) works within this rubric of photography-as-foreign, admitting that 'photography is not part of the traditional Indian cultural heritage' before proceeding to make a case for the medium as an opportunity to 'breath[e] in other traditions'.[55] Aside from the conviction in the camera's irrevocably colonial status, most criticisms of photography within Indian art pedagogy are unsurprisingly reminiscent of earlier anxieties about the camera in Europe and the United States. Early criticisms of photography within art practice frequently deployed disembodiment as a metaphor for incompletion; the photograph was said to entail an inherent lack, a removal from human intactness for its introduction of a mechanical eye.[56] In this iteration of modernism in a former colony, then, photography was largely unwelcome. In contrast, the Baroda-based participants of *Painters with a Camera* were interested in the camera's ability to 'bring about aspects of the original that can be accessed only by the lens ... and not by the human eye ... [capturing] images that are quite simply beyond natural optics'.[57] Turning the status of the camera as a 'mere tool' on its head, the photographers celebrate the photographic plane as a site of physical and imaginative labour, disrupting the mechanical expectations of camera apparatus through ingenious manual intervention.[58]

Dispersing the Frame

It is tempting to suggest that the seven photographers in *Painters with a Camera* were not only protesting the narrowness of the curriculum in their native Baroda, but also making a case for the camera *itself* as being able to produce its own specific

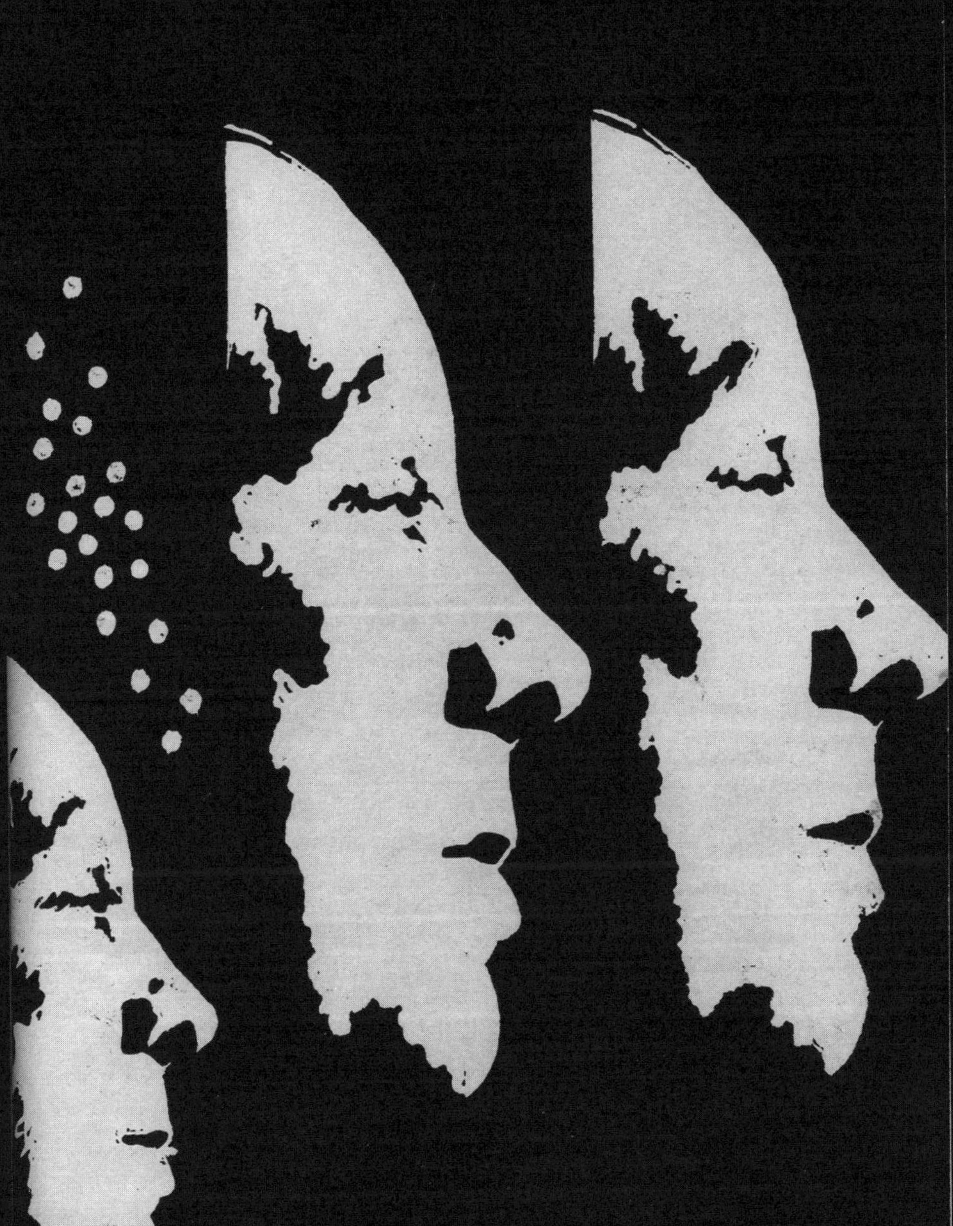

responses to modernism through the machine. It was perhaps for its presentation of the many ontological possibilities of the photograph in relation to time and trace that V.S. Patel's photograph of Vinodray was chosen to represent the exhibition as its title image. In Patel's photograph, the repetitions of the face and its abstraction into motif creates a chain of motion against an unvarying black background. He likely began by creating a high contrast print of Vinodray's face on fine photographic paper. Multiple renderings of the face were printed repeatedly and then laboriously arranged from left to right to create the effect of a chain, before transferring the now-composite print onto lith negative film in order to render it against a deep black background. Although Patel's prints of the face begin uniformly, reproducing the same portion of the face at regular intervals, the centre of the frame features an aberration – a systemic kink – that creates a cluster of dense, merged-together contortions of the silhouette. Here Vinodray Patel's likeness is obscured by the intensity and number of its own reproductions and the imperfections of manual repetition, dispersed into fragments of multiple viewpoints that overwhelm and evade simple recognition. The central aberration lends the photograph a dizzying quality as it alters the presumed relationship among the facial fragments: are they mutations in a series of infinite reproductions, or staggered manifestations of a face as it briefly turns away from the camera? In its gradual unfolding across the space of the composition, the image brings to mind Moholy-Nagy's mobilization of repetition as a 'space-time organisational motif, which ... could be achieved only by means of the technical, industrialized system of reproduction characteristic of our time'.[59]

The precise purpose of Patel's camera in his composite photograph of Vinodray is to create tension between appearance and disappearance, blurred and repeated into an assembly-line motif that reconciles mechanical movement and motions of the hand. Reminiscent of Moholy-Nagy's black-and-white photograph *The Law of Series* (1925), a composite that superimposes five near-identical portraits of Bauhaus student Marcel Breuer, here the dissolution of the individual face in favour of dispersion and repetition tilts the exploration of the camera's distinct potentialities precisely away from its machinic quality. This is interestingly echoed in a later linocut by Vinodray Patel, published on the cover of Gulammohammed Sheikh and Bhupen Khakhar's monthly magazine *Vrishchik* in November 1971, which features a linocut adaptation of a photograph of Jorge Luis Borges that is similarly abstracted by repetition. Although the imperfect reproductions of the linocuts and their spatial arrangement may allude to Borges's elaboration upon simultaneous temporalities in his fiction, the work tests the limits of seriality, reproduction and medium-specificity.[60]

This was a promise of photography that had come to be recognized in the Baroda artists' own generation. Closer to home, the Indian art critic and photographer Richard Bartholomew,[61] roughly contemporary to the artists and a proponent of their artistic practices, had extolled a similar purpose for the photographic medium in a 1960 article, writing: 'what photography has to fight against is the commonplace, the mundane, the workaday, the rejected, spent images which the eye ... cannot ignore.'[62] Through his panoramic suggestion of motion, Patel taps into a broader history of photography, wherein the image faithfully registers the motion and duration of which it is forged. In the case of Patel's photograph, however, this motion appears not before the lens but behind it; the photograph is a register of the photographer's own repeated manual reworking of the central motif as it oscillates repeatedly between positive and negative space, echoing the composite nature of Bhatt's *Untitled (A Face)*. The rehabilitation of the machinic image through intensive manual collaging has specific temporal connotations for the image: time in the photograph is connoted as a stutter, unfolding severally and simultaneously across the frame. Whereas the unseen lines that divide the face into alternating components of negative and positive space seem to suggest the multiple states in which the image is impressed upon the photographic plate, the repeated prints suggest the photograph's own infinite reproducibility. The placement of Patel's photograph at Jehangir Art Gallery indicates both the group's intentional alignment with machinic images for their ability to produce an assertive aesthetic of fracturing and displacement, and the simultaneous appropriation of those machinic images to manual ends. Here painstakingly rendered distinct both from vernacular studio-based practices and from the mechanical expectations of photographic modernism, the composite photograph is achieved and articulated as a site of multiple disorderings, expanding the scope for photographic vision in Indian artistic practice.

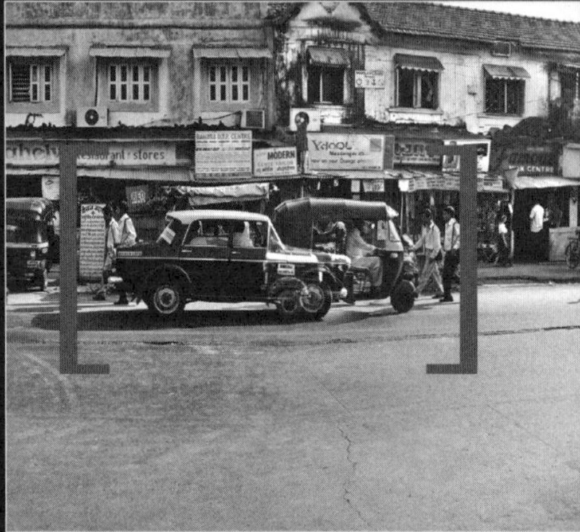
MODERN

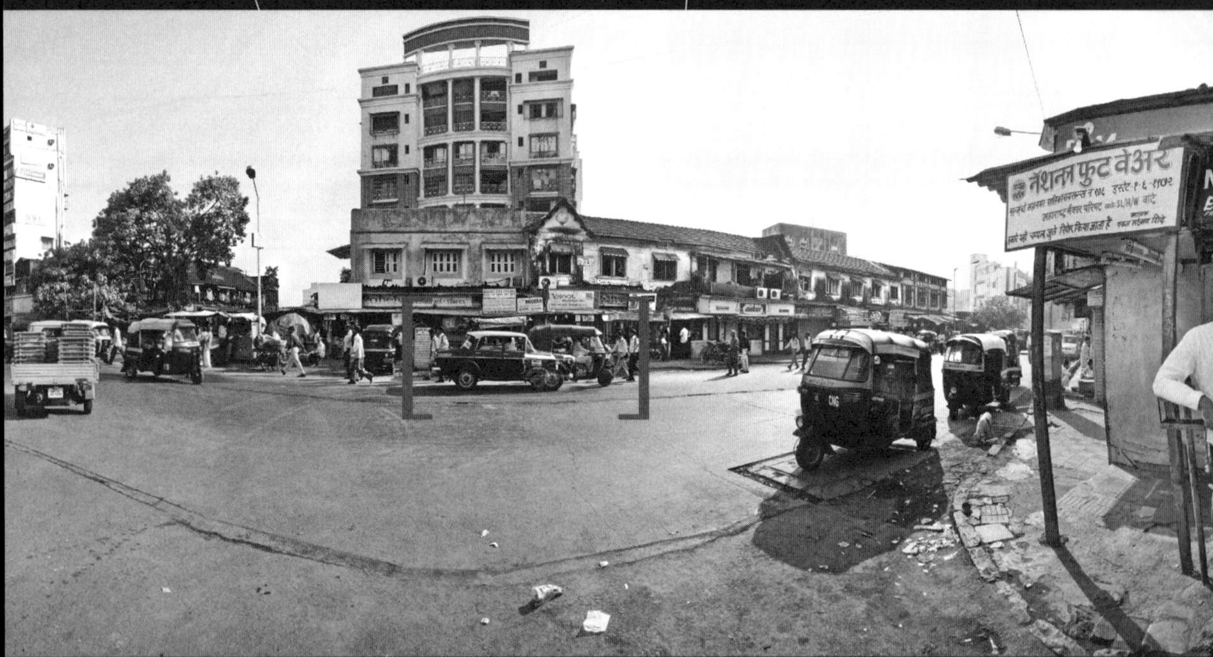
नॅशनल फुट वेअर
CNG

7 # Photography and Inherited History in India

2015

I **Jodi Throckmorton**

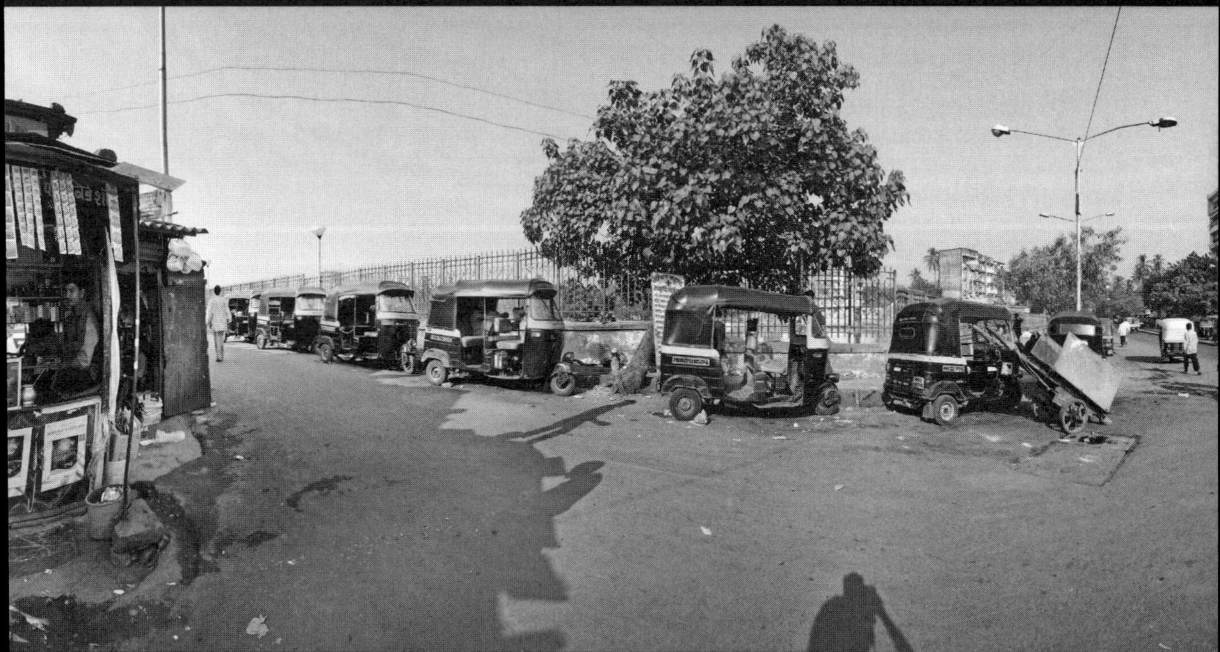

By the 1990s, photography had become a part of a wider arsenal of new media now practiced by a range of 'researchers, collectors, activists, genealogists, performers and documentarians', notes Jodi Throckmorton. These were new actors committed to creating art 'that reflects the complex hybridity inherent to a globalized India', and to a re-reading of colonial legacies through 'shifting ethnographies of practice' and 'shifting lineages of postcolonial cultural identity'. Throckmorton assesses the relationship of local and global trends in image-making, including the lens-based production of contemporary artists using traditional and digital media to disrupt canonized understandings of the image as a fixed, evidentiary document, and to radically deconstruct notions of 'authenticity' through the manipulation of found material.

This essay was earlier published in *Postdate: Photography and Inherited History in India*, University of California Press and San Jose Museum of Art, 2015, pp. 14–23. Reproduced with permission from the author and University of California Press. Images referenced within this essay can also be seen as plates in *Postdate.*

Keywords and Names

Lala Deen Dayal, *Partition of India*, *Pushpamala N.*, *Raqs Media Collective*, *Umrao Singh Sher-Gil*, *Vernacular mode*, see Keywords at the back of this volume.

Images

pp. 120–21: Jitish Kallat, *Artist Making Local Call*, 2005, digital print on vinyl mesh, 94 x 411 inches. Grateful acknowledgement to the artist for permission to reprint.

p. 125: Raqs Media Collective, images from the film *The Surface of Each Day is a Different Planet*, 2009. Grateful acknowledgement to the Raqs Media Collective.

p. 127: Madhuban Mitra and Manas Bhattacharya, photographs from *Through a Lens, Darkly,* 2009. Series on the ruins of India's first and only still camera factory, National Instruments Ltd., in Jadavpur, Kolkata. Courtesy Madhuban Mitra and Manas Bhattacharya, and PHOTOINK.

p. 129: Surekha, *Fragments of a Wedding Diary*, 2000, image from original photo installation of 33 photos, archival print, 13 x 10 inches each. Grateful acknowledgement to the artist for permission to reprint.

p. 131: Pushpamala N., being made up in her Mother India costume as she is interviewed in Avijit Mukul Kishore's film *To Let the World In*, vol. 1, 2013. Grateful acknowledgement to Avijit Mukul Kishore for permission to reprint.

Two generations after the exultation of hard-won Independence in 1947 and the concurrent horrors of the partition of the subcontinent into India and East and West Pakistan, the artists represented in *Postdate: Photography and Inherited History in India* (San Jose Museum of Art, 2015) are paving the way for a new generation of Indian thinkers who are reclaiming and reappraising the history of their country. These artists look closely and critically at the distinct history of Indian photography from the early days of the medium and at the height of the British occupation of the subcontinent in the nineteenth century to contemporary digital practices. Their sources are diverse: panorama photographs that document the development of Mumbai (then Bombay) in the mid-nineteenth century; hand-painted studio portraits from the early twentieth century; stills from Bollywood movies. The artists take history into their own hands, redefining iconic images of India and investigating the complex relationship between traditions of representation and contemporary practices of image-making. This group critically consider the nature of historical methods and whether or not the results can be trusted; the influence of the global and the draw of the local; and, through the use of digital technology, alternate ways of thinking about history and its relationship to today. Their observations are particularly germane to understanding global contemporary art practices that embrace tradition and innovation as covalent rather than competitive forces.

There are artists around the world who are interested in history - addressing history in artistic practice is neither a new mode of working nor a phenomenon that exists only in India. However, the way these artists are considering the weighty issues of colonialism and its relationship to a wide span of the history of Indian photography warrants a specific look.

This increased interest in understanding and organizing the history of photography in India occurred concurrently with the rise of the contemporary art market in the country and globally. Increasingly engaged in the international market, artists are acutely aware that the representation of India is often limited to photographs of the Taj Mahal or of disconcerting poverty in urban slums. Also, as Ram Rahman[1] noted:

> There has been a growing debate in Indian art circles on a 'Biennale aesthetic'[2] being imposed on art practice here which is leading to production of work that is slick, easily slotting into a new Orientalism, now in its consumerist global market avatar. In photography circles, the previous generation was accused of being purveyors of an 'exotic' fakir-filled India steeped in colourful riverside rituals, or quaint

> Bollywood – that was the India in demand around the world. Is it then surprising that the demand for images now is for the 'new' middle class and elite young India – consumers of Chanel, Nokia, Honda, readers of Indian editions *of Elle, Condé Nast Traveller* or *L'Officiel*? Do these images provide a reassurance that the world is becoming less complex and differentiated and more comfortably mono-cultural?[3]

The artists in *Postdate* are well aware of the whiplash-inducing debate between globalized aesthetics and images that perpetuates a one-dimensional understanding of Indian culture such as Rahman described. As a consequence, they seek to go beyond simplistic delineations and definitions such as global versus local and Western versus non-Western by including their commitment to located histories in India within their engagement in transnational discourse.

Inherited History

Photography was invented in 1839 in Europe, and by the 1850s it was firmly established commercially and artistically. Driven by the population of British colonials in India and the desire of their compatriots at home for images of this foreign and 'exotic' land, photographers (both British and Indian) focused their lenses on indigenous populations and customs, architecture and monuments, and street scenes and landscapes. Indians often worked for the British. They learned photography from them and later opened their own studios (for example, Lala Deen Dayal) or used the medium for creative expression (Umrao Singh Sher-Gil). India's First War of Independence in 1857 was one of the earliest extensively photographed wars in the world.[4]

Though photography has been present in India since its invention, critical writing and attempts to chronicle its history have been made in earnest only within the last thirty years. Concurrently, in the 1990s the Alkazi Foundation for the Arts[5], a trust that owns over 90,000 nineteenth-and early-twentieth-century photographs from South and Southeast Asia, began to archive its vast collection.

Photography makes history visible. It taps into our innate need to look at each other face-to-face. Likely due in large part to the burgeoning scholarship and recent attempts to categorize and collect archival images, many of the artists in this exhibition are mining the rich tradition of photography in India in order to rethink dominant historical narratives, share hidden stories and, ultimately, to make a

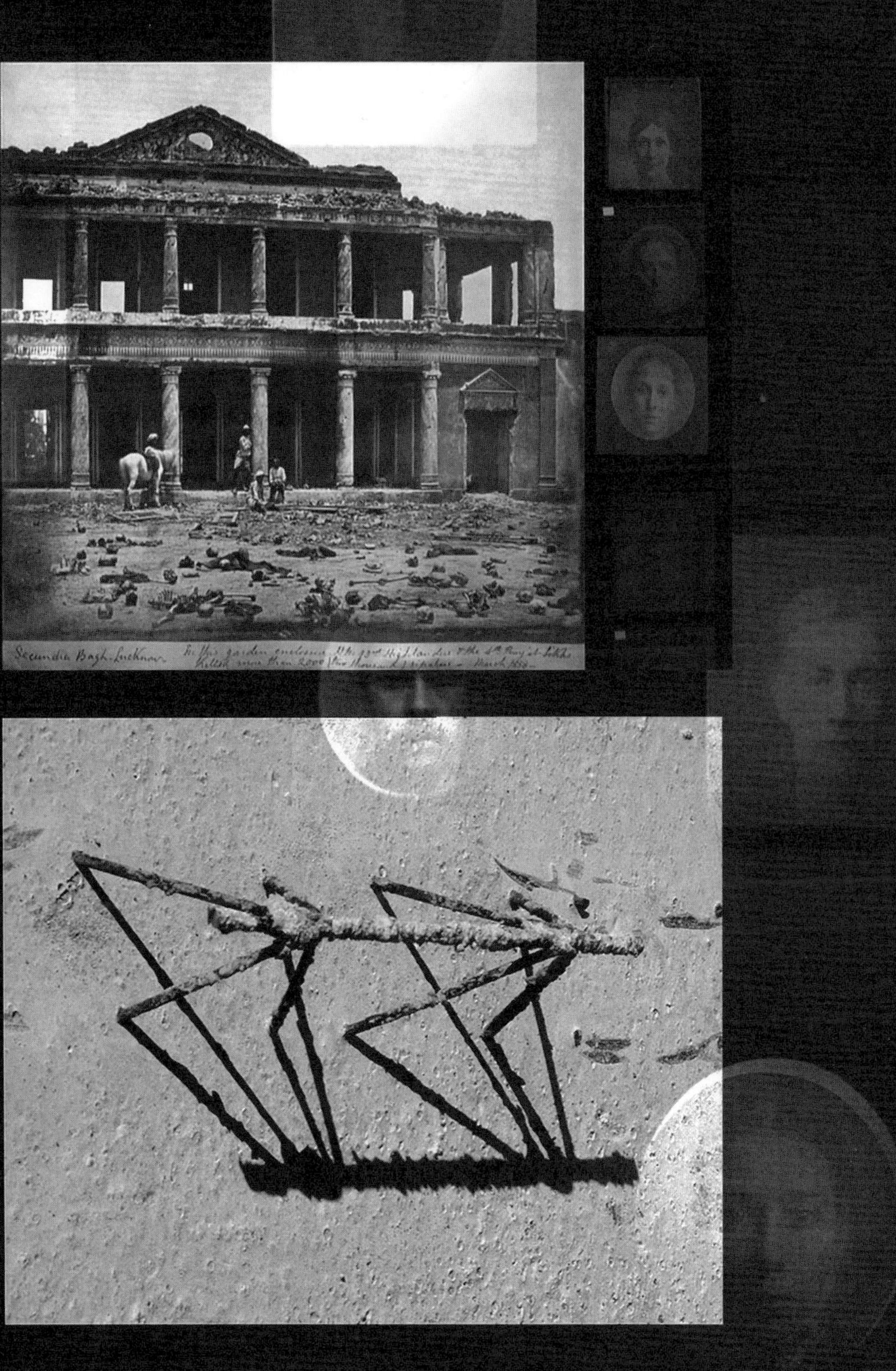

personal connection with the history of their country. This human connection to history is often at the forefront of their work. However, instead of assuming that a photograph is a representation of truth, they often take to task the structure through which history is validated and question the motives underlying the image. Although all history is 'inherited', these artists seek to better understand what has been passed on and move forward with it into the future. In the case of this project, the term 'postdate' refers to the artists' marking vestiges of the past with ideas from the present. This approach is an unmooring of history that, in the artists' movements both backward and forward in time, reveals the unsettled nature of this history.

Raqs Media Collective's[6] work has been very important in defining the key concepts of this exhibition. They have been at the forefront of artists working globally with photographic archives and are engaged specifically with the history of photography in India. Their considered extension of the role of the artist into archival science and historical fields of study finds expression in the multimedia and multi-genre nature of their installations. They dismantle existing historical frameworks to question our understanding of past events and to suggest alternative narratives. Hal Foster stated that this type of work

> not only draws on informal archives but produces them as well, and does so in a way that underscores the nature of all archival materials according to a quasi-archival logic, a matrix of citation and juxtaposition, and presents them in a quasi-archival architecture, a complex of texts and objects (again, platforms, stations, kiosks ...).[7]

Raqs noted that *The Surface of Each Day is a Different Planet* (2009), a video piece in which they combined historic photographs from archives in London and New Delhi with contemporary imagery and animation, is purposefully anti-documentary, as well as non-narrative. They asked, 'Can there be a time made of juxtapositions, a time never experienced, but made serendipitously manifest by interpretative accidents? By the careful cultivation of chance encounters in scattered archives?'[8] Though Raqs's practice is grounded in historical research, the ideas, objects, photographs or statements they choose to extract or derive from the archive are creatively combined and considered to engender new theories and histories.

Whereas Raqs Media Collective works from existing material, Madhuban Mitra and Manas Bhattacharya[9] very intentionally label their photographs and videos of the empty National Instruments Ltd. camera factory an archive. This factory in the Jadavpur neighbourhood of southern Kolkata marks a national

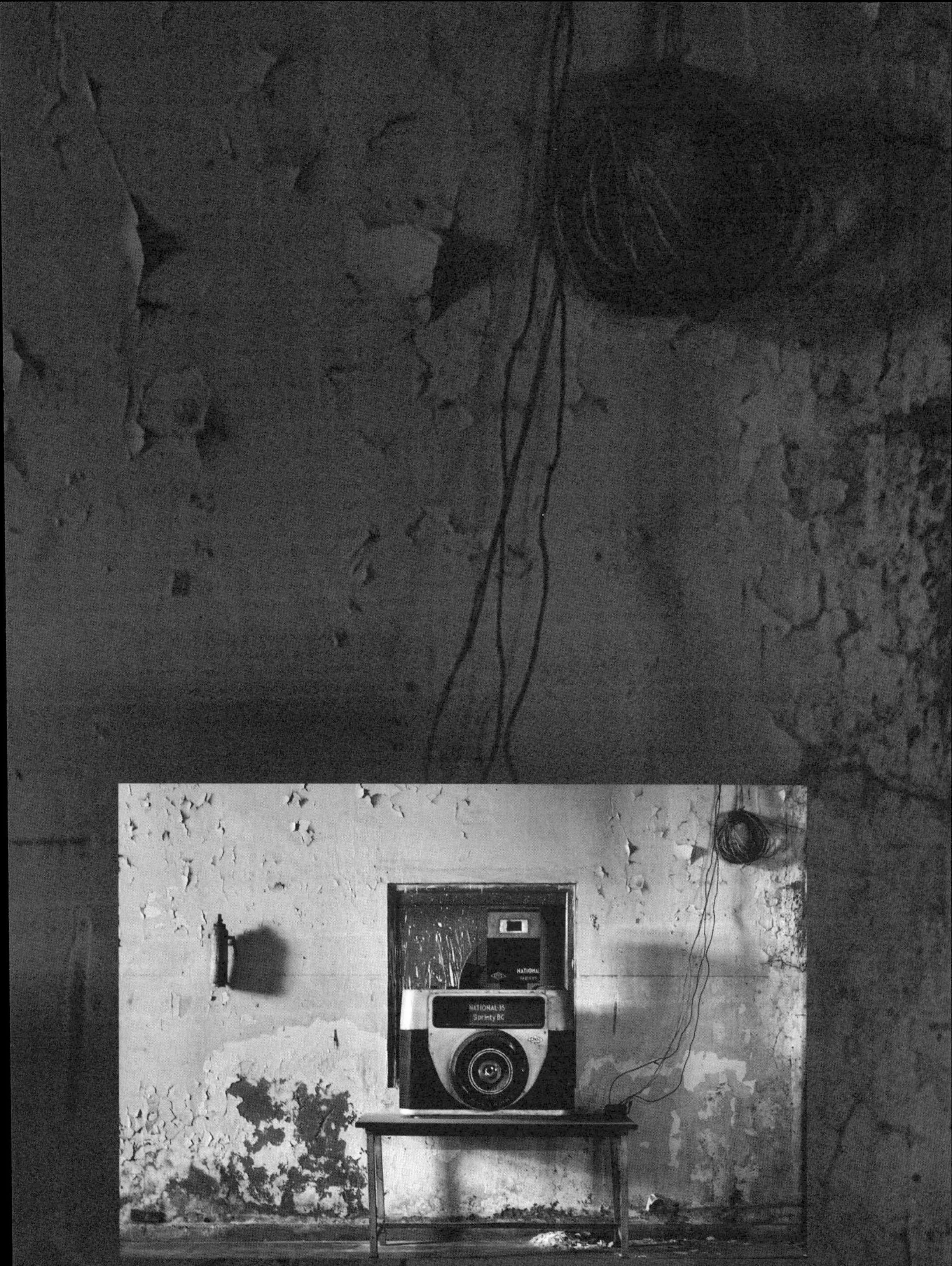
NATIONAL 35
Sprinty BC

attempt to democratize image-making in India. The National 35 was India's first locally made, low-cost camera. It was popular throughout the 1980s, but the factory, a government-owned venture, began to decline and was closed in the 1990s.[10] Mitra and Bhattacharya's images of the factory tell the story of an important moment in Indian photography. Their pictures reflect upon the histories of labour, photography and technology in India. Furthermore, they exemplify the act of photography looking at itself – in this case, specifically, digital photography looking at its analogue version. The artists are less interested in the photograph as document (though they intend their archive to be a lasting record of the factory) than in technological development within the medium. In using digital tools, they simultaneously embrace the newest developments in the medium and nostalgically mourn the failure of a camera company.

Surekha and Pushpamala N.[11] both use old photographs to examine the photographic representation of women in India. While Pushpamala is interested in the iconic images of Indian womanhood, Surekha creates installations from vernacular studio and wedding photographs that she finds in Bangalore, the city where she currently lives. In *Fragments of a Wedding Diary* (2001), Surekha digitally reframed and coloured fragments of found wedding photographs and negatives from the 1960s–90s in order to highlight the ritual and physical aspects of a wedding. By fragmenting these photographs she removed them from a specific personal context and created an installation that reflects upon the place of wedding photography in collective memory. Additionally, in regard to the artifice of photography, she noted that 'the common people become the lead actors during their auspicious wedding day. The marriage photographs or/and the marriage videos document a specific culture of people. It is also a document of what they essentially are not in their true life'.[12]

Rochona Majumdar's question about nineteenth-century wedding photography in Christopher Pinney's *The Coming of Photography in India* (2008) strikes a similar chord: 'How [are we] to understand Bengali wedding portraits, most of which show the bride and bridegroom ... often with their limbs touching, their images frozen in a gesture of togetherness when other histories seem to suggest that these sentiments were far more contested in everyday life?'[13] This contradiction between photographic convention and the history of married relationships in India is at the core of Surekha's investigation into this particular vernacular photography in South India. The contrived nature of wedding and portrait photography, in this instance, is a barrier to clearly understanding the position of women in this region. Her emphasis on the formal similarities of these

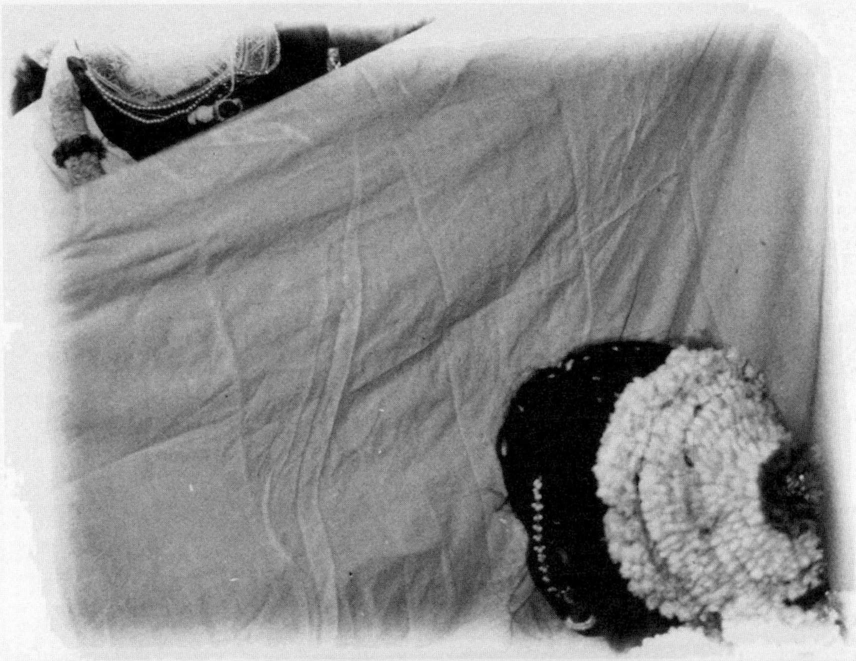

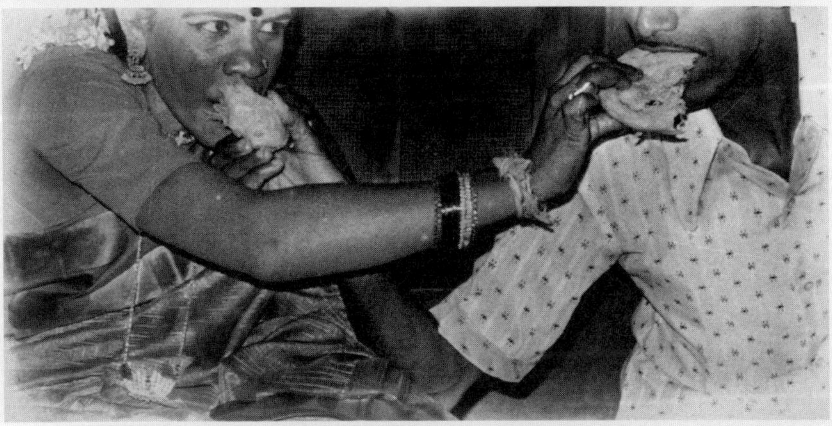

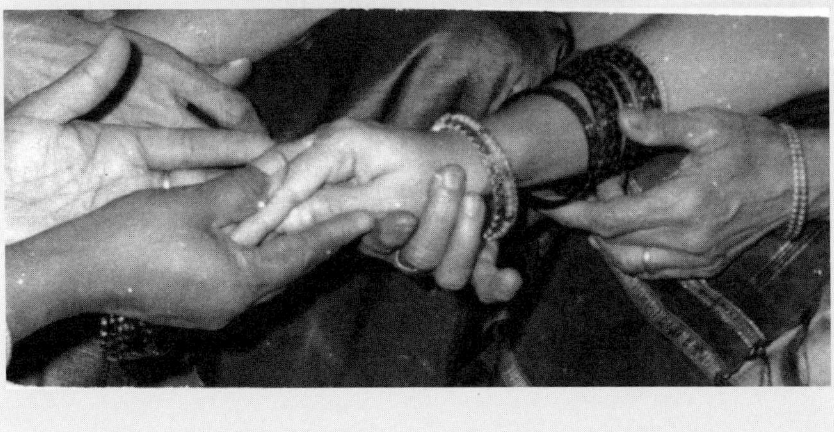

photographs prompts a consideration of past and present women's rights issues.

In her series *Native Women of South India: Manners and Customs* (2000-2004), Pushpamala N. investigated the roles of subject and photographer by enacting historical images such as Raja Ravi Varma's nineteenth-century paintings of graceful, sari-clad women and 1920s film stills featuring mysterious ingenues. In collaboration with Clare Arni, a British photographer who has spent most of her life in India, Pushpamala carefully created sets that replicated scenes from these quintessential images, casting herself in costume as the posed archetypes. As Pushpamala intended, this exactness leads to a final photograph that is obviously artificial. Geeta Kapur noted in reference to this series: 'An obsessive mimesis can render the repetition in mimicry a measure of calibrated *difference* - visual, cultural, anthropological - mocking yet enhancing representation.'[14] In so deliberately performing these tableaus, the artist calls attention to the artificial nature of the conception and creation of the source images. For example, *The Native Types - Toda*, part of the *Native Women* series, refers to British colonial ethnographic photography from the nineteenth century, specifically a series by Maurice Vidal Portman[15] in which he measured and photographed people of the Andaman Islands against black-and-white chequered backdrops. One may initially assume that the hands holding the backdrop in *Toda* were an addition by Pushpamala to emphasize the artifice and demonstrate the control that the British colonial photographer would have had over the native, but hands were also present in Portman's 1893 photograph. In re-enacting such a wide span of Indian photographic history in this series, Pushpamala called attention to the consistent and continued presence of colonial legacies in photographic practice.

Beyond Global Influence and Local Perspectives

In specifically looking back at India's photographic past - images that reflect important moments of local history and customs while simultaneously recalling the legacy of colonialism - the artists in this exhibition assert the necessity of engaging with both the global and the local in their work. As Frederick Gross suggested in his essay 'Contemporary Photography between the Global and the Local', we need 'a new model of interpretation based upon [Homi K.] Bhabha's situation of a "vernacular cosmopolitanism" in which an artist is critically aware of the effects of globalization within the distinctive worldview of his or her own localized cultural identity'.[16] The artists presented here seek to acknowledge but

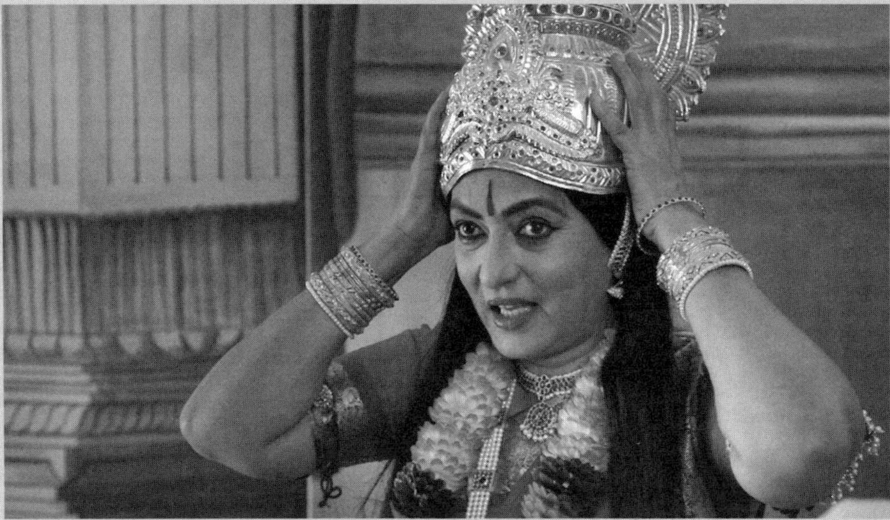

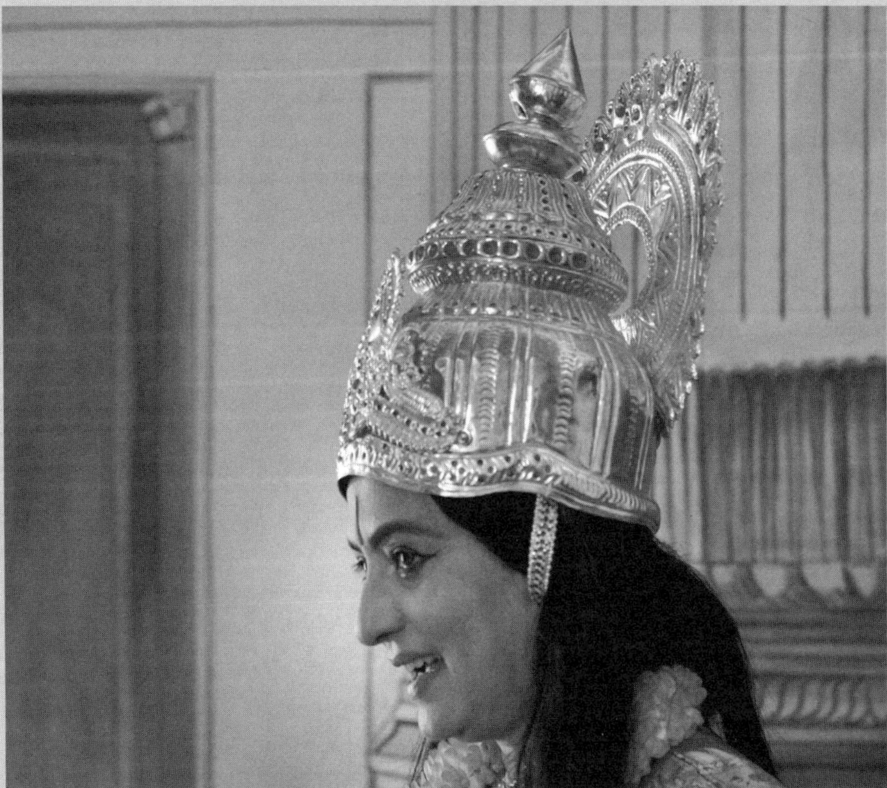

deconstruct this narrow representation to create work that reflects the complex hybridity inherent to a globalized India.

With awareness of the global art world and keeping in mind the inclinations of past photographers in India toward the exotic, these artists take a personal approach to determining cultural identity from both global and local perspectives. Gauri Gill,[17] for example, who is based in New Delhi, is conscious of her outsider status when addressing the complicated and contradictory elements of contemporary life in rural Rajasthan. She explores these issues by engaging with the problematic history of representation in rural Indian portrait photography. Her approach is collaborative and activist. In 2003, she set up a makeshift studio for young women and girls at a Rajasthani fair, and invited them to be photographed 'as they are, or as they see themselves, or to invent new selves for the camera'.[18] This attitude is in striking contrast to the methods of the photographer in nineteenth-century India who, as Christopher Pinney outlined in *Camera Indica: The Social Life of Indian Photographs* (1997), often carefully controlled the costumes, poses and props of his subjects so as 'not to capture in his negatives the complex contemporary hybrid reality he encountered, but rather to stage a vision of an authentic primitiveness salvaged from imminent extinction'.[19] Gill, on the other hand, in allowing the natural hybridity of rural Rajasthani culture to come through in her photographs, refuted historical and contemporary photographic practices that emphasize the exotic 'otherness' of their subjects. Traditional *salwar kameez*es appear alongside modern t-shirts and blue jeans - indicative of the tensions of change but also of coexistence. Moreover, initially Gill took only black-and-white photographs of Rajasthan with the idea that eliminating colour would likewise reduce the romanticized identity of the region. Anita Dube pointed out that Gill's photographs are a much-needed counterpoint to the visions of Rajasthan promoted by travel campaigns such as 'Incredible India'.[20] Gill's decision demonstrates that she (along with many other artists in this exhibition) is alert to how her photographs are interpreted both inside and outside India. As David Batchelor[21] argued, Western culture has long rejected colour and associated it with 'the feminine, the oriental, the primitive, the infantile, the vulgar, the queer or the pathological'.[22]

Jitish Kallat[23] is also interested in how global culture has shaped local experience. Like Gill, he seeks to show India's complex relationship with globalism. The changes to India's cities - both good and bad, from better housing to air and water pollution - reflect the changes of pace and ideology of the country, and Kallat's work demonstrates these complexities. Inspired by the panoramic documentation of the development of Mumbai in the boom time of the 1800s,

Kallat created a modern-day panorama of Mumbai by digitally layering multiple time-frames within a single image. Whereas the early panoramas sought to capture the changing skyline and the erecting of colonial-style buildings, Kallat sought to capture the pace of a twenty-first-century city. The title of the photograph *Artist Making Local Call* (2005), for example, refers to the fact that the photograph's exposure time matched that of the average local call on a pay phone - one-and-a-half minutes - an act performed by the artist and recorded in the centre of the photograph. Kallat's phone call provides the focal point within the surrounding chaos and comments on how a global impetus affects a city. He collapses time and space in his panoramic cityscapes in order to catch a glimpse of the present before it fades speedily into the past. His digital layering offers an apt metaphor for the convergence of years passing and the changing architecture of a city. Unlike the historic 'frozen' panorama, Kallat's photograph reels forward into the future with people and rickshaws meeting and colliding across time around him.

Though she spent much of her life in India, Annu Palakunnathu Matthew[24] is the only artist in the exhibition who does not currently live there. Matthew uses performance in her photography to better understand her experience as an immigrant to the United States and to reveal the connections and similarities between the photographic histories of the two countries. In her series *An Indian from India* (2001–03), she investigates the connection between the representation of native Indians and Native Americans in photography from the nineteenth and early twentieth centuries. With a distinctively South Asian and female perspective, she re-enacts iconic photographs of Native Americans - including famous examples by Edward S. Curtis- and prints them directly next to the original image on a sheet of paper. Her titles for the photographs comment further on stereotypes and bring this historic discussion into the present. For example, in *Feather/Dot* (2001), she paired a photograph of a Native American wearing a feather headdress with an image of herself wearing a symbolic *bindi* dot. As Matthew noted, 'It seems strange that all this confusion started because Christopher Columbus thought he had found the Indies and called the native people of America collectively as Indians.'[25] Matthew's work reminds us that 500-year-old 'confusions' can still influence global identity politics. Like Pushpamala N.'s, her mimicry points to the artificiality of photography and the heavy hand that photographers such as Curtis had in manipulating their supposedly 'documentary' photographs of native people.

Digitally Connecting Past and Present

Digital technology has proved to be a strong force in the globalization of culture. India has become one of the countries most often associated with the 'digital divide' – a disparity between those who have access to information and communications technologies and those who do not. Though this is a worldwide issue, the striking difference between the secure privileges of India's elite and the multiple disenfranchisements of its poor makes the disparity here especially conspicuous. The artists in *Postdate* use digital technology to connect past and present concerns, as well as to consider its impact on local cultures. Their work reflects the formation of a new aesthetic language that has been greatly influenced by our near-constant interactions with computers and smart phones.

Organizations such as the non-profit, crowd-sourced, community-based 1947 Partition Archive,[26] based in Berkeley, California, use digital technology and the internet to collect, preserve and share the stories and experiences of Partition. As fewer and fewer Partition survivors remain today, capturing their first-hand testimonies becomes more urgent. Digital technology has created the opportunity for these stories to be collected, translated and edited by volunteer 'citizen historians' for the archive on a massive scale – to date, numbering over 1,000 oral history interviews.[27]

Matthew's recent work echoes this desire to capture these experiences; and also, through digital technology, to connect generations. Despite having spent the majority of her childhood in India, Matthew felt vastly uninformed about Partition. In an effort to better understand the impact of this historic moment on the citizens of India and East and West Pakistan, in 2012, as part of a Fulbright fellowship, she began to collect portraits from the late 1940s from families who were affected by the division. She then photographed subsequent generations of these families and digitally brought the images together into one morphing animation. The animations conflate past and present and connect the personal with the political – a connection emphasized by the placement of the personal video stories in an English-language encyclopaedia that discusses the geopolitical impact of Partition. Matthew creates a memory that exists only in the digital world. She 're-orient[s] the viewer's connection to time as [she] collapse[s] the presumed progression of its borders, so the past and present appear here in the same virtual space',[28] and calls attention to the shifts between generations by making the family photograph into a conduit through which geopolitical shifts can be observed.

Vivan Sundaram[29] uses digital means to expand upon and create new narratives from his family's photographic archive. Sundaram's family history is deeply intertwined with the history of art in India. His aunt Amrita Sher-Gil[30] was a prominent modern artist and his grandfather Umrao Singh Sher-Gil was a noted scholar and pioneer of photography. In his *Re-Take of Amrita* series (2001–02), Sundaram collaborates posthumously with his grandfather by digitally layering family images taken at different times and placing these into single photographs. He creates new narratives for the family, chiefly around Amrita Sher-Gil. Nicolas Bourriaud applied the term 'postproduction' to artwork that has been created from already existing pieces, noting that, 'This art of postproduction seems to respond to the proliferating chaos of global culture in the information age. ...'[31] He likened the artist to a DJ – remixing parts and pieces to create a new work of art. Certainly this is true for Sundaram's series, albeit filtered through a much more personal lens. As he warps time and space, Sundaram also disrupts the notion that a photograph is a fixed, and thus truthful, document. In fact, he calls these photographs 'future' works of art[32] – perhaps because they cannot be anchored to a specific time or place. The artist pushes even further, calling into question the entire narrative by purposefully leaving footprints of his digital tools – blurring or colour variation – to show that changes have been made.

Nandan Ghiya similarly emphasizes the traces of his tools. He paints nineteenth-century studio portraits to make them look as if they have been digitally manipulated, then groups them in salon-style installations. For example, in *The Chairmen* (2012–14), he brings together photographs of Indian men in business attire posing in front of commercial studio backdrops. Like Surekha's installations of found photographs, Ghiya's groupings sort specific categories of vernacular photographs and thereby call attention to cultural connections, as well as stylistics related to studio portraiture. Ghiya, however, uses the now global language of digital technology to further separate the viewer from the people in the portraits. For example, by painting pixels on the faces of the individuals he obscures their identity and creates a sense of anonymity. In doing so, he intentionally frustrates the viewer and calls attention to the unknown or unreachable aspects of history. Given our access today to unlimited information thanks to the internet, such frustration feels particularly acute. Ghiya's barriers of pixels and 'download errors' (this descriptor is also the title of his 2012 series satirizing internet-enabled distortions and manipulations of data and visual cultures) raise questions about the idea that one can fully understand the world through digital means.

Taking on the Future

India's history of photography has proved to be a bountiful source for artistic investigation. The artists represented in this exhibition take a multidisciplinary approach to exploring cultural representation, methods of chronicling history, and the effects of globalism on their country. In old photographs and archives they find stylistic similarities that reveal larger questions about Indian society and make surprising, thoughtful juxtapositions that call into question the authority of historical structures. By engaging with both local history and the larger world, they reveal complex intersections between the past and present; rural and urban; and Western and Indian cultures. Using new digital tools, they find ways to suggest narratives that offer alternatives to dominant historical perspectives and stereotypes.

Pushpamala N. succinctly summarized the demanding roles of contemporary artists in India:

> In a postcolonial country like India, artists have seen their role as developmental and have worked to build institutions and the infrastructure for creative life to flourish. The artists I admire are scholar-writer-teacher-artists. I believe the creative subjectivity and the anarchic individualism of the artist resist the homogenous culture demanded by both a feudal society and by a globalizing world![33]

Ultimately, the artists in *Postdate* exemplify this model: they are researchers, collectors, activists, genealogists, performers and documentarians. They engage with the history of photography in their country in order to better understand the lasting legacy of colonialism on contemporary culture. Engaged globally and locally, they have a large role and considerable responsibility in defining and developing the postcolonial artistic culture in India and representing the history of their country to the world.

8 No Ordinary Darkness

2010

Sandhini Poddar

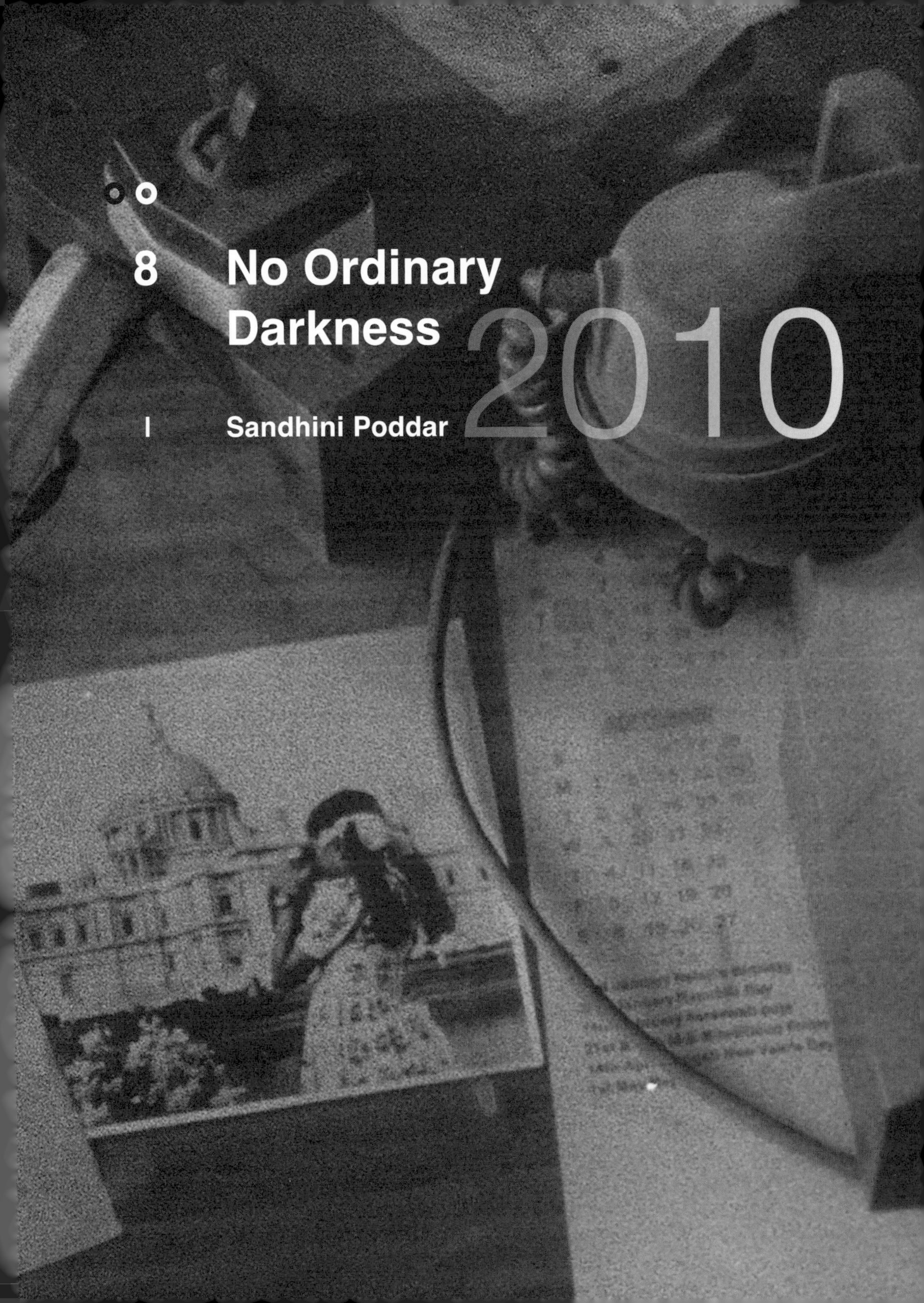

As photographic art expanded into new media, digital technology enabled visual artists to challenge ostensibly watertight compartments such as 'fiction and nonfiction, art and cinema, documentation and poetry, and the still and moving image', and spectators were challenged by 'new modes of phenomenological and physiological address'. Sandhini Poddar's essay draws on philosopher Jean-Luc Nancy's observation that the screen is a 'sensitive membrane' between the observer and the world, and that the creative act of 'voiding'/emptying out of normative representational frames in different ways enables new aesthetic experiences that defy empirical calibration, yet are valid 'evidence' of the 'real'. She analyses the trajectories of four contemporary practitioners in the exhibition *Being Singular Plural* (2010): Shumona Goel and Shai Heredia's film *I am micro,* about an abandoned camera factory in Kolkata; Kabir Mohanty's four-part epic, *Songs for an ancient land*; Amar Kanwar's *The Torn First Pages*; and Desire Machine Collective's films and site-specific project titled *Periferry*.

Keywords, Names

Babri Masjid/Ram Janmabhoomi violence 1992, *Gujarat Riots 2002*, *Moving Images*, *Partition of India*, see Keywords at the back of this volume.

Images

pp. 137, 141: Images from *I am micro*, 2012 (dir. Shumona Goel and Shai Heredia, cinematography: Avijit Mukul Kishore), 35-mm celluloid film. Images courtesy the filmmakers.

p. 145: *Song for an ancient land – Part 2*, 2009 (dir. Kabir Mohanty, cinematography: Setu and Kabir Mohanty), 51 mins, colour, stereo sound, digital video. The opening sequence of the work, assembled and shot a series of still images taken in Bombay during December 1992–January 1993, some by unknown photographers and from the archives, following the destruction of the Babri Masjid.

p. 149: Amar Kanwar, part 2 of *The Torn First Pages*, 2004–08. 7 channel digital colour video, sound (24 min. 53 sec., synch, looped) and 7 sheets of blank paper. Installation view, Haus der Kunst, Munich, Germany (2008). Photo: Marino Solokhov. Co-commissioned by Thyssen-Bornemisza Art Contemporary, Vienna, and Public Press, New Delhi. Image courtesy Amar Kanwar.

p. 153: Desire Machine Collective (Sonal Jain and Mriganka Madhukaillya), *25/75, Guwahati, India*, 2007. Image courtesy the artists.

Being Singular Plural: Moving Images from India[1] is oriented toward co-producing new work, facilitating research and assembling a community of practitioners. A resolutely heterogeneous and ultimately unresolved exhibition, it attempts to avoid some of the pitfalls of surveying contemporary production in a given region. While recent international exhibitions of contemporary Indian art have celebrated artistry as an end product, often in light of the country's economic boom and the concomitant strength of the art market,[2] artists and filmmakers such as Sonal Jain and Mriganka Madhukaillya of Desire Machine Collective,[3] Shumona Goel, Amar Kanwar and Kabir Mohanty[4] reveal a craft that is based on the principles of practice, process and perception.

Being Singular Plural brings together a number of moving-image works by a select group of media practitioners who currently live in India and who are working in film or video rather than 'new media'.[5] All of their works refer to cinema or employ an expanded notion of the cinematic apparatus. They conceive of video as an interlaced but separate category from film. Their images do not serve as windows onto the world, nor point to any transcendent truths, but are presented as they are, distinguished by their *evidence*. As Jean-Luc Nancy states:

> The recurring attempt to compare cinema with Plato's cave is inaccurate: precisely, the depths of the cave attest to an outside of the world, but as a negative, and this sets up the discrediting of images, as we know, or it demands a consideration for images that are loftier and purer, named 'ideas'. Film works the opposite way: it does not reflect an outside; it opens an inside onto itself. The image on the screen is itself the idea.[6]

Although discussing the work of Abbas Kiarostami, Nancy's observations have import for the artists under consideration here. He formulates the screen as a

> sensitive membrane ... [that] stretches and hangs between a world in which representation ... [is] in charge of the signs of truth, of the heralding of a meaning, or of the warrant of a presence to come; and another world that opens onto its own presence through a voiding where its thoughtful evidence *realizes* itself.[7]

The act of 'voiding' or emptying out of representation, which is the resting place of *evidence*, points ontologically to the moving image as an end in itself rather than a means to an end that may lie outside of its surface. This embodiment of truth as it resides within the very structure and materiality of the image (or idea) overturns previous expectations of how the moving image communicates with the world. Nancy continues:

> Other arts can present evidence of a truth, of a presence, in brief, of a 'thing in itself'. ... Cinema too takes up this gesture, this *presentation*. But what it adds as that which is its own ... is the linking, the indefinite sliding along of its presentation. Where does it slide to indefinitely? In a certain way, toward *insignificance* (there where the other arts appeal to an excess of *significance*). Toward the insignificance of life that offers itself these images, always in movement, going toward no mystery, no revelation, only this sliding along by means of which it leads itself from one image to another (exemplary, subliminal, banal, grotesque or naive, tampered with, sketchy or overloaded). Life that invents its own cinema.[8]

The textural correlation between life and the moving image is crucial. As with life, the moving image is distinguished by flux and ephemerality, an endless process of sliding along. This seemingly futile movement can become the strongest testimony to the present, both on and off screen.

Cognizant of this evidential nature of film and video, the practitioners in the current exhibition posit new modes of phenomenological and physiological address for the viewer. They embrace ambiguity with an unusual mixture of simplicity and complexity, and test the resilience between the boundaries of such ostensibly watertight compartments as fiction and nonfiction, art and cinema, documentation and poetry, and the still and moving image, thereby short-circuiting our conditioned expectations. Furthermore, whereas non-fiction filmmaking is often geared toward the object, in these artists' work the location of the subject (the image-maker himself or herself) in relation to this visual field is mutant and warrants discovery. Accordingly, Desire Machine Collective, Goel (along with Shai Heredia, her co-director for *I am micro*), Kanwar and Mohanty each occupy a different location. The subject or self in these contexts can be disembodied and subterranean but is always present, animated through voiceovers, cast in an interview, or felt through an alter ego. In each instance, the *singularly plural* and *plurally singular* nature of being and of art remains central.[9] In asking pertinent questions about the how, why and who of the moving image, the artists offer us works that circulate and communicate in ways that are inherently contingent, mirroring their multiple existences.

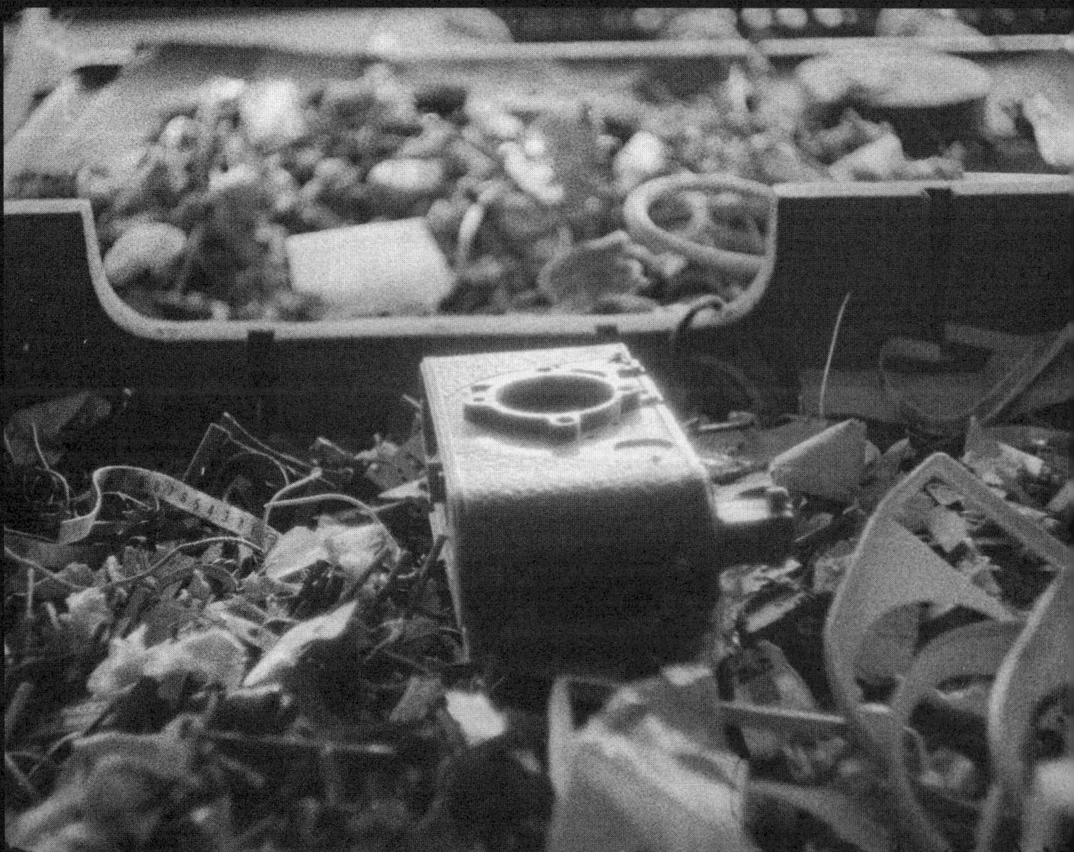

The first part of *I am micro*, Goel and Heredia's new 16 mm film, is presented as a work-in-progress in the current exhibition. The motivation to include an unfinished work was a deliberate curatorial strategy aimed at opening up and sharing the creative process of filmmaking, including its conditions and politics of practice. *I am micro* is a film that celebrates small-scale independent filmmaking and a devotion to radical cinematic practices that involves a rethinking of conventional film techniques, formats and content. This attitude of experimentation is also evident in Goel's previous site-specific film and sound installation, *Family Tree* (2008), a work of 'expanded cinema'.[10] Installed for three days in an apartment in the neighbourhood of Colaba in Mumbai, the installation involved a number of visual components, such as still photographs, two VHS tapes played on TV monitors, a 16 mm projection, and slides shown on a carousel.[11] In choosing a disused, transient, domestic space over a pristine white cube, Goel resisted the collapse of film into traditional art spaces.[12] When completed, *I am micro* will consist of a number of portraits of people whose lives normally go undocumented and who struggle to carve out a place for themselves in society.

Goel and Heredia started sketching out *I am micro* in 2008. 'We wanted to make a series of short portrait films,' Goel recounts.

> When I became pregnant, we decided to focus on a Mumbai-based character, 'Kamal'. This led to a series of interviews. I started shooting on Ashim's [Ahluwalia, Goel's then husband] set [for his upcoming Hindi fiction film *Miss Lovely*] and *I am micro* emerged ... *I am micro* honours the small, almost invisible forms of cinema. It features filmmakers whose personal voices do not make money or history, but celebrate the beauty of the world.

The first part consists of a voiceover by director and screenwriter Kamal Swaroop, whose debut Hindi film *Om Dar-B-Dar* (1988)[13] received wide critical acclaim, soon accompanied by an almost mythic aura. Goel and Heredia's interview with the filmmaker strays from overarching biographical information and offers instead a rumination on the slow death of independent filmmaking in light of the lack of infrastructural support available in India. The images in the film are culled from two different sources – a film shoot around National Instruments Limited (NIL), a now defunct Kolkata-based company that was once involved in the design, manufacture and development of optomechanical and optoelectronic instruments (and which is now under the purview of Jadavpur University), and behind-the-scenes footage from the set of Ahluwalia's *Miss Lovely*[14] (ongoing). By focusing on these micronarratives, Goel indirectly comments on her own difficulties as a woman in a field dominated by male filmmakers. The second part of *I am micro* will revolve around another Mumbai-based character, 'Lauren', a man who has spent his life working in the shipyards and has created a community for himself by opening up his home to prostitutes and bystanders. Taken together, this series of short films will reveal the innards of filmmaking by problematizing the position of the subject and exposing the conditions of creativity.

Whereas Goel and Heredia experiment with the language of film, Mohanty's approach to his moving-image practice stems from a 'filmmaker's sensibility',[15] but moves beyond this framework to develop an innovative vision for video. Having worked in both film (35 mm and 16 mm) and video (analogue and digital) over the past twenty years, Mohanty is a practitioner whose journey to the surface of the moving image is nestled within a deep ontological inquiry. In his work, philosophy is not a passive process but an action that dictates the conditions of sight, touch and other modes of perception. The spaces for his video and sound installations, which have developed with some consistency since 2001, are demarcated mental landscapes that have the capacity to slowly transport viewers into meditative zones. Reality (or non-fiction) is a thin veil that coexists with the unreal (or fiction). The screen or surface of the moving image is the closest approximation of this coexistence. By adopting non-fiction as a mode of storytelling, Mohanty's exploration of his surroundings and his study of Indian history and philosophy reveal the limits of these inquiries and point instead to where the world ceases to exist. 'I am least interested in observing, commenting, or having opinions about the world,' says Mohanty. 'I feel that the quest [as a moving image practitioner] is to realize that there is no world. The human questions arising from this feeling, the ethical questions, are crucial.' Mohanty's position lies at the very heart of the notion of evidence, which is necessary for the moving image to exist on its own terms.

The artist draws inspiration from a number of historical and contemporary figures in the arts and humanities in India, including G. Aravindan, Ritwik Ghatak, Ashis Nandy and A.K. Ramanujan,[16] to name a few. He muses: 'They are all saying that the world is a story, an impression.' For Mohanty, this impressionistic character of the world manifests itself in the porosity and plasticity of his images. His voiceover in part one (2003–06) of the digital video *Song for an ancient land* (2003–) emerges intermittently. One such passage about Diwali (the festival of lights) expresses his ideas concerning connectedness and transmogrification:

'And then it was Diwali. A plane galloped across the sky. Trees were light. Smoke was a cloud of grain. Noise was breath. Video was me.' Mohanty's absorption of the world around him through video reveals a subterranean being that is constantly questioning, feeling, reacting and reflecting. He uses the screen of the moving image as an extension of his body, his breath.

For Mohanty, the choice of video over film resides in a number of motivations. Whereas film is an inherently collaborative process (a fact that questions the validity of the idea of the 'auteur'), video gives the artist an opportunity to work more spontaneously, often alone. The scales are also different: film has a predetermined scale set in relation to the viewing conditions of a black box. 'Why is one showing then in the museum?' asks Mohanty. 'Video, with its more recent history and intersecting disciplines of practice, has yet to find its permanent scale. There will probably be many scales in video for some time to come. This I find of immense interest.' The indeterminacy of video enables the artist to experiment and improvise with various formats of image making and viewing. In some short digital video studies or sketches he utilizes tiny 4-inch LCD monitors that fit into the palm of a viewer's hand (*handheld*, 2003–08). In others, he builds impermanent spaces that are imbued with natural light during the day and that come alive at selected screening times late in the evening in order to experience video essays epic in length and scope (*Song for an ancient land*, whose four parts, when completed, will run approximately 250 minutes in full).

All of Mohanty's videos and installations demand vigilant attention to nuance. The works and the rooms in which they are placed are sites of rest and quiet vibration. This description stems in part from the artist's engagement with traditions of Hindustani classical music such as *dhrupad* and *khayal* (both vocal genres). Mohanty's approach to building a sequence of shots in his videos is akin to the progressively developed slow, unmetred, improvised sounds of the *alap* (opening section of a *raga*), of *dhrupad* especially. His keen interest in sound has been further catalysed by a long-term collaboration with sound designer Vikram Joglekar.[17] In *Song for an ancient land* they have pushed the limits of what can be experienced through video. A work such as this resides on the very edge of perceptual experience, both visually and acoustically. It compels viewers to distinguish multiple blacks from Black, grays from Gray, and whites from White, and employs a full spectrum of auditory pitches from high to low. These sounds have the ability to carry us out of our bodies and cast us onto external realities, or to reside deep within our inner bodies and consciousness. The sounds can come very close or seem faint in the distance. In fine-tuning our senses with the

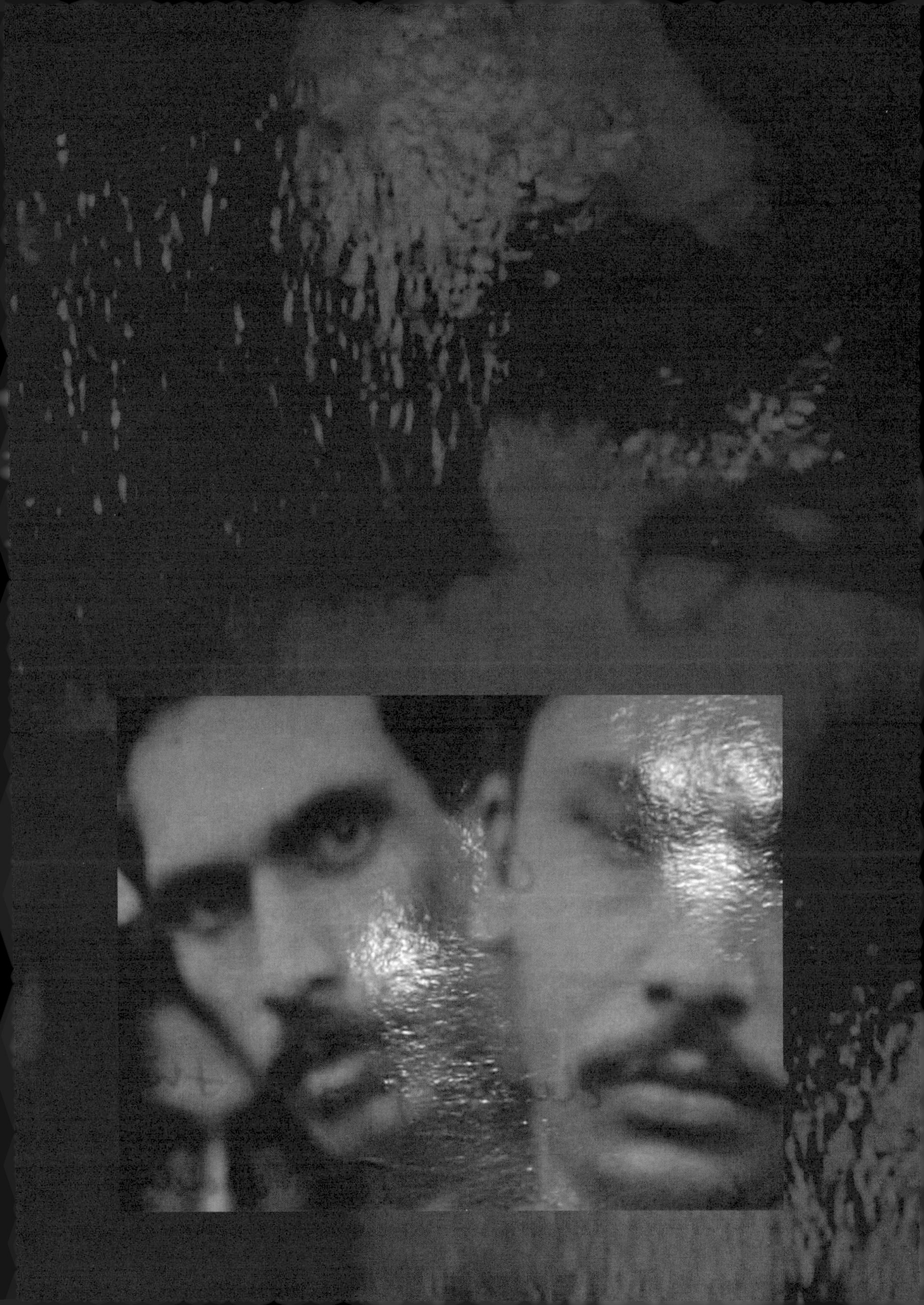

most minimal of means, Mohanty invites us to charge our own immense, static energies through our acts of looking and perceiving.

Filmed around Mumbai, part one of *Song for an ancient land* meditates on the multivalent idea of *dharma* (from the Sanskrit root *dhr-*; that which upholds or supports, literally meaning law or duty in Indic religions). Referencing the streets where fruit and clock sellers, vendors and cobblers exchange their wares, Mohanty states in his voiceover: 'Only on these banks where every day one comes to buy, and others to sell, is equality momentarily possible.' Much later, he says: 'The end is always moving towards the shore. Today he thinks of the middle, and repair, and of tradition, and *dharma*.' The video is built up through a number of sequences that together form a spacious whole, enveloped in air, light and breath. The artist's gestures are sweeping, expressionistic and even painterly at times, orchestrated through continuous, unedited footage that captures the result of every tiny movement of his hand. This feature is reminiscent of the video sketch *shape* (2004), one of the five videos in the *handheld* installation. Mohanty employs other optical devices, which may be found in sketches such as *6'58"* (2003) and *mountain* (2005, also from *handheld*). In these latter works, by controlling the aperture of his digital camera Mohanty is able to saturate his images with darkness, bleach them completely or leave them suspended in between. They can be in sharp focus or blurred, each deliberate nuance affecting our sense of time and place while paying homage to the craft and intimate joy of moving-image work.

Part two of *Song for an ancient land* (2003–10) consists of a number of invisible stepping stones used by the artist to navigate the video. While explaining the compositional structure of the work to me in New York, Mohanty jotted down a number of keywords, including 'stills sequence', 'pinhole', 'Panch Pir', 'police station', '*dargah*' (tomb of a Muslim saint), 'matte surfaces', 'video', '*ustad*' (maestro/teacher of a classical art), 'New York' and 'Gustav Klimt'. The thoughts surrounding each of these ideas, places, objects or persons are used to orchestrate the work.[18] The video begins with close-ups of a number of black-and-white photographic strips, images taken during the Mumbai riots in 1992 and 1993 in the aftermath of the Babri Masjid destruction in the town of Ayodhya. The artist amassed a vast archive of images from this time and acknowledges each photographer in the video credits. While slowly panning across these strips (made into larger contact sheets by the artist to approximate the size of the camera lens), Mohanty at times exposes the material edge of the photographic reel, situating us back in the present, in our act of looking, and preventing us from engaging in false nostalgia. At another instance, the video suddenly cuts (with ease) from these still images to street children playing at night, drenched in colour. This sudden transition is unexpected and completely liberating. Finally, the camera moves diagonally across a large set of stills in one quick, violent gesture, which is accompanied by an equally discomforting soundtrack. This movement matches the chaotic content of the photographs themselves. For Mohanty, each image demands a different response from the camera.

In a subsequent pinhole sequence, Mohanty's voiceover emerges: 'The history of the moving image has been one of upheavals, each epoch defining, replacing the previous. Talkie the silent, colour the monochrome, the lens this pinhole that can be held. Yet the camera still has to be panned, the colours chosen.' Later in the video, Mohanty adopts a special lens (also used in the video *curve*, 2005, from *handheld*) to investigate the interiors and surroundings of the Mahim police station in Mumbai. The lens distorts the image and creates a curve or a bend along each side, mimicking how our peripheral vision actually works while also investigating the world that remains unseen behind us. A revelatory moment comes at the fifteenth-century *dargah* of the Sufi saint Makhdoom Ali Mahimi in Mumbai. For a blink of an eye, Mohanty carves out the innermost sanctum of the saint's tomb and replaces it just momentarily with a shot of a church interior, complete with pews and a figure of Christ. In so doing, the artist gestures toward the shared origins of these two great religions and to the complex spiritual inheritances of most people in the subcontinent. Toward the end of the video, he muses: 'The nature of the subcontinental self is multiple ... saw difference as life.' Taken together, parts one and two of *Song for an ancient land* prefigure the third and final part of the video (Mohanty has already worked on the fourth part, the epilogue), which will be loosely centred on the notion of *karma* (from the Sanskrit root *kri-*; literally action or deed, and the law of cause and effect in Indic religions).

In this exhibition, Mohanty and Kanwar exemplify divergent artistic voices through their individualistic approaches toward their chosen mediums. Kanwar's *The Torn First Pages* (2004–08) is a complex nineteen-channel video installation that envelops the viewer in multiple spatial, emotional and temporal zones. The intimate drama of the projections unfolds on several fragile pieces of paper attached to steel armatures, together forming a large *granth* (text or book). Composed of three distinct parts in which images and words emerge and mirror one another, each fragment of the installation reflects and refracts the next, creating panoplies of sounds and moving images that attest to the simultaneity in which we experience time. Kanwar is an artist-filmmaker who is deeply interested in conflating accepted genres in order to open up new relations. He attempts to destroy any solitary system of address (his trilogy of films, *A Season Outside* [1997], *To Remember* [2003] and *A Night of Prophecy* [2002], uses prose, silence, and poetry and song, respectively); adopts more than one venue for display (film festival, museum, gallery, community space or university); and employs multiple methodologies of seeing (by shifting between a multichannel video installation and a single-channel cinematic screening, as in *The Lightning Testimonies* (2007), which complicates both by collapsing its eight screens into a single channel toward the end of the video cycle). Like his work, Kanwar himself is a moving target. No token description of 'activist' is acceptable either for his craft or his person. The work is better situated within 'the politics of aesthetics'[19] rather than the aesthetics of politics. For Kanwar, aesthetic decisions arise from the ethical dilemmas he faces, as he continues to interrogate the self and the meaning of political engagement. This is in stark contrast to political works of art that often suffer from an overly illustrative or representational quality.

In art, the role of the interrogator or the interlocutor comes with a risk and may be misconceived as carrying too high a moral pitch. Yet, when this interrogation stems from an internalized understanding of the issues at hand and an active participation in the conditions it seeks to analyse, it opens these polemical spaces onto larger conceptual fields wherein the subject can be grasped obliquely and multiple histories can unfold. The alarming current sociopolitical situation in Burma serves as the context for *The Torn First Pages*. The State Peace and Development Council (SPDC) or military junta of Myanmar (the name given to Burma by the junta) mandates that every single publication include certain state objectives (slogans). The installation of *The Torn First Pages* includes a cross-section of such materials, including a fashion magazine, classic Burmese novel, Western novel, recipe book, folktale book and a book of poems. Each one's first page contains the state manifesto. In December 1994, Ko Than Htay, a Mandalay-based bookshop owner, was arrested and imprisoned for tearing out the first page of every book and magazine that he sold. In commemorating this private act of courage and resistance, Kanwar transforms the bookseller into the heroic Everyman. The artist extends his study beyond the nation's borders to include the lives of Burmese exiles in Oslo, New Delhi and Fort Wayne, Indiana; and looks further afield to the global circulation of images of the Burmese struggle on the internet. Filmmakers and artists in Burma continue to struggle to survive, and few open systems of circulation and distribution exist. *The Face* (2005), a short video shot on 25 and 26 October 2004, and one of the six channels[20] that form part one of *The Torn First Pages*, records the rare public appearance and visit of Senior

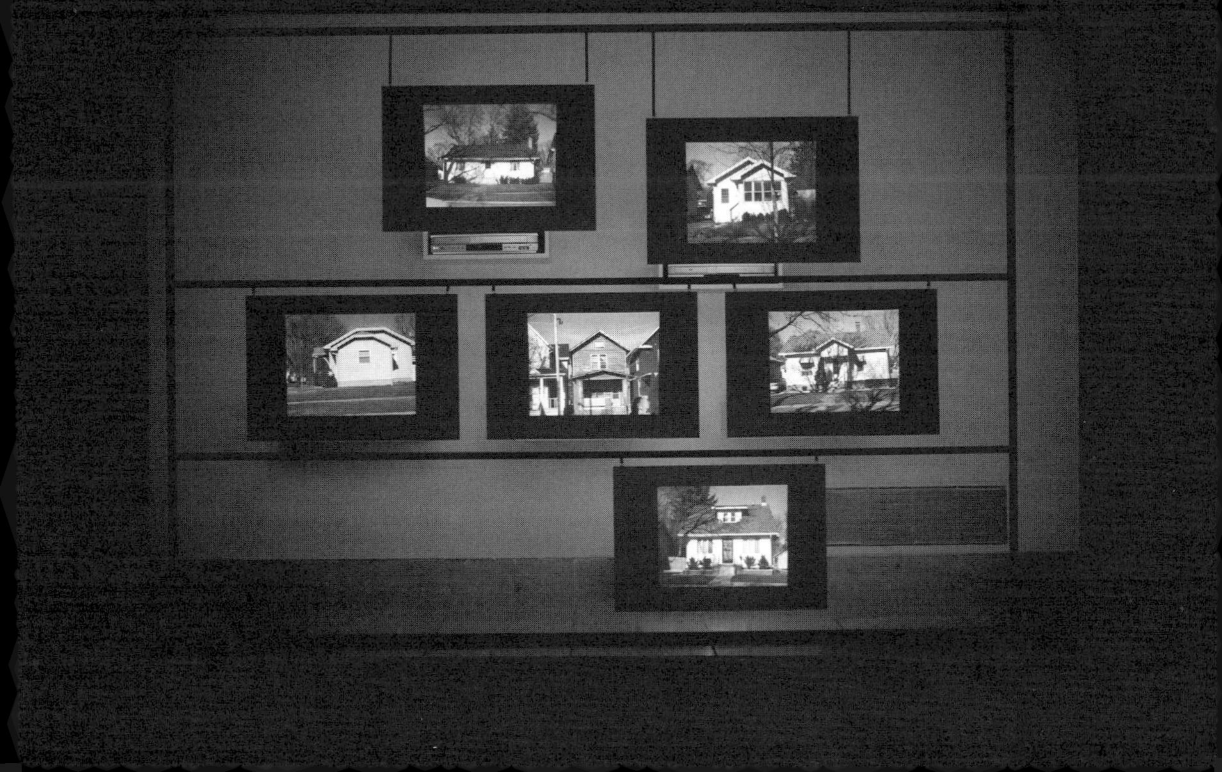

General Than Shwe, head of the Burmese military junta, to Mahatma Gandhi's memorial site at Rajghat, New Delhi. In an act calculated to expose this vacuous gesture, Kanwar accelerates the footage of the general throwing pink rose petals on the cremation site and repeats this act *ad absurdum*. Petals explode into blood, calm faces turn into masks of horror, and a chronic, hysteric sound takes over. A symbolic unseeing witness looks on.

Kanwar's *oeuvre* as a documentary filmmaker has been criticized on occasion for its subjective and aesthetic overtones. Rather than see these as shortcomings, we should make a case for how his images interact with our material culture (the aesthetic realms in which we live) and media culture (how we communicate agendas). Kanwar's interest in aesthetics and the critique of traditional views of non-fiction filmmaking does not rest with the work of art alone. He is more interested in the trajectories images can take as they enter the public domain and assume a life of their own, interfering with our expectations about material culture and piggybacking on the mechanisms of media culture. Kanwar will often find ways to show a new work as it is being made, rather than wait for it to be seen as a completed entity, in order to set his images free as soon as possible. A Burma solidarity group screened the video *Thet Win Aung* (2005) at the Nobels Fredssenter (Nobel Peace Center) in Oslo as early as 2006, before the work was incorporated into *The Torn First Pages*. In February 2007, an image from *The Face* found its way onto the cover of the South Asian magazine *Himal* (Kanwar had written a cover story titled 'Gandhi and the General' for the issue).[21] It is under these independent circulatory conditions that Kanwar considers art as having agency and thus great potential to affect change.

The videos *Thet Win Aung* and *Ma Win Maw Oo*[22] (2005, also part of *The Torn First Pages*) both detail the injustices enacted upon the bodies of Burmese people. In choosing precisely what to show and for how long, as well as to what degree focus is used, Kanwar utilizes the eyes of a non-fiction filmmaker to scan subject matter whose ethical dimensions demand an astute sensibility. Imprisoned in 1999 for having participated in ongoing students' protests for an improved educational system and the release of political prisoners, Ko Thet Win Aung died prematurely due to torture and disease in Mandalay Central Prison on 16 October 2006. The video attempts to catch the thirty-four-year-old student between a portrait and a landscape, a still and a moving image. The reverberations between hundreds of silent frames enable us to acutely sense the lapse between an immeasurably prolonged jail sentence (59 years) and the seconds it takes to forget. In his tribute to this brave young man, Kanwar adds a second adjacent screen of the same video, reversing the image to create a mirroring effect. This device is a simple yet poetic rumination on differing considerations of time and visual evidence. On a neighbouring screen, Kanwar's lens zooms in and out of a pixellated image of sixteen-year-old Ma Win Maw Oo, an unsettling digital document of the dead student being carried by two medical students through the streets of Rangoon on 8 August 1988 after she was killed by soldiers during the 8888 Uprising[23] – a series of nationwide marches, demonstrations and riots by people protesting against the totalitarian regime's social and economic agendas; the mass agitation was brutally suppressed by the army. By examining ambiguous areas of the surface of the pixellated image and hovering over them for a while, the filmmaker creates an abstraction, full of gaps and holes. As T.J. Demos states: 'The documentation of bare life ... can take place *negatively*, that is, indicated through the lacuna, blurs, and blind spots that mar the image, but also open up possibility within it, which parallels the condition of the subject stripped bare of political representation.'[24] The image of Ma Win Maw Oo circulated widely through the media, but remained newsworthy for only a day.

Underlying this visual information is a subterranean material layer – Kanwar exposes the technical limits of video as well as the digitized provenance of this mediated image by transitioning to an empty green video-frame, a split second at a time. 'It is a disintegrating digital image,' he says. 'I received it like that and felt there was a meaning behind it, that I must try and revive it, bring it back to life ... live with it and let it live as it wants to.'[25] The pixellated composition lays bare the ruse of the enduring, significant image, as well as the limitation of Kanwar's own ability to fully recount its history.

Images can be active or passive, empty or full, meaningless or meaningful, authored or anonymous. The seven untitled channels of part two of *The Torn First Pages* embrace an emptiness that is full. Several of the floating screens become embalmed with a still darkness at varying intermittent moments in the work's progression. These black-screen sequences intercut sections of moving colour images and sounds, which, taken together, create a cinematic effect that distinguishes part two. Kanwar shifts his gaze from the suppressed struggle within Burma to the Burmese communities living in exile in Fort Wayne, to map their psychic topographies. The absurdity of the shots of nameless, faceless houses and automobile factory lines in Fort Wayne becomes a metaphor for the suspended displacement of those cast away from their home country. Here, documentation becomes intervention as Kanwar explores the quotidian, anonymous lives of the artists, poets, writers and musicians he encounters, affording them an opportunity to recount their stories. On occasion, he even journeys with them as they embark on new voyages, as in the case of Sein Myint and his long-desired visit to the Statue of Liberty in New York. As Kanwar states: 'Everyone archives differently, everyone recalls differently – individuals and communities.'[26]

The first three untitled channels of part three of *The Torn First Pages* consist of found archival VHS footage of General Ne Win and his coterie of Burma Socialist Programme Party (BSPP) members. Kanwar's manipulations draw a dark caricature of these powerful men, as their images appear upon the state-mandated political, economic and social slogans, as well as the four main 'People's Desires' printed on the floating sheets. Three other adjacent untitled channels offer an open archive of the Burmese resistance, as documented on the internet on sites such as the Democratic Voice of Burma (DVB) and through videos posted to YouTube. The channels carry found amateur and professional footage ranging from the September 2007 non-violent uprising led by Buddhist monks in Rangoon to political rallies and speeches by Aung San Suu Kyi, and from images of ethnic minorities fleeing the SPDC and taking refuge in the forest to child labour and junta recruitments. When talking about the circulation routes that images adopt, Kanwar observes: 'There are several anonymous networks of Burmese groups. Images are very porous and move very fast.' Taken together, the three parts of *The Torn First Pages* provide an insight into the questions that arise from an individual's engagement with politics, and the possibilities of political resistance through art. Appealing to different audiences and subjects around the world, each with their own historical moorings, Kanwar's work aims at disturbing the status quo of image acceptance.

Jain and Madhukaillya also deal with sociopolitical subject matter, but in a manner that is entirely different from Kanwar's approach. The two artists have been collaborating as Desire Machine Collective on films and videos since 2004. After the Gujarat communal riots in 2002, which centred on the Godhra train burnings, they made a conscious decision to leave the city of Ahmedabad and move back home to the northeast region of India. This contested space has witnessed military violence and ethnic insurgencies for decades. Colonialism's legacy of treating India's border regions (especially the northwest and the northeast) as unruly buffer zones against powerful neighbours has had dire results. Both these zones of conflict suffer from border wars and occupations (from Pakistan and China respectively) and ambivalent states of governance, and both fall under the Armed Forces (Special Powers) Act (1958), which confers exceptional powers to armed forces to act against civilians and suspected militants and 'terrorists' in such areas.

LIC. NO. 1542
FORECAST
F.C. DIV. 10 Rs. = Rs.
5 Rs. = Rs.
2 Rs. = Rs.
1 Re. = Rs.
SINGLE DIV.
1st ROUND 1Re
TAXI
LUCKY

In this arena of pathological mutual mistrust, all the certain lines drawn between witnessing and intrusion, recording and surveillance, become unclear.

Desire Machine Collective's praxis examines the roles that moving images play in recording social histories and asks what the limits of this involvement can be. In 2007, they established *Periferry 1.0*, a migratory artists' project utilizing the *M.V. Chandardinga*, a government-leased ferry docked on the Brahmaputra river in the heart of Guwahati. Negotiations involving the Inland Water Transport Department over the ferry continue to run the constant risk of dissolving the initiative at any moment. Given this fact and the limited opportunities and platforms that exist for interstate or interregional exchange (with Southeast Asia) in the North East, Jain and Madhukaillya's context-based practice operates against state sanctions and bureaucracy. Ultimately, their aim is to dislodge the ferry from the city proper and conduct community-based workshops along the Brahmaputra. As an act of cultural resistance that deconstructs centre-periphery biases, *Periferry 1.0* extends praxis to incorporate flux and nomadism as essential components of a contemporary vision. To project their 'idea of nowhere', Desire Machine Collective will dissipate and 'deterritorialize' *Periferry 1.0* to re-create similar river-based projects around the world.[27] This liberation from any developmental model can be seen as a positivist and 'schizophrenic' revolutionary practice: a model delineated in Gilles Deleuze and Felix Guattari's radical 1972 text *Anti-Oedipus: Capitalism and Schizophrenia*, from which the artists derive their name and critical methodology.

In his decoding of a number of Deleuze and Guattari's ideas, Michael Hardt notes: 'There is no such thing as desire, only desiring-machines. ... Desire as desiring-machine is not a thing but a process, an act of producing. ... Desiring-machines can thus never be "satisfied" or come to a completion.'[28] Jain and Madhukaillya's artistic output, primarily in digital video, has undergone a number of shifts and transformations since their collaboration began (they shoot their videos independently, but support each other on sound design and editing). Certain themes have emerged in their process of self-interrogation, brought about through a maturation of experience and a deep interest in critical theory. Whereas an early video such as *Alfa Beta* (2005) resides squarely within issues of representation (of the self, as well as the North East), later works such as *Passage* (2006), *Nishan* (2007), *Noise Life* (2008) and *Residue* (2009–10), move beyond the mechanisms by which culture enacts itself (through references to archival documentation and the history of cinema) to display a complicated relationship with violence and control.

Alfa Beta consists of spliced-together pirated footage from director Mani Shankar's Bollywood film *Tango Charlie* (2005)[29] which was banned in the North East for its controversial portrayal of the Bodo ethnic community in Assam, and Dinesh Gogoi's *Surya Tejor Anya Naam* (Sun Is Blood's Other Name, 1991),[30] an Assamese film that sympathized with the insurgents and was also subsequently banned by the government. 'I wanted to expose all the clichés associated with this region,' says Madhukaillya of the work. The video also includes found archival photographs as well as raw footage from a handheld camera that catches partial glimpses of the artist's portrait and surrounding urban environment in order to develop an epistemological relationship between private and social histories.

By subsequently preferring to portray abstract and perceptual processes to communicate their inner lives rather than showcase any visible signifiers of violence, the artists excavate a repressed public life through their own private experiences and symptoms of fear. Madhukaillya asks, 'What is the construction of India? Which community do I belong to? I need to recognize my symptoms; it is a form of therapy. I am looking for an expanded, formless time.' This search for timelessness and the process of recognizing neurotic symptoms on an individual level is not unlike Kanwar's own self-interrogation in his early film *A Season Outside* (1997). By speaking in the first person, Kanwar turns the documentary into a set of deliberations on violence and non-violence in the Indian subcontinent, cast against the biography of his own family at the time of the Partition of India/ creation of East and West Pakistan in 1947. However, whereas Kanwar often utilizes different styles of text (prose in this case) to speak for the subject, Jain and Madhukaillya opt for a non-textual strategy. Underneath the thin veneer of their images, the subject is disembodied and unidentifiable, no longer engaged with any autobiographical elements. The move away from representation (expression or meaning) to production (process or usage) in the artists' modus operandi also undergirds *Anti-Oedipus*. Hardt explains: 'In *Anti-Oedipus*, expression is related to representation and signification, and thus it designates precisely what is not immanent to the term or thing. ... As such expression is the primary enemy of production.'[31] For Jain and Madhukaillya, this philosophy of focusing on process and usage instead of the nuances of expression is of the utmost importance.

The artists' new work *Residue* is framed from the perspective of the schizophrenic. 'The human, the machinic, and the natural are all one,' says Hardt. 'The first great advantage of the schizophrenic is its recognition of this unity.'[32] In *Residue*, this unity is proclaimed through a series of shots in and around a redundant coal power plant in the outskirts of Guwahati. The plant was abandoned due to the high costs of production, which outweighed the beneficial outcome in electric output. The history of the Assam agitation is closely entwined with the control and flow of natural resources such as coal and oil. The artists recall the time when the gross domestic product (GDP) of Assam in pre-Independence India was higher than the rest of the country, whereas it has now assumed a negative value owing to the lack of royalties due from oil lobbies in the city of Kolkata in neighbouring West Bengal. Composed in 16 mm film and transferred to digital video, *Residue* embodies several key notions found within *Anti-Oedipus* and distils them to an essence. Nestled within an encroaching forest, the power plant lies dormant. The artists focus our attention on the generative and regenerative processes of nature as it slowly claims its ground. A machine turns into a butterfly. At times the camera zooms in on meters that lie powerless at zero watts. At other times these machines assume anthropomorphic qualities and quasi-human forms. Madhukaillya states:

> I am interested in constructed signs that can never be replicated or remembered and in the relationship between matter and memory. I am also interested in endless circularity, in unbearable silence – the pause – and in looking at other possibilities of the site. In the end, it is a perception-image.

In this no man's land of continual flux, capital is unable to reterritorialize.

A related work, *Trespassers Will Be Prosecuted* (2008/10), is a multi-layered sound installation that is currently being remodelled into a site-specific intervention for the Deutsche Guggenheim presentation of *Being Singular Plural*. The work consists of a number of speakers with ambient and directional sounds that interact with passers-by. The sounds are drawn from the sacred forests of Mawphlang in the North East state of Meghalaya. According to local animistic beliefs, spirits or 'U Ryngew U Basa' guard the area, and the taking of any objects from the forest or the destruction of plant or animal life is taboo. By lifting sound recordings from the forest and inserting them into the consumerist space of the street, the artists run the risk of 'trespassing' the sacred area. These autonomous, isolated sounds exist beyond agency. Through suggestive recall, the sounds will, in the artists' words, 'summon false memories' of a pre-urban natural existence and effectively displace passers-by at the Berlin venue into a faraway forest. 'Circulation – or eternity', says Nancy,

> goes in all directions, but it moves only insofar as it goes from one point to another; spacing is its absolute condition. From place to place, and from moment to moment, without any progression or linear path, bit by bit and case by case, essentially accidental, it is singular and plural in its very principle. It does not have a final fulfilment any more than it has a point of origin.[33]

The moving-image works presented in this exhibition, like life itself, are a compendium of endless static moments without origin or completion, and which point only to the relentless unfolding of immanence, of the 'now'.

केन्द्रीय फ़िल्म प्रमाणन बोर्ड
CENTRAL BOARD OF FILM CERTIFICATION

Certificate Detail

Film Name	: VIKRAM VEDHA	**Links for more information**
Language	: Hindi	
Duration	: 139.55 MM.SS	Synopsis of the movie
Applicant Name	: GOLDMINES TELEFILMS PVT LTD- MUMBAI	
Producers	: GOLDMINES TELEFILMS PVT LTD - MUMBAI	Cast and Credit Details
Name of Signatory	: Anurag Srivastava, CEO, CBFC, Mumbai	
Name of EO / PO	: Sheetal Tandel (E.O.)	

Endorsement

File No. : 1A012304201892563

Film Name : VIKRAM VEDHA (HINDI) (Color) (2-D)

Applied Running Time : 139.55 MM.SS

Cert No. DIL/2/175/2018-MUM Dated 24/05/2018

Insertions / Excisions/ Modifications carried out by the applicant to comply with the law in force **Duration (MM.SS)**

Cut No.	Description	Deleted	Replaced	Inserted
1	Muted the words "Gandhi" and "Ghodse" (as it is found defamatory)	00.00	00.00	00.00
2	Replaced the word "Bambai" with "Mumbai"	00.00	00.00	00.00
	Total :	00.00	00.00	00.00

Actual Duration of the film after the aforesaid deletions and replacements will be **139.55** MM.SS in 1 cassette(s).

9 Between Sedition and Seduction

Thinking Censorship in South Asia

2009

William Mazzarella and
Raminder Kaur

Insertions / Exclusions / Modifications carried out by the applicant to comply with the law in force

Cut No.	Description
1	Muted the words "Gandhi" and "Ghodse" (as it is found defamatory)
2	Replaced the word "Bambai" with "Mumbai"

'The harder one looks at censorship, the stranger it becomes', say Raminder Kaur and William Mazzarella. At one level censorship takes place almost clandestinely, conducted in the popular imagination by a 'nondescript functionary, seated at an anonymous desk in some minor alleyway of the corridors of power, wielding his pen and scissors with smug pedantry'. At another level, however, it is not just *in* but also *of* the public sphere. The censor's work is 'curiously dependent upon that which it would silence', not only structurally but also in terms of public morality, for 'a society without obscenity would no longer require censors'. As a result, 'no one pays the provocative word or image as much careful, detailed, even loving attention as the censor'. What this leads to is a curious duality: there seems to be a 'correlation between the regulation of cultural production and the proliferation of provocative forms'.

Referencing location-specific dimensions of religion and politics, Kaur and Mazzarella discuss how the cosmopolitan media establishment in South Asia has combined consumerism with religious nationalism in staging the contradictions of public culture within the ethos of globalization. Tracing the meta-history of censorship from the colonial era into the present, and scrutinizing popular forms of expression (cinema and print publications) banned or manipulated by the state under pressure by social conservatives and right-wing vigilantes, the authors narrate how national institutions strategically mediate between sacred and secular, public and private claims in the fraught realm of public culture.

A longer version of this essay appeared in Raminder Kaur and William Mazzarella, eds, *Censorship in South Asia: Cultural Regulation from Sedition to Seduction*, Bloomington: Indiana University Press, 2009. Republished with permission from Indiana University Press.

Keywords and Names

Babri Masjid/Ram Janmabhoomi violence, 1992, *Citizenship*, *Doordarshan*, *Emergency*, *Maoist movement (Nepal)*, *Modernism*, *Press censorship*, see Keywords at the back of this volume.

Images

pp. 158–59, 167: Instructions from the Central Board of Film Certification (CBFC) to producers of major films of 2018 listing sequences that needed to be cut, muted, or replaced with 'approved' content.
The Board's approach as something far more interventionist than merely that of 'certification' – as it gives clear instructions on what filmmakers need to do to get their certificates – also splits its duties into two halves: one is its public face, namely the certificate itself, and the other a confidential document listing the actual cuts that need to be made. These images are taken from *Vikram Vedha* (Hindi version of Tamil film directed by Pushkar-Gayathri, 2017) and *Kaala* (Tamil, directed by Pa. Ranjith, 2018).

Shutting Up/Shutting Down

Over the past two decades, politically-enabled censorship in South Asia has aggressively moved centre stage. The newly 'liberalizing' India of the 1990s and the newly 'globalized' India of the 2000s surged and stuttered across the line between the acceptable and unacceptable in public culture. The mid-1990s alone saw a veritable carnival of controversies. By way of example, one might point to the uproar in 1994 over the alleged obscenity of Madhuri Dixit's song-and-dance sequence, *Choli ke peeche kya hai?* (What lies behind the bodice?) in Subhash Ghai's film *Khalnayak*;[1] to Shekhar Kapur's *Bandit Queen* (1994) which ran afoul of caste sentiment, the film censor board and its real-life protagonist, outlaw-turned-parliamentarian Phoolan Devi;[2] to Mani Ratnam's feature *Bombay*, a dramatization of the Bombay riots of 1992–93, that managed to offend Hindu groups, Muslim groups and secular intellectuals alike; to the extraordinary intensity of protest (including one self-immolation) and policing that surrounded the Miss World 1996 pageant in Bangalore, an event traditionalists condemned as a form of 'cultural imperialism'; to the Bombay ban on Salman Rushdie's *The Moor's Last Sigh* (1995), which, in the wake of the national ban on *The Satanic Verses* (1989),[3] desecrated Indian political idols old and new by featuring a dog named Jawaharlal Nehru and an unflattering, thinly-veiled portrait of Maharashtrian strongman Bal Thackeray; to Mira Nair's feature adaptation of the *Kamasutra*, whose Hindi version was in 1997 subjected to more stringent cuts than its English-language equivalent;[4] to the cinema-smashing, homophobic protest, legal challenges and extra-legal harassment that greeted Canadian director Deepa Mehta's *Fire*, depicting an erotic relationship between married sisters-in-law in a traditional middle-class joint family, in 1998 – not to mention the direct physical violence that ended her first attempt at filming *Fire*'s successor *Water*,[5] set in colonial-era Banaras and focusing on the plight of Hindu widows, in 2000 before it had even properly begun.[6]

And that is just India. In November 2007, Pakistani President Pervez Musharraf's State of Emergency suspended the 1973 Constitution for a third time. Independent news stations were forced off the air, hundreds of protesting journalists and lawyers were arrested and the Supreme Court was stacked with clients of the regime. But this relatively dramatic move – in some ways reminiscent of the much more extended Emergency imposed by Indira Gandhi in India in 1975–77 – was not Musharraf's first experiment with censorship. Sporadic official interference with the media as well as 'disappearances' of media professionals had marked his rule since its beginnings in a 'bloodless' coup in 1999.[7] As in other parts of the world, the internet presents wholly new challenges to official regulation. 'Cyber-cops' working for the Pakistan Internet Exchange[8] assiduously filter pornography, blasphemy and 'anti-Islamic' content from online circuits. More generally, as Asad Ahmed shows,[9] Islamic orthodoxy is regularly asserted in the form of blasphemy accusations. Popular culture is by no means immune: Islamist parties have been involved in incidents such as the 2003 provincial banning of music by the pop band Junoon. And in the wake of the murder of three journalists in October of that year, self-censorship has exerted a tighter hold on the press.

Bangladesh emerged onto the world map of censorship when Taslima Nasreen's[10] Bengali novel *Lajja* (Shame, 1993), a response to the anti-Hindu riots in Bangladesh that followed the destruction of the Babri Masjid in India in 1992 by Hindu mobs, was banned in the same year. As with Salman Rushdie's *The Satanic Verses*, the banning of *Lajja* only heightened the adulation with which it was greeted in the 'liberal' West. Nasreen's more recent books, *Ko* and *Dwikhandito* (2003),[11] personal memoirs that identify the author's sexual partners in Bangladesh and West Bengal, have provoked lawsuits and bans in both cross-border regions. Nasreen had by then gone into exile after mass protests provoked by death threats from religious fundamentalists. She relocated to the West in 1994 when her Bangladeshi passport was revoked, returned to the subcontinent in 2004 to live in Kolkata, a city she called 'home', under a temporary renewable residence permit, but was pressurized by the West Bengal government to leave India in 2007 after similar threats from orthodox clerics demanding her expulsion and the burning of her books. In Nepal, two major incidents stand out since 1990 (prior to that year, under the Panchayat regime, strictly enforced press censorship prevailed). First, there was the deafening silence consequent upon the Narayanhiti massacre of 2001,[12] when the editor-in-chief, general manager and publisher of the Nepali language daily newspaper *Kantipur* were arrested for publishing an editorial by Baburam Bhattarai, the second-in-command of the Maoists, alleging that the king's brother Gyanendra[13] was implicated in the deaths.[14] Second, there was the more dispersed regime of press censorship imposed along with the State of Emergency from November 2001 until August 2002. While not as brutal as other Emergencies in the region, it involved comparable restrictions on the press: all pro-Maoist publications were raided and shut down the day before the Emergency was declared. As for Sri Lanka, censorship has generally focused on narratives about the prolonged civil war between the state and the separatist Liberation Tigers of Tamil Eelam.[15] While some aspects of President Chandrika Kumaratunga's[16] media censorship have now been revoked, it is still illegal to report on any proposed operations or military activity by the security forces, or on the acquisition of arms, ammunition or other equipment by the armed forces or the police.

The incidents we have listed here are only some of the best-known, most publicized controversies of recent years. By no means a comprehensive list, they nevertheless give some indication of the complex political and cultural terrain with which we are concerned. Our intention in bringing them together under the rubric 'South Asia' is to explore their commonalities in terms of a shared history of colonial subjugation, to account for their differences in terms of their locations in distinct national polities, and finally to examine the more recent connections and contestations brought about by regional liberalization in the 1990s and beyond. Even though the primary emphasis of this volume is on Indian materials, our underlying ambition is comparative.

The very fact that these and other similar controversies were taken up and circulated by the cosmopolitan media establishment in South Asia (and often beyond) is itself an important social fact. Superficially, part of what made them compelling as public dramas was the way that they seemed to stage the contradictions of South Asian public culture in an age of globalization, a period that combined effervescent consumerism with surging religious supremacism, communitarianism and ethno-nationalism. From the mid-1980s, and especially after 1991, the deregulation of consumer goods markets joined hands with an explosion in new commercial media. In the 1980s, India saw the expansion of colour television (already established in the rest of South Asia) and the coming of video and cable; in the 1990s, South Asians began absorbing the influence of transnational satellite broadcasting and the internet.

In this context, the relationship between the public interest and the interests of publicity inevitably became more complicated. Marketers, politicians, cultural producers and social movements all sought to establish a media presence and a profile, to realize the value-creating possibilities of these new affect-intensive fields of public identification, as well as to proclaim their dangers.[17] Structurally, the labile lure of what one might call 'profitable provocation' meant that the boundaries of public civility and decorum were constantly being challenged. Key areas included the public representation of sex, the supposed irrationality of religious appeals in an ostensibly secular democracy, and the line between legal and illegal forms of political action – this last paradigmatically represented by the popular rise of hypermasculinized, often violent political organizations like Bombay's Shiv Sena.[18]

With so much publicity, many of these controversies actually became less rather than more intelligible. The media reportage quickly imposed a kind of discursive hardening, a sort of dramaturgical standardization. It was the pre-scripted urban drama of cultural globalization, the overdetermined clash between the cosmopolitans and the localists, between modernity and tradition, iconically fungible and readymade for nightly summary on CNN. At the same time, it would certainly be a mistake to suggest that we might reach the 'truth' of these events by stripping away the 'distortions' and 'biases' imposed upon them by the media. These were struggles that, in a very fundamental way, lived and breathed in the media, found their distinctive forms and their conditions of possibility in the space provided by a particular configuration of media and publics.

From Censorship to Cultural Regulation

As with many social phenomena, the harder one looks at censorship, the stranger it becomes. At the most elementary level, it quickly becomes clear that the common understanding of censorship as the repressive action of states and state-sanctioned institutions will not get us very far. One might even say that there seems to be something of a correlation between the regulation of cultural production and the proliferation of provocative forms.

Repression first: By attending to censorship only as a matter of silencing and of denial, we risk missing what several scholars have identified as its productive aspects. On one level, we are referring here to the relatively obvious point that any kind of utterance or discourse, indeed the very possibility of language, depends upon a kind of constitutive foreclosure.[19] This foreclosure is, as Judith Butler argues, 'a kind of unofficial censorship or primary restriction in speech that constitutes the possibility of agency in speech'.[20] In this sense, censorship does not act upon a sovereign subject from 'outside'; rather, it is one of the very preconditions of the expression of subjectivity itself.

In practice, the relation between explicit and implicit forms of censorship is often ambiguous. We see this in Lakier's analysis of the self-censorship at work in the (lack of) representations of the massacre of Nepal's royal family in the indigenous media.[21] And Tejaswini Ganti shows how, in the world of Mumbai film production, self-censorship is inextricable from personal dispositions towards controversial themes.[22] An open question – both empirically and theoretically – is the extent to which the positive meanings allowed or encouraged by a certain linguistic or semiotic configuration are haunted by the possibilities that they must disavow, but which remain crucial to their intelligibility. By attending to the particular politics of disavowal that structure particular events or sites we may well understand something important about the dialectic of fascination and loathing that seems to characterize so much in the realm of censorship.

On another level, some have theorized censorship as productive according to a Foucauldian schema. Classically, we imagine the censor, as Dominic Boyer reminds us, as the very embodiment of the anti-intellectual.[23] The endangered act or enunciation (lively, inventive, poetic, audacious) confronts the complacent philistinism of the censor (sluggish, pedantic, literal-minded). But censorship may also be understood as a generative technology of truth. Far from only silencing, censorship can be read as a relentless proliferation of discourses on normative modes of desiring, of acting, of being in the world. Censorship, then, would be not so much a desperate rearguard action as a productive part of the apparatus of modern governmentality.[24] We find, for example, that the discourses on Indian women's sexuality that emerge out of censorship practices are internally contradictory in interesting ways.[25] Moreover, as many recent public controversies over obscenity in the media have demonstrated, these discourses are routinely brought up against equally normalizing but quite different narratives of Indian sexuality – the compulsory invocation and valorization, by 'cosmopolitan' critics of censorship, of Vatsyayana's *Kamasutra* and the erotic temple carvings at Khajuraho and Konarak as an integral part of South Asian civilizational heritage, is a case in point.[26]

Then there is the issue of censorship as the action of states or state-sanctioned institutions. This raises two questions. The first is one of location: Where is censorship? What are its sites? Where should we look for its logic and its motivation? Should we be examining the utterances and ideologies of those individuals authorized by states to intervene into the public field? To what extent does it make sense to say that the person who enacts censorship is better placed to comment on it than the person who is subjected to it? The Foucauldian commandment would of course encourage us, at the very least, to situate the deliberate utterances of practitioners within a wider institutional field. But what is the best way to discern the play of censorship in the textual traces left by its operation? How should we read the relationship between the carapace of case law and the relatively ephemeral rhythms of public debate?

The second question: What 'counts' as censorship? Are we stretching the term too far if we force it to accommodate not only the operations of official regulatory authorities (the courts, the police, censor boards), but also various 'extra-legal' or 'extra-constitutional' initiatives and interventions? Some critics, for example, speak of the 'silent censorship' that market forces (or, better, the social relations that are reified as such) exert on the contents of the media.[27] Does violent action against the screening of a film count as censorship? Or indeed any of the many 'non-violent' tactics by which activists in South Asia often seek to prevent particular events from unfolding – *bandh, hartal, dharna, gherao, morcha* and so forth?

What about the connections between legal and extra-legal forms of censorship? Does it matter if violent or non-violent 'extra-legal' protests are linked, either by alliance or overt sympathy, to those who in fact do control the official machinery of regulation? Such, for instance, was the case at the time of the Shiv Sena's agitations against Deepa Mehta's *Fire* in Bombay and Delhi in 1998. The smashing of theatres and intimidation of actors by the Shiv Sena, recently ousted from political power in Maharashtra, was greeted ambiguously by the national government. National political leaders deplored the 'lawlessness' of the violence, but regionally affiliated allies at the centre expressed solidarity with and approval of the Sena actions against a public product deemed an immoral denigration of 'Indian cultural values' by self-appointed custodians of 'Indian culture'. And the then-Minister for Information and Broadcasting was in fact, to the dismay of many, persuaded to return the film to the Censor Board for recertification (a practice that the Indian Supreme Court declared illegal in December 2000).

On occasion, conversely, the Indian Supreme Court has effectively acknowledged the social force of an unofficial ban. In mid-2006, after Aamir Khan, the lead actor in the feature film *Fanaa* (Annihilated) publicized his support for the rehabilitation of people displaced by the Narmada dam project in Gujarat, cinemas were subjected to violent, government-supported protests in that state.[28] Constitutionally-guaranteed freedom of expression was thus pitted against the repressive practices of a state government claiming to be acting in the interests of the people. The deadlock was only partly resolved when a public interest litigation filed in the Supreme Court yielded the verdict that while nothing could be done against the unofficial ban, individual theatres would receive protection if they decided to screen the film. In this way, in the language of the ruling, 'any untoward incident' might be avoided. Certainly, 'extra-legal' or 'extra-constitutional' forms of censorship, particularly when backed by local leaders, often seem to carry more social force than official decrees.

Censorship is not just *in* but also *of* the public sphere. The censor's work is generally figured as semi-clandestine, shy of – indeed perhaps structurally opposed to – publicity. We might imagine a nondescript functionary, seated at an anonymous desk in some minor alleyway of the corridors of power, wielding his pen and scissors with smug pedantry (and, yes, it does seem to us that the

केन्द्रीय फ़िल्म प्रमाणन बोर्ड
CENTRAL BOARD OF FILM CERTIFICATION

Certificate Detail

Film Name	: KAALA	**Links for more information**
Language	: Tamil	
Duration	: 162.48 MM.SS	Synopsis of the movie
Applicant Name	: Dhanush Kasthooriraja- CHENNAI(WUNDERBAR FILMS PVT LTD)	
Producers	: DHANUSH KASTHOORIRAJA - CHENNAI(WUNDERBAR FILMS PVT LTD)	Cast and Credit Details
Name of Signatory	: M Leela Meenatchi, RO, CBFC, Chennai	
Name of EO / PO	: M Leela Meenatchi (E.O.)	

Endorsement

File No. : 1A032203201805325

Film Name : KAALA (TAMIL) (Color) (2-D)

Applied Running Time : 167.40 MM.SS

Cert No. DIL/2/38/2018-Che Dated 02/04/2018

Insertions / Excisions/ Modifications carried out by the applicant to comply with the law in force **Duration (MM.SS)**

Cut No.	Description	Deleted	Replaced	Inserted
1	Muted the word 'Arasu' in Shot No.63. (Reel 1) (Defamation)	00.00	00.00	00.00
2	Muted the word 'Kundi'. (Shot 202) (Reel 1) (Public decency)	00.00	00.00	00.00
3	Muted the word 'Yerikkavum' in the dialogue 'Engala miditcha thookki pottu yerikkavum theriyum. (Shot 223) (Reel 1) (Defamation)	00.00	00.00	00.00
4	Removed the dialogue 'Raanuva veerargalukku katra paadaiyila irundhu'. (Shot Nos.263, 264) (Reel 3) (Defamation)	00.02	00.00	00.00
5	Muted the word 'Cheri'. (Shot 302) (Reel 3) (Defamation)	00.00	00.00	00.00
6	Trimmed the visuals of hitting a person with Umbrella in Shot Nos.171,172 & 173. (Reel 4) (Violence)	00.01	00.00	00.00
7	Deleted the word 'Muslim'. (Shot 23) (Reel 5) (Religious)	00.01	00.00	00.00
8	Muted the word 'Saala' in Reel 5 & 6. (twice) (Public decency)	00.00	00.00	00.00
9	Distorted the visual of pork head in Shot Nos.9,10 & 11. (Reel 8) (Religious)	00.00	00.00	00.00
10	Muted the word 'Thulukkan'. (Shot 26) (Reel 8) (Religious)	00.00	00.00	00.00
11	Muted the word 'Naaye' in the dialogue 'Policekaara naaye' in Shot No.44. (Reel 8) (Defamation)	00.00	00.00	00.00
12	Removed & Replaced the visual of hitting Valiappan with the rod in Shot No.174. (Reel 8) (violence)	00.03	00.03	00.00
13	Removed the visual of Lenin hitting the other person in Shot No.190. (Reel 8) (violence)	00.05	00.00	00.00
14	Trimmed the shots from 90 to 95 which is related to the visuals of Police removing the dress of the girl Puyal. (Reel 8) (vulgarity)	00.02	00.00	00.00
15	Trimmed by 20% the fight sequence in the climax. (Reel 8) (violence)	00.18	00.00	00.00
16	Removed & Replaced the ticker 'Pakistan beat India' which was shown in the TV channel. (Reel 8) (Defamation)	00.02	00.02	00.00
17	Removed & Replaced the visuals of showing Police burning the vehicles in Shot No.82 & later in news clipping. (Reel 8) (Defamation)	00.17	00.05	00.00
	Total :	00.51	00.10	00.00

Total Deletions at the Time of Examination : **00.51** MM.SS

Total Replacement at the time of Examination : **00.10** MM.SS

Actual Duration of the film after the aforesaid deletions and replacements will be **166.59** MM.SS in 1 cassette(s).

censor, despite all evidence to the contrary, is generically imagined as a man). But censorship, as we have suggested, often actually courts the full glare of publicity. And its agents are by no means always impersonal bureaucrats. Moreover, the censor's work is, it turns out, curiously dependent upon that which it would silence. Not just structurally – a society without obscenity would no longer require censors – but also sensuously: no one pays the provocative word or image as much careful, detailed, even loving attention as the censor.

We are all familiar with this compulsive dependency from the drama of legal process, where the forbidden word must be aired again and again precisely to establish its unspeakability and reinforce its malignity. And we recognize it in marketing strategies that court bans in order to heighten the desirability of a product by marking it as controversial. Official censors will themselves often dismiss the indignant objections of their 'victims' as nothing but publicity stunts. Directors Shekhar Kapur in the field of commercial cinema (*Bandit Queen*; *Elizabeth*) and Anand Patwardhan in that of political documentary (*Father, Son and Holy War*; *War and Peace*) have both been accused of this in recent years.[29]

In this age of liberalization and proliferating media, the singular centralized authority of government film censorship is increasingly coming to be supplemented by self-regulatory councils and professional advisory bodies, such as the Advertising Standards Council of India[30] and the Press Council of India.[31] Such independent organizations respond to and act upon public complaints against already circulating images and texts. But when it comes to the cinema, there has long been a sense that pre-censorship is necessary. The Government of India's Central Board of Film Certification retains the tradition established in 1920 when the first regional film censor boards were founded: moving images are censored before they reach the viewing public.

Richard Burt points out that censorship sometimes even becomes quite flamboyant, as keen and as media-savvy a participant in the great game of publicity as its ostensible quarry.[32] In this mode, censorship competes quite keenly for the conviction and attention of its publics. 'Censorship not only legitimates discourses by allowing them to circulate, but is itself part of a performance, a simulation in which censorship can function as a trope to be put on show.'[33] Book-burning, then, is not simply about getting rid of the books, but equally about 'staging an opposition between corrupting and purifying forces and agencies'.[34] This publicity-seeking side of censorship is evident across the spectrum of regulatory action. Few cultural protests, whether on the left or the right, whether peaceful or incendiary, commence these days before newspaper and television reporters are in place, and before press releases have been distributed. But the official organs of censorship are equally conscious of the need to perform their efficacy and their relevance through compliant agents. When film actor Anupam Kher[35] took over as chairman of the Central Board of Film Certification in India in late 2003, the board was quick to promote a new clampdown on indecency in Hindi film-song remix videos and film trailers on television.

All this points to the fact that any claim to authority or power via regulatory action in the field of public culture necessarily involves some kind of active participation in the poetics and politics of publicity. Calculated interventions into the play of publicity – in the name of protecting the sentiments or cultural integrity of a particular constituency – are now a standard feature of contemporary South Asian politics. Such forms of 'censorship' – calling for the withdrawal or ban of this or that film, book, image or newspaper article – are obviously not just silencing tactics; rather they rely, for their political efficacy, on harnessing and mobilizing the public energy of the very artefacts that they appear to be trying to suppress. It is not surprising that such wagers on mass attention should be a matter of some ambivalence. The ideal of communicative rationality in public debate frowns upon the affective, spectacular tactics of publicity – the performance of this distinction becomes particularly evident during elections, when candidates' speeches are closely monitored for potential boundary-breachings. Publicity is by definition an affect-intensive game. It touches upon the embodied and the intimate; its mode of persuasion is one of affective resonance. It often seems dangerously close to disorder and chaos, to the nightmare transformation of the enlightened democratic public into the rampaging crowd. But this ambivalent aesthetics is, we are suggesting, the condition of any effective appeal to identification and authority. Public culture may be seen, then, as a field of contest between competing experiments, often improvised and volatile, with the profitable/productive harnessing of this volatile substance. That such experiments, sometimes extraordinarily compelling to their constituencies, are always inconclusive, provisional and even dangerous, goes without saying.

The affective intensity of images and the unstable corporeal energy of volatile public participation are captured in Jean-Francois Lyotard's notion of the 'figural'; the censored objects scrutinized as speech acts or texts are closer, perhaps, to Lyotard's notion of 'discourse'.[36] Our aim is not to pre-judge the relation between image and text in the work of censorship, but rather to offer a provocative juxtaposition of situations that, taken together, might open up new ways of thinking about the libidinal economies of South Asian public cultures.

From one perspective, censorship seems designed to moderate the excessive force or perceived violence that such experiments in public cultural action may involve, as in the case of 'hate speech', 'obscenity' and – a particularly important one in India – incitement to communal violence.[37] But from another perspective, censorship also seems to routinize transgression. Michael Taussig, developing Elias Canetti's aphorism about the secret at the heart of power,[38] argues that social orders are based on 'public secrets': that is, forms of knowledge and/or representation that are generally, even obsessively, known precisely insofar as they must not be overtly acknowledged.[39] Everyday social dynamics, then, depend upon the institutionalization or management of transgression, the normalization of a system of taboos and their breaking. In India, this dynamic has recently become particularly evident around the phenomenon of the screen kiss. For the first fifty years of Independence, Indian commercial filmmakers rigorously observed an unwritten (but nevertheless incessantly discussed) 'ban' on hero-heroine kissing. The prohibition began to be breached with some regularity in the 1990s, but always with a *frisson* that effectively reinstated the power of the prohibition. Director Govind Menon's Hindi romance *Khwahish* (Desire, 2003)[40] was marketed primarily on the premise that it contained seventeen kissing scenes; meanwhile, critics complained that Indian actors looked 'unnatural' and 'awkward' kissing in films; and via an avid film press, female stars keen to be seen as respectable tactically publicized their visceral dislike of screen kissing.[41]

Madhava Prasad has developed an interesting argument about the prohibition on the screen kiss being an index of the impossibility of a bourgeois space of conjugal privacy and intimacy in the context of a social order that continues in large measure to idealize a patriarchal-feudal model of the family and, by extension, of social relations in general. It might be assumed that such idealization, internalized as the social 'norm', found expression in the collective assault on Mehta's film *Fire*, where taboo sexuality radically disrupts conjugal patterns within the bourgeois household.[42] We do think that the question of the intimate and its possible relations to public culture is crucial. But we are also interested in exploring the ways in which the compulsive assertion and foregrounding of a prohibition serves to routinize a pattern of incitement, a fraught relation of desire and transgression. Here, too, censorship is not only or even primarily a mechanism of denial and repression; rather, it serves to articulate an equivocal language of the concealed and the revealed in which everything is 'out in the open' even if it is not 'shown'. We are of course well aware of this dynamic when it comes to marketing or to show business: the strategic deployment of the tease, of provocation as a means of focusing attention, realizing profits and attracting audiences. However, mainstream politics is no less performative, no less dependent upon a volatile calculus of provocation and respectability, defiance and dignity.[43]

Independence and Ambivalence

The coming of Indian Independence in 1947, with the parallel creation of West and East Pakistan, was marked by a characteristic ambivalence vis-à-vis public culture. On the one hand, the very fact of an Indian nation state was supposed, by definition, to mark the historical overcoming of the split between 'inner' and 'outer' domains.[44] On the other hand, the Nehruvian formula for secularism,[45] convinced of its universal validity, imposed a stringent filter on what kind of affect-intensive, embedded representations and practices would be allowed to participate in public culture. These two faces of Nehru are evident in his own writings. There is the Nehru who, with some eloquence, sought in his *Glimpses of World History* (1934) and in prison writings like *The Discovery of India* (1946) to fuse a world-historical rapprochement between the commandments of modernity and the density of Indian tradition.[46] But, as noted by Shashi Tharoor, there is also the Nehru who exasperatedly writes to a (Muslim) friend that all Indians should be required to immerse themselves in the rationalist atheism of Bertrand Russell.[47]

Freitag observes that the consolidation of a nationalist visual repertoire around the turn of the twentieth century made patriotism the new mediator between the sacred and the profane.[48] This mediation was, as Arvind Rajagopal describes, predicated upon a political compromise between the secular nationalist leadership and the custodians of cultural/religious tradition.[49] Its resolution was projected onto the future, onto the moment of Independence. For that reason, the actual achievement of Independence brought the leadership of the new nation face to face with the need to make good on the promise of integrating prosaic policy with the transcendent truth of the nation often informally deployed as a punitive parallel code of 'law'.

Under Nehru, Republic Day parades, government craft emporia, official cultural festivals and other government-staged events and spectacles harnessed a state-driven and rigorously secularized understanding of 'Indian tradition' to the great projects of modernization and development.[50] At the same time Nehru famously referred to his monuments of modernism, the hydroelectric dams and the steel mills as the 'temples' of modern India,[51] thus perhaps also acknowledging the potential for a serious affective deficit at the heart of the developmentalist dispensation. The question was never simply one of whether secularism should mean a complete evacuation of religious commitments from public life or, alternatively, a pluralistic recognition of religious values in political and legal processes.[52] Rather, as a formally empowered cultural regulator, the state after Independence always struggled with the tension between a recognition of the importance of an affective grounding for any successful polity and a fear of what such an affective grounding might mean in practice for a self-consciously 'modern' and 'developing' nation, particularly vis-à-vis sentiments and commitments that might be defined as 'religious'. After Nehru's death in 1964, this early dilemma became a justification both for a stream of attacks, from the right, on the supposed cultural inauthenticity and alienation of the Nehruvian model (Nehru as the 'last Englishman'), and for the increasingly assiduous manipulation of communal 'vote-banks' by national political leaders.[53]

Much has been written on the stunning expansion of commercial entertainment-based television in India in the 1980s – how it brought together, in a volatile compact around the affect-intensive television image, a range of new middle-class aspirations, the blandishments of consumerism and a mass acceptance for an overtly and frequently aggressive religious nationalism.[54] From a regulatory point of view, these were, in some ways, peculiar days.[55] In the form of the state television service, Doordarshan,[56] the government retained sole proprietorship over this boisterously mushrooming medium, constantly striving to reconcile its habituated 'fear of the image'[57] with highly profitable content that was often lustily corporeal. With programming increasingly farmed out to the private sector but control still centralized in the hands of the government, television in the 1980s became a kind of tug-of-war between state and commercial interests.[58]

But it also doubled as a laboratory for new experiments in cultural regulation. By this we mean not only the often heavy-handed blackouts that Doordarshan imposed on particular news items or on the doings and sayings of political critics. We are also thinking of experiments in the profitable mass mobilization of affect, whether commercial, religious or political. Indeed, one of the defining features of this period, as many have noted, was the increasing televisual interpenetration of devotional viewing, political propaganda and consumer goods advertising.

These developments laid the foundations for the media scandals listed at the start of this essay. Today the dawning consumerism and televisual politics of the 1980s are almost invariably read as a prequel to the full-tilt tryst with liberalization that started with the economic reforms of 1991. In subscribing to this teleology, however, we may miss something equally, if not more important about the new televisual dispensation: namely, the ways in which it was a response to the failure of Indira Gandhi's experiment with dictatorship during the Emergency of 1975–77.[59] In histories of the media, the Emergency has come to stand as the exception that proves the rule of Indian democratic freedom, and as an object lesson in the political dangers of censorship. After all, the story goes, was it not precisely Mrs Gandhi's totalizing approach to information control that isolated her from 'public opinion' to such a degree that she mistakenly believed that she would have no trouble winning the national election in 1977?

The style of information management that prevailed during the Emergency was exceptionally heavy-handed. Press materials generally had to be submitted for pre-screening under official categories such as 'pre-censorship', 'news management' and the starkly simple 'banned'. As Soli Sorabjee[60] notes, although overt political critique was of course almost impossible, the restrictions also extended to such topics as strikes, the nuclear programme, reports on family planning/vasectomy follow-up centres, and even the arrest of legendary Hindi film actress Nargis[61] for shoplifting in London.[62] Under the Defence of India Rules and the Maintenance of Internal Security Act,[63] thousands were jailed and silenced, and – in a kind of perfect sovereign recursivity – any reference to censorship in the media was itself banned. Troubling bodies were incarcerated (political opponents, editors, activists) or physically transferred (recalcitrant judges); power supply to newspapers was cut; and a comprehensive range of 'directives' were issued to the media from Samachar, the central government news agencies.[64] Mrs Gandhi's son and heir apparent, Sanjay, is said to have personally demanded substantial cash 'contributions' in return for permission to premier new films in the capital.

To be sure, although Mrs Gandhi's second period in office (1980–84) did see some highly controversial blanket bans on media reportage during regional eruptions of political turmoil (for example in Punjab and in Assam), the crudely repressive measures of the Emergency were not repeated in India. But by identifying these crude tactics with censorship *per se*, there is a risk of losing sight of some of the subtler forms of cultural regulation that were developed in tandem with the expansion of the commercial media in the early- to mid-1980s. As Shiv Visvanathan puts it, the Emergency was not so much an embarrassing aberration as 'a pilot plant, a large scale trial for the totalitarianisms and emergencies that were to come later'.[65] One could argue that cultural regulation under the sign of liberalization, particularly after Mrs Gandhi's assassination in late 1984, required a rapid reinterpretation of the kind of state-centric authoritarian populism that the Emergency had come to typify.

Emphatically consigning Mrs Gandhi to a superseded past, mere months after her death, was of course never going to be an easy or an uncontested process.[66] As a project, it involved something far more comprehensive than the dismissal of the Emergency as a historical anomaly, a dismissal that she herself had already propounded during her last years in office. Rather, what was required was the impression of a more dispersed affective field, one not so tightly cathected onto the singular image of the charismatic leader. The new, liberalized mode of citizenship was one in which the energies of public participation should be seen as coming from below rather than from the 'commanding heights' of the Planning Commission. It located the nation's destiny less in the heroic agency of a leader and more in the embodied and embedded impulses of everyday life. The language of faith and tradition, of consumerist desire, and of regionally chauvinist identifications might still at times trouble the sovereignty of the national project, but they attained, in this period, a new image of authenticity, the dignity of affective truth as compared to the alienating abstractions and the grand schemes of the Nehru years.

We are certainly not suggesting that liberalization in fact brought about some kind of authentically democratic revival. Rather, what is visible in debates over the media from this period is a diffuse consciousness, expressed in many different idioms by many different interest groups, of a tension between sovereignty and control in public communications, and an increasingly complex set of claims on representation and recognition in public culture. At times, the government clamped down and silenced dissent in the old, crude way. At other times, however, the myriad voices emerging from inside and around the government seemed to be advocating the possibility of a more subtle co-optation, one in which consumer choice, religious assertion and regional pride might perhaps still be harnessed to a collective national project. By the same token, of course, the legitimacy of the state as the final arbiter in public cultural matters, in matters of value, identity and desire was increasingly being called into question. After Bollywood star Manisha Koirala decided that she had been deceived by director Shashilal Nair in the making of *Ek Chhoti Si Love Story* (A Little Love Story, 2002) through the insertion of provocative, partially nude scenes featuring a body double,[67] her actions reflected a perfect understanding of the ambiguities and ambiguous reaches of the new dispensation. Hedging her bets, she appealed in quick succession to the Censor Board, to the Ministry of Information and Broadcasting, and to Shiv Sena chief Bal Thackeray, for justice.

Messy, Unequal, Trans-local ... and Real

We are now in a very different situation from that which prevailed in the 1980s. Strategies of regulation have diversified in proportion to the proliferation of new media. The coming of commercial satellite television in the early 1990s has shifted television away from state control. In response, government has sought to reassert its authority. In addition to making regular - if relatively ineffectual - noises about bringing television directly under the authority of the Central Board of Film Certification, a 2006 decision of the Mumbai High Court made it illegal for any television station broadcasting in India to screen films with 'A' (for audiences aged 18 and above) censor certificates. The liberalization and globalization of consumer markets has intensified competition in the field of visual publicity, requiring Indian advertisers to 'keep up' with international benchmarks in profitable provocation. And the increasing regionalization of both television and the press has allowed a far wider range of local identities to find their aspirations and their reification in the mass media.

At the time of the TV *Ramayana* in the late 1980s,[68] controversy raged around the fact that Doordarshan, the broadcast medium of a self-avowedly secular state, was both presiding over and profiting from such blatantly 'religious' content.[69] In response to this accusation, Philip Lutgendorf reminds us that recitations and performances of the epics have always enjoyed and depended upon political patronage in India.[70] And one could even add that from a certain perspective, the landscape of the 1990s and after might even look like a return to something like a pre-modern diversity of cultural patrons and publics, each presiding over their own regional turf, their own chosen 'traditions'. But what such an analysis would miss, in its neoliberal enthusiasm, is the tension that persists between a diversity of claimants to cultural sovereignty and the singular regulatory authority represented by the state and, in particular, by the language and institutions of the law. We are all familiar with this tension as it pertains to the antinomies and limits of liberalism. One thinks, for example, of the Shah Bano case of 1986,[71] which pitted a particularist appeal to Muslim personal law against the putative universalism of the Uniform Civil Code.

This is also a question of publics and the forms of media that constitute them. It has become *de rigueur* to insist that we have transcended the age of 'the masses', and that the diversification of markets and media have consigned the age of standardization and massification to the dustbin of history. But in South Asia, such a diversification continues to coexist with a developmentalist narrative which constitutes precisely 'the masses' as the prime beneficiaries of state action, both redistributive and regulatory. It is 'the masses' that are the objects (and intended future subjects) of the process of modernization. And it is 'the masses' that may most typically be injured or misled by provocative, obscene or seditious public communications. On the one hand, we may sympathize with Ashis Nandy's call for an approach to Indian politics that captures the messiness, ambiguity and unpredictability that a more rationalist *Realpolitik* elides.[72] And certainly an ethnographic approach would seem to be ideally suited to such a pursuit. On the other hand, we would suggest that the politics of cultural regulation are played out at the intersection between pragmatist politics of the concrete and the reified terms of administration.

This tension also plays itself out as a crisis of temporality. Against the perpetual 'not yet' of Third World Time, the permanent deferral of the full realization of modernity, the big movements of the last couple of decades have all been premised on a big immediacy, on a sensuous immersion. This dream of immediacy is present in the often-violent identitarian politics of regional and religious chauvinism, in the promise of instant consumerist gratification, and in the fullness of devotional absorption upon which contemporary political spectacle is so often premised.

We began with the juxtaposition of censorship and publicity, in order to ask what it might mean that practices of cultural regulation seem to have become so central to contemporary South Asian public cultures. We suggest that this is not only a matter of what does or does not 'go into' public circulation, but also points to the political centrality of discourses on and around practices of regulation. Regulation is self-reflexive: it cannot help but articulate the terms and foundations of its own legitimacy. For this reason, regulation is performative too: the silencing gesture is not only often quite public, but also simultaneously invokes and supports an entire socio-cultural dispensation.

The conventional language that attaches to censorship and its refusal – 'security', 'freedom of speech', 'diversity', 'choice' and so forth – must itself be read as a political technology that helps to negotiate what we referred to earlier as the tension between the public interest and the interests of publicity. Naturally, in an era of globalization and rapidly exploding commercial media networks, the stakes of profitable provocation are immeasurably heightened. But it is absolutely crucial that we understand the politics of the relationship between a generalized discourse on censorship and the specificities of long-standing local histories of media and performance. This is never simply a matter of 'localizing' abstract or universalizing claims. Rather, cultural regulation is in some sense the attempt to forge an authoritative relationship between the energy of embedded and embodied phenomena and that of trans-local categories distributed along a much wider arc of normativity.

Typically, mainstream discussions of censorship in South Asia, as elsewhere, are stolidly steadfast in declaring censorship a 'bad thing'. We would agree that the repressive aspects of censorship do need to be noted. It is perfectly possible to acknowledge, in a Foucauldian mode, the perverse productivity of various forms of cultural regulation while still recognizing that censorship does silence even as it speaks. But the interesting question is not '*Censored ke peeche kya hai?*' (What lies behind the censored?). Rather, our hope is to indicate that there is nothing self-evident about censorship, nor about the worlds it makes. Censorship is not merely a constant forge of discourse; nor is it only a ruthless mechanism of silencing. As a generative gamble, cultural regulation is, for all its apparently routinized banality, an uncertain, affect-laden and open-ended venture. In that paradoxical instability/predictability lies its fascination, and its importance as a node for cultural analysis. We hope that readers will dwell with the censors, look twice, and refuse to grant them the obviousness to which they aspire.

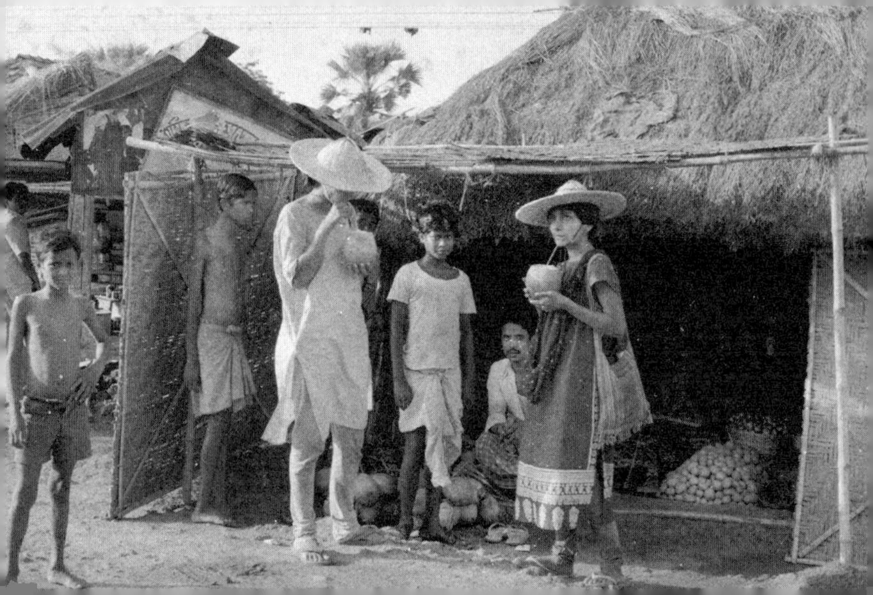

10 Mimicking Anthropologists

Re-Membering a Photo Archive via *Pata* Paintings, Performative Mimesis and Photo-Performance

2019

I Parul Dave Mukherji

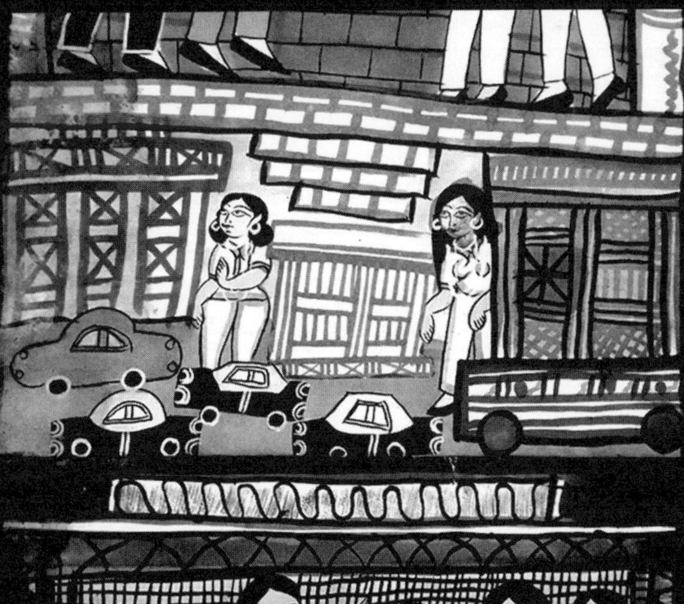

In 1985, art students Parul Dave Mukherji, **Pushpamala N.** (see Keywords) and Ayisha Abraham travelled to a village in Bengal to photo-document the art of renowned *pata* (folk scroll) painter, Dukhshyam Chitrakar. As part of their training they also lived with the community for some days. Much later, Pushpamala scrawled 'Visiting Anthropologists!' on the back of one of the photographs, providing the catalyst for Dave Mukherji's provocative inquiry. Revisiting that experience using the photographs Pushpamala discovered decades later in her personal archive, the author raises sharp questions about the ethnographic turn in art practice, the ethics of artistic intervention and the limits of participant observation as an anthropological method. The images further engage in the radical act of what she terms 'performative mimesis' – Dukhshyam returning the ethnographic gaze through a commissioned *pata* scroll depicting his vision of the city and the three researchers in a contemporary urban pedagogical environment.

An earlier version of this essay was published in Sasanka Perera and Dev Nath Pathak, eds, *Intersections of Contemporary Art: Anthropology and Art History in South Asia: Decoding Visual Worlds*, Palgrave Macmillan, 2019. Reprinted with permission of the author.

Keywords/Names

Adivasi, Navjot Altaf, Mulk Raj Anand, Faculty of Fine Arts Maharaja Sayajirao University Baroda, Festivals of India, Marg, Modernism, Pushpamala N., Gulammohammed Sheikh, see Keywords at the back of this volume.

Images

p. 178: Pushpamala and Parul Dave Mukherji sipping coconut water in front of a vegetable shop in Naya Village, Midnapore, 1985. Photographer unknown. Image courtesy Pushpamala N.

pp. 179, 193: Dukhshyam Chitrakar, The documentation scroll. *Our arrival in Calcutta and our negotiations with the city traffic to catch a bus to visit the Naya Village, Midnapore, West Bengal, India,* 1985. Image courtesy Parul Dave Mukherji.

p. 185: Pushpamala N., *The Ethnographers #1*, 2017. Village Naya, Midnapore District, West Bengal. Colour photograph printed from a scanned 1985 negative on aluminium compressed panel, 40 x 60 inches. Photographer unknown. Image courtesy Pushpamala N.

p. 189: Pushpamala N., *The Ethnographers #2*, 2017. Village Naya, Midnapore District, West Bengal. Colour photograph printed from a scanned 1985 negative on aluminium compressed panel, 40 x 60 inches. Photographer unknown. Image courtesy Pushpamala N.

p. 197: *The Native Types/Toda*, from the project *Native Women of South India: Manners and Customs* (2000–04). Pushpamala N. in collaboration with Clare Arni. Image courtesy Pushpamala N.

In 1985, as a graduate student of the Faculty of Fine Arts, Maharaja Sayajirao University, Baroda[1], I was part of a research trip and visited Naya Village in Midnapore district of West Bengal to document the art and life of Dukhshyam Chitrakar.[2] He was a *patua* (folk scroll painter)[3] who lived in this village, located about 130 kilometres from Calcutta (now Kolkata). I was accompanied by two researchers along with two of my friends from the same art school, Pushpamala N. and Ayisha Abraham,[4, 5] who were later on going to embrace photography in their own practice in interesting ways. This visit was part of a documentation project mentored by Professor Gulammohammed Sheikh,[6] head of the painting department at M.S. University, established in 1949 as India's first postcolonial art school. Its aim was to address the existent wide gulf between folk artists and art school-trained artists and art historians. While our textual and photo documentation were submitted to the painting department on our return, the photographs were subsumed into archival oblivion as subsequently our little group dispersed into the pursuit of individual careers. Only recently were these decades-old images 'excavated', through Pushpamala's chance discovery of their negatives in her personal collection. When developed, they elicited a powerful response from us – not only suddenly returning us back in time to our younger selves, but also for confronting us with the dramatic contrast between the folk artist/his extended family and us, the urban trio in a 'native' context.[7] This stark visual difference prompted Pushpamala to scribble 'Visiting Anthropologists!' on the back of one of the photographs.

In this essay, I deploy Pushpamala's self-mocking, parodic descriptor as a heuristic device to stage a conversation between the 'real', almost always European and male, colonial-era anthropologists who followed particular parameters and set a particular pedagogical tradition, and us 'brown', female, 'visiting' anthropologists attempting to deconstruct that methodology in a postcolonial context. In parallel, I explore questions raised by these excavated photographs that had triggered a self-reflexive opportunity to see a possible connection between our collective ethnographic experience and our individual trajectories in the field of art history and art practice.[8] How does one revisit this past moment of an earlier research 'visit' through memory and visual trace, and re-engage with the questions of difference across various registers such as the urban–rural, folk artist–urban artist/art historian, among other divides? What does it mean to document folk art across various modes of unequal relationship between the 'Visiting Anthropologists' and their 'native others', and to consider the impact of this encounter on Pushpamala's later project *Native Women of South India* and on my interest in the concept of performative mimesis?[9] Can this encounter serve as a prism through which to diffract major questions about the experiential and discursive interfaces between art history, contemporary art practice and anthropology?

The first section of this essay attempts to set up a conversation between art history and visual anthropology via a specific genre of group photography that features in every anthropologist's fieldwork documentation. This genre is further narrowed to group photos in which the anthropologist is also present posing with the 'natives'. Using a cross-disciplinary lens, I offer a close formalistic analysis of these group photographs to try and understand the implacable asymmetries between 'them' and 'us' - something that we did not contemplate at the time the photographs were taken in Naya Village, and paid full attention to only after we encountered them as recovered images three decades later. I was haunted by the way we three had slipped into and upheld the classic position of 'objective' researcher, seemingly oblivious to the radical differences between us and our 'native' subjects.

The second section deals with a more recent moment. In 2015, *patua* Dukhshyam Chitrakar, by then aged and impoverished, contacted me out of need, requesting a commission to make a scroll painting. On learning about the excavated photos of our 1985 visit to his village, he decided to paint a scroll depicting that experience from his point of view. The commission eventually turned out to be an occasion for him to himself become an informal documentarian, to turn his gaze on us, the 'Visiting Anthropologists', and delineate the kind of urban life he imagined us to embody. In the process he offered a subtle critique of the privileged urban art world and its simultaneous commercialization of folk art/ marginalization of folk artists.

The third section scrutinizes the 1985 photographs in relation to Pushpamala's emerging art practice and her foray into photo-performance. Moving towards this medium in the late 1990s, she collaborated with British photographer Clare Arni to produce the now famous series *Native Women of South India: Manners and Customs* (2000-04)[10] in which she refashions her own appearance after various ethnic and tribal 'types' of natives classified for the colonial knowledge project. How does her satiric visual exploration of the taxonomic colonial archive in which she places herself as the (in)authentic 'native' compare with her person/a in our excavated village photos? What effects arise from her performative scrutiny of the ethnographic turn in contemporary art in India?

Through these three sections I argue for the continued critique of a particular strand of analysis that continues to 'other' and denies full visibility and legibility to the marginalized internal 'other': a seemingly intractable problem that infiltrates even the most politically engaged and progressive postcolonial arts discourse.

Margi/Desi: Coercing the Gap[11]

> [T]wo uses of photographic archives: to provide 'a record as complete as it can be made ... of the present state of the world' and to provide 'valuable documents' for the future.
>
> – Terence Wright[12]

Taking as a point of entry Pushpamala's satiric scribble on the back of one of the photos[13] referring to us – the urban art students – as 'Visiting Anthropologists', I raise a crucial question: what particular pedagogical tensions led to this particular photographic moment and prompted her to use this descriptor? The folk-art documentation project that we were a part of was funded by the central government's Ministry of Culture;[14] it was mentored by Gulammohammed Sheikh, an eminent artist and art teacher, to address the immense disparity between the life-world and art practiced in the Baroda art school and that of the traditional folk artists in their villages. The project was conceptualized in two stages. First the folk artists were invited for a residency at the art school; then students from the art school were to live with the folk artists in their villages, observe them at work in their 'native' environments, and explore the possibility of dialogue – quite in line with what renowned anthropologists such as Malinowski would call 'participant observation' in field research. We three 'Visiting Anthropologists' stayed in Naya Village for less than two weeks, and took turns to photo-document our 'native others'.

Compared to countries in Latin America, where anthropology had a different status through being extended beyond academia and actively enlisted in nation-building,[15] in India, nationalists preferred to invoke, reiterate and reinforce the Indic-/Sanskrit-based classical tradition that dominated cultural discourse during the first quarter of the twentieth century.[16] Folk and tribal art did play a crucial role in early nationalist art – in paintings by Jamini Roy,[17] for instance – but quite often it served as a visual vocabulary appropriated by male urban artists as a way to significantly indigenize Western modernism. Seldom did the figure of the folk or tribal artist per se emerge as a legitimate maker of modern art – much in the way women artists and their representations of gendered realities remained confined to the margins of art history, despite female figures having a strong presence in symbolic and mythopoetic realms through images of goddesses and the ultimate allegorical figure of idealized femininity: Bharat Mata ('Mother India'), co-opted by the nationalists and expanded into a permanent trope that has since then been aggressively wielded to inculcate and promote patriotism and various kinds of religio-supremacist doctrines.[18]

It was largely during the 1980s that folk and tribal art began to gain recognition and become an object of research and critical discourse: a belated post-Independence acknowledgment from the state.[19] At that time India was attracting international attention through large-scale cultural interventions in the form of the Festival of India, organized across the West. At these spectacular events, folk and tribal art best captured a purported 'Indianness' and became the 'authentic' hallmarks of 'national identity'. Folk and tribal art had in fact begun to gain wide cultural visibility as far back as 1946 with the founding of *MARG*, India's first arts magazine, by the socialist writer and poet Mulk Raj Anand (1905–2004) who ensured the equal exposure of folk/tribal and Indic/classical arts in this influential journal.[20] However, the tension between these two categories was manifest in the respective oppositional descriptors *margi* and *desi*, first used in modern arts critique by Coomaraswamy.[21] These two terms have a long history in the visual and performing arts, their genealogy traceable to the twelfth century when the distinction was about style and aesthetic principles rather than about the underlying social and cultural hierarchies. From 1982, *desi* entered an institutional frame with artist J. Swaminathan (1928–1994) setting up Bharat Bhavan in Bhopal[22] – an art institute envisaged to bridge the gap between urban/metropolitan art and indigenous art traditions in the large tribal areas of central India. So today when I look back at our visit to the Naya Village, our exploration may be seen to fall under the *desi* rubric even though we ourselves were thoroughly urban.

As mentioned earlier, while revisiting the recuperated Naya Village photographs after a lapse of three decades it became clear to me that the set of differences between 'us' and 'them', as encapsulated in the self-parodic/satiric label 'Visiting Anthropologists', did produce a complex emotional effect that nudged me towards a close visual study of those images. I felt compelled to undertake a deeper formal analysis using art-historical tools, and to thus go beyond the obvious incongruities – our clothing (we expressed a certain 'urban chic', as it were), our stance vis-à-vis the material environment, and our tourist-like activity such as posing in our *tokas* (local hats) while drinking coconut water. I decided to compare these photographs with those taken in 'native' settings by 'real' anthropologists. The field photographs taken by Bronislaw Malinowski (1884–1942), who

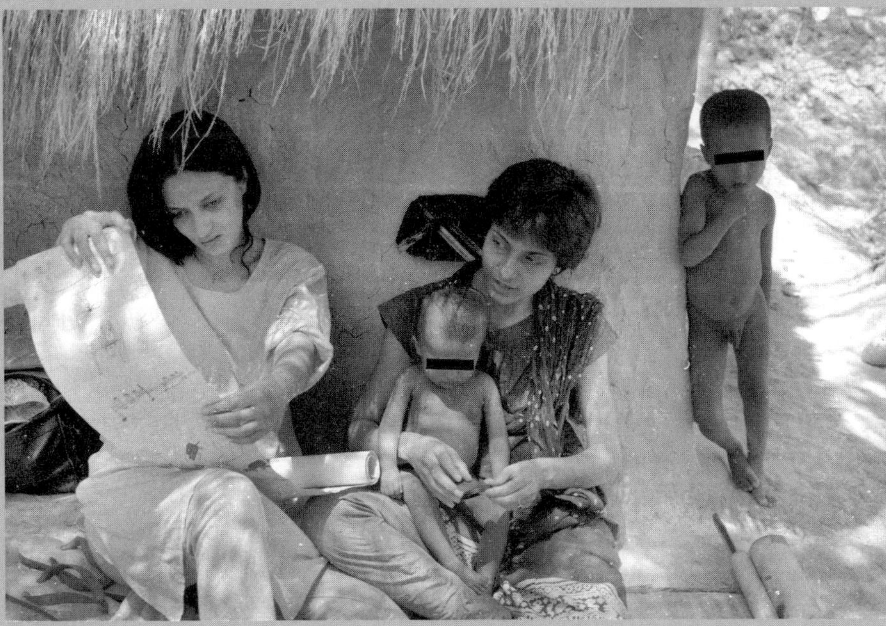

pioneered the method of participant observation, was an obvious starting point.[23]

My endeavour was to investigate the possibility of staging a dialogue between anthropology and art history, and move into visual anthropology but yet remain within the vectors of the latter. In terms of disciplinary rethinking, art history had learned many of its lessons about the politics of representation from anthropology, and redressed its own disciplinary blind spots. But could art history also offer anthropology – a domain that from habit still valorized the earlier research ideal of 'objectivity' in research – the tools to deepen self-reflexivity, as well as offer a way to overcome disciplinary anxiety with regard to visual representation? Taking genre[24] as a way to understand the fashioning of a group photograph, I intended to visually read the 1985 photographs both in their specific experiential 'photographic moment'[25] and also in terms of later reception as recuperated images, in order to make sense of their emotional effect on us, and to closely examine the visual order/s they make apparent (it is worth noting here that Ayisha is now well known for using photographs, especially family albums, in her own practice as a contemporary artist; hence, any rigid distinction between creative and realist photography[26] seems irrelevant here).

Turning to the visual genre of the group photograph that anthropologists typically take of themselves with the natives who are the objects of their study, I take as my point of departure the well-known photograph captioned 'Malinowski with Trobriand Islanders, 1918'.[27] I will read this photo against the grain of the current anthropological reading of Malinowski's photographs that swerves towards political correctness and ascribes the self-reflexivity of participant observation to his fieldwork photographs.[28] In this image, despite the horizontal format Malinowski preferred due to its enabling of non-hierarchical poses, the anthropologist seems to inhabit a more exalted position through being centrally placed, much like the figure of Christ in Leonardo da Vinci's celebrated painting *The Last Supper*. Four native men are featured, two on either side of him, seated on felled logs that serve as a high platform. All five men hold identical traditional musical instruments. Malinowski's white skin, accentuated by his white shirt, forms a sharp contrast to the bare torsos flanking him. His balding head is a counterpoint to the natives' dense black hair. A further sign of overt difference is signalled by Malinowski's trousers and shoes set against the natives' bare legs and bare feet that, like his, dangle above the ground.

Within this genre of the anthropologist photographed with a group of natives is the sub-genre of images of the anthropologist posing with native children. Take for instance the well-known photograph of Malinowski with native children in the

Trobriand Islands, *c.* 1918; two adult native men are also in the frame, the loincloth-clad man on the right a stark visual foil to the anthropologist protectively clad in sola hat, long sleeves and high boots.[29] The group formation in this photo, set against a background of huts and trees, follows a different logic from the previously discussed image. Here the native children, arranged in a loose ascending order, are gathered in one mass in the centre, flanked on one side by Malinowski and on the other a native man standing at a slight distance; a second man stands close behind the central mass of small bodies. Much has been written about the anthropologist's crouching at the eye level of the children and his preference for the horizontal format as a way to neutralize obvious differences in height and age. However, Malinowksi's posture can also be seen as one that further enhances his role and authority as a 'real' anthropologist studiously observing indigenous children who have been posed as if playing a game. Does this static, supervised arrangement signify the occlusion of difference, and successfully project the 'insider' status and authentic close connection with native 'others', so keenly desired by anthropologists? Even if Malinowski crouches to reduce the distance between himself and the children, his posture, along with his formal 'outsider' clothing from head to foot, accentuates the staging of a necessary interaction rather than a moment of genuine integration into native life as an empathetic participant observer.

Quite strikingly different is an image of Malinowski's contemporary, the Brazilian anthropologist Edgar Roquette-Pinto (1884–1954) posing with native children.[30] Here, 'native' has a different resonance – as a scientist connected to the National Museum in Rio de Janeiro between 1905 and 1935, Roquette-Pinto was involved in ethnographic anthropological research on the formative racial characteristics of the country within the context of Brazilian nationalist activism. In the frontal photograph taken by his friend Antonio Pyreneus de Souza against the backdrop of a stone wall, a cheerful Pinto holds four wary native children in an intimate, choreographed embrace: his arms go around in an 'S' shape, forming two semicircles to support the children on either side, and ensure all four are in direct contact with his body. The arm of two of the children is laid diagonally so as to cover their nakedness. Even while he is the masterly pivot of this striking configuration, Roquette-Pinto, unlike Malinowski, does indeed successfully collapse the distance between 'participant' and 'observer'.

Closer to home, the English former missionary and self-trained anthropologist Verrier Elwin (1902–1964)[31] too partakes of this sub-genre, as seen in these two similar images of him posing with five children from the Gond and Pardhan tribes of central India, *c.* 1940s. Rather than crouch in order to be at the children's eye level, Elwin sits informally on a chair, holding the youngest child in his lap; turning his head, he meets the eyes of a little girl on one side of him; two children stand on the other side, and one child, back to the camera, squats at Elwin's feet, looking up at him, closing the circle. Of the group, only the child in his lap looks directly, curiously, at the camera. In the second image, the little girl is replaced by a smiling boy.

It is highly instructive to compare these field photos by/of the 'real' anthropologists with two images from Pushpamala's Midnapore documentation album.[32] In the first image, a group photograph of Pushpamala and I with two *patua* children, the frame is partly infused with the gendered perspective of us 'brown' female anthropologists. Squatting on the ground, and resting our backs against a thatched mud hut, Pushpamala and I examine the scroll she holds open. While Pushpamala strikes a pose, gazing intently at the scroll, I glance at it somewhat distractedly, using a lens cap to hold the attention of the child protectively supported in my lap. The awkward stance of the child leaning against the side of the hut appears to be more of a happy coincidence captured by the camera, rather than a deliberate pose. The bystander boy is naked; and due to the placement of my hand it is difficult to tell but likely that the child I hold is naked too. This was what led me to pay attention to the careful orchestration of the arms of two of the children in the Roquette-Pinto photograph described earlier. One might assume that this strategy reveals the anxiety of the 'outsider' anthropologist – whether 'real' or 'Visiting' – around the issue, and that in contrast, the nakedness of young children causes neither discomfort nor embarrassment to Indian and Brazilian 'natives'.

The second group photograph, taken against the mud wall of a thatched hut, offers an intriguing elision of art history and anthropology. Here, two of the 'mimicking anthropologists' quite easily blend with Dukhshyam and his extended family while the third is behind the camera. The naked infants in this frame are held by men who have opted to pose with their children. Notably, the artist Dukhshyam, who poses standing in a white shirt, has his son Rohin propped up on his waist. So while men proudly pose with their children, the women stand unencumbered but have covered their heads with their saris, a socially coded gesture that fifteen years later will inform Pushpamala's purposive self-fashioning as a 'native woman'. Pushpamala and I are sitting on a raised platform towards one end and are joined by a boy while the rest of the group either stands or squats on the mud floor. The eldest among the extended family are two *patuas* in the

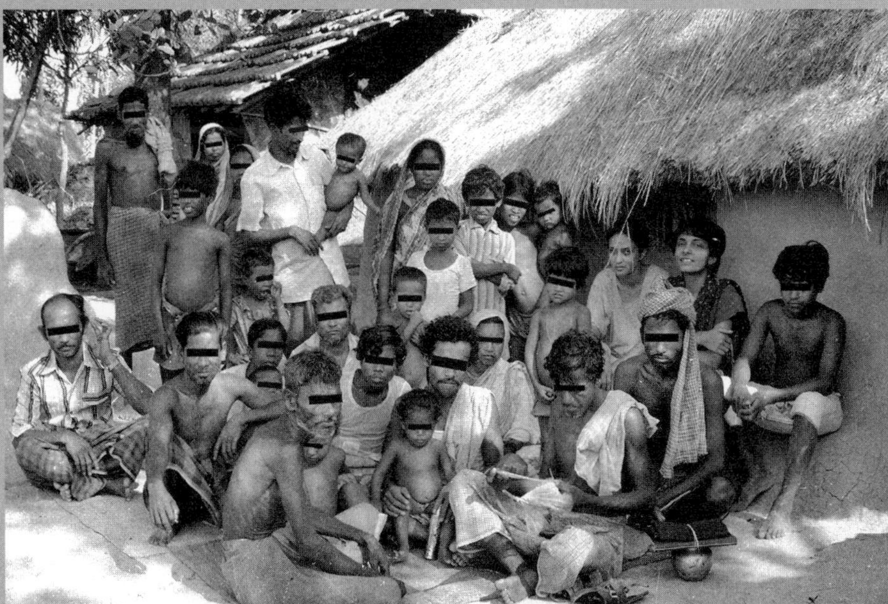

foreground. One holds a scroll in his hands, and a couple of notebooks in which the songs are written down rest on an aluminium pot. As this photo was most likely taken by one of my friends [author's note: given the lapse of four decades between the event and its recall, it is not possible to remember exactly who the photographer was for every photograph during this trip], it is possible that we followed her instructions regarding our positioning; she ensures that in visual terms we 'Visiting Anthropologists' are integrated into the group that extends back like a rough quadrilateral, echoing the shape of the roofs in the frame. However, quite extraordinary was the recent transformation of these photographs when Pushpamala turned them into artworks in 2017, titled *The Ethnographers #1* and *#2*. In deference to copyright image regulations that prohibit showing the face of a photographed subject without explicit permission, or to make an artistic intervention on a 'found' photograph, she devised a visual strategy of covering the eyes of the adults in the frame with black strips: an ethical practice otherwise that ended up visually segregating 'us' from 'them'. Whereas the two 'outsiders' among the massed 'insiders', Pushpamala and I – privileged with resources, education, agency and autonomy – have unobstructed faces. Reading the image in symbolic terms that underscore the earlier discussed *margi/desi* divide: we 'Visiting Anthropologists' are empowered to freely see (and by implication, discursively and artistically represent) ourselves and our 'native others', whereas they, due to the imposed black strips, are unable to look at each other or at us. They cannot see, they can only be seen. (Actually the black strips are used to protect vulnerable subjects like rape victims, etc. – one could also see the image in another way, that our exposed faces make us vulnerable.)

How does one define the gaze of the positioned 'brown' ethnographers, outsiders to Naya village and its *patuas* but insiders to broader Indian culture? And is it primarily our gender that enables us 'Visiting Anthropologists' to conceive of the category of a 'soft' gaze? After all, we have photographic evidence that Verrier Elwin, a male 'real' anthropologist who straddles the colonial/postcolonial moment, regards the tribal children around him with deep tenderness. Our 'soft' gaze notwithstanding, are we women documentarians involved in non-reciprocal transaction, rather than authentic relationship, with the village community? And are the tribal women with sari-covered heads posed in our photographs in any way actually empowered through Pushpamala's later ironic reconfiguring of them as ethnographic 'types' of the female 'native other'?

Object/Subject: Facing the Mirror

> ... I am, as a 'European type', brought to confront my cultured self in the form of an Indian figurine [carved by the Cuna indigenous people of Panama for shamanic healing rituals]. ... What magic lies in this, my wooden self, sung to power in a language I cannot understand? Who is this self, objectified without my knowledge, that I am hell-bent on analyzing as object-over-there ... Something trembles in the whole enterprise of analysis and knowledge-making here: the whole anthropological trip starts to eviscerate ... I am honor-bound to respond to the mimicry of myself in ways other than the defensive maneuver of the powerful by subjecting it [the figurine] to scrutiny as yet another primitive artifact, grist to the analytic machinery of Euroamerican anthropology. The very mimicry corrodes the alterity by which my science is nourished. For now I too am part of the object of study. The Indians have made me alter to myself.
>
> - Michael Taussig[33]

I now jump-cut to a recent scroll painting by Dukhshyam based on what he could recall of our 1985 visit to his village, the home of many *patua* families. He was still living there, and like many of his fellow painters was struggling to make ends meet, finding it difficult to solely survive on the traditional practice of scroll painting. Lack of state patronage and ill health prevented him from travelling to nearby villages to earn his living. In 2015, he called me, asking me if I wanted to buy a scroll from him. On being informed about the rediscovered photographs of our 1985 visit, he astutely came up with the idea of basing his commissioned scroll on our 1985 'anthropological' experience. His proposition appealed to me. He completed the scroll over three months and sent it to me by post, along with a DVD recording of himself performing the scroll in his village.

Unlike traditional scroll paintings that drew on mythological stories about Hindu gods and goddesses, this scroll had an unusual theme: inscribing the habitus, as perceived by Dukhshyam, of the three women 'ethnographers' who had visited his village some three decades ago. While remaining within the ambit of his traditional visual language, he found ways to fuse the past with the present. He depicted not just the moment we set out as students to travel to his village, but also our current professional activity. The other remarkable feature of this scroll is his engagement with photography and its function in mechanical reproduction. In other words, the camera is inserted into the story both as an object and as a form of representation. I found I could best interpret this aspect of Dukhshyam's rendering through the idea of performative mimesis, a concept and critical methodology that I have been engaging with for some time. In the context of the *pata* tradition, the scroll is mimetic in that it delineates the painter's perceived or imagined reality; it is performative in that the scroll is unwound in front of an audience and the *patua* sings out its story. Thus inserting himself into the narrative that he himself has created, he transforms the work's fixed frame into a flexible, immersive, fully relational experience, repudiating the neat separation of viewing subject/viewed object that undergirds standard concepts of representation.[34]

The opening frame depicts the 'Visiting Anthropologists' preparing to leave Baroda for Naya Village. It has two sub-frames. On the right, the three of us, clad in trousers and sturdy shoes, are ready to travel by train from Gujarat to West Bengal, our destination right across the country. One of us holds a camera for project documentation; it looks more like a video recorder, a device that in the past two decades had become a familiar sight in rural India. On the left, Professor Gulam Sheikh, shown with his characteristic beard and moustache, is seated on the classroom floor, painting; he glances up at us while we take his leave.

In the next set of frames, the three of us are shown navigating the city with its high-rise buildings, taxis and buses, and with an aircraft passing overhead.

In one frame, Dukhshyam depicts me as a professor taking class in Jawaharlal Nehru University, standing in front of a blackboard before a group of students, all women. Did the artist single me out from our group of three because I had commissioned this scroll? As I scrutinized the image closely, my attention was drawn to the blackboard that bears the words *Pater Katha* (Bengali: 'The Story of a Scroll') written in English, in large letters; below it, in smaller font, were the same words in Hindi. This was a remarkable, skilful, orthographic intervention that served two purposes - by making *pata* painting the main topic of my class, he was not only exercising his agency as a folk artist, but also symbolizing the mainstream art world's neglect of his genre of painting. Was this how he viewed our 1985 documentation trip? Was this his way of critiquing the marginalization of folk art practice within cultural discourse that is almost wholly dominated by urban professionals and pedagogues?

The final frame shows our return to Baroda - to Gulam Sheikh's very classroom from where our trip had begun - thus bringing the narrative full circle. Sheikh reviews our photo documentation, which is shown vertically much like a *pata* painting, except that the same figure is shown within each frame. Here, as read through the concept of performative mimesis, a folk rendering effectively

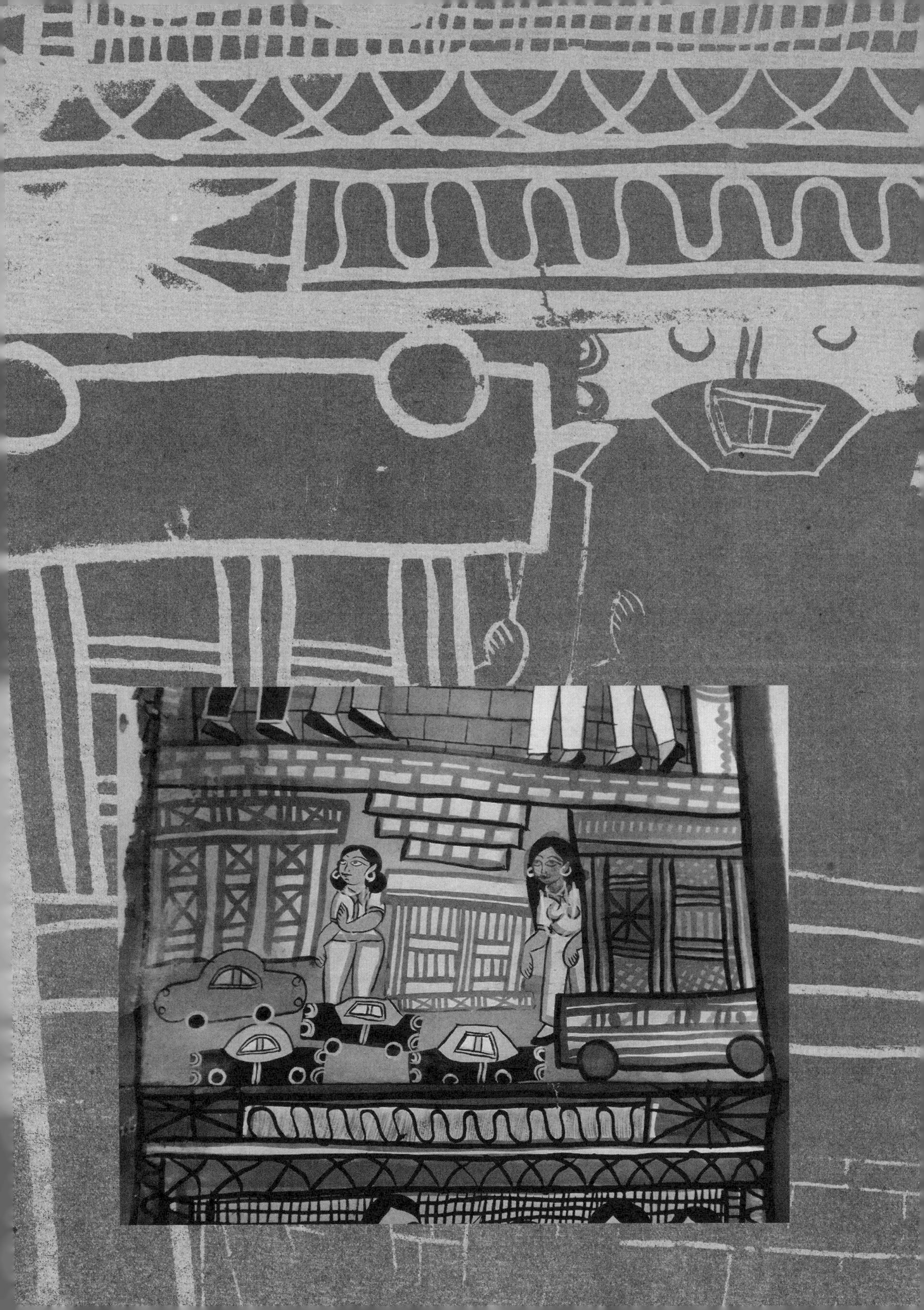

comments on a key principle of photography: the replication of an image. In this frame, mimesis does not function as a one-to-one correspondence between an object and its copy but rather invokes the technical principle/property of indexical repetition promised, enabled and delivered by photography. In other words, the reiteration of the same figure in five frames signifies the enigmatic allure and power of photographic reproduction. Adding his own feminist touches, in a closing comment on his largely woman-centric narrative, Dukhshyam depicts women security guards flanking the main gate of the Faculty of Fine Arts.

Is there anything 'soft' about the gaze Dukhshyam the outsider/artist-ethnographer has turned on us 'Visiting Anthropologists' who are 'natives' of the city? His remarkable scroll narrative may at first be read less as an assertion of self-empowerment and more his desperate effort to find contemporary creative relevance in a technologically dominated era/ethos of cultural production where most traditional artisans/craftspeople are barely surviving. His articulation remains fully traditional, yet he adapts his style to successfully present a radically different, modern theme. A village classroom appears to have worked well as a model for his delineation of a university classroom. To what extent does his reversal of our gaze transform him into a valid and knowledgeable ethnographer of academia, of the urban, and of urban academia? Beyond our particular encounter with Dukhshyam, how does any such radical subversion of the gaze empower this disenfranchised folk artist, and countless others like him, in actual material terms? Dukhshyam, who had acquired a certain visibility in the Baroda art world during the 1980s through a residency programme, now languishes in oblivion and is struggling to find buyers for his scrolls. His ingenious critique of our 1985 visit also alludes to the failed promise of state and institutional support for rural artists. Despite the voluminous research done on *patua* painting, the folk producers of this art are relegated to anonymity. They only find adequate patronage in the city (Kolkata) during Durga Puja. Their relationship to the urban is unidirectional, and cultural institutions such as the Gurusaday Museum in Kolkata[35] hold the key to their visibility in the art world. Did the Naya Village *patuas* benefit from our 1985 visit? Or was our presence in their village extractive, non-reciprocal, mere spectacle?

Sonal Khullar was the first art historian to draw attention to our 1985 encounter with Bengali folk artists, referring to this moment as an example of a 'translation between local and regional cultures that was a hallmark of modernism in India'.[36] Pushpamala's rediscovery of our Naya Village photographs revived our memories of the 1985 field trip and, equally, demanded that we now completely rethink that experience from a practitioner perspective. Gulam Sheikh had wanted us to live with *patua* painters and their families in order to connect their life with their work. What at the time of our visit seemed to us urban outsiders to be an organic, cohesive traditional social formation is today undoubtedly a community left behind. The *desi* artist, once a potent symbol of postcolonial cultural politics, has indeed, and most unjustly, been pushed to the occluded, under-researched and under-served fringes of the contemporary art world.

Fact and Fiction: 'Selving the Other'[37]

> I remember that morning in Bastar vividly. I had woken up in a green haze. Shantibai had collected the intoxicating mahua flowers that had fallen on the ground and was laying them out to dry at the Dialogue Center. We had planned a trip to Chitrakoot Falls. Before motoring down to the Falls, we had walked through the clearing of gorgeous Sal trees, the air ringing suddenly with the laughter of children jumping up to cradle themselves in a tangle of vines.
>
> – Nancy Adajania[38]

This section explores a possible connection between our 'Visiting Anthropologists' experience and Pushpamala's *Native Women* series (2000–04), a major work consciously/self-consciously aligned with the ethnographic turn in contemporary art in India. Until the 1990s, the discourse on modern Indian art was largely driven by the interlocking energies of the past and the present. Geeta Kapur captures the dynamics of the Indian modern by suggesting it be examined through a complex quadripartite equation of nationalism, secularism, tradition and modernity:

> ... nationalism in our experience is at the very least a foil to the universal modern. It helps resist imperial hegemony up to a point; it serves as environmental testing ground for unheeding modernism. Just as modernism, a cultural and specifically modern category, interrogates through its formalist means, through its negative dialectic and valorized transgressions, the dangerously totalizing ideology of nationalism.[39]

The relationships discussed in Kapur's pathbreaking study *When Was Modernism* (2000) fissured and fractured over the 1990s, while a particular construct of postcolonial discourse that pitted the Indian modern against the West began to sound increasingly elitist. This construct left little room to address the post-Independence 'internal colonization' that had taken root and was asserting itself as a factor in arts production. Additionally, over the next fifty years the terrain of contemporary Indian art grew far more challenging, negotiating the impact of globalization on the one hand and the rise of aggressive religious/caste/gender politics on the other; and with many diverse internal/internally colonized 'others' finding voice through the cracks manifesting in the Nehruvian model of a secular and democratic social contract. While art historians and critics attempted to analyse these complexities, artists experimented boldly with new mediums and materiality; this served to not only overturn the standard notions of form but also to hold up for scrutiny the very question of 'representation' itself, this term now interpreted as simultaneously aesthetic and political.

Navjot Altaf[40] pioneered a move in the *desi* direction in the late 1990s when she 'surprised many of her contemporaries in the Indian art world by walking away from a successful career in Bombay and retreating to Bastar, in the tribal heartland of central India'.[41] Altaf and Pushpamala applied Sheikh's pedagogic vision to contemporary art practice in different ways. Framed within Hal Foster's incisive and influential 'artist-as-ethnographer' argument that explains the shift in radical cultural politics from Marxism (class) to culture (race and other signifiers) in the 1990s, Navjot's and Pushpamala's engagement with tribal communities – the former's actual participation with the community and the latter's re-versioning of the colonial archive of the Toda tribe – can be read as creative engagements with notions of history as linear time and of identity as essential/fixed; such projects serve to question the modernist notion of 'progress'. While Pushpamala interrogated the colonial photo archives that had objectified tribal bodies, Altaf moved her studio to Bastar and successfully initiated material collaboration with tribal artists in alignment with their traditions and world-view.[42] The ethnographic and the archival approach emerged as two key axes along which diverse contemporary art practices, including Pushpamala's foray into ironic photo-performance, could be mapped. Her *Native Women* series combined both these concerns: art as a form of ethnography, and the static archive as a dynamic form of history.

At a time when postcolonial arts discourse was rapidly building momentum, Pushpamala revisited colonial photo archives and found their representation of native women to be a suitable subject for an embodied form of critical scrutiny. The term 'performative mimesis' seems to best encapsulate her adept strategies of presenting herself in diverse costumes as diverse 'authentic' native women, scrutinized by postcolonial audiences just as India's races, ethnicities and tribes were objects for the colonial gaze and photo-documented for the colonial

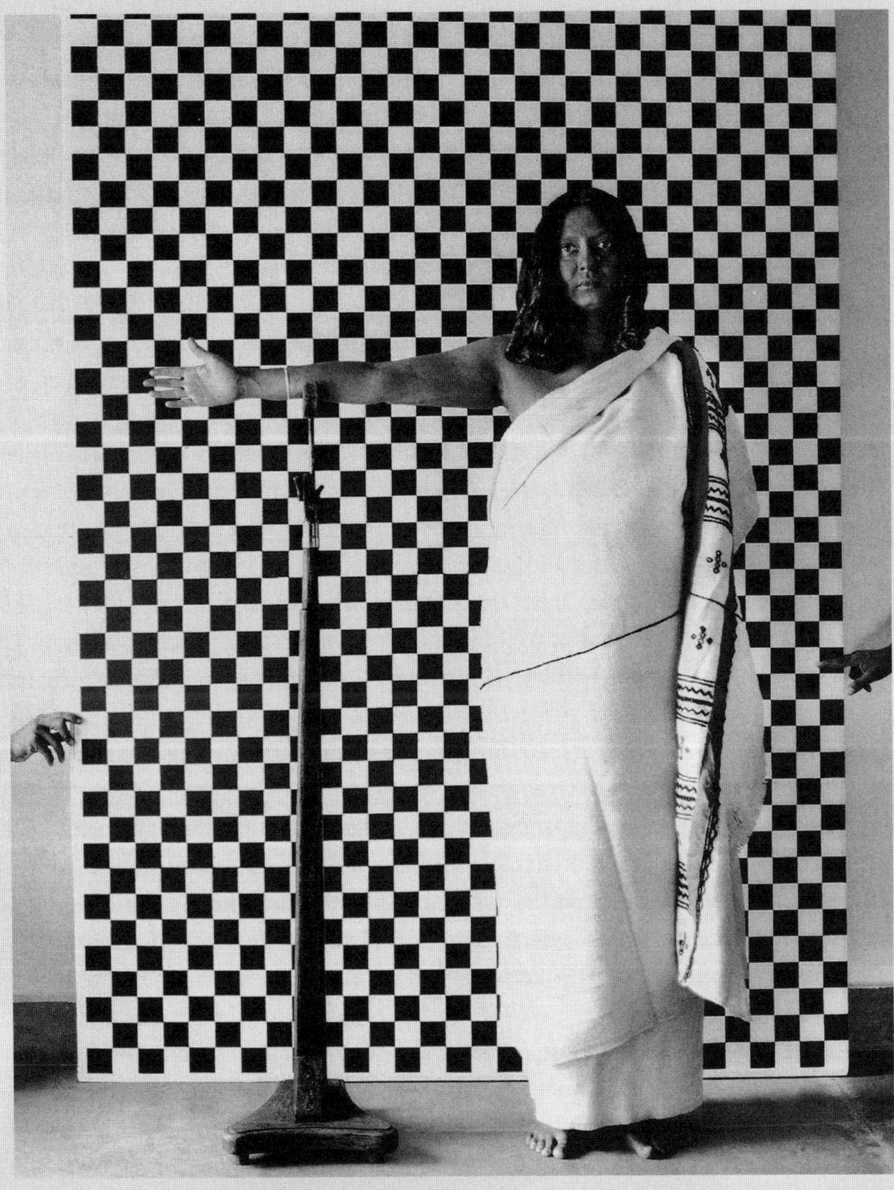

knowledge project.[43] Here, mimicry expands into full-blown, edgy masquerade as the impersonator-artist builds her new mode of representation via postmodern citationality from the existent formal lexicon of colonial photography.[44] Each meta-fictional, contextualized, staged 'native' self is, of course, starkly different from the casual 'Visiting Anthropologist' Pushpamala photographed with the 'native women' of Naya Village in 1985. Yet in both cases the personae are the result of a carefully plotted and orchestrated *mise-en-scène*.

Moving beyond these epistemic ruptures, we need to engage with the political implications of this deliberate self-fashioning through the 'artist-as-ethnographer' formulation, and of art thus passing 'into the expanded field of culture that anthropology is thought to survey'.[45] Given India's diverse demography and the innumerable complexities of the colonial interlude, the figure of the artist/art historian as an ethnographer has a longer history here than in the Euro-American world.[46] The oppositional terms *desi* and *margi* referenced earlier in this essay capture the millennia-old deep social and cultural disparities across class, caste, religion, ethnicity, etc. Hence, Foster's tracing of the 1960s' ethnographic turn to the Marxist model of avant-garde arts practice being displaced by another activist model – postmodern artists' engagement with subaltern alterity – does not really apply to the Indian context. However, in the context of this essay, Foster's concept of the-artist-as-ethnographer permanently complicates our relationship to our younger selves as we appear in the 'Visiting Anthropologists' images, as well as to the 'native others' with whom we share those frames. The concept can also be usefully applied to examine contemporary Indian artists' engagement with ethnography. The way we pose in our Naya Village photos and Pushpamala's later mode of photo-performance both manifest what Foster castigates as the artist's 'ethnographic self-fashioning' that can easily fall into the trap of 'promote[ing] a presumption of ethnographic authority as much as a questioning of it'.[47] The sari-clad village woman in our 1985 photos, present as our contextual 'other' in her own environment and looking at the camera, would later have her 'native' gaze appropriated by the artist-ethnographer, and have her 'native' personhood mimicked through the costumed, staged portrayal of an ethnic 'type', hyper-real and parodic in equal measure.

If narcissism is a possible trap within Pushpamala's performative practice, Altaf, despite relocating her practice from an urban to a rural context, risks inhabiting the position of what Foster terms 'ideological patronage',[48] vis-à-vis the tribal artists who are collaborators and co-creators in her socially engaged art projects. Thus situated, it is difficult for the privileged practitioner, no matter how well intentioned or immersed in the ground realities of his/her 'other', to speak *with* the subaltern subject – invariably, the artist finds himself/herself speaking *for* the latter. This entrenched mode of privilege is also reflected in contemporary art-historical critique, for instance Nancy Adajania's excellent study *Navjot Altaf: The Thirteenth Place* (2016), commissioned by a private gallery and taking the form of a monograph – a market-friendly yet circumscribed genre that focuses on highlighting individual achievement.

Any juxtaposition of the career of Dukhshyam and the careers of Pushpamala and Altaf dramatizes the intractable divide between folk artists and contemporary artists in India. The very issue that had so deeply troubled Gulam Sheikh in the mid-1980s continues, more or less without alleviation, into the present. At best, the bold moves by these two urban artists to actively engage with their social and cultural 'others' affirm very different forms of political and cultural radicalism. While these artists have successfully reinvented their practice through the ethnographic turn, postcolonial theory also needs to be reconfigured so that rather than habitually reiterating the fatigued trope of the East–West encounter, it develops greater responsiveness to the meta-histories and psychological truths of internal colonization. As discussed at the end of the first section of this essay, our obscuring the eyes of the adult villagers in our 1985 photographs with black strips, which on the one hand is evidence of best practices/upholding photography's ethical codes, on the other hand also deeply enhances the disturbing asymmetry of the relationship between our anonymous, disenfranchised 'native others' and ourselves as elite, empowered urban 'Visiting Anthropologists'. Those opaque signifiers imposed on our 'others' faces occlude, obstruct, deflect, distract, disrupt, negate and annul our invasive scrutiny – but also, in effect, achieve an erasure of the signified.

Dukhshyam Chitrakar *does* return our gaze, however, and speaks for innumerable erased, internal/internally colonized 'others' through his commissioned scroll. With visual audacity he levels that unequal relationship via his clever depiction of us in his traditional *pata* style, and also via his clever inscription of *Pater Katha* on the classroom blackboard – written not in Bengali but in English and Hindi, languages more audible in the elite corridors of the art world and art market. And while for Dukhshyam this scroll reflects his desire to embed his traditional art/its 'native' producers within the contemporary, for me this extraordinary art object becomes the uncompromising site of a new, and unsettling, pedagogic responsibility, one mandating a far more radical politics of inclusion. However, given the networked solipsism that pervades much of current cultural discourse, how do we effectively build theoretical and material spaces that would secure and make fully legible this marginalized folk artist's seemingly impertinent act of self-affirmation?

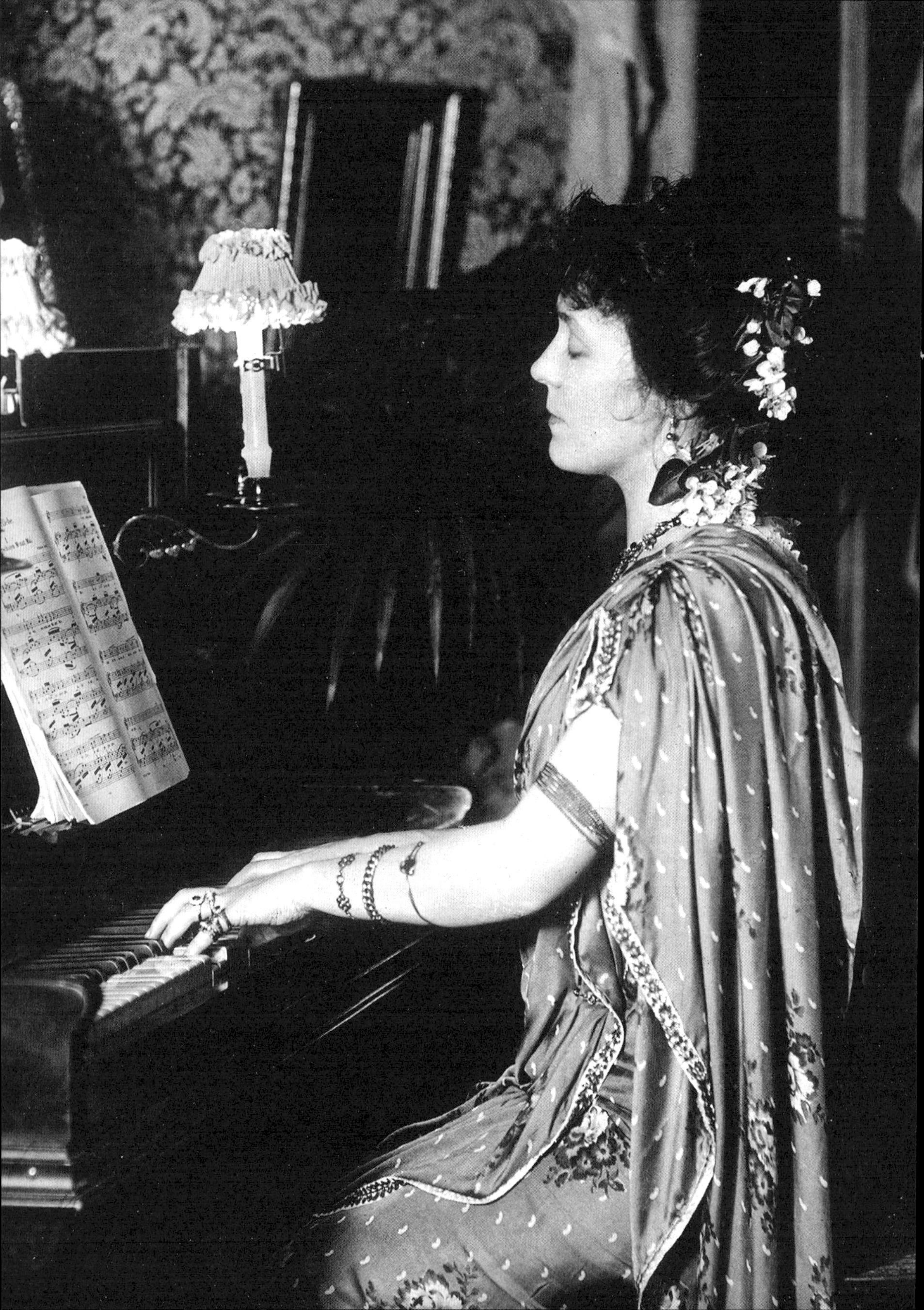

11 *Re-take of Amrita*

Re-configuring the Past in the Age of Digital Imaging

Ruth Rosengarten

2019

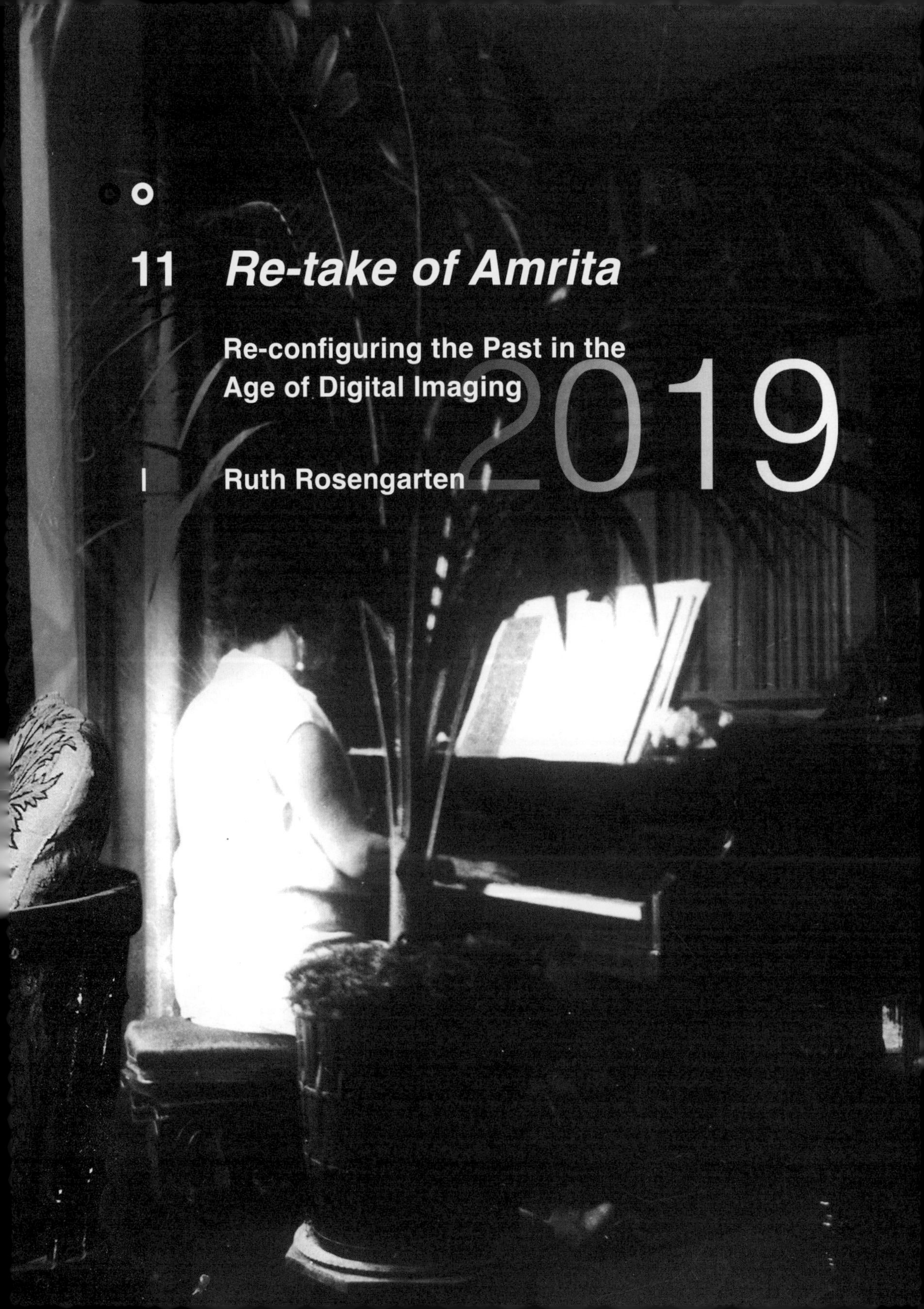

The artist **Vivan Sundaram** creates photomontages reconstructing the photographic work of his grandfather, **Umrao Singh Sher-Gil**, and the paintings of his aunt, the artist Amrita Sher-Gil. Moving between the factual and the biographical, to the scripted, the performed and even the illusory, Sundaram produces a refined, intense and vivid aesthetic psychodrama. Much of this is produced by digitization, even though historically Sundaram returns to montage forms with long histories going back to Dada and Surrealism.

It is, says Ruth Rosengarten, now commonly acknowledged that digital image production (or the capabilities of digitization to which pre-existing analogue photographs are exposed) is able to dismantle the causal link between ostensibly unadulterated reality and image, while maintaining the 'smoothness and continuity' of the surface so that the 'real and the fantastical' are allowed to converge into an idealized, dreamlike universe. What the form produces is narcissism and desire playing out alongside stylized therapeutic self-delineation, all against the historical backdrop of an idealized elite cosmopolitanism.

A longer version of this essay appeared as 'Reconfiguring the Past in the Age of Digital Imaging', in Ruth Rosengarten, *Vivan Sundaram Is Not a Photographer: The Photographic Works of Vivan Sundaram*, New Delhi: Tulika Books, 2019, pp. 46–131. This essay references images from the volume.

Keywords/Names

Decolonization, *First Indian War of Independence 1857*, *Moving images*, *Postmemory*, *Vernacular mode*, see Keywords at the back of this volume.

Photographic effect references the reception of the material nature of the photograph and its process, to understand its place in the history of image-making. In the case of analogue photography, this becomes a product of light, photosensitive film and chemicals that result in the construction of the photograph in a conventional sense. However, as evident in Sundaram's work, digital photography has complicated both the construction and the reading of images.

Images

pp. 200–01: Vivan Sundaram, *Piano Duet*, 2001. Based on two photographs by Umrao Singh Sher-Gil: *Marie Antoinette, Lahore* (1912); *Marie Antoinette, Simla* (1940s).

p. 207: Vivan Sundaram, *Presenting Papa*, 2001. Based on two photographs by Umrao Singh Sher-Gil: *Umrao Singh, Paris* (early 1930s); *Amrita, Paris* (early 1930s)

p. 213: Vivan Sundaram, *Doppelgänger*, 2001. Based on two photographs: *Amrita, Simla* (1937) by Umrao Singh Sher-Gil; *Amrita, Budapest* (1938) by Victor Egan.

p. 219: Vivan Sundaram, *Café-talk*, 2001. Based on two photographs: *Amrita with art school friends, Paris* (1932), photographer not known; detail of painting by Amrita Sher-Gil, *Spanish Girl* (1933).

> Postmemory is a powerful form of memory precisely because its connection to its object or source is mediated not through recollection but through an imaginative investment and creation. Postmemory characterises the experience of those who grow up dominated by narratives that preceded their birth, whose own belated stories are evacuated by the stories of the previous generation, shaped by traumatic events that can be neither fully understood nor re-created.
>
> – Marianne Hirsch[1]

Convergence

Re-take of Amrita is a series of 55 black-and-white photographic images made in 2001–02 by the late Vivan Sundaram (1943–2023).[2] Framed and hung in a grid in no specific chronological or narrative order, the images feature a small cast of characters rendered in elegiac chiaroscuro. Elegant and inscrutable, these characters move in and out of the works, addressing the camera with quiet poise. The images unite different temporalities and geographies in a death-defying time warp: seamlessly, different places and periods are granted immediacy and coincidence.[3] The work's title prepares us for this disorientation of time, space and psychological engagement: 're-take' points first to a photographic and cinematographic metaphor, and then to a hesitation, a turning back or reiteration. It thus announces the ceaselessly renewed pleasures and pains of revision and repossession that underpin this body of work.

The digital photomontages comprising *Re-take of Amrita* transport the viewer into a glamorous, cosmopolitan, aristocratic-bourgeois world in the first half of the twentieth century: a world nuanced by art and intellect. Books, paintings and musical instruments jostle together in carelessly sumptuous interiors. Staging scenes from the life of a prosperous, multi-talented family, these images seem more like enlarged film stills than the leaves of a family photograph album. Yet, clearly, they also gain their meaning from a rehearsal of the conventions and tropes of such albums: the studied arrest, the pose, an address to the camera. They also participate in the evolving transformations of a family narrative, much as photograph albums do.

Photograph albums are objects of exchange and conversation in collective and family life. The composition and constitution of such albums are subject to criteria of selection in accordance with ideas of presentation, narrative and, sometimes, a more elusive quality we call the photogenic. Martha Langford has argued persuasively that we should consider the album as a whole, an object that participates in an ongoing performance of group identity (family, peers, interest group, etc.), immersing its participants and users, present and future, as much in a visual regime as in a verbal one. In its life and afterlife, she urges, the album extends oral consciousness through the conversations that it engenders.[4]

While employing what is essentially a process of montage (with its historical origins in Dada and Surrealism), *Re-take of Amrita* immerses itself, technically, in the capabilities offered by digitization. This immersion does not mean, for Sundaram, simply the passage from the use of one technology to another. While the concept of the 'digital photograph' obscures the informational format of a digital image, its potential for invention speaks to Sundaram's innate tendency to embrace new tools and materials for their transformative capability. Nevertheless, this body of work relies heavily on the more traditional notion of 'the photographic' that grants historical unity to various technologies of image production, grouping together 'technically produced indexical images of various sorts, supplemented, more recently, by digital images in which such indexical effects are simulated in various ways'.[5]

'Photographic effect' – the fact that each image, on first glance, appears to be the product of a conventional photographic capture – is the outcome of Sundaram's annexation of an ostensibly vernacular mode into the realm of the aesthetic.[6] This has coincided with the inception of the digital age, a time during which photography as we had previously known it 'is both ending and enlarging, with an evolving medium hidden inside it as in a Trojan horse'.[7] In the vast quantity of apparently photographic images circulating in the public domain, and because of the contexts in which they are disseminated, finer and older distinctions between genre and provenance are often blurred. An elision of categorical boundaries is nourished by the very process of digitization, and by its ready availability to professionals and amateurs alike. The limitless possibilities for artful invention offered by sophisticated post-production software or readymade filters are widely accessible, at greater or lesser cost (and, at the more automated end, on platforms such as Instagram at no cost at all). Such a palette of possibility has not only undermined the unique status of photography – the epistemological privilege gained through its much-vaunted indexicality – but has also frequently collapsed the distinction between vernacular and 'art' photography, if such a distinction could ever have been made by formal and technical means alone.

It is generally assumed that vernacular photography privileges the documentary/testimonial mode and the truth effect born of its indexicality. This happened. I was here. We own that.

Yet, as Christopher Pinney has convincingly argued, many such photographs in family or peer albums capture not so much an event as the micro-event[8] of gathered family members and friends, set up as actors and posing for the camera.[9] The ensuing 'shot' is characterized not only by the fixity of the photograph as artefact, but also by the stillness of its founding moment, in opposition to the dynamic happenstance of the 'decisive moment' of street or other kinds of documentary or journalistic photography. This frozenness of the pose is especially evident in studio photographs, so popular in India in the nineteenth and twentieth centuries. Against the background of the obsession with the personal and the autobiographic that has marked cultural production across the globe at the end of the twentieth century and the beginning of the twenty-first, digital photo-sharing has brought this species of vernacular photography into focus. With this autobiographic turn, the self is rehearsed as a series of performances directed at the camera (or the camera function on a smart phone), whose very aim is to ratify the self thus appointed and to grant it status through consensual tropes of success or gratification (my body, my girlfriend/boyfriend, my work, my pleasure, my meals, my glamorous evening out, my holiday, my ethical and political integrity, my popularity, and so on).

Although the performative and self-legitimizing aspects of portrait photography on social networks and photo-sharing websites – not unlike swagger portraits of earlier times, though perhaps in a less grand manner[10] – are now commonly acknowledged, important cultural continuities with the old analogue photographs are still at work.[11] One symptom of such continuity is the sustained insistence on photographic transparency, a concordantly held untruth whereby the image is considered to be candidly evidentiary, carrying the full burden of empirical proof. Another symptom is nominal: on social software, groups of photographs are still bundled into 'albums'. A material photograph album is a finite collection of images gathered according to a criterion, theme or chronology, and, arguably, its constituent elements (the individual photographs) must be regarded as co-productive parts in the whole cultural artefact designated as album. On social media, the metaphor of the album sustains a powerful link with the good old days when the physical artefact (whether family, peer or themed albums such as travel, work or hobby) provided the viewer with a sense of intimate possession, not only of the images but also, at a remove, of their referents. 'As you turn the pages and look at the images,' writes Verna Posever Curtis of such albums, 'you imbibe the maker's experience, invoking your imagination and prompting personal memories.'[12] The physical photograph album to which the digital one points, in short, is not only a mnemonic trigger for its maker/s, it also serves to unleash mnemic reverie in the viewer.

Crucially, and not unpredictably, it is at the very point of its obsolescence - just when the photograph album has divested itself of its materiality - that it has become an object of nostalgia, providing a blueprint for artists and writers who explore personal experience against the backdrop of history, collective memory and the ideologically freighted images already circulating in the public sphere. The confrontation between obsolescence and nostalgia is not news: most famously and brilliantly, Walter Benjamin articulated this encounter in multiple observations concerning the tautological nature of novelty, particularly in commodity culture. For Benjamin, it is at the point when a technology is eclipsed by the foregone conclusion of its own obsolescence that it unleashes the memory of its earlier, possibly utopian, promises. This accounts for the ways in which digital images on platforms such as Instagram simulate the process of ageing and corruption of their analogue material counterparts, while social software offering users the ability to upload images and have them printed in bound books frequently delivers not only the mounting conventions of physical photograph albums (for example, facsimile photo-corners), but also a simulation of their passage through time in fake ageing (for instance, the simulation of craquelure, or paper printed with a marbled, deteriorated or scuffed effect).

As vernacular artefacts within the history of nostalgia, historical photograph albums have been the focus of specialized academic attention in recent years,[13] and various writers - usually falling between several disciplinary stools - have mined personal family albums in hybrid collections of texts and essays that meld memoir, criticism, theory and social history.[14] Moreover, numerous contemporary lens-based artists have probed the photograph album in general, and the family album in particular, as guarantors of personal memory. These practitioners generally fall into two camps: on the one hand, those whose work is based on the underlying assumption of the indexicality of the photograph, establishing an inherent link between photography and memory (Doug Dubois, Teirney Gearon, Lydia Goldman, Colin Gray, Terry Kurgan, Paddy Summerfield); and on the other hand, artists whose work more allusively explores the notion of the family album, its sometimes tenuous or falsifying link to memory, its quaint formal and material qualities, the nostalgic depths it sounds, and its inherently or potentially constructed nature (Christian Boltanski,[15] Renée Cox, Rafael Goldchain, Erik Kessels,[16] Jeff Eugene Meatyard,[17] Lorrie Novak, Peter Watkins). Vivan Sundaram falls into the second camp.

In *Re-take of Amrita*, the family album/archive that Sundaram appropriates

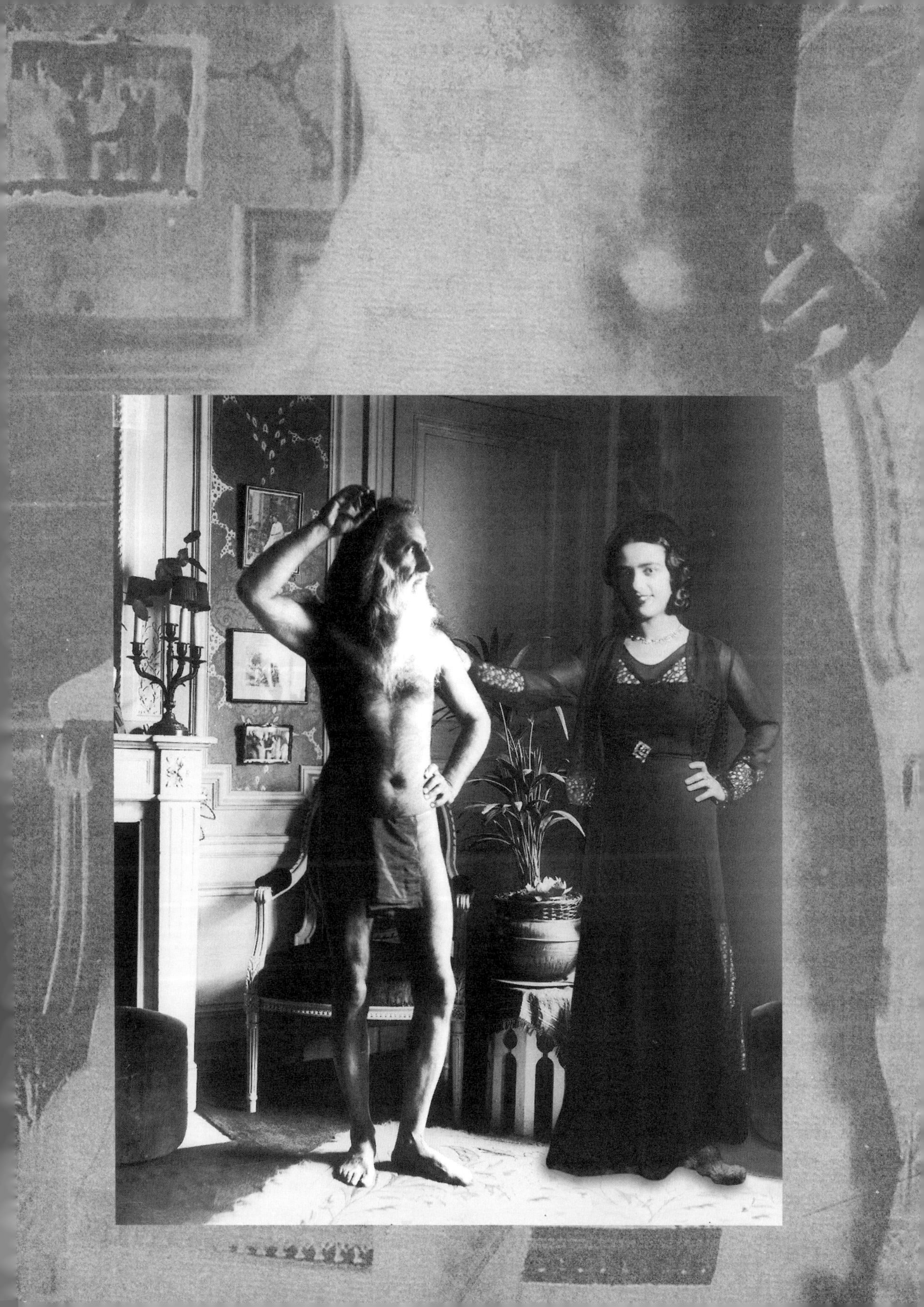

consists mostly, though not exclusively, of photographs taken by his grandfather, Umrao Singh Sher-Gil.[18] The story of this family has been much rehearsed, but warrants reiteration here. Born in 1870 as the eldest son of a Punjab chieftain, Umrao Singh[19] was a Sanskrit scholar with wide-ranging interests, including philosophy, yoga, carpentry, calligraphy, astronomy, music and (not least) politics – his sympathies lying with India's anti-colonial movement for independence. He found intellectual and spiritual kinship with Leo Tolstoy's idiosyncratic blend of asceticism and anarchism; we see in many of his self-portraits how his sartorial self-fashioning was based on Tolstoy's. Umrao Singh's second wife, Marie Antoinette Gottesman, was a flamboyant Hungarian opera singer whom he met and married in Lahore, which at the time was a part of India. The couple moved to Budapest in 1913 for the birth of their first daughter, Amrita, who was to become the renowned modern painter Amrita Sher-Gil; and then the birth in 1914 of their second daughter, Indira, the mother of Vivan Sundaram. At the outbreak of World War I the family remained in Budapest, returning to India in 1920 and setting up home in Simla. In 1929 they moved again, this time to Paris, to enable the precocious Amrita to attend the École des Beaux Arts. In 1934, at Amrita's behest, the family relocated yet again, now back to India. Having enjoyed the attentions of several lovers in Paris, in 1938 Amrita married her Hungarian cousin Victor Egan, a medical student. Tragically, in December 1941, on the eve of a major exhibition in Lahore, she died suddenly at the age of twenty-eight.

The cause of her untimely death has provoked rumour and speculation, ranging from dysentery, through peritonitis following an abortion, to a recurrence of syphilis. Her mother accused Victor of having murdered her. The day after Amrita's death, England declared war on Hungary and Victor was sent to jail as an enemy national. Marie Antoinette made two suicide attempts before finally succeeding, shooting herself with Umrao Singh's shotgun in his study in Simla in July 1948 – a scene that is figured in *Re-take of Amrita* in the image titled *Ghost* (99) – thus redoubling the trauma of the two surviving members of the family. Umrao Singh lived with his daughter Indira, her husband Kalyan Sundaram and their two children, Vivan and Navina, in Simla and Delhi until his death in 1954.

In Umrao Singh's small, now often faded prints, we see a family that delights in and performs its own talents and theatricality: a cosmopolitan family of intelligence, beauty and wealth, seemingly at home everywhere. The hybrid identities of the family members are staged within the context of an opulent, multi-textured domestic sphere, arrayed as a set. We see the diva mother, usually swathed in orientalizing robes, playing out all the evocative charms and anxieties of Mitteleuropa; we see the beautiful daughters in their similarities and differences (the one flamboyant, the other reserved), variously bedecked as 'European' or 'Indian'. These three female principals in Umrao Singh's arrested and arresting tableaux gravitate around his lens, posing variously. Their inner lives, like his, are nowhere explored: making visible a subjectivity was clearly not in Umrao Singh's range of intentions.

Together with the three female *dramatis personae* or reflexively drawing apart from them, the husband/father, with his combination of worldliness and spirituality, takes his position in this family quartet. Photographed over a period of six decades, Umrao Singh's self-portraits show a lean, austerely handsome man with erect posture and a self-possessed, reserved, patrician demeanour; a man impassioned with appliances that prosthetically extend the territory into which he projects himself; a man obsessed with himself both spiritually and physically. Umrao Singh depicts himself as both thinker and tinkerer. 'For someone who spent a lifetime tinkering with modern gadgetry,' Deepak Ananth suggests, 'photography was the happiest medium of all, given the visual record it offered of the manual activity that is the bricoleur's pride.'[20] The inclusion of his camera (naturally a familiar device in self-portrait photography) in some of the images brings into focus photography as both the medium of his work and the practice in which he was engaged. Through Umrao Singh's obsession with staging and recording his family and himself, and via these inevitable appearances of the camera in his work, we are made aware of the extent to which, for him, photography and self were intimately entwined. Many years later, his grandson put it this way: 'What I find amazing in these images is Umrao's unwavering conviction in the camera, on the one hand, and in his physicality, on the other.'[21]

Umrao Singh's photographs are always impeccably deliberated. As in the paintings of Manet or Vermeer, portraits are frequently given to view through the device of a frame: whether the intricately carved door frame of the home in Budapest, the simpler windows in Simla, the inclusion of so many of Amrita's canvases purposefully brought into view, or in the ubiquity of mirrors, enabling each family member in turn to take his or her position as both subject and object of the gaze. Their every detail – formal arrangement, depth of field, props and accoutrements, positioning and address – is selected in accordance with ideas of presentation, composition and that elusive but distinct quality we call the photogenic.[22] But more than this, each of Umrao Singh's photographs accords with a range of recognizable criteria – compositional and aesthetic – constituting a mythologized account of his family's exceptionality. In view of these particular qualities, Sundaram suggests that far from being simply a paterfamilias with an amateur interest in photography, Umrao Singh might well be considered one of the invisible pioneers of modern Indian photography.[23]

Diffraction

The sustained fascination that the photographs of Umrao Singh exerts upon his grandson hyperbolizes the way photographs more generally serve as transitional objects and conversation pieces in family life, nourishing individual imagination and in turn shaping the commonly held memories and myths that weave together family narratives, particularly in the face of subsequent loss. Umrao Singh's photographic output served Vivan Sundaram for more than one body of work, most notably in the conceptual precursor to *Re-take of Amrita*, the installation titled *The Sher-Gil Archive* (1995).[24] The autobiographic title points to an elision between the documentary (evidentiary) and the fictional (aesthetic) that is then differently explored in *Re-take of Amrita*. At the same time, this installation exposes one of Sundaram's enduring work strategies, that of incorporating photography – in this instance, pre-existing or 'found photographs' – in multimedia installations. This signals an interest in the relationship between photography and three-dimensional objects, one that has persisted through his practice. Here, Sundaram mines the family archive in order to probe the nature of his own practice as both archivist and artist.[25] 'In India at the time,' he observes, 'the word "archive" did not have the currency that it has now. I used the word "archive" for this piece quite unselfconsciously' (Sundaram, in conversation, November 2016).

In other words, the absorption of 'archive' into 'art' in Sundaram's work was undertaken in the 1990s without the degree of conceptualization that adheres to the use of the term 'archive' today, in the context of a widespread and multi-pronged archival impulse or archival turn in artistic and curatorial practice. David Houston Jones uses the term 'archivalism' for such practice, and Ernst van Alphen speaks of 'archival artworks' where the archive has replaced narrative as the dominant symbolic and cultural form.[26] Not for the last time, Sundaram evinces an instinct for the intellectual *Zeitgeist* at the brink of its emergence. In *The Sher-Gil Archive*, the relationship between strong spatial presence and detailed archival information manifests one of the ways in which such an archival impulse might be played off against an aesthetic deriving from minimalist sculpture.

Probing his maternal ancestry, Sundaram reclaims his grandfather's archive album as document and representation while making visible his legacy: the memory of a genealogy now mediated through a multi-part installation. This enables him to gain a distance that, while not ironic, grants him leverage with regard to truth claims. Out of Umrao Singh's album, Sundaram has created metonymic family 'portraits' through an assemblage of replicated archival photographs, letters in facsimile and 'simulated family possessions in small wooden boxes'[27] and presented these as both (pseudo)documents and *objets trouvés*. The authentic objects of which the copies are simulacra would, by their contiguity to the original users, be close to the notion of a document. They would, in other words, operate as the consolidation or realization, over time, of a trace. In this evocation – simultaneously counterfeit and representation – Sundaram lays bare the vexed and incommensurable relationship between trace, document and archive, undermining the stability of each term as the definitive guarantor of empirical truth.

In its dependence on his grandfather's photographs, *The Sher-Gil Archive* conflates album and archive, allowing them to dissolve into each other, redoubling their historical roles. The fact that, by virtue of their unique means of mechanical and photochemical reproduction, photographs began to be regarded as authenticating and evidentiary documents, also meant that they were granted the status of quintessential archival records.[28] Significantly, then, album and archive share a typology. The archive generates historical meaning by storing and filing unique events, not as a formless mass of random incidents at the mercy of happenstance but as statements organized in conformity with a conditioning structure, an articulated mechanism of interconnected categorical criteria. This is a reformulation of Michel Foucault's famous definition of the archive, whose rules are not imposed from the outside but, rather, constitute themselves simultaneously with that which they formulate: 'It is that which, outside of ourselves, delimits us.' In the same way that official archives contain documents that are outside of current/contemporary bureaucratic requirements – 'paperwork that has lapsed and become garbage'[29] – Foucault's more abstract, philosophical consideration of the archive entails obsolescence and loss: 'The description of the archive deploys its possibilities (and the mastery of its possibilities) on the basis of the very discourses that have just ceased to be ours; its threshold of existence is established by the discontinuity that separates us from what we can no longer say.'[30] Loss and obsolescence, in short, are intrinsic to the meaning of the archive, while indexicality – the trace of the unique, the differentiating imprint, fulcral in the theorization of photography – also govern the formation of an archive, determining that which is *archivable*.

An archival object is, by definition, possessed of a predicament of singularity; and it is this singularity that is embedded in its status as the trace, and thereby the proof, of a unique event existing - axiomatically, and like the event or micro-event of classic analogue photography - in the past. The earliest photographs in the published book of Umrao Singh's photographic work, *Umrao Singh Sher-Gil: His Misery and His Manuscript*,[31] show distinctive signs of their materiality.[32] Far from glossy reprints, the plates reproduce the photographs not as pure images but as just such unique items: scuffed, sometimes torn, cropped or folded archival objects. These reveal the extent to which the archival value of a photograph might reside in equal measure in the image it bears, and in the forensic evidence it supplies as a physical, material object bound by time and place.

In *The Sher-Gil Archive*, Sundaram uses some of the 'well-worn devices of presentation'[33] frequently employed in installation art: display boxes, illuminated vitrines, etched glass plates, photographs mounted in grids or rows. Within the installation, *Four Black Boxes for the Family* flaunts a clean, minimalist aesthetic, but this austerity is undermined by the etched glass covers and contents: autochromes by Umrao Singh. The process of making autochromes, invented by the Lumière brothers and marketed in 1907, was the first viable technique for colour photography to become commercially available. It was the principal form of producing colour photographs before the advent of subtractive colour film. For thirty years or so, this remained the most widely used means of capturing colour on film. The chromatism of autochromes appears, as Max Kozloff evocatively puts it, as though 'time-released': it is at once saturated and tentative. While promoting the illusion of actual colour recall, autochromes, Kozloff urges, are 'suspended between the conviction of impassive finish, given as in the manner of photography, and the artifice of touch and fantasy, familiar in the mode of painting. At times, their colour seems to exist tremblingly, only to evoke another colour, the colour of dream.'[34] Alfred Stieglitz and other Photo-Secessionists enthusiastically adopted the autochrome and considered its invention to have been as important as that of photography itself.[35] Umrao Singh's early adoption of a new and potentially revolutionary system of image-making also supports Sundaram's claim that his grandfather, nominally an amateur photographer, was one of the unsung pioneers of modern photography in India. The distinct, sooty, grainy quality of Umrao Singh's autochromes, here illuminated in their black boxes, grants them a chiaroscuro, painterly effect. The inscription of the names of the four family members - Umrao Singh, Marie Antoinette, Amrita and Indira - on the glass overlaying each box distils the commemorative suggestion borne by the boxes themselves.

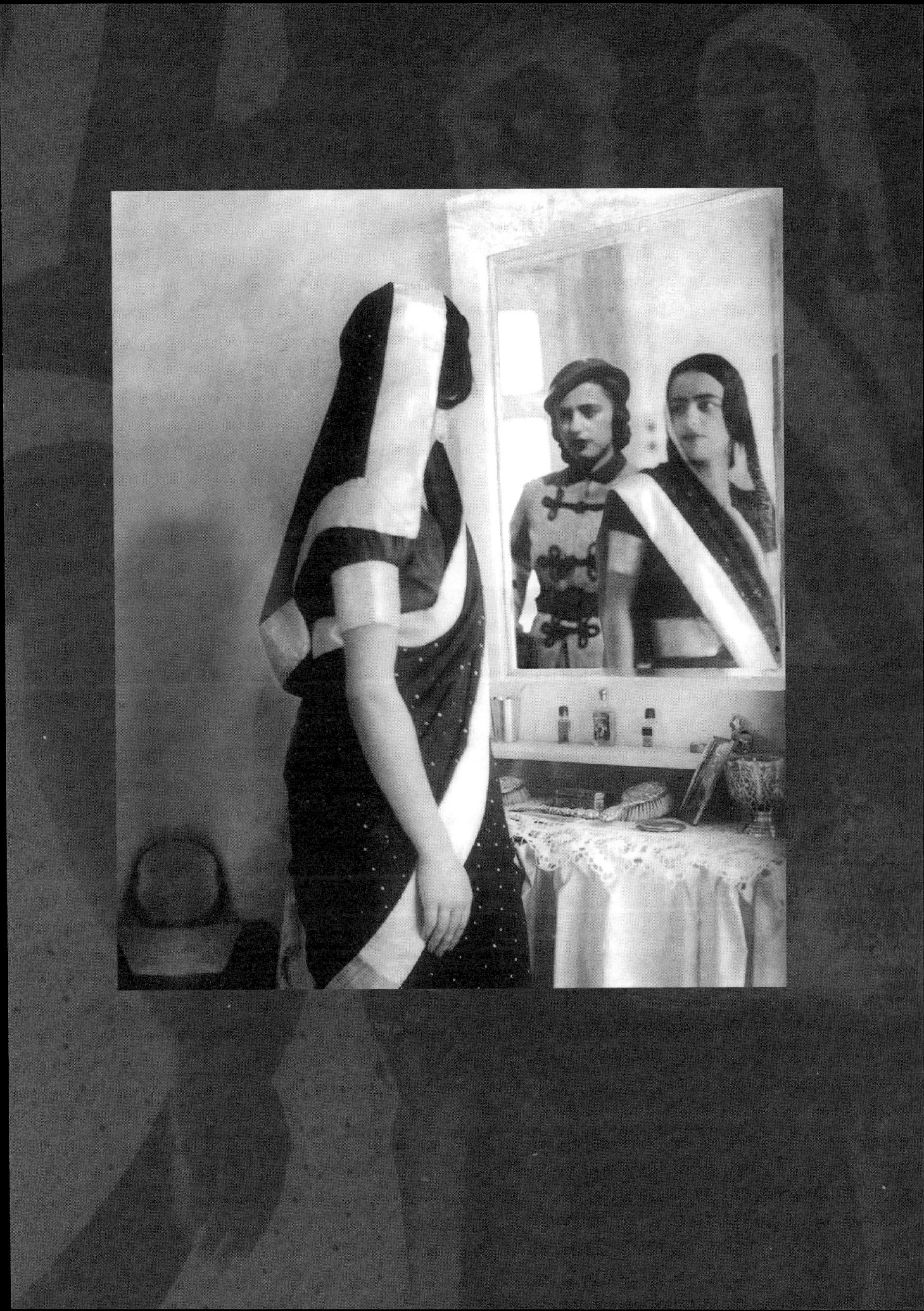

In another section of the installation, objects in glass-topped boxes are convened to evoke different aspects of the family history, captioned *Mother, Father, Sisters, Home* and finally, with a self-conscious twist, *Family Album*. Umrao Singh's photographs, (re)printed and (re)presented, at times mounted on cubes within the presentation boxes, simultaneously showcase the family narrative as historical document in facsimile – simulating the kinds of display we might expect in documentary exhibitions – and explore art-making's capacity to absorb, mediate and re-present the personal. Together, these boxes anticipate *Re-take of Amrita* in purveying a portrait of a cosmopolitan family whose intellectual and artistic endeavours 'crossed continents, languages, philosophies and cultures'.[36] It is through the lens of such cosmopolitanism that Martha Meskimmon considers *The Sher-Gil Archive*. Clearly, the photographs that Sundaram appropriates exemplify the notion of cosmopolitanism as a form of 'elite cultural movement undertaken in the main by artists, writers and intellectuals with sufficient financial resource and/or social and political connections to move freely across geographical and social boundaries'.[37] However, Meskimmon suggests, the four cities that became the sites of the singular, pluri-local Sher-Gil home[38] – Lahore, Budapest, Simla, Paris – were generally places of sanctuary and exile, serving as a background to both conflict and innovation. These are cities marked by complex histories of migration, and incorporating intercontinental trade and cultural exchange, European imperialism and decolonization.[39] While Sundaram is alive to the politics of migration, it is on the dimension of the personal and its positioning in the home, first in the family and only then in the world at large, that he focuses in this work.

Nevertheless, to the extent that subjects are never external to political contexts, arguably, such an exploration of subjectivity as we see in *The Sher-Gil Archive* might be regarded as constituting a political statement. This, convincingly, is how Geeta Kapur considers Sundaram's collation of the documentary and the aesthetic. She leans, no doubt, on the relationship explored within feminist and Marxist discourses alike – between the spheres of the personal and the political. She persuasively links the 'immanent expression of individual subjectivity'[40] to the (confining) norms of a civil society, a relationship that is often disrupted by the liberatory practices of artists. She nevertheless recognizes that this equation – this mediated relay between a radical art and a radical politics – remains, in part, elusive or tendentious. In this context, it might be useful to consider the relationship between aesthetics and politics as Jacques Rancière does, in terms of 'the plurality of ways in which they are linked'.[41]

Kapur provides an account of the ways in which artists in India have slotted into – or stood outside of – accredited power structures, highlighting how 'the courage and imagination of Indian artists' at two historical junctures (during the Indian Emergency of 1975–77 declared by Indira Gandhi, when the government became increasingly authoritarian, and again during the ascendancy of right-wing parties in India from the early 1990s) spawned a generation of artists who broke away from 'a largely classical/modernist art scene'. Alongside Sundaram, Kapur names Nalini Malani, N.N. Rimzon, Rummana Hussain and Navjot Altaf as artists who, from the early 1990s, 'articulated the rupture in the democratic equation between the state and the polity' by 'incorporating documentary photography, by switching over to sculptural and video installations, the language-in-use, and, more important, the subject position of the artist', whereby the works were made 'intentionally unstable, volatile, radical'.[42]

One of the ways in which *The Sher-Gil Archive* bypasses stable categorical definitions resides in its self-conscious exploration of the continuities and slippages that exist in the archive between fact and fiction, or the event and its reconstruction. Simultaneously, we witness the transformation of archive from repository to medium where that medium is installation art, itself a practice that covers many different constituent mediums.[43] Kapur observes that installation art in India has been linked to the positive connotations of the fragment, and also to the migration or displacement of objects, within a society that still boasts a rich artisanal culture and an 'active tradition of magic, fetish and ritual'. She outlines the complex nature of such oscillations in the status of objects, which, in the hands of 'Asian artists', signals an 'in-between stage of use and exchange value. In a situation of incomplete modernization and uneven market economy, there is something like quasi commodification at work: older forms of fetishism survive within new form of reification in the consumer culture.'[44]

In 1997, faced with the challenge of transporting works in a suitcase for his installation at the Sixth Havana Biennale where the theme was 'The Individual and Memory',[45] Sundaram expanded the repertoire of archival objects in *The Sher-Gil Archive* and took three coats, copies of the 'Tolstoy' coat Umrao Singh habitually wore, whose labels included copies of Umrao's autochromes. The second part of the Havana installation was *Portrait of Self and Daughter*, in which 65 small photographs of Umrao Singh and Amrita from Umrao Singh's archive were hung in two stacked rows, reading as a double strip. In this way, two asymmetrical timelines and their years of overlap were rendered visible, illustrating the prematurity of Amrita's death and the number of years that her father survived her. In the double row of images, Sundaram also suggested an analogy with individual frames in a film strip, as though unreeling the lives of Umrao Singh and Amrita as separate but contiguous films.

This encounter between images of father and daughter served as a precursor to what, several years later, Sundaram effected digitally in *Re-take of Amrita.* Wu Hung observes that while Umrao Singh also photographed his daughters in adolescence, it is mostly on Amrita's short life as an adult that Sundaram focuses.[46] In this body of work for which Sundaram is probably best known outside India, he considers the family album, that repository of (quasi) vernacular photography, as an evocative object: not only an object through which both affect and thought are mediated, but also one in which a self-state is stored and explored. Psychoanalyst Christopher Bollas has been particularly instrumental in underlining the ways in which real objects (as against – but also continuous with – the psychic objects of object-relations theory) constitute a lexicon for each individual's aesthetic and emotional experience of self. And because objects are most evocative when they are lost – no longer present – such evocative objects are also charged with nostalgia, 'the emotion of love lost, grief sustained and gratitude for the evocative power of memory that allows us to hold on to the lost object'.[47]

Time and its paradoxical operations lie at the heart of *Re-take of Amrita.* If *The Sher-Gil Archive* is a kind of fetish – a substitute for the lost object in which that very loss is enshrined – *Re-take of Amrita* is the space of a more integrated endeavour. For it envisages the mediation between two opposing forms of temporal engagement: history and memory. Episodes are stitched together in invisible sutures that render an 'entirely constructed space' as 'seemingly real'.[48] The spaces thus fabricated and the characters thus dislocated bind history and memory to fiction and fantasy. Where the fixity or finitude of the archive might hinder new mnemic elaborations, I suggest that the techniques of digital montage employed here enable Sundaram not only to contemplate his family, to grant its members renewed aliveness and sensuousness, but also to probe its invisible trajectories. In this process, other futures are imagined for us, the viewers: other lives in place of past fatalities. The body of digitally constructed 'photographs', in other words, turns away from the traumatic trace and its evidentiary teleology, allowing instead for the (re) inscription and (re)invention of memory.

What was a staged and static pose in Umrao Singh is, in Sundaram, newly narrativized through juxtaposition. The photographic pose has occasionally been likened to a kind of death. Its stasis seems to amplify almost to caricature – the future death that Barthes describes as the *eidos* of photography.[49] Through it we see 'across the surface of [the] body photography's "mortification" of the flesh'.[50]

But the pose is not only the mortal entrapment of flesh as photographic image. Although it enjoys a particular status in photography, the static pose is not unique *to* photography. It is that which lays the ground for what the photographed subject connotes: the pose is connotation incarnate. Such connotation rests upon a store of 'readymade elements of signification' circulating within the culture at large, constituting a historical grammar of iconographic elements derived from 'painting, theatre, associations of ideas, stock metaphors'.[51]

To this list one might add dance, fashion, yoga, TV chefs, the sign language of traffic police or flight attendants, and so forth.[52] In splicing together poses garnered from the different settings and contexts in which their connotations accrue and interrelate, Sundaram's images both acknowledge and distort the signification residing in the images of origin. So, in works such as *Dressed Couple, Man with Pipe* and *Distance*, each composed of two separate, conjoined photographs of Amrita and Victor taken by each other, the couple – thus made of distinct constituent parts – seem unsettlingly disjointed, each partner contained in her/his own solitary world.

Further, in digitally cutting and pasting, Sundaram raises an important question in the name of the album-as-archive. While, in supporting the truth claims of certain historical events, the archive says nothing of how those events are remembered, the album might say less about historical truth and more about how events are memorialized. Functioning also as *objets trouvés*, the images in Umrao Singh's archive suggest to Sundaram that memory itself might be regarded as something found and capable of being integrated into new narrative frames. In this sense, Sundaram is not engaging in an intellectual game, a postmodern appropriation of existing images to dismantle their status. He is, rather, using the existing album/archive in order to open out something hidden, if not forgotten, reiterating the past in order to reclaim or redeem it, reconfiguring the scope of its fatal determinations.

Aberration

Let us look, then, at a work from *Re-take* that has a relationship to time embedded in its content and enshrined in its title, *Remembering the Past, Looking to the Future*. This work hyperbolizes the relationships present in *Re-take of Amrita* at large. Swathed in a sari, immaculately coiffed and adorned, Amrita holds sway as the beautiful figure shadowing her father and occupying the apex of a triangular composition. She casts a pensive sideways glance away from a bearded and aged Umrao Singh, sitting at a desk. His presence is commanding, but his mental retreat is palpable. With the central figures of father and daughter psychologically withdrawn, the gazes that address us more engagingly occupy the periphery of the composition: at bottom right Indira, in softer focus, holding a cat and seemingly innocent of distress; and further back, reflected in a mirror on the mantelpiece, Marie Antoinette looks up from the letter she is reading at an escritoire, as though interrupted by the photographer. The interior is organized as a series of frames and frames-within-frames (dados, doors, a mirror, pictures), refracting and articulating the space while rendering it ambiguous. The work is also replete with art-historical allusions, not least the cat that Indira holds and the letter in Marie Antoinette's hand, both traditional and feminine props in Western painting.

The full nuclear family is figured as a staged gathering of players where – with the seams joining discreet photographs rendered invisible – we are left to consider the solitude, or even alienation, of each of the figures, none engaging with any of the others. In fact, this solipsistic view of the self is, as we saw in *Dressed Couple, Man with Pipe* and *Distance,* one of the consequences of Sundaram's montage procedure.[53] Stripped away from historical time, the composite image articulates the temporalities of the constituent photographs into a hypothetical present. In this context, the contemplative expressions of father and first-born daughter embody the descriptor 'remembering the past', while the direct, frontal gazes of mother and younger daughter configure 'looking to the future'. Yet, the future to which the picture itself gestures is of course, for the contemporary viewer, already a *fait accompli,* always already in the past. It is an 'anterior future'[54] in which familial coherence is shattered by tragedy.

This foreboding of something that has already happened is everywhere in *Re-take of Amrita.* Speaking of this work, Sundaram observes:

> Umrao Singh is the 'essential' photographer; I will orchestrate the images with a digital wand half a century later. In excavating the photograph of the artist as a boy with a Voigtlander camera, I signal a provocative relationship. An artist using his family archive of photographs to make 'future' works of art: what kind of ... narcissistic relay does this unwind?[55]

With the wand that is digital post-production processing, Sundaram pieces together this triptych, tipping a hat in the direction of a well-worn compositional

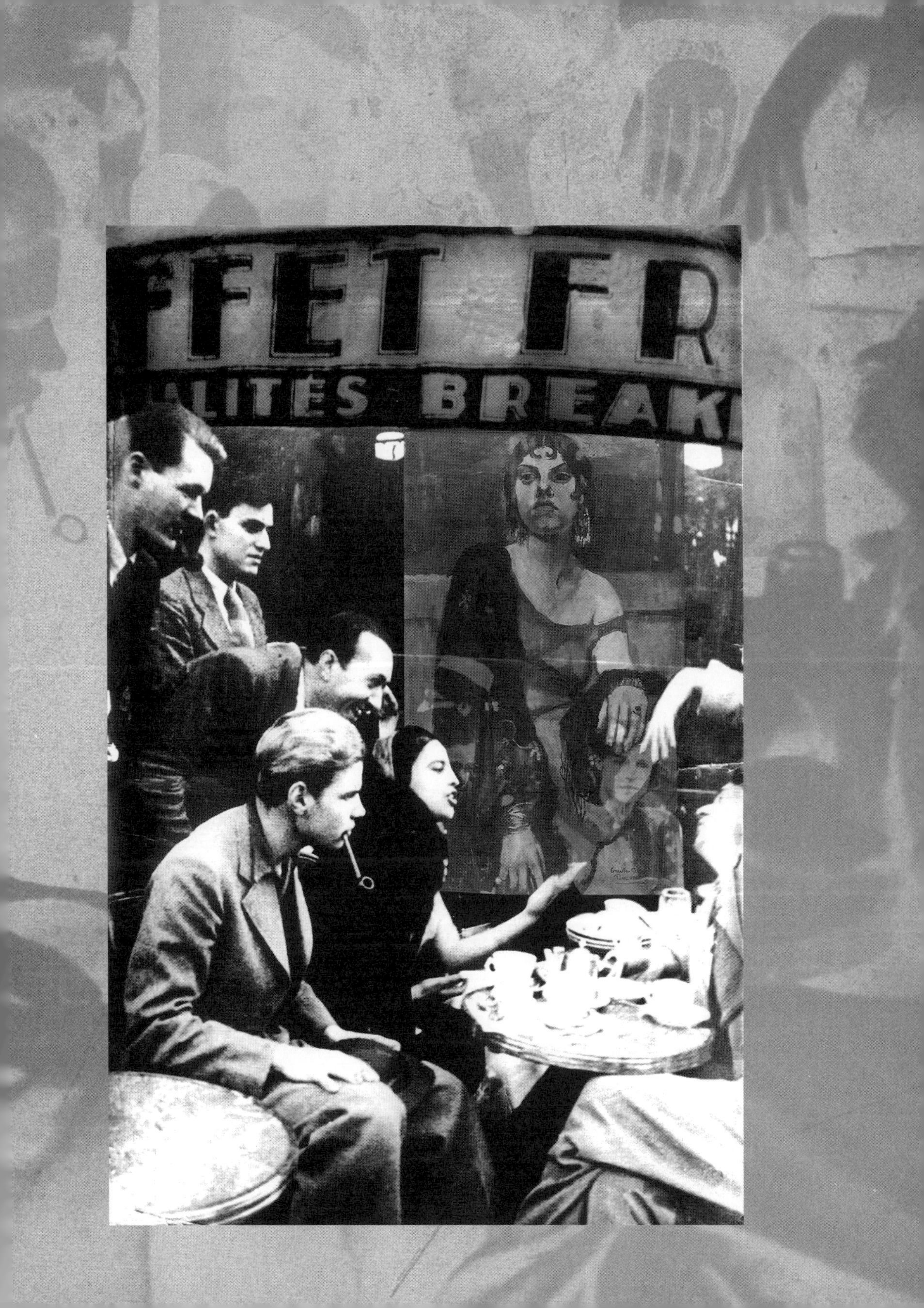
FFET FR
LITÉS BREAK

form used for centuries in painting and carving. As in all the works in *Re-take*, this one too collates figures convened from different locations and times. Along with the affecting image of grandfather and grandson, we see Marie Antoinette pregnant with Amrita; an adult Indira in Western gear; and an equally grown-up Amrita split into the two figures that sartorially describe her culturally mixed heritage, and that also constitute *Doppelganger*, an autonomous work within *Re-take of Amrita* and hence a meta-picture within a meta-picture.[56] With this layering of allusions and temporalities, Sundaram delivers an archaeology of his family. Yet that description does not explain the sense of unease which the uncanny conflation of temporalities provokes. Sundaram appears to recognize that unease in his interrogation of the appearance of his young self in this picture: 'An artist using his family archive of photographs to make "future" works of art: what kind of ... narcissistic relay does this unwind?' This question entails not only the relay between Vivan the child and Sundaram the adult artist, now retrospectively tapping into a family narrative. It also addresses the reflexive loop of self-rapture in which all the characters are caught. In *Bourgeois Family: Mirror Frieze*, such narcissism appears in programmatic form, not – for once – in the figure of Umrao Singh, but in the three women entranced by their own specular images, and in the little boy discovering the paradox and joy of directing a camera at a mirror.

It is, I have argued, digitization that has enabled the suturing that gives full aesthetic form to Sundaram's hauntings. It is now commonly acknowledged that digital image production (or the capabilities of digitization to which pre-existing analogue photographs are exposed) dismantle the causal link between ostensibly unadulterated reality and image. But in effect, digitization highlights the representational status of all photographic images. This notion was explored by some of the earliest practitioners and theorists of digital imaging. In the early 1990s, at what we would now perhaps call the dawn of the digital age, Mexican photographer Pedro Meyer was busy shattering the photographic pact – the truth effect of photography – by digitally altering images in Photoshop, rendering them in a quasi-documentary style that brought together temporally disjointed photographic images in a deadpan, apparently factual fashion. And in 1996, Florian Rötzer wrote:

> At the moment, photography is suffering the fate of all analogue media whose independence is eliminated with their integration into the digital code. Photographs or the photographic apparatus merely provide digitizable data which can be processed by a computer and thus altered at will. ... Naturally, photography also offered sufficient

> possibilities of circumventing the documentary effector exploiting it in an underhanded manner. It is claimed that the digitization of photography completes the deception, as interventions into the image are no longer visible.[57]

Photomontage, in other words, has existed for a long time,[58] but digitization enables the cuts and junctures to occur not materially but at the level of the image, while having no effect on the surface of the material object (the digital print), so that the printed photograph is granted smoothness and continuity. It is, then, the invisibility of the sutures between constituent parts of distinct and discreet analogue images that grants Sundaram, and the numerous other artists employing similar technological means, an expanded palette of possibility.

While cinema was the first medium to share photography's relationship with reality via the indexical, and also to show moving images of the real world, it was also, historically, the medium of optical illusion, of magic and the supernatural. The idea of special effects was introduced into cinema not long after its invention, and an early filmmaker like George Méliès has been celebrated as the author of 'non-actuality' or 'trick' films, whose origins point to the illusionism of the fairground or amusement park. This capability of allowing the real and the fantastical to converge has also rendered cinema an ideal medium for the evocation of dreams, and this is something that *Re-take of Amrita* invokes.

Sundaram raises the idea of the oneiric in a roundabout way, in discussing his inclusion of Amrita's work in *Re-take of Amrita*. Incorporating many images of Amrita's paintings in his digital montages, he elaborates on Amrita playing out the trope of the artist posing while painting. He describes it thus: '[T]he artist can slip between and behind the paintings, the painted figure can be seen to be real, as real as the artist or the model. ... Amrita as the photographer's model melts into her figural compositions like a dream sequence in cinema.'[59] Here Sundaram is alluding to the visual devices used to create the notion of a dream sequence cinematographically, within the diegesis of a given film. But clearly, he also taps into that critical tradition which has seen the art of cinema, from its earliest inception, as a cultural equivalent of dreaming: Roland Barthes, Christian Metz and Jean-Louis Baudry have all, in different ways, thrown light on this analogy.

With its play of light and shade, and its ability to give equivalent form and movement to both the real and the fantastical, cinema has been particularly fecund in dream imagery. Aside from the formal and rhetorical devices that have been used to designate dream sequences in film, it is also the viewer's immersion in a dark room, within which moving images are projected as flickering light, that acts as a physical analogue to the projection of dreams in the dark recesses of the sleeping subject's mind. 'According to a true metonymy,' writes Barthes,

> the darkness of the theatre is prefigured by the 'twilight reverie' (a prerequisite for hypnosis, according to Breuer-Freud) which precedes it and leads [the viewer] from street to street, from poster to poster, finally burying himself in a dim, anonymous, indifferent cube where that festival of affects known as a film will be presented.[60]

Christian Metz takes this one step further by yoking together cinema and dreams through the psychic processes that they both mobilize. He argues that both dreams and cinema encourage narcissistic withdrawal and the indulgence of fantasy. Both entail 'withdrawal of the libido into the ego, temporary suspension of concern for the exterior world as well as the cathexis of object, at least in their real form'.[61] And finally, in his formulation of 'apparatus theory', which sees all cinema as ideological (a critical stance that has become so prevalent as now to be considered a given), Jean-Louis Baudry establishes further points of contact between dreams and film. These include a 'capacity for figuration, translation of thoughts into images, reality extended to representations', as well as a sense of intensity and hyper-reality that both impart upon the subject. Baudry sees the cinematic apparatus as a response to a wish that can be traced back as far as Plato: 'the wish to construct a simulation machine capable of offering the subject perceptions which are really representations mistaken for perceptions'.[62]

The slippage between representation and perception that Sundaram underlines by setting off photographic and painted image – for instance, in the works titled *Self as Tahitian, Style, Artist with 'Fruit Vendors', Sisters with 'Two Girls'* – is further nuanced by his inclusion of many images containing mirrors. Mirrors are, of course, old standbys in self-portraiture, frequently used knowingly to explore identity to probe sameness and difference. Sundaram harnesses 'the specular ruse by which resemblance ricochets back a self-same otherness'.[63] The identification entailed in the meeting of self with self-as-other in the reflection also turns the self into an idealized other. Where he juxtaposes father and daughter, Sundaram presses upon us the notion that together they rehearse, claim, and then collapse different versions of self and other, exploring the relationship between narcissism, idealization and desire. If (self-)idealization occurs first in relation to the corporeal image in which the subject aspires to see him/herself, crucially, to idealize is also to posit the image as a desired mirror. Here, the ghost of 'the lover' (father/daughter) appears, to borrow Julia Kristeva's formulation, as a narcissist with an object.[64]

While constantly taking (re)possession of a past that is over but not done with, Sundaram's *Re-take of Amrita,* I am urging, also repeatedly – obsessively – works through a double legacy: the haunting effects of parental/adult narcissism on Vivan the child (where both Amrita and Umrao Singh stand as parental substitutes), and the prolonged repercussions of identification and idealization that shape familial seduction. With this in mind, we may consider the mirror in *Re-take of Amrita* not only as a kind of magnet for idealization/identification, but also, to use Kaja Silverman's formulation, as a 'mirage' preventing the subject from 'apprehending his or her fundamental nothingness ... a lure encouraging him or her to pursue endlessly that imaginary plenitude whose unavoidable sequel is the fantasy of bodily fragmentation'.[65] Shattering of self, annihilation, the sense of a death to come: these are prefigured and held at bay by the narcissism and idealization for which the mirror stands.

Amrita and Umrao Singh, in Sundaram's retelling of the family narrative, ceaselessly play out this route between narcissism, idealization, love and the *loss* that is love's inevitable aftermath. But in eschewing a linear narrative arrangement of these processes, Sundaram refuses to grant the family history a teleology. In the oneiric cinematographic co-presence of the adult Amrita and the aged Umrao Singh who survived and now mourns her, Sundaram reconfigures the future death that haunts all analogue photography, and that, in the complex temporality of *Re-take of Amrita,* has of course already occurred. Granted a second life in Umrao Singh's portraits of her, Amrita is more fully revived in Sundaram's *Re-take*: a revivification that remains, nonetheless, melancholic and conjectural. In this sense, *Re-take of Amrita* gives form to the simultaneity of all temporalities in the psyche also epitomized by the way the dead and the living so readily cohabit in dreams. *Re-take* throws light, then, on the uncanniness[66] of dreams, the way they represent a perceptual (if chimeric) form to the desire as already fulfilled.

As though possessed, the kar sevaks work with demonic energy and, with the help of pickaxes, hammers, shovels and iron rods, flatten the entire structure in just 5 hours and 45 minutes.

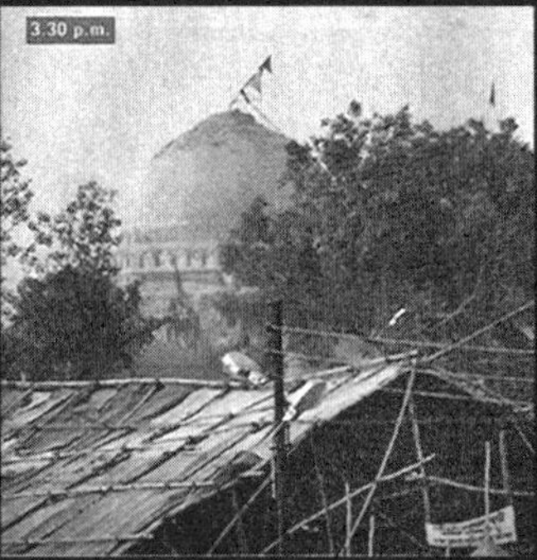

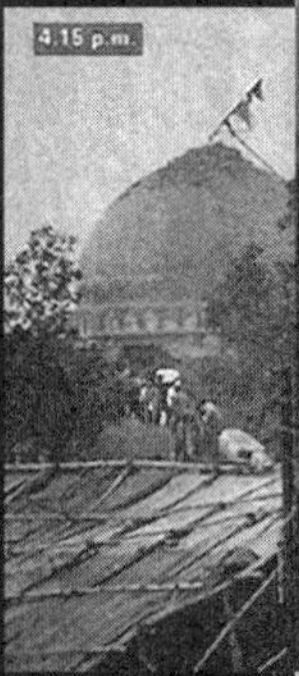

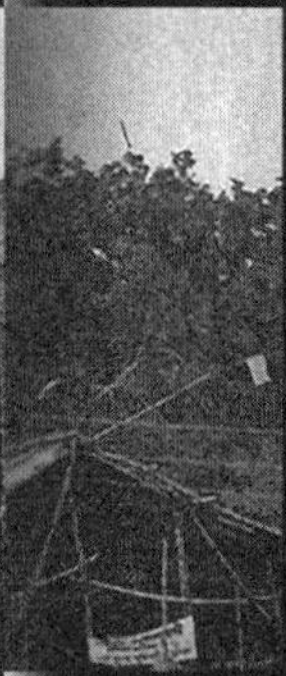

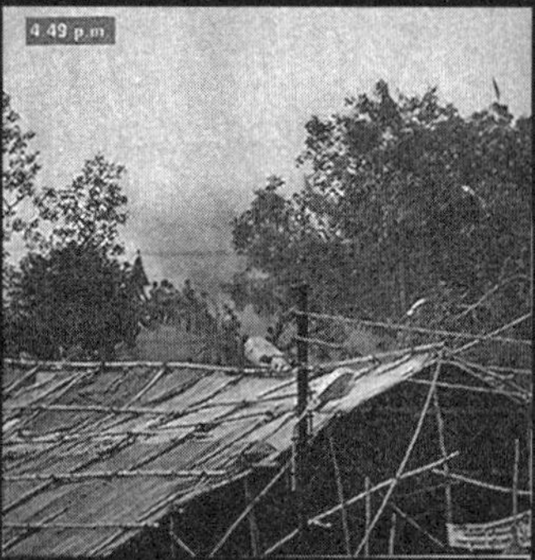

gent believed that before sundown, and in the space of a few hours, the triple domes that loomed so securely on the horizon would be razed to the ground. The mood among the kar sevaks had been sullen but not overly aggressive and even the occasional outbursts of anger or militant slogans seemed like aberrations against the backdrop of the solemn rituals and the singing of bhajans. Kar sevaks were even frisked and made to pass through metal detectors before entering the temple area.

But the inaction of the past few days as they waited for D-Day, December 6, had made them restive. By December 5, the mood had started to change, the indecision of the leadership on whether to allow construction, had stirred the hornets' hive. Harcharan Singh, 32, a strapping kar sevak from Haryana, echoed an increasingly held view when he flatly stated: "After all this if the leaders do not allow kar seva, they will face our *'maar seva'* (beating)."

"It is the most blissful day of my entire life, I keep pinching myself to see if I am awake."
UMA BHARATI

■

The afternoon of December 5 was the turning point. That was when it was finally announced that there would be a symbolic kar seva. Ayodhya simmered with suppressed anger and frustration. Hundreds of kar sevaks stormed the Maniram Chavani where two of the religious leaders—Mahant Ram Chandra Paramhans and Mahant Nrit Gopal Das—were subjected to a volley of angry questions. In the narrow, serpentine lanes of Ayodhya, the slogans were becoming more menacing. *"Jis Hindu ka khoon na khaula, khoon nahin wo paani hai"* (If a Hindu's blood doesn't boil, then it's water, not blood). In the Karsevakpuram area, thousands converged to express their wrath against the leadership. The Frankenstein's monster had been born. And its creators were now its immediate victims.

Ashok Singhal, general secretary of the VHP, pleaded with the mahants to bridge the ominous chasm that had suddenly opened up between the Janki Mahal Trust—the camp headquarters of the leaders—and Karsevakpuram, where angry kar sevaks were clustered in open defiance. The mahants, sensing the ugly mood, stayed put. Only Vinay Katiyar, Bajrang Dal chief and Faizabad MP, dared to cross over to Karsevakpuram, where the hostile mob immediately surrounded him demanding that the leaders reconsider their decision of a symbolic kar seva. Katiyar's message about the militant mood was passed on to L.K. Advani and company. But by now, the movement had been clearly hijacked by the hotheads. As a worried Paramhans said: "Who except Ram Lalla can know about the kind of kar seva which will be undertaken tomorrow."

"Hindu sentiments in this country cannot be subjugated for long. This has been proved today."
ASHOK SINGHAL

■

Sunday, December 6. The count down to disaster begins.

6 a.m. The steady stream of kar sevaks and journalists start arriving at the disputed shrine. Straddling the security wall were PAC constables armed with batons and RSS volunteers with armbands. Overnight, additional barricades encircling the 2.77-acre plot had been erected. Most of the mediapersons gather around the platform constructed during the July kar seva, instead of the roof-top of Manas Bhavan, the official press enclosure.

10 a.m. Sadhus, mahants and various leaders including Advani and BJP President Murli Manohar Joshi arrive at the platform to review the arrangements for the 'symbolic' kar seva.

10.30 a.m. VHP and BJP leaders move to the dais at the Ram Katha Kunj, 200 yards away from the designated kar seva site, where they are scheduled to address a public meeting. The objective was to avoid the angry crowd building up at the kar seva site. Within a matter of minutes, small but defiant groups of kar sevaks start pushing at the security cordon surrounding the main entrance to the disputed area. The PAC jawans and RSS volunteers struggle to hold back the crowds.

11 a.m. The first of the kar sevaks break through the cordon. Within seconds, a few more follow as the barricades are breached in three places directly in front of the shrine. Solitary and shrill shouts of *"Mandir yahin banayenge"* (We'll build the temple at this very spot) puncture the atmosphere. The police are standing idle, but the RSS volunteers in charge of security continue to try and stop the kar sevaks, chasing them and even physically removing them from the secured platform area. Among the throng of mediapersons there is nervous laughter at the comical sight.

11.15 a.m. The kar sevaks had breached the barricades in at least half a dozen places but there is still no definite indication of an impending storm. Faizabad Superintendent of Police, D.B. Rai, tells the media contingent: "It is all under control. Go and relax, you are only wasting your time." So it seems.

11.35 a.m. The sadhus, headed by Mahant Paramhans and Nrit Gopal Das, are scheduled to start a puja ceremony on the newly-built platform. But elsewhere, the floodgates have opened. Towards the rear of the disputed structure, 50-odd kar sevaks slither across the security wall. As RSS volunteers and PAC personnel try to stop them, a hail of stones thrown

(Clockwise from left) Post-destruction jubilation; Demagogue Sadhvi Rithambara raises her arms towards the crowds in triumph; Acharya Dharmendra (left) ecstatically hugging BJP MP S.C. Dixit.

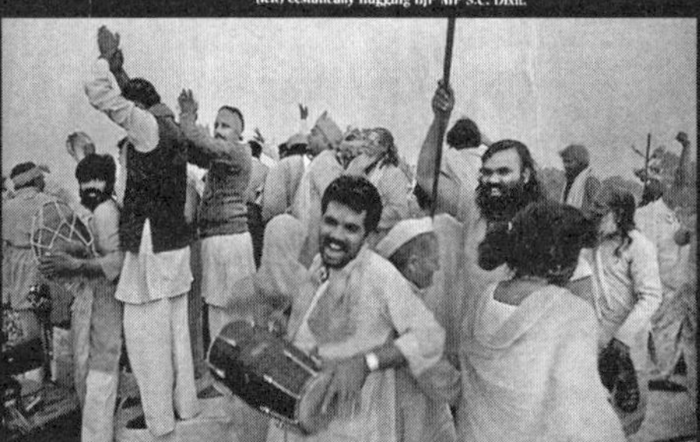

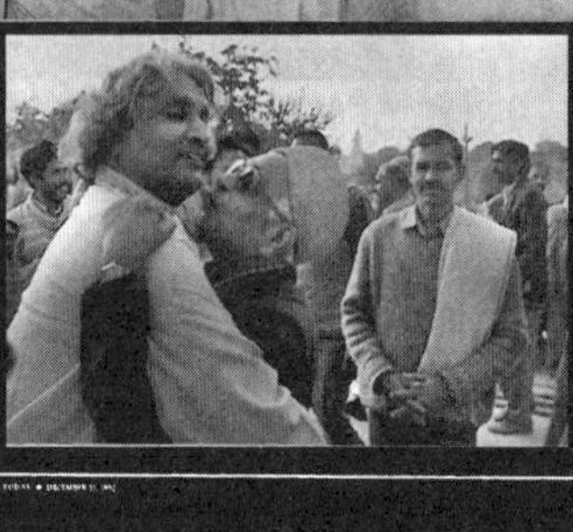

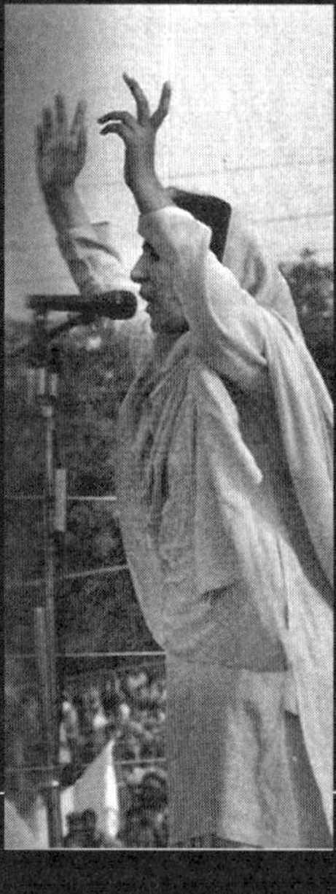

"Leaders who don't allow ka[r] seva, will face our 'maar sev[a]' (beating)."
A kar sevak

■

"The demoliti[on] has erased a 4[...] year-old blot."
TARAKANT JHA
BJP leader

■

"It is Hanuma[n's] mace at work."
VINAY KATIYA[R]

■

12 Zooming In

2020

Rahaab Allana in conversation with Prashant Panjiar

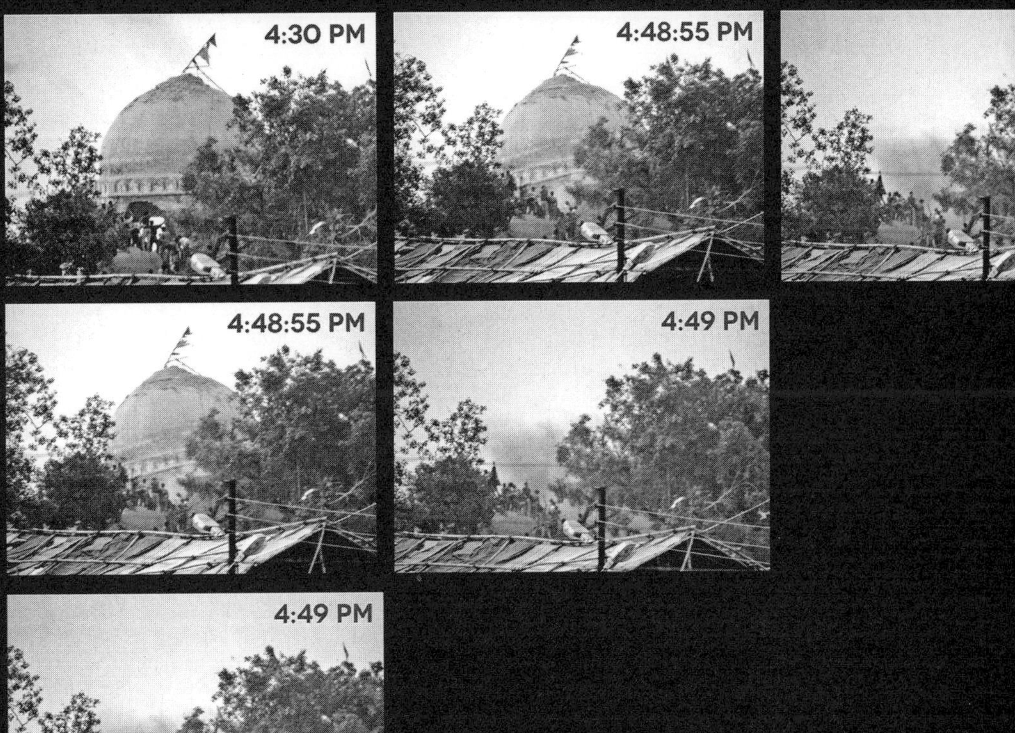

Veteran photojournalist Prashant Panjiar discusses his career and the significant shifts and turns in the Indian media industry over the past four decades. Drawing on his experience as a photographer for *The Indian Express*, a major national daily, and for two mainstream news magazines *India Today* and *Outlook*, he describes, among other subjects, the exponential development of media culture and the transformation of editorial and publishing practices with the advent of cable television and digital technology in the post-liberalized India of the 1990s and 2000s. Panjiar also identifies the influence of corporate culture and its singular, coercive view of media as a 'business' rather than as a platform for diverse voices; and the ongoing pressure on journalists due to the aggressive hegemony of right-wing politics and a simultaneous erosion of leftist ideologies. He is known for some of the most iconic images of post-Independence political history, many of which feature in his recent book, *That Which is Unseen* (Ahmedabad: Navjivan Trust, 2021).

Interview conducted by Rahaab Allana in 2020. Published with permission of Prashant Panjiar.

Keywords and Names

Picture Editor: Relatively recent position of prominence in journalism, tasked with the responsibility to conceive visuals to accompany stories, commission photographers, select and edit images, position them in the layout, and sign off on publication. Key figure in determining how the narrative is communicated through complementary relationships between image and text.

Babri Masjid/Ram Janmabhoomi violence (1992), *Dalit*, *Documentary photography*, *Emergency 1975–77*, *Left movement in India*, *Photojournalism*, see Keywords at the back of this volume.

Images

pp. 224–25: *Demolition of Babri Masjid, Ayodhya*, 1992. Prashant Panjiar – *India Today* / from the publication *That Which Is Seen*. Cover story spreads from the feature dated 31 December 1992.

p. 231: 'Arms for the Asking', *India Today*, 31 July 1989, special feature by Shekhar Gupta with images by Prashant Panjiar on the arms bazaar at Dara Adam Khel, Pakistan.

p. 235: *Kunti Devi, Shankarbigha, Bihar*, 1999. Prashant Panjiar – *Outlook* / from the publication *That Which Is Unseen*. Image taken while covering the assassination of 23 **Dalits** (see Keywords) in Shankarbigha village in Bihar's Jehanabad district. The prime accused of the carnage were members of the Ranvir Sena, a militia of Bhumihar landlords. Later that year most of the accused were acquitted.

Images courtesy Prashant Panjiar

> Early on in my career, I had a discussion with a senior editor ... and asked if as journalists we were supposed to be unbiased and objective. He said, no, whether you'd like it or not, the truth is biased. That kind of stuck with me ...
>
> I think it's important for us photographers to have a worldview. You might call it an ethic, a politics, whatever you like – to have a view of what you believe in is important. Writers and reporters bring their opinion into their work. Why shouldn't we as photojournalists not have that right too?
>
> – Prashant Panjiar[1]

Rahaab Allana (RA): When did you actively begin your career?

Prashant Panjiar (PP): I started as a professional photographer in 1978, and began working as a photojournalist in 1981. I joined a newspaper in 1984, after about six years of independent freelance photographic work.

RA: You say that the 1990s were not the 'heyday of photojournalism' ...

PP: The 'heyday of photojournalism' ... Do you mean in India, or internationally?

RA: In the 1990s, photojournalism in the international context was benefiting from technological advances and wider orbits of image distribution. What do you consider to be a significant marker of the evolution of photojournalism in India?

PP: Generally speaking, the 'heyday of photojournalism' in both contexts was shaped through the arrival and success of popular illustrated magazines. Post World War II, the West produced magazines such as *Look*[2] and *Life*, and that mode of print culture was already very active before the mid-twentieth century. In India we only had the *Illustrated Weekly of India*[3] as such, and specific magazines with a journalistic focus were quite rare. Here the illustrated magazines took off as a genre post-Emergency. *India Today*[4] was more or less born during the Emergency; *Sunday* came after the Emergency; and there were many others, including regional and vernacular publications. And that's when you actually saw the rise of photojournalism in India.

RA: How did technological changes influence production processes and the quality of photojournalism in the 1990s?

PP: The biggest shift happened in the 1990s – namely, that we started working with computers. Prior to that, our processes were more or less manual. Phototypesetting, layout, even the cover, which was made on cellophane paper with the colours, the headline, mastered, layered on top of that. The team would output what they called the 'chromaline'[5] for us to check and approve, and then it was ready for printing. All this changed when we were able to get information from the computer, actually design pages, design the cover, on the computer. This was a major, major change.

RA: *India Today* was one of the most influential news magazines at the time - what kind of circulation would it have had in the early 1990s?

PP: As far as I remember the figures, circulation varied from about 2,75,000 to 3,50,000 - the approximate range. Multiply that by three or four and you get the overall readership. What sets magazines apart from newspapers, and the reason why magazines are fundamental for photojournalism, is that the newspapers in general relied on the single image and magazines relied on photo series.

RA: Can you describe the newsroom culture of the 1980s and 1990s? What was it like to go through the process of a photo editorial on a typical working day - for instance, how did the editors treat your story on the Gulf War?

PP: Well, in those days newsroom culture used to be completely personality-driven. I have worked in *Patriot*,[6] a small newspaper, which was different. Here I'm talking about my experience of two major publications: *India Today* and *Outlook*. Raghu Rai[7] was Picture Editor when I joined *India Today*. At that time it was a fortnightly. The photo editing process at the magazine was entirely conditioned by his personality. When Raghu was in charge he had the principal say - he decided how many, and whose, images should appear in each issue, and he had very definite ideas about how the pictures should be edited. Raghu had left *India Today* by late 1989, so I'm describing the post-Raghu period: the 1990s onwards. The photo department had a darkroom, a processing lab, light tables and those kinds of accessories, as well as a projector for slides. For the choice of cover image, senior editors would come into the department; we would project images on the wall in the darkroom and there would be a discussion. Someone from the art department would place an outline of the *India Today* cover over the projected image to create mock-ups of what the final cover might look like. The picture was selected in this way - through a conglomeration of five to six people, along with the art director. But for any major story, as was the case with my Gulf War story, the reporter would focus only on the text, and we photographers would participate in image selection through creating a shortlist of options that the picture editor would then show to the senior editors.

Our input in the photo-editorial processes had to do with the personas of the chief editors. Aroon Purie[8] of *India Today* and Vinod Mehta of *Outlook* were very different, and had very different ways of looking at stories. Regarding images for a story, Vinod Mehta didn't have the patience to deal with minute details. He would only engage with us at the layout stage.

RA: Who were some of your prominent colleagues in the 1980s and 1990s?

PP: At *India Today* there was Pramod Pushkarna,[9] Bhawan Singh, Sharad Saxena, Saibal Das, Namas Bhojani, Fawzan Husain.[10] At *Outlook* I worked with T. Narayan,[11] Jitender Gupta,[12] Gireesh GV, Gauri Gill, Tribhuvan Tiwari,[13] Sushobhan Rakshit (Photo Research), Atul Loke, Abhijit Bhatlekar, Swapan Nayak and many others. They were my immediate colleagues. In the wider professional sphere Pablo Bartholomew, Sondeep Shankar and Raghu Rai were active; Dayanita Singh was still slightly connected to journalism. Arko Datta came later.[14]

RA: The 1980s and 1990s were so volatile, politically and socially. During this period you covered major events, including the Sardar Sarovar/Narmada Bachao Andolan,[15] Babri Masjid/Ayodhya,[16] the Gulf War ... And then you found yourself within the sudden rush of media stories oriented towards marking fifty years of Independence. What did this mean to you as a professional?

PP: By that time I was working at *Outlook*. There I was not just a photographer, I had a slightly different position – I was very much part of the editorial team that decided the magazine's content.

In earlier decades, if you look at leftist movements or the Naxalite movement, these took the form of rebellion outside the system, challenging the authority of the state. Whereas after the 1980s all the movements we have seen are within the so-called system and trying to change the nature of our society by participating in politics. In the 1990s, whether it was the rise of the Dalit political parties, or the right-wing Hindutva movement, the intention was to grab political power through the mainstream political process.

I entered journalism in the 1980s, so media people who witnessed earlier decades might have viewed these power-grabbing politics in a different way. But through the mandate of working on stories to reflect fifty years of Independence, journalists of my generation had the opportunity to look at what had happened earlier. Our work was almost a kind of assessment of where and how we began evolving as a nation, what we had imagined, and the kind of social vision held by those who had fought for our freedom and self-rule. One had not really thought about those things till now.

These concerns were reflected in the media - for instance, *Outlook* produced its Partition issue, Independence issue - and those themes remained in place till the end of the 1990s and the start of the new millennium. We did a lot of Special Issues - one cover story was titled 'The Idea of India', drawing on the title of Sunil Khilnani's book.[17] Through my work at that time I was able to learn what I had not understood well earlier - current happenings in relation to their roots in the history of modern India, and the tactics being used by right-wing parties to grab power.

RA: You have documented major 'national' events and crises, including the general election of 1998, the Kargil War in 1999, the Dalit movement in 1999, Naxal politics in 2001, the Gujarat riots in 2002.[18] Today, so much contemporary media production is aligned along a definite political arc - it feels as if very particular, singular, ideologically legitimated concepts of 'nation', 'nationality', 'national identity', 'nationhood', etc., are being pressed into the minds of journalists as well as the reading and viewing public. In your view, what impact does such pressure have on the culture of journalism? With all your experience, could you have foreseen this mode of pressure, exerted on both the media and consumers of media?

PP: I was then working at *Outlook*, and the editor, Vinod Mehta,[19] can best be described only as a liberal anarchist. He had no patience for the right-wing at all and therefore the magazine was very critical of what was happening, even in the Vajpayee government.[20] So we were actually targeted by the state. And at the same time one could observe the start of fissuring and divergence within newspapers and magazines - not based on ideological differences but on the differing concepts about the nature and functions of media. I don't think newspapers like *The Times of India*[21] and others became right-wing because they believed in the ideology; this happened because they became just businesses, rather than being just newspapers.

The 1990s were also the start of liberalization and globalization in India, with Narasimha Rao[22] as Prime Minister and Manmohan Singh[23] as Finance Minister, and the opening up of the economy. By the end of the 1990s much of the Indian media was switching its focus. They realized that the readership, mainly from the upper-middle and middle classes, were more concerned with their own lives and their own surroundings, and were not necessarily interested in events outside the metro cities, or in the villages. This was a sharp shift, and therefore a lot of reporting after the mid-1990s moved towards lifestyle; and the first malls were set up in big cities at that time. And at the same time many publications started defining and advertising themselves as 'products'. Some newspapers, like *The Indian Express*[24] and *The Hindu*,[25] and magazines like *Outlook*, stayed on their earlier path

DARRA ADAM KHEL

Arms for the Asking

Just 50 km south of the Pakistani frontier city of Peshawar, in an area governed by tribal laws, lies the world's most unusual arms bazaar frequented by the subcontinent's extremists. Here lethal weapons sell openly alongside narcotics.

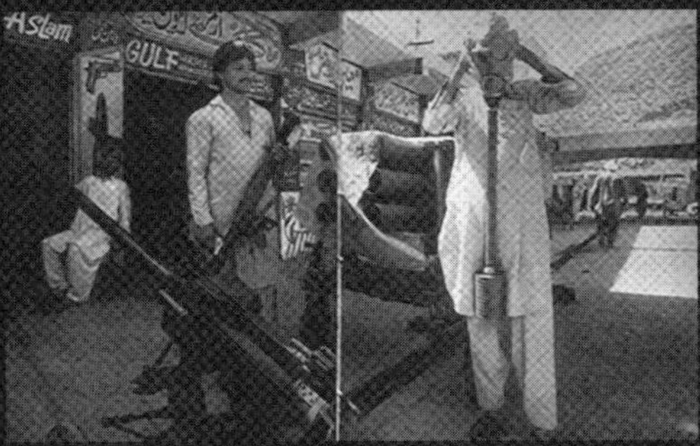

This is the ultimate arms bazaar. No one asks the buyer's name, address or intentions. What matters is the bulge in the pocket.

PRICE LIST

Item	(in Rs)
Kalashnikov rifle (Russian)	13,000
Kalashnikov (Chinese)	10,000
Kalashnikov (local remake)	3,000
RPG-7 rocket launcher	20,000
Anti-aircraft gun	45,000
Stalin's Organ (multi-barrel rocket-launcher)	55,000
Chinese BM-1 rocket-launcher	28,000
Anti-Personnel mines (per dozen)	1,000
Anti-tank mines (per dozen)	5,000
Mine sweeping equipment	10,000
Gas Mask	500
Kalashnikov bullets (local per hundred)	60
Kalashnikov bullets (Soviet per hundred)	90

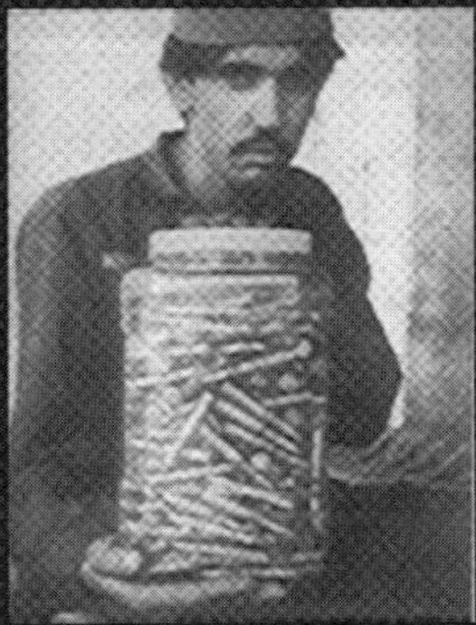

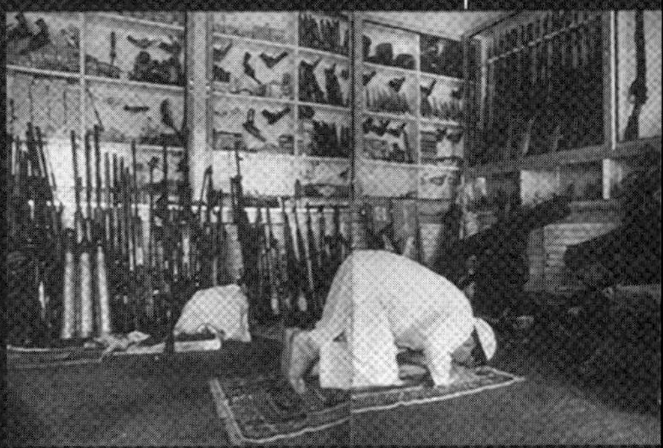

The tribals are fiercely proud of their "freedom", and despite international pressures Pakistani regimes have refused to curb their businesses.

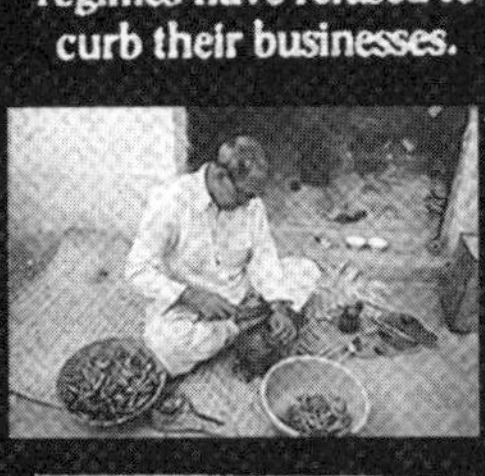

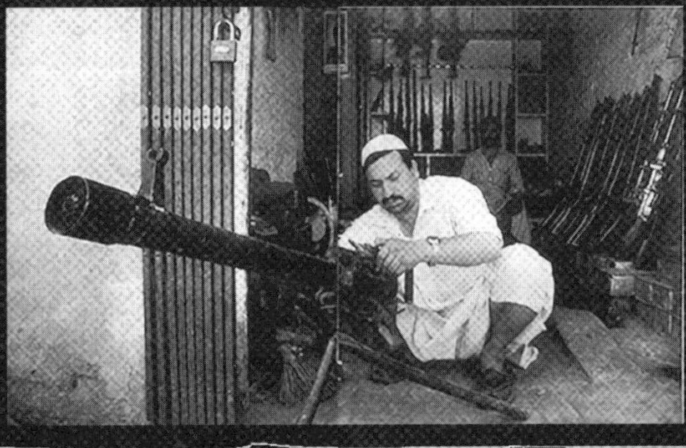

because of their editors. Whereas other publications, now thinking of themselves primarily as businesses, or with their owners seeing themselves as media tycoons rather than as editors, reoriented themselves to the new consumerism. I saw the beginnings of this kind of cosying up to the establishment, to particular business and political powers, and to the regime as a whole.

In the past, we had newspapers and magazines that were sympathetic to a certain cause at certain times; and party-oriented newspapers have always existed. I have worked for a left-wing paper which was very sympathetic to the CPI. Such movement has always been there, but the real turns take place when allegiances are no longer based on ideology but on other factors. And today you see the extreme end of this. A large part of the media is now in bed with today's rulers.

RA: Earlier, the whole point of investigative journalism was to go out into the field to get the story. It has changed dramatically; today the preference seems to be to just reflect on what is out there, rather than actually being out there, in real time, on the ground ...

PP: The problem is deeper than that. When a right-wing regressive mindset dominates the country, our sense of outrage at social injustices and violence recedes. And everywhere in the world the sense of 'outrage' has always been the driver of good journalism. So, till the 1990s, if there was an atrocity committed against common or defenceless people, there would be a sense of outrage in the media. And as an individual, as a photographer or a journalist, you would feel that sense of outrage and it would fuel your work. That existed even till 2000, but after the early 2000s it started changing. Since the proprietors and owners of media outlets did not express outrage, many of the journalists also suppressed it; and even if they didn't, they were often not allowed to go out into the field to report and document. And if you scrutinize television or print media today, that sense of outrage has not just receded – it is actually missing. Instead there is apology and even defence of the perpetrators, especially on TV channels.

RA: Can you describe one of your shoots from the 1990s that really stayed with you, and from which the images you created had a strong impact on journalism?

PP: There are two different things to be considered here – what stands in terms of journalism, and what stands for me personally. Right through the 1990s I had wanted to move away from 'in-your-face' news photography. I needed to narrate what people 'felt', rather than to merely 'show' what was happening to them, through my pictures. I was floundering, trying to redefine how I should take photographs, trying to reconsider my way of looking, and thinking about what viewers might want to see.

I came to my turning point, my own moment of transition, during an assignment about caste-war widows in a Bihar village called Shankarbigha where a massacre had taken place.[26] Three of us – reporters Soutik Biswas,[27] Amarnath Tewary and I – landed up there to cover the story. We were talking to this girl, Kunti Devi, a fourteen-year-old widow. She had just got married a few days ago and had gone to her home in a nearby village. While she was away, the Ranvir Sena killed ten people in the village, including her new husband. Soutik asked her, 'Now that all this has happened, will you stay here?' And she said, '*rahibe padhi*', which means 'I will have to stay'. However, the way she said it made me realize that it was not a fatalistic answer but actually a terrified question: 'Will I have to stay?' She was terrified, and I thought to myself: here we have a victim of such a tragedy, how do you photograph someone like that? How do you ever manage to convey in a picture what she might be feeling, or what might happen to her? It's almost impossible to do it. I mean, if someone has been beaten up you can show the physical injury, but what do you do with this ...?

That's when something was triggered in my mind – the understanding that one has to step back, one has to think not just about *what* one photographs, but *how* one photographs ...[28]

RA: What was the process of putting together, thematically and editorially, your book *King, Commoner, Citizen*, a collection of photographs offering a subaltern view of modern India?

PP: To trace my process I have to go back a little bit in terms of my own history, both personal and professional. I came to journalism through commitment to left-wing politics. In college I was involved in theatre and interested in cinema, and began learning about photography. In 1977 I took a gap year and worked on a research project on the Naxalite movement in Bihar.[29] I moved to Delhi in 1981, and immediately started looking for a career in photojournalism; during that time I began a book on dacoits in Chambal. I was always interested in society and polity. This interest has stayed with me, and a focus on people who were fighting for their rights was always part of my being and continues to be reflected in my work. In my whole career as a photojournalist and editorial photographer, I have no work in the areas of fashion, celebrities, sports, wildlife – none of that.

While I was at university I saw Satyajit Ray's 1958 film *Jalsaghar*[30] that explores the inner world of privileged people who become marginalized through reduction of their circumstances, and consequently have retreated from the world, become recluses. This film stayed with me, and stoked my interest in developing a book about our former maharajas in contemporary conditions, including states of decline. I had imagined a coffee-table book - a genre that was a big thing back in the 1980s. Each photographer's ambition was to create one of those books, and usually the theme was 'exotic India'.

I worked on this project for quite some time. Along the way, I started looking at all the other work I had done so far, and realized that how I photographed the maharajas was very similar to the way I had been documenting who you would call the 'ordinary people' of India. I have always wanted to be politically correct, and always accord my subjects the respect they deserve. In 2000, I exhibited this photo series under the title *Kings and Commoners*. For me the experience was rooted in my awareness of the complexities of documentary work in a society as class- and caste-divided as India. We photographers have to be acutely aware of our own position in relation to our subjects. It is a very important question: when you photograph people right across the social spectrum, how much agency are you according to them? Hence the title, suggesting that a commoner can be a king, and a king can be a commoner.

The same images, with the addition of more recent pictures, were published by Mahatta Multimedia in 2007 as *King, Commoner, Citizen*, edited by Sanjeev Saith.[31]

RA: Did you ever engage with video crews in the field? Did you think about television and the impact of television news/video culture on photojournalism, and on the media in general?

PP: Interestingly, in 1995 my wife, who was a researcher and archivist in ethnomusicology, moved on to working in a television channel. But I never wanted to move to television. Of course, in the field one was always working alongside video people, they were shooting at the same time as photojournalists. The influence of television on print journalism in the 1990s is very interesting. If you ask photojournalists of that era, they will say they were very often told, 'Oh but the television guys have this image, why don't you have it?' So instead of trying to depict events differently, a lot of us - the photographers, the media houses, the magazines, the newspapers - started imitating the visual style and the manner of television reporting. This had a detrimental effect on photojournalism to quite an extent, in the sense that at a time when we should have been creating nuanced imagery, we instead repeatedly pressured ourselves into more mechanical

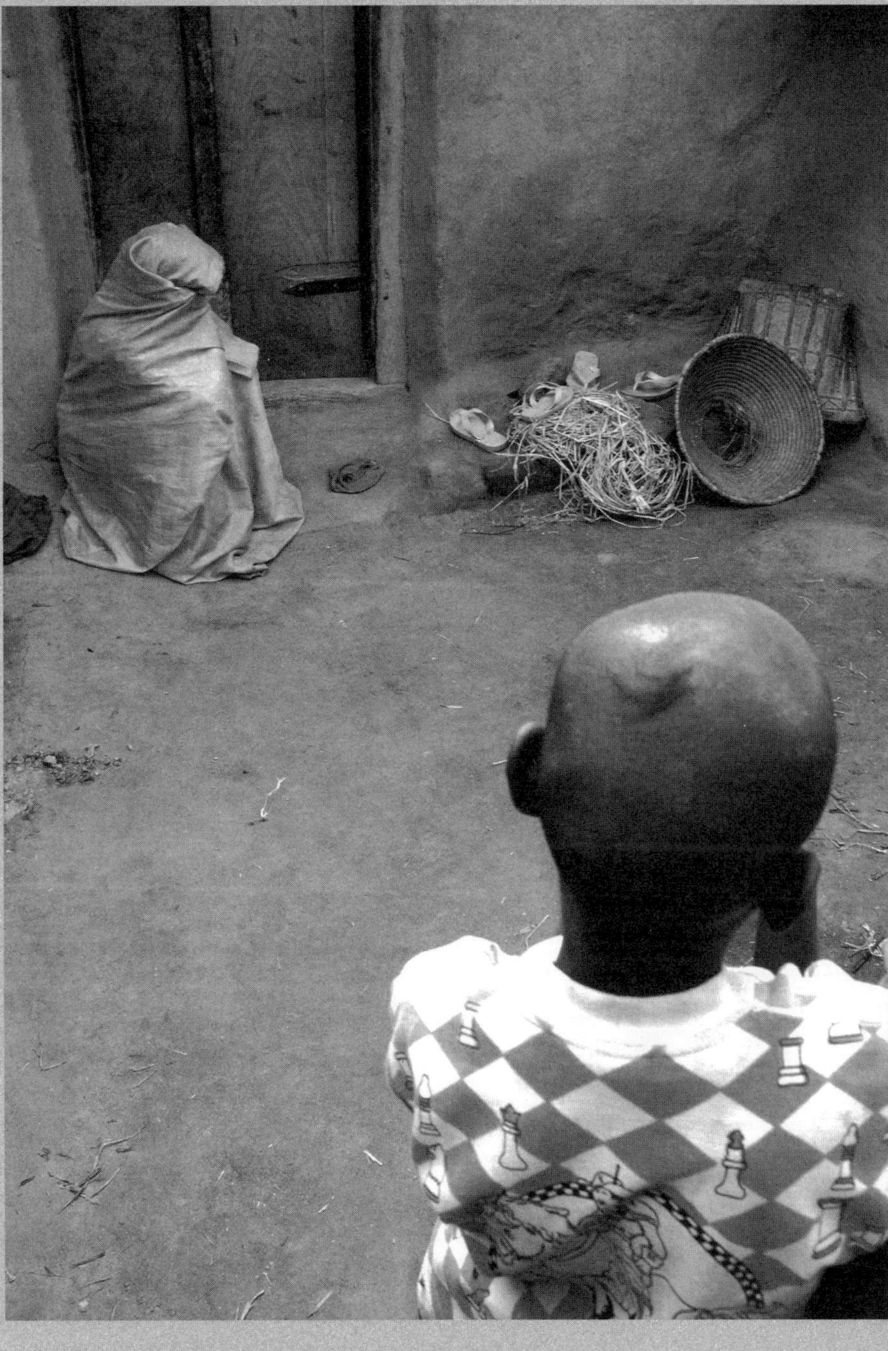

documentation. A lot of this was due to insistence by our editors. It led to a kind of pushing and shoving within the media pack, as we would say, along with a kind of need to replicate each other's work. This has been problematic for Indian media, especially for photojournalism.

RA: Seen from our digital vantage point, what strikes me about 1990s media is that unlike in the current unlimited and uninterrupted information flow and unlimited global circulation, images from earlier decades carried a particular impact because they were not over-analysed and then 'left behind', as we do today – our attention always in pursuit of more, moving, migrating, distracted, hooked to the next option. In terms of documentation of social injustice and violence, etc., we have become desensitized; overwhelmed by images, our blunted outrage is further blunted – or, as you say, actually missing ... Additionally, our capacity to filter these image cascades has also radically diminished because we can no longer view or depict India in isolation from the rest of the world – technology urges us to create simultaneous narratives that can be instantaneously shared across time and space, so whatever we produce now is by default 'international' ...

How does this compare with your international experience in the 1990s? Were your editors committed to publishing international stories, supporting your work and enabling access – seen for instance in your images of the Gulf War, and the North West Frontier Province arms bazaar?

PP: The late 1980s and the 1990s were also an important transition period in India, between the 1960s and 1970s with their ideologies of rebellion, the left-wing and student movements in Europe, etc., and the right-wing ideologies that are currently dominating the world after generally crushing the left-wing ideologies that prevailed in the 2000s.

I was lucky that I worked with *India Today* at a time when they became interested in international stories, and also had the resources to spend on the international stories. So from 1989 to about 1992 I got to do a lot of stories outside India, especially in the subcontinent, and in China post the Tiananmen Square protests. *India Today* was covering all these historical events – the fall of the Berlin Wall, the collapse of the Soviet Union, the Sri Lanka civil war and the IPKF,[32] and several others. I was lucky to get such assignments. All photojournalists did not get the chance.

This was really a big learning curve for me – how does one report in depth on major aspects of an unfamiliar country within a very short time?

The aspect of photojournalism which still excites me is the actual chasing of a story. The arms bazaar assignment is a good example.[33] You are forbidden to go there, denied access – you are bullshitting your way through, there's danger and subterfuge, and eventually somehow you manage to get the story against these odds. It is the thrill of chasing that matters. Half the fun and the excitement come from being able to do *that*, more than from getting the story itself. It was the same in the case of that story on exporting terror – and it led to Pakistan banning *India Today*. Most photojournalists are junkies for that kind of stuff!

An aspect of photojournalism that needs to be more deeply studied is how the media started using the internet when it came into India in 1995–96. At *Outlook* we were quick to do this. In 1995 Gauri Gill had to go and shoot when Amitabh Bachchan took over the Miss World contest in Bangalore.[34] We actually moved those pictures through the internet and published digitally for the first time. I remember the first digital cameras and the first use of floppy drives in computers. When Atal Bihari Vajpayee visited Pakistan, in order to beat *India Today* I had to send out a photo very quickly – I had to rush to a lab, process the image, scan it, put it on a floppy disk, take it to the NICNET[35] guys and upload it.

So, all that transformation started happening around 1996. It was an interesting time technologically, and also in terms of what started happening to the media ...[36]

In the 1990s the Indian media sphere began to radically open up but we also identified a certain kind of conformism taking hold within society. Even the fashion industry typified it, in a particular way. Anyone who thinks about that decade will be able to recognize this conformism as a marker of a particular time.[37]

Shifts in journalism here have always taken place in parallel with political change ... I remember discussions with colleagues, raising the question: what is this age that we are living through ...?

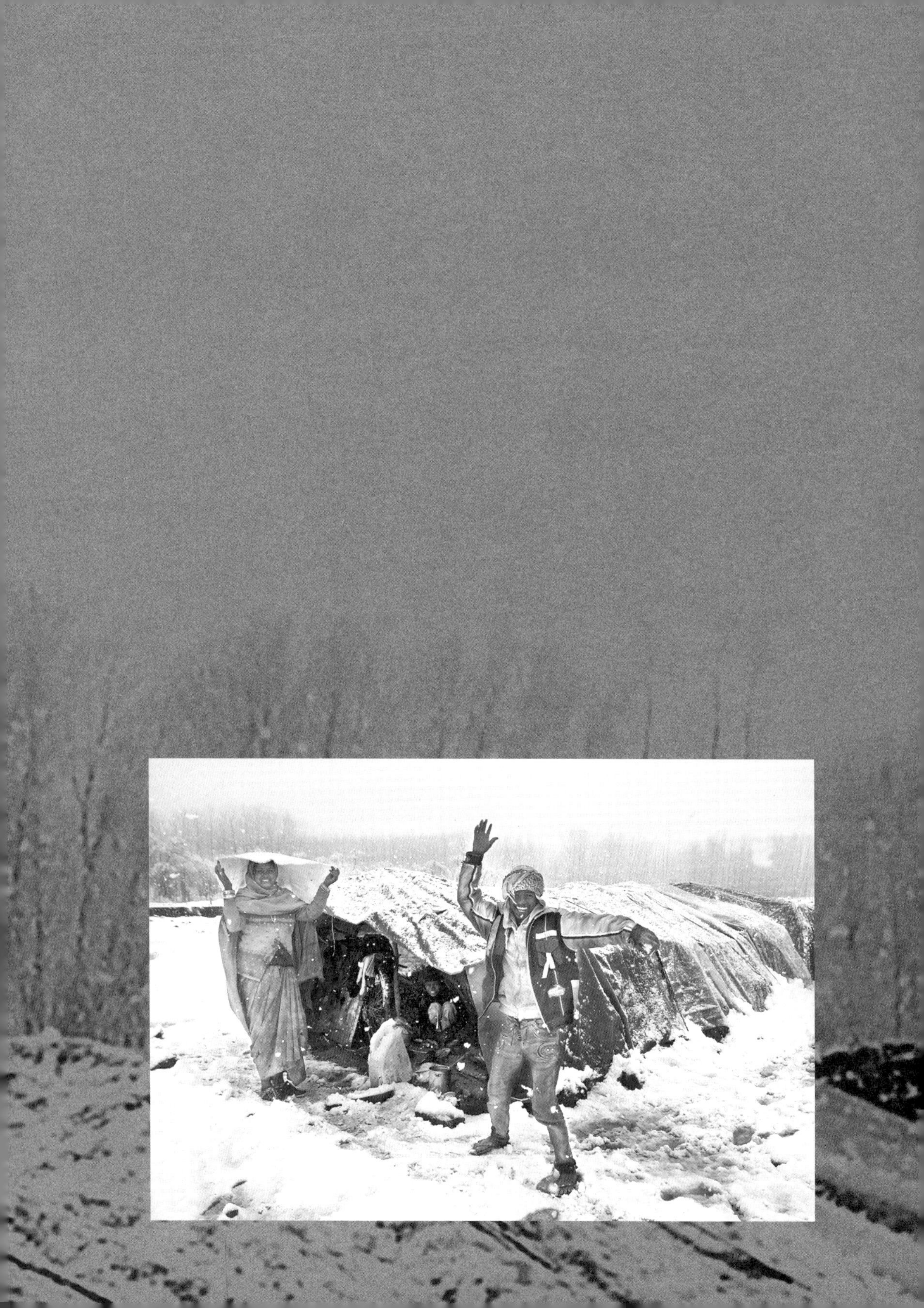

13 The Making of *Witness: Kashmir 1986–2016 / Nine Photographers*

2017

Majid Maqbool in conversation with Sanjay Kak

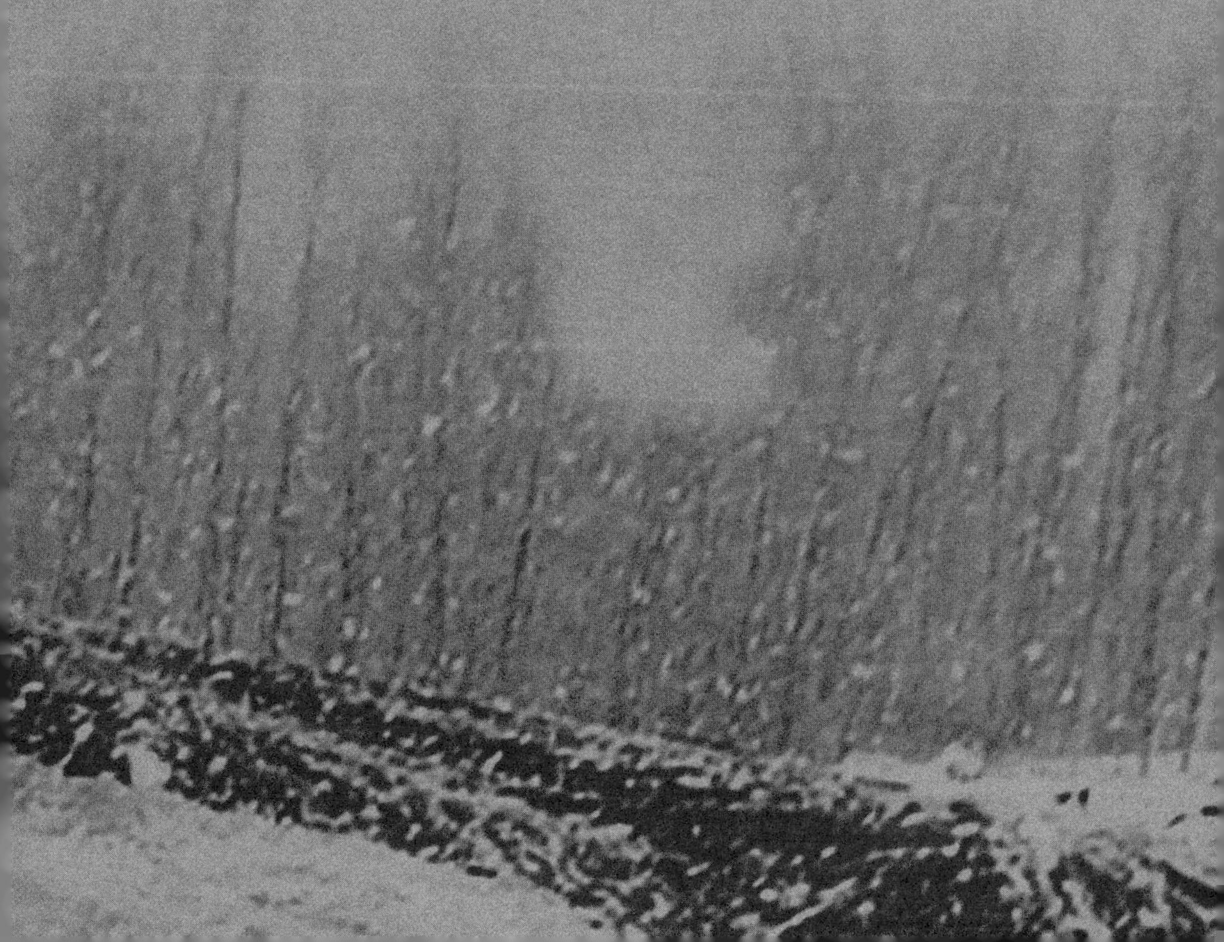

Filmmaker and author Sanjay Kak's *Witness: Kashmir 1986-2016/Nine Photographers* offers images ranging from vintage prints to photojournalism, many inscribing a period dominated by state violence, human rights abuses, occupation, censorship, militancy, and a resistance movement rooted in demands for civil liberties and independent governance.

The book is as much an assemblage as it is a unitary object (it has an open spine, bound together with a cord). It invokes what scholar-curator Ariella Aïsha Azoulay terms the '**civil contract of photography**' – namely, a condition of citizenship enabled by an expanded definition of the relationship between who takes the picture, who is in it, and how that relationship expands into a new political domain analogous to, but also beyond, the domain of state operation. *Witness* brings new significance to the role photography has played in the Valley, as 'evidence' that can be read in multiple and complex ways, and where what is missing becomes as important as what is manifested.

In this conversation, Sanjay Kak explains his aesthetic choices, the unusual design, the choice of images and the nature of representation itself in the region. *Witness* reflects Kak's interest in the material and social conditions in which art is made as a form of protest; such art-making is now even more critical, given the abrogation of Article 370 ('special status'/semi-autonomy of Kashmir) in 2019, and the related punitive lockdowns, extreme militarization, surveillance regimes and the carceral norms of daily life in the Valley.

An earlier version of this interview was published online on *Sbcltr*, 24 May 2017; https://www.sbcltr.in/interview-with-documentary-film-maker-and-publisher-sanjay-kak/

Keywords and Names

Citizenship, *Civil contract of photography*, *Documentary photography*, *Kashmir/ Kashmir insurgency*, *Photojournalism*, see Keywords at the back of this volume.

Images

pp. 238–39: Javed Dar, *Migrant Worker Family, Anantnag* (2015). Dar is a photojournalist who has covered the conflict in Kashmir for over a decade.

p. 243: Meraj Ud Din, *Kuka Parray and Ikhwan, Sumbal* (1995). Meraj Ud Din is a Srinagar-based photographer and videographer who has worked for several news agencies and news magazines, including Reuters, *Kashmir Times*, *India Today* and Associated Press.

p 247: Cover of the book *Witness: Kashmir 1986–2016/Nine Photographers* (2017).

Both images are from *Witness: Kashmir 1986–2016/Nine Photographers* (New Delhi: Yaarbal/ Octave Communications, 2017). Permission to reproduce courtesy Sanjay Kak and the photographers.

Majid Maqbool (MM): *Witness: Kashmir 1986–2016/Nine Photographers* (2017) features very diverse work that presents the complex and unsettling realities of life in the valley. Was putting together a book of photographs on Kashmir a challenging task for you as a documentary filmmaker? How and when did this idea come to you?

Sanjay Kak (SK): I think it was more than ten years ago that I first became aware of the remarkable body of images that have been created by photojournalists in Kashmir. I was actually looking for ways to illuminate the very dark period of the 1990s in Kashmir for a film that I was working on, and it was in the work of news photographers that I began to find the first traces ... Eventually, I didn't use still photographs in that film, but the sense that there was an important historical archive, one that opened out a largely unseen emotional landscape, stayed with me.[1]

MM: How do you respond to the work of photojournalists in Kashmir who work in difficult circumstances, and are among the first to reach the spot to cover a protest, an encounter, a funeral or any violent confrontation between people and the government forces?

SK: The work of these photographers is all that you say, certainly, but it is much more too. Those flashpoints will dominate our visual memory – that first, on-the-spot, dramatic picture will always mark certain moments; our minds retain those impressions, and sometimes the accompanying emotional shock as well. But the book offers much more – it contains the essence of these past thirty years in Kashmir. It could be a picture of a flower-laden shikara that is weighed under with a sort of desolation. Or even a picture of a young child walking past an abandoned bunker.

Every great image need not be made under grave personal risk, or in exceptionally difficult circumstances. But you could definitely say that the outstanding picture will always come from a lot of thought, and from familiarity with the ground, and from a passion to tell a story.[2]

MM: At a book release in Srinagar, you described *Witness* as not only about photographs but also about photographers. What influenced your decisions with regard to the eventual selection of these nine particular practitioners?

SK: *Witness* does not lay claim to representing the nine best photographers in Kashmir, although each one featured in the book is certainly an outstanding photographer. I have seen and admired the work of several other photographers who could also quite easily have been a part of the book. But despite my best efforts I don't think I was persuasive enough ... ! The final choice of these nine practitioners was also ultimately shaped by the larger narrative that the book tries to map – not just of Kashmir in these last three decades, but also of the photographers' own concerns and, eventually, of photography itself. We were guided by which photographers' work best signposted both the past and the future of image-making in Kashmir.[3]

MM: Why did you limit the number of featured photographers featured in the book to just nine? Did you at any stage feel that your final choice could/should be expanded in order to enrich the range of the work?

SK: I would have liked to feature a dozen photographers. But a photo-book is not just a collection of pictures – that would be more like an encyclopaedia. Quite early into the curation we realized that in order to provide an authentic sense of the range and depth of an individual photographer's vision we would need to present at least twenty to twenty-five pictures from each. That logic took us close to 200 images, and with the additions of text and index we eventually had a 400-page book on our hands ... That alone made the book financially non-viable for publishers, which is why I decided to publish it myself, as Yaarbal Books. To have added any more photographers would have made it an impossible book to publish.

MM: *Witness* contains a substantial amount of text. Is this because you felt the photographs in themselves would be insufficient in terms of conveying the story?

SK: The photographs in the book have very little accompanying text – only the tersest of captions. A longer accompanying text is about the photographers – each person's work is followed by a brief profile, and this personalized text was integral to the intention of the project. I always remain interested in the material and social conditions in which any art, including photography, is made. Who are these people who take pictures? Where do they come from? Why did they turn to photography? *Witness* is a book about Kashmir, yes, but it's also about nine Kashmiris, closely linked by the fact that they are all photographers. That is what the text tries to unwrap ...

Also, I'm not sure that photographs without any accompanying words would be enough to fully convey the story. I do believe giving context is important: for example, where the photograph was taken, which is specified by the caption. And why the photographer does what he/she does: this can only be answered through the text of his/her profile.

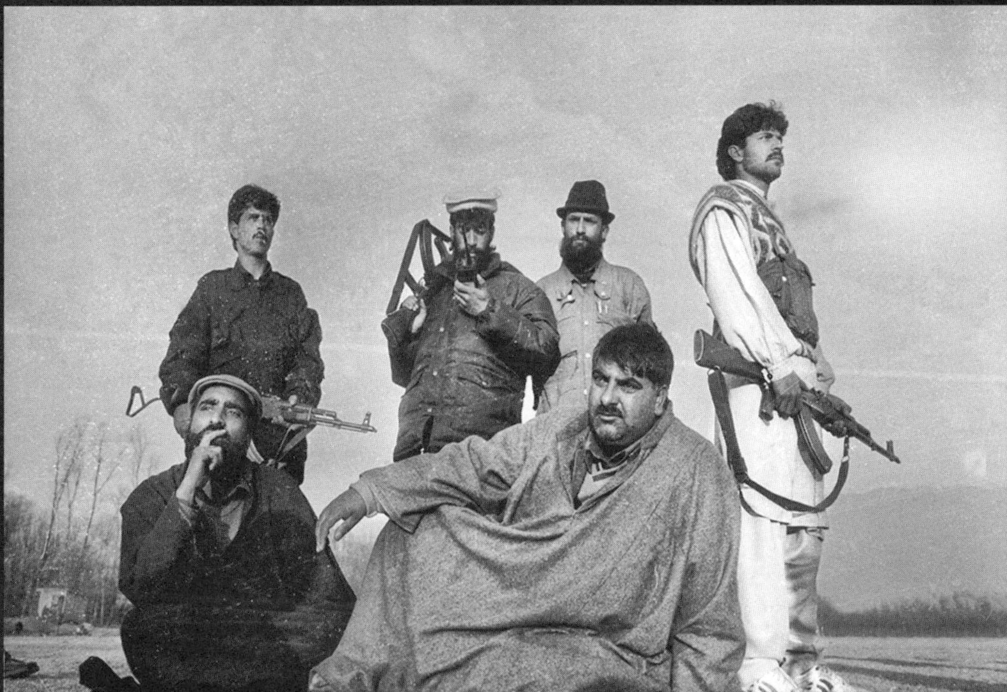

I was looking through *Witness* with a photographer - a very eminent one - and I made a reference to one of the practitioner profiles ... 'What profile?' she asked. 'The one that accompanies the work of each photographer,' I answered. She flipped through the book, and found one. And admitted that she had completely missed them, even though she had been through the book several times!

So each reader will pick up on some particular thing. And ignore or overlook others. Which is how it should be: let our readers rely on their own volition.

MM: *Witness* has a very interesting and unique design - the spine is open, and a string holds the book together. Who took the major design decisions - for instance, which photograph would feature as a double-spread? Did the personal style of individual photographers influence the design choices and the aesthetic 'look'?

SK: Each physical detail of *Witness* has obviously been carefully worked out, and is an integrated part of its design: that is why it is a photo-book, and not a book of photographs. Itu Chaudhuri Design, one of the most outstanding design practices in India, poured hundreds of hours of careful consideration into the design ... So, from the idea of having a string to bind the folder-like cover, to the open spine, to working out the logic of placing an image as a double-bleed, or as a small inset, or as a series of continuous images - these insights come from the designers. There are also certain patterns in the way the pictures are laid out, and these patterns recur across the work of all the photographers - like an invisible rhythm that you set, and then the work of the individual photographers, very different from each other, develops its own visual trajectory within that rhythm.

MM: There's a gradual change of visual style as *Witness* progresses. The vintage look of the photographs of late 1980s/early 1990s are followed by more gritty photojournalistic images. A little later we see more artistic images, mostly in black-and-white, where black dominates the frame. Then suddenly, once again there are colour images. Was there a special focus on the narrative flow?

SK: Some of the visual shifts come from the material itself - the early work by Meraj Ud Din[4] is shot on negative film, some of which had suffered extensive damage during the 2014 flood,[5] so it ends up giving what you call a 'vintage' look. Javeed Shah's[6] work in the book is mostly from his digital material, but you can see how the new technology is subservient to his own style, developed in the pre-digital era. In the middle of the book we have the work of three exceptional wire-service photographers - Dar Yasin,[7] Javed Dar,[8] Altaf Qadri[9] - and you can see a very high standard of sharp, pictorially eye-grabbing photojournalism. Quite a few images in the last section of *Witness* are in black-and-white, more experimental, often pushing the limits of what constitutes news photography. Obviously, these are personal aesthetic choices made by Sumit Dayal[10] and Showkat Nanda,[11] and by the much younger Syed Shahriyar[12] and Azaan Shah,[13] and made possible because this is independent work, and not done as an assignment, or for a wire service ...

Yes, we did think very deeply about how best to arrange the images smoothly, but without compromising on granularities within the narrative flow.

MM: *Witness* was first released in Delhi, then in Bangalore, and later in Srinagar too. How have people outside Kashmir received the book, as opposed to within Kashmir where the images featured in the book must undoubtedly trigger difficult memories and associations?

SK: It's difficult to say. How do you gauge reception ... ?

The book is selling well, given that it is self-published and even self-distributed. We've had very good press coverage, almost all of it uniformly positive, usually sensitive to the implications of what a book like this seeks to do. Responses to *Witness* at public events outside Kashmir have been very reassuring too ...

Does this mean that more Indians have begun to understand the history and meaning of the conflict in Kashmir? It might be too early to say, given the general climate in the country, but certainly the kind of people who are interested in books, yes, you could say that they are increasingly more open to thinking focused around the 'Kashmir problem' ...

Within Kashmir the reaction has been very different, much more emotional, each image eliciting a whole cupboard of memories - and sometimes even the absence of memories, as someone remarked at the Srinagar release.

MM: Post the 2010 uprising, there has been a resurgence of what might be called 'creative capital' in Kashmir, especially among the youth who are producing their own stories and even registering their political protest through various art forms - prose texts, poetry, music, etc. You were the editor of *Until My Freedom Has Come - The New Intifada in Kashmir*, an anthology about the uprising/protest movement, with contributions by young Kashmiri writers as well as journalists, artists and academics. Do you see this kind of indigenous creative output making any difference, over the years, as to how the Kashmir narrative is being viewed and read by people from outside Kashmir?

SK: As a somewhat unlikely parallel, I would like to recall the land reforms in the Kashmir of the 1950s which played a major part in releasing the productive capacities of Kashmiris by the very revolutionary act of giving land to the tiller, land to the landless. In many ways the arrival of the internet has done something like that for the generations that came to adulthood within the last three decades. They have found a voice, and despite distance and the restrictions imposed by the terrible conditions of daily life, they have found a way of sharing with each other. They have found humour and irony, music and poetry, and just as significantly, analysis and understanding. And they have deployed all of these in a combative, joyous way. I have no doubt that the slight shifts in public opinion about the 'Kashmir problem' in India and across the globe have been strongly shaped by this vibrant creative capital.[14]

MM: Do you think *Witness* will help to generate meaningful discussions about what Kashmir has gone through in the last thirty years and about what is happening there in the present?

SK: Why else would one make such a book? Sometimes even one image can help destabilize long-held beliefs. The very first photograph in the book is a 1986 image of young Kashmiri activists marching in support of Palestine, and it includes many well-known faces of the resistance. I know that image has had a deep impact on many people in India and abroad.[15]

To think that those were the protests thirty years ago ... and to think about where Kashmiris find themselves today ...[16]

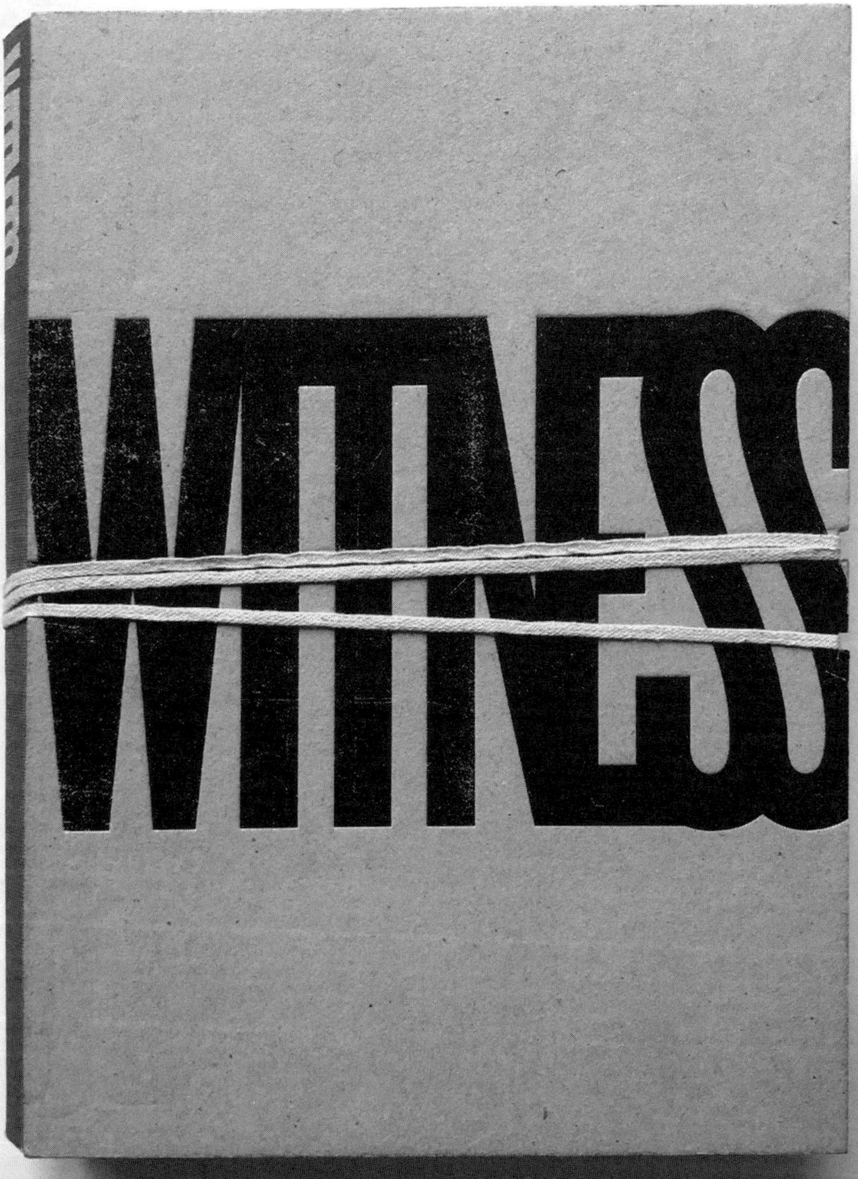

PUBLISHED WITH THE SUPPORT OF

C Fonds
Prince Claus Fund for Culture and Development

20 Years of Celebrating the Arts
India Foundation for the Arts
IFA

YAARBAL

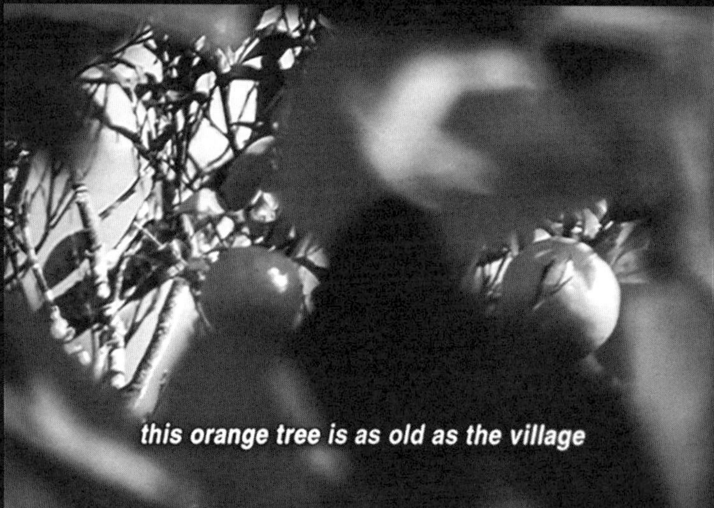
this orange tree is as old as the village

14 Embracing Doubt

2018

Amar Kanwar

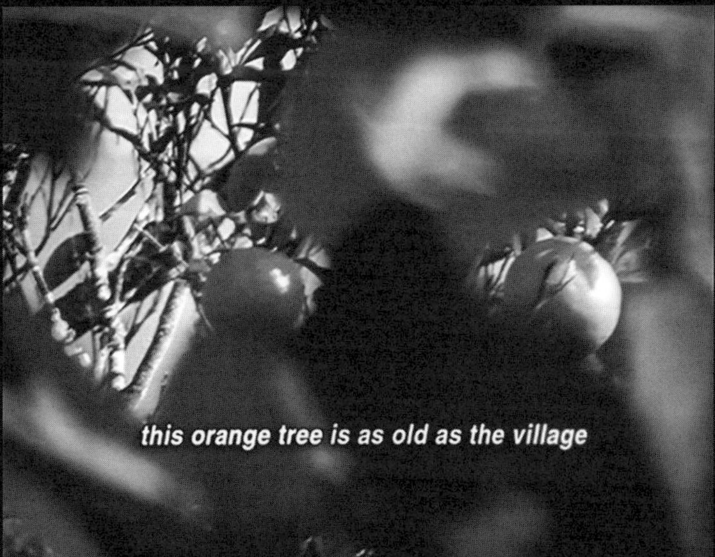

Section IV
Politics/Aesthetics

Filmmaker and artist Amar Kanwar reflects on the several contingent factors that define his lens-based documentary practice, in relation to contemporary meta-histories of the moving image. Over the years, Kanwar's art has addressed indigenous resistance movements, military dictatorship, ecological devastation, and the perennial, and perennially urgent, issues of identity, nationhood, labour and caste. His works have made ethical demands upon the authorial task of bearing witness.

Here he asks if it is possible to make a film 'where there is no defined position': 'Yearning for the zero position is like a freefall', Kanwar writes, 'where the absence of control can be terrifying.' However, it is only in the 'momentary delusion of such an aspiration' that 'method emerges'. Aligning various lyric/poetic, introspective trajectories, Kanwar argues that visually compelling narratives may be woven around subjects that are invisible, ephemeral, dispersed and elusive.

This essay first appeared in *MARG*, 'Documentary Now', ed. Ravi Vasudevan, vol. 70, no. 1, September–December 2018.

Keywords and Names

Adivasi, *Citizenship*, *Civil contract of photography*, *Dalit*, *Decolonization*, *Documentary photography*, *Gujarat riots 2002*, *Modernism*, *Moving images*, *Partition of India*, *Postmemory*, see Keywords at the back of this volume.

Images

pp. 248–49: *The Lightning Testimonies*, 2016. Detail from installation with eight synchronized video projections, 32 min., Goethe-Intitut, Max Mueller Bhavan, Mumbai, 23 January–6 March 2016. Photograph: Philippe Calia.

pp. 252–53: *The Sovereign Forest*, 2011–2023. Films, projections on handmade books, seeds, photographs. Installation view, Thyssen-Bornemisza Art Contemporary–Augarten (TBA21–Augarten), Vienna, 23 November 2013–23 March 2014. Photograph: Stephan Wyckoff.

pp. 258–59: Still from *A Love Story*, 2010. Short film, 5 min. 37 sec.

All images courtesy Amar Kanwar.

The 'document' of the documentary has for long been thrown up into the air. Is illusion more real than fact? What vocabulary is appropriate for a dream? Can a pamphlet be a poem, a poem be the story of a murder, the murder be recalled as a ballad, and the ballad then become an argument? Can the expression of this argument become a vulnerability which negates the argument itself? Would this lead to shifts in our internal positions ... ?

My work has always seemed to be about doubt. Doubt about the method, about my own inadequacies and the repeated experience of losing voice and finding it again.[1]

Almost every film would leave me with a conundrum of difficult feelings and questions. Sometimes the absurd expense of the medium while filming issues about poverty would become a crippling contradiction. At another moment, even speaking on someone else's behalf seemed to become incorrect. In the earlier films I would often be confused by expert opinions about the 'mind of the common man', entangled by the aspirations and insecurities of revolutionaries, tossed around by dramatically varied audience responses and occasionally stung by the scornful and perhaps deliberate indifference of a few peers. Much later I began to squirm at my own expertise in gaining the trust of participants, the interviewees, the fascinating characters that filled the world around me. But most disturbing was the heightened stress of going out to film motivated by the moral fervour of a particular conception, only to come back with pieces of reality that had a mind of their own, and then having to put the excruciating jigsaw together with the desperate hope that it would cohere and receive appreciation.

What a waste of time all this felt, sometimes. Surely there must be another way to do this.

Perhaps the very premise was faulty, coming from some preconfigured route assembled over decades, geographies and histories by champions of the colonial anthropological gaze and the Leninist school of agitation and propaganda. Add to this the distortion of mainstream television channels, the film-festival matrix of what works and what doesn't, and the expectations to represent the charming, beautiful and diverse underbelly of the third world. Sometimes making without fear seems impossible as flavour replaces flavour, anxieties become invisible and the need to earn a living becomes crucial. And then the jigsaw begins all over again.

After the assassination of Shankar Guha Niyogi in 1991,[2] another set of questions emerged for me. I knew the film I made was useful to the Chhattisgarh Mukti Morcha[3] labour union, then and much later. I also knew immediately that it could have been made much better. Niyogi had predicted his assassination, and I

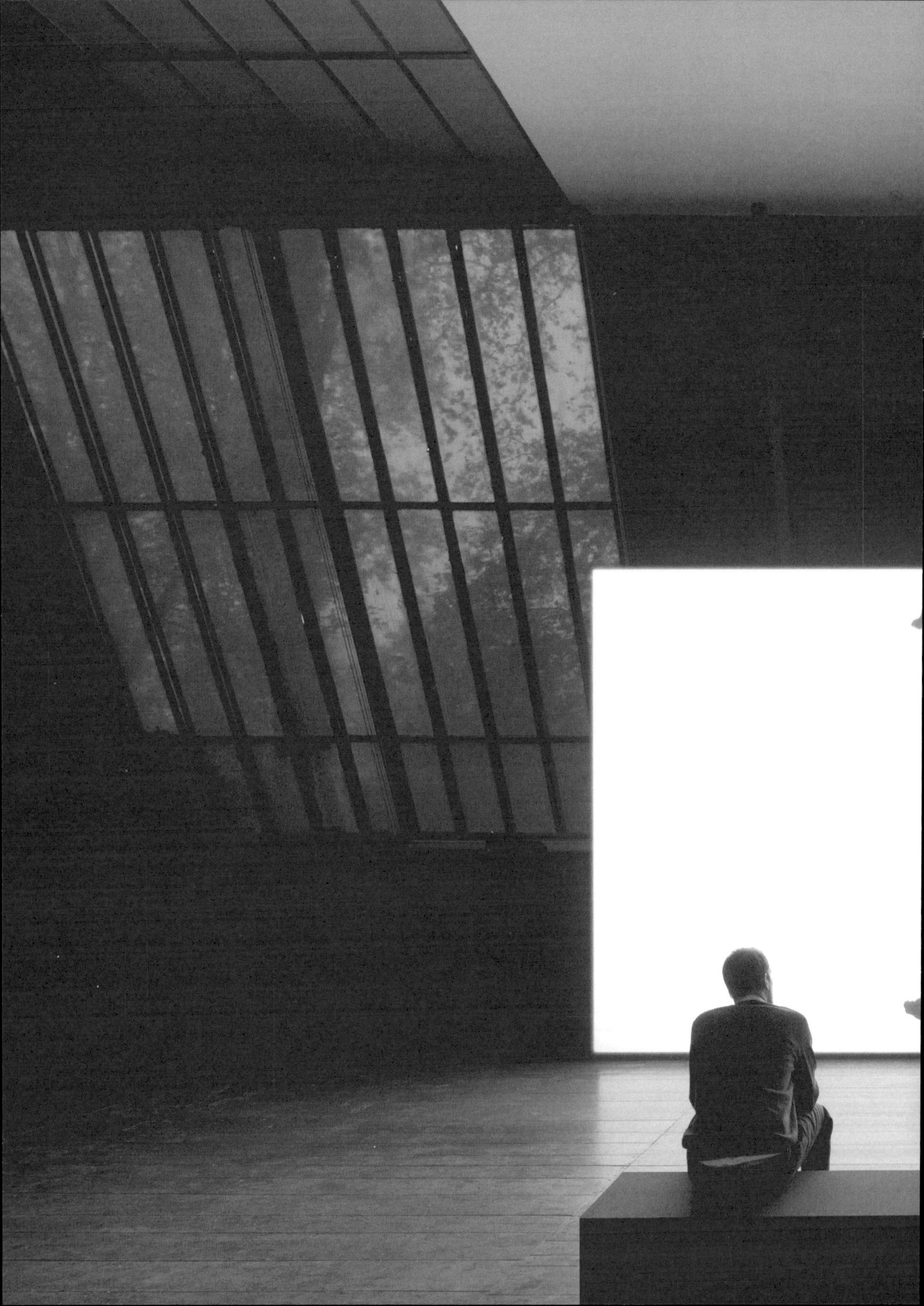

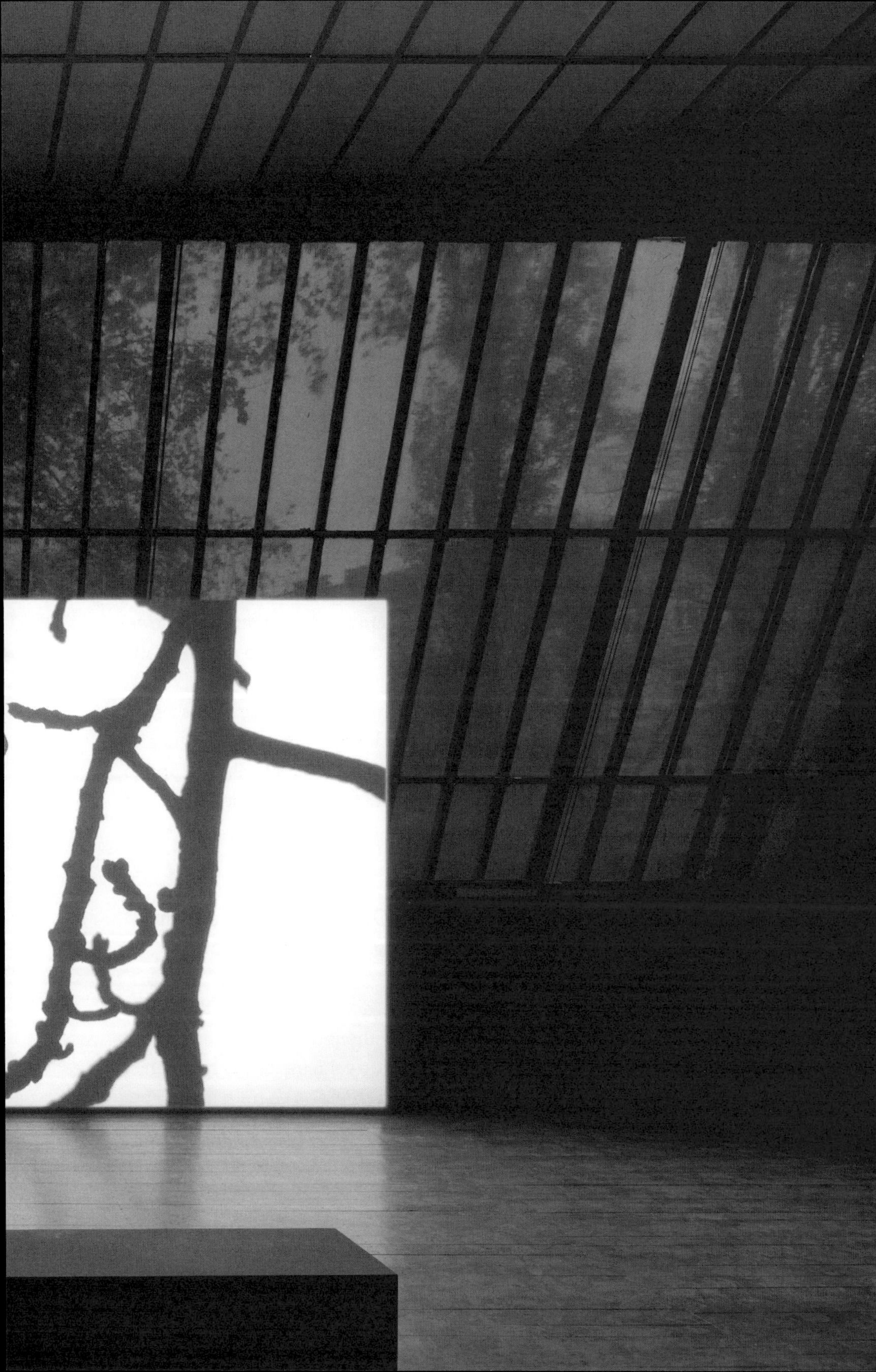

was shaken to find that he had wanted a filmmaker, rather than a security guard, to be present. Perhaps to be witness to what would unfold. I was grateful for the union's invitation and for the welcome I received from the most inspiring political mass movement I had ever seen. Beautiful, powerful, vulnerable men and women involved in a unique process of creation and struggle. Almost every shot I took then, twenty-seven years ago, is still imprinted as if straight from the viewfinder into my brain. I had even rolled the camera for long stretches in almost complete darkness as it was heartbreaking to cut just because of low light. Later there was an abiding sense that I had been unable to express much of what I saw, felt and experienced. These were stories that I did not have a vocabulary for.

Many of the films I made at that time would leave me with a deep awareness that I had in fact left behind the most important experiences. Perhaps there was another way of looking or comprehending, a way that could create another kind of telling.[4]

Drop falling in ocean everyone knows, ocean falling in drop, a rare one knows.

'Now listen!' Kabir shouted, 'Who calls out your name, is it life or is it death, who calls out your name ...'[5]

Here is a select chronology that skips several films but delineates the essential trajectory of doubts, questions and temporary resolutions.[6] I am deeply grateful to a small group of friends, teachers and professionals who have helped, and to the activists, writers and human rights organizations who have guided me along the way.

1997–98: Prior to the Making of *A Season Outside* (1997),[7] a Film about Understanding Violence and Finding a Way to Respond

If the author's presence is crafted to be minimal, then does it really make the author minimal, or is this just a matter of perception? If all thoughts – random, coherent or fragmented but integrated and interconnected – are valid inside my mind, then can they also be valid and presented as such in the film? Can I go from my mother to the tree to the politics on the street? How can I speak about but not represent the other? Can I film in zones rather than in points of view? What is the difference between research and preparation? Would I see in a particular way if I researched and see in another way if I prepared – would my instincts be different in either case? How to test this out? How best to compare the results? Is there a way to prepare for the unexpected? Is there an unseen line through the centre of the dancer's body?

What happens to the audience when she finds it during a performance? If I find meaning, then does my audience find meaning too? And is it the same meaning or different for each? And should it be the same, or is it better that it be different?

1997–2002: Prior to and during the Making of *The Many Faces of Madness* (2000),[8] *Freedom* (2001),[9] *Baphlimali 173* (2001),[10] *King of Dreams* (2001)[11] and *A Night of Prophecy* (2002)[12]

During this period, I travelled extensively within India, often alone, researching and then making a set of films about ecological devastation, police repression and the forcible takeover of lands and forests by governments and corporations, and local resistance by farmers, fisherfolk and indigenous communities. Briefly: I attempted to make a set of films with three distinct intentions – useful for a campaign; for a negotiation with an opponent; and to create a terrain of analysis about political resistance for those with no access to data. I also made a film about masculine sexuality, experimenting with compressing several personal narratives into one voice.

However, these travels filled me with a deeper sense of the extreme inequalities and despair caused by violence generated both by the state and social actors in different regions. I felt everyone was bursting forward with arguments and distinct points of view, an extreme super-articulation seemed to be taking place, but no one was really listening to the other. It was from this intractable setting that *A Night of Prophecy* came into being, a film that sought to address the faultlines of caste, labour, nationality and self-determination. The film was shot in Maharashtra, Andhra Pradesh, Manipur, Nagaland and Kashmir. I had two key questions in mind before I started shooting: Is it possible to understand the passage of time through poetry? And if that were so even momentarily, then would it be possible to see the future?

Additionally: Could I use poetry to cut through the super-articulation of ideological positions and prejudices and bring opponents into a zone of comprehension? Would I be able to predict the social/political map of the South Asia of 2040? There were also less lofty questions: Why do some images seem sterile and others potent? Could it be because the latter holds a continuously oscillating time? Does such an oscillation of time allow the possibility of multiple interpretations of the image?

Another unstated objective was to counter the politics of non-violence earnestly advocated in *A Season Outside*. To counter - not necessarily to disagree but to test and confront it with the scale and complexity of the violence coiled in the underbelly of the nation. Was I wrong? The sophisticated and systemic daily violence of untouchability and caste continues to this day. The killings and disappearances continue in Kashmir,[13] regardless of the open lessons of the Palestinian-Israeli conflict. Perhaps we are all destined to a future scenario of cyclical massacres.

2003-07: Prior to and during the Making of *To Remember* (2003)[14] and *The Lightning Testimonies* (2007)[15]

After the sweeping electoral victory of the Bharatiya Janata Party (BJP) in Gujarat in 2003,[16] following the Godhra attack and the anti-Muslim riots and killings, it seemed that Mahatma Gandhi's assassination would need to be commemorated differently. This led to the silent film *To Remember* and also the completion of the trilogy addressing violence: one an essay with spoken prose, the second with eleven languages in poetry, and the third in silence - a formal decision inspired by the *maunvrat* or vow/fast of silence, a tradition practiced by Mahatma Gandhi who observed silence each Monday, never broke this rule for any reason, and used the time to finish work pending from the previous week.

However, the Gujarat riots also threw up another horror: the celebration of brutality, the public spectacle and approbation of sexual violence against Muslim women. How does one respond? How can one talk, show, share anything about this kind of pain? How, while making a film, to not cause survivors and families to revisit the pain?[17]

A few key dilemmas from a long list of concerns: How can one identify the gaps in the available narrative? How does one see and represent the different methods of the archiving and recalling of pain? Could there be different images for different kinds of silences? Can a tree, pattern, window be a witness to a crime? How do secrets and testimonies travel, mutate, transform over decades? What is the difference in the nature of comprehension - when time travels chronologically within a narrative and when the viewer has to relate to disparate time but simultaneously? How to tell the process of going along with, through and also beyond the narrative of suffering towards the meaning and strength of resistance?

The Lightning Testimonies finally included narratives from Punjab, Delhi, Gujarat, Manipur, Nagaland, Maharashtra, Kashmir and Bangladesh, from 1947 to 2006.

2004–08: Prior to and during the Making of *The Torn First Pages*[18]

There were many motivations to explore Burma: the strength and charisma of several Burmese activists in exile, embarrassment at my own ignorance about the nation's incredible students' movement, the challenge of trying to understand a courage that persisted regardless of extreme brutality by the security forces and the terrible personal consequences of opposing the state. Thet Win Aung, a student leader in his early thirties, was arrested in 1998 and sentenced to 59 years in prison, several spent in solitary confinement. How could I even try and respond to the most terrible of punishments, solitary confinement in prison? What image could possibly represent the meaning of that experience of isolation?

And finally, as always, the difficulty of filming a political movement ... There were several ethnic communities, nationalities within Burma with varied histories, and complex and even contradictory political positions. No single story could even come close to telling the scale and spectrum of this epic struggle. I explored three possible routes of comprehension, comprising three parts of the film installation. The hypothesis that developed may be summed up as follows:

> Part 1: What if the viewer were to see time separated in its various forms – in real time, slow time, static time, living time, accelerated time and the time of exile?
>
> Part 2: What would happen if it became possible to experience the passage of multiple moments in time simultaneously? Would the simultaneous experience of the absences and interconnections awaken an enhanced and different ability to comprehend?
>
> Part 3: Archival time – the old-older-oldest presented alongside the new-newer-newest time. Would a heightened sense of the present moment becoming instantaneously and continuously the past, trigger a reactivation of much older archival time, bring it alive in a certain way, make it suddenly part of the present moment?

The conclusions of this experiment with time became *The Torn First Pages*. In the process, a certain kind of comprehension that was not explicit in the work emerged. It allowed me to hazard another speculation: the viability of poetry as evidence in a war-crimes tribunal.

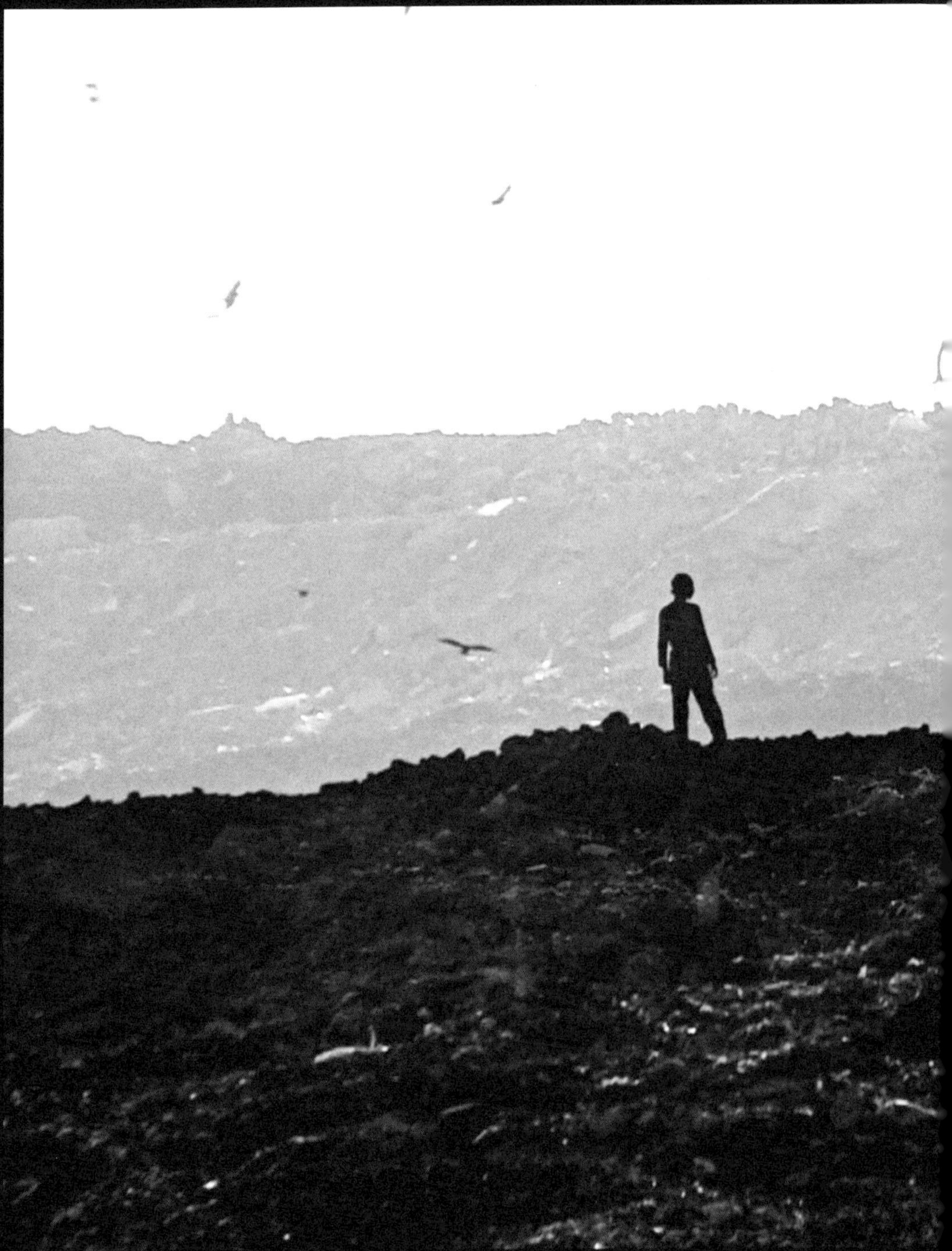

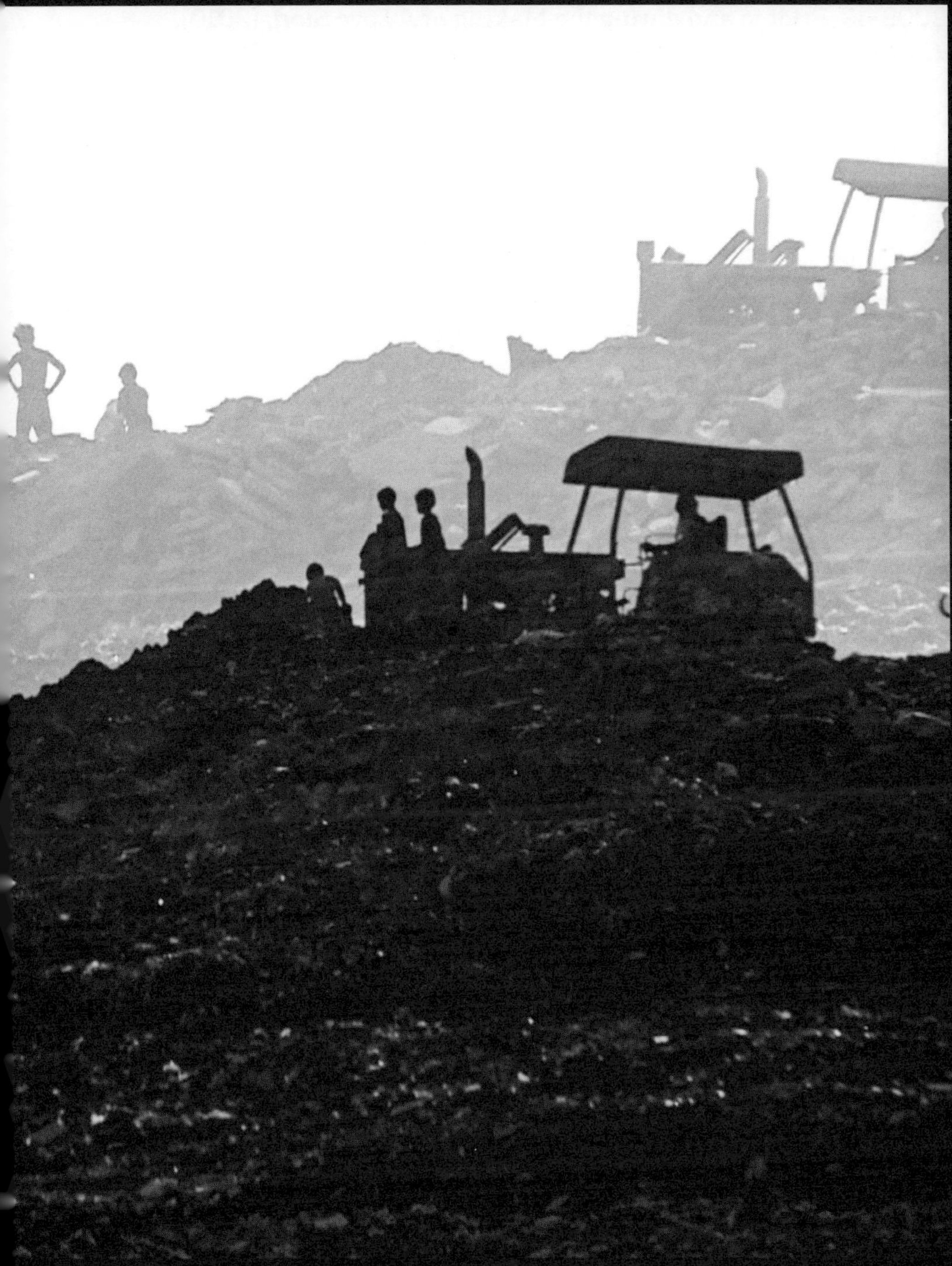

2009–12: Prior to and during the Making of *A Love Story* (2010), *The Scene of Crime* (2011) and *The Sovereign Forest* (2012)[19]

Can I make a film where there is no defined objective, no subject, the content of the film is unknown on the first day of the first shoot, and so on?

Yearning for the zero position is like a free fall, the absence of control can be terrifying. In the momentary delusion of such an aspiration, method emerges: by making the decision to shoot, for instance, only light in its varied forms, a certain distillation of the image became possible. Black-and-white could be shot in colour, the eye could be prepared to see in a certain way, the human form became distant and the embedding of any narrative became organically possible. In the resulting film, *A Love Story*, it felt as if only in the deep core of separation could one comprehend the meaning of life. In order to enter this core, perhaps, we needed to slip into a state of mind where we could momentarily see the bareness of the image, of human beings, of the inner life of nature. In the interconnected web of this bareness it suddenly became possible to exist, to express. Almost any narrative embedded here would integrate and find resonance.

A Love Story opened the door to *The Scene of Crime*. What if I could look without hierarchies? How to practise that? If the concentrated separation of every inhalation and exhalation could create a sense of unity, then could a separation of every glance also dissolve all divisions, integrate every being, trigger a dramatic awareness of our own existence and transform the way we see the world around us? Again, an impractical aspiration led to looking carefully at the terrain of the crime rather than the crime, and to then film, for instance, every physical movement within it. But for what purpose?

Central to the notion of crime is the question of evidence. All crimes are investigated by the police or the criminal justice system. Subsequently, only evidence that is defined as permissible by the law is allowed to be presented in court – all other evidence is dismissed as invalid. The carefully crafted text of the law tells us what is permissible, how to understand and what to conclude. But what happens if a crime continues to occur regardless of the enormous evidence available? Then is the crime invisible or the evidence invisible, or are both visible but not seen? The moment you ask this question a new set of questions emerge. Perhaps we do not comprehend the crime fully. Is legally valid evidence adequate to understand the meaning and extent of a crime? What if the definition of valid evidence is itself incorrect? What is the scene of crime, what is its footprint? Is the crime always a single cataclysmic event, or is it an expanding, accumulating process as well? Which vocabulary can adequately comprehend the scene and extent of a crime?

If I do not understand the meaning of loss, its scale, its extent, its multiple dimensions, then how could I even know what it is that is lost? Loss must have, it seems, its own unique language. Be it the loss of land, of voice, of life, or of freedom.

These were some of the questions that led to *The Sovereign Forest*, within which the poetics of multiple forms of evidence were formally presented. Doubt interrogated intent, which created content, which in turn triggered form. Many interconnected routes opened into the scene of crime. A deeper sense of the unknown lay in the chance encounters between inner narratives. A constellation of different comprehensions became possible.

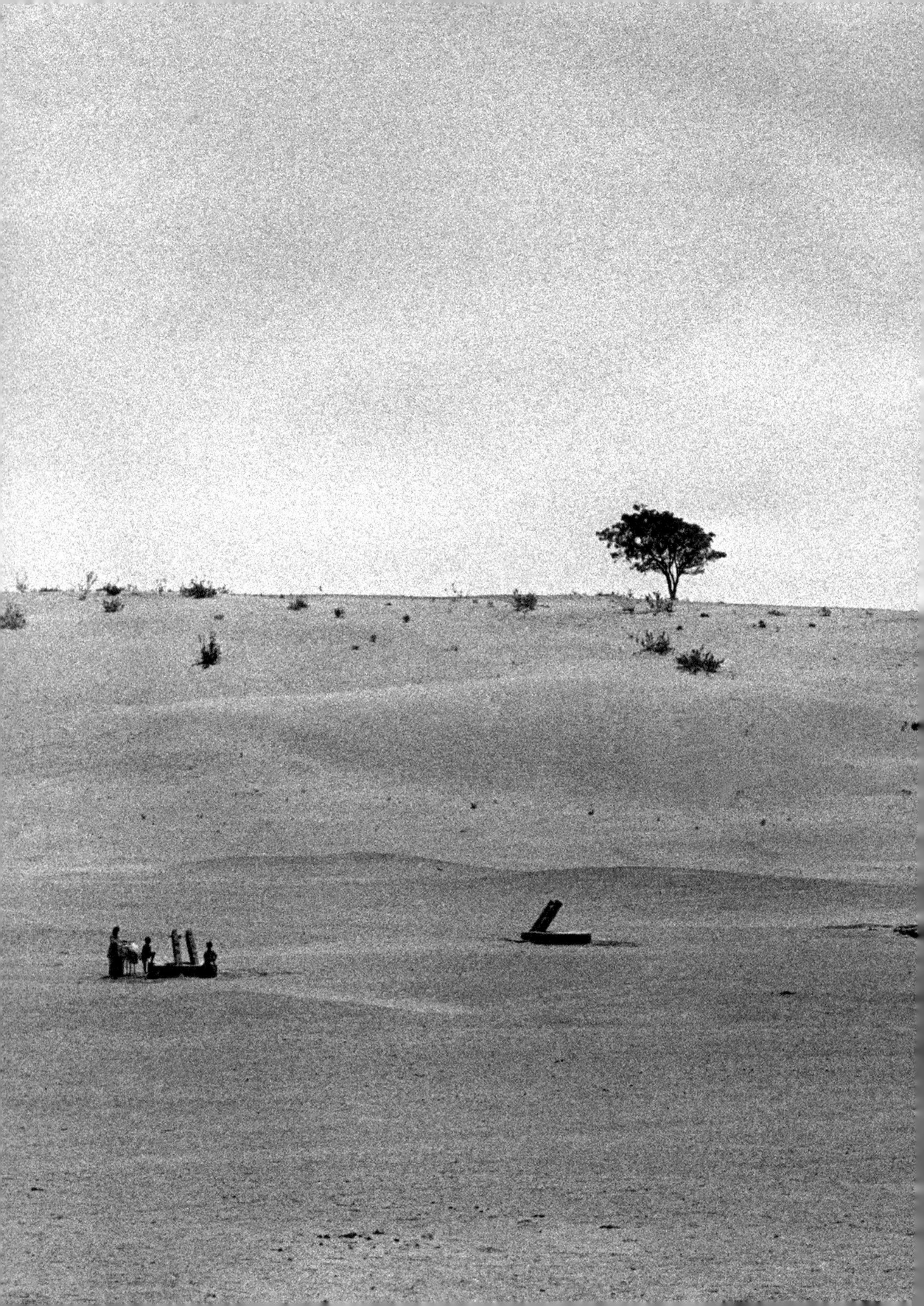

15 On Seeing 2023

I Gauri Gill

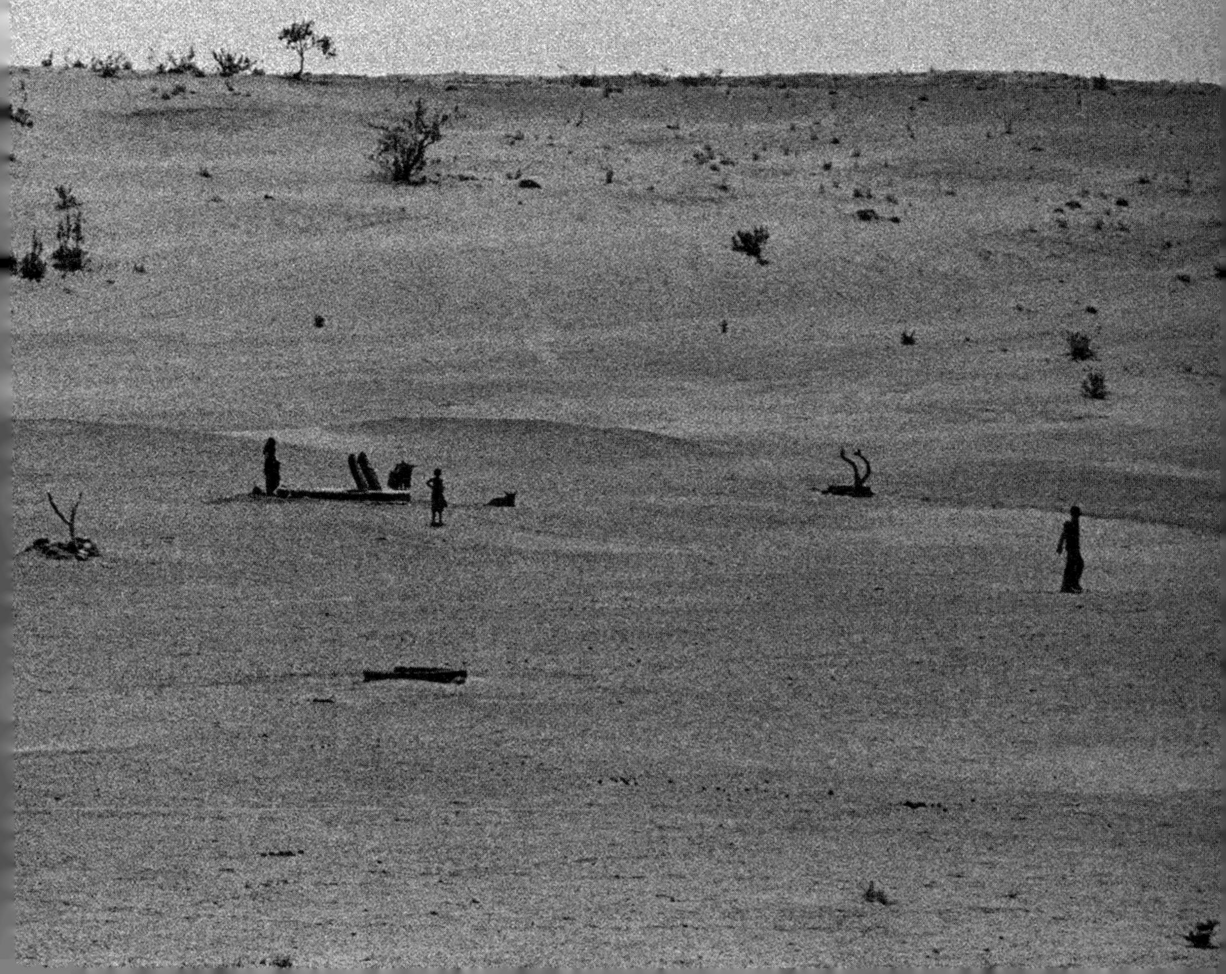

Artist-photographer Gauri Gill invites us into a deeply immersive photographic practice through projects she has developed across rural India over the last twenty five years including within Rajasthan and Maharashtra. She has lived and worked in different places, where she has met, collaborated with and photographed diverse protagonists such as Jannat, a young woman, her sister Hoora and their mother Izmat in Barmer; members of the NGO Urmul Setu Sansthan and their Balika Mela (fair for girls) in Lunkaransar town; the *dai* or midwife, Kasumbi Dai, in Motasar; the Warli Indigenous artist Rajesh Chaitya Vangad in Ganjad; and the Indigenous *papier-mache* artists, brothers Subhas and Bhagvan Dharma Kadu, sons of the legendary artist Dharma Ram Kadu in Jawhar.

Gill emphasizes the psychological, social and aesthetic value of deep engagement with locations along with participatory creation with local communities, as well as the need to show work in the context in which it was made. She delineates her choices, her methodologies, her commitment and her sustained effort to get herself 'out of the way in order to see more clearly, and collectively', so that her acts of image-making enable her to 'privilege all the ingenuous ways people find to swim, or to stay afloat, despite fragile or precarious circumstances'.

Published for the first time in this volume, with the permission of the author.

Keywords and Names

Adivasi, Documentary Photography, see Keywords at the back of this volume.

Images

pp. 262–63: *Waterwells*, from the series *Notes from the Desert*, 1999–ongoing.

p. 267: *Jannat, Barmer*, from the series *Notes from the Desert*, 1999–ongoing.

p. 269: *Indira and Kumari*, 2003, from the series *Balika Mela*, 2003/2010.

p. 271: (Above) *Untitled (20)*, (Below) *Untitled (39)*, from the series *The Mark on the Wall*, 1999–ongoing.

p. 273: *Building the City*, 2016, from the series *Fields of Sight*, 2013–ongoing.

p. 275: *Untitled (4)*, from the series *Acts of Appearance*, 2015–ongoing.

In April 1999, I set out to photograph village schools in Rajasthan. Some months earlier, I had happened to witness a girl being beaten by her teacher in a small government school some hours from Jodhpur, and had been dwelling upon it. When I came back to Delhi, I proposed an essay to the political weekly where I worked at the time, about what it was like being a girl in a village school. I was told the story lacked a suitable 'news peg', or one that more urban readers of the magazine might relate to, and my idea was set aside. I decided to take a month-long sabbatical from work and to spend it in rural Rajasthan.

I started by travelling randomly from school to school, criss-crossing the state through Jaipur, Jodhpur, Osiyan, Bikaner, Barmer, Phalodi, Baran and Churu districts, photographing mainly in the villages, from government schools to experimental set-ups to NGO-organized community events. I met students, teachers, officials and activists. They were surprisingly tolerant of my ignorance, endeavouring to answer my many questions as an English-speaking person from Delhi.

In the town of Lunkaransar, I visited a Marushala or experimental school run by Urmul Setu Sansthan[1] for nomadic Jogi children, whose ancestry, it is said, connects them to the Romas of Europe. I met Urma and Halima, who took me home with them, and I was introduced to the family of Bhana Nathji, father of Urma and respected community leader. We sat in their mud home, on the bed with the snakes and chameleons and rooster underneath it, with Urma's brothers and their hunting dogs around us, and Bhana Nathji invited me to travel with them. I did. He was to become my friend and sage guide over these many years since, until he passed away at the end of 2019. I miss him greatly.

In Barmer district, lost, I came upon a group of women fully covered in large dark *ajrak* (textile block-printed) shawls standing around the corpse of a little girl. They looked intimidating but when I ventured to ask for directions to the village school, I was interrupted by one who grasped me by my hands and told me all that was wrong with her life. With the conviction borne of great suffering, Izmat impressed upon me that on my return to Delhi I must tell people of the troubles of those in Barmer. Her older daughter Jannat was terrified of me in my jeans and short hair with my camera. She thought I must be a boy. But Izmat took my address, and in subsequent letters that she dictated to literate acquaintances, and posted to me, urged me to return. I did.

Looking at those rural schools opened out a world. I realized that school was only a microcosm of a complex reality that I knew nothing about, having grown up mainly in the cities. My own grandfathers both left their villages to join the army, and slowly our ties with the rural were severed. Over the past two decades my visits to western Rajasthan, to meet with essentially the same people in the same places, have encompassed various parts of life, and changes that have occurred over time. I have witnessed the seasons: drought years and the year of a great monsoon – when Barmer became Kashmir, dust storms that could give you a fever, and a flood that wreaked enough havoc to require the rebuilding of Urma's home. I have followed the farming cycle, migration, men travelling to work as labour in Gujarat and Maharashtra, Food for Work programmes, MGNREGA[2] and other government schemes, nomadic journeys, illness, epidemics, cerebral malaria, tuberculosis, overwhelmed hospitals and understaffed schools, death from snakebite, from accidents, from being burned alive for providing inadequate dowry, from growing old, the death of a camel in a year that is remembered as the year of the death of the camel, births, marriages, child marriages, moneylenders, civil society interventions, dharnas, rallies, national and panchayat elections, festivals, feuds passed down over generations, celebrations, prayers ... and through it all, my friends, by whom I was led.

This large archive now embeds various narratives and stories within it, as well as different forms of image-making, from posed studio pictures to *cinéma vérité*-style images. I hope to eventually make a series of books – each one a note from the desert.

Made between 1999 and 2007, the series *Jannat*[3] is based upon the life of Jannat, her younger sister Hoora and mother Izmat. After Jannat and Hoora's father abandoned them, the small and imperilled family of three, living in a remote hamlet near Barmer, were fused together as one symbiotic being. I spent days and weeks with them, over the course of years. In the form that I have struggled to create, as much as it is a story about growing up in a village, one I wish to tell for city-dwelling children like my niece, it is also a story about love. Jannat died of illness in 2007, at the age of 23, although as with many in the village her exact birth date is uncertain. Hoora has just completed a college degree, as well as studying computers, practically unheard of in her peer group of local young Muslim women. When Izmat was in the courts struggling to gain access to her own land from her ex-husband, the judge would not believe that she had once been the poorest person in her village. These photographs were used as evidence.

The series *Ruined Rainbow*[4] was created from rolls of film taken by children in the same village as Jannat and Hoora. After I had been visiting for some years, several of the children – who were always avid followers of where I was going and what I was doing, and in a sense my first collaborators – decided they too would

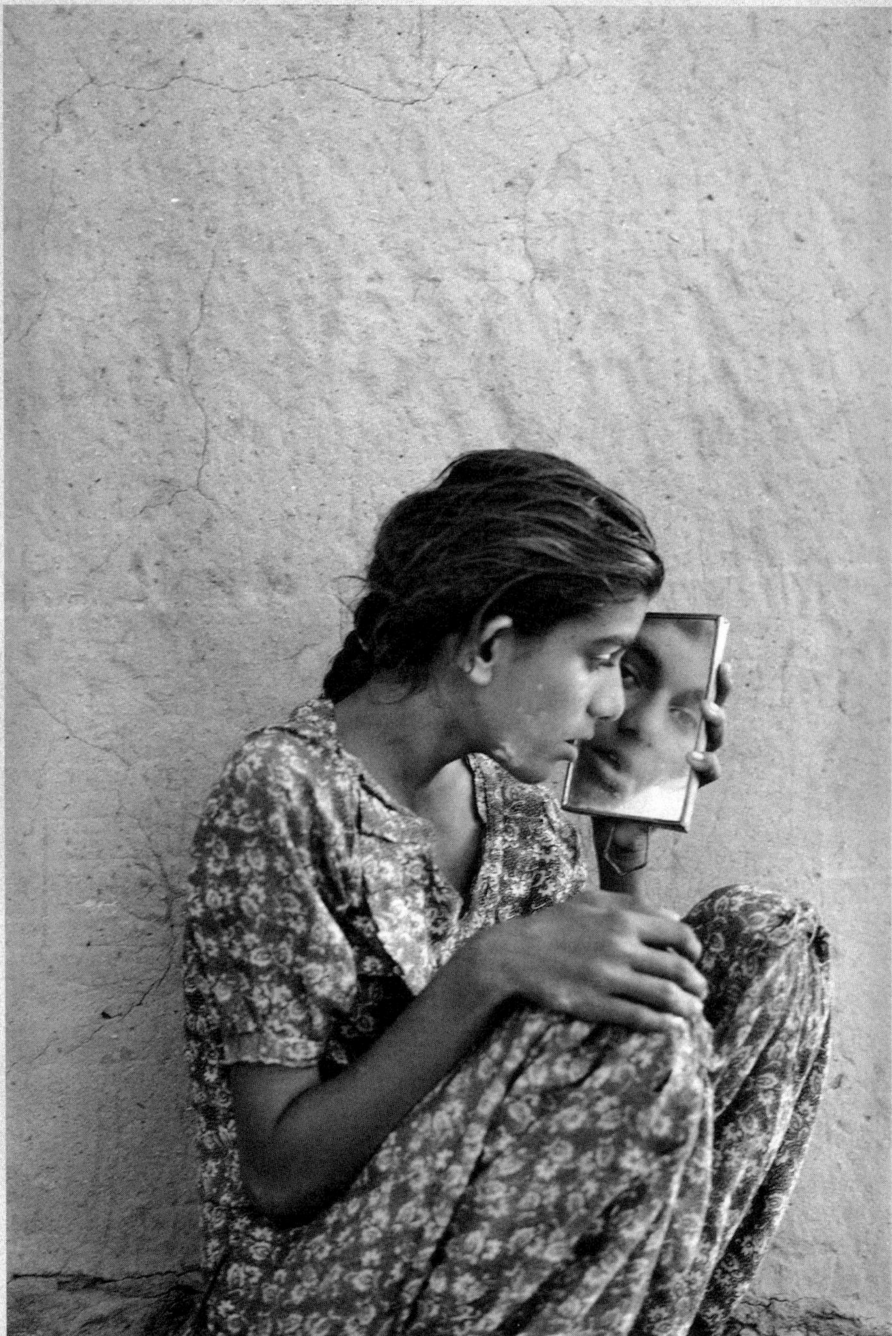

like to take pictures. I asked if they were serious, and as they insisted they were, I brought them some Kodak cameras. These now belonged to them. They could decide, for instance, whether they wished to photograph in colour or in black-and-white. In the initial years, the children would photograph and give me the rolls to develop and print in the lab in Barmer or Delhi, and bring back to them. They were excited and enthusiastic, and photographed widely. In the process of learning, they also made 'mistakes'. On one occasion they were horrified to see flashes of light streaked across the prints I brought them - the unidentified photographer among them had accidentally opened the back of the camera and exposed the film to light. No one would claim the film as theirs, and it was instantly discarded as failed - but I kept it in my bag. Years later, in 2010, when I was editing my own contact sheets for the exhibition *Notes from the Desert*, I found these rolls. I looked at them anew, and was moved to see long-familiar faces and places appear in the photographs. I wondered which particular child had made the images, and at the precise exchange that might have occurred at that moment. I thought about photography, and its inherent subjectivity, and how there are as many possible narratives as there are narrators. As with life, the medium of technology introduces its own presence through chance and accidents. I played with the prints, and when I looked at them again, the exposed images had formed an unexpected rainbow. A *ruined rainbow*, if you will.

Visiting Rajasthan so frequently, I formed close relationships with local activists. Although I saw myself as an independent artist, having studied painting and documentary and fine art photography, and later funding my projects through journalism in my twenties and teaching in my thirties, I would sometimes live at local NGOs, and spontaneous ideas would arise from our mutual conversations. In early 2003, Urmul Setu Sansthan organized a Balika Mela (fair for girls) in Lunkaransar town, attended by almost fifteen hundred adolescent girls from seventy surrounding villages. The *mela* (fair) had various stalls, food, performances, a Ferris wheel, magicians, puppet shows, games and competitions, similar to any other small-town fair. Urmul Setu invited me to 'do something with photography'.

I created a photo-stall for anyone to come in and have their portrait taken, and later buy the silver gelatin print at a subsidized rate if they wished. I had a few basic props and backdrops, whatever we could get from the local town studio and cloth shop on a very limited budget, but it was fairly minimal, and since it can get windy out in the desert everything would keep getting blown around, or periodically struck down. The light was the broad, even light of an open sky, filtered through the cloth roof of our tent. Many of the more striking props - like

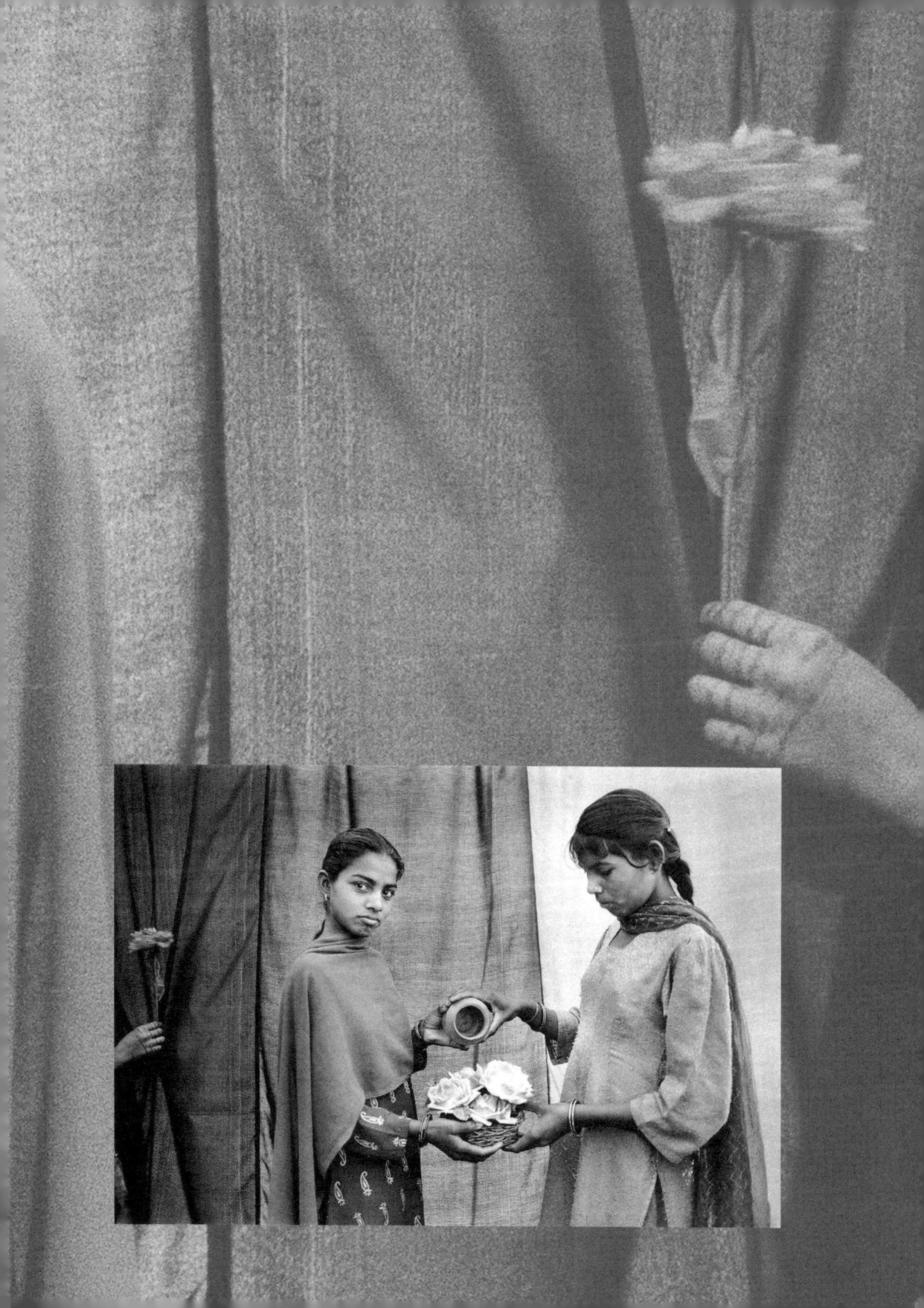

the peacock and the paper hats – were brought in by the girls themselves. Girls came in, and decided how and with whom they would like to be photographed – best friends, new friends, sisters, the odd younger brother who had tagged along, girls with their teachers, the whole class, the local girl scouts. Thirteen of those who posed for the pictures went on to learn photography in the workshops that I began there with Urmul Setu that summer, and two years later they photographed the fair themselves. One of them, Manju Saran, ran Shiva Photo Studio in village Kalu for five years before her marriage, a rare occurrence in deeply patriarchal Rajasthan. The second essay in the book *Balika Mela* (Edition Patrick Frey, 2012) is written by her.

In 2005 I met a great *dai*, or midwife, Kasumbi Dai, at a birthing workshop organized by NGO friends. She invited me to photograph her work, to be there when she delivered her grandchild in the remote village of Motasar, in Ghafan. I lived with her for ten days before the baby came, and I ended up assisting with the birth. An indomitable feminist, someone who became a midwife after she lost her own husband at a young age, Kasumbi Dai had delivered all the children in the surrounding areas for miles around. I see her as the 'Mother of Mothers'. The set of pictures became the *Birth Series*.[5]

Izmat took me to visit her father's grave, and those of other family members. Created from materials found in nature, I was struck by how lightly the graves exist upon the earth's surface, and in time I began to photograph the graveyards. *Traces*[6] memorializes both marked and unmarked graves. They belong to people with relatively few economic resources, and from both the Muslim and Hindu communities, including Bishnois, Jats and Meghwals, pointing to a more heterogeneous complexity of the local population and contradicting the conservative formulations of nationalist politics in India today. Using stones, shards of pottery, hand-inscribed gravestones or personal items such as fabric or medicine bottles, each site is marked with the available materials to pay homage and cultivate memory. Slowly, these are reabsorbed by the landscape as they are assimilated by other creatures of the earth, or erased by sand and the elements, to become one with the emptiness and silence of the desert.

Through all of this time, I continued to photograph in schools. *The Mark on the Wall*, its title drawn from a short story by Virginia Woolf in which a woman in a rocking chair gets obsessed with a mark on the wall, documents drawings made by local artists, children and teachers in government schools in Rajasthan, under the Leher Kaksha and other subsequent government schemes[7] initiated by the state to help children learn visually from the walls in their classrooms. In the

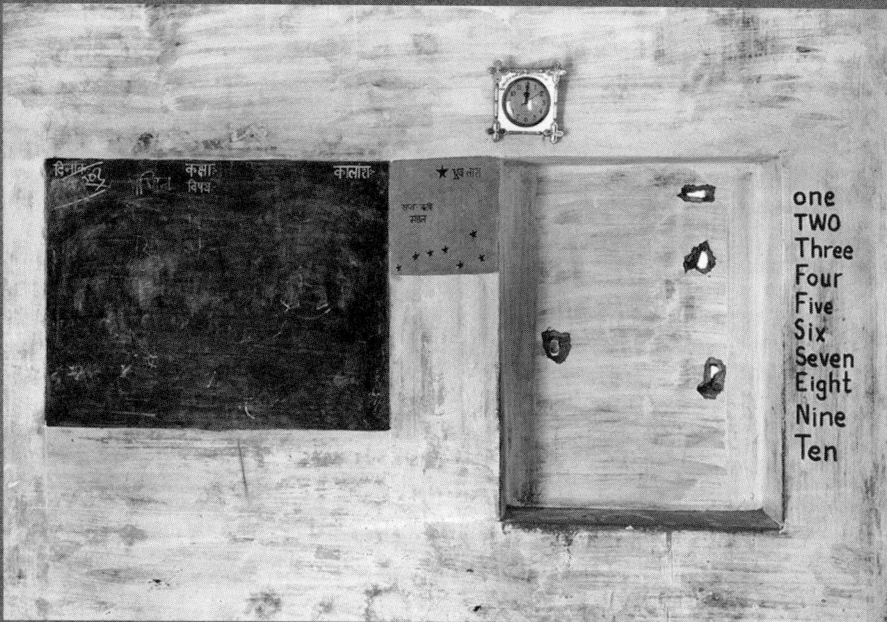
one
TWO
Three
Four
Five
Six
Seven
Eight
Nine
Ten

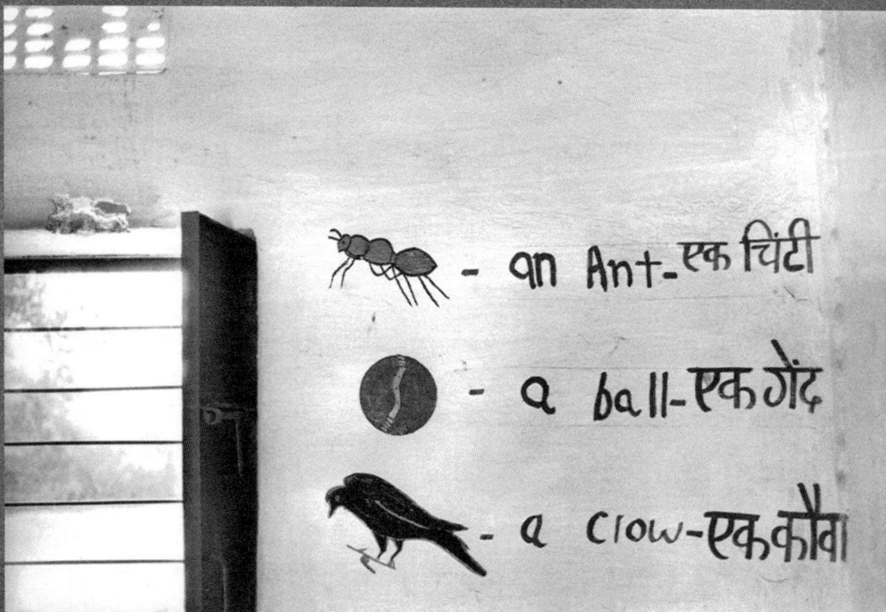
- an Ant - एक चिंटी
- a ball - एक गेंद
- a clow - एक कौवा।

starkest of villages, in bare concrete schools, using the most meagre resources, I found rich, imaginative traces of the human hand. From the most tentative marks to those more sophisticated, from depictions of determined children making their way to school to individualistic expressions of nature, from maps of the village to symbols of the state, these fragments offered glimpses of the collective mind of local communities.

In early 2013, I was invited by an NGO organizing a festival of the arts in Ganjad, Maharashtra to live in the home of a Warli indigenous artist, Rajesh Chaitya Vangad,[8] who was also participating in the festival. I was to create a photo-studio followed by an exhibition in the local primary school. It was loosely based on Balika Mela.

In the course of my time, living and working on the school project in Ganjad, I began to appreciate the landscape; only some hours away from Bombay, it was nonetheless completely distinct. We were living within nature, which, chameleon-like, had so many faces - changing even as one took a turn. There was no electricity for hours and nights altogether, and my Airtel phone only worked when I climbed a little hill.

Undistracted, my awareness was sharpened. I wished to try and record the landscape, but my images felt distant, even opaque. Perhaps the beauty obscured the reality of the place, or perhaps I simply did not know it well enough. In conversations with Rajeshji, whose family has lived for generations in Vangad Pada, working as artists, we began to discuss his village.

Any place looks entirely different to different eyes. I was made acutely aware, once again, of how a place is assigned meaning only by its viewer, determined perhaps by her relative distance or proximity to it; and of how viewing itself is an essentially solitary act. What we see is only a projection of what we know, have already seen, or experienced. As someone wise once said, to the Brahmin's eye the pond is full of beautiful lotuses to admire; to the Adivasi fisherwoman it appears as the host of fish and living creatures, the very source of sustenance.

Tentatively, I decided to photograph places significant to Rajeshji - often with him present in the frame. He would take me to these special places, and I would decide where and how to construct the image, what to include, how to work with or against the light, how best to place him within the landscape, and so on. It was a set of pictures about his place, a map determined by Rajeshji, and formally constructed by me - photographer as cartographer.

When I later viewed my contact sheets, I realized that so much of the narrative that I had received from Rajeshji, the great stories which had made it come alive

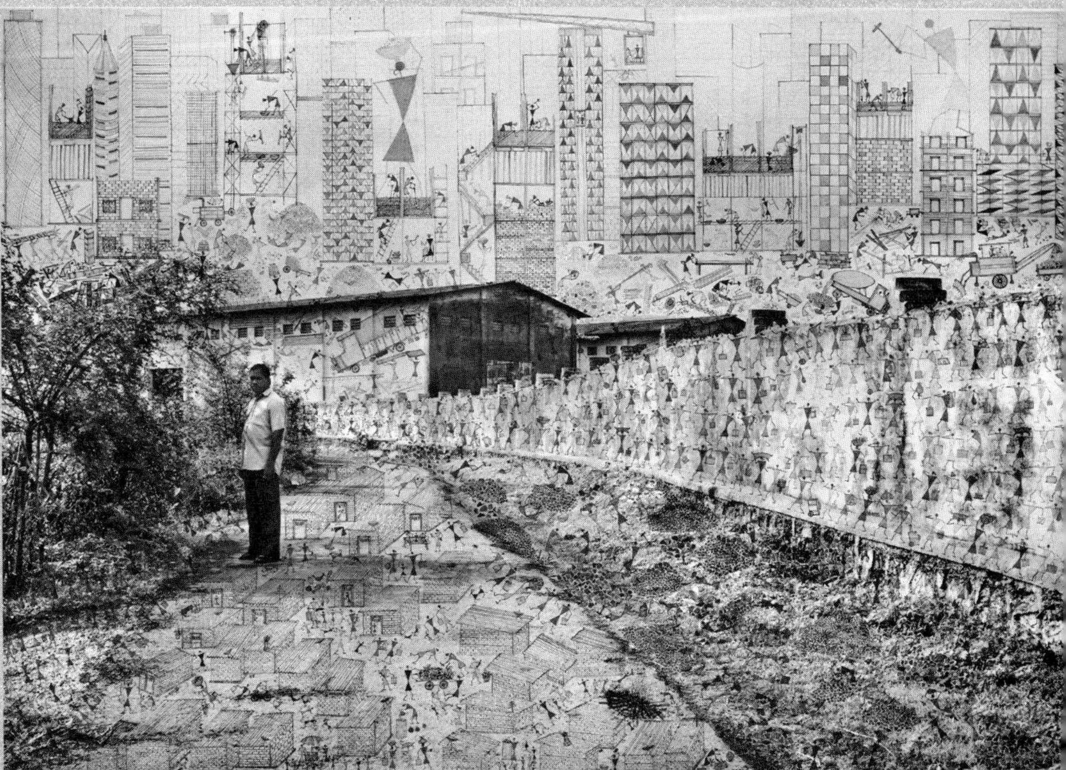

for me, was missing. Part of it, I understood, was the limitation – and perhaps, the unique quality – of photography, which brings our attention via the image to the immediacy of the present moment, but which also thereby erases all that came before. How could I convey what happened in those months in the 1970s when the violent mobs of a powerful political party raided the village and the locals fled and fell upon each other in terror; or the particular full moon night in October when a great forest on one hill comes alive, and all the people who spend that night in the forest see shining eyes glitter around them, as even the most dangerous animals are known to turn benign when everything glows from the special aura of the moon; or the stories of great overlords who come calling in secret to the homes of innocent, hospitable men, bringing gifts and drink and returning with deeds of land; or the mythical stories that encompass everything that has been, or is yet to be.

I had an idea. We would extend our collaboration to make it more explicit: Rajeshji would inscribe his drawing over my photographs, meet my visual text with own graphic response. As Warli art is monochromatic, and in order to make the encounter intense and precise, we decided to restrict our work to a black-and-white palette. Initially autobiographical, the work has grown to become more abstract, and to encompass larger themes.

This commingled work may be seen as an encounter between two artists, of about the same age, using entirely different languages – one with ancient antecedents, the other with more recent origins, and the histories, politics and worldviews embedded within the expression of both of those forms. Rajeshji's language, constructed with stick and brush, unfolds entirely from an encyclopaedia of forms in his mind, which emerge to reflect the world, memory and myth; wind, disease, apocalypse – everything is summoned forth at will. In my own language, constructed by camera and negative, the world itself is the encyclopedia, and I recognize and edit existing structures to reflect what arises in my mind. The final work contains parallel projections of place; using perspective, negative and positive space, tonal values and relative dimensions, it merges fields of sight, and of perception. If you stand here, you might see it this way; move to one side just a little, and another world unfolds. Or as someone put it to me: 'It's as though you were photographing an old home, and the resident of the house came out, and began to speak.'

In Dahanu, spending time in Rajeshji's village, I learned of the Bohada procession,[9] held once a year in many Adivasi villages, in which the entire community participates in a ritual performance over several nights, in order to enact a mythological tale. *Acts of Appearance*[10] assumed its form within a village

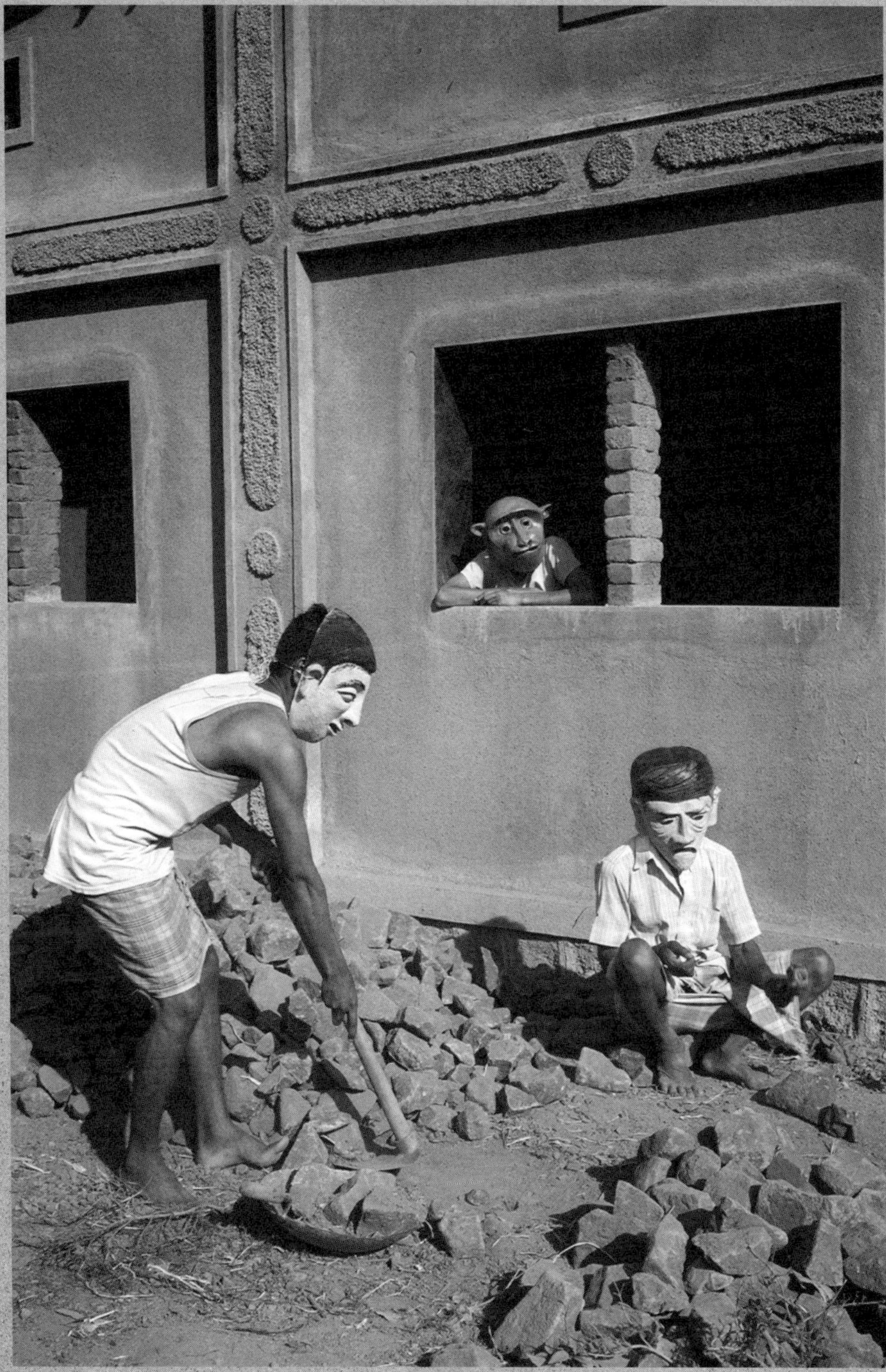

of *papier-mache* artists from the Kokna and Warli tribes in Jawhar district, further inland from Dahanu.[11] The performers for the Bohada are chosen from among the residents and wear elaborate masks made by artists to represent different gods, demons and ancillary figures. These masks take weeks to make, are sacred and consecrated, and constitute a moral and imaginative universe, but must also conform to strict rules of creation as they represent powerful archetypes refined over generations of storytelling. Spending time in the area, I began to wonder about the incongruity between these idealized mythic masks and the reality I saw all around me. After initiating a dialogue, in 2015, I made a proposal to the acclaimed brothers Subhas and Bhagvan Dharma Kadu, sons of the legendary artist Dharma Ram Kadu.[12] I wished to commission them, along with their families and fellow volunteers (eventually almost forty people in total), to create a new set of masks – not of gods or demons as per local tradition, but rather representing beings existing in contemporary reality. The interpretive creations were to come from them, with the suggestion that they embody familiar or known individuals of different ages, the varied *rasas* – love, sadness, fear and anger and those experiences common to all humans, such as sickness, relationships or aging. In the course of dialogue, animals were naturally understood to be a part of this universe. Later, precious objects entered the frame, as they are believed to have sentience too. Inhabiting these masks, a cast of volunteer 'actors', including some of the artists, would later improvise and enact different 'real' scenarios, across dreaming and waking states, in and around the village.

I imagined using the freedom afforded by the masks as a way to create distance from and reflect upon the self; as a possible means to explore one's life and circumstances in the lived present rather than the distant past of historical memory. We are all heterogeneous beings, constituted of as many different selves as moments in time, inhabiting varying contexts, and others read us in their own subjective ways, often different from how we imagine ourselves to be. The question also arises: To whom does my face belong – me, or the world that views me? Although these enactments were mediated by the camera (and me behind it), the viewer is denied access to the physical likenesses of the subjects, to be replaced instead by their art.

In a sense, my endeavour has involved learning to listen more deeply, to get myself out of the way in order to see more clearly, and collectively. While photography is a democratic medium in some respects, as almost everyone today has access to some form of camera, there is disproportionate power in terms of who gets to tell the story. My own small attempt has been to try and cede control of representation, and individualization. Photography can help us not only to broaden monolithic representations, but also to expand the closed and self-referential circles of power and visibility, who gets to be included, and who is excluded. Where and towards whom we direct our attention is an act of love, and belief. Offering this attention might also reveal the so-called extraordinary to be quite banal, and the so-called ordinary to be endlessly fascinating. And when I focus only on the explicit object – which itself is constantly changing – I fail to pay heed to all of the processes and players embedded in it. Even in attempting to deconstruct the process I end up creating new centres of focus. In truth, there is a multitude behind any singular act – or any solidified convergence of acts – that appear in the form of an object. And there is an ever-flowing continuum, each instant following naturally from what came before.

Finally, as much as the work engages with conditions that are unjust in the world, I have wished to privilege all the ingenuous ways people find to swim, or to stay afloat, despite fragile or precarious circumstances. These small acts of resistance and beauty by individuals or communities are all we have in the end, and wherein lies hope.

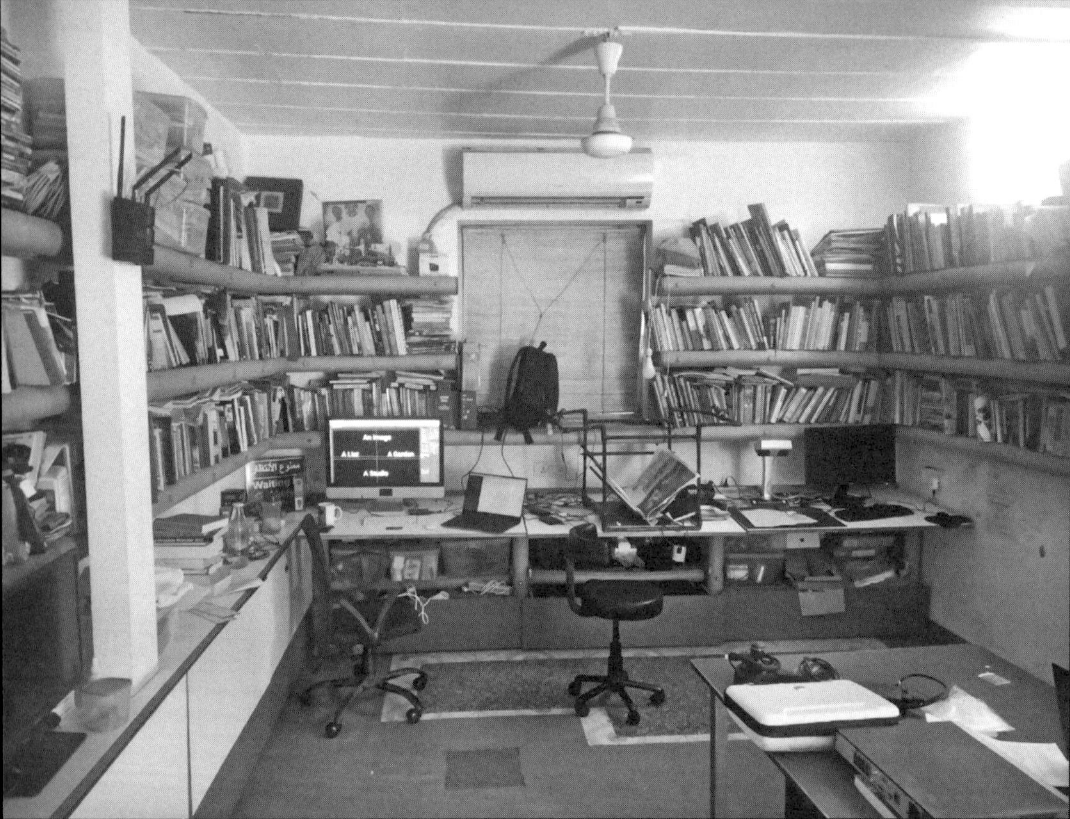

Afternoon Scene

CAMP studio, late 2018

Two book scanners, four computers, an NVR recorder, a PTZ joystick, microphones, salad, water, biscuits, coffee on the tables. Bookshelves, routers, awards, air conditioning and fan above the tables. Inventory of electronics + museum of Jurassic technology below the tables. Person taking photograph behind.

16 CAMP on CAMP

2022

CAMP

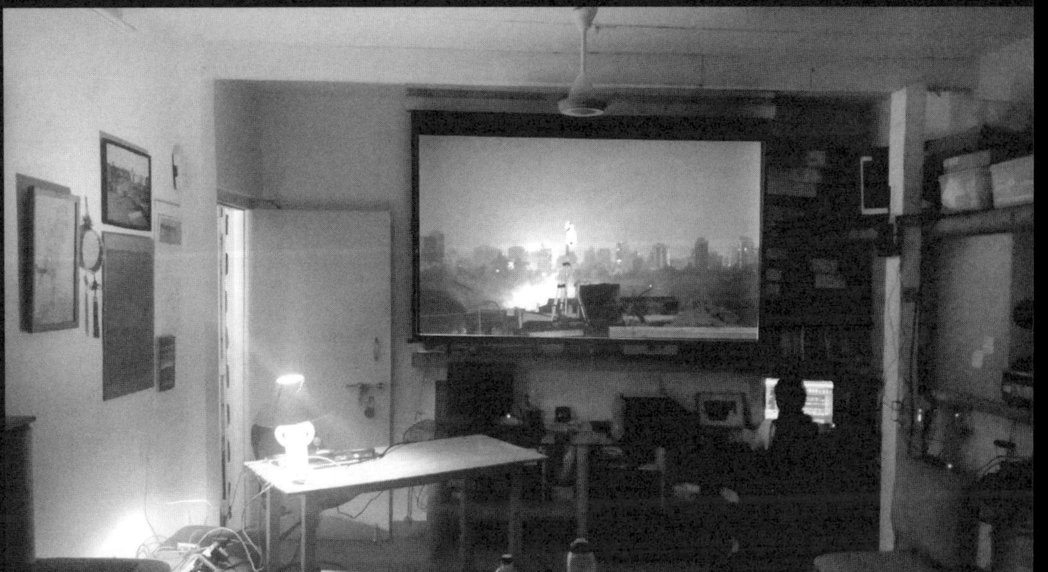

Evening Scene

CAMP Studio, late 2018

From left to right: Dickinson Survey 1812 map of Bombay, photograph by Dharavi Art Room, silkscreen print by Amol Patil, Styrofoam iPad on wall, ethernet switch and spike buster on seating, mascot table lamp, PTZ controller and video switcher on table top, live image from a rooftop on the projection screen, glass-top table with paper rolls for legs, person on http://indiancine.ma, router, HDD cabinet and post-its with wifi passwords, reading glasses in foreground, some persons taking a break, a person taking the picture.

In 2006, a small group of practitioners with diverse skills came together in Mumbai to start work with materials that included electricity, cable TV, FM radio, miniature cameras, php code, sunlight, kitchen utensils, chunks of philosophy, film and media theory. This would come to be known as 'new' media, but to them it included a century-old history, defined as much by the city as by the different classes of individuals who survived in it. These materials were, say CAMP, 'instruments and sensoriums of the possible, the extendable, the sayable and the hearable, the everywhere-present and yet vanishing-while-at-work'.

CAMP focuses on imaging practices, local media and technology infrastructures, and the flux of the cultural economy. Convinced of art-making as a means to distil new sites of political possibility, the artists critique an expanded art market dominated by what they experience as 'a pyramid scheme of commercially-driven art growing taller, and certainly more unstable', with the 'main artistic developments' seeming to involve 'the propagation of a kind of large-scale artistic irony'.

Originally written in 2006, a revised version of this essay appeared in Partha Mitter, Parul Dave-Mukherji and Rakhee Balaram eds, *20th Century Indian Art: Modern, Post-Independence, Contemporary.* London and New York: Thames & Hudson, 2022.

Keywords and Names

Citizenship, *Documentary photography*, *Gujarat riots 2002*, *Modernism*, *Moving images*, see Keywords at the back of this volume.

Images

p. 278: *Afternoon Scene, CAMP studio*, late 2018.

p. 279: *Evening Scene, CAMP Studio*, late 2018.

In 2006, the group of people who set up CAMP (Shaina Anand, Sanjay Bhangar, Ashok Sukumaran) worked with a list of materials that included: electricity, cable TV, FM radio, miniature cameras, php code, sunlight, kitchen utensils, chunks of philosophy, film and media theory. The important thing for us (the above-mentioned group) was not whether this list, a product of a sometimes century-old electric/domestic world, should be thought of as 'new media', or whether these were phenomena of 'the city', or even expressions of a particular social class. Rather, they were instruments and sensoriums of the possible, the extendable, the sayable and the hearable, the everywhere-present and yet vanishing-while-at-work. They were points of turning and transformation in relation to 'progress' and social imagination, and a provocation to cinema and spatial practices. Such technologies and carriers that were widely and deeply present in our environment, but were always kept at a safe/middle/referential distance and rarely accounted for in political theory and post-medium artistic thought, had in fact become our intimate media.

How had this happened? Shaina and Sanjay had worked together since late 2001, after 9/11 and through the Gujarat pogrom and its effects in Bombay.[1] Sanjay had described Shaina's video practice as 'fierce'. Shaina had declared pre-emptively to Sanjay's mother that he was a 'self-taught computer programmer'. Ashok and Shaina shared, among other things, a history of intense and often traumatic encounters with turn-of-the-century technologies: crashing computers, lost data, expensive and eerily unreliable hardware, the smell of solder, burning wires and CPU dust. Meanwhile Sanjay, a young administrator of the Indymedia Bombay website in the early 2000s, was also experiencing crashing computers, toxic right-wing trolls and other signs of the times.

Yet, let's not give too much credit to this technologized milieu, or to the city of Bombay for the artistic practices that would emerge at CAMP. Our activities and questions were 'of their time and place' in a roundabout and antagonistic sense. Some of the main questions had been generated earlier and elsewhere – for example, in Shaina's 1999 book-length text (co-authored with filmmaker/curator Shai Heredia)[2] about being part of a documentary film crew travelling with the filmmaker Saeed Mirza[3] through India, or Ashok's abandonment, that same year, of an intellectually-minded architectural practice in the faraway Himalayas. Shaina and Sanjay had both dropped out of college, in different contexts. Ashok had tried to glean a retroactive art education at University abroad, from such esoteric figures as (media historian and magic lantern collector) Erkki Huhtamo and (*How We Became Posthuman* author) N. Katherine Hayles. The original group of three was a peculiar and unlikely one, even as its overall nerdiness, political orientation and unfamiliarity with art gallery protocols set a tone and also a limit to what it could produce, and underscored its relationship with the art world of its time.

There is probably elsewhere in this book (*20th Century Indian Art*), an account of what was going on in the Bombay/Mumbai art world from 2004 to 2008. It should be enough for us to say that the established galleries or Bodhi-like startups showed scant interest in our work. But that is something every young Baroda- or J.J.-graduating artist, bar a lucky few, could say as well.[4]

So let us instead put it this way, in terms of a 'media landscape' that we were increasingly sensitive to:

In the early years of liberalization when the airwaves were 'freed', a dozen startup TV channels ran their operations out of three-star hotels near Juhu beach. Some readers will remember BI-TV,[5] and fewer still may know of one of its unrealized serials, *Hum Bambai Nahi Jayenge* (We Will Not Go to Bombay),[6] that was modelled around a group of theatre actors from the National School of Drama in Delhi,[7] who didn't want to sell out to Bombay. Of course, the opposite happened, quite literally. And Indian television went from two to one hundred channels in a matter of a few years.

The early 2000s were a time of a booming 'creative economy' in Mumbai. And a generation of young creative practitioners – filmmakers, 'applied' artists, musicians, web coders, writers, video activists – found their place in a milieu that was also going through its first dot.com boom. Those brought up in Bombay in that decade would have had a memory, for example, of the 1993 riots as teenagers.[8] But for even younger people, and for so many coming to the city afterwards, Mumbai appeared as a post-industrial and post-liberalized city, largely freed of the older social antagonisms, resistances and solidarities. Its competitive creative economy meant that visibility, eyeballs and other such measures of success were, quite simply, measures of having made it. Survival in the city was never easy for those who were not from Bombay, but in the 'creative' metropolis, the fight for visibility was literally the path to security. This situation was a backdrop, 'an elephant in the room', in the oversized gallery shows that we began to see in the years after 2005 or so. One could sense a pyramid scheme of commercially-driven art growing taller, and certainly more unstable. There were immediate benefits for some artists, but the long-term effects of the boom period, even for the art market, and certainly in terms of the expansion of art as a discourse, are debatable. The main artistic developments, it seemed to us, involved the propagation of a kind of large-scale artistic irony. By which we mean that the encounter between art and the rest of the world was an increasingly ironized, winked-at, blown-up cartoon caricature of what such encounters could have been. In the worst cases, of course, the oversizing and endless multiplication of objects were present without any irony at all. It seemed to us that an opportunity to deploy art as a sharp-edged, tough-nosed, not-just-wink-wink reflection on contemporary questions was largely lost, at a time of increased patronage and visibility for art.

At the same time, city-based collectives with new ways of working, such as Open Circle,[9] had split up and were no longer active. For us, there were thus multiple moves involved in entering this 'creative space': staying out of the millennium bubble, not 'going to Bombay', not being part of the new bound-script/call-sheet efficiency of productions that a new breed of assistant directors were bringing to film and Bollywood; not being part of the 'community-media-for-change' of NGOs and other structural adjustment-like programmes either. We were drawn to invisible and subterranean aspects of what was surrounding us, to materials and their assemblies in society, to systems and energies and capacities of people and things. We often found these capacities shackled to old but boosterist ideas, or to governmental logics, or to profitability. We parasited them, re-dreamed them, broke them up and found other uses for them. This was our idea of art.

CAMP was born in late 2007, as a way of sheltering and organizing this peculiar artistic practice in the midst of a burgeoning scene that had everything to do with us (in terms of our decision to be artists), and yet very little. None of us showed work in a Mumbai gallery from 2002 to 2008, while living and working there. Not for lack of trying, but because of excuses that were easily made on either side, approaches or imaginations that did not fit into a room, ephemerality, unsaleability, and our own general grumpiness. There is a line in our first website from 2007 which said that CAMP is not an artist's collective.[10] To us, there was no real difference in the way an individual artist or a collective was received or understood in the art world. There may have been some residual ideological value, but by this point the differences were not worth making any claims about. So instead we chose to say that we were a collectively-run studio, a space for production, a unit of undetermined future function. This was more descriptive in a way, where windows were left open, soon to be entered, for other people to join in, and for things that may or may not be art.

These rhetorical callisthenics around naming and defining oneself become less important over time. And yet, we can now see that some of our intentions or the words we used were not only our guides, but gathered new meanings along the way. They have become things beyond our words, and sometimes beyond us.

In what follows, we expand on three such terms that now have a certain weight and depth of function beyond CAMP the sign. They are, or could be, of general interest. They are ideas chasing possibilities and piercing descriptions. Or concepts diving into a reality which opens out to old or new imaginations from time to time.

Studio

Since 2009 our studio is on the third and terrace floor of a building in Chuim Village, Khar, on the border between what were the Portuguese and British colonies, midway in height between nearby residential towers and older bungalows that surround it below. This building, among others like it, does not exist in municipality records - or, to be more precise, exists as two small houses and a meat shop. From our terrace you have a view of suburban Bandra's apartment towers, many of which were made under Slum Rehabilitation Authority schemes,[11] and thus split between super-expensive tower flats and 225-square-foot 'rehabilitation' flats. Our building and its terrace exists as a kind of suspended middle ground between these types of habitation. The older houses directly surrounding us are part of a Christian-majority village called Chuim, now fragmented into scooter and car garages, flats for renting single mothers and small families, airline flight crews and small-scale factories, a situation largely unchanged for the past two decades. Visitors to the studio pass through some of this diversity on the way to the terrace, where three rooms full of books and computers can be found.

The studio has been from the beginning a space that could on short notice turn into a public space, not only for 'friends' but for a general and unknown public. This switching has happened more or less continuously over the years in the context of film or footage screenings on our terrace, public discussions, or in-progress presentations of our own work. This idea - of a place where things are made neither secretively nor in a constant publicity but in a rhythm that has little to do with formal exhibiting - is something we cherish. To us this is an evolution of 'studio artists': namely, towards those for whom the studio is a site for a hospitality to all manner of encounters, and who can at the same time conduct direct public performances in the studio, without mediation of the 'art world'.

Before 2009, our studio was in a flat where some of us also lived, and so these public moments could be quite intimate. From the current studio, a wire goes out to the adjacent building where Zinnia, a fourth long-standing member of CAMP lives; and through which she remotely accesses computers and hard drives.

If you turn off all the usual lights in our studio, there would be several dozen blinking lights still left, a hint of digital materials in storage, in transit, or being processed in one way or the other. The studio is our way of modulating our own space-time, and is a kind of organism that stores and digests information at different speeds, processes our intuitions, and occasionally breaks out into collective speech or acts. Perhaps any 'post-contemporary' artistic practice needs such an extra-bodily structure, social interface and processing machine, to support aims similar to what ours were: to sustain long-term projects, to achieve a certain scale and intensity of interventions, to work collaboratively in deep and different senses of the term.

Cinema

Cinema, to quote philosopher Alain Badiou's recent book on the subject, is 'the most impure of arts'. It is impure in relation to the arts, but also impure in relation to non-art, to everyday experiences, to aesthetic encounters that are banal and numerous. In other words, cinema is an art of assembling into shape diverse forces and pieces that one could not easily imagine joined, or montaged. Cinema doesn't begin, in this account, from Stéphane Mallarmé's blank page but rather from a material chaos that it seeks to purify and distil. This impure and flexible cinema precedes politics by suggesting new sites of political possibility, and 'points from where the world can be transformed'.[12]

Such a cinema, as such a backdrop and a meta-practice, is very close to activities at CAMP. Our departures from mainstream film culture and practice could be briefly described in four ways:

First, as Shaina once described as a *Rock-Paper-Scissors* game,[13] we are interested in the instability of the mutual triangular relations between authors, subjects and intervening technologies such as the camera, in any act of cinema. This has meant, for example, a number of projects and works where the traditional author or editor withdraws, or the subjects or technologies assume an authorial and outward-looking role, and so on.

Second, we have worked with, written about and built systems (the online archive Pad.ma is one example);[14] with other collaborators, to test cinematic questions more broadly, we could say, following the democratizing processes of digital video. Video's 'general economy', or video in the time of more cameras than people, which appears to be the case today, is something we have tried to address via the category of footage. Footage, not only as part of films, but conceived as encounters, intentions and media in its own right. Not just 'found' footage, but extracted or catalysed. That which is filmic, but not 'the film'.

Third, and at the same time, we are simultaneously concerned with film as something that lives today alongside the internet. In the work around the Radia tapes,[15] for example, film is deployed retroactively and in a very minimal way (without images, only sound and text) as a way of creating an intermediate form of attention, of concern, between the television-byte treatment of a subject and its vast online data dump or leak. In these ways, among others, cinema's basic questions of montage, experimentation, time and even ethics are for us elements that travel into (and coalesce within the templates of) other media.

Fourth, cinema in its vast and diverse forms of time-based experience is also part of a public screening practice at CAMP. Last year's series of public screenings were composed of very long films, the shortest of which was about seven hours long, and included classics like *Shoah* to new work by the Filipino director Lav Diaz,[16] for example.

Infrastructure

CAMP has used the term 'infrastructure' since about 2007.[17] Our interest in 'media' has meant a sensitivity to the infrastructural quality of contemporary expressions, support and agency. For us the term 'media' applies not only to visual or sound media, but also to water and ships. Thus we are on board with Ravi Sundaram's description of an infrastructural mesh of media that 'determine our situation' in ways that are often unacknowledged. Sundaram also describes a split in postcolonial governance thinking between the social and the medial - in which the social is demarcated by welfare and the management of a population's health, while the media occupied an 'upper' realm of leisure ... supplied by a different infrastructure (cinema, radio, etc.). For us, following our expanded sense of the medial, there is also a split along another axis: between the social and the 'lower' realms of material production, supply chains, financial and surveillance networks, and the like. Here infrastructure is what disappears, and what recedes from the senses. Thus it is not only that we have what Sundaram describes as an 'affect-driven' 'postcolonial media modernity', but also another vast one in which lies below affects, and in a sense excludes the human sensorium.[18] Even as, like in surveillance, it 'sucks' at humans.

Our interest in the ship's hold, oceans, databases, the insides of containers and CCTV control rooms comes from this curiosity and engagement with that infrastructure that tends towards disappearance. Which is the subterranean mirror of the sensorial and social infrastructures of texting, video and sound events, social media and the like. Art, in this case, crafts a kind of bridge or (a) break between these different modes of infrastructure: the ones above and below the ground level of our senses. Affect can emerge from strange places in the network, and we are looking for it in the back-ends of systems, in the archives, in leaks, in cameras mounted on homes, in walks around factories ... and, in general, by crafting encounters between the ever-blackening boxes of infrastructures and our senses and intelligences which could be taught (or trained) or teased to respond in turn.

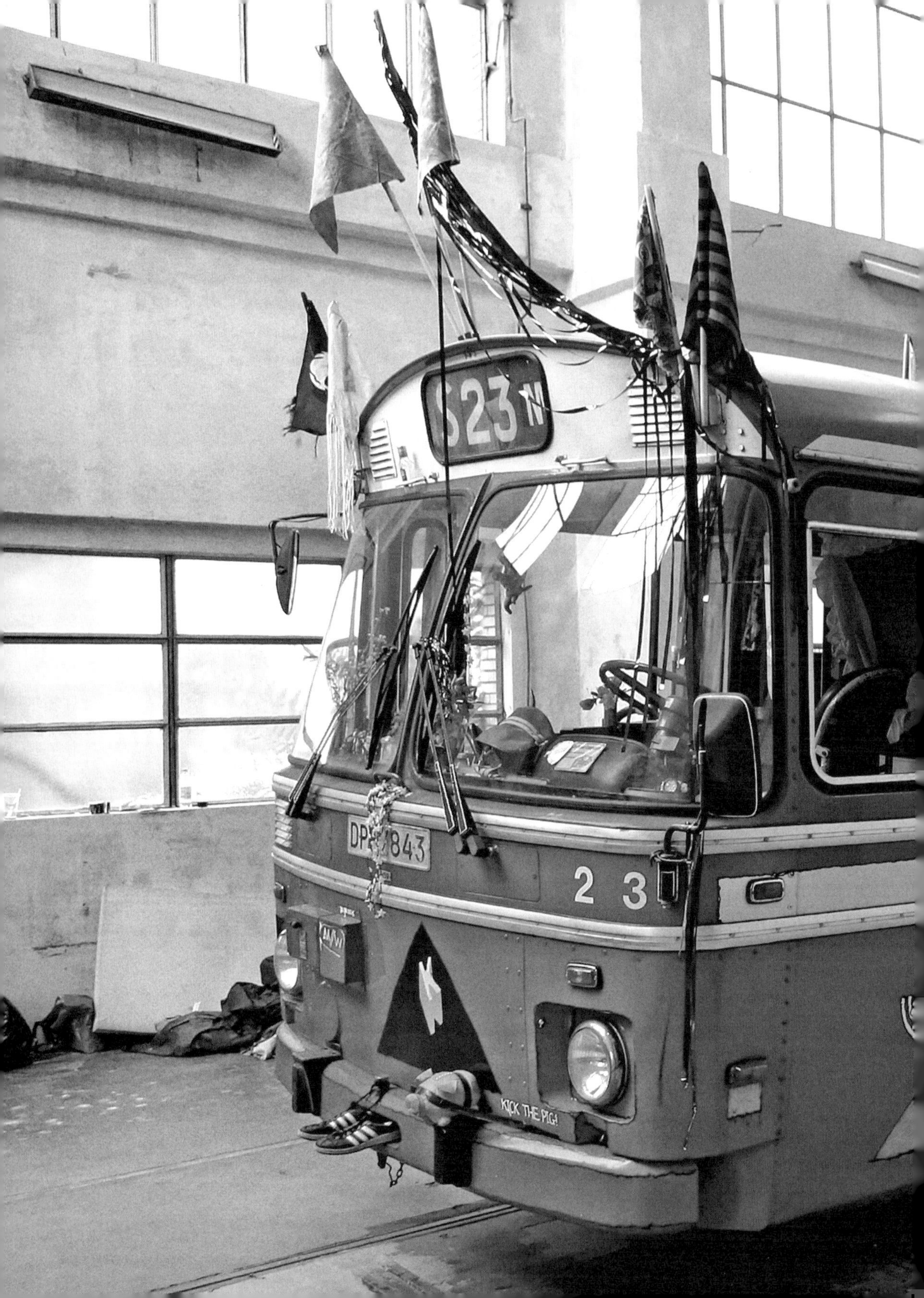
2 3
KICK THE PIG!

17 Centres/Peripheries: Complex Constellations

2019

Francesca Ceccherini & Noriko Yamakoshi in conversation with Raqs Media Collective

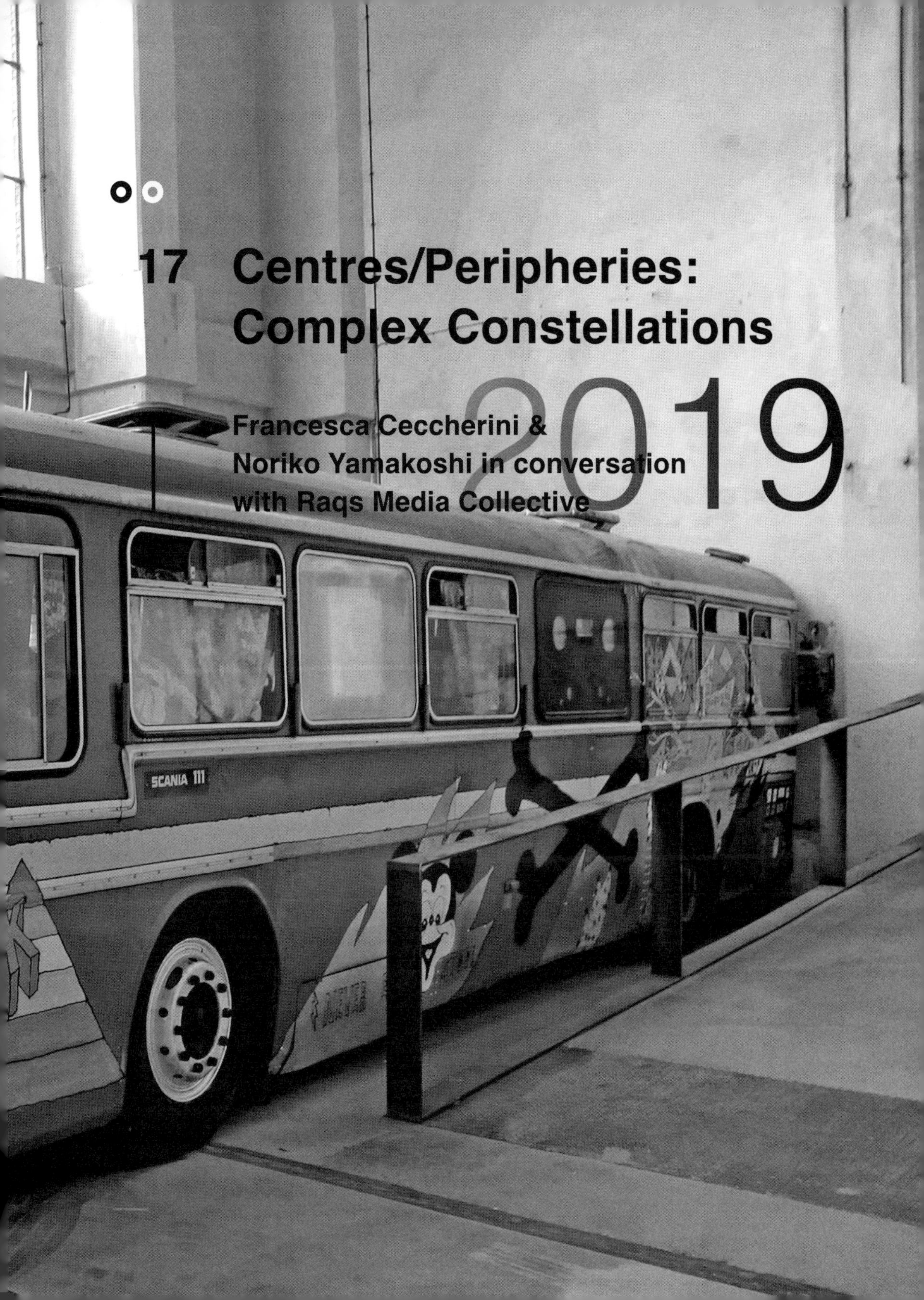

The Raqs Media Collective create within a broad and complex art-space: one where notions of 'centre–periphery' suture together much of postcolonial art-historical critique within the expanding orbits of the global art market. Raqs moved into curation in 2006, although as they point out, some element of this activity – a kind of 'playing together' – has always been a part of their art-making. Key moments in their curatorial trajectory, discussed here, include *The Rest of Now* (2008) exhibited at Manifesta 7 in Bolzano, *Sarai Reader 09: Projections* (2012–13), an exhibition in Gurgaon associated with the themed print *Reader 09* published by Sarai-CSDS, and *51 Personae* (2016–17) at the 11th Shanghai Biennial.

Describing their co-creative, co-curatorial practice as 'kinetic contemplation', Raqs traces how contemporary theoretical discourses are today emerging from multiple sources and through multiple sites across the global South – thus shaping new networks and dislocating conventional nodes of knowledge creation and representation, such as the traditional archives, galleries and museums long accepted as the singular and legitimate custodians of cultural property.

An earlier version of this interview was published in *On curating: Centres/ Peripheries – Complex Constellations*, Issue 41, 2019, pp. 90–96. Grateful acknowledgements to Francesca Ceccherini and Noriko Yamakoshi for their support.

Keywords and Names

11th Shanghai Biennale (2016–17): Titled *Why Not Ask Again? Arguments, Counter-Arguments and Stories*, this biennale, curated by Raqs Media Collective, was held from November 2016 to March 2017 at the Power Station of Art, Shanghai. The event hosted 92 participants from forty countries in the global South who were tasked with re-imagining the world. The title is inspired by Chinese author Liu Cixin's science-fiction trilogy *The Three-Body Problem* (2016), and by director Ritwik Ghatak's Bengali film *Jukti, Takko aar Gappo* (Reason, Debate and a Story, 1974). The biennale operated through multiple structures of engagement, with sections such as 'Terminals', 'Infra-curatorial Platforms', 'Theory Opera', '51 Personae' and 'City Projects'.

Centre–periphery: A theory of dependency based on a political geography of the world wherein advanced industrial societies constitute the 'centre' and postcolonial/underdeveloped societies form the 'periphery'. The spatial model was popular in the 1970s as a descriptor of the extractive trajectory of capitalism and unequal structures of power.

Images

All images from the exhibition *The Rest of Now*, curated by Raqs Media Collective, at a former aluminum melting factory in Bolzano, Italy, as part of Manifesta 7, July–November 2008.

pp. 288–89: Piratbyrån, *Please Join The Party*, 2008. © Manifesta 7/Wolfgang Träger.

p. 293: Work by Reinhard Kropf, Siv Helene Stangeland.

p. 297: Nikolaus Hirsch, Michel Müller.

All images courtesy Raqs Media Collective.

Francesca Ceccherini and Noriko Yamakoshi (FC+NY):[1] In Arabic, Farsi and Urdu, the word *raqs* translates as 'dance' – it refers to the ecstatic whirling of Sufi dervishes, and also invokes something that is capable of being an engine of energy ... a dynamic process, a ritual that asks people to form a mutually responsive circle through which to listen, act, observe, relate, take part, discover old meanings and build new ones. In terms of the essence of your practice, what first motivated this energy, and what has sustained your creative process for the past twenty-five years?

Raqs Media Collective (RMC/Jeebesh Bagchi, Monica Narula, Shuddhabrata Sengupta): We wanted to give to ourselves an image that allowed us to rethink continuously who we are – not as a fixed idea or image, but as something mobile and in transformation. So we came up with this specific name – 'Raqs' – that suggested a form of 'dancing' together, whirling, relaying an inner joy to one another. It was a way to give ourselves a philosophical principle. We didn't write a document or a manifesto; we tried to figure out a way of writing the self and the collective through our practices. We translate the word as 'kinetic contemplation'. It's an idea that you can be with others, as a collective, where others are a part of you, in movement with you.

Two natural elements are symbolized through the dance of the dervishes – the earth and the sky, invoked through the medium and posture and momentum of the whirling body. With one hand held upwards, the dancer draws energy from the sky; the other hand, held downwards, conducts that energy onto the earth. To us this becomes a way to rethink the relationship between any two forces, dimensions, positions, etc.; between the individual and the collective; between thought and action. It represents the continuous rethinking that we have been doing through our practice in our twenty-five years together. Rethinking, and also acting on/reacting to ideas of what collective life is, and what it means to cultivate – and to question – the capacities and the relationships that we build in the world.

Through our practice we contribute to a certain way of thinking our name: our effort is for it to remain vital, to not turn into a thing written in stone; and for us to not become imprisoned by our own words. Also, for us, this self-reflexive mode of investigation acts as a horizon.

FC+NY: How did you develop this kind of 'kinetic' co-curatorial practice?

RMC: We were born as a collective through writing and filmmaking, and through undertaking long-term research projects on the histories of cinematography and anthropological photography. We wanted to do many things, and we did not define ourselves as artists or curators. On some level we are still media practitioners who remain active via curatorial and artistic processes, by writing, by teaching, setting up institutions and scenarios, and by being engaged in conversations with the coming generations. Our 'kinetic' practice is something we always keep testing between us, and with other people. In not following the certainty of any script, the idea is to keep moving and testing new terms.

At Sarai, we realized that our practice had already had curatorial dimensions.[2] Our first formal experience of curation was in 2006 when we were invited by Hans Christ and Iris Dressler at the Württembergischer Kunstverein in Stuttgart to curate a section within an exhibition titled *On Difference #2*. Not long after that we started actively working as curators - through an awareness of our curatorial agency - in specific contexts and situations.

We enjoy working with a lot of people. Like in a game of football, where many play together. This 'playing together' is very important for us. That's what makes curating a continuously lively process — rethinking collective cultural and intellectual life and an enlargement in the number of people coalescing and colliding in one's head, and in reality. A seasoned football player has over a thousand players in their mind at all times. In that sense, curation is akin to creating unlikely processions with many figures and movements; it is an act of co-creation that opens out new journeys and itineraries.

FC+NY: As Indian/international artists and curators, coming from a country where art history is shaped by strong traditions and strong contradictions, how do you perceive the so-called 'centre-periphery dichotomy' in artistic and curatorial practices, as you move between the East and the West?[3]

RMC: The 'centre-periphery' dichotomy was produced after World War II. It was the result of a thinking about development as something that goes through stages, and that certain societies and economies were at the 'centre' of the global economy while others, still waiting to be developed, were at the 'periphery'. After the 1970s, this understanding broke down because the world economy became very unstable and volatile. And now, in terms of GDP, the world economy has shifted from about 5 trillion USD in the 1970s to 85 trillion USD in 2019.[4] What we see now is an intensification, a reorientation of capital, and a massive rerouting of the production and circulation of both material and immaterial goods and wealth around the world.

The world - including the cultural world - can no longer be described in terms of the 'centre-periphery dichotomy' - or indeed any such polarities. With respect to cultural production and custodianship, what we have to notice is the

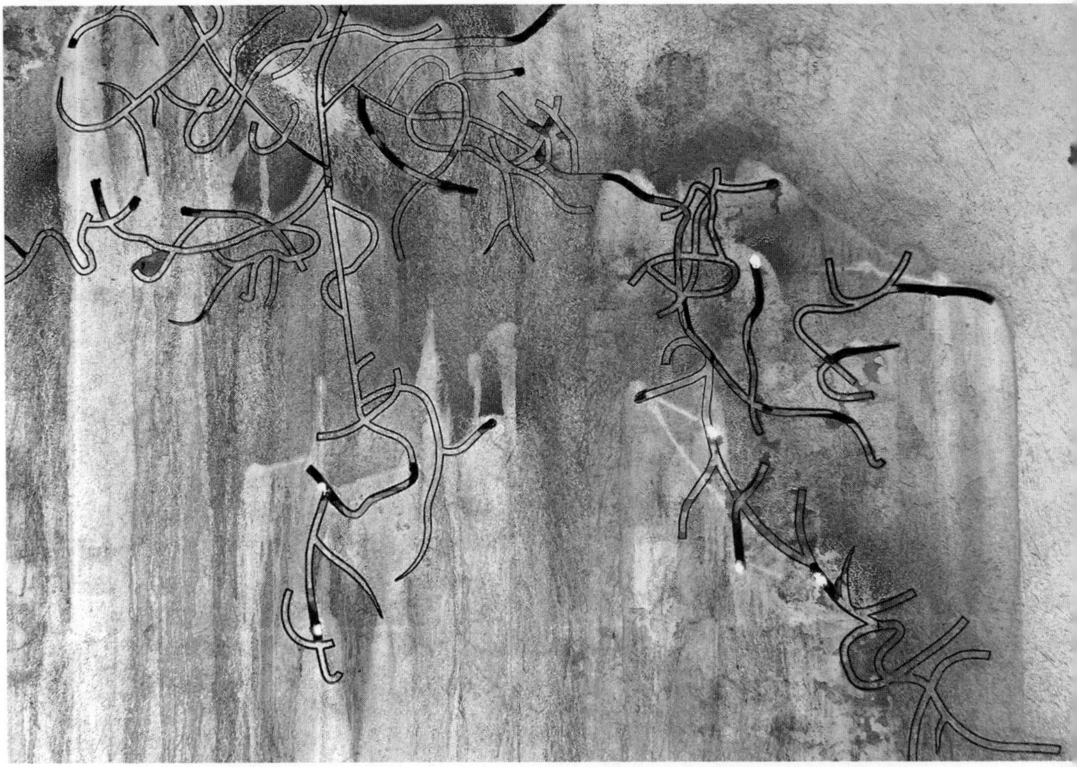

entry of some new power blocs, cutting into the earlier solidity and locations of power. Institutional spheres, such as museums, leverage a high quotient of hold on discourse. Fixed geographical locations of museums, earlier highly valued as stable nodes of cultural property, are increasingly facing a challenge from the multiplicity and mobility of other locations and their claim on discourse.

Over the last twenty years, the density of traffic of artworks, artists and people encountering art – the diverse and dispersed new 'publics' – has shifted away from the so-called 'old centres'. Just look at Asia, at the biennales and triennales, and also consider new museums and other temporary shows, and you'll see that the traffic is very intense – and that there is much more traffic of European artists to Asia than there are Asian artists travelling to Europe or America. The big problem is that this traffic is not represented, is not registered, is not comprehended as an occurrence that is here to stay. Rather, these flows of practitioners and products are seen as aberrations and distractions from the 'real' world of art, and they are dismissed as a consequence and effect of neoliberalism. So while the contemporary West-to-East flow is indeed a major reality, it remains minor in terms of discourse. However, in a subterranean way these 'minor' discourses are multiple and multiplying from many sites, and will emerge as a significant force that will upset the confidence of conventional cultural institutions and canonized art-historical modalities.

New intellectual resources have to be built to do justice to the demand of these new densities and traffic, and we, as Raqs, try to argue for and build these resources, to be actively part of and contributing to the emergent polyphony – a polyphony that is poly-axial, generous and spacious in how it sees and accommodates the proliferating tensions and pressures of the world. When ideas are drawn from different resources – from what we, in our practice, call 'sources' – then the questions we have will be different, as will be the ways in which we understand this world. Otherwise a lot of the time sources get drawn from histories of Europe and America. Now these are very dense histories, but when they are drawn on to try and encapsulate all that is happening in the world, they begin to thin. And then ideas of 'colonialism' and 'nationalism' keep getting reconfigured over and over again to try to accommodate 'other' histories.

So then, the question is of traffic and densities between many nodes. A good way to think about this is through biological diversity. One finds that the density of biological diversity is in the so-called global 'South'. That is, the centres of biological diversity are far distant from the financial centres of the world, in the so-called global 'North'. Now, there are fantastic bio-labs in Europe and America, but the main mass of biological diversity might be elsewhere, maybe in India or

Indonesia, in South Africa, in Brazil, or somewhere else in the 'South'. Today, the normative mapping of the world, primarily conducted in terms of West-centric institutional economics, onto other territories is not possible. Similarly, dispersed centres of culture no longer map onto the institutional order of the world. We need to keep imagining and pursuing a different way, a recalibration.

One way to do this is by rethinking these densities, asking questions about traffic in a different way, and by making an argument for multi- and poly-axial sources that allow this new geography to grow in us intellectually and discursively, to not be kept dependent on West-centric categories and concepts that are explaining away the cultural assertions/contributions from the 'South'. That is, we need to produce concepts and categories that then enable us to read the world not just in the framework of certain local or specific conditions, but in ways that generate a capacity to ask of the world a different set of questions. There is a certain idea of categories that works in the world presently, which is to make us think about the world in terms of so-called 'universal categories' on the one hand, and 'regional experience' on the other. What we must accept is that there are 'contending universalisms' in the world, and they ask us to think about a multi-axial, multi-source world.[5]

FC+NY: And where do you see yourselves on the spectrum between centre and periphery?

RMC: We live in Delhi, a dense, rapidly and continuously expanding city with an economy that is amongst the fastest growing in the world. It is a highly unequal city, with staggering levels of toxicity in its air, water, soil. It has an economic and political climate that is going to throw up a lot of questions about the world. It is, you could say, at a cusp from where it may turn in any direction. In other words, a vectorial space that is dynamic and volatile. It can – in as few as ten years – change the intellectual and political terrain of the world. So, in that sense, it isn't peripheral to anything, whether one is considering global questions of economics, or politics, or climate. It is axial; it is mobile; it is volatile in all matters. And yet, it is not at the centre of anything. Neither the word 'centre' nor the word 'periphery' capture the specificity of Delhi embedding many intersecting trajectories and forms of difference, or capture the decisive impact and effect it has on the 'South' and the world.

And, though in an opposite way, it's the same for America. It is no longer the centre of the world, even in its self-image. Its new politics is based on the idea – and fear – that it is becoming marginal, that it has to reposition itself, and that the rest of the world has become too independent, volatile and diverse to further submit to American hegemony. So then, basically, the situation has changed in the world, and we need a different description. With the descriptors 'centre' or 'periphery', one is still holding on to a very odd and perhaps increasingly irrelevant, inept idea of economy, institutions and geo-political relationships.[6]

FC+NY: Your work often links to one of your main areas of interest – cross-disciplinary, participatory urban research. For instance, *The Rest of Now* (2008)[7] exhibited at Manifesta 7 in Bolzano was a reflection on the concept of urban 'residue'; *Sarai Reader 09: Projections* (2012–13),[8] an exhibition in Gurgaon associated with the themed print *Reader 09* published by Sarai-CSDS, involved many practitioners interacting with the public during an extended process of creating work; *51 Personae* (2016–17) at the 11th Shanghai Biennial re-imagined different facets of ordinary lives in that city. How did the specific location and context influence your vision of each project?

RMC: Locations and contexts always change things for us. For example, at Manifesta 7 we presented work at the Ex-Alumix, a defunct aluminium factory complex in Bolzano in northern Italy. Bolzano is a very small town, but with a fascinating history in the twentieth century. The factory – today transformed into a space for hosting contemporary art – was a very important site in the context of World War II. Apart from production, there was also the symbolic power of aluminium for the Fascist regime in Italy. Aluminium is still a very important material in all our lives. The thing to do was to investigate, materially and conceptually, the venue and this history; to create possibilities that we then shared with artists, both established and emerging, to realize works.

Sarai Reader 09 was based on a completely different impulse – to create an open format that would allow over a hundred artists and practitioners to interact and produce works in public view, with public conversations. It was a nine-month-long process, which invented its rules and protocols as it went along on its course.

Shanghai is a city of twenty-three million people and has a turbulent history in the twentieth century. It built more skyscrapers in twenty years than New York built in a hundred. Here we were encountering a very different set of questions. We travelled through the city, and *51 Personae* emerged as we started to articulate the question of the life-force of the inhabitants, their ideas and skills, their intensities, their life-worlds. The challenge was to make sense of Shanghai's interstitial, edge-consciousness in its different manifestations.

Places change the questions we start with. Places interrogate us, and our ideas of the world. They interrogate us about who we are, and our assumptions, positions, directions and movements.

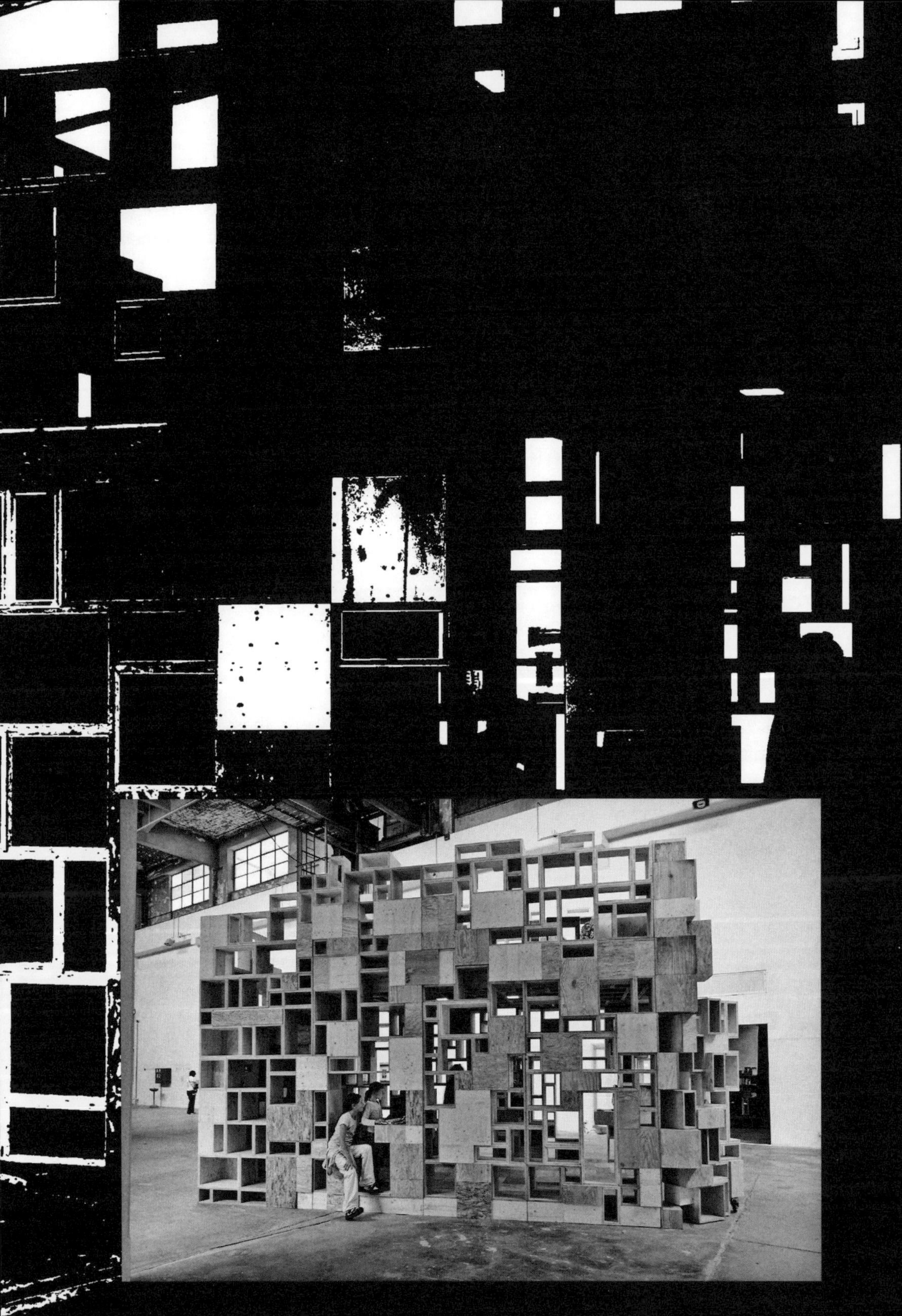

FC+NY: How do you relate through your practice to your native country and its social, political and cultural contexts? Have you faced any big problems or challenges in this respect?

RMC: India has more than one billion people, and five to six thousand years of recorded history. That means a very complicated landscape and cosmology, and a multi-millennial archive of contradictions and conflicts. This temporal and spatial vastness is inspiring, but it is also marked by profound inequality, entrenched prejudice and phobia, and inflexible codes of social relating that justify this inequality and ensure that it is violently reinforced. Establishing equality is perhaps the biggest challenge for the Indic civilization.

One of the things that we have learned in our travels - whether to Europe, Mexico, China or Vietnam - is that equality, as an ideal, an aspiration and a practice, can be a kind of material force of life. It is a surge; it is an infrastructure; it seeks expression in every encounter, with every form of labour. We keep on observing this: there is and can be a beautiful poetics of equality. The politics and poetics of equality are being intensely fought, and fought for, here. This fight is changing the dynamics of all lives.

Also, there are questions of time and place. In our work, these come from our confidence in, and disquiet with, staying in Delhi, as well as the exuberant experiences of travelling in India, surely one of the most diverse nations in the world, even while it is bound by customs and beliefs unchanged for millennia. A lot of our works, both curatorial and artistic, are inflected by our thinking on the incongruous nature of time and place that we encounter.

In our practice we try to give a play to a sense of time, whether to lighten it, to dilate it or to make detours from known chronologies. Places change the way we look at artworks, change the tonality of our speech and the boundaries of our bodies. We enjoy curating in this sense - this heightening of our relationship with places, this becoming entangled and enveloped in uncharted dimensions ...

To operate as practitioners, we need this 'kinetic' open-endedness. It's how we find ways with which to narrate the world we live in, possibly dislodging habitual ways of seeing it. We need to reimagine and rearticulate in order to produce new values.

18 FotoFest 2018 and Other Curatorial Practices

2019

Rahaab Allana in conversation with Sunil Gupta

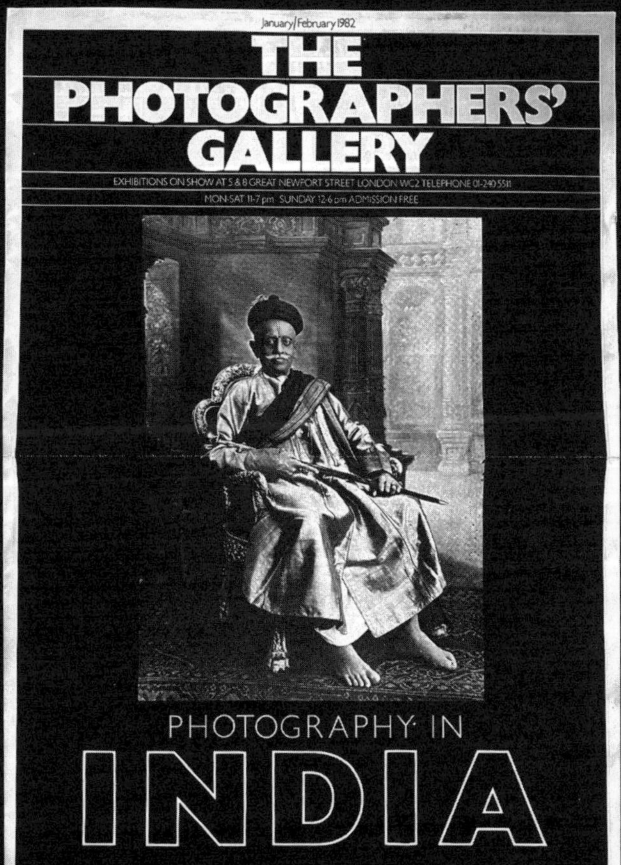

In this interview, photographer, activist and curator Sunil Gupta traces a long and diverse diasporic career that began in London in the 1980s, as a student at the Royal College of Art and then as part of the radical British Black Arts Movement. A founder-member of the collective Autograph ABP (Association of Black Photographers), Gupta has organized and curated international exhibitions on themes of migration, identity, sexuality and social marginalization, and is a recognized contributor to the shaping of new cultural policy in the UK. Here he comments on the business and politics of emergent art markets; power relationships in the now globalized sphere of cultural production; and the work of building networks and creative collaborations across borders.

An earlier version of this interview appeared as 'Talking About FotoFest 2018 and Other Curatorial Experiences': Rahaab Allana in conversation with Sunil Gupta, Parts 1 and 2, PIX Posts online: http://www.enterpix.in/pix-post/fotofest-2018-india-contemporary-photographic-and-new-media-art/; http://www.enterpix.in/pix-post/talking-about-fotofest-2018-and-other-curatorial-experiences-with-sunil-gupta-part-2/

Keywords and Names

Decolonization, *Festivals of India*, *Johannesburg Biennale*, *Lalit Kala Akademi*, see Keywords at the back of this volume.

Images

p. 299: Exhibition ephemera, *Photography in India*, The Photographers' Gallery, London, 1982.

p. 303: Cover of the catalogue *INDIA/ Contemporary Photographic and New Media Art* (FotoFest 2018 Biennial India exhibition). Cover image: Sandip Kuriakose. Published by Fotofest, Houston and Schilt, Amsterdam.

p. 307: 'Divided Britain': Photo commission for *Good Housekeeping* magazine (1986). Image courtesy Sunil Gupta.

p. 311: Self-published catalogue from *Exiles* (1987; booklet 1999), a series about gay men in Delhi, commissioned by The Photographers' Gallery. Image courtesy Sunil Gupta.

Rahaab Allana (RA): FotoFest, the oldest photographic art festival in the US, focused on India for the FotoFest Biennial held in Houston from 10 March to 22 April 2018.[1] When and how were you approached to curate this exhibition, *INDIA/Contemporary Photography and New Media Art*?[2]

Sunil Gupta (SG): I was first approached about the festival three years ago. The Houston FotoFest's previous biennial themed around climate change and an earlier biennial with a focus on Arab culture both had external curators, so I wasn't the first 'outside' one to be brought in. Fredrick Baldwin and Wendy Watriss,[3] Founder Directors of FotoFest, and Executive Director Steven Evans[4] asked, 'What if we make the Indian subcontinent the focal show in 2018?' They were familiar with *Where Three Dreams Cross: 150 Years of Photography from India, Pakistan and Bangladesh* (2010),[5] and they were clearly interested in representations of a certain geography.[6] But as festival organizers, they wanted to show contemporary rather than historical works at FotoFest 2018.

That perspective triggered the same wheels in my mind from *Where Three Dreams Cross* (*WTDC*) left off. I suggested that we approach Hammad Nasar, Shahidul Alam and, potentially, Radhika Singh, my great collaborator in Delhi. So that's how it started – the idea of taking the frame of *WTDC* and making it about the contemporary, with more or less the same co-curators.

RA: The show featured forty-seven artists of Indian origin, and the accompanying publication raises questions around how an artist's identity might be construed – or misconstrued – in cultural spaces outside his/her 'home' country. As a diasporic practitioner yourself, are you guided in your curations by particular understandings of the complex relationships between subjectivity, location and practice?

SG: For budgetary reasons the spectrum of the Houston exhibition was narrowed down from the entire subcontinent to just India, so we immediately lost all the neighbours. This drastic reduction was also necessary because of organizational time constraints. Then I began a discussion that the exhibition couldn't be about the 'place' India, because then we'd have a very different kind of show. A lot of people, those who live there and those who don't live there, Indian or non-Indian, go and shoot pictures in India. And if 'ethnicity' (in a very specific sense) has been left out of photo history as it identifies practices by geographical location only and not by race, we need to keep bringing it back in. So we decided to exclude all the non-Indian-origin contributors and retain only those with origins from India, regardless of whether or not they lived there.

I also wanted to feature people I had already worked with, and they tended to be the older, more established practitioners. And I wanted them to somehow be brought together with younger photographers, even students about to emerge from college. I wanted to reference the diversity of the Indian diaspora, their trajectories having taken them to opposite ends of the globe – Fiji in one case, Trinidad in another ... I also pondered whether there was such a thing as a 'global' Indian identity. For instance, there are enormous differences between me here in England where I now live and work, compared with a lot of second- or third-generation local residents of Indian, Bangladeshi and Pakistani origin. Although people say identity politics has been on the wane in the 2000s, it seems to be making a comeback within the current politics of Trump and Brexit ...

Looking back on FotoFest 2018 now, it seems to me that the exhibition was a very big success in the sense that it fulfilled many of the requirements of 'inclusive' photography: the diversity of approaches and techniques, the diversity of gender – there was almost an equal balance in terms of practitioners – and the diversity of age range.

And the spectrum of works successfully manifested what in the West is accepted and appreciated as dynamic critical practice – an almost 'academic' practice, but without the overt theorizing associated with the formal academy. This was also interesting because we seem to be short of such practice in India.

RA: What sorts of challenges did you encounter in terms of selecting the photographers featured in FotoFest 2018?

SG: The whole notion of 'who's in' and 'who's out' of the exhibitions, who gets to select and how the works get selected, and all of that ... is all apparently a mystery! I once met a French collector in Paris, and to him the logic of selection was very clear – it was just about 'good taste', and that's how he justified what he bought – basically what he liked, and as a wealthy man and a patron that's how he set the tone for things. We shouldn't forget that some aspects of what the arts establishment reinforces as 'good' taste originate from that kind of entitlement and privilege.

'Good' is not a word that I personally like to use about art. It's so subjective – who's to say what's 'good' about a work? For me, it's more a question of which works are more successfully trying to say something new or different; and which works fully come into themselves when 'in conversation' with other works. As the organizer of group shows, I always pay attention to specific criteria vis-à-vis the display. One has to think about all four walls of the space together, so juxtapositions become very important – how a work relates with whatever is positioned next to it ...

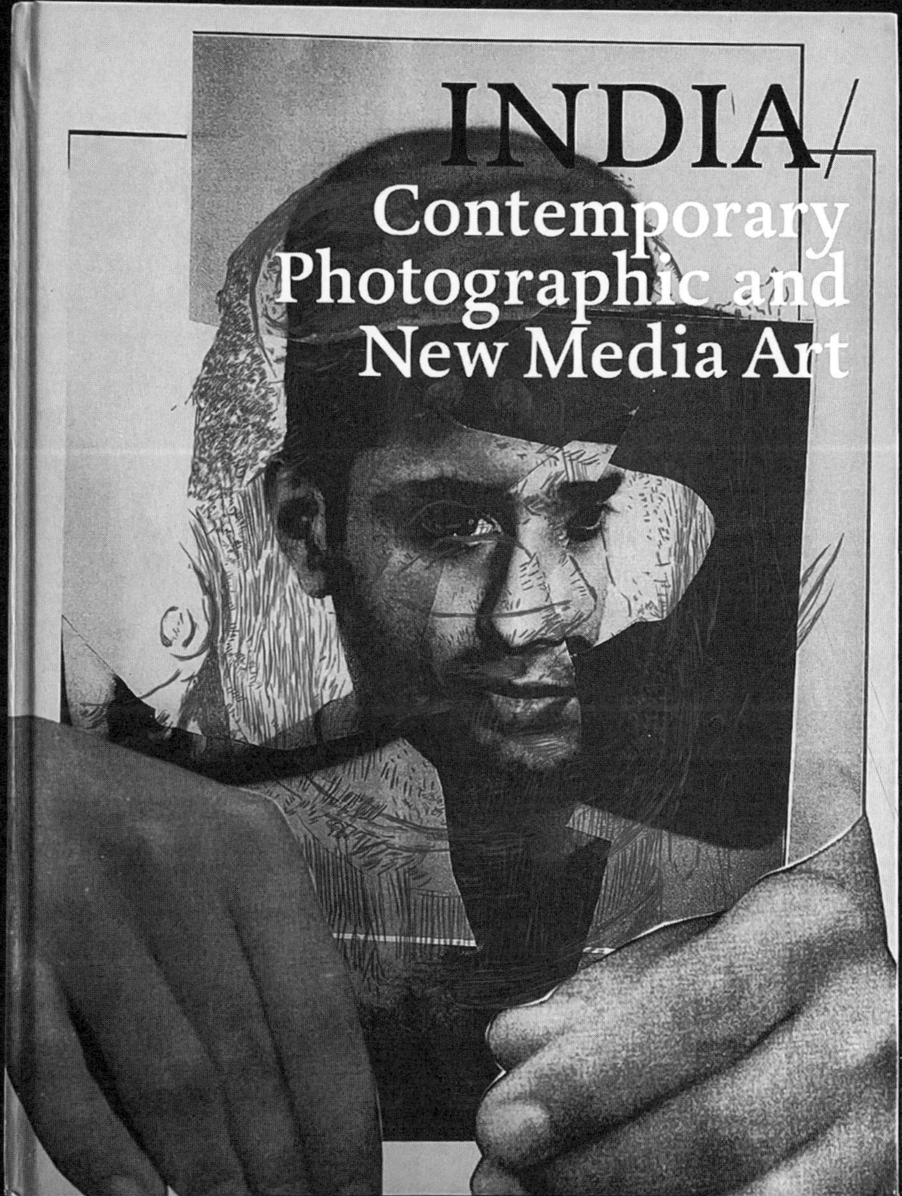
INDIA/
Contemporary
Photographic and
New Media Art

RA: How was this selection of photography from India received in America?

SG: My sense is that Americans found the exhibition quite engaging. American audiences, unlike UK audiences, tend to be less informed about contemporary India and are therefore more intrigued by ideas generating from location. Hence I feel that in terms of a historical moment, this was the right time for such an exhibition. Had we done it ten years ago it might have been a shade too early, and twenty years ago would have been far too soon. But as we know from the Western art world, after China the next region of interest is India. An interest that may or may not be on the wane now, but commercially has woken up.

Media response to the exhibition was phenomenal. It was covered by major outlets such as the *New York Times*, the *Washington Post*, and the *Guardian* (in the UK); the story was also picked up by all kinds of regional press. It was a bit like the reporting and reviewing of *WTDC*, which was a benchmark for the Whitechapel Gallery because the exhibition, which was ticketed, was packed all the time and the catalogue sold out a couple of weeks before the show concluded! By those kinds of press and attendance markers, FotoFest 2018 was clearly a 'success', but I always find it hard to judge what such so-called 'success' actually implies ...

Another marker of 'success' for people critically observing the exhibition was the fact of sales. The auction that was held offered about fifteen works from the Indian contributors, which were eventually bought for hundreds and sometimes well over a thousand dollars. This tangible exposure to the marketplace was an eye-opener, especially for the Indian artists who were present at the auction dinner.

I know now that a number of American museums, having viewed FotoFest 2018, are looking to acquire works of Indian lens-based artists. America is full of local museums and hardly any have an 'Indian' photography collection. I think this could be the beginning of a trend, with some museums seeing FotoFest 2018 as an opportune moment to step in and start making some acquisitions. But apart from budgetary considerations, they're also looking at the works via a particular logic - namely, assessing which ones are likely to have longevity, and which images *should* and *can* serve a museum's purpose as the basis for a collection that might grow in time. American museums seem to like the experimental, but they also appreciate classic photography, and large-format landscapes.

And I certainly think Americans prefer to collect photography more than the British do. The British like their text-based arts too much!

RA: Your essay in the FotoFest publication references the exhibition *Photography* *in India*[7] held at the Photographers' Gallery[8] in London in 1982. What was the significance of that show?

SG: *Photography in India* was held during the Festival of India, so it was a little bit like 'India Shining', a promotional tool for the nation, not for the medium. I'm not sure if that was entirely helpful for our purposes because it felt like something that was 'foreign', and it came and went ... People who had connections with and sympathies towards the subcontinent went to see it and those who didn't, didn't. Also, India was not the emerging economic powerhouse on the global stage that it is now.

I don't think that show had much of a lasting impact on the photography scene here in the UK. And it did not have an accompanying publication – which meant, as I discovered later when I began teaching, that since there was no linked textual source, the exhibition virtually disappeared. But during the show I did meet some of the featured artists, like Pablo [Bartholomew]. Also, I myself hadn't been to India after leaving for Canada in 1969, and the exhibition provoked me to begin returning to India in the early 1980s. I would go straight to Rajasthan to shoot and didn't really have much to do with the Delhi scene.

RA: How does your own practice influence your curatorial work, particularly the researching and shaping of survey exhibitions and large themed shows that bring together meta-histories of image production and visual cultures?

SG: I'm a product of what used to be called 'Black Arts' in Britain in the 1980s.[9] At that time the term 'Black' also included non-African/Afro-Caribbean people of colour, South Asians, other ethnicities. So my sense of cultural practice is very wide. I primarily thought of myself – and probably still do – not as a fine artist or a photographer but as a cultural activist. For me, such activism includes making work, curating shows, editing books, teaching and writing.

I graduated from the Royal College of Art (RCA), London in 1983, and went straight into the Town Hall of the Greater London Council, and got involved with multicultural policy making and learnt how the arts fit into that. I learnt to appreciate how, in Europe and the UK, the arts and politics work together, and how they serve marginalized communities and include their stories in the larger cultural narrative. These communities were seen as not just the subject and the audience of those stories, but also as citizen 'makers' who had the right to agency and self-representation.

In parallel, with regard to my own creative work I soon realized that despite my having come out of a very 'elite' institution as part of a very elite group (only six photography students were admitted each year), no curators were beating a path to my door. So, if I was going to have a show, I was going to have to organize it myself ... and if you were a person of colour, getting noticed through your work was simply about survival.[10]

In the 1980s, museum curators in the UK were called 'keepers'. They were actually the custodians of the collections. They were meant to be the people who knew everything there was to know about their collections. In France, I believe, to become a 'keeper' you had to pass an incredible IAS-type of exam where you were even asked to indicate where pieces of art 'lived' – in such-and-such place in the museum – along with having to give extremely in-depth knowledge about the work. The 'keepers' were experts in organizing objects and events in a managerial way, but they made no effort to reassess their collections – in terms of postcolonial critique, for instance.

If in the 1980s you had discussions with full-time curators in art institutions, museums and cultural spaces such as the Whitechapel Gallery, you very soon realized that they had never heard of a 'Black' photographer, or an 'Indian' one, for that matter ... because there was no mention of non-white practitioners in books or historical surveys. Quite simply, image-making by people of colour had never been represented or taught. I too learned a photography history that was completely 'white' ... The British and the French brought it to us in India in the nineteenth century. So I learnt about Bourne & Shepherd, Felice Beato, etc. I had no idea there were any Indians taking pictures until I saw a private collection, the Alkazi Collection of Photography and met an expert, Sophie Gordon who maintained the collections in London.

In the early 1980s there were various informal attempts by practitioners of colour to familiarize the London public with Black Arts. For instance, a group called the Caribbean Craft Circle would put up stalls on weekends at popular sites like the Covent Garden market and display whatever they made. I once had a stall with my photographs, but it soon became obvious that this casual mode wasn't the ideal way to sell something like photo prints. It took another decade for photography to be accepted as a serious art form and for prints to be valued as significant art objects.

In 1986, we had the first show of works by Black photographers, *Reflections of the Black Experience*,[11] at the Brixton Art Gallery in London, curated by artist Monika Baker and supported by the city hall. It featured ten practitioners of colour (mainly Afro-Caribbeans and South Asians). It led to a series of discussions and realpolitik strategies in relation to getting funds for Black arts. We knew that we had to be activist 'organizers' as well as curators, because we were trying to

DIVIDED BRITAIN:

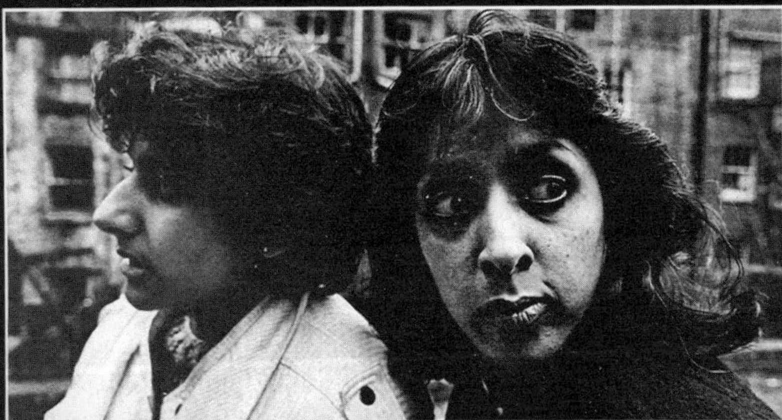

ASIANS UNDER ATTACK

Photographs/Sunil Gupta

One in every 56 Britons live in fear of racial harassment: they may be publicly reviled, spat upon, beaten up by gangs, their homes burnt down. Hardly surprising, then, that the Asian community is losing faith in this country. *Naseem Khan* reports

GOOD HOUSEKEEPING SIG 3.

foreground the absence of arts-related skills in our communities – so many people from our background had not formally studied visual art or art history. So we went marching off across the Thames to the Arts Council and said: 'Four percent of the UK is non-white, and so we want four percent of your arts budget, and definitely four percent of your photo budget, whatever it is, however small it is ... and we want it because that's who we represent. Who are you giving it to now ... ?'

Our presence, and our pressure, seemed to work – in 1988 the Council gave us £2,000 to write a report, *Are There Any Black Photographers in the UK?* So that's really what our organizing was about. But it also had a larger purpose – that purpose being to unseat Margaret Thatcher ... ![12]

RA: While shaping the Houston show, did you draw on your collaborations and networks and curatorial experience of the 1990s?

SG: Yes ... The first group show for which I did deep research was *An Economy of Signs* (1990),[13] held at the Photographers' Gallery in London, featuring eight artists – four women, four men. But I had begun my work in 1988, when there was no primary research on contemporary Indian photography or much published material on photography from India at all, in general. I was trying to prove a point to the London audience and arts management that if you commissioned eight Indians from India, they would give you quality work of an international standard – something the institutions here were not really convinced about, initially.

I actually had a budget for the commissioning of new works for the proposed exhibition. So I'd fly from London to my hometown Delhi, and visit a smattering of people, and city venues like Triveni Kala Sangam that had been cultural nodes since the 1960s. And that's when I met Radhika Singh, who ran a photo agency. It seemed like a very remarkable thing at the time, because I hadn't come across any photo agencies till then. So we went through her inventory of photographers, moving from person to person ... this is how we identified artists for the show.

Between 1988 and 1990 I was also working with a group of people in London to establish Autograph ABP (Association of Black Photographers), a collective supporting photographic practices by people of colour.[14] Autograph, that later developed into a commercial agency/archive/gallery space, brought together a wider pool of practitioners who also connected through sharing their skill sets. This was a great benefit when we started to do group shows. For instance, when people turned up with impossibly thin negatives, I was able to take over the printmaking because I was a trained analogue printer – I had been through a rigorous, technically oriented photo-school education at the University for the

Creative Arts and the Royal College of Art. Our first show *Autoportraits* (1990)[15] at Camerawork, London critically examined the genre of self-portraiture through works by eight selected photographers and visual artists – four men, four women; four South Asian, four Afro-Caribbean.

Meanwhile, I left my teaching job to take up curating. My experience as a franchisee curator began with the photography show *Disrupted Borders* (1993),[16] a collaboration between my company OVA (Organization for Visual Arts), London,[17] the Arnolfini arts and cultural space, Bristol[18] and The Photographers' Gallery, London. I also began working with INIVA (Institute of International Visual Art, London), an organization founded in 1994 and funded by Arts Council England, that focuses on arts education, exhibiting and publishing, with a remit to explore and reflect cultural diversity in the arts. As a franchisee curator I've had to negotiate one of the continual tensions of the job – namely, that you've in fact *got* to keep finding something new, either a practitioner, or a work/body of work …

In 1994, as a preamble to the Johannesburg Biennial I was invited for an entertaining curators' tour. I was representing the UK. At that time very little was known about South Africa's contemporary art practices because of the international cultural boycott of the apartheid regime. The organizers took a number of us on a three-week tour of the country in order to introduce us to collections and artists. In return, we agreed to feature one of their artists in shows in our respective countries (I featured the artist Clive van den Berg[19] who made spectacular fire drawings on mine dumps). Our group of about 60 curators from across the globe would emerge from the tour bus and fan out to discover the 'new thing'! And we competed – I *had* to find something 'better' than you, which meant beating you in a race to discover the exciting 'new' artist or work. That was an interesting exercise. … And to a certain extent, this kind of aggressive searching does go on even today.

One principle I've followed in my curating career is to not always look for the 'newest' and the 'latest', but to understand who you can carry to the next level – namely, which practitioner has longer potential. So I took Sheba Chhachhi out of the Indian context and featured her in *Disrupted Borders* along with twelve other international artists. Sheba became my connecting thread, and she's been in all of my exhibitions. She's certainly disproved the male critics who in 1988 told me that she was 'not a photographer'.

RA: Another exhibition that you highlighted at FotoFest 2018 is *Click!* (2008).[20] What was the significance of its inclusion?

SG: *Click!* was a big exercise, in the sense that there was a time commitment to researching it. We (Radhika Singh and I) had an important conversation with Vadehra Art Gallery[21] in Delhi to see if they would commission the research. They operated with the fixed idea that artists wanting to exhibit came with ready-made works; the concept of funding the research behind a show was not present in their thinking at all. And here I was insisting: 'If there's no research funding, there's no exhibition.' This impasse was a bit of a stumbling block because that was not the way things worked in the private sector, and neither was there any accessible public sector support. But finally they agreed to fund some research.

We'd send out word before travelling to different cities that we were going to select works by as many people as possible. This messaging was done through word of mouth and local networks. People came in person to meet us, and some sent in their work on CDs. And it became a very complicated exercise because of a two-way communication gap. People brought too much work, asking what genre we were looking for; to them the whole selection exercise seemed like a totally new experience. At our end, we tried to explain what we meant by a 'portfolio review' to the many practitioners who didn't know how to present their work for selection. But we persevered – we met several hundred people, looked at the work of twice as many via the CDs posted to us. ... And in time, this mode of research became an integral aspect of the larger *WTDC* methodology for selecting contemporary work.

With *Click!* we were trying to include as many artists as possible, so we only chose one or two pictures per person. The exhibition wasn't about the expression of diverse practices, per se. Rather, we wanted to emphasize the fact of so many people making good photographs, since we hadn't yet seen a show in India that featured so many names. The gallery then wanted to reinforce their investment through sales of the works, so they introduced a commercial criterion – not an area in which I had any competence. So nobody really knew how it would go. ... Selling photos was really difficult in India at that time. I don't know if things have changed a lot, but my guess is that collectors weren't used to buying photographs, and they were certainly not used to buying from multiples, or from edition series; collectors seemed more at ease with unique works of art. The gallery did bring a version of *Click!* to the UK, and here the sales experience was quite different ...

At the time of FotoFest 2018, some of the contributors to *Click!* had stopped practising and were no longer involved in photography, and therefore couldn't be featured in the show since it was themed around 'contemporary' production. For instance, Sanjeev Saith was not especially represented because by then he'd become more of a publisher and less of a photographer, although I think we did manage to get a picture of his father from him.

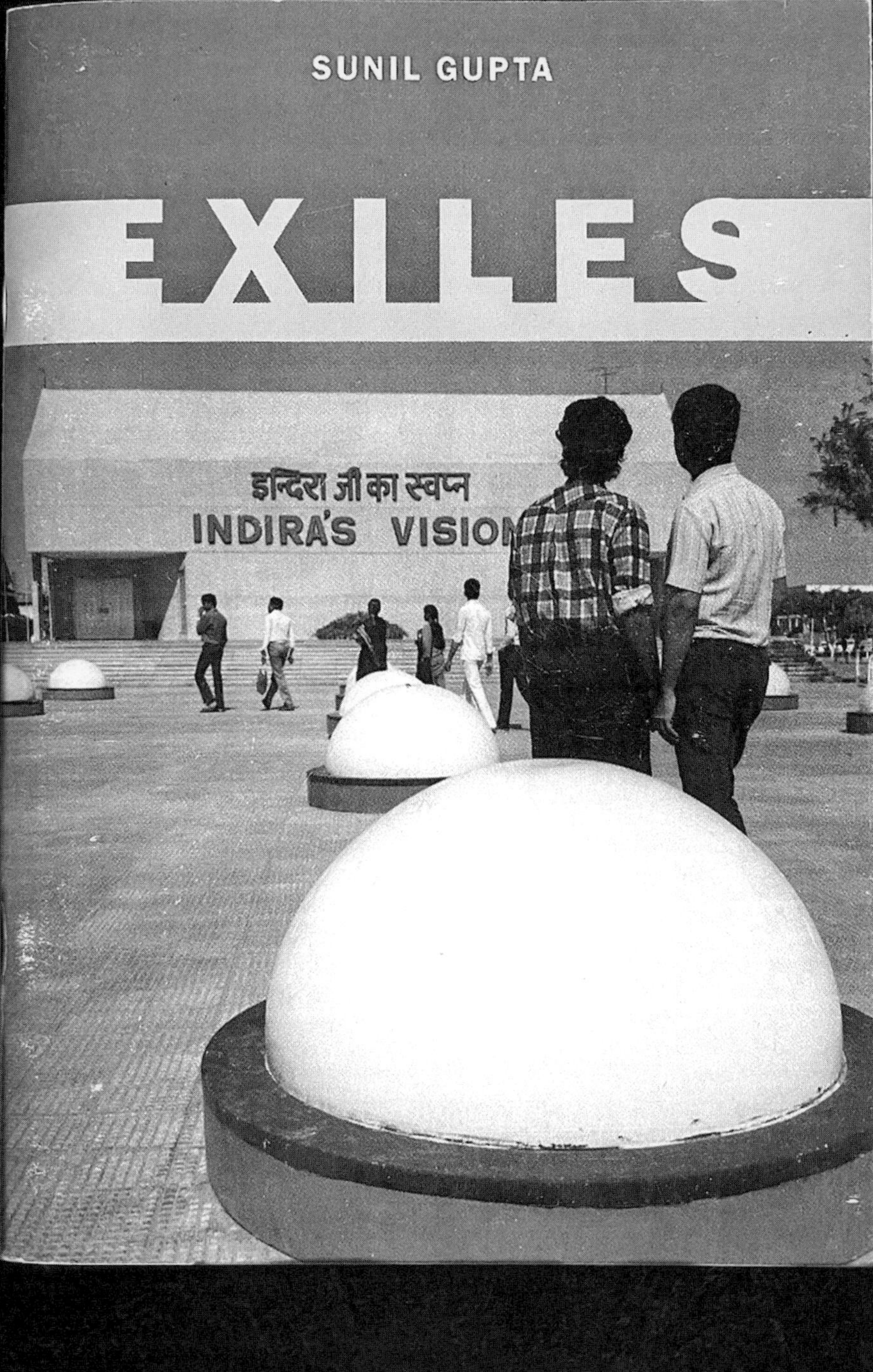
SUNIL GUPTA
EXILES
इन्दिरा जी का स्वप्न
INDIRA'S VISION

RA: *Where Three Dreams Cross* was displayed differently in London and in Winterthur, and there was also some curatorial variance. What was the underlying logic?

SG: No two exhibits, even of the same material, ever look the same at different locations. Initially *WTDC* was devised only for the Whitechapel Gallery, which is a smaller venue than Fotomuseum. We had about 550 works on display at both sites, but Whitechapel seemed more crowded. In Winterthur, we suddenly had more space for the display, so it physically expanded. The show was bigger – pictures were added; there was more colour (the gallery had coloured walls); the captions were highlighted and translated; the *WTDC* publication was revised, with a German translation and a new cover for the hardback edition.

In London, I worked very closely with my co-curators throughout the research for the show. But in Winterthur, Urs Stahel,[22] the director at that time, had a very strong singular influence. I had a minimal role, partly because of the distance between the two venues, and partly because *WTDC* had not been conceived for the Winterthur space. I think I made one trip to confer with Stahel at a planning stage, but he was very much in control of everything on site. This reflects the way such collaborations are set up in managerial terms. I had been employed by the Whitechapel over a long period of time so I had a sense of ownership vis-à-vis the project, but I was an 'outsider' at Winterthur. So after the Whitechapel show opened, I essentially felt that my job was over.

Winterthur is located just outside Zürich and is very much in the European photography scene/mode. In the UK, *WTDC* was seen by photo enthusiasts and the large general public drawn to the Whitechapel generally, rather than the 'art' people. The Houston experience was different, and more complicated because I spent a lot of time there. I sort of just let it happen, let the exhibition unfold organically, but this is not something that one can often do.

I sometimes feel like an interloper who has come full circle. I'm from a photography background, but became involved in fine art through my curatorial work; and now photography is part of fine art in all the teaching institutions, so I'm back to teaching it as well. ... Critics may deny it, but the earlier 'photography versus art' debate is still going on in photography circles today. For example, Photo London, the photography fair, features galleries that specialize in photography where the works are at a much lower retail price point, unlike major art fairs like Frieze London or Art Basel. At the same time, the art world is focused on conceptual art photography and has no capacity to understand the ways in which photography works in many disciplines like science and technology, etc., thereby focusing on just a handful of practitioners.

It's a bit like that in India too – the way the Kochi Biennale and the Delhi Art Fair are just impossibly large. I mean, photography fairs are not ever going to be at that scale, are they?

I have to say that *WTDC*, not for lack of trying, couldn't travel to India because a problem with India and big exhibitions is that they can only be shown in large spaces, which tend to be government-run institutions – and these are really hard to work with, especially if you're not used to them. Also, the kind of lead times that Western arts management insists upon, and the kind of time the works would be on hold for, are limited. So *WTDC* fell victim to that – the Whitechapel said they're not going to pay for more storage time.

I did go to a meeting in Delhi in 2011, a joint one involving both the public sector and the private sector, at Lalit Kala Akademi, where the public sector representatives said something like: 'Hands up, we surrender, we can't do it. You guys do it.' I was quite shocked, and I'm surprised actually that our Indian art world, which is so critical in its artwork, is not haranguing the government to give them a better public art sector, because otherwise we are at the whimsy of the private art gallery or rich patrons – rendering us vulnerable to their moods and conditions.

I'm well trained in the system of a public sector – there is policy-making in the ministry and that's where you can effect change. That's where you have the discussion, a civilized exchange that's all on record. There's a process that we can go through as concerned citizen artists. If it's all private, how can we appeal to anyone?

RA: If you were given completely free rein to curate an exhibition that expanded the idea of 'India' and photography from India, and could bring together whichever artists you wished to for this purpose, what would you visualize?

SG: This hypothetical exhibition would present curators with the same challenges as actual exhibitions do, because India is so problematically full of red-flagged 'issues'. This is also true of the UK – for example, I'm working with a research group at my university on the subject of women in photography. A lot of discussion happens within the group – it is also a lobbying group – and I'm still waiting for them to delineate what a 'woman' is. Are trans women to be included, for instance? The broadest discussions about gender and queer intersectionalities haven't really taken place yet.

And outside India, my problem is always that the perspective on photography is colonial, and that one is looking at it within a certain history of photography, which is also colonial, and which doesn't have any significant actors other than the usual suspects from here. I think that has something to do with what now is all being lumped together as a necessary process of 'decolonizing'. One might find this definition somewhat incorrect. But no doubt some 'decolonizing', some unlearning of what 'they' and 'we' both know, *has* to take place ...

I think any contemporary show should be within and about what has transpired/is transpiring regionally. And in India, we need to have many more advanced courses on photography, and research in image histories and image cultures, in higher educational institutions – right now there seems to be just the one, NID [National Institute of Design, Ahmedabad]. More formal teaching and learning is the way to generate more critical discourse. Otherwise, people from India will keep coming here [the UK] to study photography, and the risk is that their perspectives might become over-globalized and distracting.

And now, whenever you think about 'India' as a photographic subject, you think 'gender violence' – that's such an important topic. As is 'caste'. It makes me nervous, because I wonder how one would go about imaging these. It's such a minefield.[23]

I think there's a big critical tidal wave coming in India, and I don't know if the arts world there is ready for it. Artists will have to confront complicated, deeply unsettling, controversial issues vis-à-vis their choices. For instance, a universal question: *How can privileged artists make work about the underprivileged ... ?* The Whitney Biennial[24] in New York in 2017 included Dana Schutz's *Open Casket* (2016) – a white artist's oil painting based on the funeral photographs of fourteen-year-old Emmett Till, an African American boy savagely murdered in Mississippi in 1955 after he had been falsely accused of flirting with a white woman. 'Till's mother insisted on having an open casket funeral so people could see the brutality of the lynching, exposing the horrific extent of American racism. The press images of Till's mutilated body, along with the fact that his murderers were subsequently acquitted, are often credited as having galvanized the civil rights movement in the US.'[25] There was a huge emotional backlash: *How can she interpret that experience ... ? Should she even be allowed to ... ?* Would that be 'censorship' ... ?[26]

These are the kinds of discussions that are unavoidably coming towards artists everywhere ...

Discussions about who has a voice ...[27]

KEYWORDS

A list of terms – including names of people, technologies, events and institutions – that have specific conceptual significance to this volume. Several are likely to be familiar to readers, but these are being revisited here, in part as a ready primer, and in large measure to draw attention to how they have been used here, and to their shifting and open-ended definitional status.

Adivasi: Translates as 'original inhabitants', a collective descriptor of the Indian subcontinent's indigenous people. First used politically in 1938 with the formation of the Adivasi Sabha in Bihar which demanded a separate tribal homeland called 'Jharkhand'. The Constitution uses the term 'Scheduled Tribes' to identify communities that are historically considered 'backward', systematically neglected and denied opportunities. Also see Keywords in *The Hunger of the Republic: Our Present in Retrospect*, edited by Ashish Rajadhyaksha, *India Since the 90s*, vol. 1, New Delhi: Tulika Books, 2021, p. 367. See, in this volume, Emilia Terracciano, 'Beyond or in Emergency?'; Gemma Scott, 'Putting Women in the Picture'; Gauri Gill, 'On Seeing'; Parul Dave Mukherji, 'Mimicking Anthropologists'; Prashant Panjiar/Rahaab Allana, 'Zooming In'.

Alam, Shahidul (b. 1955): Dhaka-based photojournalist, teacher and social activist who has documented social and political upheavals in Bangladesh for over three decades. Founder of the Drik Picture Library, Dhaka (1989); Pathshala South Asian Media Institute, Dhaka (1998); and the Chobi Mela International Photography Festival, Dhaka (2000). Arrested and detained in August 2018 after giving an interview and posting live videos that appeared to criticize the government's violent response to protests over police crackdowns. Granted bail on 20 November 2018 after humanitarian organizations and news media around the world called for his release. See, in this volume, Sunil Gupta/Rahaab Allana, 'FotoFest 2018 and Other Curatorial Practices'.

Altaf, Navjot (b. 1949): Visual artist, working in painting, photography, sculpture, installation art, video and other forms of public art. Worked in Bastar in the late 1990s with indigenous artists and communities. See image in *The Hunger of the Republic: Our Present in Retrospect*, edited by Ashish Rajadhyaksha, *India Since the 90s*, vol. 1, New Delhi: Tulika Books, 2021, pp. 326–27. See, in this volume, Ruth Rosengarten, '*Re-take of Amrita*'; Parul Dave Mukherji, 'Mimicking Anthropologists'.

Anand, Mulk Raj (1905–2004): Author, critic, editor, journalist and political activist, torchbearer of the twentieth-century Progressive Writers' Movement. Founded the arts journal ***MARG***. In 1968, during his term as chairman of the **Lalit Kala Akademi** (1965–70), he laid the foundation for India's First Triennale of Contemporary Art. See, in this volume, Parul Dave Mukherji, 'Mimicking Anthropologists'.

Babri Masjid/Ram Janmabhoomi violence (1992): On 6 December 1992, 1,50,000 people gathered at the Babri mosque led by the Bharatiya Janata Party and Vishwa Hindu Parishad (see **Hindutva**, below). A mob of *karsevak*s (religious volunteers) then stormed the compound and demolished the entire structure, leading to multiple riots and protests across India. On 5 August 2020 the foundation-laying ceremony for the monumental Ram *mandir* (temple) was conducted at the site. The new temple is being inaugurated on 22 January 2024. See **Ayodhya**, in *The Vanishing Point: Moving Images After Video*, edited by Rashmi Devi Sawhney, *India Since the 90s*, vol. 3, New Delhi: Tulika Books, 2022, p. 327. See, in this volume, Prashant Panjiar/Rahaab Allana, 'Zooming In'; William Mazzarella and Raminder Kaur, 'Between Sedition and Seduction'; Sandhini Poddar, 'No Ordinary Darkness'; Suryanandini Narain, 'The Camera Tours the City'.

Bartholomew, Pablo (b. 1955): Independent photographer. Started as a photojournalist and in 1975 received his first World Press Photo award for a series on morphine addicts. He received the Padma Shri in 2013. Known for deeply personal, even autobiographical form of work. His popular series include: *Chronicles of a Past Life: Bombay* (New Delhi: Photoink, 2012); *Outside In: A Tale of Three Cities* (New Delhi: Photoink, 2013); and *The Calcutta Diaries* (New Delhi: Art Heritage, 2012). See, in this volume, Sunil Gupta/Rahaab Allana, 'FotoFest 2018 and Other Curatorial Practices'; Sabeena Gadihoke, 'Journeys into Inner and Outer Worlds'.

Beato, Felice (1832–1909): Nineteenth-century Italian–British war photographer, worked in India, China, Japan, Korea and Burma. Recorded the Crimean War (1855–56), the aftermath of the Sepoy Mutiny in India (see **First Indian War of Independence, 1857**) and the Second Opium War (1860). Alleged to have dressed up documentary images. Emilia Terracciano writes, 'Dug up by order of the photographer, the skeletal remains of slaughtered Indian *sepoys* and prosthetic additions of dubious provenance were arranged across the grounds of the villa's interior pavilion for a macabre photo opportunity in Lucknow' ('Beyond or in Emergency?' p. 42, in this volume). Ruth Rosengarten writes of how he 'arrived on the scene several months after the Mutiny ended', and arranged for buried remains to be disinterred and placed in order to locate the event of his making of the photograph mimetically closer to the event of the fighting ('*Re-take of Amrita*', p. 379, note 28, in this volume). See, in this volume, Sunil Gupta/Rahaab Allana, 'FotoFest 2018 and Other Curatorial Practices'; Sabeena Gadihoke, 'Journeys into Inner and Outer Worlds'.

Bedi, Mitter (1926–1985): Photographer. Worked in early years in the film industry, later specializing in industrial photography covering public sector corporations and private enterprises in steel and oil, hospitality, mines, sugar, pharmaceuticals, etc. Several images are now classic icons of industrialization under Nehru. See, in this volume, Suryanandini Narain, 'The Camera Tours the City'; Sunil Gupta/Rahaab Allana, 'FotoFest 2018 and Other Curatorial Practices'.

Bengal Famine (1943): Major famine in pre-Independence eastern India. A key event featured in nearly all the arts practices, especially those by pro-Communist artists, its representations took place in the play *Nabanna* by Bijon Bhattacharya, the first important play of the newly formed **Indian People's Theatre Association**, and in the film *Dharti Ke Lal* (*Children of the Earth*, by K.A. Abbas, 1946). Important for music with several songs emerging from or alluding to the famine. It was photographed by Sunil Janah. Mrinal Sen's film *Akaler Sandhaney* (*In Search of Famine*, 1982) is referenced by Emilia Terracciano, 'Beyond or in Emergency?', p. 25, in this volume. Also see Sabeena Gadihoke, 'Journeys into Inner and Outer Worlds'.

Bourke-White, Margaret (1904–1971): American photojournalist, *Life* magazine's first female staff photographer, the first Western photographer permitted to enter the Soviet Union during the 1930s' industrial revolution, and the first accredited female photographer to cover the combat zones of World War II. Interviewed and photographed Mahatma Gandhi for *Life* shortly before his assassination. Sixty-six of Bourke-White's previously unpublished photographs of **Partition of India** were included in a reissue of Khushwant Singh's 1956 novel, *Train to Pakistan* (2006). See, in this volume, Emilia Terracciano, 'Beyond or in Emergency?'; Suryanandini Narain, 'The Camera Tours the City'; Sabeena Gadihoke, 'Journeys into Inner and Outer Worlds'.

Bourne, Samuel (1834–1912): Nineteenth-century photographer known for work in India from 1863 to 1870. He produced one of the largest collections of nineteenth-century landscape images from South Asia. With Charles Shepherd he set up the photographic studio Bourne & Shepherd in Simla in 1863, and later in Calcutta; the company closed in June 2016. See, in this volume, Suryanandini Narain, 'The Camera Tours the City'; Sabeena Gadihoke, 'Journeys into Inner and Outer Worlds'; Sunil Gupta/Rahaab Allana, 'FotoFest 2018 and Other Curatorial Practices'.

Cartier-Bresson, Henri (1908–2004): Revered French photographer, considered a paradigmatic master of candid photography. Famous for his theory of the 'decisive moment', i.e. the instant when everything comes together and is successfully captured as an image. Photographed the **Partition of India** and **Mahatma Gandhi**'s funeral. See, in this volume, Sabeena Gadihoke, 'Journeys into Inner and Outer Worlds'.

Chhachhi, Sheba (b. 1958): Photographer, installation artist, writer and activist based in New Delhi, known for creating large-scale multimedia installations incorporating light, sound and the moving image. Gender is an important focus of her work. Chhachhi has exhibited widely, and her works are part of several prominent private and public collections. Her notable work includes *Seven Lives in a Dream* (1980–91, printed 2014), *Ganga's Daughters: Meetings with Women Ascetics* (1992–2002), *Neelkanth: Poison/Nectar* (2000/2003/2008), *The Water Diviner* (2008), *Record/ Resist* (2012) and *Temporal Twist* (2017). In collaboration with Sonia Jabbar, she created the photography installation *When the Gun is Raised the Dialogue Stops* (2000), documenting voices of ordinary women during the Kashmir conflict in the 1990s. See Nancy Adajania, 'The Ecologies of Technological Experimentation', in *The Vanishing Point: Moving Images After Video*, edited by Rashmi Devi Sawhney, *India Since the 90s*, vol. 3, New Delhi: Tulika Books, 2022, pp. 143–65. See, in this volume, Sunil Gupta/Rahaab Allana, 'FotoFest 2018 and Other Curatorial Practices'.

Citizenship: Complex concept in India with an evolving history. Defined in Article 5 of the Constitution after Independence and later by the Citizenship Act of 1955, it has been viewed largely within a post-Partition frame in its original emphasis on the rights of residents as against those defined by birth or ancestry. The Act was amended in 2004 and then, controversially, in 2019, leading to major protests since it was seen as targeting the Muslim community. See Keywords in *The Hunger of the Republic: Our Present in Retrospect*, edited by Ashish Rajadhyaksha, *India Since the 90s*, vol. 1, New Delhi: Tulika Books, 2021, p. 370. As used across the *India Since the 90s* series, the concept also has an aesthetic dimension. See with specific reference to the cinema, *The Vanishing Point: Moving Images After Video*, edited by Rashmi Devi Sawhney, *India Since the 90s*, vol. 3, New Delhi: Tulika Books, 2022, p. 330. Citizenship in photography has become a major issue after the work of Ariella Azoulay (see **civil contract of photography**, below). Photography historian Christopher Pinney and the Photo Demos Collective explore the concept globally in *Citizens of Photography: The Camera and Political Imagination*, Durham: Duke University Press, 2023. See, in this volume, Sabeena Gadihoke, 'Journeys into Inner and Outer Worlds'; Suryanandini Narain, 'The Camera Tours the City'; William Mazzarella and Raminder Kaur, 'Between Sedition and Seduction'.

Civil contract of photography: Concept introduced by Israeli-Palestinian photography theorist Ariella Azoulay. In her 2008 book of the same title, Azoulay argues for a theory of citizenship and even a fully formed civil contract that exists autonomously of the state, as a particular set of relations between individuals that govern as well as constrain power. Anyone, even a stateless person, who addresses others through photographs or is in the position of a photograph's addressee, is or can become a member of the citizenry of photography. See, in this volume, Emilia Terracciano, 'Beyond or in Emergency?'

Civil Disobedience Movement (12 March 1930–7 April 1934): Extensively filmed and photographed political movement started by **Mahatma Gandhi** with the Dandi Salt March, wherein nationalists broke the law by refusing to pay the colonial tax on salt. Its second phase began following failed talks at the Second Round Table Conference with the continuation of anti-tax and anti-rent campaigns. Emilia Terracciano suggests that this movement, along with the Non-Cooperation Movement in the early 1920s and the Quit India campaign of 1942, were 'all events in which processional marches, prayer meetings and public rallies became affective theatrical performances'; see 'Beyond or in Emergency?' in this volume, p. 31.

Dalit: Political descriptor and category for oppressed groups and sub-groups who were declared 'untouchable' under the caste system, and who now have organized political movements demanding rights, equality and social justice. B.R. Ambedkar led protests such as the Mahad Satyagraha and mass conversion of Dalits to Buddhism in order to address the discrimination historically experienced by Dalits on every level and in every sphere. The 1970s saw the formation of the Dalit Panthers in Maharashtra as a social and cultural organization seeking to combat caste discrimination. The term **Dalit/Dalitbahujan** is annotated in all the previous volumes of the *India Since the 90s* series: see *The Hunger of the Republic: Our Present in Retrospect*, edited by Ashish Rajadhyaksha, *India Since the 90s*, vol. 1, New Delhi: Tulika Books, 2021, p. 370; *Improvised Futures: Encountering the Body in Performance*, edited by Ranjana Dave, *India Since the 90s*, vol. 2, New Delhi: Tulika Books, 2021, p. 332; and *The Vanishing Point: Moving Images After Video*, edited by Rashmi Devi Sawhney, *India Since the 90s*, vol. 3, New Delhi: Tulika Books, 2022, p. 331. See also, in this volume, Prashant Panjiar/Rahaab Allana, 'Zooming In'.

Deen Dayal, **Lala** (1844–1905): Major turn-of-the-century photographer who began his career in the mid-1870s as a commissioned photographer, eventually setting up studios in Indore, Bombay and Secunderabad. Official photographer to the Nizam of Hyderabad (1884) and the Viceroy of India (1885). In 1892, Deen Dayal started a *zenana* (gender-segregated, women only) studio in Hyderabad, run by the American photographer Mrs. Kenny-Levick whose husband was a correspondent for *The Times*. A valuable biographical account is presented in *Raja Deen Dayal: Artist-Photographer in 19th-Century India*, The Alkazi Collection of Photography & Mapin, 2013. See, in this volume, Jodi Throckmorton, 'Photography and Inherited History in India'; Suryanandini Narain, 'The Camera Tours the City'.

Decolonization: Controversial concept in India. Usually imagined as a critical process challenging (or subverting) the lingering effects of colonialism through an inquiry into historical legacies and power imbalances that persist as a residue of the colonial era. The question has remained open as to whether India's Independence has, or has not, led to the furtherance of decolonization. See, e.g., **Adivasi** and **Dalit**; Hamza Alavi, 'India and the Colonial Mode of Production',in *The Hunger of the Republic: Our Present in Retrospect*, edited by Ashish Rajadhyaksha, *India Since the 90s*, vol. 1, New Delhi: Tulika Books, 2021, pp. 121–38.

In this volume, Diva Gujral, '*Painters with a Camera*'; Gemma Scott, 'Putting Women in the Picture'; Ruth Rosengarten, '*Re-take of Amrita*'; Sunil Gupta/Rahaab Allana, 'FotoFest 2018 and Other Curatorial Practices'.

Delhi Durbars (1877, 1903, 1911): Major spectacles of imperial splendour seen as produced mainly for purposes of being photographed and filmed. The 1903 Durbar was held to celebrate the succession of Edward VII as emperor, and organized by Lord Curzon with meticulous detail as a display of pomp. The 1911 Durbar was held to commemorate the coronation of King George V. The 1903 Durbar was photographed, among the world's press, by **Bourne & Shepherd** and by **Lala Deen Dayal**; and the second and third Durbars were filmed by pioneering Indian filmmakers H.S. Bhatavdekar, Madan Theatres and Hiralal Sen. Suryanandini Narain writes that these were 'opportune moments for the camera to document the pomp and splendour of the Raj … [they] re-imagined the city as a makeshift entity, with sprawling grounds hosting tents, administrative buildings, shops and spaces for celebration'; 'The Camera Tours the City', p. 72, in this volume

Documentary photography: Popular form used to capture reality – whether historical events or the minutiae of everyday life – as objectively as possible. A lynchpin of photojournalism, this genre is often deployed to speak about and for marginalized communities, to raise social consciousness, and to advocate for social change. Practitioners' embrace of the documentary was evident in the seminal exhibition *Images of India* (1960), and documentary realism developed into a mainstay of Indian photography through the work of photographers such as **Kulwant Roy**, **Homai Vyarawalla**, Kishor Parekh, **S. Paul**, **Raghu Rai**, **Raghubir Singh**, **Pablo Bartholomew**, Gauri Gill (see 'On Seeing', in this volume), Prashant Panjiar (see 'Zooming In', in this volume), etc.

Doordarshan: Indian public service television broadcaster set up as an experimental service on 15 September 1959. Initially operating under All India Radio, by April 1976 it was constituted as a separate department under the Ministry of Information and Broadcasting, with broadcasts to seven Indian cities. Initially experimented with satellite technologies as a tool to accelerate 'development'. By 1982, national telecasts had been initiated. Remembered for its production of popular dramas, soap operas and mythological serials from the 1980s. Also see *The Vanishing Point: Moving Images After Video*, edited by Rashmi Devi Sawhney, *India Since the 90s*, vol. 3, New Delhi: Tulika Books, 2022, p. 332. See, in this volume, William Mazzarella and Raminder Kaur, 'Between Sedition and Seduction'.

Emergency (1975–77): In a landmark judgement on 12 June 1975, the Allahabad High Court found Prime Minister **Indira Gandhi** guilty of electoral malpractices, thereby invalidating her seat in the Lok Sabha and banning her from office. Citing political instability, Gandhi recommended that President Fakhruddin Ali Ahmed declare a state of Emergency on 25 June 1975. These granted the Prime Minister extraordinary powers, resulting in the suspension of the democratic process, extreme censorship, suppression of dissent, incarceration of political opponents and an array of human rights violations, including forced sterilization. See, in this volume, Gemma Scott, 'Putting Women in the Picture'; William Mazzarella and Raminder Kaur, 'Between Sedition and Seduction'; Prashant Panjiar/Rahaab Allana, 'Zooming In'.

Faculty of Fine Arts, Maharaja Sayajirao University, Baroda: Founded in June 1950, envisioned as a pedagogical and practice-enabling unit concerned with the future of art education in newly independent India. Distanced from the traditionalism of the prevalent Bengal School and Santiniketan, primarily associated with art trajectories and formal experimentation defined by aesthetic **modernism**. The curriculum offered courses in applied arts, painting, printmaking, sculpture, art history and aesthetics, with Fine Arts Fairs being held annually to showcase student work. Notable alumni include Jyoti Bhatt, **Gulammohammed Sheikh**, Nilima Sheikh, **Nasreen Mohamedi**, **Vivan Sundaram** and **Pushpamala N.** See, in this volume, Diva Gujral, '*Painters with a Camera*'; Parul Dave Mukherji, 'Mimicking Anthropologists'.

Festival(s) of India: Series of major international arts festivals held in the UK (1982), followed by the USA and France (1985–86), USSR (1987–99), and later, Germany, Japan, Sweden, China and other countries. Associated primarily with **Indira Gandhi**'s re-election in 1980 on a new post-**Emergency** electoral platform based on economic liberalization, and with her main cultural adviser, Pupul Jayakar, it combined a strong civilizational claim with a futuristic emphasis on science and technology and 'modern' India's artistic achievements. It included shows of photography including the 1982 exhibition *Photography in India* at the Photographers' Gallery, London (see Sunil Gupta/Rahaab Allana, 'FotoFest 2018 and Other Curatorial Practices' in this volume) and *Pratibimba* in 1987 at The Pushkin State Museum of Fine Arts, Moscow (see Introduction in this volume). Also see Parul Dave Mukherji, 'Mimicking Anthropologists'.

Films Division: Established in 1948 as India's first official documentary film production and distribution unit, operating under the Ministry of Information and Broadcasting, its forebears include the Film Advisory Board (FAB) and Information Films of India (IFI). As a state-funded body, its objective was to make films for public information/education as well as for cultural purposes. From 1965 to 1975 experimental forms replaced the didactic approach – a shift evident in the works of filmmakers such as Pramod Pati, S.N.S. Sastry and S. Sukhdev. In January 2023, it was brought under the National Film Development Corporation (NFDC). Also see Keywords in *The Vanishing Point: Moving Images After Video*, edited by Rashmi Devi Sawhney, *India Since the 90s*, vol. 3, New Delhi: Tulika Books, 2022, p. 334. See, in this volume, Diva Gujral, '*Painters with a Camera*'.

First Indian War of Independence, 1857: Also known as the 1857 Mutiny/ Sepoy Mutiny and the Uprising. In March 1857, a sepoy from the Bengal Native Infantry named Mangal Pandey is believed to have shot a British officer as an act of rebellion, for which he was hanged. Soldiers from the 3rd Bengal Light Cavalry revolted and it spread from Meerut to Delhi, where the rebels declared Mughal descendant Bahadur Shah Zafar to be the Emperor of India. Known as the primary cause for the end of the East India Company's authority and the beginning of Crown rule over India. Important event for photography history in the works of **Felice Beato** (see above) and for his controversial reconstructions of the actual events. Sabeena Gadihoke writes, 'As photographers could not be physically present at sites of violence, the excesses of the Mutiny (for the British) came to be represented through fictional reconstructions, such as lithographs that could fill in for what was missing, or the more famous examples of staging by early commercial photographers – for instance Felice Beato': 'Journeys into Inner and Outer Worlds', p. 361, note 35 in this volume. Also see, in this volume, Emilia Terracciano, 'Beyond or in Emergency?'; Ruth Rosengarten, '*Re-take of Amrita*'; Sunil Gupta/ Rahaab Allana, 'FotoFest 2018 and Other Curatorial Practices'.

Gandhi, Indira (1917–1984): Politician and stateswoman who served as India's Prime Minister in 1966–77 and 1980–84. Declared the **Emergency** in 1975. See, in this volume, Emilia Terracciano, 'Beyond or in Emergency?'; Gemma Scott, 'Putting Women in the Picture'. Assassinated by her Sikh bodyguards in 1984, leading to major anti-Sikh riots (see, in this volume, Sabeena Gadihoke, 'Journeys into Inner and Outer Worlds'; Suryanandini Narain, 'The Camera Tours the City').

Gandhi, Mohandas Karamchand (1869–1948): Popularly known as Mahatma Gandhi, regarded as the Father of the Nation. One of the most filmed and photographed political leaders of the pre-war era, famously by **Margaret Bourke-White** when running his *charkha* (spinning wheel). She provides remarkable detail about how she went about photographing him (see Emilia Terracciano, 'Beyond or in Emergency?' in this volume). His funeral, which was a major state event, was photographed by **Henri Cartier-Bresson**.

Gedney, William (1932–1989): A key figure in the genre of American black-and-white street photography. His photographs of India were taken during two extensive trips – as a Fulbright scholar from 1969 to 1971 when he lived in Benaras for fourteen months with a local family, and later during a four-month stay in Calcutta. These were showcased in the exhibition *The Life and Work of William Gedney* at the Jehangir Nicholson Gallery, Chhatrapati Shivaji Maharaj Vastu Sangrahalaya (CSMVS), Mumbai, in 2017. See Sabeena Gadihoke, 'Journeys into Inner and Outer Worlds' in this volume.

Gujarat riots (2002): Also known as the Godhra riots after the city where they began. On 27 February 2002, a train full of Hindu *karsevak*s (volunteers to the religious cause) returning from

Ayodhya caught fire, resulting in the deaths of 59 people. Though the cause of the fire is disputed, the act became a trigger for politicized rioting across Gujarat, with the Muslim community subjected to gruesome assault, rape and murder. The complicity of authorities, especially the police, was central to the state-sponsored pogrom in which an estimated 2,000 Muslims were killed. Media coverage was used by the state to fuel its electoral ambitions. See Keyword **2002 Gujarat Riots** in *The Vanishing Point: Moving Images After Video*, edited by Rashmi Devi Sawhney, *India Since the 90s*, vol. 3, New Delhi: Tulika Books, 2022, p. 326. See, in this volume, Sandhini Poddar, 'No Ordinary Darkness'; 'CAMP on CAMP'; Amar Kanwar, 'Embracing Doubt'; Prashant Panjiar/Rahaab Allana, 'Zooming In'.

Hindutva: While the organized form of the Hindu right-wing movement may be traced to the relatively obscure Hindu Maha Sabha, in 1906 the ideology of Hindutva started to gain prominence via the works of V.D. Savarkar, was actively promulgated by K.B. Hedgewar and M.S. Golwalkar, and inspired Nathuram Godse to assassinate Mahatma Gandhi in 1948, after which the RSS was banned for a year. Hindutva dominated the Jan Sangh, formed in 1952; in 1980 it became the Bharatiya Janata Party (BJP) and from then on muscled a place for itself in the political arena and the popular political imagination. The **Babri Masjid** demolition of 1992 and the **Gujarat riots** of 2002 were pivotal moments of right-wing dominance. The BJP surged to power in the 2014 elections, and since then have enabled aggressive public articulation of Hindu nationalism and condoned Hindu supremacist violence against minorities. See **Hinduism/Hindutva** in *The Hunger of the Republic: Our Present in Retrospect*, edited by Ashish Rajadhyaksha, *India Since the 90s*, vol. 1, New Delhi: Tulika Books, 2021, p. 372; *Improvised Futures: Encountering the Body in Performance*, edited by Ranjana Dave, *India Since the 90s*, vol. 2, New Delhi: Tulika Books, 2021, p. 334; and *The Vanishing Point: Moving Images After Video*, edited by Rashmi Devi Sawhney, *India Since the 90s*, vol. 3, New Delhi: Tulika Books, 2022, p. 334. See, in this volume, Prashant Panjiar/Rahaab Allana, 'Zooming In'.

Indian National Congress: Often called the 'grand old party', founded on 28 December 1885 as an organization of social reformers, journalists and lawyers, in response to British colonial rule. Became the primary mass-based organization driving the Indian national movement. After Independence in 1947, the Congress formed the government with Jawaharlal Nehru as the first Prime Minister, and it continued to remain dominant till late 1970. Internal schisms weakened the Congress, as did the anti-**Emergency** mass mobilization campaign led by Jayaprakash Narayan. This helped to galvanize an anti-Congress united front that defeated the Congress in the 1977 national elections. The post-Emergency boom in print media served to launch a new era in photojournalism. The Congress returned to power in 1980, and formed alliances with smaller regional parties as a way to expand electoral gains in the 1990s. United Progressive Alliance formed the government from 2004 to 2014. See **Congress/Congress-I** in *The Hunger of the Republic: Our Present in Retrospect*, edited by Ashish Rajadhyaksha, *India Since the 90s*, vol. 1, New Delhi: Tulika Books, 2021, p. 370. See, in this volume, Emilia Terracciano, 'Beyond or in Emergency?'; Gemma Scott, 'Putting Women in the Picture'.

Indian People's Theatre Association (IPTA): Theatre initiative formally associated with the Communist Party of India, formally started in 1943. For more details, see Keywords in *Improvised Futures: Encountering the Body in Performance*, edited by Ranjana Dave, *India Since the 90s*, vol. 2, New Delhi: Tulika Books, 2021, p. 335, and *The Vanishing Point: Moving Images After Video*, edited by Rashmi Devi Sawhney, *India Since the 90s*, vol. 3, New Delhi: Tulika Books, 2022, p. 335. See, in this volume, Emilia Terracciano, 'Beyond or in Emergency?'.

Jallianwala Bagh Massacre (1919): Towards the end of World War I, the British introduced the Rowlatt Act (1919), a draconian legislation authorizing the colonial regime to arrest any person in India without a warrant. On 13 April 1919, people gathered in Amritsar to celebrate Baisakhi (the spring festival) and to peacefully protest against the arrests of nationalist leaders Satya Pal and Saifuddin Kitchlew under the Rowlatt Act. General Dyer ordered his troops to fire. Having blocked the only route out of the grounds, the soldiers continued firing till they ran out of ammunition. An estimated 379 Indians were killed and 1,200 injured. The aftermath was documented by Narayan Virkar who arrived the next day, his photographs featuring witnesses and survivors pointing to bullet holes marked with chalk. See, in this volume, Sabeena Gadihoke, 'Journeys into Inner and Outer Worlds'; Emilia Terracciano, 'Beyond or in Emergency?'.

Janah, Sunil (1918–2012): Revered photojournalist and documentary photographer best known for photographs of the **Bengal Famine**, the evolving Indian Independence movement, post-Independence industrialization, and **Adivasi** communities. Mentored by close family friend and leading photographer Shambhu Saha. See, in this volume, Emilia Terracciano, 'Beyond or in Emergency?'; Sabeena Gadihoke, 'Journeys into Inner and Outer Worlds'; Suryanandini Narain, 'The Camera Tours the City'.

Johannesburg Biennial: First organized in 1995 (28 February–30 April), a year after South Africa's first free elections. Envisioned as an opportunity to restore dialogue with the rest of the world through art. Sixty-three countries, forty-three from outside Africa, participated in the exhibition. See, in this volume, Sunil Gupta/Rahaab Allana, 'FotoFest 2018 and Other Curatorial Practices'.

Kashmir/Kashmir insurgency: Region of the northwestern Indian subcontinent with a predominantly Muslim population. Following the Partition of India, in October 1947, Hari Singh, Maharaja of Kashmir, signed an Instrument of Accession to the Indian Union. In July of that year, India and Pakistan defined a ceasefire line (see, in this volume, Sumathi Ramaswamy, 'Midnight's Line') that divided the administration of the territory as a temporary solution through Article 370 of the Indian Constitution. With many conflicts associated with military intervention and insurgency, the most recent unrest began after the Bharatiya Janata Party (BJP) swept elections across India in 2014. Exploiting a constitutional provision that allowed the Union government to integrate Jammu and Kashmir upon the approval of a no-longer-extant elected body, it suspended Jammu and Kashmir's autonomy and applied India's Constitution fully to the territory. It also passed legislation in October 2019 to relegate the state to a union territory – thereby allowing the Union government full control over its governance – and to split off the Ladakh region into a separate union territory of its own. Photography in Kashmir has had a specific significance, discussed in Sanjay Kak/Majid Maqbool, 'The Making of *Witness: Kashmir 1986–2016/Nine Photographers*' in this volume. Photography has maintained an archival memory of people who have 'disappeared', as – to quote Amar Kanwar ('Embracing Doubt', p. 256, in this volume) – the 'killings and disappearances [that] continue in Kashmir regardless of the open lessons of the Palestinian–Israeli conflict' also keep alive memories of an era that might precede but also follow the darkness of the present. See the same Keyword in *The Vanishing Point: Moving Images After Video*, edited by Rashmi Devi Sawhney, *India Since the 90s*, vol. 3, New Delhi: Tulika Books, 2022, p. 335.

Kumbh Mela: Spectacular and widely photographed festival, based on the myth of the churning of the ocean and the *kumbh* (pot) filled with nectar, from which drops fell on the four sites of Allahabad, Ujjain, Nasik and Haridwar. The festival is celebrated with mass pilgrimages to these sites. The month-long *mela* (fair) draws *sadhu*s (ascetics) of different persuasions from all over India, who gather to take a ritual dip in the sacred rivers at these sites at propitious times. Most are male *sadhu*s, but *sadhvi*s (female ascetics) also have a presence at this much-photographed event that becomes a dramatic world unto itself. The *mela* also serves as a site for commercial ventures, welfare activities and recruitment to *akhada*s. Sheba Chhachhi's well-known *Ganga's Daughters: Meetings with Women Ascetics* (1992–2002) features this festival. See, in this volume, Sabeena Gadihoke, 'Journeys into Inner and Outer Worlds'.

Lalit Kala Akademi (est. 1954): India's national academy for fine arts, mandated to preserve and project contemporary art. It has always had a founding contradiction, part of a larger conceptual battle over what 'contemporary' art meant, whether it was restricted to 'fine' arts – painting, sculpture, graphics – or had a wider mandate in the arts as a whole. A related question was whether it was the domain of 'elite' arts, or whether support for indigenous crafts, or what came to be known as 'folk' or 'tribal' (see **Adivasi**) art, would be included. In 1968, when the Art Triennale was launched, the rules of participation explicitly stated that 'folk', 'tribal' and 'tradition' would not be allowed as they were not within the ambit of the 'contemporary'. See, in this volume, 'Introduction'; Diva Gujral, '*Painters with a Camera*'; Sunil Gupta/Rahaab Allana, 'FotoFest 2018 and Other Curatorial Practices'. Also see **Akademi** in *Improvised Futures: Encountering the Body in Performance*, edited by Ranjana Dave, *India Since the 90s*, vol. 2, New Delhi: Tulika Books, 2021, p. 339.

Left movement in India: The history of India's Left is complex: associated with its Communist Parties, the Congress and with Socialist parties, divided along political priorities and emphases on issues such as caste. The Communist Party of India (CPI) entered parliamentary politics to form the largest opposition in the 1952 elections. Following differences between the Soviet Union and China, in 1964 the CPI split into two factions – the CPI and the CPI-M (Marxist). In 1967, peasants rose up against landowners in the Naxalbari area of West Bengal, initiating what became known as the **Naxalite** movement (see **Naxalite/ Urban Naxal** in *The Hunger of the Republic: Our Present in Retrospect*, edited by Ashish Rajadhyaksha, *India Since the 90s*, vol. 1, New Delhi: Tulika Books, 2021, p. 376; and **Naxalite/ Naxalism** in *The Vanishing Point: Moving Images After Video*, edited by Rashmi Devi Sawhney, *India Since the 90s*, vol. 3, New Delhi: Tulika Books, 2022, p. 339). This caused a further schism leading to the formation of the CPI-ML (Marxist-Leninist), advocates of armed struggle. Since the 1970s, the CPI-M has periodically held power in West Bengal, Tripura and Kerala. See, in this volume, Prashant Panjiar/ Rahaab Allana, 'Zooming In'.

Mahatta, Madan (1932–2014): Photographer working mainly in black-and-white and on architectural photography. Closely associated with major architects such as Charles Correa and Habib Rahman. Mahatta's work exhibited in *Delhi Modern (1950s–1980s)* curated by **Ram Rahman** in 2012, focused on the building of New Delhi at the height of Nehruvian modernism. See, in this volume, Suryanandini Narain, 'The Camera Tours the City'; Prashant Panjiar/Rahaab Allana, 'Zooming In'.

Maoist movement (Nepal): Movement that originated in 1994 in Nepal, a traditional monarchy, with the schism in the Communist Party of Nepal (Unity Centre) and the formation of the Communist Party of Nepal (Maoist Centre). In 1996, the Maoists launched an armed struggle calling for a People's Liberation War against the government, resulting in the ten-year civil war in Nepal. Following the revolution in 2006 which ended the monarchy, they formed a parliamentary party and have formed the government several times. See William Mazzarella and Raminder Kaur, 'Between Sedition and Seduction', in this volume.

MARG (est. 1946; Hindi: 'path'): Began as a publication of the Modern Architectural Research Group, taking its name from the acronym. The group members were artists, writers and architects, including **Mulk Raj Anand**, Otto Keonigsberger, Minette De Silva, Minoo Mistry and J.P.J. Billimoria, who were inspired by the Modern Architectural Society (MARS) in London. A quarterly magazine with a related book publication programme that has maintained an ideal of progressive cosmopolitanism in documenting the arts and architecture over nearly seven decades. See, in this volume, Diva Gujral, '*Painters with a Camera*'; Parul Dave Mukherji, 'Mimicking Anthropologists'.

Modernism: A complex, multivalent, equivocal signifier, closely associated with a specific period of Western art history that nurtured avant-garde ideologies and forms. With reference to India, Geeta Kapur has argued (in *When Was Modernism: Essays on Contemporary Cultural Practice in India*, New Delhi: Tulika Books, 2000) that modernism constitutes a double, even paradoxical, discourse with nationalism, with the two converging via attempts at self-determination. Contextualized within 'third world' decolonization, modernism resists the de-politicization of narratives and simultaneously proposes an engagement with the avant-garde. The modernist turn in photography emphasized formal aspects over themes, with a move towards abstraction and a hybridized vocabulary that referred to both contemporary Western ideas and traditional (i.e. influenced by ideas of the 'nation') form, seen in the work of photographers such as **Mitter Bedi** and **Raghubir Singh**. See detailed entry on **Modernism** in Keywords, in *The Hunger of the Republic: Our Present in Retrospect*, edited by Ashish Rajadhyaksha, *India Since the 90s*, vol. 1, New Delhi: Tulika Books, 2021, pp. 374–75. See, in this volume, Diva Gujral, '*Painters with a Camera*'; Gemma Scott, 'Putting Women in the Picture'; William Mazzarella and Raminder Kaur, 'Between Sedition and Seduction'; Parul Dave-Mukherji, 'Mimicking Anthropologists'.

Mohamedi, Nasreen (1937–1990): Avant-garde Indian artist, best known for abstract paintings and line drawings based on grid patterns. Her style challenged the very categorization of contemporary art, and her deep engagement with abstraction and preference for a minimalist aesthetic distinguished her from her contemporaries. Also a major photographer continuing the abstract aesthetic. Member of the path-breaking **Vision Exchange Workshop** (1969–72). Worked in **Faculty of Fine Arts, Maharaja Sayajirao University, Baroda**. Major retrospectives include *Nasreen in Retrospect* (Jehangir Art Gallery, Mumbai, 1991); *A Retrospective: Nasreen Mohamedi* (Chatterjee & Lal, Mumbai, 2004); *A View to Infinity: A Retrospective* (1937–90) – *Part of Difficult Love* (Kiran Nadar Museum of Art, Delhi, 2013); and, most recently, *Nasreen Mohamedi* (The MET Breuer, New York, 2016). See Diva Gujral, '*Painters with a Camera*', in this volume.

'Mother India': The personification of the nation as 'Mother India'/'Bharat Mata' can be traced back to the late nineteenth century. The concept emerged as form of anti-colonialism in texts such as in Bankim Chandra Chatterjee's book *Ananda Math* (1888). Major Hindi film *Mother India* (1955) featured movie star Nargis in the title role. One of the earliest visual portrayals of Mother India is Abanindranath Tagore's 1905 painting which depicts Bharat Mata as a simply dressed Bengali woman with four arms and a halo. Sumathi Ramaswamy (see

'Midnight's Line' in this volume) traced the manner in which the cartographic form of the nation and the anthropomorphic mother goddess figure become fused in a bid to generate patriotic fervour (*The Goddess and the Nation: Mapping Mother India*, 1997). Recent artists who have worked on the theme include Nalini Malani and **Pushpamala N**. Contemporary scholarship has taken note of the recent militaristic, coopting propagation of the image, now generally aligned with the current government's majoritarian and supremacist worldview.

Moving images: A term referring to lens-based modes that present images sequentially to create the illusion of motion and a continuity of meaning. Functioning as an umbrella term for film, video, television and related media that comprise durational images, it has gained traction through digital technology and new media forms that render increasingly porous definitions of older mediums and the boundaries between them. Such unifying terms are widely deployed within the complex, technologically driven realms of contemporary media culture. See, in this volume, Sandhini Poddar, 'No Ordinary Darkness'; Ruth Rosengarten, '*Re-take of Amrita*'; Amar Kanwar, 'Embracing Doubt'.

N. Pushpamala: See **Pushpamala N.**

Partition of India: The division of the Indian subcontinent into two independent nation-states accompanying the dissolution of the British Raj. Mainly affecting the former provinces of Punjab and Bengal, it caused large-scale loss of life and an unprecedented migration between the two dominions. Sumathi Ramaswamy (in 'Midnight's Line' in this volume) points to how the line that split the continent, known as the Radcliffe Line, produces a 'martyred map'. She also quotes Christopher Pinney as saying that 'the trauma of Partition was never visually represented by the commercial picture production industry' (p. 19). **Sunil Janah**, who photographed the Partition extensively, is quoted by Emilia Terracciano (in 'Beyond or in Emergency?' in this volume) as saying: 'For many of us, the disastrous Partition of our country, and the murderous communal riots that accompanied India's Independence, were a heartbreak from which we never recovered. Independence had not brought any beginnings of a new era, nor any remarkable changes in the country, not even the promise of any' (p. 46). Sabeena Gadihoke (in 'Journeys into Inner and Outer Worlds' in this volume) points out that it was the visual representation of the Partition and the assassination of Mahatma Gandhi, 'defined largely by the images of two "outsider–insider" photographers, **Henri Cartier-Bresson** and **Margaret Bourke-White**' that captured this history. See Sandhini Poddar, 'No Ordinary Darkness' in this volume, on Amar Kanwar's references to Partition. Also see Jodi Throckmorton, 'Photography and Inherited History in India', for more on the 1947 Partition Archive, initiated in 2010 as a crowd-funded, crowd-sourced digital museum that collects witness accounts of the Partition of India/creation of Pakistan. The archive hosts over 10,000 interviews in twenty-two languages from across twelve countries. Partition Museums have been set up in Amritsar (2016) and Delhi (2023), based on oral histories, objects and photographs. See www.partitionmuseum.org. Dhaka's Liberation War Museum (est. 1996) commemorates the 1971 War and the independence of Bangladesh. See www.liberationwarmuseumbd.org.

Paul, S. (1930–2017): Venerated figure in Indian photojournalism, described as 'the Henri Cartier-Bresson of India' by American publication *B&W Magazine*. Chief of Photography at *Indian Express* from 1960, retiring in 1989. In 1967, Paul became the first Indian practitioner to be profiled by the *British Journal of Photography*. See, in this volume, Sabeena Gadihoke, 'Journeys into Inner and Outer Worlds'.

Photographic societies: Societies set up in the mid-nineteenth century mainly for amateur photographers, initially restricted to leisured British and Indian upper classes, but expanded to include imperial functions like surveying, documentation and record-keeping projects in the colony. The Photographic Society of Bombay (est. 1854) was the first, and included Bhau Daji Lad, Venaik Gungathur and Ardaseer Cursetjee among its founding members. It ran its own journal modelled after the Photographic Society of London that had started one year earlier. The Society of Madras (est. 1857) included medical people since knowledge of chemistry was considered necessary. It was revived in 1932 by photography enthusiast A. Arunachalam and briefly renamed the Madras Amateur Photographic Society, returning to its former name after Independence. The Bengal Photographic Society (est. 1856) had its first exhibition in March 1857. The launch of both societies, and of the *Journal of the Photographic Society of Bengal*, coincided with the **First Indian War of Independence**. Emilia Terracciano (in 'Beyond or in Emergency?' in this volume) comments on the journal's role in disseminating the style that came to be known as 'pictorialism', a 'photographic style and type of imagery based on the application of the principles of fine art ... underpinned by an aesthetic response to the ongoing debate about photography's scientific and artistic status'. She also mentions other societies like the Brotherhood of the Linked Ring, an association of British photographers formed in 1892 with a focus on promoting photography as fine art, to which photo-artists like Shapoor N. Bhedwar who worked in Bombay from 1890 to 1900 belonged.

Photojournalism: A realist mode of visual storytelling to create compelling narratives of news events, often in real time, and of particular subject matter, often rendered in granular detail. While photographs have accompanied the news since the mid-1850s, the arrival of smaller lightweight cameras in the 1920s greatly facilitated photojournalism, and more recently digital technologies and processes have radically expanded its potential for mass public dissemination. Indian photographers such as **Homai Vyarawalla**, **Sunil Janah**, **Kulwant Roy**, N. Thiagarajan, Kishor Parekh, **S. Paul**, **Ram Rahman**, and **Pablo Bartholomew**, have all adeptly chronicled India's diverse and tumultuous modern history. The post-**Emergency** period saw a major boom in photojournalism, for example, in the work of **Raghu Rai** and Prashant Panjiar. See, in this volume, Prashant Panjiar/Rahaab Allana, 'Zooming In'; Emilia Terracciano, 'Beyond or in Emergency?'; Sabeena Gadihoke, 'Journeys into Inner and Outer Worlds'; Sanjay Kak/Majid Maqbool, 'The Making of *Witness: Kashmir 1986–2016/Nine Photographers*'.

Postmemory: Coined by Marianne Hirsch, 'postmemory' refers to the relationship second or later generations have to traumatic events that they did not personally experience, but that are a part of their personal/collective genealogies. This transmitted 'intergenerational trauma' engenders certain forms of memory that are consolidated and legitimated through narrative expression. Examining the way in which the Holocaust is remembered through certain iconic images at the expense of others, Hirsch proposes postmemory as a productive tension between the past and the present. See Ruth Rosengarten, '*Re-take of Amrita*', in this volume.

Press censorship: Under colonial rule, the growth and popularity of Indian publications that voiced dissent against the British resulted in the often draconian use of censorship through various legislations, including the Press Act of 1910. This was also the case during the **Emergency**, when there was a blanket suppression of press freedom. Today, forms of press censorship are much more complex, with new definitions of what constitutes 'sedition', interwoven social media networks, digital platforms that disseminate hate speech. See, in this volume, Emilia Terracciano, 'Beyond or in Emergency?'; Sanjay Kak/Majid Maqbool, 'The Making of *Witness: Kashmir 1986–2016/Nine Photographers*'; William Mazzarella and Raminder Kaur, 'Between Sedition and Seduction'; Prashant Panjiar/Rahaab Allana, 'Zooming In'; Gemma Scott, 'Putting Women in the Picture'.

Press Information Bureau: Under L.F. Rushbrook Williams, a cell was instituted in 1919 within the Home Department of the Government of India to prepare yearly reports on India for the British parliament. Renamed Central Bureau of Information in 1920, the unit's responsibilities were expanded to providing and overseeing the distribution of correct information on India as well as on issues of public opinion. In 1946, its name was changed to the Press Information Bureau (PIB), and it provided crucial training and employment to many post-Independence photographers. As a nodal agency of the Ministry of Information and Broadcasting, it disseminates public information on various activities of the government. See, in this volume, Emilia Terracciano, 'Beyond or in Emergency?'; Sabeena Gadihoke, 'Journeys into Inner and Outer Worlds'.

Progressive Artists Group: Creative alliance founded in Bombay in 1947 by artists Francis Newton Souza, Sayed Haider Raza, Maqbool Fida Husain, Krishnaji Howlaji Ara, Hari Ambadas Gade and Sadanand Bakre. Sometimes also known as the Bombay

Progressives. Some members were from marginalized backgrounds and were influenced by the Communist Party of India (hence the group's name, inspired by the Progressive Writers' Association). They sought to develop a vocabulary of modern Indian art befitting the international aspirations of the newly independent country. Breaking away from the nationalism of the Bengal School, the artists engaged with formal experimentation. The original group changed when Souza, Raza and Bakre left India in the early 1950s, but the number remained constant as Vasudeo Gaitonde, Mohan Samant and Krishen Khanna became members. While most were painters, Khanna experimented with photography to produce images in an abstract expressionist style. See **Nasreen Mohamedi**. See another entry on **Progressive Artists Group** in Keywords, in *The Vanishing Point: Moving Images After Video*, edited by Rashmi Devi Sawhney, *India Since the 90s*, vol. 3, New Delhi: Tulika Books, p. 339. See, in this volume, Emilia Terracciano, 'Beyond or in Emergency?'; Gemma Scott, 'Putting Women in the Picture'; Diva Gujral, '*Painters with a Camera*'.

Pushpamala N. (b. 1956): Bengaluru-based photo-performance artist who began working with photography, video and performance in the mid-1990s through costumed tableaux and stylized photo-romances featuring her in a variety of roles. Through these re-enactments she offers a postcolonial critique of entrenched stereotypes of gender, race, ethnicity and caste within the fraught ethos of Indian 'modernity'. Major exhibitions include *Phantom Lady or Kismet: A Photoromance* (1998), *Native Women of South India: Manners and Customs* (2002–04), *Paris Autumn* (2006), *The Return of the Phantom Lady (Sinful City)* (2012), *Avega: The Passion* (2013), *The Arrival of Vasco da Gama* (2015). See, in this volume, Parul Dave Mukherji, 'Mimicking Anthropologists'; Suryanandini Narain, 'The Camera Tours the City'; Jodi Throckmorton, 'Photography and Inherited History in India'.

Quit India campaign (1942–44): Political movement launched at the Bombay session of the **Indian National Congress** (above) demanding an end to British rule, following the failure of the Stafford Cripps Mission to propose a timeline for Independence and to secure Indian support for the war. The event at Mumbai's Gowalia Tank, when Congress Socialist leader Aruna Asaf Ali hoisted the Congress flag at the Gowalia Tank Maidan, leading to police firing, was extensively photographed, producing iconic moments of the latter part of the freedom struggle. See, in this volume, Emilia Terracciano, 'Beyond or in Emergency?'.

Rahman, Ram (b. 1955): Contemporary artist, photographer, curator and activist, and one of the founding members of the Safdar Hashmi Memorial Trust (Sahmat), a Delhi-based collective of artists and scholars dedicated to promoting cultural pluralism and secularism in India. His book, *Bioscope: Scenes from an Eventful Life* (Bodhi Art, 2008), features documentary images from thirty years of his practice. See, in this volume, Sabeena Gadihoke, 'Journeys into Inner and Outer Worlds'.

Rai, Raghu (b. 1942): Major photographer and photojournalist, protégé of **Henri Cartier-Bresson**, joined Magnum Photos in 1977 as a young journalist. Known as the 'father of Indian photography', renowned for documentation of major events such as the Liberation War of Bangladesh (1971) and the Bhopal gas tragedy (1984). From 1982 to 1991 Rai was Picture Editor–Visualizer–Photographer at the news magazine *India Today*, considered as having revived photojournalism in the post-**Emergency** period. See, in this volume, Suryanandini Narain, 'The Camera Tours the City'; Sabeena Gadihoke, 'Journeys into Inner and Outer Worlds'; Prashant Panjiar/Rahaab Allana, 'Zooming In'.

Raqs Media Collective: Formed in 1992, Raqs (artists/media practitioners Jeebesh Bagchi, Monica Narula, Shuddhabrata Sengupta) works in the areas of new media, conceptual art, documentary film, photography, critique, theoretical research and curation. Based in Delhi, co-founders of Sarai, the interdisciplinary media research programme of the Centre for the Study of Developing Societies. Curated Yokohama Triennale 2020; exhibited their work at the Venice, Shanghai, Sydney and Istanbul Biennales. See, in this volume, Jodi Throckmorton, 'Photography and Inherited History in India'; Raqs Media Collective/Francesca Ceccherini & Noriko Yamakoshi, 'Centres/Peripheries: Complex Constellations'.

Roy, Kulwant (1914–1984): Photojournalist known for documentation of the Indian freedom struggle. Untrained in the medium, Roy learned on the job at the Lahore studio Gopal Chitter Kuteer. Freelanced in Lahore and eventually founded Associated Press Photos in Delhi in 1943. Three decades of work featured in Aditya Arya and Indivar Kamtekar's book, *History in the Making: The Visual Archives of Kulwant Roy* (Delhi: HarperCollins India, 2010). See Sabeena Gadihoke, 'Journeys into Inner and Outer Worlds', in this volume.

Saith, Sanjeev (b. 1958): Photographer, curator and writer based in New Delhi, known for images of the Himalayas (*A Journey Down the Ganga,* Lustre Press, 1989). His projects include *King, Commoner, Citizen* (2007), an exhibition of images by Prashant Panjiar (see Prashant Panjiar/Rahaab Allana, 'Zooming In') and *Kanu's Gandhi* (2017), a collection of photographs of Mahatma Gandhi by his grandson Kanu. Also see *Happy Goodnight* (self-published, 2011), family portraits shot in the early 2000s, and *A Negative Year* (2019), on 1990s street photography. See, in this volume, Sunil Gupta/Rahaab Allana, 'FotoFest 2018 and Other Curatorial Practices'.

Satyan, T.S. (1923–2009): Renowned photojournalist known for black-and-white photographs of famous personalities, key moments in South Asian history and everyday life in twentieth-century India. Worked for *Deccan Herald* and *Illustrated Weekly of India* before freelancing, including assignments for UNICEF and WHO in the early 1960s. Autobiography titled *Alive and Clicking: A Memoir* (2005), was a first for Indian photojournalists. See, in this volume, Sabeena Gadihoke, 'Journeys into Inner and Outer Worlds'.

Sheikh, Gulammohammed (b. 1937): Renowned painter, poet, art critic and teacher whose works draw from historical visual genealogies (Mughal, Rajasthani, Pahari), and are inspired by Bhakti and Sufi traditions. Iconic figure at the **Faculty of Fine Arts, Maharaja Sayajirao University, Baroda** where he taught art history and painting. Diva Gujral (in '*Painters with a Camera*', this volume) excavates another history of his work as a photographer. Made a short film with a camera borrowed from the **Vision Exchange Workshop**. Also see Parul Dave Mukherji, 'Mimicking Anthropologists', in this volume.

Sher-Gil, Umrao Singh (1870–1954): Key figure in the history of early twentieth-century photography in India. Produced a vast corpus of photographs mostly consisting of self- and family portraits. Largely remembered as the father of painter Amrita Sher-Gil, his oeuvre first received scholarly attention in 2001 through Stuart Hall and Mark Sealy's work on the self-representational practices of non-white artists (*Different: A Historical Context*, 2001). *Re-take of Amrita* (2006) features digital photo-montages based on Umrao Singh's photographs by his grandson, the late **Vivan Sundaram**. See, in this volume, Jodi Throckmorton, 'Photography and Inherited History in India'.

Sheth, Ketaki (b. 1957): Mumbai-based photographer and author known for analogue black-and-white documentary photographs depicting life and labour in urban spaces. Began photographing in the 1980s under the mentorship of **Raghubir Singh**. *Twinspotting* (1995–98) is a series of staged photographs of twins from the diasporic Patel community in the UK and India. *Photo Studio* (2015–18) is her most recent exhibition-cum-photobook and her first in colour. See, in this volume, Suryanandini Narain, 'The Camera Tours the City'; Sabeena Gadihoke, 'Journeys into Inner and Outer Worlds'.

Sikka, Bharat (b. 1973): Photographer whose work explores themes of masculinity, regional identity, inscriptions of nationality and globalization. His latest book is *The Sapper* (Fw: Books, 2022). See, in this volume, Sabeena Gadihoke, 'Journeys into Inner and Outer Worlds'.

Singh, Dayanita (b. 1961): Celebrated photographer, archivist and curator working in cross-media modes, creating sets of work in varied forms, such as books, textual objects and boxes, and inviting the viewer to participate in the unfolding narrative. Productions include *Blue Book* (2009) and *Dream Villa* (2010). Her latest book, *Let's See* (2022), presents her work from the 1980s and early 1990s. See, in this volume, Suryanandini Narain, 'The Camera Tours the City'; Sabeena Gadihoke, 'Journeys into Inner and Outer Worlds'.

Singh, Raghubir (1942–1999): Revered photographer known for his landscapes and documentary style. Worked as a photojournalist for *National Geographic*, *Time*, *New Yorker* and *New York Times*. Known for early use of colour film. *River of Colour: The India of Raghubir Singh* (1998), accompanied a major retrospective of his work at the Art Institute of Chicago. See, in this volume, Suryanandini Narain, 'The Camera Tours the City'; Sabeena Gadihoke, 'Journeys into Inner and Outer Worlds'.

Sundaram, Vivan (1943–2023): Major Indian artist with a career spanning multiple media interests. Early interest in collage forms, focused in the 1980s on painting, and in the 1990s on various media. Made installations, and massive art projects including found material, collaborating with practitioners in theatre, traditional crafts, film and photography. Major focus on still photomontages when he began working on the photographs of his grandfather **Umrao Singh Sher-Gil** and his aunt Amrita Sher-Gil. Ruth Rosengarten says that the photomontages in *Re-Take on Amrita* 'transport the viewer into a glamorous, cosmopolitan, aristocratic-bourgeois world in the first half of the twentieth century: a world nuanced by art and intellect. ... Yet, clearly, they also gain their meaning from a rehearsal of the conventions and tropes of such albums: the studied arrest, the pose, an address to the camera' ('*Re-take of Amrita*', p. 203, in this volume). Later photomontages extensively use urban waste (*Trash*, 2008). A major installation, *Memorial* (1993/2022), is based on a found photograph of a man killed on the streets of Mumbai in 1992, taken by photojournalist Hoshi Jal.

Vernacular mode: Expanded notion of photography that takes into consideration various regional, local, minority or indigenous practices of image-making, and the diverse forms of 'ordinary' photography that may include family albums, images in lockets, scrapbooks, photographic memorials, etc., that have been ignored by dominant critical theory. Can be read as a valid and significant trajectory of self-fashioning and self-representation emerging in the postcolonial context, now embedded in the 'vernacular modernism' found in the arts discourses of many former colonies. See Ruth Rosengarten, '*Re-take of Amrita*'; Diva Gujral, '*Painters with a Camera*'; Jodi Throckmorton, 'Photography and Inherited History in India', in this volume.

Vision Exchange Workshop (VIEW): Workshop set up by painter Akbar Padamsee in 1969 when he was awarded the Nehru Fellowship. Inter-art Vision Exchange Workshop (VIEW) in Bombay promoted cross-media experiments. VIEW functioned till 1971, with participating artists, filmmakers and literary figures including Gieve Patel, **Nasreen Mohamedi**, Nalini Malani, Mani Kaul, Kumar Shahani and **Gulammohammed Sheikh**. See Keywords in *The Vanishing Point: Moving Images After Video*, edited by Rashmi Devi Sawhney, *India Since the 90s*, vol. 3, New Delhi: Tulika Books, 2022, p. 344. See, in this volume, Diva Gujral, '*Painters with a Camera*'.

Vyarawalla, Homai (1913–2012): Known by her pseudonym 'Dalda 13', Homai Vyarawalla was India's first woman photojournalist. She captured the last days of the British in India and the transformation of India into a nation-state from the late 1930s to 1970. *Three Women and a Camera* (1998), a documentary by photo-historian/filmmaker Sabeena Gadihoke, featured her work and that of two other women photographers (**Sheba Chhachhi**, **Dayanita Singh**). Retrospective at the National Gallery of Modern Art in New Delhi, Mumbai and Bengaluru in 2010–11. See, in this volume, Sabeena Gadihoke, 'Journeys into Inner and Outer Worlds'.

NOTES & REFERENCES

Introduction

1 K.K. Nair, *Pratibimba*, catalogue of a photographic exhibition organized by the Ministry of Tourism, Government of India in Moscow as part of the Festival of India in the USSR, January 1987, p. 88.

2 **Editor's note**: See **Festival(s) of India** in Keywords.

3 See also Sanjay Srivastava, 'Urban Spaces, Post-Nationalism and the Making of the Consumer Citizen in India', in Partha Chatterji, Tapati Guha-Thakurta and Boddhisatva Kar, eds, *New Cultural Histories of India*, Oxford University Press, 2014.

4 Chaitanya Sambrani, *Edge of Desire: Recent Art in India*, London: Philip Wilson Publishers, 2005. The catalogue was published in conjunction with the exhibition of the same name showcased in various countries including Australia, the United States, Mexico and India.

5 **Editor's note**: See **Babri Masjid/Ram Janmabhoomi violence** and **Gujarat riots** in Keywords.

6 Saloni Mathur, *India by Design: Colonial History and Cultural Display*, University of California Press, 2007, p. 165.

7 **Editor's note**: **Lalit Kala Akademi**, see Keywords.

8 Art Heritage: Founded in 1977 by Ebrahim and Roshen Alkazi, the Art Heritage gallery is committed to promoting both established and emerging artists. Located in the renowned Triveni Kala Sangam cultural complex in New Delhi, the gallery has held over 600 exhibitions and produced over 450 catalogues celebrating the work of distinguished artists such as F.N. Souza and M.F. Husain as well as new talent. The gallery's publication, *Ebrahim Alkazi: Directing Art*, edited by Parul Dave Mukherji (New Delhi: Art Heritage and Ahmedabad: Mapin Publishing, 2016), documenting Alkazi's lifelong commitment to supporting Indian modern and contemporary art through Art Heritage, was released at the India Art Fair, Delhi in 2016; www.artheritagegallery.com

9 Holland Cotter, 'Art Review: Many Shows, Many Ideas', *New York Times*, 26 December 1997; https://www.nytimes.com/1997/12/26/arts/art-review-many-shows-and-many-indias.html, accessed 2 February 2020.

10 **Editor's note**: *Images of India*, photography exhibition held at the Jehangir Art Gallery, Bombay, in February 1960, inspired by *The Family of Man* (1955), curated by Edward Steichen at the Museum of Modern Art, New York and shown at the Jehangir Art Gallery, Bombay in 1956. See note 23 in Sabeena Gadihoke, 'Journeys into Inner and Outer Worlds', and note 31 in Diva Gujral, '*Painters with a Camera*'.

11 **Editor's note**: Pictorialism: See note 31 in Emilia Terracciano, 'Beyond or in Emergency?', and note 56 in Diva Gujral, '*Painters with a Camera*'.

12 See *MARG: Photography as an Art Form*, vol. 14, no.1, December 1960.

13 **Editor's note**: **Sunil Janah**: see Keywords. R.J. Chinwalla: Indian photojournalist who had a column in the *Times of India* in the 1950s–60s; contributor to *MARG's* special issue, *Photography as an Art Form* (December 1960). Richard Lannoy (1928–2016): British photographer and writer known for research on India. Jitendra Arya (1931–2011): Chief Photo-editor at *The Times of India* (1960–85); known as a master of portraiture, his work was extensively published in *Filmfare*, *Femina* and *The Illustrated Weekly of India*.

14 For instance, see Gemma Scott, 'Photography and the Presentations of Women during the Emergency in India, 1975–77', Newsletter: Women I Photography II, The Alkazi Foundation for the Arts, 2021; https://alkazifoundation.org/photography-and-representations-of-women-during-the-emergency-in-india-1975-1977/, accessed 2 June 2022. See, in this volume, Gemma Scott, 'Putting Women in the Picture'. Also see PIX: *Citizen Issue*, 2019; http://www.enterpix.in/issue/citizen-issue/

15 **Editor's note**: *Vrishchik*, see note 17 in Diva Gujral, '*Painters with a Camera*'.

16 This subject is explored in the exhibition *Crafting Subversion: DIY and Decolonial Print*, The Brunei Gallery, School of Oriental and African Studies, University of London, 28 April–3 September 2022, curated by Pragya Dhital; https://www.soas.ac.uk/about/event/craftingsubversiondiy-and-decolonial-print. For more on literary magazines, see Asia Art Archive, https://aaa.org.hk/en/collections/search/archive/gulammohammed-sheikh-archive-vrishchik; Scribd, https://www.scribd.com/document/366899839/damn-you-a-magazine-of-the-arts-all-6-issues-of-the-1967-self-published-poetry-mag-run-by-poet-Arvind-Krishna-Mehrotra. **Editor's note**: Arvind Krishna Mehrotra, renowned poet and translator, makes a mention of Indian 'little magazines' in *The Book of Indian Essays: Two Hundred Years of Indian Prose* (Black Kite, 2020). One such was *damn you*, started by Mehrotra with Amit Rai and Alok Rai, grandsons of litterateur Munshi Premchand. See http://permanent-black.blogspot.com/2020/12/the-arvind-krishna-mehrotra-interview.html; and https://scroll.in/article/1055197/when-we-speak-of-the-secular-in-india-these-days-poetry-literature-cinema-do-not-come-into-play

17 **Editor's note**: **Faculty of Fine Arts, Maharaja Sayajirao University, Baroda** and **Emergency**: See Keywords. Indian Radical Painters and Sculptors Association: Commonly known as the Kerala Radicals, a group of artists who came together in Baroda, led by sculptor K.P. Krishnakumar. See Anita Dube, 'Questions and Dialogue', in *The Hunger of the Republic: Our Present in Retrospect* , edited by Ashish Rajadhyaksha, *India Since the 90s*, vol. 1, New Delhi: Tulika Books, 2021, pp. 357–65.

18 **Editor's note**: **Emergency** and **Indira Gandhi**: See Keywords.

19 The blueprint for establishing the National Museum in Delhi was prepared by the Maurice Gwyer Committee in May 1946. *Exhibition of Indian Art*, consisting of selected artefacts from various museums of India, was organized by the Royal Academy, London with the cooperation of Government of India and Britain, on display in the galleries of Burlington House, London in 1947–48. The same collection was displayed at the Rashtrapati Bhavan (the President's residence), New Delhi, in 1949. This event proved responsible for the creation of the National Museum.

20 **Editor's note**: **Festival of India**: See Keywords.

21 Programming Leaflet, *Festival of India*, 1982. Reference material available at The Photographers' Gallery, London. Also see the report of the 1982 exhibition prepared by the Visual Arts Committee, including Geeta Kapur, Akbar Padamsee and Richard Bartholomew. Two exhibitions were mounted at the Royal Academy of House, Burlington House, London: *The Gesture and Motif* and *Stories, Situations*; https://aaa.org.hk/en/collections/search/archive/k-contemporary-indian-art-an-exhibition-of-the-festival-of-india-london-1982/object/contemporary-indian-art-the-royal-academy-of-arts-london-festival-of-india-1982-report, accessed 2 February 2020.

22 See Ken Barrett and Suresh Sharma, eds, *The Indian Experience,* Hong Kong: Thomson Press, 1982.

23 **Editor's note**: Raja Deen Dayal, aka **Lala Deen Dayal**: See Keywords.

24 *Lala Deen Dayal: The Eminent Photographer 1844–1910*, catalogue of an exhibition presented by the London Borough of Camden in association with Air India as part of Festival of India, United Kingdom, 1982.

25 For further reading, see Yaduendra Sahai, *Maharaja Sawai Ram Singh II of Jaipur: The Photographer Prince*, Jaipur: Dr. Durga Sahai Foundation, 1996. Also see Giles Tillotson and Mrinalini Venkateswaran, eds, *Painting & Photography at the Jaipur Court*, New Delhi: Niyogi Books, 2016.

26 Ebrahim Alkazi and David Elliott, eds, *India, Myth and Reality: Aspects of Modern Indian Art*, Oxford: Museum of Modern Art, 1982.

27 Press Release, *Festival of India*, 1982. Reference material available at The Photographers' Gallery, London. **Editor's note**: Also see Sunil Gupta/Rahaab Allana, 'FotoFest 2018 and Other Curatorial Practices'.

28 **Editor's note**: Mani Kaul (1944–2011), major avant-garde filmmaker. Govind Nihalani (b. 1940), cinematographer and film director. R.K. Laxman (1921–2015), cartoonist best known for his daily cartoon strip 'You Said It', started in 1951 in *The Times of India*. Tyeb Mehta (1925–2009), major painter. T.S. Nagarajan, photojournalist; see note 22 in Sabeena Gadihoke, 'Journeys into Inner and Outer Worlds'.

29 **Editor's note**: Nissar Allana: Stage and lighting designer, and director of a production company, Theatre & Television Associates. Saryu Doshi: Art historian and curator, former director of the National Gallery of Modern Art, Mumbai.

30 'Heritage: Pathways to Eternity' included work by artists Avinash Pasricha, Sandeep Shankar, R.R. Bhardwaj and Satish Sharma; 'Life Cycle: Moving Towards Enlightenment' featured Swapan Parekh, Jyoti Bhatt, **T.S. Satyan** and **Pablo Bartholomew**; 'Rural: Images of Change' featured **Dayanita Singh**, **Madan Mahatta**, Kishor Parekh and his son Manu Parekh; 'Birth of a Nation, 20th Century' featured Aman Nath and Francis Wacziarg; and 'Urban: A Tradition in Transition' included now-iconic work by **Mitter Bedi** and Bhagwan Singh, Karan Kapoor, N. Thyagarajan, Muthuraman, Dilip Chatterjee, **S. Paul**, Ashok Dilwali and Jagdish Agarwal. **Editor's note**: For names in bold, see Keywords.

31 **Editor's note**: **T.S. Satyan**, **Raghu Rai**: See Keywords.

32 Sankho Chaudhuri, Preface, *First Indian Biennale of Photography*, exhibition catalogue, New Delhi: Lalit Kala Akademi, 1989.

33 From the mid-1850s onwards the Photographic Society established in each Presidency (Bombay, Calcutta and Madras) mounted exhibits of photographic works by resourceful royal 'native' patrons who were themselves enthusiastic and skilled lensmen, and had created their own private circuits of image dissemination.

34 **Editor's note**: Art Triennale (est. 1968), run by **Lalit Kala Akademi.** Started with internationalist ambitions and initially defined by **Mulk Raj Anand**'s approach, it ran into controversies. **Vivan Sundaram** led a rebel group who called themselves 'Six Who Declined to Show at the Triennale' in 1978.

35 See Nancy Adajania, 'Globalism before Globalization: The Ambivalent Fate of Triennale India', in Rahaab Allana, ed., *Unframed: Discovering Image Practices in South Asia*, New Delhi: HarperCollins Publishers India and The Alkazi Foundation for the Arts, 2023, pp. 555–77.

36 **Editor's note**: *Artists Alert:* Exhibition and public auction of painting, sculpture, graphics and photography organized by the Safdar Hashmi Memorial Trust (Sahmat), 12–15 April 1989.

37 **Editor's note**: Safdar Hashmi (1954–1989): Activist and playwright, best known for his work with street theatre in India. Founder member of the Jana Natya Manch in 1973, inspired by the **Indian People's Theatre Association (IPTA)**.

38 **Editor's note**: Safdar Hashmi Memorial Trust (Sahmat): Independent arts organization founded in the wake of the murderous assault on Hashmi on 1 January 1989, when writers, painters, scholars, poets, architects, photographers, designers, cultural activists and media persons came together to support a space for secular art.

39 For a photograph of Hashmi performing a street play, see Arushi Vats, 'The Sahmat Collective: Art and Activism in India since 1989', ASAP (Alternative South Asian Photography), 18 January 2021, https://asapconnect.in/post/24/singleevents/the-sahmat-collective; Khushmi Mehta, 'Street-theatre as a Form of Protest: Safdar Hashmi and JANAM', MAP Academy, 29 November 2021, https://mapacademy.io/street-theatre-as-a-form-of-protest-safdar-hashmi-and-janam/. For more information, see sahmat.in. Also see the script of Jana Natya Manch's famous play, *Halla Bol!*, in *Improvised Futures: Encountering the Body in Performance*, edited by Ranjana Dave, *India Since the 90s*, vol. 2, New Delhi: Tulika Books, 2021, pp. 73–92.

40 **Editor's note**: Krishen Khanna (b. 1925): Painter, associated with the **Progressive Artists Group**. Manjit Bawa (1941–2008): Painter with a distinctive style often using mythological themes. **Ram Rahman**: See Keywords. Madan Gopal Singh (b. 1950): Composer, singer, film theorist. **Vivan Sundaram**: See Keywords.

41 *Artists Alert*, exhibition catalogue, New Delhi: Safdar Hashmi Memorial Trust, 1989. Participants included Raghavendra Rao from *The Indian Express*, Jyoti Bhatt, Tejbir Singh, Prashant Panjiar, Parthiv Shah, Raghubir Singh, Sooni Taraporevala, Satish Sharma and Pushpamala N.

42 Geeta Kapur, introductory essay, ibid.

43 Jessica Moss and Ram Rahman, eds, *The SAHMAT Collective: Art and Activism in India since 1989,* Chicago: Smart Museum of Art, The University of Chicago, pp. 76–81. This catalogue accompanied an exhibition of the same name at the University of Chicago's Smart Museum of Art, 14 February–9 June 2013.

44 Ibid., p. 60.

45 **Editor's note**: **Pushpamala N.**: See Keywords. Orijit Sen (b. 1963): Graphic artist and designer, author of *River of Stories* (1994), considered India's first graphic novel. Mukesh Parpiani: Photojournalist,

formerly photo editor of *The Daily*, *The Indian Express* and *Mid-day*, later worked on archives and exhibitions at the Piramal Art Gallery, National Centre for Performing Arts.

46 **Editor's note**: Praveen Jain: Renowned photojournalist, photo editor of *The Indian Express*.

47 See the book version of the exhibition, https://issuu.com/sahmat-india/docs/hum_sab_ayodhya_book_dec_2012_pdf_jpeg. Also see Moss and Rahman, eds, *The SAHMAT Collective*, pp. 110–22. **Editor's note**: *Hum Sab Ayodhya* (Hindi: 'All of Us Are Ayodhya'), exhibition in 1993 of photographs, paintings, drawings and text in the context of the destruction of the **Babri Masjid** (see Keywords). First exhibited at Nehru Memorial Museum and Library, New Delhi, where it was forcibly taken down by the police on orders of the Lieutenant Governor of Delhi. Paramjit Singh (b. 1935): Painter associated with hyper-real images usually drawn from nature. Samar Singh Jodha: Photographer and installation artist, who has often worked with marginal communities.

48 Moss and Rahman, eds, *The SAHMAT Collective*, pp. 128–41. **Editor's note**: *Tribute to Gandhi* (1994–95), a year-long series of events organized by Sahmat on the 125th anniversary of Mahatma Gandhi's birth. Habib Rahman (1915–1995): Well-known architect. *Manas Bana*: Exhibition organized by Sahmat as part of Gandhi's 125th birth anniversary celebrations.

49 Satish Sharma, 'In Search of an Identity', *2nd Indian Biennale of Creative Photography*, exhibition catalogue, New Delhi: Lalit Kala Akademi, 1993.

50 Artists in the 'General/Competitive' category included Ravi Agarwal (see notes 39 and 44 in Sabeena Gadihoke, 'Journeys into Inner and Outer Worlds' in this volume), Sharad Apte, Veeresh Babu, Pavan Mahatta and Partha Mitra, among others, while artists in the 'Invited' category included Ipshita Barua, Achinto Bhadra, Pradeep Dasgupta, Ashim Ghosh, T. Kashinath, Sudhir Kasliwal, Dinesh Kumar, **Madan Mahatta**, Paresh Maity, Asit Poddar, **Sanjeev Saith**, Parthiv Shah and O.P. Sharma. In contrast to the large exhibitions mentioned earlier in this essay, the main selectors/jurors were Avinash Pasricha and **S. Paul**, experienced professional photographers from the field of journalism. For names in bold, see Keywords.

51 The Biennale showcased solarizations (Rajan Babu), alternative printing techniques (Asit Ray), fashion (Rohit Chawla, Syed Rafique), performance, photojournalism, montage (Asit Mandal, Madhu Sarkar), wildlife and colour photography, industrial photography (S. Kumar), and even images of nudes (Asit Poddar, known through his association with Satyajit Ray).

52 **Editor's note**: Satish Sharma: See note 16 in Suryanandini Narain, 'The Camera Tours the City'.

53 B.P. Kamboj, 'Introduction', *2nd Indian Biennale of Creative Photography*, exhibition catalogue, New Delhi: Lalit Kala Akademi, 1993. Kamboj was the secretary of the Lalit Kala Akademi, New Delhi at the time.

54 **Editor's note**: **Homai Vyarawalla**: See Keywords.

55 Satish Sharma, 'In Search of an Identity', *2nd Indian Biennale of Creative Photography*.

56 Practitioners showing work via salon and club circuits included: Surendra Patel, who would be president of the India International Photographic Council and chair of the Colour Division, Federation of India Photography; Jaiteg Singh Anant, who organized the first Photo Salon in Chandigarh and worked as a photographer for the Department of Culture and Photography in Chandigarh; Bandi Rajan Babu, an honorary fellow of the Andhra Pradesh State Akademi of Photography and recipient of awards by the India International Photographic Council, New Delhi; Kasinath Basu, later winner of a Lalit Kala Akademi photography award; Samar Mondal, a graduate of the Sir J.J. School of Art, Bombay and member of the Photographic Society of India, who later became a photographer at Rashtrapati Bhavan, and taught at the Indian Institute of Photography and the Indian Photo Academy; Jayanta Saha, who taught photography at the Ramakrishna Mission; Madhu Sarkar, who founded the National Academy of Photography in Calcutta; Gautam Sen, who later worked for the photo unit of the Indian Museum; Shiv Narayan Joshi, who later founded the Gurukul School of Photographic Art, Jodhpur; and the list goes on. See Anasuya Basu, 'Calcutta through the lens of a photographer', *The Telegraph*, 1 September 2019; Bishali Khati, 'Understanding the Beauty of Nature', *The Statesman*, 16 February 2016; and Dinesh Maneer's interview with photographer Shiv Narayan Joshi, https://dineshmaneer.com/the-incredible-rajasthani-photographer-shivji-joshi/, accessed 3 February 2020.

57 **Editor's note**: **Babri Masjid**: See Keywords.

58 Ram Rahman, 'Photography: A Sharper Focus', in *Bioscope: Scenes from an Eventful Life,* exhibition catalogue, New Delhi: Bodhi Art, 2008, pp. 191–94. **Editor's note**: Mahatta, Delhi Photo Studio, Kinsey Brothers: among the earliest and popular photo studios that emerged in New Delhi during the 1930s–40s.

59 **Editor's note**: **Bengal Famine**, **Henri Cartier-Bresson**, **Margaret Bourke-White** and **Sunil Janah**: See Keywords.

60 **Editor's note**: **Homai Vyarawalla**, Prem Prakash, Baldev Kapoor, R. Satakopan, P.N. Sharma, Ram Dhamija, **Raghubir Singh** and **Kulwant Roy**: For names in bold, see Keywords. *The Illustrated Weekly of India*: See note 3 in Prashant Panjiar/Rahaab Allana, 'Zooming In'.

61 Ram Rahman, 'Photography: A Sharper Focus'. **Editor's note**: Kishor Parekh, see note 10 in Suryanandini Narain, 'The Camera Tours the City'; **S. Paul**, **Raghu Rai**, see Keywords; Prashant Panjiar, see Prashant Panjiar/Rahaab Allana, 'Zooming in'; Pramod Pushkarna, see note 9 in Prashant Panjiar/Rahaab Allana, 'Zooming In'.

62 Francesco Zanot, Walter Guadagnini and Urs Stahel, *Photography: From the Press to the Museum: 1941–80*, Milan: Skira, 2014.

63 **Editor's note**: **Ketaki Sheth**, **Dayanita Singh**: See Keywords. Sunil Gupta: See Sunil Gupta/Rahaab Allana, 'FotoFest 2018 and Other Curatorial Practices'. Mary Ellen Mark: See note 18 in Suryanandini Narain, 'The Camera Tours the City' and note 18 in Sabeena Gadihoke, 'Journeys into Inner and Outer Worlds'.

64 **Editor's note**: See Prashant Panjiar/Rahaab Allana, 'Zooming In'.

65 Nadja-Christina Schneider, 'More Than a Belated Gutenberg Age: Daily Newspapers in India, an Overview of the Print Media Development since the 1980s, Key Issues and Current Perspectives', *Global Media Journal* (German edition), vol. 3, no. 2, 2013.

66 Ibid., p. 18.

67 **Editor's note**: **Gujarat Riots 2002**: See Keywords. For Kargil war, see note 18 in Prashant Panjiar/Rahaab Allana, 'Zooming In'.

68 See *India: A Celebration of Independence, 1947 to 1997*, New York: Aperture, 1997. The publication constitutes an unprecedented gathering of the most significant photographs to be made in India over the past five decades. It was the culmination of a quest to capture the country's essence in visual terms, and to depict the unique attachment binding both native-born and foreign artists to India for their lifetimes.

69 Victor Anant, 'The Sacred and the Secular', *India: A Celebration of Independence, 1947 to 1997*, New York, p. 39.

70 The exhibition here also included a compelling array of material – views of cosmopolitan life in Mumbai (Pamela Singh); labour in Bihar and Mumbai (Sebastião Salgado); trans-sexualism, and upper- middle-class family portraits (Dayanita Singh); industrial complexes (Charles Lindsay); Calcutta (Rosalind Solomon); rural child marriage, and the families of deemed 'terrorists' of Operation Bluestar (Swapan Parekh); Mandal Commission violence in Delhi (Robert Nickelsberg). Also featured were works by William Gedney, Raghu Rai, Mary Ellen Mark, Prashant Panjiar and Thomas Kelly. A notable omission was photographer Raghubir Singh, and several artists now recall how the selection process by the then editor Michael Hoffman was quite pre-meditated.

71 For further reading, see the exhibition catalogues of *Out of India: Contemporary Art of the South Asian Diaspora*, Queens Museum of Art, New York, 9 December 1997–22 March 1998, and *Women Artists of India: A Celebration of Independence*, Mills College Art Gallery, Oakland, 10 September–26 October 1997. *Out of India* was curated by Jane Farver, and *Women Artists of India* by Mary-Ann Lutzker. Also see Holland Cotter, 'Art Review: Many Shows, Many Ideas'.

72 **Editor's note**: Ayisha Abraham's (b. 1963) work includes installations, short digital films and artist's books. See her exhibition '... Looks the Other Way', New Delhi, 1998; www.ayishabraham.wordpress.com.

73 **Editor's note**: Zarina Bhimji (b. 1963) works across a wide range of media including installation, photography, film and sound. She was nominated for the Turner Prize in 2007.

74 **Editor's note**: Mohini Chandra's (b. 1964) work deals with articulations of identity and globalized spaces, and the role of the photographic in relation to memory and migration; www.mohinichandra.com

75 **Editor's note**: Poulomi Desai (b. 1966), multimedia artist and activist based in the UK. In 2010, she started Usurp Art gallery and studios, the first and only artist-led creative space in the London Borough of Harrow.

76 **Editor's note**: Shahzia Sikander (b. 1969), Pakistani artist working in drawing, painting, printmaking, animation, installation, performance and video. Known for returning to the traditional miniature form and reinterpreting themes of romance within contemporary political frames.

77 **Editor's note**: **Pushpamala N.**: See Keywords.

78 **Editor's note**: Anita Dube (b. 1958): Artist and curator, trained as an art historian, associated with the Indian Radical Painters and Sculptors Association (see note 17 above).

79 **Editor's note**: Sonia Khurana: See note 36 in Suryanandini Narain, 'The Camera Tours the City'.

80 **Editor's note**: Naveen Kishore's *Performing the Goddess: The Chapal Bhaduri Story* (1999) was a documentary and video installation about an actor who played female characters in *jatra* (Bengali folk theatre).

81 William Mazzarella and Raminder Kaur, 'Between Sedition and Seduction: Thinking Censorship in South Asia', in Raminder Kaur and William Mazzarella, eds, *Censorship in South Asia: Cultural Regulation from Sedition to Seduction*, Indiana University Press, 2009, p. 29; also in this volume.

82 **Editor's note**: **Sheba Chhachhi**: See Keywords.

83 *Women of the Cloth: Photographic Conversations*, catalogue of solo exhibition by Sheba Chhachhi, New Delhi: Nature Morte, 2007. The catalogue comprises photographs from ten years of the artist's work with women ascetics.

84 Personal communication with Sheba Chhachhi, 23 March 2020. **Editor's note**: See image on p. 77 of this volume.

85 Diva Gujral, '*Painters with a Camera* (1968/69): In Search of an Indian Photography Exhibition', *Object*, vol. 20, 2019, p. 49; also in this volume. Also see Anisha Baid, 'Magic of Coincidence: Subcontinental Flows in Photography – In Conversation with Diva Gujral', PIX online; http://www.enterpix.in/pix-post/magic-of-coincidence-subcontinental-flows-in-photography-in-conversation-with-diva-gujral

86 Diva Gujral, '*Painters with a Camera* (1968/69)'.

87 **Editor's note**: **Faculty of Fine Arts, Maharaja Sayajirao University, Baroda**: See Keywords.

88 See *Mastering the Lens: Before and After Cartier-Bresson in Pondicherry*, Mapin Publishing and The Alkazi Collection of Photography, supported by the Embassy of France in India and Alliance Française de Delhi, 2012. Also see https://incarnateword.in/documents/last-photographs-of-sri-aurobindo

89 The first Pondicherry Salon of Photography, conducted according to the recommendations and approval of the Photographic Society of America and the International Federation of Photographic Art, opened to the public on 15 August 1955 (Independence Day).

90 **Editor's note**: **Raqs Media Collective**: See Keywords.

91 For instance, the 2nd International Asian-European Art Biennale, Ankara 1988 (painting); 4th Asian Art Biennale, Dacca 1989 (painting and sculpture); 3rd Biennale, Havana 1989 (painting and sculpture); 3rd International Asian-European Art Biennial, Ankara 1990 (painting, sculpture, graphic arts); 6th Asian Art Biennale, Dacca 1993 (painting), etc.

92 **Editor's note**: Dilli Haat (est. 1994) is a ticketed open-air market, food plaza and craft bazaar run by the Delhi Tourism and Transportation Development Corporation.

93 Saloni Mathur, *India by Design*, p. 168.

94 Intellectuals included art historians and writers Geeta Kapur, Gayatri Sinha, Yashodhara Dalmia, Partha Mitter, Tapati Guha-Thakurta, Parul Dave-Mukherji, Vidya Dehejia, Kavita Singh and others.

95 Art Heritage, see note 8 above. Sepia International (1995–2006): A commercial art gallery focused on contemporary photography.

96 **Mitter Bedi**, Arun Kumar Mukherjee, Yog Joy, **Mulk Raj Anand**, North India Accredited Press Photographers Association. **Editor's note**: For names in bold, see Keywords.

97 **Editor's note**: India International Photographic Council: International photography organization established in 1983 in New Delhi.

98 See Shailaja Tripathi, 'Lens and the man', *The Hindu*, 27 September 2013; https://www.thehindu.com/features/friday-review/art/lens-and-the-man/article5175522.ece, accessed 2 February 2020. Also K.B. Goel, 'The Hidden Text in Photography', *O.P. Sharma Photographs*, exhibition catalogue, Art Heritage, 1998–99, pp. 22–24.

99 **Editor's note**: Pamela Singh (b. 1961): Photographer and beauty queen, works with self-portraiture.

100 Peter Nagy, 'A Compelling Narrative', *Pamela Singh Photographs*, exhibition catalogue, Art Heritage, 1998–99, pp. 109–10.

101 **Editor's note**: **Ketaki Sheth**, **Raghubir Singh**: See Keywords. Sooni Taraporevala: See note 11 in Sabeena Gadihoke, 'Journeys into Inner and Outer Worlds'.

102 **Editor's note**: **Sanjeev Saith**: See Keywords.

103 Sanjeev Saith, 'Different Lives: Photographs 1992–93', exhibition catalogue, Art Heritage, 1993–94, pp. 89–90.

104 K.G. Subramanyan, 'Jyoti Bhatt: Photographer, Conserving a Precious Heritage', exhibition catalogue, Art Heritage, 1994–95, pp. 105–06.

105 **Editor's note**: **Vivan Sundaram**, **Umrao Singh Sher-Gil**: See Keywords. Amrita Sher-Gil: See note 30 in Jodi Throckmorton, 'Photography and Inherited History in India'.

106 For further reading, see Vivan Sundaram, *Umrao Singh Sher-Gil: His Misery and His Manuscript*, New Delhi: Photoink, 2008. Also see Ruth Rosengarten, *Vivan Sundaram Is Not a Photographer: The Photographic Works of Vivan Sundaram*, New Delhi: Tulika Books, 2018.

107 **Editor's note**: Navroze Contractor (1944–2023): Cinematographer and photographer, major figure in India's New Cinema movement, associated with the feminist collective Yugantar.

108 **Editor's note**: Akbar Padamsee's experiments with photography: **Vision Exchange Workshop** in Keywords.

109 *Stone Column Enclosing the Gaze* (1992): This work belongs to the series *Collaboration/Combines*. For an image of the work, see https://aaa.org.hk/tc/collections/search/archive/geeta-kapur-and-vivan-sundaram-archive-collaboration-combines-1992/archive/geeta-kapur-and-vivan-sundaram-archive-collaboration-combines-1992/sort/title-desc/object/untitled-stone-column-enclosing-the-gaze-10118; and https://www.icp.org/interviews/vivan-sundaram

110 See *Re-take of Amrita*, Sepia International and The Alkazi Collection, 2006, published in conjunction with the exhibition *Vivan Sundaram: Re-take of Amrita*, 25 May–28 July 2006, New York.

111 *Kashmir: A Passage in Time* (2005), installed for the Ministry of Information and Broadcasting, Government of India at the Indira Gandhi National Centre for the Arts, New Delhi, depicted 50 years of Kashmir's social history.

112 *Woman/Goddess* (1998–2001), curated by Gayatri Sinha and supported by a series of gender-related films, seminars, performances, etc., was exhibited in Delhi, Bangalore, Chennai, Kolkata and New York.

113 *Middle Age Spread: Imaging India 1947–2004*, curated by Gayatri Sinha, exhibited at the National Museum, New Delhi (28 July–18 August 2004). It featured works by **Dayanita Singh**, **Henri Cartier-Bresson**, **Ketaki Sheth**, Kishor Parekh, **Raghu Rai**, Rajesh Vora, **Ram Rahman**, Romesh Dutt Chopra, **S. Paul**, **Sheba Chhachhi** and Swapan Parekh. **Editor's note**: For names in bold, see Keywords.

114 **Editor's note**: Tasveer (est. 2006, now closed): Organization committed to promoting contemporary photography in travelling shows in Bangalore, Delhi, Kolkata, Mumbai and Ahmedabad. Photoink (est. 2001 by Devika Daulet-Singh): Photo agency and publication design studio and photography gallery in Delhi.

115 **Editor's note**: **Deen Dayal, Raghubir Singh**, **Raghu Rai**, **Dayanita Singh**: See Keywords. Gauri Gill: See 'On Seeing' in this volume. Prabuddha Dasgupta (1956–2012): Self-taught photographer, known for controversial collection of portraits and nudes of urban Indian women titled *Women* (1996).

116 Sanjukta Sunderason, 'Freedom by Other Means: Art as Archives of Decolonization', Aditi Chandra and Sanjukta Sunderason, eds, 'Living Archives': *Third Text*, May 2023; https://www.thirdtext.org/livingarchives-sunderason

117 **Editor's note**: Bandung Conference (April 1955): Postcolonial Afro–Asian Conference attended by twenty-nine newly independent nations in Indonesia, representing 54 per cent of the world's population.

118 **Editor's note**: Chittaprosad Bhattacharya (1915–1978): Communist artist and cartoonist working with water colour and printmaking. The publication *Hungry Bengal* was about the **Bengal Famine (1943)**.

119 See Saloni Mathur, 'Ends and Means: A Conversation with Geeta Kapur', *October*, vol. 171, Winter 2020, pp. 115–38.

120 Ibid.

121 Anoli Perera, 'Theertha: A Journey by a Collective of Restless Artists', Asia Art Archive; https://aaa.org.hk/en/like-a-fever/like-a-fever/theertha-a-journey-by-a-collective-of-restless-artists, accessed 3 February 2020. Also see Anoli Perera, 'Collectivism in Contemporary Sri Lankan Art: The History of an Unusual Case of Artists', in Sasanka Perera and Dev Nath Pathak, eds, *Intersections of Contemporary Art, Anthropology and Art History in South Asia: Decoding Visual Worlds*, Palgrave Macmillan and Cham (Switzerland), 2019.

122 **Editor's note**: Stephen Champion: London-based photographer and author known for his work on Sri Lanka in the late 1980s–early 1990s.

123 **Editor's note**: Dominic Sansoni (b. 1956): Sri Lankan art collector/gallerist and photographer whose photographs have appeared in *Time*, *Newsweek*, *Asiaweek* and *Meridiani*. Recent projects focus on the recording of vernacular architecture in south India, and the documentation of festivals and 'Sacred Space' in Sri Lanka. The Harold Peiris Gallery was opened in 2000 to celebrate the 100th birth anniversary of Lionel Wendt. The gallery is situated at the Lionel Wendt Centre for the Arts, a major art hub in Sri Lanka. See www.lionelwendt.org for more.

124 Interview with Sangeeta Thapa, Liverpool John Moores University, https://www.ljmu.ac.uk/-/media/files/ljmu/microsites/qualitative-analysis-in-action-nepal-project/art/interview_with_sangeeta_thapa.pdf, accessed 3 February 2020. Also see Christian Schicklgruber and Swosti Rajbhandari Kayastha, eds, *Nepal Art Now*, Weltmuseum Wien, 2019.

125 Kiran Man Chitrakar: Kathmandu-based photographer whose lineage personifies the history of Nepalese photography with three generations involved. His grandfather, Dirgha Man Chitrakar (1877–1951), was the royal painter and first court photographer. And his father, Ganesh Man Chitrakar (1916–1985), the royal painter and photographer, founded the first photography lab in Nepal – Ganesh Photo Lab. Accompanying the royals, Ranas and the ministers on their foreign visits, the Chitrakars captured some of the most momentous events of the country. Also see catalogue for the exhibition *Capturing a Legacy, Four Generations of Nepalese Photographers*, East-West Center Gallery, Honolulu, 30 September–6 January 2019.

126 **Editor's note**: Philip Blenkinsop, first Western photographer to document Nepal's Maoist guerrilla insurgency and its effects on the people of Nepal. His photographic work is centred around atrocities in Laos, Nepal and Burma, amongst others.

127 'Aye Ko: From Silence Is Golden', *DVD Magazine*, vol. 1, Aura Mekong Art Project, https://auraart-project.com/en/artists/aye-ko-from-silence-is-golden-dvd-magazine-vol-1/, accessed 1 February 2020. Also Ellen Pearlman, 'An Artist-Run Nonprofit Helps Open Up Myanmar to Contemporary Art', *Hyperallergic,* 1 September 2017, https://hyperallergic.com/384403/myanmar-contemporary-art-new-zero/, accessed 3 February 2020.

128 **Editor's note**: **Shahidul Alam**: See Keywords. Rahnuma Ahmed: Author and columnist, and Alam's partner. Drik Picture Library (est. 1989): Independent Bangladeshi media organization, provides diverse multimedia services for advocacy and awareness campaigns.

129 **Editor's note**: Manzoor Alam Beg (1931–1998): Considered father of the photography movement in Bangladesh; founded the Beg Art Institute of Photography in the 1960s, the first of its kind in Bangladesh. Bijon Sarkar (1935–2012): Pioneering Bangladeshi photographer; a founding member of the Bangladesh Photographic Society (BPS) and later its president in the 1990s. Jahangir Kabir (1986–1991): Bangladeshi politician and journalist. Naib Uddin Ahmed (1925–2009): Bangladeshi photographer best known for his work during the Bangladesh Liberation War. Mohammad Ali Salim (b. 1959): First recipient of the AFIAP award (Artist Fédération Internationale de l'Art Photographique) in Bangladesh, 1987. Shafiqul Alam Kiron: First Bangladeshi photographer to receive the World Press Photo award in 1998 and 2000 for his work on acid survivors. Rashid Un Nabi: Bangladeshi photographer who received Excellence (EFIAP) from International Federation of Photographic art, Luxembourg in 1996.

130 Kaamil Ahmed, 'Shifting the Lens: Shahidul Alam's Radical Ways of Seeing Bangladesh', *The Caravan*, 6 December 2018; https://caravanmagazine.in/media/shahidul-alam-bangladesh-ways-of-seeing

131 **Editor's note**: Pathshala (est. 1998): Started as an institute of photography with particular emphasis on photojournalism. Became an institute for visual storytelling in 2010 with a new department of broadcast and multimedia. Now called Pathshala South Asian Media Institute.

132 **Editor's note**: Chobi Mela (est. 2000): International photography biennale widely viewed as Asia's largest photography festival.

133 Rashmi Sawhney and Lucia King, 'Artists' Moving Image: South Asian Trajectories', *Moving Image Review and Arts Journal*, vol. 7, no. 2, July 2018, pp. 191–201.

134 **Editor's note**: Iftikhar Dadi: Professor in art history at Cornell University, author of several books (more recently, *Lahore Cinema: Between Realism and Fable*, 2022), visual artist and photographer.

135 See Iftikhar Dadi and Hammad Nasar, eds, *Lines of Control: Partition as a Productive Space,* London: Green Cardamom and Ithaca: Herbert F. Johnson Museum of Art, 2012. This catalogue accompanies an exhibition of the same name presented at the Herbert F. Johnson Museum of Art, New York, 21 January–1 April 2012, and the Nasher Museum of Art, Duke University, Durham, 19 September 2013–2 February 2014. **Editor's note**: Shahzia Sikander: See note 76 above.

136 Iftikhar Dadi, 'BioScopic and Screen Studies of Pakistan and of Contemporary Art', *BioScope: South Asian Screen Studies*, vol. 1, no. 1, 2010, pp. 11–15.

137 **Editor's note**: Huma Mulji (b. 1970): Pakistani artist known mainly for sculptural installation, also works with photography, collage and drawing. Rashid Rana (b. 1968): Pakistani artist trained as painter, now works in complex technologically driven collages using photography and video performance.

138 **Editor's note**: Yash Raj Films (est. 1970): One of India's most high-profile film studios, started by filmmaker Yash Chopra. Known for several of Hindi cinema's biggest blockbusters. Established as a corporation in 2005, it went global in 2011 with an office in Los Angeles and was publicly listed in 2013.

139 See, in this volume, William Mazzarella and Raminder Kaur, 'Between Sedition and Seduction'; Rashmi Sawhney and Lucia King, 'Artists' Moving Image'.

140 **Editor's note**: *Bandit Queen* (dir. Shekhar Kapur, 1994) and *Bombay* (dir. Mani Ratnam, 1995). See William Mazzarella and Raminder Kaur, 'Between Sedition and Seduction'.

141 **Editor's note**: *Kama Sutra: A Tale of Love* (1996), *Fire* (1996), *Earth* (1998) and *Water* (2005); see notes 4 and 5 in William Mazzarella and Raminder Kaur, 'Between Sedition and Seduction'.

142 Salman Rushdie's *The Satanic Verses* (1988); see note 3, ibid.

143 **Editor's note**: Taslima Nasreen, see notes 10 and 11, ibid.

144 **Editor's note**: For more on Amar Kanwar and his films, see 'Embracing Doubt' in this volume.

145 Sandhini Poddar *et al.*, *Being Singular Plural: Moving Images from India*, The Solomon R. Guggenheim Foundation, New York, 2010, p. 21. This publication accompanies the first exhibition at the Deutsche Guggenheim, Berlin from 26 June to 10 October 2010, focusing exclusively on artistic production in India. See, in this volume, Sandhini Poddar, 'No Ordinary Darkness'.

146 **Editor's note**: For Kabir Mohanty and *Song for an ancient land*, see note 4 in Sandhini Poddar, 'No Ordinary Darkness'.

147 Sandhini Poddar *et al.*, *Being Singular Plural*, p. 21. See ibid. in this volume.

148 **Editor's note**: *Camerawork Delhi* (2006–2011): An independent non-profit quarterly newsletter put together by 'photographers, curators, editors, collectors, students and others interested in establishing a discourse around the photographic print'. The original statement was signed by Gauri Gill, Sunil Gupta, Radhika Singh/Fotomedia and Pooja Sood/Khoj. For Gauri Gill, see in this volume, 'On Seeing', and for Sunil Gupta, see Sunil Gupta/Rahaab Allana, 'FotoFest 2018 and Other Curatorial Practices'.

149 **Editor's note**: *Punctum* (2008–2010): An independently published magazine with international distribution focusing exclusively on photography by Asian image-makers and with the involvement of photography nominators from the region. *Vislumbres* (2010–2013): A publication supported by the Embassy of Spain which explored the connections between the photographic image and the written word.

150 **Editor's note**: Archival project initiated by historian Malavika Karlekar at the Centre for Women's Development Studies (CWDS), New Delhi, as a by-product of her 1986 research project on nineteenth-century Bengali women's narratives, published as *Voices from Within: Early Personal Narratives of Bengali Women* (1993). This led to a significant archive, presented as a photo exhibition, *Re-presenting Indian Women 1875–1947* (2001), curated by Karlekar, Leela Kasturi and Indrani Mazumdar, and later the book *Re-Visioning the Past: Early Photography in Bengal 1875–1915* (2005).

151 **Editor's note**: Centre for Studies in Social Sciences, Kolkata: A research centre with major holdings on the social history of modern Bengal including microfilms of periodicals and non-conventional historical sources from nineteenth and early twentieth centuries.

152 Sen's reference is to lines from Blake's long religious poem, *The Everlasting Gospel* (*c.* 1818): 'This life's five windows of the soul / Distorts the heavens from pole to pole / And leads you to believe a lie/ When you see with, not thro-, the eye.' See Aveek Sen, 'Photography – A Promiscuous Life', in the series 'What We Talk about When We Talk about Photography', 29 February 2012; http://blog.fotomuseum.ch/2012/02/1-photography-a-promiscuous-life-part-i/, accessed 17 June 2020.

Sumathi Ramaswamy

1 Adapted from Nicholas Mirzoeff, *The Right to Look: A Counterhistory of Visuality*, Durham: Duke University Press, 2011, p. 242.

2 For the role of cartography in 'geo-coding', see John Pickles, *A History of Spaces: Cartographic Reason, Mapping, and the Geo-Coded World*, London: Routledge, 2004.

3 Ibid., pp. 17–18.

4 Attributed to Italian sculptor Gilberto Zorio. See Richard Flood and Frances Morris, eds, *Zero to Infinity: Arte Povera, 1962–1972*, Minneapolis: Walker Art Center, 2001, p. 327.

5 Michael Taussig, *Mimesis and Alterity: A Particular History of the Senses*, New York: Routledge, 1993. The referenced *Time* cover image can be viewed at https://content.time.com/time/subscriber/article/0,33009,854810,00.html

6 'INDIA–PAKISTAN: The Trial of Kali', *Time*, 27 October 1947. The tenor of this lengthy analysis frequently mirrors the dramatic quality of the cover image that features a voracious demonic Kali. For instance: 'Thus, not in spite of innocence but because of it, blood appeared; and not the jubilant blood of birth alone, but blood more especially pleasing to Kali, who is both mother and demolisher. India tore herself in two in the womb as a condition to being born at all. Even in the womb, the two unborn nations tore at each other, and from the instant they were born they fell upon each other in maniacal fury.' See https://content.time.com/time/subscriber/article/0,33009,854810,00.html

7 Sumathi Ramaswamy, *The Goddess and the Nation: Mapping Mother India*, Durham: Duke University Press, 2010, pp. 108–10.

8 I thank Lucy Chester for drawing my attention to this image, which can be viewed at https://content.time.com/time/covers/0,16641,19460422,00.html

9 I thank Lee Schlesinger for help in translating the Marathi title.

10 Raminder Kaur, *Performative Politics and the Cultures of Hinduism: Public Uses of Religion in Western India*, Delhi: Permanent Black, 2003, pp. 239–42.

11 W.H. Auden, *Collected Poems*, edited by Edward Mendelson, New York: Random House, 2007, pp. 803–04. There is virtually no discussion of why Auden might have written this poem at this point, in the critical scholarship on the Partition, which invariably cites this poem.

12 Sunil Khilnani, 'India's Mapmaker', *The Observer*, 22 June 1997, p. 7.

13 For a complication of this argument see Lucy Chester, *Borders and Conflict in South Asia: The Radcliffe Boundary Commission and the Partition of Punjab*, Manchester: Manchester University Press, 2009, pp. 83–88.

14 Quoted in ibid., p. 85.

15 Ibid., p. 86.

16 Yasmin Khan, *The Great Partition: The Making of India and Pakistan*, New Haven: Yale University Press, 2007, p. 106, also p. 88. It is important to note that the so-called Radcliffe Line, as with many such boundary-making exercises, was a collective act rather than a one-man exercise.

17 Quoted in ibid., p. 104

18 Quoted in Lucy Chester, *Borders and Conflict in South Asia*, p. 119. In a subsequent interview with Lucy Chester in February 2000, Beaumont vehemently denied such accusations.

19 Ibid., p. 66.

20 Ibid.

21 So, unlike Chaliapin and the editors of *Time*, this image holds Nehru as well responsible for the destruction of the map of India.

22 Quoted in Sankaran Krishna, 'Cartographic Anxiety: Mapping the Body Politic in India', in Michael J. Shapiro and Hayward R. Alker, eds, *Challenging Boundaries: Global Flows, Territorial Identities*, Minneapolis: University of Minnesota Press, 1996, p. 195.

23 **Editor's note**: **Mother India**: See Keywords.

24 Sumathi Ramaswamy, *The Goddess and the Nation*.

25 John Pickles, *A History of Spaces*, p. 3.

26 Quoted in Peter Hardy, *Muslims of British India*, Cambridge: Cambridge University Press, 1972, p. 250.

27 David Gilmartin, 'Partition, Pakistan, and South Asian History: In Search of a Narrative', *Journal of Asian Studies*, vol. 57, no. 4, 1998, p. 1081.

28 For a recent discussion of Rahmat Ali's cartographic productions, see Alyssa Ayres, *Speaking Like a State: Language and Nationalism in Pakistan*, Cambridge: Cambridge University Press, 2009, pp. 25–27, 105–23. **Editor's note**: Choudhry Rahmat Ali (1897–1951): Pakistani nationalist generally credited for coining the name 'Pakistan' (Urdu: 'Land of the Pure') for a separate Muslim homeland. Played a key role in founding the Pakistan National Movement. Published the pamphlet 'Now or Never: Are We to Live or Perish Forever?' (1933), also known as the 'Pakistan Declaration', while studying law at Cambridge University. Returned to Pakistan in 1948 but was expelled by then Prime Minister Liaqat Ali Khan.

29 See entry for Choudhary Rahmat Ali on the Open University webpage, 'Making Britain: Discover How South Asians Shaped the Nation, 1870–1950', https://www.open.ac.uk/researchprojects/makingbritain/content/choudhary-rahmat-ali. Also see Tahir Kamran, 'Choudhary Rahmat Ali and His Political Imagination: Pak Plan and the Continent of Dinia' (2017), a study that draws on Choudhary Rahmat Ali's original writings archived as part of the Foster Papers at the Centre of South Asian Studies, University of Cambridge, https://www.researchgate.net/publication/325953542_Choudhary_Rahmat_Ali_and_his_political_imagination_Pak_plan_and_the_Continent_of_Dinia

30 British Library, India Office Records, L/P&J/8/689, ff. 494–95.

31 Thongchai Winichakul, 'Maps and the Formation of the Geo-Body of Siam', in Hans Antlov and Stein Tonnesson, eds, *Asian Forms of the Nation*, London: Curzon Press, 1996, p. 76.

32 Yasmin Khan, *The Great Partition*, p. 43.

33 British Library, India Office Records, L/P&J/8/689, ff. 422–27.

34 Thanks to David Gilmartin for alerting me to this map, and for discussing it with me.

35 Ayesha Jalal, *Self and Sovereignty: Individual and Community in South Asian Islam since 1850*, London: Routledge, 2000, p. 400.

36 Sumathi Ramaswamy, *The Goddess and the Nation*.

37 For other examples, see http://tasveergharindia.net/cmsdesk/essay/116/index.html

38 Kashmir, however, is claimed for India, as is the case in many such productions.

39 Sumathi Ramaswamy, *The Goddess and the Nation*, p. 51.

40 For another example, see http://tasveergharindia.net/cmsdesk/essay/116/index.html, figure 8.

41 **Editor's note**: **Kashmir**: See Keywords.

42 **Editor's note**: Line of Control (LoC): A 725-kilometre-long ceasefire line between Indian-administered Kashmir and Pakistan-administered Kashmir.

43 Ananya Jahanara Kabir, *Territory of Desire: Representing the Valley of Kashmir*, Minneapolis: University of Minnesota Press, 2009, pp. 8–9.

44 Christopher Pinney, *Photos of the Gods: The Printed Image and Political Struggle in India*, New Delhi: Oxford University Press, 2004, p. 146.

45 Ananya Jahanara Kabir, *Territory of Desire*, p. 187.

Emilia Terracciano

1 *In Search of Famine* (Mrinal Sen, 1982) is a film within a film. In the opening scene, a young, Calcutta-based film director arrives at a village in Bengal with his crew to make a film about the 1943 Bengal Famine. The optimistic director hopes to expose the privations besetting contemporary rural India on the big screen. Following his summary welcome introduction, the jaded crew members participate in a light-hearted memory quiz which involves identifying Indian twentieth-century famines by looking at a variety of famine photographs, including those of the Bengal Famine.

2 The photograph was originally taken by Janah in July 1943; he subsequently captioned it '1944'. These temporal inconsistencies are frequently encountered when one is assessing Janah's remarkable portfolio.

3 Twentieth-century Russian photographers were often compared with the figure of the engineer who

designed and built the basic structures of the new revolutionary society. For this reason, the world was no longer merely interpreted so much as radically (re)constructed in the image. See Graham Clarke, *The Photograph*, Oxford: Oxford University Press, 1997, p. 191.

4 Smith, quoted in Zahid R. Chaudhary, *Afterimage of Empire: Photography in Nineteenth-Century India*, Minneapolis: University of Minnesota Press, 2012, p. 173. See Adam Smith, *The Theory of Moral Sentiments*, New York: Penguin Classics, 2010, p. 140.

5 Zahid R. Chaudhary, *Afterimage of Empire*, p. 175.

6 Ibid.

7 Ibid., p. 184. For *affectus* (translated as emotion or affect – the composite of perception and mental image), see Samuel Shirley, trans., and Seymour Feldman and Baruch Spinoza, eds, *The Ethics: With the Treatise on the Emendation of the Intellect and Selected Letters*, Indianapolis: Hackett Publishing Co., 1997, p. 119 (II, Prop. 27, proof).

8 Zahid R. Chaudhary, *Afterimage of Empire*, p. 175.

9 Ibid., p. 10.

10 Merleau-Ponty, quoted in ibid., p. 25. See Maurice Merleau-Ponty, *Phenomenology of Perception*, London and New York: Routledge, 2002, p. 166.

11 Theodor W. Adorno, *Negative Dialectics*, London: Routledge, 1996, p. 362.

12 For famine and the visual politics of mobilization, see Margaret Kelleher, *The Feminization of Famine: Expressions of the Inexpressible?* Cork: Cork University Press, 1997, p. 174.

13 Allen Feldman, 'On the Actuarial Gaze', *Cultural Studies*, vol. 19, no. 2, 2005, p. 216.

14 Lefort, quoted in ibid., p. 217.

15 Hal Foster, 'Death in America: Shocked Subjectivity and Compulsive Visual Repetition', in R. Krauss, ed., *October: The Second Decade, 1986–1996*, Cambridge: MIT Press, 1997, p. 336.

16 The subject of famine was foregrounded in the nationalist fashioning of the so-called 'drain theory', which advanced the idea that famine was a product of British rule. One of its leading proponents was Parsi politician Dadabhai Naoroji (1825–1917), a founder of the Indian National Congress and a member of the British House of Commons during 1892–95. Naoroji frequently referenced the famine phenomenon in his book *Poverty and Un-British Rule in India* (London: S. Sonnenschein & Co., 1901). While touring England, he gave lectures to critique and oppose the Malthusian logic (favoured by most administrators) which held that India's poverty was rooted in overpopulation rather than British exploitation and mismanagement. For more on the 'drain theory', see Birendranath Ganguli, *Dadabhai Naoroji and the Drain Theory*, New York: Asia Publishing House, 1965.

17 Amartya Sen, *Poverty and Famines: An Essay on Entitlement and Deprivation*, Oxford: Clarendon, 1981, p. 78. Scholars have noted that the massive famines in colonial India were part of a global pattern. See Mike Davis, *Late Victorian Holocausts: El Niño Famines and the Making of the Third World*, New York: Verso, 2001, pp. 6–9.

18 Historical accounts concerned with the theme of famine include David Arnold's *Famine: Social Crisis and Historical Change*; David Ludden and David Washbrook on the commercialization of agriculture in India; and David Hardiman, *Feeding the Baniya: Peasants and Usurers in Western India*, New Delhi and Oxford: Oxford University Press, 2000.

19 **Editor's note**: Jawaharlal Nehru (1889–1964): First prime minister of independent India, prolific writer noted for *Glimpses of World History* (1934) and *The Discovery of India* (1946).

20 'The tragedy of Bengal and the famines of Orissa, Malabar, and other places, are the final judgment on British rule in India.' See Jawaharlal Nehru, *The Discovery of India*, London: Meridian Books, 1951, p. 264.

21 Ibid., pp. 4–6.

22 Winston Churchill, quoted in Madhusree Mukerjee, *Churchill's Secret War: The British Empire and the Ravaging of India during World War II*, New York: Basic Books, 2010, p. 5.

23 Ibid.

24 Achille Mbembe, 'Necropolitics', *Public Culture*, vol. 15, no. 1, 2003, p. 40.

25 Churchill, quoted in Mukerjee, *Churchill's Secret War*, p. 36.

26 Sumit Sarkar, *Modern India, 1885–1947*, New Delhi: Macmillan, 1983, p. 413.

27 Ian Stephens, *Monsoon Morning (A Picture of India in 1942–44)*, London: Ernest Benn, 1966, p. 185; emphasis added.

28 Sabeena Gadihoke, 'Journeys into Inner and Outer Worlds: Photography's Encounter with Public Space in India', in *Where Three Dreams Cross: 150 Years of Photography from India, Pakistan and Bangladesh*, Göttingen, London and Winterthur: Steidl, Whitechapel Art Gallery and Fotomuseum Winterthur, 2010, p. 39.

29 Christopher Pinney, *The Coming of Photography* in India, London: British Library, 2008, p. 137.

30 A. Arya and I. Kamtekar, eds, *History in the Making: The Visual Archives of Kulwant Roy*, New Delhi: HarperCollins, 2008.

31 Pictorialism was a photographic style and type of imagery based on the application of the principles of fine art, especially on ideas of beauty and nature related to the picturesque. Although specifically identified in the late nineteenth and the early twentieth centuries, pictorialist photography was underpinned by an aesthetic response to the ongoing debate about photography's scientific and artistic status. For this reason, Henry Peach Robinson defined the term 'pictorial' in his *Pictorial Effect in Photography: Being Hints on Composition and Chiaroscuro for Photographers to Which is Added a Chapter on Combination Printing* (London: Piper & Carter, 1869), as 'adherence to the systemized aesthetic of the contemporary painting Salon'. During World War II, however, Post-Impressionism pulled avant-garde photography away from pictorialist concerns and towards abstraction. But the manipulation of photographic media, subjectivity and symbolism which had been crucial to the pictorialist aesthetic tradition remained important principles in photography. See Hope Kingsley, 'Pictorialism', in *The Oxford Companion to the Photograph*, Oxford: Oxford University Press, 2009, pp. 739–40. Amongst the Indian photographers influenced by Pictorialism was Bombay-based A.L. Syed (1904–1991). Sophie Gordon cites the work of Shapoor N. Bhedwar, who worked in Bombay from 1890 to 1900 and was part of the Brotherhood of the Linked Ring, an association of British photographers formed in 1892 with a focus on promoting photography as fine art; Robinson was a founding member. Gordon also mentions the important role played by the Photographic Society of India, which reproduced pictorial examples in the pages of its journal during the 1920s. See Sophie Gordon, 'The Colonial Project and the Shifting Gaze', *MARG: A Magazine of the Arts*, vol. 59, no. 4, 2008, pp. 40–53.

32 **Editor's note**: Non-Cooperation Movement (September 1920): Nationalist campaign to boycott machine-manufactured foreign cloth. Gandhi advocated the mass use of *khadi* (handspun cloth).

33 Although the Leica (85 mm) camera was first marketed in 1925, appearing in India shortly thereafter, photographers did not use it due to its small-format negative. On the other hand, the Speedgraphic, first developed in the early twentieth century, was sold in second-hand markets in the aftermath of World War II, when American soldiers left the country. But the Rolleiflex, with its twelve or twenty-four exposures, continued to be the most popular camera amongst press photographers until the 1960s. See Sabeena Gadihoke, 'Journeys into Inner and Outer Worlds', pp. 39–40.

34 Pinney mentions the work of commercial studio photographer Nasik Vinayak Virkar (1890–1968). Virkar, who trained in Lahore, had moved to Bombay where he set up his own private commercial studio. He became a successful film still and studio portrait photographer. In 1919, following the Jallianwala Bagh massacre in Amritsar, Virkar moved with his camera beyond the studio to the site of atrocity to document the forensic traces of 'the event' for posterity. See Christopher Pinney, *The Coming of Photography in India*, p. 83.

35 Sunil Khilnani, *The Idea of India*, London: Hamish Hamilton, 1997, pp. 109, 125; emphasis added.

36 Pinney cites two examples, which both took place in the 1920s within a few years of each other in Amritsar. See *The Coming of Photography in India*, pp. 83–95.

37 Dissident political leaders, including Bombay-based Bal Gangadhar Tilak, brought politics into the street. However, it was Gandhi who radicalized this public space for political expediency. By organizing mass dawn prayer meetings, Gandhi implicitly undermined the rules of colonial public meeting. Ibid., p. 109.

38 Ibid., p. 125.

39 Lisa Trivedi, 'Visually Mapping the "Nation": Swadeshi Politics in Nationalist India, 1920–1930', *The Journal of Asian* Studies, vol. 62, no. 1, 2003, pp. 11–42.

40 Ibid., p. 15.

41 Ibid., p. 37. **Editor's note**: **Jallianwala Bagh massacre**: See Keywords.

42 Sudipta Kaviraj, 'Filth and the Public Sphere: Concepts and Practices about Space in Calcutta',

Public Culture, vol. 10, no. 1, 1997, pp. 83–113. See also Sumanta Banerjee, *The Parlour and the Streets: Elite and Popular Culture in Nineteenth Century Calcutta*, Calcutta: Seagull Books, 1989.

43 Sunil Khilnani, *The Idea of India*, p. 126.

44 In 1920, on Gandhi's advice, the Congress declared that all parades, receptions and celebrations in honour of the Prince of Wales were to be strictly boycotted in view of the 1919 Jallianwala Bagh massacre and the postponement of Home Rule. As a result, the prince was greeted with empty streets in all major Indian cities. See Sumit Sarkar, *Modern India.* Pinney observes that the importance of a sovereign's public visibility began to fade by 1858; see his *The Coming of Photography in India*, p. 46.

45 For photographs documenting the mass meetings instigated by Gandhi in 1908 in Durban, as well as the mass campaign he called for in 1913 to challenge the ban on Indian migration, see Peter Rühe, *Gandhi: A Photo Biography*, London and New York: Phaidon, 2001, pp. 41, 43. For indigenous photographic surveillance, see Judith Mara Gutman, *Through Indian Eyes*, New York: Oxford University Press, 1982.

46 The Press Act was implemented after the Partition of Bengal (1905) to curb the rise of revolutionary and seditious press. See Christopher Pinney, *'Photos of the Gods': The Printed Image and Political Struggle in India*, London: Reaktion, 2004, pp. 11, 56, 109–16, 121, 131. See also R. Kaur and W. Mazzarella, eds, *Censorship in South Asia: Cultural Regulation from Sedition to Seduction*, Bloomington: Indiana University Press, 2009.

47 **Editor's note**: Muhammad Jinnah (1876–1948): Barrister, politician and the founder of Pakistan. He served as the leader of the All-India Muslim League from 1913 until the inception of Pakistan on 14 August 1947, and then as the Dominion of Pakistan's first Governor-General until his death in September 1948.

48 **Editor's note**: Aurobindo Ghose (1872–1950), aka Sri Aurobindo: Philosopher, poet and nationalist persecuted for anti-colonial activities. Founded the Aurobindo Ashram in Pondicherry in 1926.

49 **Editor's note**: Bal Gangadhar Tilak (1856–1920): Nationalist and advocate of *swaraj* ('self-rule').

50 **Editor's note**: *The Bombay Chronicle*: Bombay-based English newspaper started in 1910 by Sir Pherozeshah Mehta, president of **Indian National Congress** in 1890. Closed in 1959. *Young India,* weekly paper in English founded by Lala Lajpat Rai in 1916, later published by Mahatma Gandhi until 1931. *The Leader,* started in 1909, founded by Madan Mohan Malaviya, was one of India's most influential English-language newspapers in the British period. It closed in 1967. *The Hindustan Times* was founded in 1924 in Delhi by Sunder Singh Lyallpuri, associated with the Akali movement. It is still one of northern India's leading newspapers.

51 Christopher Pinney, *The Coming of Photography in India*, p. 137.

52 Kanu Gandhi, Gandhi's grand-nephew, lived in Gandhi's Sevagram Ashram in Ahmedabad and in central India near Wardha. In 1936, he acquired his first camera and a roll of film. He was thus able to document the last ten years of Gandhi's life. According to Rühe, Gandhi allowed Kanu to photograph him on three conditions: 'he was not to use flash, the ashram would not finance his photographic equipment and Gandhi would never pose'. See Peter Rühe, *Gandhi: A Photo Biography*, p. 310.

53 William Mazzarella, 'Branding the Mahatma: The Untimely Provocation of Gandhian Publicity', *Cultural Anthropology*, vol. 25, no. 1, 2010, p. 17.

54 Ibid.

55 Mahatma Gandhi, *The Gandhi Reader: A Source Book of His Life and Writings*, Bloomington: Indiana University Press, 1956, pp. 129–30.

56 In this connection, see also Claude Markovits, *The Un-Gandhian Gandhi: The Life and Afterlife of the Mahatma*, New Delhi: Permanent Black, 2003; Emma Tarlo, *Clothing Matters: Dress and Identity in India*, London: Hurst, 1996; Suchitra, 'What Moves Masses: Dandi March as Communication Strategy', *Economic and Political Weekly*, vol. 30, no. 4, 8 April 1995, p. 745; and Dipesh Chakrabarty, 'Clothing the Political Man: A Reading of the Use of Khadi/White in Indian Public Life', *Journal of Human Values*, vol. 5, no. 1, 1999, pp. 3–14.

57 Naidu, quoted in Tariq Ali, *The Nehrus and the Gandhis: An Indian Dynasty*, London: Picador, 2005, p. 38. In a print published in the *Civil and Military Gazette*, Lahore, on the occasion of Gandhi's seventieth birthday, the Mahatma is depicted as Mickey Mouse. In a birthday broadcast on All India Radio, Sarojini Naidu had referred to the Mahatma as 'this tiny creature whom once in a mood of loving irreverence I called a Mickey Mouse of a Man'. In the print, the Mahatma, mimicking Mickey Mouse, is confronted by the real Mickey Mouse. The latter, arms akimbo, looks reproachfully at the giggling impostor. See Durga Das, *Gandhi in Cartoons*, Ahmedabad: Navjivan Publishing House, 1970, pp. 1529–53.

58 Gandhi used textile as a non-violent protest tool that had strong economic and semiotic implications during the Independence movement. By 1944, the weaving and wearing of *khadi* became a powerful instrument of resistance, conveying both identity and status. See Susan S. Bean, 'Gandhi and Khadi, the Fabric of Indian Independence', in A.B. Weiner and J. Schneider, eds, *Cloth and Human Experience*, Washington, DC: Smithsonian Institution Press, 1989; Peter Gonsalves, *Clothing for Liberation: A Communication Analysis of Gandhi's Swadeshi Revolution*, New Delhi: Sage India, 2010; and Emma Tarlo, *Clothing Matters*.

59 Rahaab Allana and Pramod Kumar, *Painted Photographs: Coloured Portraiture in India*, Ahmedabad: Mapin, 2008, p. 7.

60 Ibid.

61 For a compelling account of *khadi* as both political symbol and commodity in pre- and post-Independence India, see Lisa Trivedi, *Clothing Gandhi's Nation: Home-spun and Modern India*, Bloomington: Indiana University Press, 2007, p. 72. For Gandhi's dislike of colour and use of white as a source of nationalist redemption, see Natasha Eaton, *Colour, Art and Empire: Visual Culture and the Nomadism of Representation*, London: I.B. Tauris, 2013, pp. 259–60. Eaton writes: 'Colour is too heterogeneous, too rebellious (indigo), too traditional and (as anilines) too foreign – and what's more, it didn't photograph effectively. Like the modern technologies of the telegraph and the microphone, Gandhi orchestrated his self-image through black-and-white photography, newspapers, film and newsreel – exemplified by Bourke-White's assignment for *Life* magazine' (ibid., p. 260).

62 This was especially the case during the Salt March to Dandi (1930), an occasion on which thousands of followers wore iconic *khadi* clothes and *topi*s (caps). The march excited not just the whole of India but also millions of spectators around the world, thanks to the press who reported the daily progress of the march. For photographs of the Salt March, see Peter Rühe, *Gandhi: A Photo Biography*, pp. 79–90.

63 **Editor's note**: **Margaret Bourke-White**: See Keywords.

64 Richard Pollard, quoted in Vicki Goldberg, *Margaret Bourke-White: A Biography*, London: Heinemann, 1987, p. 189. For Bourke-White's Dust Bowl photographs, see Erskine Caldwell and Margaret Bourke-White, *You Have Seen Their Faces*, Athens: University of Georgia Press, 1995.

65 Bourke-White struggled with many of Gandhi's ideas on industry and agriculture. She wrote: 'This conviction of Gandhi's that machinery was intrinsically evil particularly disturbed me because of my love of the machine and my belief of what it could do for man'; see Margaret Bourke-White, *Portrait of Myself*, New York: Simon and Schuster, 1963, p. 273.

66 Contrary to what Bourke-White writes in her memoirs, the photographer took several pictures of the Mahatma. This suggests that she moved around him undisturbed and that the sitter, while paying no attention to her, was cooperatively and performatively motionless. She would later write: 'Photography demands a high degree of participation'; see Margaret Bourke-White, *Portrait of Myself*, p. 84. In *Halfway to Freedom*, an account of her travels in India in 1947 and 1948, she narrates a tense experience of photographing Gandhi in his hut. His assistant Pyarelal told her that the Mahatma would pay no attention to her as it was his weekly day of silence; and that she was not to use flashbulbs as it disturbed Gandhi's concentration and vision. She was 'overjoyed' upon hearing that Gandhi would ignore her: 'If he paid no attention to me, he would not stop me.' However, the ban on flash was a 'serious' problem as she 'could see from the outside of the hut that there would be very little light within'. Persistent, she 'finally won permission to use three flashbulbs' and went into the hut with all her equipment. 'It was even worse than I had imagined. A little daylight came in, but it couldn't have been in a more unfortunate spot. From an uncovered window directly above Gandhiji's head a single dazzling beam shone directly into my lens. His nut-brown body sank into the indistinct background in a dense fog of halation, which no shading of maneuvering seemed to cure. He was reading a large pile of newspaper clippings, bowed over them so his features disappeared in the shadows. As Pyarelal had predicted, he paid no attention to me, for which I was grateful.' As Bourke-White arranged the shot, her shutters and synchronizers began to malfunction: 'I tried loosening up the equipment by taking some slow time shots before using up my flashbulbs. The shutter began catching on the automatic release device, gaping wide open and refusing to close. When I coaxed that into action, the blade-arrester gadget thrust itself in the way. The film adapters kept slipping in crooked and sticking. The paper pulls on the film pack tore in half when the films were only partly drawn. As I turned to my tripod, two legs stuck at their shortest position while a third became wedged at its maximum length. Then Gandhi laid aside his clippings and started to spin. I decided to risk the first flashbulb. It was quite plain from the span of time

between bulb flash and shutter click that the camera hadn't synchronized. The second shot sounded perfect and I was overjoyed, only to observe in the next second that I had forgotten to pull the slide.' Bourke-White 'checked everything' before the third shot, watching Gandhi carefully; 'and when he touched the fine cotton thread with his brown hand, gathered it up skillfully and beautifully, I caught him on the upstroke, and the camera sounded perfect. I threw my arms around the equipment and rushed out of the hut, feeling I wasn't so sold on the machine age after all. Not till I held the finished photograph in my hand did my faith return completely.' See *Halfway to Freedom: A Report on the New India in the Words and Photographs of Margaret Bourke-White*, New York: Simon and Schuster, 1949, pp. 84, 85.

67 Edward Weston, 'Entry for 10 March 1924', in *The Daybooks of Edward Weston*, Millerton: Aperture, 1973, quoted in N. Newhall, ed., *Edward Weston: The Flame of Recognition: His Photographs Accompanied by Excerpts from Daybooks & Letters*, Millerton: Aperture, 1975, p. 12.

68 While the ever-optimistic technophile Bourke-White disagreed with Gandhi over the issue of industrialization in India, she was sensitive to the leader's ambivalent behaviour towards machinery. Confessing her difficulty as 'an American, to hurdle his antiquated ideas on the machine age ... because to me the machine has always been a glorious thing', Bourke-White observed how Gandhi's anti-machine references at prayer meetings were especially disturbing when 'delivered through a modern microphone.' Hence she found Gandhi's professed views on industry at odds with his own lifestyle. For the photographer, the final irony was that at the end of the talk, 'Gandhi would step off his prayer platform into the milk-white Packard car belonging to the richest textile manufacturers in India. I was not satisfied by these inconsistencies.' Margaret Bourke-White, *Portrait of Myself*, pp. 278–79.

69 **Editor's note**: P.C. (Puran Chand) Joshi (1907–1980): Joined the Communist Party of India (CPI) in 1929, and was general secretary from 1935–47.

70 Vladimir Lenin, quoted in S.I. Morozov and V. Lloyd, eds, *Soviet Photography 1917–1940: The New Photojournalism*, London: Orbis, 1984, p. 8. In pre-Soviet Russia, Maxim Dimitriev was the first Russian photographer to record mass suffering under the Tsarist regime during the 1881–82 Volga Basin Famine. Dimitriev documented the terrible conditions of the peasants, many of whom were suffering from severe malnutrition, typhoid and cholera.

71 C. Vaughan James, *Soviet Socialist Realism: Origins and Theory*, London: Macmillan Press, 1973, p. 13. See also Margarita Tupitsyn, *Gustav Klutsis and Valentina Kulagina: Photography and Montage after Constructivism*, New York and Göttingen: International Center of Photography and Steidl, 2004.

72 Vicki Goldberg, *Margaret Bourke-White*, p. 300.

73 Bipan Chandra, 'P.C. Joshi and National Politics', *Studies in History*, vol. 24, no. 2, 2008, p. 248.

74 Antonio Gramsci, *Selections from the Prison notebooks of Antonio Gramsci,* London: Lawrence & Wishart, 1971, p. 3.

75 Debates on critical realism and the function of art were common in India since 1935 and frequently voiced at the Progressive Writers' Association. These discussions integrated an anti-imperialist rhetoric with that of a broader opposition towards the rise of Fascism. From the early 1940s the progressive cultural initiatives of the CPI took over these debates. The Anti-Fascist Writers' and Artists' Association (1941) was resolutely left-wing. See Sanjukta Sunderason, 'As "Agitator and Organizer": Chittaprosad and Art for the Communist Party of India, 1941–48', *Object*, vol. 13, 2011, pp. 76–95. See also Sunderason's unpublished doctoral thesis, 'The Nation and the Everyday: The Aesthetics and Politics of Modern Art in India, Bengal c. 1920–c. 1960', University College London, 2012; and Sudhi Pradhan, *Marxist Cultural Movement in India: Chronicles and Documents, 1936–1947*, Calcutta: National Book Agency, 1979. **Editor's note**: Also see **Progressive Artists Group** in Keywords.

76 Benjamin Francis Bradley (1898–1957) was a British Communist who was sent to India in 1927 by the Communist Party of Great Britain to promote militant trade unionism. In 1931, he was sentenced to ten years penal transportation in the infamous Meerut Conspiracy Trial (1929–33). Among the thirty-two prisoners was the twenty-two-year-old P.C. Joshi. See J. M. Bellamy, J. Saville and D.E. Martin, eds, *Dictionary of Labour Biography*, vol. 10, Basingstoke: Macmillan, 2000; also see Jean Jones, *Ben Bradley: Fighter for India's Freedom*, London: Socialist History Society, 1994.

77 The strategy of colonial Communists resulted in a significant debate between Mexico-based Bengali revolutionary M.N. Roy and Lenin at the Second Congress of the Communist International (1921). While Lenin

encouraged the broad support of the bourgeois-led national movements in the colonies, Roy argued that the Indian masses were already disillusioned with bourgeois leaders like Gandhi. See Sumit Sarkar, *Modern India*, p. 247.

78 In 1935, the Seventh Congress of the Comintern switched to supporting a united front of all anti-Fascist forces in capitalist countries and the alliance of Communist and nationalist forces in colonial and semi-colonial countries. India was thus compelled to adopt the Dutt–Bradley thesis, its Communist British authors urging the necessity of working within Congress and converting the latter into an anti-imperialist people's front. Joshi implemented this thesis successfully, with left-wing Congress members from both the Indian National Congress and the Congress Socialist Party welcoming all Communists. His success had been further sustained by Jawaharlal Nehru's sympathy towards and admiration for the Left, expressed in the 1936 National Congress presidential address. At this time, Nehru supported the formation of an Anti-Imperialist People's Front, criticizing the Congress's isolation from the masses. However Joshi's theorizing began to waver between 1939–40, when the new pro-Soviet defection caused the Indian Communist movement to be associated with the Soviet-German pact and with the *People's War* ideological line. Although the about-turn in Comintern policy after the Soviet-German Pact represented an embarrassment for European Communists, it represented an asset for their comrades in India, allowing an easy synchronization of 'internationalist' support to Soviet policies with nationalist hostility to Britain's war. Upon Hitler's invasion of Russia in 1941, this situation would be exactly reversed. In September 1939, the Viceroy arbitrarily subscribed India to the British declaration of war on Germany as a supporter and without consulting prominent Indian Congress leaders. For more on the role of the Comintern, Communism and nationalism in India, see Bipan Chandra, 'P.C. Joshi and National Politics', p. 251; Irfan Habib, 'The Left and the National Movement', *Social Scientist*, vol. 26, nos. 5–6, 1998, p. 18; Anil Rajimwale, *Life and Works of P.C. Joshi*, New Delhi: People's Publishing House, 2007, p. 44; John Patrick Haithcox, *Communism and Nationalism in India: M.N. Roy and Comintern Policy, 1920–1939*, Princeton: Princeton University Press, 1971, p. 382; and D.N. Gupta, *Communism and Nationalism in Colonial India, 1939–45*, Thousand Oaks: Sage Publications, 2008, p. 56.

79 Anil Rajimwale, *Life and Works of P. C. Joshi*, p. 46; Bipan Chandra, 'P. C. Joshi and National Politics', p. 251.

80 The All India Kisan Sabha (All India Peasants Union) was formed during the Lucknow and Faizpur Congress sessions in 1930. The movement incarnated the new spirit of unity advocated by the Dutt–Bradley thesis among Left-nationalists, Socialists and Communists. The greatest triumph of the Left during this period was represented by the re-election of Subhas Chandra Bose as Congress President in 1939. This victory signalled the short-lived high tide of Left influence within Congress. See Sumit Sarkar, *Modern India*, p. 340. **Editor's note**: **Indian People's Theatre Association**: See Keywords.

81 Bipan Chandra, 'P.C. Joshi and National Politics', p. 249. **Editor's note**: Ali Sardar Jafri (1913–2000): Urdu writer, poet, critic and film lyricist. Faiz Ahmad Faiz (1911–1984): Celebrated poet and author, major national figure in Pakistan. P.C. (Prasanta Chandra) Mahalanobis (1893–1972): Scientist and statistician and major figure in founding Indian statistics. Bishnu Dey (1909–1982): Major Bengali modernist poet.

82 The CPI became further discredited after adopting the problematic Adhikari thesis on 'Pakistan and National Unity' in 1942. While pleading for an agreement between Gandhi and Jinnah, it came very close to endorsing the Pakistan demand as an opportunistic means to strike an alliance with the Muslim League and undermine Congress hegemony. See Sumit Sarkar, *Modern India*, pp. 411–12.

83 Irfan Habib, 'The Left and the National Movement', p. 23.

84 For Gramsci's influential concept of 'hegemony' and the role of the organic intellectual in the context of Fascist Italy, see Antonio Gramsci, *Selections from the Prison notebooks*, pp. 12–13.

85 Sunil Janah, *Photographing India*, New Delhi: Oxford University Press, 2013, pp. 8, 11.

86 Ibid., p. 12.

87 Ibid., p. 8.

88 A.D. Coleman, *Depth of Field: Essays on Photography, Mass Media, and Lens Culture*, Albuquerque: University of New Mexico Press, 1998, pp. 36–37. Newspaper photographers in both Europe and the Soviet Union would usually (though not always) go for the single image, while magazine photographers opted for sequences.

89 Sunil Janah, in conversation with the author, 12 March 2009.

90 See N. Ganguly, ed., *Somnath Hore*, New Delhi: Lalit Kala Akademi, 2010; and Sanjoy Kumar Mallik, *Chittaprosad: A Retrospective 1915–1978*, New Delhi: Delhi Art Gallery, 2004. For more on the work of Zainul

Abedin, see Iftikhar Dadi, *Modernism and the Art of Muslim South Asia,* Chapel Hill: University of North Carolina Press, 2010; and Sanjoy Kumar Mallik, 'Responses in the Art of Bengal to the 1943 Famine and the Tebhaga Movement', paper delivered at the 'Culture and Democracy' workshop organized by the Centre for Studies in Social Sciences (Kolkata) in Gwalior, 1–5 February 1997. See also Sanjoy Kumar Mallik, 'Social Realism in the Visual Arts: "Man-Made" Famine and Political Ferment, Bengal 1943–1946', in G. Sinha, ed., *Art and Visual Culture in India, 1857–2007*, Mumbai and New Delhi: MARG Publications in collaboration with National Cultural Fund, Government of India and Bodhi Art, 2009. **Editor's note**: Chittaprosad Bhattacharya (1915–1978): Major Communist artist working in water colour and printmaking. Zainul Abedin (1914–1976): Bengali painter, later in Bangladesh, painted the Bengal Famine in 1943; helped start the Institute of Arts and Crafts, University of Dhaka. Gobardhan Ash (1907–1996): Indian artist and early modernist; co-founded Art Rebel Center in 1933 in Calcutta; employed as Chief Artist at the Indian Institute of Arts and Industry in Kolkata in 1946, and from 1953 as Senior Teacher at the Indian Art School of Kolkata. Somnath Hore (1921–2006): Major sculptor and printmaker associated with radical movements of the Communist Party (e.g., the Tebhaga movement); later taught at Santiniketan. Quamrul Hassan (1921–1988): Bengali artist associated with folk styles; a major figure in Bangladesh.

91 See Sanjukta Sunderason, 'As "Agitator and Organizer"'. In 1942, at a conference devoted to the role of art and literature during China's liberation war, Mao had urged Party members 'to investigate, to observe, to study, and to analyze the various personalities, the different classes, the various social groups, and the various active forms of life and struggle.' Mao Zedong, *Problems of Art and Literature*, New York: International Publishers, 1950, pp. 17–18.

92 Janaki Nair, 'Cultural Production in an Age of Retreating State Patronage', unpublished paper delivered at a conference in Jawaharlal Nehru University, New Delhi, 1996, not paginated. I am grateful to Professor Nair for sharing this paper with me in Delhi.

93 P.C. Joshi, 'Who Lives If Bengal Dies?', *People's War*, 14 November 1943, p. 17.

94 Sunil Janah, *Photographing India*, p. 10.

95 **Editor's note**: Soli S. Batliwala (d. 1986) was a freedom fighter who worked for the Congress Socialist Party and the Communist Party for over two decades.

96 Natasha Eaton, *Mimesis across Empires: Artworks and Networks in India 1765–1860*, Durham: Duke University Press, 2013, p. 236.

97 **Editor's note**: **Felice Beato**: See Keywords.

98 This image continues to be fruitfully theorized by cultural historians, photography scholars and arts/media practitioners. See, for instance, Christopher Pinney, 'Seven Theses on Photography', in Rahaab Allana, ed., *Unframed: Discovering Image Practices in South Asia*, New Delhi: The Alkazi Foundation for the Arts and HarperCollins Publishers India, 2023, pp. 72–91. For an appraisal of Beato's staged photograph and the politics of the archive, that is, the tension between the claim to truth and the 'ruses' necessary to the making of this claim, see Raqs Media Collective, 'In the Theatre of Memory: The Work of Contemporary Art in the Photographic Archive', *Lalit Kala Contemporary*, vol. 52, 2012, pp. 85–95.

99 Felice Beato (1832–1909) specialized in the depiction of conflicts, including the Crimean War (1853–56) and the Second Opium War in China (1856–60). His aftermath coverage of the 1857 Mutiny catered to the endless craving of the British public for images related to the event. Beato arrived at Sikandar Bagh in Lucknow five months after the revolt. See David Harris, 'Topography and Memory: Felice Beato's Photographs of India, 1858–1859', in Vidya Dehejia *et al.*, *India Through the Lens: Photography 1840–1911*, Washington DC, Munich and New York: Freer Gallery of Art and Arthur M. Sackler Gallery, Smithsonian Institution in association with Mapin Publishers and Prestel, 2000.

100 In relation to the collapse of governmentality, see the work of Zahid R. Chaudhary, 'Phantasmagoric Aesthetics', p. 99; and Narayani Gupta, 'Pictorializing the "Mutiny" of 1857', in M.A. Pellizzari, ed., *Traces of India: Photography, Architecture, and the Politics of Representation, 1850–1900*, Montreal and New Haven: Canadian Centre for Architecture, Yale Center for British Art, Yale University Press, 2003, pp. 216–39.

101 P.C. Joshi, 'Who Lives If Bengal Dies?': p. 19

102 Henry Luce, founder and editor-in-chief of *Life*, assured his subscribers that 'Britain was ready to pass the mantle of leadership to America.' Quoted in Vicki Goldberg, *Margaret Bourke-White*, p. 300.

103 Sunil Janah, *Photographing India*, pp. 30–31. For an image of Janah with Bourke-White, see

Rituparna Ray, 'Photographer Margaret Bourke-White and Sunil Janah: The Story of a Rare Collaboration', *Outlook*, 6 March 2022; https://www.outlookindia.com/culture-society/photographer-margaret-bourke-white-and-sunil-janah-the-story-of-a-rare-collaboration-news-185485

104 Jacques Derrida, 'The Deaths of Roland Barthes', in H.J. Silverman, ed., *Philosophy and Non-Philosophy since Merleau-Ponty*, Evanston: Northwestern University Press, 1997, pp. 266–27.

105 Sunil Janah, in conversation with the author, 12 March 2009.

106 Irfan Habib, 'The Left and the National Movement', p. 25.

107 Ibid., p. 26.

108 Under the (Stalinist) leadership of B.T. Ranadive, Communists resolved to continue fighting for a 'free India'; ibid., p. 28. In 1964, the Communist Party split into two: the Communist Party of India (Marxist)/CPI(M) and the Communist Party of India/CPI. See D.N. Gupta, *Communism and Nationalism in Colonial India, 1939–45.*

109 Sunil Janah, *Photographing India*, pp. 36–37.

110 Although scholars cite the importance of Janah in the history of photography in India, no substantial study has been published on his work to date. The following essays expound upon particular aspects of Janah's career: Atreyee Gupta, 'Developmental Aesthetics: Modernism's Ocular Economies and Laconic Discontents in the Era of Nehruvian Technocracy', in S. Ray and V. Maddipati, eds, *Water Histories of South Asia: The Materiality of Liquescence,* New Delhi and London: Routledge, 2019; Ranu Roychoudhuri, 'Documentary Photography, Decolonization, and the Making of "Secular Icons": Reading Sunil Janah's Photographs from the 1940s through the 1950s', *Bioscope: South Asian Screen Studies*, vol. 8, no. 1, 2017, pp. 46–80. See also Roychoudhuri's unpublished doctoral thesis, 'The Public Lives of Photographs: Aesthetic Conventions and Sociocultural Change in Twentieth-Century India', University of Chicago, 2015; and Ankan Kazi, 'Making New Images: On the Exhibition *Making a Photograph* by Sunil Janah', ASAP I Art, 5 May 2022, a discussion of Janah's industrial photographs – images that 'reflect something crucial about Janah's practice during those early years after independence. They reveal the tactile world of freedom, of new possibilities, emerging out of older ideological scars and struggles and the power of the photographic image to reveal the ambivalent promise of the future'; https://asapconnect.in/post/405/singleevents/making-new-images

111 **Editor's note**: J.R.D. Tata (1904–1993): Indian aviator and pioneering industrialist. Known as the father of civil aviation in India, he built the national airline, Air India. He was chairman of the Tata Group of companies. G.D. (Ghanshyam Das) Birla (1894–1983): Businessman and scion of the Birla group of industries.

112 Bourke-White writes (in *Portrait of Myself*, p. 33): 'To me, fresh from college with my camera over my shoulder, the Flats were a photographic paradise. The smokestacks ringing the horizon were the giants of an unexplored world, guarding the secrets and wonder of the steel mills. When, I wondered, would I get inside those slab-sided coffin-black buildings with their mysterious unpredictable flashes of light leaking out the edges?'

113 For a different reading of this image, see Rebecca M. Brown, *Art for a Modern India, 1947–1980*, Durham: Duke University Press, 2009, pp. 128–29.

114 **Editor's note**: Verrier Elwin (1902–1964): English-born self-trained anthropologist, ethnologist and tribal activist, becoming an authority on the Baigas and Gonds of central India. Began his career as a Christian missionary; worked with Gandhi and the Indian National Congress; converted to Hinduism in 1935; and served as the deputy director of the Anthropological Survey of India in 1945.

115 Notable works of Verrier Elwin are *Leaves from the Jungle: Life in a Gond Village* (London: John Murray, 1936); *The Baiga* (London: John Murray, 1939); *The Muria and Their Ghotul* (Oxford: Oxford University Press, 1947); and *The Tribal World of Verrier Elwin: An Autobiography* (London: Oxford University Press, 1964).

116 Photograph originally titled *Malabar, Kerala, 1940s. Peasant Girl, Malabar Coast, Kerala 1945.*

117 Joshi, in Bipan Chandra, 'P.C. Joshi and National Politics', p. 250.

118 Sunil Janah, *Photographing India*, pp. 10–11. Bourke-White, who photographed the effects of famine in south India, remarked (*Halfway to Freedom*, p. 149) that the 'fear of starvation is always hanging over the Indian peasant', and that the Bengal Famine's 'horrible losses – which spread far beyond Bengal – were due less to actual food shortages than to the cornering of food for inflationary profit and to the tragic inadequacy of transportation, which was never planned with the peasants' needs in mind. In 1943 the roads and railroads served the Indian people even less than usual, because of the prior claims of the military. While the outside world was losing its hundreds of thousands of lives on the battlefield, India was losing them from starvation. As prices

rose, rice disappeared into the black market, and multitudes of peasants marched to the towns. When more than a million dead clogged the streets of Calcutta and other millions of bodies lay strewn over the fields of several provinces, censorship within India kept the world outside from appreciating the ghastly extent of the tragedy. The Western world is apt to regard mass starvation as the inevitable fate of the crowded Orient, the certain accompaniment of dense population. But many of the food difficulties arise from the outmoded methods of land tenure, the layers of rural parasites – landowners and moneylenders – who live on peasants' labor without any responsibility of looking after the irrigation or improvement of the land.'

119 For a compelling discussion on the relationship between photojournalism and fine art photography in the work of Brazilian photographer Sebastião Salgado, see Julian Stallabrass, 'Sebastião Salgado and Fine Art Photojournalism', *New Left* Review, vol. 223, 1997, p. 131. Stallabrass contends that in the case of Salgado's photographs of the inhabitants of the Sahel, there is great difficulty in successfully ascribing agency to his subjects, since their sole preoccupation is the need to find food.

120 Joshi, in Bipan Chandra, 'P.C. Joshi and National Politics', p. 263; emphasis added.

121 Sunil Janah, *Photographing India*, p. 110; emphasis added. Janah is here referring to a passage from Sontag's Preface to *Don McCullin* (London: Jonathan Cape, 2001, not paginated). In his obituary for Janah, photographer Ram Rahman, author of *Sunil Janah: Photographs 1940–1960: Vintage Prints from the Swaraj Art Archive* (Noida: Vijay Kumar Aggarwal, 2014), writes that Janah's work 'is the defining epic document of the last decade of the freedom struggle and the first decade of free India'; and that the huge Janah retrospective, 'an informal exhibition of 600 vintage prints' that Rahman mounted at Gallery 678 in New York in 1988, 'created a sensation. A full-page review in the *New York Times* brought scores of people to the gallery, many older Indians left sobbing, so moved were they by the history they saw.' See Ram Rahman, 'Portraitist of the Nehruvian Era', *The Hindu*, 23 June 2012, http://www.sacw.net/article2712.html.

122 Julian Stallabrass, 'Sebastião Salgado and Fine Art Photojournalism', p. 29; emphasis added.

123 See Sunil Janah, *The Second Creature: 64 Photographs*, Calcutta: Signet Press, 1949; and the posthumous *Photographing India*.

124 James Clifford, 'The Others: Beyond the "Salvage" Paradigm', *Third Text*, vol. 3, no. 6, 1989, p. 74.

125 Eduardo Cadava, *Words of Light: Theses on the Photography of History*, Princeton: Princeton University Press, 1997, p. 11. See Walter Benjamin, *Charles Baudelaire: A Lyric Poet in the Era of High Capitalism*, New York and London: Verso, 1983, p. 87; and his 'Trauerspiels', in *GesammelteSchriften*, vol. 2, Frankfurt am Main: Suhrkamp, 1972, p. 136.

Gemma Scott

1 These protests included a three-week-long railway strike in May 1974, led by socialist activist/trade union leader and president of the All India Railwaymen's Federation George Fernandes, a fiercely anti-Gandhi crusader who was jailed during the Emergency for allegedly attempting to dynamite railway bridges; the women's Anti-Price Rise Movement in Maharashtra and Gujarat; and student agitations in Gujarat and Bihar led by veteran freedom fighter Jayaprakash Narayan. For further discussions, see Ramachandra Guha, *India after Gandhi: The History of the World's Largest Democracy*, London: Macmillan, 2007, pp. 477–78.

2 **Editor's note**: Jayaprakash Narayan (1902–1979): Socialist and social reformer best known for leading the opposition against Indira Gandhi in the mid-1970s, calling for 'total revolution'.

3 **Editor's note**: Jagmohanlal Sinha (1920–2008): Judge in the Allahabad High Court who ruled in the *State of Uttar Pradesh v. Raj Narain* lawsuit (1975) invalidating the election of Indira Gandhi.

4 Ramachandra Guha, *India after Gandhi*, pp. 493–522.

5 Ibid. Also see Bipan Chandra, *In the Name of Democracy: JP Movement and the Emergency*, New Delhi: Penguin, 2003.

6 Emma Tarlo, *Unsettling Memories: Narratives of the Emergency in Delhi*, Los Angeles: University of California Press, 2003. A post-Emergency denunciation of the regime's barbaric sterilization campaign (a 'massive body-snatching exercise' that was 'implemented on a national scale' with 'brute force' while Indira Gandhi 'pleaded ignorance') lists the following violations: 'the forcible sterilization of bachelors, young married men and women,

persons with no children, old persons, hospital patients (also charging extra money from outdoor patients who could not produce sterilization certificate), inmates of jails and night-shelters, and pavement dwellers; catching hold of passers-by, passengers in buses and persons returning home after late-night cinema shows; stopping the salaries of school teachers and administrative staff members; transfers as punishment (for non-procurement of sterilization cases); non-renewal of all manner of licences; rejection of applications of non-sterilized persons for loans, fertilizers, water and electric connection; cutting off water and electricity supplies; forcible collection of money from shopkeepers by the so-called youth leaders on the pretext of organizing sterilization camps; threat of arrest under MISA [Maintenance of Internal Security Act, 1971]; and, finally, lathi charge and police firing and death of scores of persons.' See Ashish Bose, 'How Did the Emergency Get Mixed Up with Sterilization?', *India Today*, 15 February 1978 (updated 10 February 2015); https://www.indiatoday.in/magazine/guest-column/story/19780215-how-did-the-emergency-get-mixed-up-with-sterilization-822855-2014-11-07

7 Patrick Clibbens, '"The Destiny of This City is To Be the Spiritual Workshop of the Nation": Clearing Cities and Making Citizens during the Indian Emergency, 1975–1977', *Contemporary South Asia*, vol. 22, no. 1, 2014, pp. 51–66; Rebecca Jane Williams, 'Storming the Citadels of Poverty: Family Planning and the Emergency in India, 1975–1977', *Journal of Asian Studies*, vol. 73, no. 2, 2014, pp. 471–92.

8 Rajeswari Sunder Rajan, *Real and Imagined Women: Gender, Culture and Postcolonialism*, London: Routledge, 1993; Trina Nileena Banerjee, 'Political Iconography and the Female Political Leader: The Case of Indira Gandhi, Some Initial Questions', *Humanities Underground*, 2 October 2012, http://humanitiesunderground.org/political-iconography-the-female-political-leader-the-case-of-indira-gandhi-some-initial-questions/

9 Guha mentions the poor prison conditions in which authorities kept two female detainees: Socialist Party leader Mrinal Gore and Snehalata Reddy, film star and friend of Socialist Party leader George Fernandes; he also discusses Snehalata's death after authorities failed to provide her adequate medical treatment (Ramachandra Guha, *India after Gandhi*, pp. 499, 506). This analysis focuses more on the mistreatment, positioning them exclusively as victims, rather than considering their contribution to the resistance movement.

10 Jennifer Tucker and Tina Campt, 'Entwined Practices: Engagements with Photography in Historical Enquiry', *History and Theory*, vol. 48, no. 4, 2009, p. 1.

11 James R. Ryan, *Picturing Empire: Photography and the Visualization of the British Empire*, Chicago: University of Chicago Press, 1997.

12 Patricia Hayes, Jeremy Silvester and Wolfram Hartmann, 'Photography, History and Memory', in Patricia Hayes, Jeremy Silvester and Wolfram Hartmann, eds, *The Colonizing Camera: Photographs in the Making of Namibian History*, Cape Town: University of Cape Town Press, 1998, p. 5.

13 Annu Palakunnathu Matthew, 'An Indian from India', 2013, http://www.annumatthew.com/gallery/an-indian-from-india/#3. **Editor's note**: Annu Palakunnathu Matthew, photographer and artist, draws on old photographs to re-examine historical narratives and marginalized histories in both the US and South Asia. Published *The Answers Take Time* in 2022.

14 Trina Nileena Banerjee, 'Political Iconography and the Female Political Leader'.

15 Paul Frosh, 'The Public Eye and the Citizen-Voyeur: Photography as a Performance of Power', *Social Semiotics*, vol. 11, issue 1, 2001, p. 43.

16 Robert Rapstein, 'Creating and Using Photographs as Historical Evidence', *History in Africa*, vol. 17, 1990, pp. 248–49.

17 Jennifer Tucker and Tina Campt, 'Entwined Practices', p. 4.

18 None of the photographs referenced in this chapter included information about their origins. *Socialist India* usually, although not always, included a small caption explaining images, but rarely credited them to a particular photographer except for a handful of instances. In its 21 June 1975 issue, the bulletin featured images of Gandhi giving speeches with the following information accompanying the captions – 'Photos: Gopal Chitra Kuteer' (18a). This Delhi-based private studio was also credited with photographs that appeared in the 3 January 1976 issue depicting the 75th Plenary Session of the Indian National Congress (28a–28d). On 10 April 1976 the party credited another studio, 'PANA', for photographs showing the Congress president D.K. Barooah's visit to Sikkim that graced its front cover. *Socialist India* also attributed a small number of images to an individual photographer, 'R.D. Rawal' (21 June 1975: 36; 5 July 1975: 2). The Congress did credit external photographers

where its bulletin used their images. In all other instances where it provided no detail the images can only be assigned to the Congress Party, as this bulletin's publisher.

19 Diego Maiorano, *Autumn of the Matriarch: Indira Gandhi's Final Term in Office*, London: Hurst & Co, 2015, pp. 109–10.

20 Indira Gandhi, *Selected Speeches and Writings of Indira Gandhi, 1972–1977*, New Delhi: Ministry of Information and Broadcasting, Government of India, 1984, p. 189.

21 'PM's Candid Replies to Frank Questions from Mexican Journalists', *Socialist India*, 2 August 1975, p. 29.

22 Diego Maiorano, *Autumn of the Matriarch*, p. 109.

23 On her election as Prime Minister in 1966, she famously asserted, 'I am not a feminist. I am simply doing a particular job and would do it wherever I was placed.' See Tariq Ali, *The Nehrus and the Gandhis: An Indian Dynasty*, Bombay: Popular Prakashan, 1983, p. 182. Throughout 1975 to 1977, she spoke at a number of women's conferences but often denounced them – in one instance in August 1975 she opened her address with the statement 'I am a bit allergic to such conferences', and in another in February 1976 she decried them as 'repetitive and costly' (Indira Gandhi, *Speeches and Writings*, pp. 523, 753).

24 'PM on Women's Status', *Socialist India*, 14 June 1975, p. 23.

25 'PM: Days of License over for Good', *Women on the March* (*WOTM*), December 1975, p. 6.

26 *WOTM*, July 1975, p. 1.

27 'Women's Aid in Family Planning Programme Sought', *WOTM*, August 1975, p. 30.

28 *WOTM*, October 1975, p. 1.

29 'Smt M Chandrasekhar's call to Kerala Women for Implementing PM's 20-point Programme', ibid., p. 2. See also 'PM asks women to lead consumer movement', January 1976, p. 19; 'PM tells women to play role in revolution', March 1976, pp. 17–18; 'Exhibition on Twenty Point Economic Programme', June 1976, p. 36, which was organized by women; 'Women's Consumer Vigilance Committee', September 1976, p. 26.

30 Kumkum Mathur, 'Welfare Plans Galore for Women', *Socialist India*, 21 August 1976, p. 36.

31 Ramachandra Guha, *India after Gandhi*, p. 467.

32 *Socialist India*, 5 June 1975.

33 **Editor's note**: Dev Kant Barooah (1914–1996): Politician and Assamese poet, president of the Indian National Congress during the Emergency (1975–77).

34 Ibid., p. 1.

35 **Editor's note**: Press Trust of India (PTI): Delhi-based news agency registered in 1947 as a non-profit cooperative created by multiple newspapers. Merged during the Emergency with United News of India, Hindustan Samachar and Samachar Bharati, into Samachar.

36 '*Smt*', *the* abbreviation of '*srimati*', is a standard respectful term of address for women, especially married women, in several Indian languages, akin to 'Mrs' in English.

37 *Mangal kalash* refers to a clay or metal pot or vessel used in Hindu rituals or on important occasions as a sign of auspiciousness and/or welcome.

38 'Women Know Their Sisters', *Socialist India*, 5 June 1975, p. 6.

39 In its January 1975 report, the Committee on the Status of Women, established by the government to investigate gender inequality, highlighted the problematic practice of women eating last in the family and the negative impacts of this on their health. See *Towards Equality*, New Delhi: Government of India, 1975, p. 311. Gandhi did not suggest change to this practice of unequal food distribution within the family; rather, she posited it as an acceptable solution to the problems caused by rising prices and shortages.

40 'The People's Tryst with the Prime Minister', *Socialist India*, 5 July 1975, 18–18d.

41 Ibid., 18a.

42 Ibid., 18b.

43 Ibid., 18c.

44 Ibid.

45 Ibid., 18d.

46 *Socialist India*, 12 February 1977, 18c.

47 *Socialist India*, 5 March 1977, p. 3.

48 This image of an Adivasi woman voting while breastfeeding also featured in *The Patriot*, the mouthpiece of the Communist Party of India. Initially pro-Emergency, by the 1977 elections this party publicly revoked its support. The image is one of the few images published in *The Patriot* not credited as a 'Patriot Photo', strengthening my suggestion that these photographs, uncredited in *Socialist India*, were the Congress Party's own. See *The Patriot*, 18 March 1977, p. 4.

49 'Spotlight on Elections', *Socialist India*, 26 March 1977, p. 14.

50 **Editor's note**: For **Adivasi**, see Keywords.

51 Ibid., pp. 15–18.

52 Ibid., p. 16.

53 Ibid., p. 19.

54 Ibid., pp. 17–18.

55 Ibid., p. 15.

56 Ibid., p. 16.

57 Anirudh Deshpande, 'Films as Historical Sources or Alternative History', *Economic and Political Weekly*, vol. 39, no. 40, 2004, p. 4456.

58 Paul Frosh, 'The Public Eye', p. 47.

Suryanandini Narain

1 Homi K. Bhabha, interview with Neelam Raj, *The Times of India,* Crest Edition, 22–28 January 2011.

2 **Editor's note**: Archaeological Survey of India: Major arm of the Ministry of Culture, in charge of over 3,000 monuments. Founded in 1861 by oriental archaeologist Alexander Cunningham.

3 **Editor's note**: See **Photographic societies** in Keywords.

4 **Editor's note**: **Samuel Bourne** (1834–1912): See Keywords.

5 **Editor's note**: **Lala Deen Dayal** (1844–1905): See Keywords.

6 One of Beato's Mutiny images has become notorious, and remains a focus of critical debate vis-à-vis the photograph as a trustworthy signifier of empirical/historical 'truth'. See, for instance, Christopher Pinney, 'Seven Theses on Photography', in Rahaab Allana, ed., *Unframed: Discovering Image Practices in South Asia*, HarperCollins Publishers India and Alkazi Foundation, 2023, pp. 72–91. **Editor's note**: **Felice Beato**: See Keywords.

7 **Editor's note**: **Delhi Durbars**: See Keywords.

8 **Editor's note**: Walter Bosshard (1892–1975): Swiss photojournalist and reporter prominent in the 1920s; key figure in modern photojournalism. **Margaret Bourke-White**, **Kulwant Roy**, **Henri Cartier-Bresson** and **Homai Vyarawalla**: See Keywords.

9 **Editor's note**: **Sunil Janah**: See Keywords.

10 **Editor's note**: Kishor Parekh (1930–1982): Influential photojournalist, worked as chief photographer of the newspaper *Hindustan Times*, covering the 1962 India–China war and India's 1965 war with Pakistan. Best known for his coverage of the 1971 Bangladesh War; see the book *Bangladesh: A Brutal Birth* (1972).

11 **Editor's note**: Debalina Mazumder (1919–2012) and Manobina Roy (1919–2001): Twin sisters, both amateur photographers. Commemorated in a major exhibition, *Twin Sisters with Cameras*, by Sabeena Gadihoke, Mallika Leuzinger and Tapati Guha-Thakurta (2022–23).

12 **Editor's note**: **Raghu Rai** (b. 1942) and **S. Paul** (b. 1931): See Keywords.

13 **Editor's note**: **Raghubir Singh** (1942–1999): See Keywords.

14 **Editor's note**: **Kulwant Roy, Mitter Bedi** and **Madan Mahatta**: See Keywords.

15 **Editor's note**: **Ram Rahman**: See Keywords.

16 **Editor's note**: **Satish Sharma**: Independent photographer, writer, cultural critic and curator. Has worked as a freelance photojournalist since 1975 and as a documentary photographer for UNICEF. Curated *Street Dreams: Contemporary Indian Studio Photographs from the Satish Sharma Collection* (1997–1999).

17 **Editor's note**: Sooni Taraporevala (b. 1957): Photographer, screenwriter and filmmaker. Known for working with the Parsi community; see her book *Parsis, the Zoroastrians of India: A Photographic Journey,*

1980–2000 (2000). Known for screenwriting collaborations with Mira Nair and for adapting Rohinton Mistry's novel, *Such A Long Journey*, to the screen (1998). Directorial work includes *Yeh Ballet* (2020). Shahid Datawala (b. 1974): Mumbai-based artist-photographer known for several solo exhibitions often using the city of Mumbai, e.g., *Where the City Rests* (2010) and *I Once Was Alive* (2015).

18 **Editor's note**: American photojournalist Mary Ellen Mark's *Falkland Road: Prostitutes of Bombay*, Steidl, Thames & Hudson, 2005 [1978)], is a well-known work on sex workers in Kamathipura, Mumbai.

19 **Editor's note**: Sudharak Olwe (b. 1966) is a noted Mumbai-based photojournalist working on human rights issues, often in collaboration with NGOs in rural and urban communities. *11th Road, Kamathipura* (2017) is based on an exhibition of photographs inspired by the poems of major Dalit poet Namdeo Dhasal, who grew up in that red-light district. Olwe was present when Dhasal organized a *morcha* by sex workers in 1995. 'Kamathipura was the world that Namdeo grew up in' says Olwe. 'He called it *do number ki duniya* ... the bottom of the world.'

20 **Editor's note**: *Seven Lives and a Dream* is a group of black-and-white photographs taken between 1980 and 1991 and printed in 2014, including staged and documentary images spanning decades of engagement with, and participation in, the feminist movement in India. **Sheba Chhachhi**: See Keywords.

21 **Editor's note**: Anti-Sikh riots in Delhi: See note 5 in Sabeena Gadihoke, 'Journeys into Inner and Outer Worlds'.

22 **Editor's note**: Sondeep Shankar is a major photojournalist known mainly for his work during the Emergency years and after. Has published in, among others, *The Times of India, India Today, Hindustan Times, Asian Age* and *Deccan Chronicle*. **Pablo Bartholomew**, **Ram Rahman**: See Keywords.

23 **Editor's note**: **Babri Masjid/Ram Janmabhoomi violence (1992)**: See Keywords.

24 **Editor's note**: See, in this volume, Prashant Panjiar/Rahaab Allan, 'Zooming In'. Nitin Rai: Acclaimed photojournalist and son of **Raghu Rai**; remembered especially for his photographs of the **Babri Masjid** demolition.

25 **Editor's note**: Citizenship Amendment Act 2019: Second amendment to the Act of 1955, specifically excluding Muslims from the 'persecuted minorities' who would be eligible for Indian citizenship.

26 **Editor's note**: Shaheen Bagh, Delhi: A women-led protest against the Citizenship Amendment Act.

27 **Editor's note**: Ravi Agarwal: See notes 38 and 44 in Sabeena Gadihoke, 'Journeys into Inner and Outer Worlds'.

28 **Editor's note**: **Vivan Sundaram**: See Keywords.

29 **Editor's note**: Dhruv Malhotra (b.1985): Photographer focused on urban areas and especially cities at night. Major work is the *After Dark* trilogy: *Noida Soliloquy*, *Sleepers* and *After Party*, spanning a decade's work between 2007 and 2015.

30 **Editor's note**: Jagori: Feminist NGO established in 1984.

31 **Editor's note**: Gauri Gill: See 'On Seeing' in this volume.

32 **Editor's note**: Nirbhaya gang rape: The 2012 gang rape and murder, commonly known as the Nirbhaya case, involved a rape and fatal assault that occurred on 16 December 2012 in Munirka, a neighbourhood in south Delhi. It led to a major protest movement; a judicial inquiry in December 2012 submitted a report which indicated that failures on the part of the government and police were the root cause behind crimes against women.

33 **Editor's note**: Anay Mann: Photographer known for staged portraits of young urban Indians including *Generations in Transition*. Since 2001, has widely exhibited photographs of wife titled *About Neetika*.

34 **Editor's note**: Bharti Kher (b. 1969): Artist working with painting, sculpture and installation.

35 **Editor's note**: *Paris Autumn* (2006): Short film using still images, edited 'in the style of a gothic thriller', telling the story of the artist's stay in Paris in the autumn of 2005. The room she lives in turns out to be in the outhouses of a mansion that had once belonged to Gabrielle d'Estrées, King Henri IV's favourite, who died due to poisoning at the age of twenty-six, just as she was about to marry the king.

36 **Editor's note:** Sonia Khurana, *Logic of Birds*, 2006, video/photo series. Khurana (b. 1968) is a performance artist who works with diverse lens-based media.

37 **Editor's note**: *The Americans* (2000–07): Exhibition of photographs shot after a series of solitary journeys travelling from New York and New Jersey to California to the midwest and five southern states.

38 **Editor's note**: Ahmed Ali (1923–2016): Joined Bourne & Shepherd, Calcutta, aged seventeen. Set up the studio Universal Camera Arts in Calcutta, in 1948. First professional assignment was to photograph the Tata Steel Plant in 1947. Known for an astonishing body of work including tea gardens, coal mines, uranium mines,

steel plants, hotels, locomotive plants, truck and car factories, radio manufacturing factories, lamp factories, as also models for advertisements and even aerial photography.

39 **Editor's note**: Siddhartha Ghosh (1948–2002): Photography collector and prolific author on Bengal's photography history. *Chhobi Tola: Bangalir Photography Charcha* (*Taking Photographs: The Photographic Practices of Bengalis*, Ananda Publishers Pvt. Ltd., 1988) is a pioneering resource.

40 **Editor's note**: Pablo Bartholomew, *et al.*, *The Calcutta Diaries*, New Delhi: Art Heritage, 2012. Manish Chakraborti, Florian Haniq and Peter Bialobrzeski, eds, *Calcutta: Chitpur Road Neighborhoods*, Hatje Cantz/Alkazi Foundation for the Arts, 2015. *Calcutta 1940–1970: In the Photographs of Jayant Patel*, New Delhi: Niyogi Books, 2017. *City of Photos* (dir. Nishtha Jain, 2004).

41 **Editor's note**: see Madhusree Dutta *et al.*, *dates.sites: Project Cinema City Bombay/Mumbai*, New Delhi: Tulika Books, 2012 and *Project Cinema City*, New Delhi: Tulika Books, 2013.

42 **Editor's note**: Salaam Balak Trust: NGO established in 1989 to support homeless children, set up after the making of Mira Nair's film *Salaam Bombay* (1988).

43 **Editor's note**: Rahaab Allana, ed., *Delhi: Looking Out/Looking In, Aperture* 243, Summer 2021.

44 Matias Echanove and Rahul Srivastava, *ARTIndia*, vol. 15, no. 3, 2010, pp. 29–34.

Sabeena Gadihoke

1 William Gedney, 'India: Bittersweet Land', in Margaret Sartor and Geoff Dyer, eds, *What Was True: The Photographs and Notebooks of William Gedney*, New York and London: The Centre for Documentary Studies in association with W.W. Norton & Co., 2000, p. 110.

2 See Arjun Appadurai, 'Street Culture', *The India Magazine*, vol. 8, December 1987, pp. 2–23; and Dipesh Chakrabarty, 'Open Space/Public Place: Garbage, Modernity and India', *South Asia*, vol. 14, no. 1, 1991, pp. 15–31. Noting that Indian streets are often the scenes of intensely personal acts such as bathing or worship, Appadurai points out that Indian street culture did not rely on 'sharp breaks between "inside" and "outside", "private" and "public", personal and collective activities'.

3 Raghu Rai in conversation with Manoj Nair and Uma Nair, responding to their question of why so many of his images were 'off-centre'. See 'I had no love for photography', *The Economic Times*, 18 April 2011.

4 Photojournalism of the1960s was a response to the undelivered promises of the new nation-state. Kishor Parekh's photographs of the liberation of Bangladesh in 1971 represented a gritty, outdoor, guerrilla type of photography. This sensibility was inherited by Raghu Rai and his brother S. Paul who started their careers in the press in the 1960s, and later by photojournalists such as Pablo Bartholomew, Prashant Panjiar and Pramod Pushkarna who covered major political events, wars and disasters for the national and international press. All these photographers produced independent bodies of work in addition to their photojournalistic assignments.

5 **Editor's note**: 1984 was marked by two unforgettable traumatic public events. Bhopal Gas Leak: An accident at the Union Carbide India Limited pesticide plant in Bhopal, Madhya Pradesh on 2 December 1984 that led to India's biggest industrial disaster. **Pablo Bartholomew**'s image of a child being buried by her family after the gas leak won World Press Photo's 1984 Photo of the Year award. Anti-Sikh Riots: After the assassination of Indira Gandhi in Delhi, riots saw the Sikh community brutally targeted, resulting in over 8,000 deaths.

6 **Editor's note**: **Raghubir Singh**, **Raghu Rai**: See Keywords.

7 During the span of a career shortened due to his premature passing, Singh published numerous books. The works discussed in this essay include *Bombay: Gateway of India*, New York: Aperture, 1994; *Benaras: Sacred City of India*, London: Thames and Hudson, 1988; and *A Way into India*, London: Phaidon Press, 2002.

8 **Editor's note**: **Henri Cartier-Bresson**, **S. Paul**: See Keywords.

9 See Raghu Rai, *Calcutta*, New Delhi: Time Books International, 1989.

10 **Editor's note**: **Ketaki Sheth**, **Ram Rahman**: See Keywords.

11 **Editor's note**: Sooni Taraporevala, Mumbai-based photographer and filmmaker. See her *Parsis: The Zoroastrians of India, A Photographic Journey* (2000) and *Home in the City: Bombay 1977–Mumbai 2017* (2017).

12 The subtitles of Raghubir Singh's books on Benaras (*Sacred City of India*) and Bombay (*Gateway of

India) are indicative of the ways in which these cities were framed in terms of their relationship to tradition and modernity, respectively.

13 Sunil Khilnani, 'I am as I am', in *Dayanita Singh*, Penguin Studio, Penguin Books India, 2010, p. 21.

14 **Editor's note**: **Dayanita Singh**: See Keywords.

15 **Editor's note**: **Sheba Chhachhi**: See Keywords.

16 This section of the essay refers to the photographic display of these images as opposed to their subsequent use in other art installations.

17 Addressing the invisibility of gay men in public space, this body of work by Gupta, performed by a 'cast of willing gay accomplices', marks an early departure from the realist project of documentary photography at the time.

18 Mary Ellen Mark photographed extensively for publications such as *Life*, *New York Times Magazine*, *Rolling Stone*, *Vanity Fair* and *New Yorker* for over four decades. She visited India several times and her body of work on the red-light district in Bombay was published as the book *Falkland Road* (New York: Knopf, 1981).

19 See 'Sunil Janah: Documenting India Frame by Frame', an interview with Sunil Janah by Vandana Makker, *India-West*, 24 September 2000, http://suniljanah.org/sjanah/review/exsf00/india-west/india-west.htm, last accessed 21 September 2009.

20 Sunil Janah's large repertoire of work includes photographs of Gandhi's meetings, peace processions in Calcutta and peasants' movements in Punjab.

21 **Editor's note**: **Sunil Janah**, **Bengal Famine**: See Keywords.

22 **Editor's note**: **Kulwant Roy**, **T.S. Satyan**: See Keywords. T.S. Nagarajan (1932–2014): Photo-journalist, picture editor of the Planning Commission journal *Yojana* and consultant photographer to UNICEF. See his book *Vanishing Homes of India* (The HECAR Foundation, 2013).

23 The famous exhibition *The Family of Man* (1955), curated by Edward Steichen for the Museum of Modern Art, New York, was a major photographic event of its time. Its various editions toured the world, including India (Bombay, Agra, Delhi, Calcutta, Madras, Ahmedabad and Trivandrum during 1956–57). Accompanied by a catalogue, the exhibition showcased images by Cartier-Bresson. Second-hand issues of *Life* magazine could have been another way of circulating his images, though some press photographers may not have had a chance to know Bresson's work till much later.

24 **Editor's note**: **Homai Vyarawalla** (1913–2012): See Keywords.

25 **Editor's note:** *Blitz*: Sensationalist weekly tabloid paper founded on 1 February 1941 by Rustom ('Russi') Karanjia, publishing in English, Hindi and Urdu.

26 Walter Benjamin, 'On Some Motifs in Baudelaire' [1939], in Hannah Arendt, ed., *Illuminations: Essays and Reflections*, New York: Schocken Books, 1968, p. 175.

27 **Editor's note**: Filmmaker Roberto Rossellini married Ingrid Bergman in 1950. In 1957, Prime Minister Jawaharlal Nehru invited Rossellini to make a documentary and to aid the Films Division. Rossellini however had an affair with Sonali Dasgupta, screenwriter wife of filmmaker Harisadhan Dasgupta, leading to a major scandal enthusiastically covered in the Indian and international tabloid press.

28 In April 1959, naval commander Kawas Nanavati confronted and then shot dead his English wife Sylvia's lover, Prem Ahuja. The ensuing sensational trial was pictorially covered for two years in the tabloid press, led by *Blitz*, turning Nanavati into a celebrity. **Editor's note**: *Blitz* published nine pages of images and text about the murder and continued to sensationalize the case after the trial began. See image in Sabeena Gadihoke, 'Journeys into Inner and Outer Worlds', p. 93 in this volume.

29 **Editor's note**: *Illustrated Weekly of India*: See note 3 of Prashant Panjiar/Rahaab Allana, 'Zooming In'.

30 **Editor's note**: *Femina*, *Eve's Weekly*, *Filmfare*: *Femina* was founded in July 1959 and is the oldest running English-language women's magazine in India. *Eve's Weekly* was set up in 1949, and is remembered for recipes, knitting patterns, confessionals and gossip columns. *Filmfare* was founded in 1952, carrying film reviews, interviews, news about celebrities and features on rising actors.

31 Local histories of the journeys of these cameras in the region are still to be documented. The most famous of early press cameras, the Speed Graphic that was developed in the early twentieth century, became more readily available in India when it was sold in second-hand markets after American troops left the country at the end of World War II. While the compact Leica and other medium-format 35 mm cameras had made their entry,

the Rolleiflex with its 120 mm film continued to be the camera of choice for press photographers till the 1960s.

32 Field cameras developed after the 1870s enabled the panoramic views of Samuel Bourne and his fellow British photographers, but with slow exposure times they would blur easily in less controlled spaces. Deen Dayal trained as a civil engineer and draughtsman and hence was able to achieve a remarkable clarity in several planes of depth in his images of cities and landscapes, but one can only imagine the effort required to control the movement of human subjects within these frames. For a rich and detailed account of the technomateriality of early colonial photography, see Christopher Pinney, *The Coming of Photography in India*, Oxford: Oxford University Press, 2008.

33 **Editor's note**: Narayan Vinayak Virkar (1890–1968): Portrait photographer and photojournalist known for documenting the **Jallianwala Bagh massacre** (see Keywords), and for portraits of nationalist leaders.

34 See Sharada Dwivedi, 'In Pursuit of History', *Harmony Magazine*, August 2004.

35 Pinney gives fascinating examples of how the lack of camera mobility had an impact on the visual representation of the Mutiny half a century earlier. As photographers could not be physically present at sites of violence, the excesses of the Mutiny (for the British) came to be represented through fictional reconstructions, such as lithographs that could fill in for what was missing, or the more famous examples of staging by early commercial photographers – for instance, **Felice Beato**, who earned notoriety through his recreation of the massacre of rebel sepoys at Sikandar Bagh, Lucknow by arranging the exhumed bones of victims across the site. See Christopher Pinney, 'Photography as Poison', in *The Coming of Photography to India*, Oxford: Oxford University Press, 2008, p. 82.

36 Excerpted from 'Photo Fiction', Singh's post on her webpage, 'Random Thoughts on Photography, Art and Being a Soloist', 16 June 2016, https://dayanitasingh.org/

37 Discussion at a seminar on photography organized by the French Embassy at the India International Centre, New Delhi in January 2008. There was an increasing shift in focus to themes of a rapidly globalizing India, that include the middle- and upper-middle-class family, sexuality, and other forms of urban experience that tended to be captured in interior spaces.

38 This section consciously chooses to speak about practitioners who have demonstrated consistent bodies of work on outdoor-based subjects in the last decade, even while recent shows such as *Click* (Vadehra Art Gallery, New Delhi, 2008) seem to suggest an increasing diversity of practice. For instance, a photographer who has explored emerging small-town India since 2004, as seen in her *Urban Landscapes – The New Indian City* series, is Gauri Gill. Her other significant focus since 1999 is rural Rajasthan, the site for her series *Balika Mela*, P. Sainath's persistent documentation of rural India and Ravi Agarwal's photographs of migrant labour in his book *Down and Out: Labouring under Global Capitalism* (2000) are other significant exceptions to the focus on the urban experience.

39 **Editor's note**: **Pablo Bartholomew**: See Keywords.

40 Vijay and Samar Jodha's *Through the Looking Glass* (1997–2001) on the ubiquitous presence of television could be seen as a similar exploration of the outer world through an interior object.

41 **Editor's note**: Anita Khemka (b. 1972): Documentary photographer who collaborates with partner Imran Kokiloo. Since 2017, their focus has been on Kashmir. Currently with PhotoSouthAsia, dedicated to South Asian photography practices. **Editor's note:** Tejal Shah (b. 1979): Artist working with video art, photography, performance, drawing and sound work; themes include LGBTQ+ community, sexuality and gender disability.

42 **Editor's note**: **Bharat Sikka**: See Keywords.

43 **Editor's note**: Gauri Gill: See her essay in this volume, 'On Seeing'.

44 It is very difficult to summarize the complex work of Sheba Chhachhi, but I refer here to a range of work from the early *Mappings* (1997) to the more recent *Winged Pilgrims: A Chronicle from Asia* (2006). In the latter Chhachhi tells multiple stories of global migration through a series of imaginary landscapes using a variety of media, including documentary photography. Photographer Sunil Gupta's *Homelands* (2001) similarly layers the vulnerable and fragile body/self against landscapes of 'homecoming' in a mixed-media installation using video. An array of other artists, including Raqs Media Collective, Jitish Kallat, Gigi Scaria, Ravi Agarwal and Atul Bhalla, have explored public space using photographs in multimedia works. **Editor's note**: **Sheba Chhachhi**, **Raqs Media Collective**: See Keywords. Sunil Gupta: See Sunil Gupta/Rahaab Allana, 'FotoFest 2018 and Other Curatorial Practices', in this volume. Jitish Kallat (b. 1974): Artist working with painting, photography, collages,

sculpture, installations and multimedia works. Gigi Scaria (b. 1973): Multimedia artist. Ravi Agarwal (b. 1958): Visual artist, curator and environmental activist; works with photography, video, text and installation. Atul Bhalla (b. 1964): Professor of Visual Art at Shiv Nadar University in India.

45 See Patricia Hayes, 'Realism and Phantasmagoria in the Border War (Namibia), 1970s–80s', paper delivered at the International Association of Historians of Asia Conference, Jawaharlal Nehru University, New Delhi, 2008.

46 There are glimpses of this in some of Richard Bartholomew's stunning moonlit exteriors from the 1950s that have recently been published in Pablo Bartholomew and Devika Daulat Singh, eds, *A Critic's Eye*, New York: Chatterjee & Lal, Photoink and Sepia International, 2009.

Diva Gujral

1 **Editor's note**: Jyoti (Jyotindra Manshankar) Bhatt (b. 1934): Artist and photographer, studied painting at **Faculty of Fine Arts, Maharaja Sayajirao University, Baroda**, best known for his photographic work. Feroz Katpitia (b. 1926): Taught painting from 1956 to 1986, also got into experimental photography. Jeram Patel (1930–2016): Major abstract painter, part of the Group 1890. **Gulammohammed Sheikh**: See Keywords.

2 **Editor' note**: **Faculty of Fine Arts, Maharaja Sayajirao University, Baroda**: See Keywords.

3 Made accessible by Asia Art Archive, a Hong Kong-based organization that creates digital archives of artists' personal collections, photographs, essays and correspondence; https://aaa.org.hk/en

4 This essay uses the cities' former names, Bombay and Baroda, rather than Mumbai and Vadodara (changed in 1995 and 1974 respectively).

5 Fleeting references are made to this presumed ban: for example, J.N. Unwalla writes: 'In India the story of Photography ... is not very heartening. The Government has yet to give it official recognition as an expressive art form ... the next few years will undoubtedly be for this search for recognition and unity.' See J.N. Unwalla, 'Indian Photography – 50 Years', *MARG*, vol. 14, no. 1, 1960, pp. 5–10. In 1971, Jyoti Bhatt flouted the Lalit Kala's prohibition of photography in their annual exhibition by submitting *Untitled (A Face)* with the medium description 'silver gelatin print' (rather than 'photograph'), because of which it went undiscovered and was selected for display by the jury. Interview with Jyoti Bhatt, 24 January 2017.

6 This of course has parallels in interventions made in the United States and England in the late nineteenth and early twentieth centuries, when groups such as the Linked Ring and Alfred Stieglitz's Photo-Secession campaigned for the camera's status as art by staging regular photography exhibitions.

7 Simultaneous iterations of photographic modernism in other non-European nations are addressed in Esther Gabara, *Errant Modernism: The Ethos of Photography in Mexico and Brazil*, Durham: Duke University Press, 2008; Judith Keller and Amanda Maddox, eds, *Japan's Modern Divide: The Photographs of Hiroshi Hamaya and Kansuke Yamamoto*, Los Angeles: J. Paul Getty Museum, 2013; and William Schaefer, *Shadow Modernism: Photography, Writing, and Space in Shanghai, 1925–1937*, Durham: Duke University Press, 2017. In the study of Indian photography, there continues to be a prominent imbalance towards the study of nineteenth- and early twentieth-century photography, with a number of prolific engagements with colonial photographic culture and early Indian practitioners in texts such as Christopher Pinney, *Camera Indica: The Social Life of Indian Photographs*, London: Reaktion Books, 1997; and Zahid R. Chaudhary, *Afterimage of Empire: Photography in Nineteenth-century India*, Minneapolis: University of Minnesota Press, 2012. More recent literature has paid close attention to the relationship of photography and memory, such as in *Postdate: Photography and Inherited History in India*, exhibition catalogue, San Jose: San Jose Museum of Art, 2015. In the specific context of mid-twentieth-century India, monographs on photography have pertained primarily to photojournalists such as Homai Vyarawalla and Sunil Janah; see Sabeena Gadihoke, *Camera Chronicles of Homai Vyarawalla*, Ahmedabad: Mapin Publishing, 2006, and Ram Rahman, *Sunil Janah: Photographs 1940–1960: Vintage Prints from the Swaraj Art Archive*, Noida, Uttar Pradesh: Swaraj Art Archive, 2014. Studies of artists' excursions into photography are largely restricted to exhibition catalogues, such as *Nasreen Mohamedi: Waiting is a Part of Intense Living*, exhibition catalogue, Madrid: Reina Sofia, 2015, and *Jyoti Bhatt: Parallels that Meet*, exhibition catalogue, New Delhi: Delhi Art Gallery, 2008. More recent engagements with artistic practice include Rebecca Brown, *Art for a*

Modern India, 1947–1980, Durham: Duke University Press, 2009; and Emilia Terracciano, *Art and Emergency: Modernism in Twentieth-Century India*, London and New York: I.B. Tauris, 2018; however, a comprehensive, interconnected account of these photographic practices has yet to be written.

8 **Editor's note**: **Vision Exchange Workshop**: See Keywords.

9 **Editor's note**: Krishen Khanna (b. 1925): Renowned painter; in late 1940s, part of the Bombay **Progressive Artists' Group** (see Keywords). Member of Akbar Padamsee's interdisciplinary **Vision Exchange Workshop** (see Keywords), where he created the layered photographic series, *The Crows around My Studio, Made The Game*, political paintings inspired by the 1971 Bangladesh War of Liberation.

10 **Editor's note**: Akbar Padamsee (1928–2020): Major painter working with oil painting, water colour, plastic emulsion, drawings, sculpture, printmaking, photography, film and computer graphics.

11 **Editor's note**: Bhupendra Karia (1936–1994): Headed the Photography/Graphic Arts department at **Maharaja Sayajirao University, Baroda** (see Keywords) from 1964 to 1966.

12 **Editor's note**: **Nasreen Mohamedi**: See Keywords.

13 See *Murtaza Vali, Ashim Ahluwalia: Events in a Cloud Chamber*, exhibition document, Mumbai, 2016; and Shanay Jhaveri and Nalini Malani, 'Building on a Prehistory: Artists' Film and New Media in India, Part 3', *LUX*, 24 June 2014, https://lux.org.uk/writing/building-prehistory-artists-film-new-media-india-part-3.

14 **Editor's note**: S.N.S. Sastry (1930–1978) was a celebrated experimental documentary filmmaker working with **Films Division** (see Keywords).

15 **Editor's note**: *Yet in Him We Trust* (1966) is a 52-second graphic film on 'Man and His World'. *Yes, It's On* (1972) is a 12-minute film using photographs and found footage . Both were made for **Films Division**.

16 Nancy Adajania, 'New Media Overtures Before New Media Practice in India', in Gayatri Sinha, ed., *Art and Visual Culture in India, 1857–2007*, Mumbai: MARG Publications, 2009, pp. 266–81.

17 **Editor's note**: *Vrishchik* (meaning Scorpion): Art magazine started by **Gulammohammed Sheikh** in 1969 with Bhupen Khakhar (1934–2003) – major Indian painter based, like Sheikh, in Baroda.

18 A form of camera film that was known to produce particularly high-contrast images; photographs in the positive could be contact-printed on to lith film in order to yield a larger, high-contrast negative.

19 Jyoti Bhatt, Baroda, personal communication, 25 September 2017.

20 Ibid.

21 The notion of loaded, potent acts of sight and seeing, using such multivalent terms as 'nazar', 'darshan', and 'corpothetics', recurs in methodologies that unpack the specificity of visual transactions in the Indian subcontinent and their complex manifestations in public culture. See Carol Breckenridge, ed., *Consuming Modernity: Public Culture in a South Asian World*, Minneapolis: University of Minnesota Press, 1995; and Shaila Bhatti, *Translating Museums: A Counterhistory of South Asian Museology*, Abingdon: Routledge, 2012. See also Gopesa Paquette, 'Darshan and the Decisive Moment', in Rahaab Allana, ed., *Unframed: Discovering Image Practices in South Asia*, New Delhi: The Alkazi Foundation for the Arts and HarperCollins Publishers India, 2023, pp. 156–58.

22 Carol Breckenridge and Arjun Appadurai, 'Public Modernity in India', in Carol Breckenridge, ed., *Consuming Modernity*, p. 12.

23 Christopher Pinney, 'Introduction', in Rachel Dwyer and Christopher Pinney, eds, *Pleasure and the Nation: The History, Politics and Consumption of Public Culture in India*, New Delhi: Oxford University Press, 2001, p. 1.

24 Carol Breckenridge, ed., *Consuming Modernity*, pp. 4–5. The historiographies of public culture and viewing are closely intertwined in the study of twentieth-century India, and have been mobilized variously in studies of local film, cricket and urban restaurant culture, and strangely, have yet to make their way into the study of 'secular' artistic viewing. See ibid.; Rachel Dwyer and Christopher Pinney, eds, *Pleasure and the Nation*; and Martin Jay and Sumathi Ramaswamy, eds, *Empires of Vision: A Reader*, Durham: Duke University Press, 2014.

25 See Rahul Mehrotra and Sharada Dwivedi, *The Jehangir Art Gallery: Established 21 January, 1952*, Mumbai: Jehangir Art Gallery, 2002; and Karin Zitzewitz, *The Art of Secularism: The Cultural Politics of Modernist Art in Contemporary India*, London: Oxford University Press, 2014.

26 See Zitzewitz's detailed interviews with Kekoo Gandhy, whose framing business (the Chemical Moulding Manufacturing Company) and subsequent art gallery (Gallery Chemould) were physically located inside the Jehangir Art Gallery until 2007 (ibid., pp. 87–88). **Editor's note**: **Progressive Artists Group**: See Keywords.

27 Atreyee Gupta, 'The Promise of the Modern: State, Culture, and Avant-gardism in India (*ca.* 1930–1960)', unpublished doctoral thesis, University of Minnesota, 2011, pp. 106–09.

28 For a discussion of coevalness and cotemporality, see Johannes Fabian, *Time and the Other: How Anthropology Makes Its Object*, New York: Columbia University Press, 1983.

29 **Editor's note**: Dashrath Patel (1925–2010): Visionary designer, pedagogue and versatile artist in painting, sculpture, ceramics, photography, architecture and design. Played a key role in shaping the trajectory of the National Institute of Design, Ahmedabad; set up the 'Rural Design School' in Sewapuri near Varanasi in 1981.

30 Walter Benjamin, *The Arcades Project*, translated by Howard Eiland and Kevin McLaughlin, 1982; reprinted Cambridge: Harvard University Press, 2002, pp. 22–23.

31 **Editor's note**: Edward Steichen (1879–1973): Luxembourg-born American photographer and curator; co-founder of the Galleries of the Photo-Secession (later known as '291'), the first to represent European modern art in New York.

32 See *MARG*, vol. 14, no. 1, titled *Photography: Images of India*, in which details of the exhibition and its constituent works were reproduced. The relationship of *The Family of Man* and *Images of India* is briefly addressed in Atreyee Gupta, 'Belatedness and Simultaneity: A Short History of Photography from India', in *Postdate: Photography and Inherited History in India*, pp. 24–35. See also Sukanya Baskar, '"An Experience One Must Not Miss": *The Family of Man* and Modern Indian Photography', in Rahaab Allana, ed., *Unframed: Discovering Image Practices in South Asia*, New Delhi: The Alkazi Foundation for the Arts and HarperCollins Publishers India, 2023, pp. 311–52. **Editor's note**: *The Family of Man* (1955) See note 10 of Introduction in this volume. **Editor's note**: Bombay Photography Association, see **Photographic societies** in Keywords.

33 Nancy Adajania, 'New Media Overtures Before New Media Practice in India', p. 270.

34 Manu Bhagavan presents a cogent account of Maharaja Pratapsingh's grandfather Maharaja Sayajirao Gaekwad III's extended struggle to establish the University of Baroda, eventually allowing the movement to lapse in 1930, in large part because of the maharaja's fear of dethronement at the hands of the displeased imperial government. See Manu Bhagavan, 'The Rebel Academy: Modernity and the Movement for a University in Princely Baroda, 1908–49', *Journal of Asian Studies*, vol. 61, no. 3, 2002, pp. 919–47.

35 Ibid., p. 944.

36 Author unknown, *Rules of the Society for the Promotion of Industrial Art* (Calcutta, 1856), quoted in Atreyee Gupta, 'The Promise of the Modern', p. 29.

37 For a detailed account of the curricula of colonial art schools, see Arindam Dutta, *The Bureaucracy of Beauty: Design in the Age of its Global Reproducibility*, New York: Routledge, 2007, pp. 32–33.

38 See **Gulammohammed Sheikh**, ed., *Contemporary Art in Baroda*, New Delhi: Tulika Books, 1997.

39 Karen Zitzewitz, *The Art of Secularism*, p. 44.

40 Amrita Gupta Singh, 'Tradition and Innovation: The Past as Resource', in *Jyoti Bhatt: Parallels that Meet*, p. 29. See also Rebecca Brown, *Art for a Modern India, 1947–80*, Durham: Duke University Press, 2009.

41 Hansa Mehta, 'Foreword', in *Faculty of Fine Arts: The Maharaja Sayajirao University of Baroda*, university prospectus, 1953.

42 Ibid.

43 **Editor's note**: Sankho Chaudhuri (1916–2006): Renowned sculptor. Founded the Sculpture Department at the **Faculty of Fine Arts, Maharaja Sayajirao University, Baroda** (see Keywords) in 1949.

44 **Editor's note**: Ramkinkar Baij (1906–1980): Pioneering Indian sculptor and a key figure of Contextual Modernism. Studied at Kala Bhavan in Santiniketan in the 1920s under the tutelage of Nandalal Bose and Rabindranath Tagore.

45 **Editor's note**: K.G. Subramanyan (1924–2016): Artist, scholar, writer, educator and art historian. Worked as painter, muralist, sculptor, printmaker, set designer and toy maker. Graduated from Kala Bhavan, Santiniketan in 1948, having studied/trained under the mentorship of great masters such as Benodebehari Mukherjee, Nandalal Bose and Ramkinkar Baij.

46 **Editor's note**: N.S. Bendre (1910–1992): Artist and educator, briefly a member of the **Progressive Artists' Group** (see Keywords) in 1948. Helped start the Lalit Kala Akademi in 1954. Appointed head, Department of Painting at the **Faculty of Fine Arts, Maharaja Sayajirao University**, Baroda (see Keywords) in 1950.

47 Author unknown, 'Outline of Courses', in Hansa Mehta, 'Foreword', *Faculty of Fine Arts: The Maharaja Sayajirao University of Baroda.*

48 Gulammohammed Sheikh, ed., *Contemporary Art in Baroda*, p. 267, footnote 6.

49 **Editor's note**: Rabindranath Tagore (1861–1941): Iconic figure in Indian cultural renaissance, poet, writer, playwright, composer, philosopher, social reformer and painter. See Keywords in *The Vanishing Point: Moving Images After Video*, edited by Rashmi Devi Sawhney, *India Since the 90s*, vol. 3, New Delhi: Tulika Books, 2022, p. 342.

50 **Editor's note**: **Gaganendranath Tagore** (1867–1938): Avant-garde Indian painter and caricaturist, nephew of Rabindranath Tagore, founded the Indian Society of Oriental Art in 1907.

51 See Regina Bittner and Kathrin Rhomberg, eds, *The Bauhaus in Calcutta: An Encounter of Cosmopolitan Avant-Gardes*, Berlin: Hatje Cantz, 2013.

52 See Pinney's consideration of Indian photography as poison and as cure. In *The Coming of Photography in India* (2008), Pinney invoked a dichotomous distinction in camera practices of the late nineteenth century: where cure denotes the jubilant adoption of the camera in various bureaucratic capacities as a means of solving 'existing representational problems' in the imaging of India, the camera turns poisonous when the images it generates begin to favour the cause of the colonized. For the formerly colonized, I would argue, the stages of cure and poison are reversed. See also László Moholy-Nagy, 'From Pigment to Light', in Vicki Goldberg, ed., *Photography in Print: Writings from 1816 to the Present*, Albuquerque: University of New Mexico Press, 1981, p. 344.

53 Nandalal Bose, *Vision and Creation*, Santiniketan: Visva-Bharati Publications Department, 1999, p. 247.

54 Tagore, quoted in Natasha Eaton, *Colour, Art and Empire: Culture and the Nomadism of Representation*, London: I.B. Tauris, 2013, p. 240.

55 Unwalla, 'Indian Photography – 50 Years', p. 10.

56 See Mary Price, *The Photograph: A Strange, Confined Space*, Stanford: Stanford University Press, 1994, for a discussion of critics of the camera, including George Bernard Shaw, John Ruskin and Charles Baudelaire, in relation to absence or loss in the photographic plane; also see a discussion of Alfred Stieglitz's journal *Camera Work* (1903–07) in Jonathan Green, ed., *Camera Work: A Critical Anthology*, New York: Aperture, 1973, for references to debates around Pictorialism. In the context of South Asia, Bose's declaration of the camera's lack of heart (a loss of the quality of human emotion) echoes Baudelaire's argument that the photograph existed in the absence of imagination. See Baudelaire quoted in *Before Photography: Painting and the Invention of Photography*, exhibition catalogue, New York: Museum of Modern Art, 1981, p. 28.

57 Walter Benjamin, *The Work of Art in an Age of Mechanical Reproduction*, translated by J.A. Underwood, 1936; reprinted London: Penguin, 2008, p. 6.

58 See Jyoti Bhatt's conversation with K.G. Subramanyan, *Lalit Kala Contemporary*, 18, 1974, pp. 25–26: 'Personally, I do not see why mechanical devices should not be used by an artist. ... In fact all artists have used some tool or the other since the prehistoric times. Cameras, enlargers, and other mechanical devices are only more advanced types of tools. Why should he not use them if they serve this purpose?'

59 László Moholy-Nagy, *Painting Photography Film*, translated by Janet Seligman, 1925; reprint, Cambridge, Mass.: MIT Press, 1969, p. 51.

60 See Jorge Luis Borges, 'The Garden of Forking Paths' and 'Death and the Compass', in *Labyrinths: Selected Stories and Other Writings*, translated by Onís *et al.*, New York: New Directions Publishing, 1964, pp. 31–39, 79–88.

61 **Editor's note**: **Richard Bartholomew (1926–1985)**: Art critic, photographer, painter, poet and writer.

62 Richard Bartholomew, 'Seventh Members' Photographic Exhibition', *Thought*, 23 April 1960, reproduced in Pablo Bartholomew, ed., *Richard Bartholomew: The Art Critic*, Noida: Bart, 2012, p. 499. Bartholomew, a long-standing art critic, played an interesting mediating role in the New Delhi art network, at once negotiating institutional renown (as secretary of the Lalit Kala Akademi from 1977 to 1985) and counter-institutional spaces (as a firm fixture in the social circles of the Bombay Progressives and the Baroda artists).

Jodi Throckmorton

1 **Editor's note**: **Ram Rahman**, see Keywords.

2 **Editor's note**: Biennale aesthetic refers to a specific demand for/creation of art in several international art biennales that arguably fulfils Western expectations of India. Photographer **Ram Rahman** ('A Sharper Focus', *Seminar*, 2007) notes that from the late 1990s onwards international biennale and exhibition curators began including more Indian artists, as it became 'fashionable' to showcase them in the profitable market.

3 Ram Rahman, 'A Sharper Focus', *Seminar*, 2007, http://www.india-seminar.com/2007/578/578_ram_rahman.htm, accessed 13 August 2014.

4 **Editor's note**: **Lala Deen Dayal**, **Umrao Singh Sher-Gil**, **First Indian War of Independence**: See Keywords.

5 **Editor's note**: The Alkazi Foundation for the Arts: Instituted by Ebrahim Alkazi in New Delhi in 2004, devoted to the preservation and study of India's cultural history through research, curation and publishing.

6 **Editor's note**: **Raqs Media Collective**: See Keywords.

7 Hal Foster, 'An Archival Impulse', *October*, vol. 110, 2004, p. 5.

8 Raqs Media Collective, 'The Surface of Each Day Is a Different Planet', exhibition announcement, http://e-flux.com/announcements/raqs-media-collective-the-surface-of-each-day-is-a-dlfferent-planet/, accessed 23 July 2014.

9 **Editor's note**: Madhuban Mitra and Manas Bhattacharya: Artist duo based in Kolkata, working with photography and video. Their work emphasizes time and memory, archive, original and copy.

10 Anustup Basu, '"Through a Lens Starkly": An Exploration of Jadavpur University's Medialab's National Instruments Project Archive', in Rajinder Dudrah *et al.*, eds, *InterMedia in South Asia*, London and New York: Routledge, 2012, p. 101.

11 **Editor's note**: Surekha: Bangalore-based artist and curator. **Pushpamala N**: See Keywords.

12 Surekha, artist statement, http://surekha.info/fragments/, accessed 24 March 2014.

13 Christopher Pinney, *The Coming of Photography in India*, London: British Library, 2008, p. 144.

14 Geeta Kapur, 'Gender Mobility: Through the Lens of Five Women Artists in India', in Maura Reilly and Linda Nochlin, eds, *Global Feminisms: New Directions in Contemporary Art*, New York: Brooklyn Museum, 2007, p. 85.

15 **Editor's note**: Maurice Vidal Portman (1860–1935): British naval officer best known for documenting Andamanese tribes between 1879 and 1901 while posted as assistant superintendent of the Penal Colony.

16 Frederick Gross, 'Contemporary Photography between the Global and the Local', in Celina Jefferey and Gregory Minissale, eds, *Global and Local Art Histories*, Newcastle: Cambridge Scholars Publishing, 2007, p. 43.

17 **Editor's note**: Gauri Gill: See her essay in this volume, 'On Seeing'.

18 Gauri Gill, *Balika Mela*, Zurich: Edition Patrick Frey, 2012, p. 163.

19 Christopher Pinney, *Camera Indica: The Social Life of Indian Photographs*, Chicago: The University of Chicago Press, 1997, p. 46.

20 Anita Dube, 'The Desert Mirror', *ARTIndia*, vol. 15, no. 1, 2010.

21 **Editor's note**: David Batchelor: London-based artist and writer who works across media, including photography. Published titles include *Minimalism* (1997), *Chromophobia* (2000), *Colour* (2008), *Found Monochromes* (2010), *The Luminous and the Grey* (2014) and *Concretos* (2022).

22 David Batchelor, *Chromophobia*, FOCI series, London: Reaktion Books, 2000, pp. 22–23.

23 **Editor' note**: Jitish Kallat: See note 44 in Sabeena Gadihoke, 'Journeys into Inner and Outer Worlds'.

24 **Editor' note**: Annu P. Matthew: See note 13 in Gemma Scott, 'Putting Women in the Picture'.

25 Annu P. Matthew, artist statement, http://www.annumatthew.com/artist%20statement/Indian_statement.html, accessed 24 March 2014.

26 **Editor's note**: 1947 Partition Archive: Initiated in 2010 by Guneeta Singh Bhalla, based in Berkeley, California, as a crowd-funded, crowd-sourced database/digital museum that collects witness accounts of the Partition of India/creation of Pakistan. See **Partition** in Keywords.

27 1947 Partition Archive website, http://www.1947partitionarchive.org/browse, accessed 24 July 2015.

28 Annu P. Matthew, artist statement, http://www.annumatthew.com/Portfolioregeneration/Regeneration_statement.html, accessed 24 March 2014.

29 **Editor's note**: **Vivan Sundaram**: See Keywords.

30 **Editor's note**: Amrita Sher-Gil (1913–1941): Pioneering visual artist in pre-Independence India, widely seen to have founded a new direction in modernism. Daughter of **Umrao Singh Sher-Gil** (see Keywords).

31 Nicolas Bourriaud, *Postproduction. Culture as Screenplay: How Art Reprograms the World*, translated by Jeanine Herman, New York: Lukas & Sternberg, 2002, p. 4.

32 Vivan Sundaram, *Re-take of Amrita*, New Delhi: Tulika Books, 2001, p. 5.

33 Pushpamala N., *Pushpamala N.: Indian Lady*, New York: Bose Pacia, 2004.

Sandhini Poddar

1 **Editor's note**: Exhibition at Deutsche Guggenheim, Berlin, 26 June–10 October 2010.

2 The exhibitions *Urban Manners: Contemporary Artists from India*, Hangar Bicocca, Milan, 19 October 2007–6 January 2008; *Indian Highway*, Serpentine Gallery, London, 10 December 2008–22 February 2009; and *The Empire Strikes Back: Indian Art Today*, Saatchi Gallery, London, 29 January–7 May 2010, are examples of this type.

3 **Editor's note**: Desire Machine Collective (Mriganka Madhukaillya, Sonal Jain) use film, video, photography and multimedia installation in their works. In 2007 they initiated *Periferry*, an alternative artist-led space and residency programme on the *M.V. Chandardinga*, a ferry docked on the Brahmaputra river in Guwahati.

4 **Editor's note**: Shumona Goel: Experimental filmmaker and photographer Co-director of *I am micro* (2012); co-produced films directed by Ashim Ahluwalia (*John and Jane*, 2005 and *Miss Lovely*, 2012). Amar Kanwar: See 'Embracing Doubt' in this volume. Kabir Mohanty: Filmmaker and video artist, e.g. *Riyaaz* (1990) and *Home* (1996), in collaboration with Vikram Joglekar; *now i feel i don't know anything* (2001). Worked on video and sound installations: *dwelling* (2006), *handheld* (2009) and *In Memory* (2009, 2012).

5 For a discussion of the possibilities and limitations of the term 'moving image', see Tanya Leighton, 'Introduction', in Tanya Leighton and Charles Esche, eds, *Art and the Moving Image: A Critical Reader*, London: Tate Publishing in association with Afterall, 2008, pp. 11–12.

6 Jean-Luc Nancy, 'The Evidence of Film: Abbas Kiarostami', translated by Christine Irizarry, in Christine Irizarry and Verena Andermatt Conley, trans., *L'evidence du film/The Evidence of Film: Abbas Kiarostami*, Brussels: Yves Gevaert, 2001, p. 46.

7 Ibid., p. 56.

8 Jean-Luc Nancy, 'And Life Goes On: Life and Nothing More', in Christine Irizarry and Verena Andermatt Conley, trans., *L'evidence du film/The Evidence of Film*, p. 78.

9 The complex and paradoxical status of the 'first-person plural' is best explained in Nancy's text, *Being Singular Plural*, which lends its title in part to this exhibition. See Jean-Luc Nancy, 'Of Being Singular Plural', in Robert D. Richardson and Anne E. O'Byrne, trans., *Being Singular Plural*, Meridian: Crossing Aesthetics, Stanford: Stanford University Press, 2000, p. 5. For an explication of Nancy's approach to community and his views on art, see the text by Martta Heikkila in this exhibition catalogue.

10 This and all subsequent quotes by Shumona Goel: Goel, in e-mail correspondence and conversations with the author, September 2009–January 2010.

11 See Goel's artist statement in the plates section of the exhibition catalogue for more information about this work.

12 For an explication of gallery and museum-based practices, see the text by Erika Balsom in the exhibition catalogue.

13 **Editor's note**: *Om Dar-B-Dar* (1988): Iconic cult film directed by Kamal Swaroop, presents a postmodern portrait of growing up in Rajasthan, combining science, religion, myth and magic.

14 **Editor's note**: *Miss Lovely* (dir. Ashim Ahluwalia, 2012), well-known period movie set in the 1980s (when celluloid was just giving way to video) in Mumbai's low-end pornographic market.

15 This and all subsequent quotes by Kabir Mohanty: Mohanty, in written and e-mail correspondence and conversations with the author, September 2009–January 2010.

16 **Editor's note**: G. Aravindan (1935–1991): Major Malayalam filmmaker. Ritwik Ghatak (1925–1976): Acclaimed Bengali filmmaker whose best known work is set in the refugee communities following the **Partition** (see Keywords). Ashis Nandy (b. 1937): Sociologist, psychologist and public intellectual whose research interests centre on the political psychology of violence and cultures of knowledge. A.K. Ramanujan (1929–93): Poet, philologist, translator, linguist, folklorist and playwright.

17 **Editor's note**: Vikram Joglekar: Sound designer and composer, helped make Indian cinema compliant with Dolby sound technology. Collaborator with several major Indian independent filmmakers, including Kabir Mohanty.

18 In conversation, Mohanty associates passages in his video with certain terms, such as 'stills sequence', 'pinhole', 'police station'. Each of these employs a certain manoeuvre by the camera. Mohanty pans, inverts, curves or otherwise deconstructs the material bases of the images in order to reveal the artifice of his construction and the physicality of video.

19 As Slavoj Žižek states, 'The second great breakthrough of [Jacques] Rancière articulated in *Le Partage du sensible* … [is] the aestheticization of politics, the assertion of the aesthetic dimension as INHERENT in any radical emancipatory politics. … If what Rancière refers to as the police-aspect of the political, the rational administration and control of social processes, focuses [*sic*] on the clear categorization of every individual, of every "visible" social unit, then disturbing such orders of the visible and proposing different lateral links of the visible, unexpected short-circuits, etc., is the elementary form of resistance.' See Slavoj Žižek, 'The Lesson of Rancière', in Jacques Rancière, *The Politics of Aesthetics: The Distribution of the Sensible*, translated by Gabriel Rockhill, New York and London: Continuum, 2004, pp. 76, 77.

20 Part one consists of the following videos: *The Face*, two versions of *Thet Win Aung*, *Ma Win Maw Oo*, *The Bodhi Tree* and *Somewhere in May* (all 2005).

21 Amar Kanwar, 'Gandhi and the General', *Himal Southasian*, February 2007; http://www.himalmag.com/read.php?id=2214, accessed January 2010.

22 **Editor's note**: Ma Win Maw Oo (1971–88) was a Burmese student activist who was killed during the 8888 Uprising. The uprising turned violent in August 1988 and ended on 18 September 1988 after a military coup by the State Law and Order Restoration Council. Photographer Steve Lehman's image of Win Maw Oo's bloodied body became an icon of the movement.

23 **Editor's note**: 8888 Uprising: This series of protests against the dictatorship of the ruling Burma Socialist Programme Party was led by student groups in Yangon. Also known as the People Power Uprising, the agitation peaked on 8 August 1988, as hundreds of thousands joined the call for a national strike. The army crackdown resulted in martial rule under the State Law and Order Restoration Council (SLORC).

24 T.J. Demos, 'Life Full of Holes', in Maria Lind and Hito Steyerl, eds, *The Greenroom: Reconsidering the Documentary and Contemporary Art #1*, Berlin: Sternberg Press and Annandale-on-Hudson, NY: Center for Curatorial Studies, Bard College, 2008, p. 111.

25 Except where otherwise stated, this and all subsequent quotes by Amar Kanwar: Kanwar, in e-mail correspondence and conversations with the author, September 2009–January 2010.

26 Amar Kanwar, 'The Invisible Image', lecture at conference series 'Self-Rule and Non-Violence: Hind Swaraj a Century After', Mumbai, 19 December 2009.

27 This and all subsequent quotes by Desire Machine Collective: Sonal Jain and Mriganka Madhukaillya, in conversation with the author, Kolkata, 23–24 December 2009.

28 Michael Hardt, 'Reading notes on Deleuze and Guattari, Capitalism and Schizophrenia', http://www.duke.edu/hardt/Deleuze&Guattari.html, accessed January 2010.

29 **Editor's note**: *Tango Charlie* (dir. Mani Shankar, 2005): Mainstream commercial film about a paramilitary commando, controversial for its depiction of Bodo community, was briefly banned in Assam.

30 **Editor's note**: *Surya Tejor Anya Naam* (Sun Is Blood's Other Name, dir. Dinesh Gogoi, 1991): Assamese film seeking to depict history of political insurgency in the state using mainstream film language.

31 Ibid.

32 Ibid.

33 Jean-Luc Nancy, 'Of Being Singular Plural', pp. 4–5.

William Mazzarella and Raminder Kaur

1 **Editor's note**: *Choli ke peeche kya hai?* (What lies behind the bodice?): Raunchy folk song sung by Ila Arun in bandit movie *Khalnayak* (Villain, dir. Subhash Ghai, 1993) that led to a censorship controversy and controversy over theft of traditional knowledges and intellectual property.

2 **Editor's note**: Phoolan Devi (1963–2001): Well-known bandit operating from the ravines of central India. *Bandit Queen* (1994) was a controversial film on her life which she opposed and fought to get banned.

3 **Editor's note**: Salman Rushdie: His novel *The Satanic Verses* (1988) sparked backlash from the Muslim community worldwide for its fictional retelling of the birth of Islam and was banned in many countries, including India. *The Moor's Last Sigh* (1995), which traced four generations of a family in Mumbai and Kochi, was Rushdie's first novel after the *fatwa*. It was banned in Maharashtra for its parody of Shiv Sena leader Bal Thackeray via the character Raman Fielding and unofficially for reference to a dog named 'Jawahar'.

4 **Editor's note**: *Kama Sutra: A Tale of Love* (dir. Mira Nair, 1996): Erotic romance based on short story 'Utran' ('Hand Me Downs') by Wajida Tabassum. Censors refused to certify it for its explicit content.

5 **Editor's note**: *Fire* (1998) and *Water* (2005): Parts of an *Elements* trilogy by Indo-Canadian filmmaker Deepa Mehta. *Fire*, loosely based on Ismat Chughtai's Urdu short story, 'Lihaaf' (1941), featured Shabana Azmi and Nandita Das as sisters-in-law Radha and Sita. Hindu nationalist groups attacked theatres for promoting same-sex 'perversion' and insulting the Hindu religion. *Water* (2005) explores the plight of widows in ashrams in Varanasi in the 1930s. Mehta abandoned location shooting when a mob demolished her set.

6 *Water* was eventually filmed, under the false name *River Moon*, in Sri Lanka in 2003 and released in India in 2005. Mehta has described how in 2000, upon obtaining 'the requisite permissions and script approval from the Government of India', she began filming on the banks of the Ganges after six weeks of pre-production work: 'Two days into the shoot, what transpired next was unexpected and unprecedented. Overnight, violent protests by Hindu fundamentalists erupted in the city. Accusations of *Water* being anti-Hindu were cited as the cause of the film sets being thrown in the river, my effigy being burned, and protesters marching in the streets of Varanasi, denouncing the film and its portrayal of Hindu widows. Nobody had read the script. Bewildered by the turn of events, we tried to muster help from the state government who had given the script its approval, but to no avail. Amidst escalating protests and violence and personal death threats we were forced to shut down production. In retrospect, *Water* reflected what was taking place in India in some form or other; the rise of Hindu fundamentalism and high intolerance for anything or anybody that viewed it with scepticism.' Mehta 'resurrected the project' in Sri Lanka with a new cast, and the shoot there 'was a breeze' after the 'horrendous experience' in India. 'We decided not to even try to re-create Varanasi. ... Instead, our modest ghats were only one-third of a mile long peppered with the requisite Hindu temples.' See 'Director's Statement on *Water*', https://www.spiritualityandpractice.com/films/features/view/15544/directors-statement-on-water

7 **Editor's note**: Pakistan's 'bloodless' coup (1999): On 14 October 1999, Pakistan's army chief, General Pervez Musharraf, declared a state of Emergency and issued a provisional constitutional order that ousted Prime Minister Nawaz Sharif's democratically elected government. Musharraf was sworn in as President in June 2001, an office he held till his resignation in 2008.

8 **Editor's note**: Pakistan Internet Exchange (PIE): Established in 2000 to host the majority of internet traffic in Pakistan. Owned by the Pakistan Telecommunication Company Limited, this allowed for easy monitoring of incoming and outgoing internet traffic.

9 Asad Ali Ahmed, 'Specters of Macaulay: Blasphemy, the Indian Penal Code, and Pakistan's Postcolonial Predicament', in Raminder Kaur and William Mazzarella, eds, *Censorship in South Asia: Cultural Regulation from Sedition to Seduction*, Bloomington: Indiana University Press, 2009, pp. 172–205.

10 **Editor's note**: Taslima Nasreen (b. 1962): Bangladeshi author, faced censorship and forced exile.

11 **Editor's note**: *Ka* and *Dwikhandita*: *Ka*, the third part of Nasreen's autobiography, published in 2003, was banned in Bangladesh. Its Indian version, *Dwikhandita*, was banned in West Bengal for obscenity (the ban was lifted in 2003). It chronicles her life in Mymensingh, her experience as a gynaecologist, and the banning of the novel *Lajja* (1993, written in response to the 1992 Babri Masjid demolition).

12 **Editor's note**: Narayanhiti massacre: The killing of nine members of the Nepalese royal family, including King Birendra and Queen Aishwarya, by Crown Prince Dipendra on 1 June 2001. This mass

murder caused a pivotal shift in Nepalese politics, and ultimately led to the dissolution of the monarchy in 2008.

13 **Editor's note**: Gyanendra Bir Bikram Shah Dev was the last monarch of Nepal, between 2001 and 2008 when the monarchy was abolished by a Maoist elected assembly.

14 Genevieve Lakier, 'After the Massacre: Secrecy, Disbelief, and the Public Sphere in Nepal,' in Raminder Kaur and William Mazzarella, eds, *Censorship in South Asia*, pp. 206–34.

15 **Editor's note**: Liberation Tigers of Tamil Eelam (LTTE): Militant guerrilla group fighting to establish a separate homeland in northern Sri Lanka for the country's ethnic Tamils, against majority Sinhala-Buddhists.

16 **Editor's note**: Chandrika Bandaranaike Kumaratunga: Politician elected as President (1994–2005) of Sri Lanka, the country's first and only female holder of that office. Both her parents served as Prime Ministers.

17 See Christiane Brosiuse and Melissa Butcher, eds, *Image Journeys: Audio-Visual Media and Cultural Change in India*, New Delhi: Sage, 1999; Raminder Kaur, *Performative Politics and the Cultures of Hinduism*, New Delhi: Permanent Black, 2003; Purnima Mankekar, *Screening Culture, Viewing Politics: An Ethnography of Television, Womanhood and Nation in Postcolonial India*, Durham: Duke University Press, 1999; William Mazzarella, *Shoveling Smoke: Advertising and Globalization in Contemporary India*, Durham: Duke University Press, 2003; and Arvind Rajagopal, *Politics after Television: Hindu Nationalism and the Reshaping of the Public in India*, Cambridge: Cambridge University Press, 2001.

18 See Julia Eckert, *The Charisma of Direct Action: Power, Politics and the Shiv Sena*, New Delhi: Oxford University Press, 2003; Dipankar Gupta, *Nativism in a Metropolis: The Shiv Sena in Bombay*, New Delhi: Manohar Publications, 1982; Thomas Blom Hansen, *Wages of Violence: Naming and Identity in Postcolonial Bombay*, Princeton: Princeton University Press, 2001; and Mary Fainsod Katzenstein, *Ethnicity and Equality: The Shiv Sena Party and Preferential Policies in Bombay*, Ithaca: Cornell University Press, 1979.

19 See Pierre Bourdieu, 'Censorship and the Imposition of Form', in John Thompson, ed., *Language and Symbolic Power*, Cambridge, MA: Harvard University Press, 1991; Judith Butler, *Excitable Speech: A Politics of the Performative*, London: Routledge, 1997, and 'Ruled Out: Vocabularies of the Censor', in Robert C. Post, ed., *Censorship and Silencing: Practices of Cultural Regulation*, Los Angeles: The Getty Research Institute, 1998.

20 Judith Butler, *Excitable Speech*, p. 41.

21 Genevieve Lakier, 'After the Massacre', in Raminder Kaur and William Mazzarella, eds, *Censorship in South Asia*, pp. 206–34.

22 Tejaswini Ganti, 'The Limits of Decency and the Decency of Limits: Censorship and the Bombay Film Industry', in Raminder Kaur and William Mazzarella, eds, *Censorship in South Asia*, pp. 87–122.

23 Dominic Boyer, 'Censorship as a Vocation: The Institutions, Practices and Cultural Logic of Media Control in the German Democratic Republic', *Comparative Studies in Society and History*, vol. 45, no. 3, 2003, pp. 511–45.

24 See Michel Foucault, *Discipline and Punish: The Birth of the Prison*, translated by Alan Sheridan, Harmondsworth: Penguin, 1977; *Power/Knowledge: Selected Interviews and Other Writings, 1972–77*, translated by Colin Gordon *et al.*, New York: Pantheon Books, 1980; and *The History of Sexuality, Volume 2: The Use of Pleasure*, translated by Robert Hurley, Harmondsworth: Penguin, 1985. Also see Graham Burchell, Colin Gordon and Peter Miller, *The Foucault Effect: Studies in Governmentality,* Chicago: University of Chicago Press, 1991.

25 See Monika Mehta, 'Selections: Cutting, Classifying and Certifying in Bombay Cinema', unpublished PhD dissertation, University of Minnesota, 2001; and 'What Is Behind Film Censorship?: The *Khalnayak* Debates', *Jouvert*, vol. 5, no. 3, 2001, pp. 1–12.

26 William Mazzarella, *Shoveling Smoke.*

27 Sue Curry Jansen, *Censorship: The Knot that Binds Power and Knowledge,* New York: Oxford University Press, 1988.

28 Tejaswini Ganti, 'The Limits of Decency and the Decency of Limits', pp. 87–122. **Editor's note**: Movie star Aamir Khan has had controversial political positions attributed to him, including both support to and criticism of ruling governments. In 2006 he declared his support of the movement for rehabilitation of those displaced by the building of a dam across the Narmada river. As a result, screenings of his *Rang De Basanti* ('Colour Me Saffron', dir. Rakeysh Omprakash Mehra, 2006) were stopped across Gujarat and his effigies were burnt in many cities.

29 However, as shown by a recent Supreme Court verdict with regard to Patwardhan's documentary

Father, Son and Holy War, to be aired on Doordarshan after a period of ten years, some of these contestations may simply be a case of government reticence driven by personal politics.

30 Angad Chowdhry, 'Anxiety, Failure, and Censorship in Indian Advertising', in Raminder Kaur and William Mazzarella, eds, *Censorship in South Asia*, pp. 123–39. **Editor's note**: Advertising Standards Council of India (est. 1985): An industry-owned group intended to self-regulate Indian advertising.

31 **Editor's note**: Press Council of India: Statutory quasi-judicial autonomous authority originally set up in 1966 under the Indian Press Council Act, 1965. The 1965 Act was repealed in 1975 and the Press Council was abolished during the Emergency. It was re-established in 1979. Its two-fold objects are to preserve the freedom of the press by maintaining and improving the standards of newspapers and news agencies in India.

32 Richard Burt, 'Introduction: The "New" Censorship', in Burt, ed., *The Administration of Aesthetics: Censorship, Political Criticism and the Public Sphere*, Minneapolis: University of Minnesota Press, 1994.

33 Ibid., p. xviii.

34 Ibid.

35 **Editor's note**: Anupam Kher (b. 1955): Film actor, received several governmental nominations following his support of the Bharatiya Janata Party, including chairmanship of the Central Board of Film Certification.

36 Jean-Francois Lyotard, *Libidinal Economy*, New York: Continuum, 2004.

37 See Judith Butler, *Excitable Speech*, p. 41; Henry Louis Gates, *Speaking of Race, Speaking of Sex: Hate Speech, Civil Rights and Civil Liberties*, New York: New York University Press, 1997; Milton Heumann, Thomas W. Church and David P. Redlawsk, *Hate Speech on Campus: Cases, Case Studies and Commentary*, Boston: Northeastern University Press, 1997; Philippa Strum, *When the Nazis Came to Skokie: Freedom for Speech We Hate,* Lawrence: University of Kansas Press, 1999; and Samuel Walker, *Hate Speech: The History of an American Controversy*, Lincoln: University of Nebrasaka, 1994.

38 Elias Canetti, *Crowds and Power*, New York: Farrar, Straus and Giroux, 1964.

39 Michael Taussig, *Defacement: Public Secrecy and the Labour of the Negative*, Palo Alto: Stanford University Press, 1999.

40 **Editor's note**: *Khwahish* ('Desire', dir. Govind Menon, 2003) features movie star Mallika Shehrawa, associated with sexual content. Rich boy meets poor girl, they defy convention and marry, but girl gets leukaemia.

41 Commenting on Aparna Sen's award-winning Bengali feature film *Paroma* (1985), film critic T.G. Vaidyanathan observes that 'Indians look far more convincing when they are not making love. When they are, the whole business looks forced, contrived, and bloodless.' See T.G. Vaidyanathan, *Hours in the Dark*, New Delhi: Oxford University Press, 1996, p. 116.

42 M. Madhava Prasad, *Ideology of the Hindi Film: A Historical Construction*, New Delhi: Oxford University Press, 1998. After shocked audience responses to *Fire* at the International Film Festival of India, Thiruvananthapuram in 1997, Mehta remarked she had no idea why *Fire* was labelled a 'lesbian film', clarifying that *Fire* 'is about choices, the choices we make in life which may lead to alienation. By the bisexuality theme in the film, I have just shown an extreme choice. But the end result is that you cannot have everything in your life. Happiness does not fall into your lap; in fact, happiness is too ephemeral a word. ... You have to choose in life. Ultimately, you have to take a risk.' See 'I Simply Can't Understand the Stereotyping of Women as Filmmakers Who Make Soppy Family Dramas', Deepa Mehta interviewed by Suparn Verma, Rediff on the Net, 24 October 1997; http://www.rediff.com/entertai/oct/24deep.htm. For a comprehensive account of the public violence and uproar around *Fire*, and related media reportage, see Rajeev Kumarankandath's contextualization of the film (which had been released in the West in 1996 and won international awards) as a 'highly contested space with varied claims pertaining to a wide range of issues' – lesbian rights, queer politics, Hindu nationalism, the constitutionally guaranteed right to freedom of speech and artistic expression, gradual progressive changes in rigid, reified Indian 'culture' and 'tradition', representation of Indian women, patriarchy and its privileges, gender, the institution of (heterosexual) marriage, etc. 'The protesters laid down demands to be fulfilled for uninterrupted screenings to be allowed; interestingly enough, among the conditions, one required that the protagonists' Hindu names be changed to Muslim names, that is, from Radha and Sita to Shabana and Saira.' Queer activist support for the film 'should not be understood as unconditional, and there were different opinions about the film's proximity to lesbian realities to India'; feminists critiqued the film as an 'essentialist' rather than a 'social constructionist' depiction of homosexuality, and as 'subscribing to the same biological reductionism' central to 'patriarchal arrangements'. The

film was aggressively debated in both Houses of Parliament; from activists and filmmakers' groups to the Censor Board, prominent politicians, feminists, and violent male and female Shiv Sainiks, 'virtually everyone was pulled into this controversial site'. See Rajeev Kumarankandath, 'Glimpses of the Fire: Documenting the Debates around the Film *Fire*', Centre for the Study of Culture and Society, Bangalore; http://cscs.res.in/courses_folder/other-courses/papers.2008-03-17.1729485494/glimpses-of-the-fire-documenting-the-debates-around-the-film-fire. Also see filmmaker and media scholar Shohini Ghosh, *Fire: A Queer Film Classic*, Delhi: Orient Publishing, 2010.

43 See Thomas Blom Hansen, *Wages of Violence*, and 'Politics as Permanent Performance: The Production of Political Authority in the Locality', in John Zavos, Andrew Wyatt and Vernon Hewitt, eds, *The Politics of Cultural Mobilization in India*, New Delhi: Oxford University Press, 2004. Also see Raminder Kaur, *Performative Politics.*

44 Partha Chatterjee, *The Nation and Its Fragments: Colonial and Postcolonial Histories: 4*, Princeton Studies in Culture/Power/History, Princeton: Princeton University Press, 1993.

45 **Editor's note**: Nehruvian secularism: According to historian Bipan Chandra, Nehru's definition of secularism operated at four levels: separation of religion from political, economic, social and cultural aspects of life; dissociation of state from religion; treating all religions with equal tolerance; and equal opportunities.

46 **Editor's note**: *Discovery of India* and *Glimpses of World History*: Written during periods of incarceration, both books testify to Nehru's civilizational views of world and Indian history respectively.

47 Shashi Tharoor, *Nehru: A Biography*, New Delhi: Oxford University Press, 2003.

48 Sandria Freitag, *Collective Action and Community: Public Arenas and the Emergence of Communalism in North India*, Berkeley: University of California Press, 1989.

49 Arvind Rajagopal, *Politics after Television.*

50 See Arjun Appadurai and Carol Breckenridge, 'Museums Are Good to Think: Heritage on View in India', in Ivan Karp *et al.*, eds, *Museums and Communications: The Politics of Public Culture*, Washington: Smithsonian Institution Press, 1992; Paul Greenough, 'Nation, Economy and Tradition Displayed: The Indian Crafts Museum, New Delhi', in Carol Breckenridge, ed., *Consuming Modernity: Public Culture in a South Asian World*, Minneapolis: University of Minnesota Press, 1995; B.P. Singh, *India's Culture: The State, The Arts and Beyond*, New Delhi: Oxford University Press, 1998; and Srirupa Roy, *Beyond Belief: India and the Politics of Postcolonial Nationalism*, Durham: Duke University Press, 2007.

51 See Satish Deshpande, 'Imagined Economies: Styles of Nation-Building in Twentieth Century India', *Journal of Arts and Ideas*, vol. 25–26, December 1993, pp. 5–36; and Sunil Khilnani, *The Idea of India*, Harmondsworth: Penguin, 1998.

52 See Rustom Bharucha, *In the Name of the Secular: Contemporary Cultural Activism in India*, New Delhi: Oxford University Press, 1998; Akeel Bilgrami *et al.*, eds, *The Crisis of Secularism in India*, Durham: Duke University Press, 2006; and Ashis Nandy, 'An Anti-Secularist Manifesto', in *The Romance of the State, and the Fate of Dissent in the Tropics*, New Delhi: Oxford University Press, 2002.

53 Rajagopal points out a practice that seems to straddle the Nehruvian and the communal political strategies: during the Emergency, AIR (All India Radio) would broadcast readings from the *Ramcharitmanas* on the grounds that it was 'folk culture': Arvind Rajagopal, *Politics after Television.*

54 See Girja Kumar, *Censorship in India: With Special Reference to* The Satanic Verses *and* Lady Chatterley's Lover, New Delhi: Har-Anand Publications, 2005; Purnima Mankekar, *Screening Culture*; William Mazzarella, *Shoveling Smoke*; and Arvind Rajagopal, *Politics after Television.*

55 Victoria Farmer, 'Mass Media: Images, Mobilization, and Communalism', in David Ludden, ed., *Contesting the Nation: Religion, Community and the Politics of Democracy in India*, Philadelphia: University of Pennsylvania Press, 1996.

56 **Editor's note**: **Doordarshan**: See Keywords.

57 Britta Ohm, 'Doordarshan: Representing the Nation's State', in Christiane Brosiuse and Melissa Butcher, eds, *Image Journeys.*

58 Cf. Arjun Appadurai and Carol Breckenridge, 'Public Modernity in India', in Carol Breckenridge, ed., *Consuming Modernity.*

59 **Editor's note**: **Emergency**: See Keywords.

60 **Editor's note**: **Soli Sorabjee** (1930–2021): Jurist who served as Attorney-General of India (1989–

1990, 1998–2004). Defended press freedom in landmark cases in the Supreme Court and was instrumental in revoking censorship orders and bans on publications.

61 **Editor's note**: Nargis Dutt (1929–1981): A famous film star who often portrayed sophisticated and independent women characters (e.g., *Mother India,* dir. Mehboob Khan, 1955). See **Mother India** in Keywords.

62 Soli Sorabjee, *The Emergency, Censorship and the Press in India, 1975–77*, London: Writers and Scholars Educational Trust, 1977.

63 **Editor's note**: Rules created from time to time under the Defence of India Act, 1962, passed in the context of the India–China war, to 'provide for special measures to ensure the public safety and interest, the defence of India and civil defence and for the trial of certain offences and for matters connected therewith' when a 'grave emergency exists whereby the security of India is threatened by external aggression'. There have been multiple such Acts, first passed in 1915, then in1939 (in the context of World War II). The Maintenance of Internal Security Act (MISA) was a controversial law passed in 1971 giving Indira Gandhi's (see **Indira Gandhi** in Keywords) administration very broad powers including indefinite preventive detention, search and seizure of property without warrants, and wire tapping. It was mainly used during the **Emergency** (see Keywords).

64 **Editor's note**: Samachar: Governmental news agency that replaced the Press Trust of India (PTI) during the **Emergency**. See note 35 in Gemma Scott's essay in this volume, 'Putting Women in the Picture'.

65 Shiv Visvanathan and Harsh Sethi, eds, *Foul Play: Chronicles of Corruption*, New Delhi: Banyan Books, 1998, p. 45.

66 In some sense, it was of course this tension that eventually sullied Rajiv Gandhi's 'Mr. Clean' image – namely, his inability to transcend the compulsions of the party machinery that had been established during his mother's rule. More immediately, the conflict expressed itself in several incidents of sudden censorship. For example, the sudden cancellation in February 1986 of a Doordarshan screening of Jack Anderson's documentary *Rajiv's India* (1986) which some members of the Congress Party old guard apparently felt was insufficiently respectful of Mrs Gandhi's political legacy.

67 **Editor's note**: *Ek Chhoti Si Love Story* (A Little Love Story, 2002): Adaptation of Krzysztof Kieslowski's *A Short Film About Love*. Movie star Manisha Koirala took the film to court when it appeared that nude close-ups of a body double had been used without her consent, but she lost the case in 2002.

68 **Editor's note**: *Ramayana*: Mythological television series produced by Ramanand Sagar, aired by **Doordarshan** (see Keywords) between 1987 and 1988. Viewership claimed at one point to be over 80 per cent of all those with access to television; also to have been the most watched television series in the world. Controversial because it was seen to have content that aligned with **Hindutva** (see Keywords) on a state-run network.

69 As Rajagopal points out, part of the contested politics of secularism around the televised epics took the form of arguments about whether the material should be understood as 'religious' or 'cultural'; see Arvind Rajagopal, *Politics after Television.*

70 Philip Lutgendorf, 'All in the (Raghu) Family: A Video Epic in Cultural Context', in Lawrence Babb and Susan Wadley, eds, *Media and the Transformation of Religion in South Asia*, Philadelphia: University of Pennsylvania Press, 1995.

71 **Editor's note**: Shah Bano, a 62-year-old Muslim woman from Indore, Madhya Pradesh, filed a petition in court in April 1978, demanding monthly alimony from divorced husband Mohammed Ahmad Khan, a well-known lawyer, from whom she had been separated for forty-six years. Later in November, Khan granted her an irreversible *talaq* (divorce).

72 Ashis Nandy, *The Savage Freud and Other Essays on Possible and Retrievable Selves*, Princeton: Princeton University Press, 1995.

Parul Dave Mukherji

1 **Editor's note**: **Faculty of Fine Arts, Maharaja Sayajirao University, Baroda**: See Keywords.

2 **Editor's note**: Dukhshyam Chitrakar: Traditional artist painting in the Bengal *pat* scroll painting form, from Naya Village in West Bengal.

3 A *patua* is a village scroll (*pata*) painter who paints a story on sheets of paper pasted on to a cloth

backing and stored as a scroll. In performance, he unwinds the scroll in front of an audience and sings out the story. *Pata* narratives are usually based on puranic mythology, the *Mahabharata*, the *Ramayana*, and local myths involving the snake goddess Manasa. More recently a genre called the 'Babu' scroll has emerged that delineates colonial-era events and includes stories of the martyrdom of nationalist heroes who fought against the British Raj.

4, 5 Pushpamala N., being a student of the Sculpture Department in the Faculty of Fine Arts, M.S. University, was not a formal member of this research group; she, along with Ayisha Abraham, informally joined the documentation project to Midnapore in May 1985. After three decades, it was Pushpamala who found the old negatives of the photographs taken on the trip and developed them. These were to later inspire her 2017 Ethnographers' Series. **Editor's note**: **Pushpamala N.**: See Keywords. Ayisha Abraham is an artist and experimental filmmaker. Her short digital films using found footage include *Straight 8* (2005), *You are Here* (2008), *I Saw a God Dance* (2012), *Through the Dark Mine* (2013) and *Through the Gold Mine* (2023).

6 **Editor's note**: **Gulammohammed Sheikh**: See Keywords.

7 The title of this essay was inspired by Pushpamala's ironic scribble.

8 Decades later, after joining the faculty of the School of Art History and Aesthetics at Jawaharlal Nehru University, I supported a pedagogical shift towards a focus on 'new' art-historical approaches that integrated perspectives from Anthropology and Cultural Studies and emphasized the politics of representation. One outcome of this shift was a national conference, and my co-editing, with Shivaji Panikkar and Deeptha Achar, the related publication, *Towards a New Art History: Studies in Indian Art*, New Delhi: D.K. Printworld, 2004.

9 Parul Dave Mukherji, 'Towards Performance Mimesis', *Theatre India* (National School of Drama theatre journal), no. 13, 2006: pp. 178–92.

10 **Editor's note**: Pushpamala N.'s performance photography series, *Native Women of South India: Manners and Customs* (2000–04), comprised 250 photographs across four series shot along with various props, costumes and backdrops.

11 **Editor's note**: *Margi* and *Desi*: Terms widely used in art history to create a loose division between the classical and the folk, sometimes more crudely 'high and low', but also 'sacred' and 'secular' arts. Conventionally traced back to art historian Ananda Coomaraswamy's use of the terms in writings on folk and popular art.

12 Terence Wright, 'Fieldwork Photographs of Jenness and Malinowski and the Beginnings of Modern Anthropology', *Journal of the Anthropology Society of Oxford*, vol. 22, no. 1, 1991, pp. 41–58.

13 I draw from Elizabeth Edwards's definition of a photograph as a material object that has a front and a back, with anything on the back accepted as integral to the image on the front and to the wider contextual reality. See Elizabeth Edwards, 'Material Beings: Objecthood and Ethnographic Photographs', *Visual Studies*, vol.17, no. 1, 2002, p. 67.

14 **Editor's note**: Ministry of Culture: Governmental agency dealing with an anthropological definition of culture: initially part of Education and later Tourism and Sport. Now part of the Ministry of Human Resources.

15 Claudio Lomnitz, 'Bordering on Anthropology: Dialectics of a National Tradition in Mexico', in Benoit De L'Estoile, Federico Neiburg and Lygia Sigaud, eds., *Empires, Nations and Natives: Anthropology and State-Making*, Durham and London: Duke University Press, 2005, pp. 167–96.

16 For instance, '*Vande Mataram*', India's pre-Independence national anthem, was composed in Sanskrit in 1937; originally a poem written in the 1870s by the Bengali writer Bankim Chandra Chatterjee, it was turned into a song by the poet Rabindranath Tagore.

17 **Editor's note**: Jamini Roy(1887–1972): Bengal School painter who created a unique popular idiom marrying Bengal painting with a simplified, flattened-out style, influenced by bazaar art.

18 Sumathi Ramaswamy, *The Goddess and the Nation: Mapping Mother India*, Durham: Duke University Press, 2010. **Editor's note**: See Ramaswamy's essay in this volume, 'Midnight's Line'.

19 See Pupul Jayakar, *The Earthen Drum: An Introduction to the Ritual Arts of Rural India*, New Delhi: National Museum, 1981; Carmen Kagal, ed., *Votive Terracottas of Gujarat/Haku Shah*, Ahmedabad: Mapin, 1985.

20 **Editor's note**: ***MARG*** and **Mulk Raj Anand**: See Keywords.

21 A.K. Coomaraswamy, 'The Nature of "Folklore" and "Popular Art"', in *Christian and Oriental Philosophy of Art*, New York: Dover Publications, 1956, pp. 130–43. **Editor's note**: Ananda K. Coomaraswamy (1877–1947): Renowned Sri Lankan cultural historian, critic and philosopher of Indian art, and an early interpreter of Indian culture to the West during the early twentieth century.

22 **Editor's note**: Bharat Bhavan, Bhopal: Cultural centre of music, arts and theatre inaugurated in February 1982. Initially set up by the state government, now an autonomous trust. Designed by Charles Correa, it is associated with major figures such as artist J. Swaminathan, musician Kumar Gandharva, poet Ajneya, artist S.H. Raza and theatre director B.V. Karanth.

23 In his field photographs Malinowski self-reflexively depicted the power relationship between an anthropologist and his subjects. He rejected both high and low angles in favour of eye-level shots to undermine a possible objectification of the natives.

24 I use the word 'genre' less to connote and classify, and more as a link between the genesis and the production of the group photographs. Anthropologist Johannes Fabian extensively engages with the category of 'genre', tracing its emergence to eighteenth-century Europe, especially to Dutch visual practices that in some sense anticipated the invention of photography. See Johannes Fabian, *Remembering the Present: Painting and Popular History in Zaire*, Berkeley: University of California Press, 1996.

25 See the chapter 'Ethnographic Photography and Printed Text', in Sarah Pink, *Doing Visual Ethnography: Images, Media, and Representation in Research*, London: Sage Publications, 2007.

26 See Elizabeth Edwards, 'Material Beings', p. 67

27 The image can be seen at http:// blogs.lse.ac.uk/lsehistory/2017/06/13/bronislaw-malinowski-lse-pioneer-of-socialanthropology/

28 For example, Michael Young observes: 'The height of the camera was commensurate with the height of the subject. Malinowski crouched when photographing children. He neither looked up or down at his subjects. The effect is one of directness. ... Vertical framing was foreign to Malinowski's style, and horizontal framing massively predominates in the collection.' See Michael W. Young, *Malinowski's Kiriwina: Fieldwork Photography 1915–1918*, Chicago and London: University of Chicago Press, 1998, p. 17.

29 The image can be seen at https:/lcommons.wikimedia.org/wiki/File:Bronis%C5%82aw Malinowski amongTrobriandtribe2.jpg

30 The image can be seen at https://alchetron.com/Edgar-Roquette-Pinto

31 Verrier Elwin (1902–1964) was an ethnologist and tribal activist who began his career in India as a Christian missionary. He is best known for his early work with the Baigas and Gonds of Central India. Inspired by Gandhi, he allied himself with the national movement, and later Prime Minister Jawaharlal Nehru would continually seek his expertise for tribal and rural development. For the two images under discussion, see Verrier Elwin posing with aboriginal children of Patangarh, https://blogs.bl.uk/untoldlives/2014/07/can-an-englishman-become-truly-indian-.html; and Edgar Roquette-Pinto with children of the Kozarini people, during an expedition with the Rondon Commission in 1912, https://revistapesquisa.fapesp.br/en/physician-anthropologist-and-broadcaster/

32 All photographs of the 1985 documentation trip referred to in this chapter were turned into artworks by Pushpamala and were on display at the show *India Re-Worlded: Seventy Years of Investigating a Nation*, curated by Arshiya Lokhandwala, Gallery Lakeeren, Mumbai, 11 September 2017–28 February 2018. Black strips were laid over the eyes of Dukhshyam and his extended family in the exhibited photographs, so the images align with codes for the ethical use of photographs in the absence of written permission from the photographed subjects. Riddhi Doshi and Rachel Lopez note that Pushpamala had revisited those images in order 'to reflect upon how she experiences the photographs now. Those casually clicked pictures now take on a different meaning and context. ... "The visual difference in the pictures between us and the villagers mimicked records of old European colonial anthropological expeditions, and yet the photographs possessed the familiarities that we could have as insiders," says Pushpamala. The difference between the lifestyle of the artist students and villagers is stark. It almost looks like they are from different worlds, but the ease of the body language suggests the connect of being and experiencing the same nation.' See Riddhi Doshi and Rachel Lopez, 'What's your spin? Art shows that invite you to view art differently', exhibition review, *The Hindustan Times*, 16 September 2017; https://www.hindustantimes.com/mumbai-news/what-s-your-spin-art-shows-that-invite-you-to-view-art-differently/story-nTCgmKsnOuWje2tL2QMBFP.html

33 See the brief excerpt from Michael Taussig's paradigmatic study, *Mimesis and Alterity: A Particular History of the Senses*, New York: Routledge, 1993; https://imaginative-ethnography.com/2014/05/27/taussig-on-mimesis/

34 The concept of 'performative mimesis' builds on Derrida' notion of mimesis that he derived from the

French Symbolist poet Stéphane Mallarmé. See Jonathan Culler, *On Deconstruction: Theory and Criticism after Structuralism*, Ithaca: Cornell University Press, 1982.

35 **Editor's note**: Leading museum of folk arts named after the civil service officer Gurusaday Dutt (1882–1941), primarily containing his collection of folk artifacts between 1929 and 1939.

36 Sonal Khullar, *Worldly Affiliations: Artistic Practice, National Identity and Modernism in India, 1930–1990*, Berkeley: University of California Press, 2015.

37 Problematizing the implications of artists creating 'in the name' or 'for the sake' of a cultural and/or ethnic 'other', Rutten *et al.* provide a useful synopsis of Hal Foster's influential critique that urges us to ask, with regard to such practice: Is this artist constructing an 'otherness' detached from a politics of here and now? Does this artist use 'alterity' as a primary point of subversion of dominant culture? Is this artist perceived as socially/culturally other, and therefore, has she or he either limited or automatic access to transformative alterity? Is this artist 'othering the self or selving the other'? The authors also raise what is perhaps most the significant concern for and about artists who use ethnographic approaches in their work with 'othered' communities: '*Is the artist wanted there, and by whom?* ... Every artist (and anthropologist) should be required to answer this question in depth before launching into what threatens to be intrusive or invasive projects (often called interventions).' See Hal Foster, 'The Artist as Ethnographer?' in George E. Marcus and Fred E. Myers, eds., *The Traffic in Culture: Refiguring Art and Anthropology*, Berkeley/Los Angeles: University of California Press, 1995, p. 304, full text available at https://monoskop.org/images/8/87/Foster_Hal_1995_The_Artist_as_Ethnographer.pdf; and Kris Rutten, An van. Dienderen and Ronald Soetaert, 'Revisiting the Ethnographic Turn in Contemporary Art', *Critical Arts: North-South Cultural and Media Studies*, vol. 27, no. 5, 2013, pp. 459–73, full text available at https://www.anvandienderen.net/published/article-revisiting-the-ethnographic-turn-in-contemporary-art/

38 Nancy Adajania, *Navjot Altaf: The Thirteenth Place*, Mumbai: Guild, 2016, p. 273. This excerpt from the book's epilogue, reminiscent of field notes maintained by anthropologists, demonstrates the ethnographic turn in art theory and critique, complementing and developing in parallel with the ethnographic turn in art practice.

39 Geeta Kapur, 'Place of the Modern in Indian Cultural Politics', *Economic and Political Weekly*, vol. 26, no. 49, 1991, pp. 2803–06.

40 **Editor's note**: **Navjot Altaf**: See Keywords.

41 Adajania (11) summarizes Altaf's concerns that seem to resonate with Sheikh's radical pedagogy: 'Can individuals belonging to different class and ethnic backgrounds communicate, work together, create a political solidarity, and produce shared cultural meanings?'

42 Apart from Pushpamala, other contemporary artists in India across the spectrum of practice have a deep engagement with ethnography and the archive; they include Navjot Altaf, Nikhil Chopra, Naveen Mathews and Sharmila Samant.

43 Perhaps anthropology was not enlisted in India's post-Independence nation-building project because of its historical role as a crucial instrument of colonial photography that so thoroughly objectified the native body.

44 Susie Tharu, 'Notes for a Grammar of the Visual Vernacular', in Pushpamala N., ed., *Native Women of India: Manners and Customs*, Delhi: Nature Morte Gallery, 2007.

45 See 'The Artist as Ethnographer?' in Hal Foster, *The Return of the Real: The Avant-Garde at the End of the Century*, Cambridge, MA: The MIT Press, 1996.

46 Retrospectively speaking, today it is possible to understand Coomaraswamy's very entry into art history through the prism of cultural anthropology if we trace it to his first, and seminal, work, *Medieval Sinhalese Art: Being a monograph on mediaeval Sinhalese arts and crafts, mainly as surviving in the eighteenth century, with an account of the structure of society and the status of the craftsmen*, Broad Campden: Essex House Press, 1908. Another early modern example of the salience of the ethnographic lens in disciplinary studies is Jawaharlal Nehru, *The Discovery of India*, Calcutta: Signet Press, 1946.

47 Discussing the 'crisis of representation' that is a central focus in visual and cultural studies, Rutten *et al.* invoke Foster's warning about the artist carrying a sense of 'ideological patronage' in ethnography-based activist projects involving 'othered' individuals or communities (the 'oppressed postcolonial', the 'subaltern', the 'sub-cultural'). The authors assert that cultural memory is always inscribed through a mode of either 'delegation' or 'description'. The former pivots around who has the right to represent whom, in cases when a limited number of representatives decide for and speak for an entire group; the latter pivots around how different cultural and social

groups are portrayed across cultural and social discourses and images. Inevitably, those 'who are delegated to speak and act in the name of another … govern, in a way, the process of presentation and description of the other.' See Kris Rutten, An van. Dienderen and Ronald Soetaert, 'Revisiting the Ethnographic Turn', pp. 465–66.

48 Ibid.

Ruth Rosengarten

1 Marianne Hirsch, 'Past Lives: Postmemories in Exile', *Poetics Today*, vol. 17, no. 4, 1996, pp. 659–86. Editor's note: **Postmemory**: See Keywords.

2 **Editor's note**: **Vivan Sundaram**: See Keywords.

3 A singular work in *Re-take of Amrita*, and the last to be printed in the book on the series, consists of just one negative. Sundaram's only intervention, a daring one, consists simply of turning the image upside down. Vivan Sundaram, 'Illumination and Death', in *Re-take of Amrita*, New York: Sepia International and New Delhi: The Alkazi Collection of Photography, 2006, pp. 9–11.

4 The collections of photographs owned by families before digitization would often circulate from hand to hand, and instigate reveries of remembrance as well as speculation on links that time has buried, unsolved mysteries of identity and kinship. See Martha Langford, *Suspended Conversation: The Afterlife of Memory in Photographic Albums*, Montreal and Kingston: McGill-Queens University Press, 2008.

5 Peter Osborne, *Anywhere or Not at All: Philosophy of Contemporary Art*, London and New York: Verso, 2013, p. 119.

6 Other contemporary artists have done this too: Zoe Leonard, Tracy Moffat, Christian Boltanski. Daniel Blaufuks, Santu Mofokeng and Erik Kessels, to name but a few.

7 Fred Ritchin, *After Photography*, New York: Norton, 2009, p. 15.

8 Christopher Pinney compares the micro-event – which is not the event represented but its setting up, its staging – to what, in film theory, is known as the pro-filmic, that which exists in the space before the cameras start rolling. Put differently, it is everything that lies within the recording field of the camera. In cinema, the mise-en-scène describes everything that can be seen on the screen at a given moment, and presuming we are not dealing with a digitally generated image, this is equivalent to the pro-filmic setting upon which the camera is trained from a particular, consciously chosen angle and distance. See Christopher Pinney, 'Coming out Better', in *Where Three Dreams Cross: 150 Years of Photography from India, Pakistan and Bangladesh*, London: Whitechapel Gallery and Winterthur: Fotomuseum and Steidl, 2010, pp. 23–31. **Editor's note**: Micro-event: The event of the photograph distinnguished from the historical event by Christopher Pinney ('Seven Theses on Photography', *Thesis Eleven*, 2012).

9 In this formulation, the ontological status of photography is not disavowed: the analogue photograph is the outcome of a particular technology,the purpose of which is to record that which takes place before and within the range of the camera lens. Pinney's refinement simply makes the nice distinction between the event as staged (the micro-event) and the event as occurring spontaneously, what Gilles Deleuze calls the 'any-instant-whatevers'. See Gilles Deleuze, *Cinema I: The Movement Image*, translated by Hugh Tomlinson and Barbara Habberjam, London and New York: Continuum Press, 2005 [1996], pp. 4–5.

10 The exhibition, 'The Swagger Portrait: Grand Manner Portraiture in Britain from Van Dyck to Augustus John, 1630–1930', curated by Andrew Wilton, ran at the Tate Gallery, London in late 1992–January 1993. See Andrew Wilton, *The Swagger Portrait: Grand Manner Portraiture in Britain from Van Dyck to Augustus John, 1630–1930*, exhibition catalogue, London: Tate, 1992.

11 The cultural continuities – for instance, in the notion that photographs constitute evidentiary proof – are linked to but separate from arguments concerning continuities or ruptures between analogue and digital technologies. Some early writers on digital imaging had affirmed that by being essentially discontinuous, digital technologies, limited by pixellation, could not simulate the smooth continuity of the grain of analogue photography; see W.J.T. Mitchell, *The Reconfigured Eye: Visual Truth in the Post-Photographic Era*, Cambridge, MA: The MIT Press, 2001 [1992]. Contrariwise, Lev Manovich has defended the notion that digital media offer continuities with analogue technologies, noting that 'the pixel is no longer the "final frontier": as far as the

user is concerned, it simply does not exist'. Writing as early as 2001, he noted that 'current technology has already reached the point where a digital image can easily contain much more information than anybody would ever want'. See Lev Manovich, *The Language of New Media*, Cambridge, MA: The MIT Press, 2001, p. 244.

12 See Verna Posever Curtis, *Photographic Memory: The Album in the Age of Photography*, New York: Aperture Editions, 2011, p. 7; and Martha Langford, ed., *Image & Imagination*, Montreal: Le Mois de la Photo, 2005.

13 See, for example, Barbara Levine and Stephanie Snyder, *Snapshot Chronicles: Inventing the American Photo Album*, New York: Princeton Architectural Press and Portland: Douglas F. Cooley Memorial Art Gallery, 2006; Martha Langford, *Suspended Conversation,* 2008; Elizabeth Siegel, *Galleries of Friendship and Fame: A History of Nineteenth-Century American Photograph Albums*, New Haven: Yale University Press, 2010; and Verna Posever Curtis, *Photographic Memory*.

14 See Luc Sante, *The Factory of Facts*, London: Granta Books, 1998; Hervé Guibert, *Ghost Image*, translated by Robert Bonnono, Chicago: University of Chicago Press, 2014 [1982]; Marianne Hirsch, *Family Frames: Photography, Narrative and Postmemory*, Cambridge and London: Harvard University Press, 1997; much of the writing by Annie Ernaux, including in Annie Ernaux and Marc Marie, *L'Usage de la photo*, Paris: Gallimard, 2005; and Annette Kuhn, *Family Secrets: Acts of Memory and Imagination*, London: Verso Books, 2002. Roland Barthes's discussion of the photograph of his mother in the winter garden, unleashing an exploration of time in photography, is one of the most iconic passages in photographic theory of the past fifty years. See Roland Barthes, *Camera Lucida*, translated by Richard Howard, London: Vintage Books, 1997 [1980].

15 **Editor's note**: Christian Boltanski (1944–2021): Avant-garde French conceptual artist known for his photography/lens-based media installations. .

16 **Editor's note**: Erik Kessels (b. 1966): Artist, designer, curator. Author of *Missing Links* (1997), *Small Change* (2016), *In Almost Every Picture* (2022) and *Complete Amateur* (2022).

17 **Editor's note**: Ralph Eugene Meatyard (1925–1972): American photographer. Themes of staged family photographs, masks, nature photography and still life. Noted for experimental 'Motion-Sound' pieces influenced by jazz. Best known publication, *The Family Album of Lucybelle Crater* (1974).

18 **Editor's note**: **Umrao Singh Sher-Gil** (1870–1954): See Keywords.

19 I am using, for the sake of clarity and as Sundaram himself does, the first names of the members of the Sher-Gil family.

20 Deepak Ananth, 'The Gaze of the Amateur', in *Umrao Singh Sher-Gil: His Misery and His Manuscript*, New Delhi: Photoink, 2008, pp. 223–36.

21 Vivan Sundaram, *Re-take of Amrita*, p. 5.

22 Roland Barthes defines photogenia in terms of informational structure, observing that 'in photogenia the connoted message is the image itself "embellished" (which is to say in general sublimated) by techniques of lighting, exposure and printing', alerting the reader to the necessity of distinguishing aesthetic from signifying effects. See Roland Barthes, 'The Photographic Message', in *Image–Music–Text*, translated by Stephen Heath, London: Fontana Collins, 1977, p. 23.

23 Vivan Sundaram, *Re-take of Amrita*, p. 11.

24 **Editor's note**: *The Sher-Gil Archive*: Multipart installation by Vivan Sundaram, built around three generations of the Sher-Gil family. Personal and family artefacts, such as letters and photographs, integrated into an assemblage by the artist.

25 Vivan Sundaram and Geeta Kapur have, for some five decades, assiduously and systematically preserved records and documents, both personal and professional. In January 2010, the Asia Art Archive (AAA) began to digitize their archive as 'Another Life: The Digitized Personal Archive of Geeta Kapur and Vivan Sundaram', available at aaa.org.hk/CollectionSpecialCollectionsDetails/5

26 Contemporary artists engaged in archival or quasi-archival practices over the past few decades and across the globe are too numerous to itemize here, but the genesis of this interest dates, arguably, from Marcel Duchamp's *La Boîte-en-valise* ('Box-in-a-suitcase', 1913), and later, the work of Marcel Broodthaers and other artists from the 1960s. Texts, books and catalogues dealing with these trends are numerous too, and include Cheryl Simon, 'Introduction: Following the Archival Turn', *Visual Resources: An International Journal on Images and Their Uses*, vol. 18, no. 2, special issue: *Following the Archival Turn: Photography, the Museum and the Archive*, 2002, pp. 101–07; Hans-Peter Feldman, Hans Ulrich Obrist, Diethelm Stoller, Beatrice von Bismarck and

Ulf Wuggenig, eds, *Interarchive: Archival Practices and Sites in the Contemporary Art Field*, Cologne: Verlag der Buchhandlung Walther Konig, 2002; Hal Foster, 'An Archival Impulse', *October*, 110, Fall 2004, pp. 3–22; Charles Merewether, ed., *The Archive*, Documents of Contemporary Art series, London: Whitechapel Ventures, 2006; Okwui Enwezor, *Archive Fever: Uses of the Document in Contemporary Art*, New York: International Center of Photography and Steidl, 2009; Marianne Hirsch, *The Generation of Postmemory: Writing and Visual Culture after the Holocaust*, New York: Columbia University Press, 2012; Ruth Rosengarten, *Between Memory and Document: The Archival Turn in Contemporary Art*, Lisbon: Museu Coleção Berardo, 2012; Ernst van Alphen, *Staging the Archive: Art and Photography in the Age of New Media*, London: Reaktion Books, 2014; and David Houston Jones, *Installation Art and the Practices of Archivalism*, Kindle edition, London and New York: Routledge, 2016. In the introduction to his influential curatorial foray into this field, Enwezor (2009) teases out many different uses of the archive in contemporary artistic – and, in particular, photographic – practice. Ernst van Alphen (*Staging the Archive*, p. 9) relates this to the theoretical influence of Michel Foucault and Jacques Derrida, but more significantly, he stresses, as does Manovich in *The Language of New Media*, that the paradigmatic shift from narrative to database has had a profound effect on the making of meaning and the production of cultural forms.

27 Vivan Sundaram, 'Foreword', in *Umrao Singh Sher-Gil*, p. viii.

28 While the indexicality of photographs primed them for their evidentiary and forensic role, in tandem there has always existed the belief in a photograph's availability for manipulation. Hillel Schwartz has discussed the example of pioneering American war photographer Matthew Brady (1822–1896) and his assistants 'moving bodies into better light, shifting Civil War loyalties (in black-and-white, Confederate browns were indistinct from Union blues), and posing live soldiers as if in rigor mortis'. See Hillel Schwartz, *The Culture of the Copy: Striking Likenesses, Unreasonable Facsimiles*, New York: Zone Books, 1996, p. 96. Similarly, Christopher Pinney has discussed a famous image by photographer Felice Beato (*c.* 1834–1907) taken in Lucknow in March 1858 after its recapture by British troops, showing the interior of Sikanderbagh with the scattered bones of rebel sepoys – although Beato had arrived on the scene several months after the Mutiny ended and had 'arranged for buried remains to be disinterred and placed in order to locate the event of his making of the photograph mimetically closer to the event of the fighting' (Pinney, 'Coming out Better', pp. 23–24). This image is also discussed in Pinney's seminal essay, 'Seven Theses on Photography' (2012), recently republished in Rahaab Allana, ed., *Unframed: Discovering Image Practices in South Asia*, New Delhi: The Alkazi Foundation for the Arts and HarperCollins Publishers India, 2023, pp. 72–91. While the 'truth' of such photographs is in excess of their empirical truth at a (hypothetical) 'decisive moment', practically speaking, they convey the staged truth of the pro-filmic or micro-event in the service of a broader political or moral point, with its claims to truth.

29 Sven Spieker, *The Big Archive: Art from Bureaucracy*, Cambridge, MA and London: The MIT Press, 2008, p. ix.

30 Michel Foucault, 'The Historical a priori and the Archive', in *The Archaeology of Knowledge and the Discourse on Language*, translated by A.M. Sheridan Smith, London: Routledge, 2002 [1969], pp. 142–49.

31 *Umrao Singh Sher-Gil: His Misery and His Manuscript*, New Delhi: Photoink, 2008.

32 Deepak Ananth, 'The Gaze of the Amateur'.

33 Okwui Enwezor, *Archive Fever*, p. 31.

34 Max Kozloff, 'Autochromes: The Bouquet of Lighted Air', first published in *Artforum*, 1980; reprinted in Kozloff, *The Privileged Eye: Essays on Photography*, Albuquerque: University of New Mexico Press, 1987, p. 270.

35 Douglas R. Nickel, 'Autochromes by Clarence H. White', in *Record of the Art Museum, Princeton University, 51/2: The Art of Pictorial Photography 1890–1925*, 1992, p. 31.

36 Marsha Meskimmon, *Contemporary Art and the Cosmopolitan Imagination*, London: Routledge, 2010, p. 21.

37 Ibid.

38 Ibid., pp. 15–29. Meskimmon has explored the notion of the 'plurilocal home' in the work of several contemporary artists. She borrowed the term, and the idea of home as something that is not necessarily pinned to a unitary location, from anthropologists Nigel Rapport and Andrew Dawson (1998), extending the term 'plurilocal' to discuss cosmopolitan subjectivities too.

39 Ibid.

40 Geeta Kapur, 'A Cultural Conjuncture in India: Art into Documentary', in Terry Smith, Okwui Enwezor

and Nancy Condee, eds, *Antinomies of Art and Culture: Modernity, Postmodernity, Contemporaneity*, Durham and London: Duke University Press, 2008, p. 31.

41 Jacques Rancière, *Aesthetics and Its Discontents*, translated by Steven Corcoran, Cambridge: Polity Press, 2009 [2004], p. 46.

42 Geeta Kapur, 'A Cultural Conjecture', p. 37. **Editor's note**: Nalini Malani (b. 1946): Initially a painter, now does very large multimedia works, especially video works. N.N. Rimzon (b. 1957): Sculptor working in metal, fibreglass and stone. Rummana Hussain (1952–1999): Initially a painter, pioneered politically engaged conceptual art, installation and performance.

43 A discussion on the changing status of the notion of medium and the fluctuations of its fate, from Clement Greenberg's purist formalism, through Stanley Cavell's automatism and Rosalind Krauss's post-medium condition to contemporary intermediality, is outside the remit of this book, but its effects weave through my text.

44 Geeta Kapur, 'Dismantling the Norm', in Apinan Poshyananda, ed., *Contemporary Art in Asia: Traditions/Tensions*, New York: Asia Society Galleries, 1996, pp. 66–67.

45 The only other Indian artist included in this biennale was Sutapa Biswas, whose work also systematically deals with memory. **Editor's note**: Sixth Havana Biennale (1997): Founded in 1984, the Bienal de La Habana is organized by the Centro Wifredo Lam, and aims at promoting art through South–South dialogue. Sundaram's work had previously been featured in the second (1987) and fourth (1991) editions of the biennale.

46 Wu Hung, 'A Meditation on "Re-take of Amrita"', in *Re-take of Amrita*, p. 5.

47 Christopher Bollas, *The Evocative Object World*, Hove, Sussex and New York: Routledge, 2008, p. 79.

48 Vivan Sundaram, *Re-take of Amrita*, p. 9.

49 Roland Barthes, *Camera Lucida*, p. 96.

50 Craig Owens, 'Posing', in *Beyond Recognition: Representation, Power and Culture*, Berkeley and Los Angeles: University of California Press, 1992, p. 210.

51 Roland Barthes, 'The Photographic Message', pp. 15–31.

52 This kind of reading of movement and body language in static representation was launched by Michael Baxandall's ground-breaking study of Renaissance painting in Italy, with his emphasis on the multiple origins of the representation of gesture, including dance annotation and the body language of orators and preachers, 'skilled visual performers with a codified range of gesticulation not special to Italy'. See Michael Baxandall, *Painting and Experience in Fifteenth-century Italy*, Oxford: Oxford University Press, 1972, p. 64.

53 Mining the family album for images of alienation and solitude is one of the possibilities offered by software like Photoshop, and other artists have taken advantage of this. Russian-born artist Nikolai Ishchuk's *Offset* series (2011–13) pulls apart the family album (like Sundaram, he uses found photographs) through the 'offset' filter of Photoshop, which splits an image down the middle and reverses the pieces, leaving the middle of the frame awkwardly vacant. Swedish artist Eva Stenram's series *Parted* (2010) came about through her reworking of a large quantity of other people's old 35-mm slides. Stenram breaks apart a group (whether a couple or more people) and figures, each of the people singly in a frame: a photograph of three people becomes three photographs of solitary figures, each in its occupied position.

54 Roland Barthes, *Camera Lucida*, p. 96.

55 Vivan Sundaram, *Re-take of Amrita*, p. 9.

56 Other works in *Re-take of Amrita* that contain such doubled images of Amrita and/or Indira in Indian and Western dress are *Quartet*, *Young Girl Recomposed* and *Sister Indira*.

57 Florian Rötzer, 'Re: Photography', in Hubertus von Amelunxen, Stefan Iglhaut and Florian Rötzer, eds, *Photography After Photography: Memory and Representation in the Digital Age*, Amsterdam: G+B Arts, 1996, pp. 20–22.

58 Lev Manovich takes issue with W.J.T. Mitchell's association of montage with digitization and his notion that analogue photography is generally not manipulated, arguing that 'straight' photography and montage represent two pre-existing strands in visual culture, both of which existed prior to photography. 'Digital technology does not subvert "normal" photography,' Manovich writes, 'because "normal" photography never existed.' See W.J.T. Mitchell, *The Reconfigured Eye*, and Lev Manovich, *The Language of New Media*, p. 245.

59 Vivan Sundaram, *Re-take of Amrita*, p. 9.

60 Roland Barthes, 'Leaving the Movie Theatre', in *The Rustle of Language*, translated by Richard Howard, Oxford: Blackwell, 1986, pp. 345–46.

61 Christian Metz, *The Imaginary Signifier: Psychoanalysis and the Cinema*, translated by Celia Britton, Annwyl Williams, Ben Brewster and Alfred Guzzetti, Bloomington and Indianapolis: Indiana University Press, 1982 [1977], p. 107.

62 In an earlier essay, Baudry had spoken of how 'the arrangement of the different elements – projector, darkened hall, screen' – reproduce 'in a striking way the mise-en-scène of Plato's cave'. Jean-Louis Baudry, 'Ideological Effects of the Basic Cinematographic Apparatus', translated by Alan Williams, *Film Quarterly*, vol. 28, no. 2, Winter 1974–75, p. 45.

63 Deepak Ananth, 'The Gaze of the Amateur'.

64 Julia Kristeva, *Powers of Horror: An Essay on Abjection*, translated by Leon S. Roudiez, New York: Columbia University Press, 1982, p. 33.

65 Kaja Silverman, *The Miracle of Analogy or The History of Photography*, Part I, Stanford: Stanford University Press, 2015, p. 44.

66 Scholars have noted the dual meaning of *Heimlich*, the word derived from the semantic core of *Heim*, 'home': 'The first sense is the most literal: domestic, familiar, intimate. The second meaning departs from the positive, literal sense to the more negative metaphorical sense of hidden, secret, clandestine, furtive. One might say that a certain change of perspective has taken place: in the positive sense, *heimlich* takes the inside-perspective of the intimacy of the home. In the negative sense, by contrast, the walls of the house shield the interior and in the eyes of the outsider, the secludedness of the inner circle is associated with secrecy and conspiracy. *Unheimlich* in the sense of strange, unfamiliar, uncanny, eerie, sinister ... is then clearly the negation of only the first meaning of *heimlich* and as such, it almost coincides with the second, negative meaning of *heimlich*.' For Freud, the uncanny 'is in reality nothing new or alien, but something which is familiar and old-established in the mind and which has become alienated from it only through the process of repression'; he quotes Schelling's definition that '*unheimlich* is that what ought to have remained hidden, but has nonetheless come to light'. In Freudian terms, 'the return of the repressed' may lead to self-revelations of our psychic past that have the potential to disorient, frighten and sometimes disable us. See Anneleen Masschelein, 'A Homeless Concept: Shapes of the Uncanny in Twentieth-Century Theory and Culture', *Image & Narrative*, 5, special issue: 'The Uncanny', January 2003; http://www.imageandnarrative.be/inarchive/uncanny/anneleenmasschelein.htm.

Rahaab Allana in conversation with Prashant Panjiar

1 See interview by Naresh Fernandes, 'The Truth Is Biased: Prashant Panjiar on Four Decades of Photographing India', *Scroll.in*, 16 January 2022, https://scroll.in/article/1015087/the-truth-is-biased-prashant-panjiar-on-the-backstories-of-four-decades-of-photographing-india

2 **Editor's note**: *Look:* Bi-weekly American tabloid founded in March 1937, covering politics, culture, celebrities and fashion.

3 **Editor's note**: *The Illustrated Weekly of India* (1880–1993): Weekly news magazine started by the Times of India group. Sabeena Gadihoke has described its role in the first few decades of India's Independence as a forum that offered its readers a cosmopolitan vision of life in South Asia, and contributed to the vibrant culture of photography in India via a pictorial aesthetic and humanist trajectory ('The Printed World', *Aperture*, 2021).

4 **Editor's note**: *India Today*: Weekly news magazine established in 1975, known for introducing dynamic, cutting-edge photojournalism, with **Raghu Rai** (see Keywords) serving as Picture Editor from 1982 to 1991. Panjiar was a senior photographer from 1986 to 1995. Noted for frontline coverage of the 1998 Kargil War by Dilip Banerjee and Pramod Pushkarna (see notes 9 and 18 below) .

5 **Editor's note**: Chromaline: Proofs that are the end product of a process of pre-press proofing used to check the accuracy of the offset CMYK (cyan, magenta, yellow and black).

6 **Editor's note**: *Patriot*: Newspaper founded in 1958 by socialist leader Aruna Asaf Ali. *Outlook*: Launched in 1995 as a weekly news magazine with Vinod Mehta (see note 19) as founder-editor. A member of the founding editorial team, Panjiar was in charge of photography.

7 **Editor's note**: **Raghu Rai**: See Keywords.

8 **Editor's note**: Aroon Purie (b. 1944): Founder-publisher and editor-in-chief of *India Today*, managing director of Thomson Press (India) Limited, chairman and managing director of TV Today.

9 **Editor's note**: Pramod Pushkarna: Photographer known especially for war photography, currently works as Group Photo Editor, *National Herald* (where he worked between 1973–78). Was Group Photo Editor for *The Sunday Guardian*, *Aaj Samaj* and other publications of Good Morning Media. Deputy Chief Photographer of *India Today* between 1978 and 2003.

10 **Editor's note**: Fawzan Husain: Photojournalist, artist, teacher and organic farmer. Worked with *Mid-Day* and *India Today*. Author of *Between Bombay & Mumbai: 25 Years in Pictures through a Changing City* (2012) and *The Silver Screen & Beyond: Up Close and Personal with the Bombay Film Industry* (2015).

11 **Editor's note**: T. Narayan: Independent photographer. Started career as Senior Photographer for *The Times of India*, and was Photo Editor at *Hindustan Times*, *Outlook* and *India Today*.

12 **Editor's note**: Jitender Gupta: Photojournalist, covered political events for the Outlook Group, *Sunday*, *Ananda Bazar Patrika* and *Mid-Day*.

13 **Editor's note**: Tribhuvan Tiwari: Deputy Photo Editor with *Outlook India*. Earlier Senior Photographer with *India Today*.

14 **Editor's note**: **Pablo Bartholomew**, **Dayanita Singh**: See Keywords. Sondeep Shankar: See note 22 of Suryanandini Narain, 'The Camera Tours the City' in this volume. Arko Datta (b. 1969): Photojournalist, started with *The Indian Express*, covered wars in Iraq and Afghanistan. Especially known for the iconic photograph of the riots in Ahmedabad (see **Gujarat Riots, 2002** in Keywords), of a man named Qutubuddin Ansari pleading with folded hands for his life.

15 **Editor's note**: Sardar Sarovar/Narmada Bachao Andolan (1985): Protest movement led by Medha Patkar against the building of a major dam threatening ecological damage and displacement of thousands of **Adivasi** families.

16 Panjiar was the only photojournalist to capture the violent demolition of the **Babri Masjid** (see Keywords) by Hindu extremists, within a span of nineteen minutes, on 6 December 1992. He narrates how this became possible: '*India Today* had three teams tailing Bharatiya Janata Party leaders as they made their way to Ayodhya for a symbolic *kar seva*. My brief was to follow L.K. Advani. Tens of thousands of *karsevak*s had gathered in front of the Babri Masjid-Ram Janmabhoomi. That's where all the camera crews and photographers were too. But Advani and the other leaders were some distance away on the terrace of a structure called the Ram Katha Kunj, from where they were making speeches. From here, I only had a view of the [mosque's three] domes. As the *karsevak*s began to break the barricades at the site, all the journalists there were systematically attacked. All their cameras were smashed. Many colleagues were badly injured. Some were locked away by *karsevak*s so there would be no evidence of the demolition. But on top of the Ram Katha Kunj, people thought I was with the Vishwa Hindu Parishad, so I could photograph throughout. That's how I was able to take photographs of when the domes actually fell. … All I knew at that point of time was that I had to keep my head down, don't show my emotions, and just keep on photographing – because if I had shown any kind of emotion, I would have been thrown out of there.' Panjiar's paradigmatic three-frame sequence showing the collapse of the domes pierced at the top by Hindu extremist flags is time-stamped '4.30 PM', '4.48 PM' and '4.49 PM'. *India Today* used an image of jubilant *karsevak*s atop the mosque, overlaid with the words 'Nation's Shame' in large text, on the cover of its December 1992 issue; in its editorial, Aroon Purie denounced the violence in the strongest terms. Panjiar's three frames along with an image of this cover were exhibited at the seventh edition of the Indian Photo Festival, Hyderabad (2021), accompanied by a short paragraph of wall text with the stunning symbolic heading 'EK DHAKKA AUR DO' (Hindi: 'Give One More Shove'). His terse summary of the violence concludes: '… [From atop the Ram Katha Kunj] I was able to photograph through the day with impunity because it was assumed that I was one of them [*karsevak*s]. My pictures are the only ones of the domes of the Babri Masjid as they fell on the fateful day.' Panjiar's Babri images feature in his compilation of back stories from his decades as a photojournalist, *That Which Is Unseen*, Ahmedabad: Navjeevan Trust, 2021, released at the festival. See Fernandes, 'The Truth is Unbiased', and TelupuTV Desk, 'That Which Is Unseen: Prashant Panjiar's Three Images', TelepuTV, 18 November 2021, https://www.teluputv.com/photo-feature-of-prashant-panjiar-from-indian-photo-festival-hyderabad.

17 Responding to interview questions about why *The Idea of India* (New Delhi: Penguin India, 2004)

was 'such a hotly disputed subject', and how he felt about the accusation that he was a '"Nehruvian Marxist" complicit in the depredations of the Congress Party', Khilnani clarified his authorial intent: 'What I set out to do in *The Idea of India* was to reconstruct the foundations of the modern nation: to show how it was built on a political idea – which valued freedom and diversity – and not a narrow definition of culture and religion. I analysed India's democracy and its economic development, the history of its cities, and the debates around an Indian identity. And through my study, I was able to conclude that India's success as a nation state depended on its capacity to recognize and sustain different types of diversity – religious, linguistic, ethnic – rather than to impose a homogenous idea of nationalism, religious belief or cultural practice. That was an invaluable legacy of our founders: An insistence that the idea of India was founded not on a singular idea of India, but on a commitment to let many diverse ideas of India flourish – within the framework of constitutional law and democratic liberties. I could not have imagined that *The Idea of India* would become a touchstone for thinking about contemporary India, and would continue to generate so much debate. I think, for many people, it showed the logic of the Indian political project. There are some who dispute that logic or don't like that project in the first place. These include many on the left, not just on the right. I'd invite them to offer counterarguments and historical evidence for their views, rather than anoint me with labels.' See Vikram Zutshi, 'The Idea of India: Sunil Khilnani in Conversation', *Fair Observer*, 24 August 2017; https://www.fairobserver.com/region/central_south_asia/india-south-asia-latest-news-headlines-today-world-news-97102/

18 **Editor's note**: General election of 1998: Election that followed the collapse of the United Progressive Alliance led by the Congress-I. Saw the first government of the Bharatiya Janata Party-led National Democratic Alliance led by Atal Bihari Vajpayee (see note 20 below). Kargil war (1999): A short war fought between India and Pakistan between May andJuly 1999 in the Kargil district of Jammu and Kashmir, following accusations of state-supported infiltration of pro-Kashmir militants from Pakistan. **Dalit** movement (1999): See note 26 below.

19 **Editor's note**: Vinod Mehta (1942–2015): Editor-in-chief of *Outlook* from 1995 to 2012.

20 **Editor's note**: Atal Bihari Vajpayee (1924–2018): Co-founder of the right-wing Bharatiya Janata Party, the eleventh Prime Minister of India for three terms. Sometimes considered the liberal face of the Hindu right, though this view has been contested.

21 **Editor's note**: *The Times of India*, initially the *Bombay Times and Journal of Commerce*, operated by Bennett, Coleman and Co., published its inaugural edition on 3 November 1838.

22 **Editor's note**: P.V. Narasimha Rao (1921–2004): Lawyer and politician, tenth Prime Minister of India (1991–96).

23 **Editor's note**: Manmohan Singh (b. 1932): Politician and economist, fourteenth Prime Minister of India for two consecutive terms (2004–2014). As Finance Minister in the Narasimha Rao government, in 1991, he oversaw a new era of economic reforms and liberalization policies.

24 **Editor's note**: *The Indian Express* was founded in Chennai in 1932.*The Hindu* was initially a weekly newspaper, with its first issue on 20 September 1878; it became a daily in 1889.

25 **Editor's note**: *The Times of India*, *The Indian Express* and *The Hindu* have played a major role in formulating public opinion. The use of bylines was fought for by Kishor Parekh while working at *The Hindustan Times* and later by **S. Paul** (see Keywords) at *The Indian Express* in the 1960s before it became the norm.

26 **Editor's note**: Shankarbigha massacre: Massacre on 25 January 1999 in the village of Shankarbigha, Bihar, in which twenty-three **Dalit** (see Keywords) people were killed by members of the Ranvir Sena, a landlord-driven militia. Almost all the killers were acquitted.

27 **Editor's note**: Soutik Biswas: Online correspondent for BBC News in India.

28 In terms of reflection on practice/self-reflection as a practitioner, Panjiar encourages the photo-journalists he shares ideas with or mentors 'to actually move away from the physicality of the image', because in the digital era, where information is readily available, 'the reason for seeing an image is no longer for information'. It is not enough for an image to provide the information 'that this man lived in a cave or a forest. You almost need to know through the picture why does he do it or how does he feel doing that.' To achieve this, 'the physicality of the image, of just showing the man in the cave, is not enough. You need to do something more than that'. Panjiar is also critical of the canonization of 'objectivity' as the fulcrum of photojournalism: '[T]he earlier idea of journalism was that you have to be objective. Then a lot of writers started expressing opinions in their writing in mainstream news and stories. But photographers were still expected to be objective. So why not share your opinion of things?

And that is something I would encourage photographers to do. So please express your opinion in your pictures. It's no longer about being unbiased.' See Kevin Wy Lee, 'Times and Tides in the World of Photography: Interview with Prashant Panjiar', Part 2, *Invisible Photographer Asia*, 22 March 2016. Full text of both parts of the interview available at https://invisiblephotographer.asia/2016/03/22/interview-prashantpanjiar-pt2/

29 **Editor's note**: Naxalite movement in Bihar: Far-Left movement that began in Bengal in the late 1960s, and spread to Bihar in 1968. Panjiar was with the activist Kalyan Mukherjee (see Mukherjee and Rajendra Singh Yadav, *Bhojpur: Naxalism in the Plains of Bihar*, New Delhi: Rādhā Krishna, 1980) in a research project at the National Labour Institute on land reforms.

30 **Editor's note**: *Jalsaghar* ('The Music Room', dir. Satyajit Ray, 1958): Well-known film about decaying feudalism based on a short story by Bengali writer Tarasankar Bandyopadhyay.

31 **Editor's note**: *King, Commoner, Citizen* (2007): Initially mounted as an exhibition curated by photographer Sanjeev Saith, the series featured images from across Panjiar's career, from 1981 to 2007. In 2007, India Picture published 56 of these images in a monograph edited by Saith featuring 56 photographs, a series of portraits of descendants of India's erstwhile royal families alongside those of ordinary people. **Madan Mahatta** and **Sanjiv Saith**: See Keywords.

32 **Editor's note**: Indian Peace Keeping Force (IPKF): Indian military contingent instated in Sri Lanka between 1987 and 1990 at the behest of then Prime Minister of India, Rajiv Gandhi, under the terms of the 1987 Indo–Sri Lanka Accord.

33 **Editor's note:** In 1989, Panjiar and Shekhar Gupta of *India Today* travelled to Darra Adam Khel, a village in Pakistan's North West Frontier Province, to do a story on a 150-year-old arms bazaar. As it was in a semi-autonomous tribal territory, the Pakistani government did not interfere. Anyone could openly purchase lethal weapons such as Kalashnikovs, anti-aircraft guns, rocket launchers, mines and bullets by the jar. The story was published with the headline 'Pakistan: In Darra Adam Khel, Lethal Weapons Sell Openly Alongside Narcotics' (*India Today*, 31 July 1989).

34 **Editor's note**: Amitabh Bachchan (b. 1942): Major Indian movie star. Founded the Amitabh Bachchan Corporation Limited in 1995 to do event management, film production and distribution work. Company went bankrupt in 1999. Organized the extremely controversial Miss World Beauty Contest in 1996.

35 **Editor's note**: NICNET: The information and communication technology network system of the National Informatics Centre was launched in 1987, it is responsible for facilitating linkages between the various offices of the central government, state governments and district administrations.

36 Panjiar notes the effect of digital technology on lens-based media, acknowledging that while it is now easy to make an image, this factor has led to an undervaluation and neglect of the craft of photography. In addition, in the digital era certain stereotypes have become a style within photography: 'Like the blank frontal gaze of the portrait … we all started copying it. The square format, faded colours, landscape or industrial scapes that came from Europe. … Or it's this scratchy, out of focus, blur, movement, etcetera', copied by photographers across the world all the time. 'Some people do it well. These are all languages. If your language is not good, you won't be able to tell a story. … It's not enough to have these blurry pictures and write a long artist statement about them. That's bullshit, you know. This is something we are losing – this idea of knowing your craft, knowing the language, learning your language well.'

37 Elsewhere, Panjiar summarizes the decline of print photojournalism in India amidst what he calls the 'Age of Conformism' (the late 1990s and early 2000s). 'During this time, the middle and upper-middle class became more inward-looking. People became more worried about their personal finances, faith, and lives. … In the 90s, with the arrival of satellite television, news channels could publish information without verifying. It became very easy to correct reporting on the television. This was not possible for print media. Soon, editors started insisting on why photojournalists could not imitate how satellite television covered the news in a more hysterical manner. All these factors combined lowered the value of photojournalism. This resulted in the need to produce immediate images where a lot of times people's emotions, feelings, and context are removed.' However, by the late 2000s, even as print photojournalism declined, 'a new style of photography emerged in India that was not defined just by events, but brought in an element of documentary, artistic and personal vision. Luckily this "new" photography is now being recognized.' See Daniel Jamang, 'A Life in Pictures', interview with Prashant Panjiar, *PoY Asia*, 2022; full text at https://poyasia.org/on-the-record/interview-with-prashant-panjiar/

Majid Maqbool in conversation with Sanjay Kak

1 Kak recalls 'hundreds of images' archived 'in these individual, fairly haphazard collections ... the output of photographers who shot news images, as part of the everyday grind of freelancers, earning a bit of money and moving on. Yet when I first saw their images, they spoke so loudly about the 1990s and 2000s. Reaching out to these individuals, overcoming their scepticism about the historical value of the images and persuading them to see it as part of a common heritage was not easy. ... Then came the flood of 2014, which overwhelmed Srinagar city and large parts of the Kashmir valley. Several photographers – including those whose work I had seen and admired – lost work while [the work of] others suffered extensive damage. By then I was frantic that this work be secured in some way and made more public.' See Senjuti Mukherjee, 'On *Witness*: An Interview with Sanjay Kak', *ASAP* (Alternative South Asia Photography), 27 February 2021, https://asapconnect.in/post/84/singlestories/on-witness

2 Ibid.: Kak reiterates that photojournalism 'has played a remarkable part' in reinforcing public memory in Kashmir, beginning with the first surge of armed insurgency in the early 1990s. 'For several decades, it was only these images – gathered erratically in the course of routine news gathering – that survived as shared public "evidence". In those decades, a terrible silence had been imposed on Kashmir, on its journalists, writers and human rights defenders. The conflict was being described to the world by outsiders: for the most part by visiting Indians, and largely from the lens of the Indian state. Kashmiri journalists, writers and filmmakers began to step out of the shadows – to speak out about what was really going on there – much more recently. I would say they first gathered real significance from around the time of the massive public protests of 2008. But all along, it was Kashmiri photographers who had been doing what we have only now begun to recognize as the critical work of documenting contemporary history.'

3 Ibid.: 'I realized that while the book was obviously about Kashmir, it also had to be about the photographers themselves,' Kak explains. 'Who were they, where did they come from? Over three decades the photographers had also changed. Photography – and not simply images to feed the insatiable appetite of the media – had found a foothold for itself in Kashmir. This drew me to the work of the younger photographers who feature in *Witness*. For them playing a part in history was important, but the ways in which those narratives could be made was as important. ... I see the change in status following the revocation of Article 370 in August 2019 as a legal change, as the final desecration of a constitutional promise long trampled over. The fact that it was accompanied by a paranoid level of militarization, an unbearably long shutdown and an internet siege made things much worse, no doubt. But essentially what we are seeing is a continuation of the same history that *Witness* tries to evoke. If anything, the archive that we have put together within the folds of the book flows even more seamlessly into the present.'

4 **Editor's note**: Meraj Ud Din: Photographer and videographer from Srinagar. Began career in 1986. Worked for Reuters, *Kashmir Times* and *India Today*, and is currently with Associated Press.

5 **Editor's note**: 2014 Kashmir flood: Major flood when the Jhelum river overflowed following incessant rains in September 2014, leading to controversy around the government's ability to provide relief, amid questions around whether to accept aid from international sources.

6 **Editor's note**: Javeed Shah: Kashmir-based freelance photographer, worked for *The Indian Express* (1992–2009). Featured in *Time Asia*, the *Guardian Weekend* and the *Wall Street Journal*. Exhibited his work in the show *A Celebration of Life: Photographs of Kashmir* (Asia Society Museum, New York, 2008).

7 **Editor's note**: Dar Yasin: Kashmiri photojournalist working with Associated Press. Covered the Kashmir conflict extensively. Awarded the Pulitzer Prize in 2020. He has also covered the war in Afghanistan and the Rohingya refugee crisis.

8 **Editor's note**: Javed Dar: Photojournalist with the Chinese news agency Xinhua. Has covered the conflict in Kashmir for over a decade. Photographs featured in Suvir Kaul, *Of Gardens and Graves: Kashmir, Poetry, Politics*, Durham: Duke University Press, 2017.

9 **Editor's note**: Altaf Qadri: Kashmiri photojournalist with Associated Press. He has photographed the conflict in the Valley since 2004. He has also photographed the Mumbai terror attacks, the Nepal earthquake, and the conflict in Libya and Afghanistan.

10 **Editor's note**: Sumit Dayal: India/Nepal-based photographer and filmmaker. Has worked freelance

since 2007, documenting community struggles, disappearing cultural traditions and the changing landscapes of South Asia. Co-founded the Instagram page India Photo Project and Nepal Photo Project.

11 **Editor's note**: Showkat Nanda: Journalist, documentary photographer and educator based in Kashmir. Received support from the Magnum Foundation, National Geographic Society and Henry Luce Foundation. Currently a contributing photographer for *New York Times*.

12 **Editor's note**: Syed Shahriyar: Documentary photographer and filmmaker based in Kashmir. Work has been widely published in global media houses. Recent short film, *Pushed to the Wall: Kashmir on the Road to Rebellion* (2019).

13 **Editor's note**: Azaan Shah: Documentary photographer based in Kashmir. Began experimenting with photography when still a teenager, shooting on the streets of his hometown.

14 Kak recommends that 'a combination of obstinacy and flexibility' should infuse the production of these new narratives: 'We have to be obstinate in the insistence on telling the story of what has been happening in Kashmir, we have to get better and better at telling that story. And we have to be flexible in what medium we choose to tell it … there [is] a place for a feature-length essay film … there is also space for those quick five-minute videos that so many people are making and putting up online. The two must not be seen as substitutes for each other but rather as complementary … I see people using Instagram and Twitter to continuously keep Kashmir out there, and that is critical. We cannot let them [state forces] silence us. We will be obstinate. But we will not get slow and sluggish in our obstinacy. We will be supple and fluid and flexible.' See interview by Nawaz Gul Qanungo, 'Kashmir Lays India Bare: Old Clichés of Democracy, Constitution, Free Media Now Look Very Shallow', *The Polis Project*, 5 June 2020, https://www.thepolisproject.com/read/sanjay-kak-kashmir-lays-india-bare-old-cliches-of-democracy-constitution-free-media-now-look-very-shallow/

15 Ibid.: As Kak explains, 'Many things make an image "dangerous", and it is not the evidentiary value alone that makes an image potent.' The security forces frisking young Kashmiri men force them to open their phones and delete images the soldiers do not approve of; images considered mildly undesirable may bring slaps; images considered politically offensive may bring beatings. The frequent and extended shutdowns of mobile networks and the internet in Kashmir 'are not really done to prevent militants from using these channels, as we are constantly told. … These are enforced to prevent people from reaching out to each other, to sharing news, and they are meant to break affinities and solidarities. Most of all, they are meant to prevent news and images from travelling out of Kashmir … most often it's not that the memorable photographs prove something. What they do is to open windows in the minds of the viewer, even very tiny ones, make them think, make them understand for themselves what people in Kashmir are experiencing. That's what the young soldier scrolling through the phone at the barricade is looking for, too; that's what makes those images subversive.'

16 Ibid.: Kak points out that the 2020 Pulitzer Prize for feature photography awarded to Associated Press photographers – Srinagar-based Dar Yasin and Mukhtar Khan, and Jammu-based Channi Anand, three of 'our own' – for their coverage of Kashmir, was seen with great pride in Kashmir 'as a validation of the stories that had made it out of Kashmir, and it was seen as a salute to all those who report the stories that the Indian state does not want carried to the world … [The prize] was seen as given not simply to three photographers, but as if to Kashmir's truth. … And for the young journalists and photographers, who had begun to feel anxious and fearful with the charges and arrests, it was certainly a big morale booster.' He is convinced that the attempt at silencing/censoring Kashmiri voices and imaginations has been, and will continue to be, unsuccessful: 'In Kashmir this present phase of the struggle is now thirty years old. Every time we have seen a generation get exhausted by the pressure, and the constant sense of being embattled, new people take their place. That is how it is with journalists and photographers too.'

Amar Kanwar

1 As Kanwar has remarked elsewhere: 'I think quite fundamentally central to whatever I'm doing or have been doing, something that I have managed only after several years, is to be able to develop a reasonably positive attitude to one's own inadequacy. To get out of a negative attitude toward one's own inadequacy and to a productive relationship with one's own inadequacy has been quite a relief. I say this in the context of doubt:

that if one is able to embrace it fully, then you lose voice. You then do not know how to proceed. If you stare it in the face and you understand it as much as you can, it becomes very hard to proceed further and so very hard to speak.' See Amar Kanwar, Laura Raicovich, Kaelen Wilson-Goldie and Nitin Sawhney in conversation (10 December 2018) about Kanwar's *Such a Morning* (2017), on view at the Marian Goodman Gallery, New York, 14 November–21 December 2018; full transcript at https://www.moussemagazine.it/magazine/amar-kanwar-morning-marian-goodman-gallery-new-york/

2 **Editor's note**: The assassination of Shankar Guha Niyogi: The trade union leader was attacked on 28 September 1991 by a killer hired by industrialists who felt threatened by the impact of the workers' movement on their businesses. Kanwar documented the aftermath of the killing in his film *Lal Hara Lehrake* (1992) and the handmade book *The Prediction* (1991–2012).

3 **Editor's note**: Chhattisgarh Mukti Morcha (CMM): Organization formed by Niyogi in 1982 as the political front of the Chhattisgarh Mines Shramik Sangh (Chhattisgarh Mines Workers' Union/CMSS). Beginning operations from Bhilai, CMSS demanded separation from Madhya Pradesh and formation of the state of Chhattisgarh, a goal realized in 2000.

4 Kanwar on his interest 'in what we cannot see': 'I feel that it is possible, that there is a view or a vision that you can see if you enter into a zone where you see nothing. So, what is it that you see when you see nothing … I think it can be answered, and it can be discussed … I see this as a quite concrete thing. I don't see this as just a metaphorical toss in the air …'. Amar Kanwar, Laura Raicovich, Kaelen Wilson-Goldie and Nitin Sawhney in conversation (10 December 2018) about Kanwar's *Such a Morning* (2017)

5 Linda Hess and Sukhdev Singh, trans., *The Bijak of Kabir*, Delhi: Motilal Banarsidass, reprint, 2001.

6 Kanwar on his process: 'When you get in such a situation, and you face the doubt, the contradiction, then you do not know how to proceed. Then you accept not proceeding … I accept not being able to proceed further until I figure it out or figure out the first four steps. Politically, I think it's completely critical. I know it's critical to fight back, but it's also completely critical to step back and configure – and reconfigure – and try to comprehend.' See Amar Kanwar, Laura Raicovich, Kaelen Wilson-Goldie and Nitin Sawhney in conversation; https://www.moussemagazine.it/magazine/amar-kanwar-morning-marian-goodman-gallery-new-york/

7 **Editor's note**: *A Season Outside* (1997): First part of Kanwar's *Trilogy*; starting at Wagah Attari, the militarized western border between India and Pakistan. The film speaks of the historical legacy of **Partition** (see Keywords) and the personal histories of inherited trauma.

8 **Editor's note**: *The Many Faces of Madness* (2000): Explores notion of the commons as it has slowly been eroded through the wholesale move towards industrialization, erasing traditional forms of resource-sharing crucial to ecological balance. Made for the Foundation for Ecological Security.

9 **Editor's note**: *Azaadi/'Freedom'* (2001): Traces genealogies of regional protest movements through grassroots-resistance responses such as anti-mining tribal resistance in Kashipur and Gandhmaran in Odisha, mass labour and workers' rights movements in Chhattisgarh, and protests against industrial parks by coastal communities in Kutch and Umbergaon in Gujarat.

10 **Editor's note**: *Baphlimali 173* (2001): The title derives from the Baphlimali hill range in south Odisha, which contained an estimated 173 million tons of bauxite. Documents the eight-year anti-mining resistance by tribal communities of Kashipur.

11 **Editor's note**: *King of Dreams* (2001): Through anonymous first-person narratives the film examines masculinity and sexuality, bringing together perspectives on sex, desire, love and obsession.

12 **Editor's note**: *A Night of Prophecy* (2002): Second part of Kanwar's *Trilogy*. The film speculates on the possibility of understanding the passage of time and the future through poetry. It traces the work of poets from Andhra Pradesh, Nagaland, Maharashtra and Kashmir as they respond to systemic violence and forms of marginalization.

13 **Editor's note**: See **Kashmir** in Keywords.

14 **Editor's note**: *To Remember* (2003): Silent short film, third part of Kanwar's *Trilogy* made in response to the 2002 Gujarat riots. It remembers Gandhi, his way of life and ideal of non-violence, and reminds us that Gandhi's murderer Nathuram Godse was a militant Hindu nationalist. Shot in Birla House, the site of Gandhi's assassination on 30 January 1948, now functioning as a memorial museum.

15 **Editor's note**: *The Lightning Testimonies* (2007): Multi-channel video installation reflecting the

structural nature of sexual violence in situations of conflict in the subcontinent. Eight channels synchronized to present lived experiences of women from different regions, from the Partition in 1947 to the Khairlanji massacre in 2006.

16 **Editor's note**: The Bharatiya Janata Party's win in the Gujarat state elections of 2003, generally considered a direct win for future Prime Minister Narendra Modi. See **Gujarat riots 2002** in Keywords.

17 Kanwar on the difficulties of bearing witness: 'I'm still trying to comprehend. I'm still trying to respond very clearly, and I'm figuring out different methods of responding to violence. ... There are many, many real specific incidents ... and places and events – and it's not adding up ... Our responses are not making sense ... my response is not making sense... [A few years ago] I felt that I did not want to argue anymore – that I wanted to respond [but] I wanted to speak without the specificity and still speak equally clear and equally powerful and equally engaged. I felt the need for conversation, which was not in the realm that I was witnessing around me. I wondered: when all the arguments are over, what kind of conversation begins? And more so, with whom? In that conversation – at least in the preliminary part of that conversation – is there speech? Probably not. So, if there is no spoken word, and there is a conversation then what kind of conversation is it, and with whom?' Amar Kanwar, Laura Raicovich, Kaelen Wilson-Goldie and Nitin Sawhney in conversation (10 December 2018) about Kanwar's *Such a Morning* (2017).

18 **Editor's note**: *The Torn First Pages* (2004–08): Three-part, nineteen-channel installation documenting acts of oppression by the Burmese military junta and the resistance to that violence. The title honours the defiance shown by Burmese bookshop owner Ko Than Htay, imprisoned for tearing out the first few mandatory pages from the books he sold as these pages carried military propaganda. Part I: *The Face*, *Thet Win Aung*, *Ma Win Maw Oo*, *The Bodhi Tree* (2004) and *Somewhere in May* (2005). Part II documents the lives of Burmese refugees in Fort Wayne, Indiana. Part III references archival material extracted from underground sites of resistance that circulated information and images about the crimes of the dictatorship.

19 **Editor's note**: *The Sovereign Forest* (2012): Made in collaboration with Sudhir Pattnaik and Sherna Dastur, the installation explores Odisha as an ecological site, referencing questions around crime, politics and human rights. Includes video works *Scene of Crime* (2011) and *A Love Story* (2010); three handmade books, *The Counting Sisters*, *The Prediction* and *The Constitution* with projected films; books, pamphlets and photographs; and over 270 varieties of indigenous organic rice seeds.

Gauri Gill

1 **Editor's note**: Urmul Setu Sansthan (est. 1994): Community-based organization working in Western Rajasthan on drought mitigation, disaster management, livelihoods, women's empowerment, child rights, early childcare and development, and improving access to basic amenities.

2 **Editor's Note**: Mahatma Gandhi National Rural Employment Guarantee Act/MGNREGA **(2005)**: Indian legislation that guarantees 100 days of employment in a financial year to any rural household whose adult members are willing to do unskilled manual work.

3 **Editor's note**: *Jannat* (series between 1999 and 2007): Exhibition of photographs featuring a young girl who died aged 23, part of an ongoing project set largely in Western Rajasthan collectively titled *Notes from the Desert*. Central to this project is a single mother named Izmat and her two daughters.

4 **Editor's note**: *Ruined Rainbow* (2010): Also part of the *Notes from the Desert* series, comprising photographs taken by children from Barmer villages and originally discarded because they were ruined by 'mistakes' including unintended exposure of negatives.

5 **Editor's note**: *Birth Series* (2005, first shown in 2010): Another sub-series from *Notes from the Desert*, made when Gill lived some days in a Barmer village with a midwife named Kasumbi Dai, who invited Gill to photograph her delivering her granddaughter. Gill ended up both photographing, as well as assisting with the birth. Kasumbi Dai died in 2010.

6 **Editor's note**: *Traces* (1999-ongoing): Series continuing Gill's *Notes from the Desert* project, memorializing handmade unmarked and marked graves, often made by peasants, nomads and inhabitants of remote villages in Western Rajasthan, across caste and religious dominations.

7 **Editor's note**: *The Mark on the Wall* (1999–ongoing): Photographic series from *Notes from the Desert* archive in which Gill documents drawings made by local artists, children and teachers in government schools in Rajasthan under the now-lapsed Leher Kaksha and subsequent government schemes initiated by the state to help children learn visually from the walls in their classrooms.

8 **Editor's note**: Rajesh Chaitya Vangad (b. 1975): Painter who belongs to the Indigenous Warli tribe (see **Adivasi** in Keywords, also note 10) known for distinctive style of painting, which he learnt from his mother, Ladhki Devi, and acknowledged masters like Jivya Soma Mashe. Painted several public murals including at the Crafts Museum, New Delhi, Tata Memorial Hospital, Mumbai and the International Airport in Mumbai.

9 **Editor's note**: Bohada: Mask festival in Thane, Nasik and other districts in Maharashtra, held for three days in the spring, in which masks of Indian gods and goddesses are worn by local inhabitants in a ritual procession.

10 **Editor's note**: *Acts of Appearance* (2015–ongoing): Collaborative project involving the making of masks with **Adivasi** *papier-mache* artists from the Kokna and Warli tribes (see note 11) in Palghar district, Maharashtra. After encountering the Bohada mask festival, Gill commissioned well-known artists, along with their families and fellow volunteers, to create a new set of masks representing beings existing in contemporary reality, seeking to embody different ages, distinctive individuals, varied *rasa*s (emotions) like love, sadness, fear or anger, sickness, or ageing. Gill, the artists and various resident volunteers then used these masks to tell stories about the village today.

11 **Editor's note**: Kokna (also known as Kokni, Kukna): An indigenous **Adivasi** (see Keywords) tribe found in the Sahyadri mountain ranges of Maharashtra. Warli: Indigenous tribe who live in the mountainous, coastal and bordering regions of Gujarat and Maharashtra. Known for their distinctive style of intricate painting on paper and walls, often using basic geometric shapes symbolic of different elements of nature.

12 **Editor's note**: Dharma Ram Kadu: Warli tribal artist known for mask-making. Learnt his craft aged seven from Pandharinath Sonar, a famous mask maker of Jawhar.

CAMP

1 One of Shaina's projects in 2001, *Tellavision Mumbai*, followed the political left's responses to the war in Afghanistan after 9/11, which then intersected with the **Gujarat riots** in February 2002 (see Keywords).

2 **Editor's note**: Refers to *A Tryst with the People of India* (dir. Saeed Akhtar Mirza, 1998), a 13-episode series for **Doordarshan** (see Keywords). Shaina Anand and new media practitioner Shai Heredia accompanied Mirza and 'a 17-member documentary crew in three Tata Sumos and one Tempo Traveller'. The crew travelled 'without a break through most of the States comprising India'. Years later, a complete documentation of this material is available on pad.ma (https://pad.ma/grid/title/project=A_Tryst_with_the_People_of_India).

3 **Editor's note**: Saeed Akhtar Mirza (b. 1943): Noted filmmaker who made several iconic films for New Indian Cinema in the 1980s.

4 **Editor's note**: See **Faculty of Fine Arts, Maharaja Sayajirao University, Baroda** in Keywords. Sir Jamsetjee Jeejeebhoy School of Art (Sir J. J. School of Art): Oldest and best known art school in Mumbai.

5 **Editor's note**: BI-TV, aka Business-India Television: Short-lived television channel started by Ashok Advani and Malavika Singh in 1992, in an era when satellite uplinking from India was still not allowed.

6 **Editor's note**: *Hum Bambai Nahi Jayenge* (We Will Not Go to Bombay): Television series aired in 1993 on the now-defunct BI-TV, directed by noted filmmaker Tigmanshu Dhulia.

7 **Editor's note**: National School of Drama (NSD) (est. 1959): India's best known theatre training institute. Also known since the mid-1970s for several of Indian cinema's major actors.

8 **Editor's note**: Major riots in Bombay in 1992 and 1993 following the demolition of the **Babri Masjid** (see Keywords), also viewed as a key moment in the city's globalization.

9 **Editor's note**: Open Circle: Artists' initiative formed in 1998 to create a platform in Mumbai for interactions between artists at local as well as global levels, a space to share ideas of theory and praxis.

10 **Editor's note**: CAMP sees itself, to quote from their website, as 'not an artists collective but rather a studio, in which ideas and energies gather and become interests and forms. In this process we try to move

beyond binaries of art vs. non-art, commodity markets vs. "free culture", or individual vs. institutional will to think and to build what is possible, equitable, and interesting, for the future.' The 2007 statement continues: 'We wish: To consider thresholds of ownership and authority as challenging sites for artistic practice. To test the ground between aesthetics and multiple ideas of the public (or open), private (or closed), personal (about one's world), and power (about the world, and the capacity to act within it). To engage with questions, claims and potentials around infrastructure: materials, systems and tools. This means working directly with such things as electricity, transport, trade, archives, video, radio and the internet; developing ways to think about these as integrated with human life, and beyond the "network"as its representative thought-model. To develop new or reconfigured distribution platforms: cinemas, libraries, exhibitions, books, websites, performances: with both new concepts and material, sensibility and sensuality. To take opportunities, to change. To be hospitable to ideas and to people.'

11 **Editor's note**: Slum Rehabilitation Authority: Controversial project initiated by the Maharashtra government, in which property developers would take over slum land and create separate buildings for 'slum dwellers'.

12 See Alain Badiou, *Cinema*, translated by Susan Spitzer, Cambridge: Polity Press, 2013.

13 **Editor's note**: Also refers to a major series of solo exhibitions titled *As If – I – V* held across Kolkata, Delhi and Mumbai by CAMP in 2015. *Rock, Paper, Scissors* was the first in the series.

14 **Editor's note**: https://pad.ma (Public Access Digital Media Archive) was started in 2007 as an online archive of densely text-annotated video material, primarily footage and not-finished films.

15 **Editor's note**: Radia Tapes: Refers to leaked telephonic conversations in 2008–09 between a political lobbyist named Niira Radia, and ministers, bureaucrats, senior journalists, politicians and heads of corporate houses. CAMP made a series of installations and performances using these tapes.

16 **Editor's note:** *Shoah* (dir. Claude Lanzmann, 1985): A nine-hour long French documentary about the Holocaust. Lav Diaz (Lavrente Indico Diaz): Filipino filmmaker known for long-form cinema.

17 Our first use of the term was as the title of a workshop we did as part of the 'Summit of Non-Aligned Initiatives in Education Culture', Berlin, 24–28 May 2007. Theorist and curator Irit Rogoff has analysed the 'educational turn in curating' among various other 'educational turns' in today's art world, noting that any such inquiry is complicated 'by the degree of slippage that currently takes place between notions of "knowledge production", "research", "education", "open-ended production" and "self-organized pedagogies" when all these approaches seem to have converged into a set of parameters for some renewed facet of production. Although quite different in their genesis, methodology, and protocols, it appears that some perceived proximity to "knowledge economies" has rendered all of these terms part and parcel of a certain liberalizing shift within the world of contemporary art practices.' Rogoff points to the possible 'hardening' of any turn 'into a series of generic or stylistic tropes' that may not be 'capable of resolving the urgencies that underwrote it in the first place', and asks whether the 'educational turn in curating' actually addresses education or curating 'at precisely the points at which it urgently needs to be shaken up and made uncomfortable.' She suggests that the 'educational turn' might be 'the moment when we attend to the production and articulation of truths – not truth as correct, as provable, as fact, but truth as that which collects around it subjectivities that are neither gathered nor reflected by other utterances. Stating truths in relation to the great arguments, issues and great institutions of the day is relatively easy, for these dictate the terms by which such truths are both arrived at and articulated. Telling truths in the marginal and barely-formed spaces in which the curious gather – this is another project altogether: one's personal relation to truth.' See Irit Rogoff, 'Turning', *e-flux Journal* #00, November 2008; full text at https://www.e-flux.com/journal/00/68470/turning/

18 This is not the same kind of invisibility that characterizes what Ravi Sundaram calls the 'architecture of shadows' and the 'surplus of shadow networks'. He describes how 'media became the infrastructural condition of *living*, rather than existing as distinct, regulated sites like the cinema theatre, or as celluloid'; and how 'thousands of everyday acts from a media-enabled population' enabled the emergence of a 'volatile, sensory infrastructure' that combined 'pirate tactics, media forms, and paralegal space', 'blurring and confusing the distinctions between the legal–nonlegal, private–public, fact–artefact, and governmental–nongovernmental'. These 'new interventions' coalesced into an 'ever-expanding circulation engine' used by 'socio-political actors who are also media proliferators' to create a 'visceral' and 'affect-driven' media archive that 'joins the global traffic in poor images, moving away and attaching to new environments'. As Sundaram notes, 'As typical postcolonial technologies of

visibility, paper-based information systems allowed the regime to manage urban residents through systems of inclusion and exclusion … entry into one information system could co-exist with tactical invisibility in another. Small traders and migrant residents of squatter settlements moved in this shifting information ecology … In the contemporary digital era, this is a neurophysiological zone amplified by the mix of mobile computing objects, moods, and sensations. Provisional networks form around these temporary connections. See Ravi Sundaram, 'Post Postcolonial Sensory Infrastructure', *e-flux Journal*, Issue #64, April 2015.

Francesca Ceccherini & Noriko Yamakoshi in conversation with Raqs Media Collective

1 **Editor's note**: Francesca Ceccherini and Noriko Yamakoshi: Independent art practitioners and curators based in Zurich.

2 The members of Raqs Media Collective are among the co-founders of Sarai, an experimental new media initiative/research programme established in 2000 as part of the Centre for the Study of Developing Societies (CSDS), Delhi. Sarai has emerged as one of South Asia's prominent critical platforms. Focusing on the areas of urbanism, ethnography, data and information, intellectual property, language, law, media histories, free software, art practice, digital cultures and transformations in the public domain, it brings together academics and practitioners in dialogue, produces themed publications, supports independent research through fellowships and hosts conferences, workshops and performances. See https://sarai.net/about/

3 As noted by art historian Partha Mitter, 'The Western avant-garde continues to be a closed discourse, writing the art of Asia, Africa and Latin America out of art history. Marginalization of non-Western art is explained in terms of its "derivativeness". … Hence borrowings of primitive art by Western artists such as Picasso are judged as mere affinities, unlike the use of the syntax of cubism by non-Western artists, which is seen as the influence of the West.' See chapter abstract of Mitter's essay, 'Modern Global Art and Its Discontents', in *Decentring the Avant-Garde*, Leiden: Brill, 2014, pp. 33–54; https://brill.com/display/book/edcoll/9789401210379/B9789401210379-s003.xml

4 World Bank, https://data.worldbank.org/indicator/NY.GDP.MKTP.CD, accessed 15 June 2023.

5 Mitter argues for the need 'to probe more closely the epistemological framework that fuels the "universalist" claims of the Western canon. Even though Western avant-garde has inspired the rest of the world, it is still dominated by the universalism that creates asymmetrical relations between the centre and the peripheries, which is not one of geography but of power and authority, with modernism creating its own tacit exclusions and inclusions.' See Mitter, 'Modern Global Art and Its Discontents'.

6 Ibid. Underscoring the 'significant developments in non-Western art since the 20th century', with 'many of its artists engaged in creating vital modernist expressions of cultural resistance to colonialism', Mitter argues for an 'inflected narrative of global modernity' that 'offers us a possible way of restoring the artist's agency in the context of colonial empires, by analysing art practices and reception as a cultural document that is historically situated'.

7 **Editor's note**: *The Rest of Now* (2008): Hosted by the Trentino-South Tyrol region in Italy during 19 July 2007–2 November 2008, *Manifesta* was co-curated by Raqs Media Collective, Anselm Franke/Hila Peleg and Adam Budak. *The Rest of Now* was at a disused aluminium smelting factory in Bolzano, where artists were invited to make works that responded to the afterlife of extraction.

8 **Editor's note**: *Sarai Reader 09* Exhibition (2012–13): Exhibition at Devi Art Foundation in Gurgaon, adapting from a Sarai Reader. It examined the proposition, 'Art as Place'.

Rahaab Allana in conversation with Sunil Gupta

1 **Editor's note**: FotoFest Biennial: Houston-based non-profit cultural event. Inaugural edition held in 1986. From 1990 it began a programme of inter-biennial travelling shows, exchange programmes and publications. The 2018 edition featured India as a site of speculation and observation.

2 **Editor's note**: *INDIA/Contemporary Photographic and New Media Art* (2018): The 2018 edition of

FotoFest Biennial, curated by Sunil Gupta and Steven Evans, featured 48 artists. Works highlighted issues in contemporary India such as caste, class, gender, sexuality, religion, nationalism, technological development.

3 **Editor's note**: Fredrick C. Baldwin (1929–2021): American photographer known for documenting wildlife, the civil rights movement and life in rural America. Often worked in partnership with wife Wendy Watriss. In the 1980s, they co-founded FotoFest.

4 **Editor's note**: Steven Evans: Current Executive Director of FotoFest, Professor of Philosophy and Humanities at Baylor University, Waco, Texas.

5 **Editor's note**: *Where Three Dreams Cross* (2010): Landmark exhibition organized by Whitechapel Gallery, London, in collaboration with Fotomuseum, Winterthur. See note 6 for more.

6 *Where Three Dreams Cross: 150 Years of Photography from India, Pakistan and Bangladesh*, Whitechapel Gallery, London, 21 January–11 April 2010 / Fotomuseum, Winterthur, 12 June–22 August 2010. A Whitechapel Gallery–Fotomuseum collaboration, this landmark exhibition was curated by Sunil Gupta with curatorial assistance from Shahidul Alam (Drik Archive, Dhaka), Hammad Nasar (Green Cardamom, London), Radhika Singh (Fotomedia, New Delhi) and Kirsty Ogg (Whitechapel Gallery). As noted by the organizers, 'From the days when the first Indian-run photographic studios were established in the 19th century, this exhibition tells the story of photography's development in the subcontinent with over 400 works that have been brought together for the first time. It encompasses social realism and reportage of key political moments in the 1940s, amateur snaps from the 1960s and street photography from the 1970s. Contemporary photographs reveal the reality of everyday life, while the recent digitalization of image making accelerates its cross-over with fashion and film.' The exhibition featured the work of leading contemporary artists and over 70 noted modern photographers, 'along with works drawn from important collections of historic photography, including the influential Alkazi Collection, Delhi and the Drik Archive, Dhaka [and] many previously unseen images' from private family archives, galleries and individuals. See https://www.whitechapelgallery.org/exhibitions/where-three-dreams-cross-150-years-of-photography-from-india-pakistan-and-bangladesh/

7 **Editor's note**: *Photography in India* (1982): Mounted at the Photographers' Gallery, London, this large survey exhibition was conceptualized as part of the Festival of India in the United Kingdom from March to November 1982. Organized by Partha Mitter in association with Raimonda Buitoni and Dalu Jones, the exhibition featured works of prominent photographers including **Lala Deen Dayal**, **Sunil Janah**, **Mitter Bedi**, Kishor Parekh, Mahendra Sinh and **Raghu Rai** (see Keywords for names in bold). See note 4 in Sabeena Gadihoke, 'Journeys into Inner and Outer Worlds', and note 10 in Suryanandini Narain, 'The Camera Tours the City', both in this volume.

8 **Editor's note**: The Photographers' Gallery, London: Founded in London in 1971 by Sue Davies, it is the first public gallery in the UK to feature the work of photographers only.

9 **Editor's note**: Black Arts: Radical movement founded in Britain in 1982, emphasized race and gender through the politics of representation, inspired by cultural theorist Stuart Hall. Landmark event was *The Other Story* (1989), an exhibition curated by Rasheed Araeen at the Hayward Gallery.

10 A prominent diasporic artist/gay rights activist, Gupta is known for his depictions of queer life across a wide cultural arc over the past four decades. 'Photography and homosexuality, my twin pillars of wisdom, have always been my concerns but they take on different meanings in different contexts. They are continuously evolving,' he affirms. The art history he was taught as an art student in the UK 'was Eurocentric and heterosexual: if photographers like Robert Mapplethorpe were mentioned, it was entirely cloak-and-dagger, so it became a project of mine to raise those issues. To put it crudely, the gay scene seemed very white and in need of some race-awareness training.' Another problem was 'the extreme homophobia in the Black and Brown worlds – especially in South Asia. Almost every South Asian I met lived at home, which really limited their ability to come to meetings and develop consciousness.' See Tausif Noor, 'Sunil Gupta Saturates His Photographs with Love and Sex', interview with Sunil Gupta, *Frieze*, 24 January 2023, https://www.frieze.com/article/sunil-gupta-interview-2022

11 **Editor's note**: *Reflections of the Black Experience* (1986): Organized by the Greater London Council at Brixton Gallery, exhibition researched and curated by Monika Baker. One of three South Asian artists commissioned for the show, Gupta was asked to produce ten photographs to illustrate the experience of being 'Black' in London.

12 In June 2022, the Museum of London acquired Gupta's work, *Pretended Family Relationships* (1988), set to go on permanent display in 2026. This series consists of sets of photo collages 'that pair portraits of

interracial same-sex couples with lines of poetry by Gupta's then partner, the poet and academic Stephen Dodd'. The work's title 'references an incendiary phrase in Margaret Thatcher's controversial legislation Section 28, which prohibited local authorities from promoting "the acceptability of homosexuality as a pretended family relationship". This troubling clause had a far-reaching impact on LGBTQ+ communities between its inception in 1988 and repeal in 2003, legitimizing homophobic discrimination and marginalization. Thirty-four years after the declaration of this Local Government Act, Section 28's legacy still lasts today.' Press release, Museum of London; see https://www.museumoflondon.org.uk/news-room/press-releases/sunil-guptas-pretended-family-relationships-photo-series-acquired-museum-london

13 **Editor's note**: *An Economy of Signs* (1990): Edited by Sunil Gupta and published by Oram Press, this book featured the works of eight photographers – Sheba Chhachhi, Ashim Ghosh, Karan Kapoor, Amita Prasher, Ram Rahman, Sanjeev Saith, Ketaki Sheth and Sooni Taraporevala. Initially mounted as an exhibition at the Photographers' Gallery, London and then in India by Fotomedia.

14 **Editor's note**: Autograph ABP (Association of Black Photographers): Co-founded by Gupta with fellow artists, curators and activists of African, Afro-Caribbean and South Asian cultural heritage in London, 1988. This influential international non-profit arts agency/exhibition space supports and promotes the work of artists who use lens-based mediums to respond to and make visible issues of race, representation, identity, human rights and social justice.

15 **Editor's note**: *Autoportraits* (1990): Autograph's first exhibition, curated by Sunil Gupta and Monica Baker. Centred on self-representation through self-portraiture as an act of cultural activism. On view 20 March–12 April 1990 were photographs by artists Monika Baker, Allan de Souza, Joy Gregory, Sunil Gupta, Lyle Harris, Mumtaz Karimjee and Roshini Kempadoo. Introductory text by cultural theorist Stuart Hall.

16 **Editor's note**: *Disrupted Borders* (1993): Project by the Organization for Visual Arts/Institute of New International Visual Arts franchise (OVA/InIVA), in collaboration with Arnolfini, Bristol and The Photographers' Gallery, London. It proposed a new internationalism by advocating for a plurality of art-making practices.

17 **Editor's note**: OVA (Organization for Visual Arts), London: Set up by Gupta in 1992 as curatorial franchise under the Institute of International Visual Arts (InIVA), it continued to function till the mid-2000s.

18 **Editor's note**: Arnolfini, Bristol: International Centre for Contemporary Arts founded in 1961 by Jeremy Rees. By early 1990s moved towards becoming an international centre of interdisciplinary contemporary arts, exhibiting artists such as Paula Rego, Richard Long, Chantal Joffe, Jannis Kounellis and Grayson Perry.

19 **Editor's note**: Clive van den Berg, Johannesburg-based artist, curator, designer, writer and activist.

20 **Editor's note**: *Click! Contemporary Photography in India* (2008): Exhibition curated by Gupta and Radhika Singh, displayed at the Vadehra Art Gallery, New Delhi, 27 February–27 March 2008. Showcased over 100 works by 86 photographers. Sections included *Portraiture, Politics of Identity, Performance as Photograph, The Archive, Interiorscapes, Whose Body Is It Anyway?* and *What Can a Woman Do with a Camera?*

21 **Editor's note**: Vadehra Art Gallery, New Delhi: Established in 1987, it represents several artists across generations, including M.F. Husain, Tyeb Mehta, S.H. Raza, Ram Kumar, Arpita Singh, Gulammohammed Sheikh, Rameshwar Broota, Nalini Malani, Shilpa Gupta, Atul Bhalla, Sunil Gupta and N.S. Harsha. In 2006, founded the independent non-profit, Foundation for Indian Contemporary Art (FICA).

22 **Editor's note**: Urs Stahel is an independent photography curator, writer, lecturer and consultant. He co-founded Kunsthalle, Zurich in 1986; Fotomuseum, Winterthur in 1993; and Coal Mine, Winterthur in 2000. He was Director and Curator of Fotomuseum, Winterthur from 1993 to 2013.

23 Gupta has directly and personally navigated an equally threatening 'minefield' – the fight for the decriminalization/legalization of homosexuality in India – through his photography. He describes his arrival back in India in 2003, amidst the intensification of legal activism directed towards overturning Section 377, a colonial statute applied across British-ruled dominions, criminalizing voluntary 'carnal intercourse against the order of nature with any man, woman or animal' and punishing the offending 'criminals' with fines and imprisonment. Introduced into the Indian Penal Code in 1861, it remained in effect for over 150 years. As Gupta recalls: 'There was a lot of social activism around that. ... During those years of 377 activism, I went to all these meetings about sociology and the awful law. ... By that point, I had come to a conclusion. It seemed like so much was being reduced to this law and nobody wanted to touch on emotion and love.' In response, he made *Love, Undetectable* (2009), a series of photos of his queer women friends in relationships, and large-format 'very intimate' images of himself with a partner, taken during 'a kind

of honeymoon when we took the camera to bed'. To his surprise, 'the gallery put up all the images and didn't bat an eyelid, and people came and saw the show. That was a very positive change that happened right in front of my eyes: I had a bizarre experience of going to India in the 1980s, when you couldn't even mention the word "gay" [see note 5], to being there in 2010 when so many people had come out as queer.' See Sunil Gupta interviewed by Tausif Noor [see note 10]. For a summary of the extended legal contests around Section 377, culminating on 6 September 2018 when the statute was declared unconstitutional and struck down in a landmark unanimous decision by a five-member bench of the Supreme Court, with Chief Justice Dipak Misra describing the repealed law as 'irrational, indefensible and manifestly arbitrary', see Maria Thomas, 'Timeline: The Struggle against Section 377 Began Two Decades Ago', *Quartz*, 6 September 2018, https://qz.com/india/1379620/section-377-a-timeline-of-indias-battle-for-gay-rights.

24 **Editor's note**: Whitney Biennial: Organized by the Whitney Museum of Art in Manhattan, instituted as an invitational showcase by founder Gertrude Vanderbilt Whitney. Inaugural edition in 1932, briefly shifted to annual mode in 1937 before returning to the biennial format in 1973. More than 3,600 artists have been showcased at this major event.

25 Schutz's *Open Casket* catalysed petitions for its removal, picketing, opponents positioning themselves to block the painting from view, and social media denunciation of the work as culturally appropriative, as profiting from Black trauma, and as thoroughly insensitive to the complex issues of race and representation. For Hannah Black, an artist who had previously taken part in a residency at the Whitney, 'the painting is so exploitative that is requires not only to be removed, but also destroyed, so it can't circulate in the art market or be displayed in other institutions'. In an open letter to the curators and staff of the Whitney Biennial, Black asserts: 'Although Schutz's intention may be to present white shame, this shame is not correctly represented as a painting of a dead Black boy by a white artist – those non-Black artists who sincerely wish to highlight the shameful nature of white violence should first of all stop treating Black pain as raw material. The subject matter is not Schutz's; white free speech and white creative freedom have been founded on the constraint of others, and are not natural rights.' See Lorena Muñoz-Alonso, 'Dana Schutz's Painting of Emmett Till at Whitney Biennial Sparks Protest', *Artnet*, 21 March 2017, https://news.artnet.com/art-world/dana-schutz-painting-emmett-till-whitney-biennial-protest-897929. By way of response, 'Schutz countered in an emailed statement: "I don't know what it is like to be black in America, but I do know what it is like to be a mother. Emmett was Mamie Till's only son. The thought of anything happening to your child is beyond comprehension."' See Oliver Basciano, 'Whitney Biennial: Emmett Till casket painting by white artist sparks anger', *The Guardian*, 21 March 2017, https://www.theguardian.com/artanddesign/2017/mar/21/whitney-biennial-emmett-till-painting-dana-schutz

26 Gupta's series *Exiles* (1986–87), on the subject of 'cruising' in Delhi, was made with the help of local informants who took him to specific sites to photograph gay men seeking sexual encounters. *Exiles* was an obviously risky project and also risked censorship, given that homosexuality was then illegal in India; few queer people were open about their sexuality; and being accidentally or deliberately 'outed' could have dire personal and social consequences. Gupta had intended to create a documentary effect, but due to complexities on the ground he eventually posed his subjects for a set of performative images shot in public spaces. After returning to the UK, he 'actively tried to involve the men who had volunteered as subjects, printing contact sheets in London and sharing them to ensure that he had their consent to print the photographs, with the understanding that the images would not be shown at the time in India'. See Shanay Jhaveri, 'Sunil Gupta's Vision for a Queer Politics of Belonging', *Aperture*, 11 June 2021, https://aperture.org/editorial/sunil-gupta-vision-for-a-queer-politics-of-belonging/

27 Ibid.: As Gupta observes, 'Today, there is a great explosion of queer photographers and photography in a way that was not possible not so long ago. It has also become diverse in terms of gender fluidity and race. ... Whereas it has taken years for museums to notice work by me and my LGBT contemporaries, our queer graduates are appearing in major museum exhibitions. ... In the 1990s, I thought identity politics had had its day, culturally speaking, but clearly, it's having a revival. Better late than never.'

ACKNOWLEDGEMENTS

The early 2000s were a truly fortunate turning point in my nascent career as an aspiring archivist and photo-historian. At that time I had begun to do research for and assist the artist Vivan Sundaram and cultural scholar Geeta Kapur, and thus became involved in some of their pioneering projects. Decades later, their perspectives and erudition continue to resonate in my thinking and writing. I am indebted to them for so crucially deepening my immersion in the visual arts, with particular reference to the global South that has developed into a primary interest and field of inquiry.

Series Editor of the themed volumes comprising *India Since the 90s*, Ashish Rajadhyaksha, has brought invaluable finesse and rigour to my perception and articulation of the discourses around lens-based media, their intricate genealogies, elided interfaces and symbiotic meta-histories. I am grateful to him for giving me the opportunity, through this book, to re-examine our encounters with lens-based practices and production within an exceedingly complex, challenging, digitally influenced South Asian visual sphere. It has been an immense privilege to present a wide, deep, inclusive template hospitable to both traditional and contemporary lens-based cultural inscriptions. And it was indeed a great pleasure to establish new links, and strengthen existent ones, with select authors, scholars, curators and artists who have been central to South Asian visual arts production and theory from the 1990s into the present. I thank all the contributors for their generosity in sharing their work and in their responses to the many demands of the editorial process and the detailed labour involved in shaping a volume as cross-disciplinary and thematically interwoven as *Another Lens*.

This book was achieved through the sustained perseverance, commitment and skilful collaboration of the Tulika team directed by Indu Chandrasekhar and the Alkazi Foundation team of Hitanshi Chopra and Jennifer Chowdhry Biswas. Hitanshi in particular managed coordination, correspondence and the innumerable text- and archive-related tasks mandated by a volume of such broad dimension. I thank Mallika Vishwanathan for her work on the headnotes and keywords, and Smriti Vohra for her insights, meticulous copy-editing and long-term textual support for the Alkazi Foundation's varied exhibition and publication projects. I would also like to extend my appreciation and thanks to Kinshuk for her creative insight and for overseeing the production of the book till the very end.

I thank my family and numerous friends, colleagues and well-wishers whose enthusiasm and encouragement strengthened my resolve and guided me through many moments of doubt and indecision. As always, words are insufficient when it comes to thanking my wife Nandita, an ever-patient, inspiring presence and steady fellow-traveller on my journeys.

Rahaab Allana

New Delhi, January 2024

Rahaab Allana is Curator/Publisher, Alkazi Foundation for the Arts, New Delhi. A Charles Wallace grant awardee and Fellow of the Royal Asiatic Society (UK), he received his MA in Art History from the School of Oriental and African Studies, London and was Honorary Research Associate in the Department of Visual Anthropology at University College, London. He was Founding Editor of PIX, a themed digital publication that focused on South Asian lens-based creative work, and Founder of ASAP I art (Alternative South Asia Photography I Art), the region's first app for presentation and discussion of contemporary visual cultural production. Allana works nationally and internationally with museums, archives, cultural initiatives/institutions, universities and arts festivals. He was Guest Editor for the themed issue 'Delhi: Looking Out/Looking In', *Aperture* 243 (Summer 2021), and Editor, *Unframed: Discovering Image Practices in South Asia* (HarperCollins Publishers India and Alkazi Foundation, 2023), a critical Reader on lens-based practices, meta-histories of the image, and diverse trajectories inscribed by a range of practitioners in and from the region. He is on the editorial board of *Trans Asia Photography*, the advisory committees of the India-Europe Foundation for New Dialogues (Rome), and the Arts and Culture Committee, Asia Society (India Chapter). He recently received the award 'Officer of the Order of Arts and Letters' from the Government of France.

Cover images
Gauri Gill, *Waterwells*, from the series *Notes from the Desert*, 1999–ongoing, on 35 mm.
Lenses from the Kodak Brownie, Zeiss Icon Contax, Silver Summicron2 50 (1954 M3), Agfa Isoly, Asahi Pentax K1000, Nikon D810 and Sony Alpha